THOS. J. C. MADDOX.
Assistant Surgeon U.S.A.
son of
Thomas and Mary E. Maddox
Born December 12, 1832
Killed in a skirmish with
APACHE INDIANS
Near Alma, N.M.
December 19, 1855.

MADDOX

DIED 1896
DE SAUSSURE. DIED 1904
CHARLES A. DE SAUSSURE, JR. DIED 1969
KATE B. DE SAUSSURE. DIED 1964

LIEUTENANT
WILLIAM LORD
SHERWOOD,
21st REGT. U.S. INFANTRY
WHO MET HIS DEATH AT THE
LAVA BEDS, OREGON, UNDER GEN. CANBY.
1847 — 1873.

SIGISMUND
STERNBERG
DISTRICT OF COLUMBIA

2 LT. 27 U.S. INF.
AUGUST 1, 1867

No Greater Calling

A Chronological Record of Sacrifice and Heroism during the Western Indian Wars (1865-1898)

Compiled by
Eric S. Johnson

Schiffer Military History
Atglen, PA

Dedicated to all those who wore a uniform
So that the destiny of a nation might be made manifest.

"To the soldiers in blue and black campaign hats,
To the trumpet and carbine and obsolete gat,
To those fighting men cast in Uncle Sam's mold,
Who safeguarded the railroads and settlers of old" [1]

May your deeds never be dishonored,
May your names never be forgotten....

For my parents, who always believed.

Book design by Mark David Bowyer.

Copyright © 2012 by Schiffer Publishing, Ltd.
Library of Congress Control Number: 2012948053

Printed in China
ISBN: 978-0-7643-4255-4

We are interested in hearing from authors with book ideas on related topics.

Published by Schiffer Publishing Ltd.
4880 Lower Valley Road
Atglen, PA 19310
Phone: (610) 593-1777
FAX: (610) 593-2002
E-mail: Info@schifferbooks.com.
Visit our web site at: **www.schifferbooks.com**
Please write for a free catalog.
This book may be purchased from the publisher.
Try your bookstore first.

In Europe, Schiffer books are distributed by:
Bushwood Books
6 Marksbury Avenue
Kew Gardens
Surrey TW9 4JF, England
Phone: 44 (0) 20 8392-8585
FAX: 44 (0) 20 8392-9876
E-mail: Info@bushwoodbooks.co.uk.
Visit our website at: www.bushwoodbooks.co.uk

---

[1] Fougera, *With Custer's Cavalry*, 285.

— TABLE OF CONTENTS —

— **Introduction** 5

— **1865** 7
    — Platte River Bridge, Dakota Territory (26 July 1865) 21

— **1866** 29
    — Near Fort Phil Kearny, Dakota Territory (21 December 1866) 41

— **1867** 44
    — Near Fort Wallace, Kansas (26 June 1867) 53
    — Beaver Creek, Kansas (2 July 1867) 54
    — Prairie Dog Creek, Kansas (21 and 22 August 1867) 60
    — Infernal Caverns, near Pitt River, California (26 and 27 September 1867)..........64

— **1868** 72
    — Arickaree Fork of Republican River, Kansas (17 to 25 September 1868) 92
    — Washita River, Antelope Hills, Indian Territory (27 November 1868)...............100

— **1869** 104
— **1870** 126
    — Near North Fork, Little Wichita River, Texas (12 July 1870) 134

— **1871** 139
— **1872** 148
— **1873** 164
    — Lava Beds, near Tule Lake, California (17 January 1873) 165
    — Lava Beds, California (11, 15 to 17 April 1873) 170
    — Hardin Butte, Lava Beds, California (26 April 1873) 172
    — Lake Soras, California (10 May 1873) 175

— **1874** 183
— **1875** 201
    — Sand Hills, near Cheyenne Agency, Indian Territory (6 April 1875)..................202

— **1876** 225
    — Rosebud Creek, Montana Territory (17 June 1876) 229
    — Little Big Horn, Montana Territory (25 and 26 June 1876) 231

— Little Big Horn River, Montana Territory (25 June 1876)................................236
— Slim Buttes, Dakota Territory (9 September 1876)...243
— Bates Creek, North Fork of Powder River, Wyoming Territory
(25 November 1876)..249

— **1877** 252
— Little Muddy Creek, Montana Territory (7 May 1877)...................................256
— White Bird Canyon, Idaho Territory (17 June 1877)......................................258
— Cottonwood Ranch, near Craig's Mountain, Idaho Territory (3 July 1877).......260
— South Fork of Clearwater River, Idaho Territory (11 and 12 July 1877)............261
— Near Big Hole Basin, Montana Territory (9 and 10 August 1877)....................265
— Canyon Creek, Montana Territory (13 September 1877)..................................271
— Snake or Eagle Creek, Bear Paw Mountains, Montana Territory
(30 September 1877)..273

— **1878** 279
— **1879** 288
— Milk River, Colorado (29 September to 1 October 1879)................................297

— **1880** 306
— **1881** 318
— **1882** 328
— Big Dry Wash or Chevelon's Fork, Arizona Territory (17 July 1882)................331

— **1883** 335
— **1884** 337
— **1885** 339
— **1886** 344
— **1887** 348
— **1888** 351
— **1889** 353
— **1890** 357
— Wounded Knee Creek, South Dakota (29 December 1890)............................359

— **1891-1898**..365
— Sugar Point, Leech Lake, Minnesota (5 and 6 October 1898)........................372

— **Conclusion**..373

— **Appendix A:** Western Indian War Casualty Roster (1865-1898)............................374
— **Appendix B:** Medal of Honor (1865-1898)..394
— **Appendix C:** Brevets (1865-1898)..400
— **Appendix D:** Certificate of Merit (1865-1898)..404

— **Bibliography**..405

— INTRODUCTION —

We come, not to mourn our dead soldiers, but to praise them.
— Francis A. Walker, Citizen

On April 9, 1865, four years of bloody civil war came to an end with the surrender of the Army of Northern Virginia by Confederate General Robert E. Lee at Appomattox Court House. A month later, on May 23rd, the victorious Grand Army of the Republic celebrated victory and the end of war with a parade in the nation's capital, Washington, D.C. But even as a weary nation celebrated the end of war, violence continued in the West. Indians, emboldened over the past four years, continued to make war upon those pushing ever westward. The advance of civilization had been slowed, and in some case reversed. Even as resplendently uniformed soldiers paraded in Washington, state volunteers, men of the 11th Ohio Cavalry, the 11th Kansas Cavalry, the 7th Iowa Cavalry, and others, continued to fight and die.

To the two hundred thousand men who gave their lives on the battlefields of the American Civil War, monuments of marble and granite would rise up on the public squares of countless cities and small towns throughout the nation. Their graves would be marked, decorated as that of a soldier of the Grand Army of the Republic. Future generations would remember these men, these soldiers and their sacrifice. With the passage of each they would grow larger, their service and sacrifice more celebrated. In time, these men and their deeds would become part of the very mythology of their nation. For these men fought to free the slave or preserve the Union. Those soldiers who followed, men too called upon by their nation to serve and to sacrifice, their mission equally important in the writing of the history of that nation, would not be so remembered.

During the American Civil War and lasting until the turn of the century, the Army's principal mission in the West was policing the vast open expanses. From the open barren plains of Kansas to the rugged mountains of Northern California, from the desolate deserts of Arizona to the forested coasts of Oregon, all of those pushing irreversibly westward, often with little regard to Indians or treaties, demanded protection. The settler, the wagon master, the prospector, the surveyor, the track layer, the telegraph operator, and the stage driver all faced dangers that were all too real. So too the Indian faced dangers beyond a changing world. Their reservations were invaded by horse thieves and whiskey peddlers, or even those with murderous intent. Protecting the settler from the Indian and the Indian from the settler stood the men of the frontier Army.

In accomplishing their mission the soldier faced many obstacles, including a foe they little understood or respected, and who equally little respected or understood them. The clear distinction between combatant and non-combatant, between a "good Indian" and a "bad Indian" was blurred. The normal "rules of war" did not apply. Their Indian foe, capable of such bravery and brutality, asked for and offered no quarter. To fall wounded in battle or to be captured meant an often long, horrific, and protracted death. Those new to the frontier were admonished to "Save the last bullet for yourself". The nature of war in the West, a war in which innocents, both Indian and settler, were amongst the first victims, was new and foreign.

Their service took the men of the frontier Army far from the advantages of civilization, for the Army was at the vanguard of civilization and civilization followed. In these remote posts, located in some of the most distant areas of the continent, the soldier faced extremes of both terrain and climate, from the freezing temperatures of the Northern plains to the oppressive heat of the Southwest desert. Disease, fueled by poor nutrition, was rampant. Boredom was a constant foe, one which many men, both officers and enlisted, chose to fight with alcohol, the abuse of which was epidemic. A soldier was more likely to die by accident, snakebite, or suicide than an Indian arrow. All of these factors, coupled with low pay and little opportunity of advancement, contributed to desertion, which remained a challenge to the Army.

Even as the soldiers of the frontier Army went about the tasks expected of them, forcing the Indian on to protected and isolated reservations, they were undercut by the actions of those in Washington, D.C. The size of the Army was constantly diminished, even as the expectations upon it increased. Reservations were often established with little regard to suitability or the wishes and needs of the Indian. Corruption was rampant in the Bureau of Indian Affairs; many of its members were concerned not with the welfare of the Indian, but with their own gain. Promises made to the Indian were all too often not kept. Mismanagement and corruption forced Indians to choose between starvation and war. By failing to adequately oversee the reservations, the government guaranteed that more soldiers, more citizens, and more Indians would die. Those men who answered their nation's greatest calling were often victims not only of Indian arrow or bullet, but too of a failed Indian policy.

By 1900, those veterans of the frontier Army had reason to look back at their service with pride, for by their service, they had brought a nation, and with it civilization, to all corners of the West. In the stead of their passage, a nation would stretch from sea to sea. The Indian had been successfully confined to reservations where they might be acclimated to the world they were part of, for there was no going back to the open plains and endless herds of buffalo. The reservations had been successfully defended from those who sought another solution to the Indian. They and their nation should have celebrated their service and their sacrifice. Instead, a century later it stands largely forgotten and even dishonored. For men who did all their nation asked of them, for those men who willingly answered their nation's greatest calling, this cannot stand.

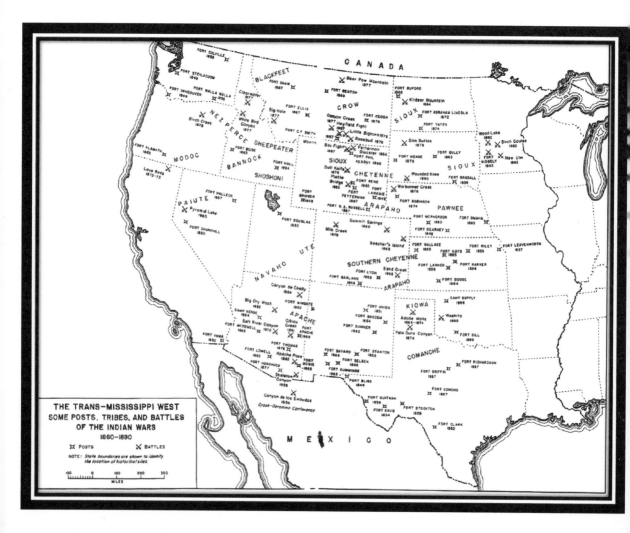

THE TRANS-MISSISSIPPI WEST
SOME POSTS, TRIBES, AND BATTLES
OF THE INDIAN WARS
1860-1890

☒ POSTS   ✗ BATTLES

NOTE: State boundaries are shown to identify the location of historical sites.

1865

"A more thankless task, a more perilous service, a more exacting test of leadership, morale and discipline no army in Christendom has ever been called upon to undertake than that which for eighty years was the lot of the little fighting force of regulars who cleared the way across the continent for the emigrant and settler. Who summer and winter stood guard over the wide frontier? Whose lives were spent in almost utter isolation? Whose lonely death was marked and mourned only by sorrowing comrade, or mayhap grief-stricken widow and children, left destitute and despairing? There never was a warfare on the face of the earth in which the soldier had so little to gain, so very much to lose... had nothing to hold the soldier stern and steadfast to the bitter end, but the solemn sense of soldier duty."

— Charles King, U.S. Army[1]

"In time of war the death of a soldier is surrounded by a certain halo, which is entirely absent in that of the poor "regular" who departs in time of peace. The former dies during a popular struggle, his death is commemorated by the poet and historian... the hands of patriotic women smooth his dying pillow; the latter, dying equally in the service of his country, his daily life a constant round of arduous duties, his end is marked by nothing of a nature to rob death of its terrors, his remains are followed to the grave by a "corporal's guard," and he dies unwept, unhonored and unsung."

— H.H. McConnell, U.S. Army[2]

---

[1] Charles King address at 1921 dinner for Order of the Indian Wars. Carter, *On the Border with Mackenzie*, 46.
[2] McConnell, *Five Years a Cavalryman*.

(0001) Operations, Canyon City Road, Oregon (January 1 to November 30, 1865)[3]
— UNKNOWN
— 1st Oregon Cavalry Detachments

(0002) Operations, near Fort Laramie, Nebraska Territory (April 1 to May 27, 1865)[4]
— UNKNOWN
— 11th Kansas Cavalry Detachment

(0003) Operations, Camp Bidwell to Antelope Creek, California (April 5 to April 18, 1865)[5]
— Captain James C. Doughty (2nd California Cavalry)
— 2nd California Cavalry Detachment Co. I

(0004) Operations, near Fort Stanton, New Mexico Territory (April 12 to 25, 1865)[6]
— 1st Lieutenant Charles M. Hubbell (1st New Mexico Cavalry)
— 1st New Mexico Cavalry Co. A and H

(0005) Operations, near Dakota City, Nebraska Territory (April 12 to 16, 1865)[7]
— Captain Zaremba Jackson (1st Nebraska Cavalry)
— 1st Nebraska Cavalry Detachment

(0006) Action, Fort Rice, Dakota Territory (April 14, 1865)[8]
— Colonel Charles A.R. Dimon (1st U.S. Volunteer Infantry)
— 1st U.S. Volunteer Infantry Detachment
— **2 KILLED**[9]
— Private John Odum (Co. B 1st U.S. Volunteer Infantry)
— Private William Hughes (Co. C 1st U.S. Volunteer Infantry)

(0007) Action, near South Fork John Day River, Oregon (April 17, 1865)[10]
— Sergeant George Garber (1st Oregon Cavalry)
— 1st Oregon Cavalry Detachment Co. G
— **1 KILLED**[11]
— Sergeant George Garber (Co. G 1st Oregon Cavalry) — d. 4-18-1865

"[Sergeant George Garber] being in advance of the train with eight men, attacked them and fell mortally wounded on the first fire… the next morning Sergeant Garber died of his wounds; an honest, upright, brave, and good soldier."
— Henry C. Small, U.S. Army[12]

(0008) Action, Dear Creek Station, Laparelle Creek, Dakota Territory (April 21, 1865)[13]
— UNKNOWN
— UNKNOWN

---

[3] Indians. *Official Records, Series 1, Volume 50, Part I*, 396-399.
[4] Indians. *Official Records, Series 1, Volume 48, Part I*, 163-164.
[5] Indians. *Official Records, Series 1, Volume 50, Part I*, 408.
[6] Indians. *Official Records, Series 1, Volume 48, Part I*, 181-182.
[7] Indians. *Official Records, Series 1, Volume 48, Part I*, 180-181.
[8] Indians. Fort Rice Post Return April 1865.
[9] Fort Rice Post Return April 1865.
[10] Indians. *Official Records, Series 1, Volume 50, Part I*, 397-398; Michno, *Deadliest Indian War*, 106.
[11] *Official Records, Series 1, Volume 50, Part I*, 398.
[12] Official Report of Captain Henry C. Small (1st Oregon Cavalry), Headquarters Canyon City Road Expedition, Cottonwood, Oregon, 21 April 1865. *Official Records, Series 1, Volume 50, Part I*, 398.
[13] Indians. *Official Roster of the Soldiers of the State of Ohio (Volume 11)*, 548, 561, 799; McChristian, *Fort Laramie*, 194; McDermott, *Circle of Fire*, 56.

— **1 KILLED**[14]
    — Private John J. Donovan (Co. E 11th Ohio Cavalry)

(0009) Operations, Dakota City to Middle Bow River, Nebraska Territory (April 22 to 27, 1865)[15]
    — Captain Zaremba Jackson (1st Nebraska Cavalry)
        — 1st Nebraska Cavalry Detachment

(0010) Operations, Deer Creek to Sage Creek, Dakota Territory (April 22 to 23, 1865)[16]
    — Major Nathaniel A. Adams (11th Kansas Cavalry)
        — 11th Kansas Cavalry Detachment

(0011) Citizens, near Fort Zarah, Kansas (April 23, 1865)[17]
    — (4) Citizens Killed

(0012) Skirmish, near Fort Zarah, Kansas (April 23, 1865)[18]
    — 1st Lieutenant Richard W. Jenkins (2nd Colorado Cavalry)
        — 2nd Colorado Cavalry Detachment

(0013) Action, Camp Marshall, Dakota Territory (April 23, 1865)[19]
    — UNKNOWN
        — UNKNOWN
    — **1 KILLED**[20]
        — Private Lenerd E. Timmons (Co. E 11th Ohio Cavalry)

(0014) Skirmish, Boggy Station, Indian Territory (April 24, 1865)[21]
    — UNKNOWN
        — Detachment of Scouts

(0015) Action, Fort Rice, Dakota Territory (April 26, 1865)[22]
    — Colonel Charles A.R. Dimon (1st U.S. Volunteers)
        — 1st U.S. Volunteer Infantry Detachment
    — **1 WOUNDED**[23]
        — Private Hiram Watson (Co. E 1st U.S. Volunteer Infantry)
          — *arrow wound, chest*

(0016) Operations, near Fort Cummings, New Mexico Territory (April 28 to May 13, 1865)[24]
    — Captain George A. Burkett (1st California Infantry)
        — 1st California Infantry Co. G

(0017) Citizens, Blue Earth Run, Minnesota (May 2, 1865)[25]
    — (4) Citizens Killed

---

[14] *Official Roster of the Soldiers of the State of Ohio (Volume 11)*, 561, 799.
[15] Indians. *Official Records, Series I, Volume 48, Part I*, 199-200; McDermott, *Circle of Fire*, 56-57.
[16] Indians. *Official Records, Series I, Volume 48, Part I*, 198-199.
[17] Indians. *Official Records, Series I, Volume 48, Part I*, 200-201.
[18] Indians. *Official Records, Series I, Volume 48, Part I*, 200-201.
[19] Indians. *Official Record of the Soldiers of the State of Ohio (Volume 11)*; McDermott, *Circle of Fire*, 57.
[20] *Official Record of the Soldiers of the State of Ohio (Volume 11)*, xyz.
[21] Confederates. *Official Records, Series I, Volume 48, Part I*, 202.
[22] Indians. *Official Records, Series I, Volume 48, Part I*, 208-209; Brown, *Galvanized Yankees*, 89; Butts, *Galvanized Yankees on the Upper Missouri*, 127-128.
[23] *Official Records, Series I, Volume 48, Part I*, 209.
[24] Indians. *Official Records, Series I, Volume 48, Part I*, 226-227.
[25] Indians. *Official Records, Series I, Volume 48, Part I*, 252-253.

(0018) Operations, Fort Churchill to Carson Lake, Nevada (May 3 to June 15, 1865)[26]
— Lt. Colonel Charles McDermit (2nd California Cavalry)
— 1st Nevada Cavalry Co. E
— 1st Nevada Infantry Co. C

(0019) Operations, Fort Laramie to Wind River, Nebraska Territory (May 3 to May 21, 1865)[27]
— Colonel Thomas Moonlight (11th Kansas Cavalry)
— 1st Nebraska Cavalry Detachment
— 7th Iowa Cavalry Detachment
—11th Ohio Cavalry Detachment

(0020) Operations, Plum Creek to Midway Station, Nebraska Territory (May 8 to 20, 1865)[28]
— Captain Thomas J. Weatherwax (1st Nebraska Cavalry)
— 1st Nebraska Cavalry Detachment

(0021) Operations, Fort Kearney to Little Blue River, Nebraska Territory (May 9 to June 2, 1865)[29]
— UNKNOWN
— 1st Nebraska Cavalry Detachment

(0022) Operations, near Fort Sumner, New Mexico Territory (May 10 to 19, 1865)[30]
— Captain Emil Fritz (1st California Cavalry)
— 1st California Cavalry Detachment

(0023) Operations, near Cottonwood, Nebraska Territory (May 12 to 14, 1865)[31]
— 1st Lieutenant Martin B. Cutler (1st Nebraska Cavalry)
— 1st Nebraska Cavalry Detachment

(0024) Skirmish, Palmetto Ranch, Texas (May 12 and 13, 1865)[32]
— Lt. Colonel David Branson (62nd U.S. Colored Infantry)
— 2nd Texas Cavalry Detachment
— 62nd U.S. Colored Infantry Detachment
— 34th Indiana Infantry Detachment

(0025) Action, Gillman's Ranch, Nebraska Territory (May 12, 1865)[33]
— UNKNOWN
— 1st Nebraska Veteran Cavalry Detachment
— **1 WOUNDED**[34]
— Private Frances W. Lohnes (Co. H 1st Nebraska Veteran Cavalry)
— *thigh and shoulder*

— Private Frances W. Lohnes (Co. H 1st Nebraska Veteran Cavalry) received MOH: Gallantry in defending government property against Indians (Gillman's Ranch, Nebraska Territory, May 12, 1865)

[26] Indians. *Official Records, Series I, Volume 50, Part I*, 409-412.
[27] Indians. *Official Records, Series I, Volume 48, Part I*, 255-256; McDermott, *Circle of Fire*, 57.
[28] Indians. *Official Records, Series I, Volume 48, Part I*, 261-262.
[29] Indians. *Official Records, Series I, Volume 48, Part I*, 280-284.
[30] Indians. *Official Records, Series I, Volume 48, Part I*, 264-265.
[31] Indians. *Official Records, Series I, Volume 48, Part I*, 269-270.
[32] Confederates. *Official Records, Series I, Volume 48, Part I*, 265-269; Hunt, *Last Battle of the Civil War*, 59-67, 172-173.
[33] Indians. *Official Records, Series I, Volume 48, Part I*, 261-262; McDermott, *Circle of Fire*, 58.
[34] McDermott, *Circle of Fire*, 58.

(0026) Action, Dan Smith's Ranch, near Julesburg, Colorado Territory (May 13, 1865)[35]
— UNKNOWN
— 1st Nebraska Veteran Cavalry Detachment
— **1 KILLED**[36]
— Commissary Sergeant Hiram Creighton (Co. A 1st Nebraska Veteran Cavalry)

(0027) Action, White's Ranch, Texas (May 13, 1865)[37]
— Lt. Colonel David Branson (62nd U.S. Colored Infantry)
— 2nd Texas Cavalry Detachment
— 62nd U.S. Colored Infantry Detachment
— 34th Indiana Infantry Detachment
— **2 KILLED**[38]
— Private Matthew F. Robinson (Co. A 2nd Texas Cavalry)
— Private John J. Williams (Co. B 34th Indiana Infantry)

— **7 WOUNDED**[39]
— Sergeant Orrin Crippen (Co. A 2nd Texas Cavalry)
— *gunshot wound, right hand, fracture, severe wound*
— Private Andrew O. Horne (2nd Texas Cavalry)
— *gunshot wound, left thigh*

— Private Wyatt Rowlett (Co. I 62nd U.S. Colored Infantry)
— *gunshot wound left groin, severe wound*
— Private Bill Redman (62nd U.S. Colored Infantry)
— *gunshot wound, severe wound*
— Sergeant Albert Crockett (62nd U.S. Colored Infantry)
— *gunshot wound, left leg, slight wound*
— Corporal Humes (62nd U.S. Colored Infantry)
— *slight wound*
— Private Ellis (62nd U.S. Colored Infantry)
— *slight wound*

— **104 CAPTURED**[40]

(0028) Skirmish, Coteau, Minnesota (May 18, 1865)[41]
— Charles Crawford (Chief Scout)
— Detachment of Indian Scouts

(0029) Action, Elm Creek Station, Nebraska Territory (May 18, 1865)[42]
— Sergeant Jefferson Fields (3rd U.S. Volunteer Infantry)
— 3rd U.S. Volunteer Infantry Detachment

[35] Indians. *Official Records, Series I, Volume 48, Part I*, 261-262; McDermott, *Circle of Fire*, 58.
[36] McDermott, *Circle of Fire*, 58.
[37] Confederates. *Official Records, Series I, Volume 48, Part I*, 265-269; Hunt, *Last Battle of the Civil War*, 68-122, 174-176.
[38] Also missing and never accounted for were Privates Augustus G. Wagoner and Henry Vance, both Co. B 2nd Texas Cavalry. Hunt, *Last Battle of the Civil War*, 125-128.
[39] Hunt, *Last Battle of the Civil War*, 125-128.
[40] Captured were (2) men 62nd U.S. Colored Infantry, (25) men 2nd Texas Cavalry and (77) men 34th Indiana Infantry. They were all paroled within days. Hunt, *Last Battle of the Civil War*, 125.
[41] Indians. *Official Records, Series I, Volume 48, Part I*, 275.
[42] Indians. *Official Records, Series I, Volume 48, Part I*, 273-274; Brown, *Galvanized Yankees*, 23-26; McDermott, *Circle of Fire*, 59.

— **2 KILLED**[43]
    — Private William J. Mers (Co. C 3rd U.S. Volunteer Infantry)
    — Enlisted Man (3rd U.S. Volunteer Infantry)

— **6 WOUNDED**[44]
    — Sergeant Jefferson Fields (Co. C 3rd U.S. Volunteer Infantry)
        — *arrow wound, left shoulder*
    — Private Peter Flynn (Co. A 3rd U.S. Volunteer Infantry)
        — *face and back*
    — Private Rinaldo Hedges (Co. C 3rd U.S. Volunteer Infantry)
    — Private John W. Twyman (Co. H 3rd U.S. Volunteer Infantry)

    — Enlisted Man (3rd U.S. Volunteer Infantry)

    — Teamster Washington Fulton (Citizen)

(0030) Operations, near Fort Kearney, Nebraska Territory (May 19 to 26, 1865)[45]
    — Captain Edwin R. Nash (Chief Scout)
        — Detachment of Indian Scouts

(0031) Operations, Sweet Water Bridge to Whiskey Gap, Dakota Territory (May 19 and 20, 1865)[46]
    — Captain James E. Greer (11th Kansas Cavalry)
        — 11th Kansas Cavalry Detachment

(0032) Operations, near Camp Plumb, Dakota Territory (May 20 to 22, 1865)[47]
    — 1st Lieutenant Jacob Van Antwerp (11th Kansas Cavalry)
        — 11th Kansas Cavalry Detachment

(0033) Operations, Three Crossings Station, Dakota Territory (May 20 to 22, 1865)[48]
    — Captain James E. Greer (11th Kansas Cavalry)
        — 11th Kansas Cavalry Detachment

(0034) Skirmish, Deer Creek Station, Dakota Territory (May 20, 1865)[49]
    — Lieutenant William B. Godfrey (11th Kansas Cavalry)
        — 11th Kansas Cavalry Detachment

(0035) Action, near Pawnee Rock, Kansas (May 20, 1865)[50]
    — UNKNOWN
        — 2nd Colorado Cavalry Detachment
    — **1 KILLED**[51]
        — Private Joseph Kuhn (Co. H 2nd Colorado Cavalry)

[43] *Official Records, Series I, Volume 48, Part I*, 273-274.
[44] *Official Records, Series I, Volume 48, Part I*, 273-274.
[45] Indians. *Official Records, Series I, Volume 48, Part I*, 279-280.
[46] Indians. *Official Records, Series I, Volume 48, Part I*, 277-278.
[47] Indians. *Official Records, Series I, Volume 48, Part I*, 287.
[48] Indians. *Official Records, Series I, Volume 48, Part I*, 286-287; Hebard and Brininstool, *Bozeman Trail (Volume 1)*, 163; McDermott, *Circle of Fire*, 59.
[49] Indians. *Official Records, Series I, Volume 48, Part I*, 286; McChristian, *Fort Laramie*, 229; McDermott, *Circle of Fire*, 59; Spring, *Caspar Collins*, 75; Vaughn, *Battle of Platte Bridge*, 14-15.
[50] Indians. *Official Records, Series I, Volume 48, Part I*, 286.
[51] *Official Records, Series I, Volume 48, Part I*, 286.

(0036) Action, near Tuscarora, Nevada (May 20, 1865)[52]
— Captain Almond B. Wells (1st Nevada Cavalry)
1st Nevada Cavalry Detachments Co. D and E
— **2 KILLED**[53]
— Private Isaac Godfrey (Co. D 1st Nevada Cavalry)
— Private James Monroe (Co. D 1st Nevada Cavalry)

— **4 WOUNDED**[54]
— Private Lewis B. Clark (1st Nevada Cavalry)
— *gunshot wound, leg*

— Enlisted Man (1st Nevada Cavalry)
— Enlisted Man (1st Nevada Cavalry)
— Enlisted Man (1st Nevada Cavalry)

(0037) Skirmish, Valley Mines, Kansas (May 22, 1865)[55]
— UNKNOWN
— UNKNOWN

(0038) Operations, Fort Ruby to Humboldt River, Nevada (May 25 to June 15, 1865)[56]
— 2nd Lieutenant John W. Tolles (1st Nevada Infantry)
— 1st Nevada Infantry Co. B
— Detachment of Indian Scouts

(0039) Operations, Platte and Sweetwater Rivers, Dakota Territory (May 26 to June 9, 1865)[57]
— UNKNOWN
— 11th Ohio Cavalry Detachment

(0040) Operations, Overland Stage Route, Platte and Sweetwater River, Nebraska Territory (May 26 to June 5, 1865)[58]
— UNKNOWN
— 11th Ohio Cavalry Detachment

(0041) Skirmish, near Plum Creek Station, Nebraska Territory (May 26 to 27, 1865)[59]
— 1st Lieutenant Morgan A. Hance (1st Nebraska Cavalry)
— 1st Nebraska Cavalry Detachment Co. A

(0042) Action, near Fort Rice, Dakota Territory (May 26, 1865)[60]
— Captain Charles A.R. Dimon (1st U.S. Volunteer Infantry)
— 1st U.S. Volunteer Infantry Detachment
— **1 KILLED**[61]
— 1st Lieutenant Benjamin S. Wilson (1st U.S. Volunteer Infantry) — d. 6-02-1865

[52] Indians. Michno, *Deadliest Indian War*, 91-92.
[53] Michno, *Deadliest Indian War*, 91-92.
[54] Michno, *Deadliest Indian War*, 91-92.
[55] Indians. *Official Records, Series I, Volume 48, Part I*, 287-288.
[56] Indians. *Official Records, Series I, Volume 50, Part I*, 412-414; Michno, *Deadliest Indian War*, 94.
[57] Indians. *Official Records, Series I, Volume 48, Part I*, 294-297.
[58] Indians. *Official Records, Series I, Volume 48, Part I*, 294-296.
[59] Indians. *Official Records, Series I, Volume 48, Part I*, 293-294.
[60] Indians. *Official Records, Series I, Volume 48, Part I*, 304; Brown, *Galvanized Yankees*, 91-92; Butts, *Galvanized Yankees on the Upper Missouri*, 130-131.
[61] *Official Records, Series I, Volume 48*, 304.

"We still have the consolation of knowing [1st Lieutenant Benjamin S. Wilson] fell in the discharge of his duties, and that he gave up his life willingly for his country, bravely contending with a common foe, and has left behind a memory we shall ever cherish, and a character for manliness, attention to duties, self-sacrifice and generosity, which few attain to...."

— E.G. Adams, Editor, *Frontier Scout*, U.S. Army[62]

(0043) Skirmish, Sweetwater Station, Nebraska Territory (May 26, 1865)[63]
 — UNKNOWN
   — 11th Ohio Cavalry Detachment

(0044) Skirmish, St. Mary's Station, Dakota Territory (May 27, 1865)[64]
 — UNKNOWN
   — 11th Ohio Cavalry Detachment

(0045) Action, Elkhorn Station, Dakota Territory (May 28, 1865)[65]
 — UNKNOWN
   — 11th Ohio Cavalry Detachment
 — 1 KILLED[66]
   — Private Alfred Curless (Co. E 11th Ohio Cavalry)

(0046) Skirmish, Austin, Nevada (May 29, 1865)[67]
 — 2nd Lieutenant John W. Tolles (1st Nevada Infantry)
   — 1st Nevada Infantry Detachment

(0047) Skirmish, Sweetwater Station, Nebraska Territory (June 1, 1865)[68]
 — UNKNOWN
   — 11th Ohio Cavalry Detachment

(0048) Skirmish, Fort Rice, Dakota Territory (June 2, 1865)[69]
 — Captain Charles A.R. Dimon (1st U.S. Volunteer Infantry)
   — 1st U.S. Volunteer Infantry Detachment

(0049) Action, Platte River Bridge, Dakota Territory (June 3, 1865)[70]
 — Lt. Colonel Preston B. Plumb (11th Kansas Cavalry)
   — 11th Kansas Cavalry Detachments Co. A and F
   — 11th Ohio Cavalry Detachment Co. G
 — 2 KILLED[71]
   — Private William T. Bonwell (Co. F 11th Kansas Cavalry)
   — Private Tilman Stahlnecker (Co. G 11th Ohio Cavalry)

[62] *Frontier Scout*, Fort Rice, Dakota Territory, 22 June 1865.
[63] Indians. *Official Records, Series I, Volume 48*, 294; McChristian, *Fort Laramie*, 229; McDermott, *Circle of Fire*, 66; Spring, *Caspar Collins*, 76.
[64] Indians. *Official Records, Series I, Volume 48*, 294; *Official Roster of the Soldiers of the State of Ohio (Volume 11)*, 548; Hibard and Brininstool, *Bozeman Trail (Volume 1)*, 161-162; Spring, *Caspar Collins*, 75-76.
[65] Indians. *Official Records, Series I, Volume 48*, 294; *Official Roster of the Soldiers of the State of Ohio (Volume 11)*, 548; McDermott, *Circle of Fire*, 67; Spring, *Caspar Collins*, 76.
[66] *Official Roster of the Soldiers of the State of Ohio (Volume 11)*, 561, 799.
[67] Indians. *Official Records, Series I, Volume 50, Part I*, 412-413.
[68] Indians. *Official Records, Series I, Volume 48, Part I*, 294.
[69] Indians. *Official Records, Series I, Volume 48, Part I*, 304-305; Brown, *Galvanized Yankees*, 93; Butts, *Galvanized Yankees on the Upper Missouri*, 131-132.
[70] Indians. *Official Records, Series I, Volume 48, Part I*, 305-306; *Official Roster of the Soldiers of the State of Ohio (Volume 11)*, 548; McDermott, *Circle of Fire*, 68; Spring, *Caspar Collins*, 77; Vaughn, *Battle of Platte Bridge*, 15.
[71] *Official Records, Series I, Volume 48, Part I*, 306; *Official Roster of the Soldiers of the State of Ohio (Volume 11)*, 569, 800; *Report of the Adjutant General of the State of Kansas (Volume 1)*, 1057.

(0050) Operations, near Fort Collins, Colorado Territory (June 4 to 10, 1865)[72]
— Captain Luther Wilson (1st Colorado Cavalry)
— 1st Colorado Cavalry Detachment

(0051) Skirmish, Fort Dodge, Kansas (June 8, 1865)[73]
— Major William F. Armstrong (2nd U.S. Volunteer Infantry)
— 2nd U.S. Volunteer Infantry Detachment

(0052) Action, Sage Creek Station, Colorado Territory (June 8, 1865)[74]
— Corporal William H. Caldwell (Co. K 11th Ohio Cavalry)
— 11th Ohio Cavalry Detachment Co. K
— **5 KILLED**[75]
— Private George Bodine (Co. K 11th Ohio Cavalry)
— Private Orlando Ducket (Co. K 11th Ohio Cavalry)
— Private Perry Stewart (Co. K 11th Ohio Cavalry)

— (2) Citizens

— **2 WOUNDED**[76]
— Corporal William H. Caldwell (Co. K 11th Ohio Cavalry)
— Private William Wilson (Co. K 11th Ohio Cavalry)

(0053) Skirmish, Chavis Creek, near Cow Creek Station, Kansas (June 9, 1865)[77]
— UNKNOWN
— 2nd U.S. Volunteer Infantry Detachment Co. K

(0054) Action, near Ash Creek, Kansas (June 11, 1865)[78]
— UNKNOWN
— 2nd Colorado Cavalry Detachment Co. K
— **2 KILLED**[79]
— Private George M. Hicks (Co. K 2nd Colorado Cavalry)
— Private Samuel J. Huestis (Co. K 2nd Colorado Cavalry)

(0055) Operations, Platte and Niobrara River, Nebraska Territory (June 12 to July 5, 1865)[80]
— Colonel Robert R. Livingston (1st Nebraska Cavalry)
— 1st Nebraska Cavalry Detachment

(0056) Action, Cow Creek Station, Kansas (June 12, 1865)[81]
— 1st Lieutenant Richard W. Jenkins (2nd Colorado Cavalry)

[72] Indians. *Official Records, Series I, Volume 48, Part I*, 307.
[73] Indians. *Official Records; Series I, Volume 48, Part I*, 308; Brown, *Galvanized Yankees*, 48-49.
[74] Indians. *Official Records, Series I, Volume 48, Part I*, 295-296; *Official Roster of the Soldiers of the State of Ohio (Volume 11)*, 548; Brown, *Galvanized Yankees*, 185; McDermott, *Circle of Fire*, 68-69; Spring, *Caspar Collins*, 77.
[75] *Official Records, Series I, Volume 48, Part I*, 295; *Official Roster of the Soldiers of the State of Ohio (Volume 11)*, 576-577, 799-800.
[76] *Official Records, Series I, Volume 48, Part I*, 295; *Official Roster of the Soldiers of the State of Ohio (Volume 11)*, 576-577.
[77] Indians. *Official Records, Series I, Volume 48, Part I*, 312-313.
[78] Indians. *Official Records, Series I, Volume 48, Part I*, 315-316.
[79] *Official Records, Series I, Volume 48, Part I*, 315-316. Official Records lists Corporal Hicks and Private Huestis, both of Co. K 2nd Colorado Cavalry.
[80] Indians. *Official Records, Series I, Volume 48, Part I*, 316-320.
[81] Indians. *Official Records, Series I, Volume 48, Part I*, 313-314.

— 2ⁿᵈ Colorado Cavalry Detachment Co. I
— 7ᵗʰ Iowa Cavalry Detachment Co. G
— **2 WOUNDED**[82]
— Private Henry C. Cutting (Co. G 7ᵗʰ Iowa Cavalry)
— *lance wound, head*
— Private William Platt (Co. G 7ᵗʰ Iowa Cavalry)
— *lance wound, head*

"I do not think that such an act of heroism has ever been displayed by six soldiers, who were surrounded by about one hundred savages, charging, arrows and lances darting from every side, and only two men slightly wounded in their heads by lances."
— Richard W. Jenkins, U.S. Army[83]

(0057) Action, Fort Dodge, Kansas (June 12, 1865)[84]
— Major William F. Armstrong (2ⁿᵈ U.S. Volunteer Infantry)
— 2ⁿᵈ U.S. Volunteer Infantry Detachment
— **2 KILLED**[85]
— Enlisted Man (2ⁿᵈ U.S. Volunteer Infantry)
— Enlisted Man (2ⁿᵈ U.S. Volunteer Infantry)

— **3 WOUNDED**[86]
— Enlisted Man (2ⁿᵈ U.S. Volunteer Infantry)
— Enlisted Man (2ⁿᵈ U.S. Volunteer Infantry)
— Enlisted Man (2ⁿᵈ U.S. Volunteer Infantry)

(0058) Skirmish, Plum Butte, Kansas (June 12, 1865)[87]
— Sergeant Cronk (2ⁿᵈ Colorado Cavalry)
— 2ⁿᵈ Colorado Cavalry Detachment
— **1 KILLED**[88]
— Private Patrick Sullivan (Co. I 2ⁿᵈ Colorado Cavalry)

(0059) Skirmish, Pawnee Rock, Kansas (June 12, 1865)[89]
— 2ⁿᵈ Lieutenant Martin Hennion (2ⁿᵈ Colorado Cavalry)
— 2ⁿᵈ Colorado Cavalry Detachment

(0060) Operations, Dun Station to Fairbank's Station, Nevada (June 13 to 26, 1865)[90]
— Lieutenant Richard A. Osmer (2ⁿᵈ California Cavalry)
— 2ⁿᵈ California Cavalry Co. B

(0061) Operations, near Camp Nichols, New Mexico Territory (June 13 to 17, 1865)[91]
— Captain Thomas A. Stombs (1ˢᵗ California Cavalry)

---

[82] *Official Records, Series I, Volume 48, Part I*, 313. Official Records identifies the men as Private Cutting and Private Platt both of Co. G 7ᵗʰ Iowa Cavalry.
[83] *Official Records, Series I, Volume 48, Part I*, 313.
[84] Indians. *Official Records, Series I, Volume 48, Part I*, 312; Brown, *Galvanized Yankees*, 49-50; Michno, *Forgotten Fights*, 212-213.
[85] "three men wounded... two captured or killed". *Official Records, Series I, Volume 48, Part I*, 312.
[86] "three men wounded ... two captured or killed". *Official Records, Series I, Volume 48, Part I*, 312.
[87] Indians. *Official Records, Series I, Volume 48, Part I*, 314.
[88] *Official Records, Series I, Volume 48, Part I*, 314.
[89] Indians. *Official Records, Series I, Volume 48, Part I*, 315.
[90] Indians. *Official Records, Series I, Volume 50, Part I*, 414-415.
[91] Indians. *Official Records, Series I, Volume 48, Part I*, 320-321.

— 1st California Cavalry Co. F

(0062) Action, Santa Fe Road, New Mexico Territory (June 14, 1865)[92]
 — Captain Thomas A. Stombs (1st California Cavalry)
  — 1st California Cavalry Co. F
— **1 KILLED**[93]
 — (1) Citizen

(0063) Action, Horse Creek, Dakota Territory (June 14, 1865)[94]
 — Captain William D. Fouts (7th Iowa Cavalry)
 — 2nd Lieutenant John Wilcox (7th Iowa Cavalry)
  — 7th Iowa Cavalry Detachments Co. A, B and D
— **4 KILLED**[95]
 — Captain William D. Fouts (Co. D 7th Iowa Cavalry)

 — Private Richard Groger (Co. D 7th Iowa Cavalry)
 — Private Edward McMahon (Co. D 7th Iowa Cavalry)
 — Private Philip Alder (Co. B 7th Iowa Cavalry)

— **4 WOUNDED**[96]
 — Private Samuel Kersey (Co. B 7th Iowa Cavalry)
 — Private Lewis Tuttle (Co. B 7th Iowa Cavalry)
 — Private James H. May (Co. D 7th Iowa Cavalry)
 — Private John Trout (Co. D 7th Iowa Cavalry)

(0064) Operations, Fort Sumner to Oscura Mountains, New Mexico Territory (June 15 to 22, 1865)[97]
 — Major Emil Fritz (1st California Cavalry)
  — 1st California Cavalry Detachment

(0065) Action, near Deer Creek Station, Dakota Territory (June 16, 1865)[98]
 — UNKNOWN
  — UNKNOWN
— **1 KILLED**[99]
 — Private Silas Hinshaw (Co. A 11th Kansas Cavalry)

(0066) Operations, near Fort Halleck, Dakota Territory (June 17 to 19, 1865)[100]
 — Captain Luther Wilson (1st Colorado Cavalry)
  — 1st Colorado Cavalry Detachment

(0067) Action, Dead Man's Fork, Dakota Territory (June 17, 1865)[101]
 — Colonel Thomas Moonlight (11th Kansas Cavalry)
  — 2nd California Cavalry Detachments Co. L and M

[92] Indians. *Official Records, Series I, Volume 48, Part I*, 320-321.
[93] *Official Records, Series I, Volume 48, Part I*, 321.
[94] Indians. *Official Records, Series I, Volume 48, Part I*, 322-324; McChristian, *Fort Laramie*, 231-235; McDermott, *Circle of Fire*, 70-73; Wagner, *Patrick Connor's War*, 43-44.
[95] *Official Records, Series I, Volume 48, Part I*, 324.
[96] *Official Records, Series I, Volume 48, Part I*, 324.
[97] Indians. *Official Records, Series I, Volume 48, Part I*, 324-325; Stanley, *Fort Craig*, 106.
[98] Indians. *Report of the Adjutant General of the State of Kansas (Volume 1)*, 1005.
[99] *Report of the Adjutant General of the State of Kansas (Volume 1)*, 1005.
[100] Indians. *Official Records, Series I, Volume 48, Part I*, 324-325; Dyer, 985.
[101] Indians. *Official Records, Series I, Volume 48, Part I*, 325-328; McChristian, *Fort Laramie*, 235-236; McDermott, *Circle of Fire*, 73-75.

— 11th Kansas Cavalry Co. L
— 16th Kansas Cavalry Detachment
— 11th Ohio Cavalry Detachment
— **2 WOUNDED**[102]
— Private Hiram Ellingsen (Co. L 2nd California Cavalry)
— *gunshot wound, head, severe wound*
— Private John M. Resoner (Co. L 2nd California Cavalry)
— *gunshot wound, foot, slight wound*

(0068) Operations, near Rock Creek Station and Seven Mile Creek, Dakota Territory (June 24 to 30, 1865)[103]
— UNKNOWN
— 1st Colorado Cavalry Detachment
— 11th Kansas Cavalry Detachment
— 11th Ohio Cavalry Detachment

(0069) Operations, Fort Bowie to Gila River, Arizona Territory (June 26 to July 6, 1865)[104]
— Lt. Colonel Clarence E. Bennett (1st California Cavalry)
— 1st California Cavalry Detachments Co. F, L and M
— Detachment of Volunteers

(0070) Action, near Red Buttes, Dakota Territory (June 26, 1865)[105]
— Lieutenant William Y. Drew (11th Kansas Cavalry)
— 11th Kansas Cavalry Detachment Co. I
— **2 WOUNDED**[106]
— Enlisted Man (11th Kansas Cavalry)
— Enlisted Man (11th Kansas Cavalry)

(0071) Action, near Fort Dodge, Kansas (June 29, 1865)[107]
— 1st Lieutenant Frederick Hubert (5th U.S. Volunteer Infantry)
— 2nd U.S. Volunteer Infantry Detachment
— **2 KILLED**[108]
— (2) Citizens

(0072) Action, Rock Creek, Dakota Territory (June 30, 1865)[109]
— UNKNOWN
— 11th Kansas Cavalry Detachment
— 11th Ohio Cavalry Detachment
— **1 KILLED**[110]
— Enlisted Man (11th Kansas Cavalry)

---

[102] *Official Records, Series I, Volume 48, Part I*, 327.
[103] Indians. *Official Records, Series I, Volume 48, Part I*, 389-390.
[104] Indians. *Official Records, Series I, Volume 50, Part I*, 415-419.
[105] Indians. *Official Records, Series I, Volume 48, Part II*, 548; McDermott, *Circle of Fire*, 78.
[106] *Official Records, Series I, Volume 48, Part II*, 548.
[107] Indians. *Official Records, Series I, Volume 48, Part I*, 390.
[108] *Official Records, Series I, Volume 48, Part I*, 390.
[109] Indians. *Official Records, Series I, Volume 48, Part I*, 390; *Official Roster of the Soldiers of the State of Ohio (Volume 11)*, 548.
[110] *Official Records, Series I, Volume 48, Part I*, 390.

(0073) Operations, Camp Lyon to Malheur River, Idaho Territory (July 2 to 13, 1865)[111]
— Lieutenant Charles Hobart (1st Oregon Cavalry)
— 1st Oregon Cavalry Detachment Co. A, B and D

(0074) Operations, Dun Glen to Fairbank's Station, Nevada (July 3 to 6, 1865)[112]
— 1st Lieutenant Richard A. Osmer (2nd California Cavalry)
— 2nd California Cavalry Co. B

(0075) Skirmish, Cottonwood Creek, Arizona Territory (July 3, 1865)[113]
— Lt. Colonel Clarence E. Bennett (1st California Cavalry)
— 1st California Cavalry Detachments Co. F, L and M

(0076) Skirmish, Cavalry Canyon, Arizona Territory (July 4, 1865)[114]
— Lt. Colonel Clarence E. Bennett (1st California Cavalry)
— 1st California Cavalry Detachments Co. F, L and M

(0077) Action, near Fort Halleck, Dakota Territory (July 5, 1865)[115]
— UNKNOWN
— UNKNOWN
— **1 KILLLED**[116]
— Commissary Sergeant Henry C. Gale (Co. A 11th Kansas Cavalry)

(0078) Action, Malheur River, Idaho Territory (July 9, 1865)[117]
— Lieutenant Charles Hobart (1st Oregon Cavalry)
— 1st Oregon Cavalry Detachments Co. A, B and D
— **2 WOUNDED**[118]
— Private Charles C. Phillips (Co. B 1st Oregon Cavalry)
— Private William R. Jones (Co. D 1st Oregon Cavalry)
— *gunshot wound, arm*

(0079) Operations, Fort Bowie to Maricopa Wells, Arizona Territory (July 10 to 21, 1865)[119]
— Lt. Colonel Clarence E. Bennett (1st California Cavalry)
— 1st California Cavalry Detachment

(0080) Action, Croton Springs, Arizona Territory (July 14, 1865)[120]
— UNKNOWN
— UNKNOWN
— **1 KILLED**[121]
— Private John L. Jones (Co. K 1st California Cavalry)

[111] Indians. *Official Records, Series I, Volume 50, Part I*, 419-421.
[112] Indians. *Official Records, Series I, Volume 50, Part I*, 414; Michno, *Deadliest Indian War*, 94-96.
[113] Indians. *Official Records, Series I, Volume 50, Part I*, 417.
[114] Indians. *Official Records, Series I, Volume 50, Part I*, 417-418; Farish, *History of Arizona (Volume 4)*, 124-125.
[115] Indians. *Report of the Adjutant General of the State of Kansas (Volume 1)*, 1001; Brown, *Galvanized Yankees*, 145; Vaughn, *Battle of Platte Bridge*, 16.
[116] *Report of the Adjutant General of the State of Kansas (Volume 1)*, 1001.
[117] Indians. *Official Records, Series I, Volume 49, Part I*, 417-421; Michno, *Deadliest Indian War*, 112.
[118] *Official Records, Series I, Volume 50, Part I*, 417-421.
[119] Indians. *Official Records, Series I, Volume 50, Part I*, 421-423; Farish, *History of Arizona (Volume 4)*, 125.
[120] Indians. Orton, *Records of California Men*, 159, 876.
[121] Orton, *Records of California Men*, 159, 876.

(0081) Skirmish, Owyhee River, Idaho Territory (July 17, 1865)[122]
— Sergeant Joseph B. Wallace (1st Oregon Cavalry)
    — 1st Oregon Cavalry Detachment

(0082) Action, Skull Valley, Arizona Territory (July 21, 1865)[123]
— UNKNOWN
    — UNKNOWN
— 2 KILLED[124]
    — Private Silas C. Long (Co. I 7th California Infantry)
    — Private John Whittig (Co. C 7th California Infantry)

(0083) Action, Huachuca Mountains, near Tubac, Arizona Territory (July 22, 1865)[125]
— Captain Hiram O. Messenger (7th California Infantry)
    — 7th California Infantry Detachment Co. E
— 2 KILLED[126]
    — Sergeant William D. Kelly (Co E 7th California Infantry)
    — Private John Henry (Co. E 7th California Infantry)

— 1 WOUNDED[127]
    — Private Abel Roe (Co. E 7th California Infantry)
        — gunshot wound, knee

(0084) Engagement, Platte River Bridge, Dakota Territory (July 26, 1865)[128]
— 2nd Lieutenant Caspar W. Collins (11th Ohio Cavalry)
    — 11th Kansas Cavalry Detachment
    — 11th Ohio Cavalry Detachment
— 5 KILLED[129]
    — 2nd Lieutenant Caspar W. Collins (Co. G 11th Ohio Cavalry)

    — Private Moses Brown (Co. H 11th Kansas Cavalry)
    — Private George W. McDonald (Co. I 11th Kansas Cavalry)
    — Private George Camp (Co. K 11th Kansas Cavalry)
    — Private Sebastian Nehring (Co. K 11th Kansas Cavalry)

— 9 WOUNDED[130]
    — Corporal Henry Grimm (Co. I 11th Kansas Cavalry)
        — arrow wound, back
    — Undercook Henry Craven (Co. I 11th Kansas Cavalry)
    — Private Henry W. Hills (Co. I 11th Kansas Cavalry)
        — severe wound
    — Private Jesse J. Playford (Co. I 11th Kansas Cavalry)
        — arrow wound, neck

[122] Indians. *Official Records, Series I, Volume 50, Part I*, 424; Michno, *Deadliest Indian War*, 113-114.
[123] Indians. Orton, *Records of California Men*, 791-792, 878, 883.
[124] Orton, *Records of California Men*, 791-792, 878, 883.
[125] Indians. Orton, *Records of California Men*, 764; Farish, *History of Arizona (Volume 4)*, 125; Hunt, *Army of the Pacific*, 143-144.
[126] Orton, *Records of California Men*, 764, 779-780, 877, 879.
[127] Orton, *Records of California Men*, 764.
[128] Indians. *Official Records, Series I, Volume 48, Part I*, 357-358; *Official Roster of the Soldiers of the State of Ohio (Volume 11)*, 548; Hebard and Brininstool, *Bozeman Trail (Volume 1)*, 167-169, 183-189; McDermott, *Circle of Fire*, 90-94; Spring, *Caspar Collins*, 81-88; Vaughn, *Battle of Platte Bridge*, 55-70.
[129] *Official Roster of the Soldiers of the State of Ohio (Volume 11)*, 567, 799; *Report of the Adjutant General of the State of Kansas (Volume 1)*, 1071; Vaughn, *Battle of Platte Bridge*, 69.
[130] *Report of the Adjutant General of the State of Kansas (Volume 1)*, 1083; Vaughn, *Battle of Platte Bridge*, 69-70.

— Private William R. Glover (Co. I 11th Kansas Cavalry)
— Private Benjamin P. Goddard (Co. I 11th Kansas Cavalry)
    — *arm*
— Private George D. May (Co. I 11th Kansas Cavalry)
— Private Harley L. Stodard (Co. I 11th Kansas Cavalry)

— Private Andrew Baker (Co. L 11th Kansas Cavalry)

"[2nd Lieutenant Caspar W. Collins] was the only son of his parents, and was a most amiable, intelligent and promising young man… Though only in his nineteenth year when he joined the regiment, he always discharged his duty with zeal and fidelity, and by his gentlemanly and kind deportment had endeared himself to all his fellow soldiers."
— Editor, *Highland Weekly News*, Citizen[131]

(0085) Action, Platte River Bridge, Dakota Territory (July 26, 1865)[132]
— 2nd Lieutenant George M. Walker (11th Kansas Cavalry)
    — 11th Kansas Cavalry Detachment
    — 11th Ohio Cavalry Detachment
— **1 KILLED**[133]
    — Private James A. Porter (Co. I 11th Kansas Cavalry)

— **1 WOUNDED**[134]
    — Farrier Joseph Hilty (Co. I 11th Kansas Cavalry)
        — *lance wound, back*

(0086) Engagement, Platte River Bridge, Dakota Territory (July 26, 1865)[135]
— Commissary Sergeant Amos J. Custard (11th Kansas Cavalry)
    — 11th Kansas Cavalry Detachments Co. H and D
— **22 KILLED**[136]
    — Corporal William H. Miller (Co. D 11th Kansas Cavalry)
    — Private William D. Gray (Co. D 11th Kansas Cavalry)
    — Private Martin Green (Co. D 11th Kansas Cavalry)
    — Private Thomas Powell (Co. D 11th Kansas Cavalry)
    — Private Edwin Summers (Co. D 11th Kansas Cavalry)
    — Private Samuel Tull (Co. D 11th Kansas Cavalry)
    — Private Jacob Zinn (Co. D 11th Kansas Cavalry)
    — Private John R. Zinn (Co. D 11th Kansas Cavalry)

    — Commissary Sergeant Amos J. Custard (Co. H 11th Kansas Cavalry)
    — Private Jesse E. Antram (Co. H 11th Kansas Cavalry)
    — Private James Ballew (Co. H 11th Kansas Cavalry)

---

[131] *Highland (Ohio) Weekly News*, 3 August 1865.
[132] Indians. *Official Records, Series I, Volume 48, Part I*, 357-358; Hebard and Brininstool, *Bozeman Trail (Volume 1)*, 168-169, 195-197; Spring, *Caspar Collins*, 88-89; McDermott, *Circle of Fire*, 94; Vaughn, *Battle of Platte Bridge*, 71-76.
[133] *Report of the Adjutant General of the State of Kansas (Volume 1)*, 1086.
[134] *Report of the Adjutant General of the State of Kansas (Volume 1)*, 1079.
[135] Indians. *Official Records, Series I, Volume 48, Part I*, 357-358; Hebard and Brininstool, *Bozeman Trail (Volume 1)*, 168-169, 189-199; McDermott, *Circle of Fire*, 94-96; Spring, *Caspar Collins*, 90-92; Vaughn, *Battle of Platte Bridge*, 77-89.
[136] *Official Roster of the Soldiers of the State of Ohio (Volume 11)*, 799; *Report of the Adjutant General of the State of Kansas (Volume 1)*, 1029, 1031, 1033, 1035, 1036, 1068, 1071, 1073, 1074, 1075, 1085; Vaughn, *Battle of Platte Bridge*, wx-yz.

— Private William Brown (Co. H 11th Kansas Cavalry)
— Private George Heil (Co. H 11th Kansas Cavalry)
— Private August Hoppe (Co. H 11th Kansas Cavalry)
— Private John Horton (Co. H 11th Kansas Cavalry)
— Private William B. Long (Co. H 11th Kansas Cavalry)
— Private Ferdinand Schaffer (Co. H 11th Kansas Cavalry)
— Private Samuel Sproul (Co. H 11th Kansas Cavalry)
— Private William West (Co. H 11th Kansas Cavalry)
— Private Thomas W. Young (Co. H 11th Kansas Cavalry)

— Private Adam Culp (Co. I 11th Kansas Cavalry)
— Private Rice B. Hamilton (Co. I 11th Ohio Cavalry)

(0087) Action, Paradise Valley, Nevada (July 26, 1865)[137]
— Sergeant James H. Stephens (2nd California Cavalry)
— Sergeant David Thomas (1st Battalion Nevada Cavalry)
    — 2nd California Cavalry Detachment Co. I
    — 1st Battalion Nevada Cavalry Detachment Co. D
    — Detachment of Volunteers
— **2 KILLED**[138]
    — Private August F. Herford (Co. I 2nd California Cavalry)

    — Joseph Warfield (Citizen)

— **4 WOUNDED**[139]
    — Private Joshua C. Murphy (Co. I 2nd California Cavalry)
    — Private Thomas J. Riehl (Co. I 2nd California Cavalry)

    — Mark Haviland (Citizen)
    — Travis (Citizen)

(0088) Action, Fort Rice, Dakota Territory (July 28, 1865)[140]
— Lt. Colonel John Pattee (6th Iowa Cavalry)
    — 1st U.S. Volunteer Infantry
    — 4th U.S. Volunteer Infantry
    — 6th Iowa Cavalry
— **2 KILLED**[141]
    — Private James Hoffman (Co. C 4th U.S. Volunteer Infantry)
    — Private James F. Hufstudler (Co. C 4th U.S. Volunteer Infantry) — d. 8-04-1865

---

[137] Indians. Orton, *Records of California Men*, 185; Michno, *Deadliest Indian War*, 99-100.
[138] Orton, *Records of California Men*, 185, 271, 876; *Deadliest Indian War*, 100.
[139] Orton, *Records of California Men*, 185, 271, 876; *Deadliest Indian War*, 100.
[140] Indians. Fort Rice Post Return July 1865; *Frontier Scout* (Fort Rice, Dakota Territory), 3 August 1865.
[141] Fort Rice Post Return July 1865; *Frontier Scout* (Fort Rice, Dakota Territory), 3 August 1865, 10 August 1865.

— **1 WOUNDED**[142]
     — Private John Blair (Co. G 6th Iowa Cavalry)
         — *saber cut, head, arrow wound, thigh, severe wound*

(0089) Action, Queens River, Nevada (August 7, 1865)[143]
     — Lt. Colonel Charles McDermit (2nd California Cavalry)
         — 2nd California Cavalry Detachment
     — **1 KILLED**[144]
         — Lt. Colonel Charles McDermit (2nd California Cavalry)

(0090) Action, near Bone Pile Creek, Dakota Territory (August 13, 1865)[145]
     — Captain George W. Williford (5th U.S. Volunteers)
         — 1st Battalion Dakota Cavalry Detachment
         — 5th U.S. Volunteer Infantry Detachment
     — **1 KILLED**[146]
         — Teamster Nathaniel D. Hedges (Citizen)

(0091) Skirmish, Powder River, Dakota Territory (August 13, 1865)[147]
     — Captain Frank North (Chief Scout)
         — Detachment of Indian Scouts

(0092) Action, near Bone Pile Creek, Dakota Territory (August 15, 1865)[148]
     — Captain George W. Williford (5th U.S. Volunteers)
         — 1st Battalion Dakota Cavalry Detachment
         — 5th U.S. Volunteer Infantry Detachment
     — **2 KILLED**[149]
         — Private Anthony Nelson (Co. B 1st Battalion Dakota Cavalry)
         — Private Orlando Sous (Co. B 1st Battalion Dakota Cavalry)

(0093) Skirmish, Powder River, Dakota Territory (August 16, 1865)[150]
     — Captain Frank North (Chief Scout)
         — Detachment of Indian Scouts

(0094) Action, near Fort Rice, Dakota Territory (August 27, 1865)[151]
     — Lt. Colonel John Pattee (6th Iowa Cavalry)
         — 1st U.S. Volunteer Infantry
         — 4th U.S. Volunteer Infantry
         — 6th Iowa Cavalry

[142] Fort Rice Post Return July 1865.

[143] Indians. Fort Churchill Post Return August 1865.

[144] Fort Churchill Post Return August 1865.

[145] Indians. *Official Records, Series I, Volume 48, Part I*, 329-389; Hafen and Hafen, *Powder River Campaigns*, 255-256, 287, 311; McDermott, *Circle of Fire*, 122-123; Wagner, *Patrick Connor's War*, 136-137.

[146] Hafen and Hafen, *Powder River Campaigns*, 255-256, 287, 311; McDermott, *Circle of Fire*, 122-123; Wagner, *Patrick Connor's War*, 136-137.

[147] Indians. *Official Records, Series I, Volume 48, Part I*, 329-389; Hafen and Hafen, *Powder River Campaigns*, 117-121, 360-362; Wagner, *Patrick Connor's War*, 109-112.

[148] Indians. *Official Records, Series I, Volume 48, Part I*, 329-389; Hafen and Hafen, *Powder River Campaigns*, 255-256, 287, 311; McDermott, *Circle of Fire*, 122-123; Wagner, *Patrick Connor's War*, 138-139.

[149] *Official Records, Series I, Volume 48, Part I*, 329-389. Orlando Sous appears on the Muster Rolls as John Rouse.

[150] Indians. *Official Records, Series I, Volume 48, Part I*, 329-389; Hafen and Hafen, *Powder River Campaigns*, 46, 117-121, 181; Van de Logt, *War Party in Blue*, 65-66; Wagner, *Patrick Connor's War*, 109-112.

[151] Indians. *Frontier Scout* (Fort Rice, Dakota Territory), 31 August 1865.

— **1 KILLED**[152]
> — Corporal Horace Jameson (Brackett's Battalion Minnesota Cavalry)

(0095) Action, Tongue River, Dakota Territory (August 29, 1865)[153]
> — Brigadier General Patrick E. Connor
>> — 2nd California Cavalry Detachment
>> — 7th Iowa Cavalry Detachment
>> — 11 Ohio Cavalry Detachment
>> — Detachment of Indian Scouts

— **1 KILLED**[154]
> — Indian Scout

— **7 WOUNDED**[155]
>> — 1st Lieutenant Oscar Jewett (1st Nevada Cavalry)
>> — *gunshot wound, left thigh, hand*
>>
>> — Enlisted Man
>> — Enlisted Man
>> — Enlisted Man
>>
>> — Sergeant Charles M. Latham (Signal Corps)
>>
>> — Private Johnson (Co. K 11th Ohio Cavalry)
>> — *arrow wound, face*
>>
>> — Enlisted Man (Co. K 11th Ohio Cavalry)

(0096) Action, near Tongue River, Dakota Territory (August 31, 1865)[156]
> — Captain Osmer F. Cole (6th Michigan Cavalry)
> — Captain Don G. Lovell (6th Michigan Cavalry)
>> — 6th Michigan Cavalry Detachment

— **1 KILLED**[157]
> — Captain Osmer F. Cole (6th Michigan Cavalry)

"[Captain Osmer F. Cole] was a young man of fine talents, brave, and genial in his manners, and was much lamented by the command...."
> — James A. Sawyer, Citizen[158]

(0097) Action, near Tongue River, Dakota Territory (September 1 to 12, 1865)[159]
> — Captain Don G. Lovell (6th Michigan Cavalry)
>> — 6th Michigan Cavalry Detachment

— **2 KILLED**[160]

---

[152] *Frontier Scout* (Fort Rice, Dakota Territory), 31 August 1865.
[153] Indians. *Official Records, Series I, Volume 48, Part I*, 329-389; *Official Roster of the Soldiers of the State of Ohio (Volume 11)*, 548; Hafen and Hafen, *Powder River Campaigns*, 46-48, 129-136, 212-214, 365-370, 373; Hebard and Brininstool, *Bozeman Trail (Volume 1)*, 255-257; McChristian, *Fort Laramie*, 244-245; McDermott, *Circle of Fire*, 112-116; Orton, *Records of California Men*, 185; Van de Logt, *War Party in Blue*, 71-73; Wagner, *Patrick Connor's War*, 156-164.
[154] Wagner, *Patrick Connor's War*, 162-163.
[155] Wagner, *Patrick Connor's War*, 162-163.
[156] Indians. *Official Records, Series I, Volume 48, Part I*, 329-389; Hafen and Hafen, *Powder River Campaigns*, 192, 260, 320-321; McDermott, *Circle of Fire*, 124; Wagner, *Patrick Connor's War*, 169.
[157] *Official Records, Series I, Volume 48, Part I*, 329-389.
[158] Official Report of James A. Sawyer. Hafen and Hafen, *Powder River Campaigns*, 260.
[159] Indians. *Official Records, Series I, Volume 48, Part I*, 329-389; Hafen and Hafen, *Powder River Campaigns*, 261, 278-279, 321-336; McDermott, *Circle of Fire*, 124-126; Wagner, *Patrick Connor's War*, 171-175.
[160] *Official Records, Series I, Volume 48, Part I*, 329-389.

— Driver James Dilleland (Citizen) — d. 09-03-1865
— Driver E.G. Merrill (Citizen)

(0098) Action, near Powder River, Montana Territory (September 1, 1865)[161]
— Colonel Nelson Cole (2nd Missouri Light Artillery)
— Lt. Colonel Samuel Walker (16th Kansas Cavalry)
    — 15th Kansas Cavalry Detachment
    — 16th Kansas Cavalry Detachment
    — 12th Missouri Cavalry Detachment
    — 2nd Missouri Light Artillery
— **5 KILLED**[162]
    — Sergeant Larkin L. Holt (Co. K 2nd Missouri Light Artillery)
    — Private Jesse Easter (Co. K 2nd Missouri Light Artillery)
    — Private Abner Garrison (Co. K 2nd Missouri Light Artillery)

    — Enlisted Man
    — Enlisted Man

— **2 WOUNDED**[163]
    — Sergeant James L. Duckett (Co. K 2nd Missouri Light Artillery)
    — Private W. Walker (Co. K 2nd Missouri Light Artillery)

(0099) Action, near Powder River, Montana Territory (September 2, 1865)[164]
— Colonel Nelson Cole (2nd Missouri Light Artillery)
— Lt. Colonel Samuel Walker (16th Kansas Cavalry)
    — 15th Kansas Cavalry Detachment
    — 16th Kansas Cavalry Detachment
    — 12th Missouri Cavalry Detachment
    — 2nd Missouri Light Artillery
— **2 KILLED**[165]
    — Enlisted Men (Co. L 2nd Missouri Light Artillery)
    — Enlisted Men (Co. L 2nd Missouri Light Artillery)

(0100) Skirmish, near Powder River, Montana Territory (September 4, 1865)[166]
— Colonel Nelson Cole (2nd Missouri Light Artillery)
— Lt. Colonel Samuel Walker (16th Kansas Cavalry)
    — 15th Kansas Cavalry Detachment
    — 16th Kansas Cavalry Detachment
    — 12th Missouri Cavalry Detachment
    — 2nd Missouri Light Artillery

[161] Indians. *Official Records, Series I, Volume 48, Part I*, 329-389; Hafen and Hafen, *Powder River Campaigns*, 73-74; Wagner, *Powder River Odyssey*, 149-153.
[162] Wagner, *Powder River Odyssey*, 265
[163] Wagner, *Powder River Odyssey*, 265.
[164] Indians. *Official Records, Series I, Volume 48, Part I*, 329-389; Wagner, *Powder River Odyssey*, 156.
[165] Wagner, *Powder River Odyssey*, 265.
[166] Indians. *Official Records, Series I, Volume 48, Part I*, 329-389; Wagner, *Powder River Odyssey*, 161-164.

(0101) Action, near Powder River, Montana Territory (September 5, 1865)[167]
— Colonel Nelson Cole (2nd Missouri Light Artillery)
— Lt. Colonel Samuel Walker (16th Kansas Cavalry)
    — 15th Kansas Cavalry Detachment
    — 16th Kansas Cavalry Detachment
    — 12th Missouri Cavalry Detachment
    — 2nd Missouri Light Artillery
— **2 KILLED**[168]
    — Private George McGully (Co. B 12th Missouri Cavalry)
    — Private James D. Morris (Co. B 12th Missouri Cavalry)

— **4 WOUNDED**[169]
    — 2nd Lieutenant Hiram L. Kelly (Co. B 2nd Missouri Light Artillery)
    — *slight wound*

    — Private Charles Elliot (Co. K 2nd Missouri Light Artillery)

    — Enlisted Man (12th Missouri Cavalry)
    — Enlisted Man (12th Missouri Cavalry)

(0102) Action, near Powder River, Montana Territory (September 7, 1865)[170]
— Colonel Nelson Cole (2nd Missouri Light Artillery)
— Lt. Colonel Samuel Walker (16th Kansas Cavalry)
    — 15th Kansas Cavalry Detachment
    — 16th Kansas Cavalry Detachment
    — 12th Missouri Cavalry Detachment
    — 2nd Missouri Light Artillery
— **1 KILLED**[171]
    — Private Elijah Bradshaw (Co. A 12th Missouri Cavalry)

(0103) Action, near Powder River, Montana Territory (September 8, 1865)[172]
— Colonel Nelson Cole (2nd Missouri Light Artillery)
— Lt. Colonel Samuel Walker (16th Kansas Cavalry)
    — 15th Kansas Cavalry Detachment
    — 16th Kansas Cavalry Detachment
    — 12th Missouri Cavalry Detachment
    — 2nd Missouri Light Artillery
— **1 KILLED**[173]
    — Private William P. Long (Co. E 16th Kansas Cavalry)

---

[167] Indians. *Official Records, Series I, Volume 48, Part I*, 329-389; Hafen and Hafen, *Powder River Campaigns*, 76-78; Wagner, *Powder River Odyssey*, 165-172.
[168] Wagner, *Powder River Odyssey*, 169, 265-266.
[169] Wagner, *Powder River Odyssey*, 170, 265.
[170] Indians. *Official Records, Series I, Volume 48, Part I*, 329-389; Wagner, *Powder River Odyssey*, 173-175.
[171] Wagner, *Powder River Odyssey*, 266.
[172] Indians. *Official Records, Series I, Volume 48, Part I*, 329-389; Dyer, 985; Hafen and Hafen, *Powder River Campaigns*, 78-80; Wagner, *Powder River Odyssey*, 177-190.
[173] *Report of the Adjutant General of the State of Kansas (Reprint)*, 546; Wagner, *Powder River Odyssey*, 265.

— **4 WOUNDED**[174]
    — Corporal John Price (Co. G 16th Kansas Cavalry)

    — Enlisted Man (16th Kansas Cavalry)
    — Enlisted Man (16th Kansas Cavalry)
    — Enlisted Man (16th Kansas Cavalry)

(0104) Action, Powder River, Montana Territory (September 10, 1865)[175]
    — Colonel Nelson Cole (2nd Missouri Light Artillery)
    — Lt. Colonel Samuel Walker (16th Kansas Cavalry)
       — 15th Kansas Cavalry Detachment
       — 16th Kansas Cavalry Detachment
       — 12th Missouri Cavalry Detachment
       — 2nd Missouri Light Artillery
— **1 WOUNDED**[176]
    — Enlisted Man (12th Missouri Cavalry)

    — *Sergeant Charles L. Thomas (Co. E 11th Ohio Cavalry) received MOH: Carried a message through a country infested with hostile Indians and saved the life of a comrade in route (Powder River Expedition, September 17, 1865).*

(0105) Action, Harney Lake, Oregon (September 23, 1865)[177]
    — Captain Loron L. Williams (1st Oregon Infantry)
       — 1st Oregon Infantry Detachments Co. F and H
— **2 WOUNDED**[178]
    — Private Alex Griffin (Co. H 1st Oregon Infantry)
       — *gunshot wound, left hip, severe wound*
    — Private Thomas Smith(Co. F 1st Oregon Infantry)
       — *gunshot wound, left foot, slight wound*

(0106) Action, Fort Laramie, Dakota Territory (September 27, 1865)[179]
    — UNKNOWN
       — UNKNOWN
— **1 KILLED**[180]
    — Private William H. Lorance (Co. L 11th Ohio Cavalry)

(0107) Action, near Alkali Station, Nebraska Territory (October 23, 1865)[181]
    — UNKNOWN
       — UNKNOWN

[174] *Report of the Adjutant General of the State of Kansas (Reprint)*, 556; Wagner, *Powder River Odyssey*, 265.
[175] Indians. *Official Records, Series I, Volume 48, Part I*, 329-389; Wagner, *Powder River Odyssey*, 194.
[176] Wagner, *Powder River Odyssey*, 195-196, 265.
[177] Indians. *Official Records, Series I, Volume 50, Part I*, 425-428.
[178] *Official Records, Series I, Volume 50, Part I*, 428.
[179] Indians. *Official Roster of the Soldiers of the State of Ohio (Volume 11)*, 799.
[180] *Official Roster of the Soldiers of the State of Ohio (Volume 11)*, 799.
[181] Indians. McDermott, *Circle of Fire*, 148-149.

— **3 KILLED**[182]
> — Private Peter Quawpaw (Co. A 16th Kansas Cavalry)

> — Enlisted Man
> — Enlisted Man

(0108) Action, near Harney Lake, Oregon (October 29, 1865)[183]
— UNKNOWN
> — UNKNOWN
— **1 KILLED**[184]
> — Private John O'Neil (Co. D 4th California Infantry)

(0109) Action, Pine Forrest, Nevada (November 17, 1865)[185]
— 1st Lieutenant Richard A. Osmer (2nd California Cavalry)
> — 2nd California Cavalry Co. B
> — Detachment of Indian Scouts
> — Detachment of Volunteers
— **1 KILLED**[186]
> — Private David W. O'Connell (Co. B 2nd California Cavalry)

— **2 WOUNDED**[187]
> — Private Alexander C. Lansdon (Co. B 2nd California Cavalry)
> — Private Moon (2nd California Cavalry)

(0110) Action, near Fort Craig, New Mexico Territory (November 22, 1865)[188]
— UNKNOWN
> — UNKNOWN
— **3 KILLED**[189]
> — Corporal George F. Edwards (Co. C 1st California Veteran Infantry)
> — Private George A. Gilmore (Co. C 1st California Veteran Infantry)
> — Private Henry Meighan (Co. C 1st California Veteran Infantry)

(0111) Action, near People's Ranch, Arizona Territory (December 11, 1865)[190]
— Captain Simon Snyder (5th U.S. Infantry)
> — 5th U.S. Infantry Detachment Co. F
— **1 KILLED**[191]
> — Sergeant Andrew Herman (Co. F 5th U.S. Infantry)

— **1 WOUNDED**[192]
> — Enlisted Man (5th U.S. Infantry)

TOTAL KILLED 1865 — 5/84/1/8 (OFFICERS, ENLISTED MEN, INDIAN SCOUTS, CITIZENS)

[182] McDermott, *Circle of Fire*, 148-149.
[183] Indians. Orton, *Record of California Men*, 628, 879.
[184] "Killed by Indians… while on a scouting expedition." Orton, *Record of California Men*, 628, 879.
[185] Indians. Orton, *Record of California Men*, 185-186, 215, 879; Michno, *Deadliest Indian War*, 133-135; Rathbun, *Nevada Military Place Names*, 86-88.
[186] Orton, *Record of California Men*, 185-186, 215, 879.
[187] Orton, *Record of California Men*, 186, 214.
[188] Indians. Orton, *Record of California Men*, 394, 396, 874, 875.
[189] Orton, *Record of California Men*, 394, 396, 397, 874, 875, 879.
[190] Indians. Chronological List, 23; Heitman (Volume 2), 426.
[191] 5th U.S. Infantry Regimental Return December 1865.
[192] Chronological List, 23.

1866

"It is unnecessary to say that the past history of our relations with the Indians has made it clear that in the settlement of new territories, the time must arrive when the Indians are so pressed upon by the whites at so many points and under such circumstances, that the security neither of white nor Indians is longer compatible with the wild life and wandering habits of the Indians. This unavoidable condition of things renders it necessary to restrict the Indian to certain limits and to buy for white settlers the districts of country thus vacated by him. This necessity has given rise to the "reservation system", to which in the future, as in the past, all Indians on the continent must be gradually subjected."

— John Pope, U.S. Army[1]

---

[1] Official Report of Major General John Pope, Fort Union, New Mexico Territory, 11 August 1866. *Annual Report of Secretary of War (1866)*, 24-25.

(0112) Action, Fish Creek, Nevada (January 12, 1866)[2]

— Captain George D. Conrad (2nd California Cavalry)
— 2nd California Cavalry Detachments Co. B and I
— **6 WOUNDED**[3]
— Private Thomas A. Duffield (Co. B 2nd California Cavalry)
— *gunshot wound, arm*
— Private John Riley (Co. B 2nd California Cavalry)
— *arrow wound, arm*
— Private Bernard Schulte (Co. B 2nd California Cavalry)
— *arrow wound, shoulder*

— Corporal Henry Biswell (Co. I 2nd California Cavalry)
— *arrow wound, head*
— Private Allen (Co. I 2nd California Cavalry)
— *arrow wound, leg*

— Jim Dunne (Indian Scout)
— *arrow wound, back*

(0113) Action, near Fort Cummings, New Mexico Territory (January 17, 1866)[4]

— Sergeant Louis Weber (1st Battalion California Veteran Infantry)
— 1st California Veteran Infantry Detachment Co. G
— **4 KILLED**[5]
— Private Thomas Daly (Co. G 1st California Veteran Infantry)
— Private Charles Devine (Co. G 1st California Veteran Infantry)
— Private Louis S. Hunter (Co. G 1st California Veteran Infantry)
— Private Thomas Ronan (Co. G 1st California Veteran Infantry)

— **1 WOUNDED**[6]
— Private Nathaniel B. Goldsberry (Co. G 1st California Veteran Infantry)
— *arrow wound, hip*

(0114) Skirmish, near Fort Grant or Cottonwood Springs, Arizona Territory (January 21, 1866)[7]

— Colonel Thomas F. Wright (2nd California Infantry)
— 2nd California Infantry Detachment

(0115) Action, near Harney Lake, Oregon (February 4, 1866)[8]

— Captain Loren L. Williams (1st Oregon Infantry)
— 1st Oregon Infantry Detachment
— **1 KILLED**[9]
— Enlisted Man (1st Oregon Infantry)

[2] Indians. Chronological List, 23; Orton, *Records of California Men*, 186-187; Michno, *Deadliest Indian War*, 136-139; Rathbun, *Nevada Military Place Names*, 23-27.
[3] Orton, *Records of California Men*, 187, 123, 216, 269; Michno, *Deadliest Indian War*, 137-138; Rathbun, *Nevada Military Place Names*, 26.
[4] Indians. Orton, *Records of California Men*, 381; Rathbun, *New Mexico Frontier Military Place Names*, 37, 131.
[5] Orton, *Records of California Men*, 414-416, 873-881; Rathbun, *New Mexico Frontier Military Place Names*, 131.
[6] Orton, *Records of California Men*, 381, 414.
[7] Indians. Chronological List, 23; Orton, *Records of California Men*, 422.
[8] Indians. *Annual Report of Secretary of War (1866)*, 37.
[9] *Annual Report of Secretary of War (1866)*, 37.

(0116) Action, Rock Canyon, Guano Valley, Nevada (February 15, 1866)[10]
    — Major Samuel P. Smith (2nd California Cavalry)
        — 2nd California Cavalry Detachments Co. D and F
    — 1 KILLED[11]
        — Private Charles Austin (Co. D 2nd California Cavalry)

    — 7 WOUNDED[12]
        — Major Samuel P. Smith (2nd California Cavalry)

        — Private Frank Belto (Co. D 2nd California Cavalry)
        — Private George Grimshaw (Co. D 2nd California Cavalry)
        — Private Edward Resler (Co. D 2nd California Cavalry)
        — Private Henrich C. Ruhman (Co. D 2nd California Cavalry)

        — Private Alexander Mills (Co. F 2nd California Cavalry)
        — Private Charles H. Smith (Co. F 2nd California Cavalry)

(0117) Action, near Jordan Creek, Oregon (February 16, 1866)[13]
    — 1st Lieutenant Silas Pepoon (1st Oregon Cavalry)
        — 14th U.S. Infantry, 2nd Battalion Co. C
        — 1st Oregon Cavalry Detachment
    — 1 WOUNDED[14]
        — Private Edward P. Miller (1st Oregon Cavalry)
        — arrow wound, side

(0118) Action, Jordan Creek, Oregon (February 23, 1866)[15]
    — Captain John H. Walker (14th U.S. Infantry)
        — 14th U.S. Infantry, 2nd Battalion Co. C and D
        — Detachment of Volunteers
    — 1 KILLED[16]
        — Corporal William Burke (Co. D 14th U.S. Infantry)

    — 1 WOUNDED[17]
        — Musician Vrooman (Co. D 14th U.S. Infantry)

"I regret to report the loss of Corporal William Burke, Company D, 2nd Battalion, 14th U.S. Infantry, killed; a brave man and a good soldier." — John H. Walker, U.S. Army[18]

(0119) Operations, between Palos Blancos and Fort McDowell, Arizona Territory (March 6 to 9, 1866)[19]
    — 1st Lieutenant Thomas Ewing (1st Arizona Infantry)

[10] Indians. Chronological List, 23; Michno, *Deadliest Indian War*, 139-140; Orton, *Records of California Men*, 187; Rathbun, *Nevada Military Place Names*, 79-81.
[11] Orton, *Records of California Men*, 187, 228, 871.
[12] Orton, *Records of California Men*, 187, 196, 227, 228, 232, 248, 249.
[13] Indians. *Annual Report of Secretary of War (1866)*, 37; Chronological List, 23; Heitman (Volume 2), 426; Michno, *Deadliest Indian War*, 144-146. Heitman lists 14th U.S. Infantry, 2nd Battalion Co. C.
[14] Michno, *Deadliest Indian War*, 146.
[15] Indians. *Annual Report of Secretary of War (1866)*, 38; Chronological List, 23; Heitman (Volume 2), 426; Michno, *Deadliest Indian War*, 146-147. Heitman lists 14th U.S. Infantry, 2nd Battalion Detachments Co. C, D.
[16] *Annual Report of Commissioner of Indian Affairs (1866)*, 188; *Annual Report of Commissioner of Indian Affairs (1867)*, 96.
[17] *Annual Report of Commissioner of Indian Affairs (1866)*, 188.
[18] Official Report of Captain John H. Walker (14th U.S. Infantry), Headquarters Superintendent District of Boise, Fort Boise, Idaho Territory, 1 March 1866. *Annual Report of Commissioner of Indian Affairs (1866)*, 188.
[19] Indians. Chronological List, 23.

— 1st Arizona Infantry Detachment

(0120) Operations, Headwaters of Salt River, Arizona Territory (March 20 to 25, 1866)[20]
— 2nd Lieutenant Primivoo Cervantes (1st Arizona Infantry)
— 1st Arizona Infantry Detachment

(0121) Action, Round Valley or Cottonwood Springs, Arizona Territory (March 22, 1866)[21]
— Captain James F. Millar (14th U.S. Infantry)
— 14th U.S. Infantry, 1st Battalion Detachment
— **5 KILLED**[22]
— Captain James F. Millar (14th U.S. Infantry)
— Assistant Surgeon Benjamin Tappan (U.S. Army)

— Private Andrew Snowdon (Co. B 14th U.S. Infantry) — d. 05-13-1866
— Private John Powell (Co. F 14th U.S. Infantry)
— Private Charles Richards (Co. F 14th U.S. Infantry)

(0122) Skirmish, South Side of Rita Mangas, New Mexico Territory (March 28, 1866)[23]
— Captain Nicholas Hodt (1st New Mexico Cavalry)
— 1st New Mexico Cavalry Detachment Co. B

(0123) Action, northeast of Pimos Village, Arizona Territory (March 31, 1866)[24]
— 1st Lieutenant John D. Walker (1st Arizona Infantry)
— 1st Arizona Infantry Co. B and C
— Detachment of Indian Scouts
— **1 KILLED**[25]
— Enlisted Man (1st Arizona Infantry) — d. 4-01-1866

— **2 WOUNDED**[26]
— Enlisted Man (1st Arizona Infantry)
— Enlisted Man (1st Arizona Infantry)

(0124) Citizens, near Sun River, Montana Territory (April 1866)[27]
— (3) Citizens Killed

(0125) Skirmish, between Fort Lincoln and Fort Whipple, Arizona Territory (April 11, 1866)[28]
— Captain Hiram S. Washburn (1st Arizona Infantry)
— 1st Arizona Infantry Co. A and E

(0126) Skirmish, Canyon de Chelly, New Mexico Territory (April 22, 1866)[29]
— Captain Edmond Butler (5th U.S. Infantry)
— 5th U.S. Infantry Detachment

[20] Indians. Chronological List, 23; Farish, *History of Arizona (Volume 4)*, 104; Thrapp, *Conquest of Apacheria*, 35.
[21] Indians. Chronological List, 23; Heitman (Volume 2), 426; Alexander, *Arizona Frontier Military Place Names*, 42-43; Altshuler, *Chains of Command*, 55; Farish, *History of Arizona (Volume 4)*, 138-139; Hamilton, Kuhn, and Ludwig, "Death in the Desert: Apache Ambush at Cottonwood Wash," *Wild West* (October 2010): 44-49. Heitman lists 14th U.S. Infantry, 1st Battalion Co. F.
[22] 14th U.S. Infantry Regimental Return April and May 1866.
[23] Indians. Chronological List, 23.
[24] Indians. Chronological List, 23; Farish, *History of Arizona (Volume 4)*, 97; Thrapp, *Conquest of Apacheria*, 35.
[25] Mortally wounded was a Pima Indian, serving in the 1st AZ Infantry. Farish, *History of Arizona (Volume 4)*, 97.
[26] Wounded were two Pima Indians, serving in the 1st AZ Infantry. Farish, *History of Arizona (Volume 4)*, 97.
[27] Indians. Killed in a series of attacks were Cass Huff, John Fitzgerald and Charles Carson. *Annual Report of Commissioner of Indian Affairs (1866)*, 202-203.
[28] Indians. Chronological List, 23; Farish, *History of Arizona (Volume 4)*, 105.
[29] Indians. Chronological List, 23.

— 1st California Cavalry Detachment
— 1st New Mexico Cavalry Detachment

(0127) Citizens, Republican River, Kansas (May 17, 1866)[30]
— (6) Citizens Killed

(0128) Action, South Canyon of Owyhee River, Idaho Territory (May 27, 1866)[31]
— Major Louis H. Marshall (14th U.S. Infantry)
— 14th U.S. Infantry, 2nd Battalion Detachments Co. A and C
— 1st Oregon Cavalry Detachment
— **1 KILLED**[32]
— Corporal William Phillips (Co. B 1st Oregon Cavalry)

(0129) Action, Stein's Mountain, Oregon (July 17, 1866)[33]
— Captain John H. Walker (14th U.S. Infantry)
— 14th U.S. Infantry, 2nd Battalion Detachment Co. C
— **1 WOUNDED**[34]
— Enlisted Man (14th U.S. Infantry)

(0130) Action, Reno Creek, Dakota Territory (July 17, 1866)[35]
— Captain Henry Haymond (18th U.S. Infantry)
— 18th U.S. Infantry, 2nd Battalion Co. D, E and F
— **1 KILLED**[36]
— Corporal Frank Livelsburger (Co. A 18th U.S. Infantry) — d. 07-19-1866

— **10 WOUNDED**[37]
— Private Thomas H. Brean (Co. E 18th U.S. Infantry)
— *arrow wound, slight wound*
— Private John A. Hartman (Co. E 18th U.S. Infantry)
— *arrow wound, severe wound*
— Private Martin B. Shirk (Co. E 18th U.S. Infantry)
— *arrow wound, slight wound*

— 7 Teamsters (Citizens)
— *arrow wounds*

(0131) Action, Snake Creek, near Malheur River, Oregon (July 19, 1866)[38]
— 1st Lieutenant Reuben F. Bernard (1st U.S. Cavalry)
— 1st U.S. Cavalry Detachment Co. I
— **1 KILLED**[39]
— Corporal William B. Lord (Co. I 1st U.S. Cavalry)

[30] Indians. *Annual Report of Commissioner of Indian Affairs (1866)*, 222; Crawford, *Kansas in the Sixties*, 267.
[31] Indians. *Annual Report of Secretary of War (1866)*, 38-39; Chronological List, 23; Heitman (Volume 2), 426; Michno, *Deadliest Indian War*, 153-154. Chronological List and Heitman both list 14th U.S. Infantry, 2nd Battalion Co. A, C.
[32] Michno, *Deadliest Indian War*, 154.
[33] Indians. Chronological List, 23; Heitman (Volume 2), 426; Michno, *Deadliest Indian War*, 161.
[34] Chronological List, 23.
[35] Indians. Chronological List, 23; Heitman (Volume 2), 426; Brown, *Fort Phil Kearny*, 77-78; Carrington, *Absaraka*, 119-120; Hagan, *Exactly in the Right Place*, 21-22; McDermott, *Red Clouds War (Volume 1)*, 94; Monnett, *Where a Hundred Soldiers*, 57-58.
[36] 18th U.S. Infantry 2nd Battalion Annual Return 1866; Register of Deaths Regular Army, 1860-1889 (Volume 1).
[37] 18th U.S. Infantry 2nd Battalion Annual Return 1866.
[38] Indians. *Annual Report of Secretary of War (1866)*, 39; Chronological List, 23; Heitman (Volume 2), 426; Michno, *Deadliest Indian War*, 161-162. Chronological List lists 18 July 1866. Heitman lists a single entry 18, 20 and 22 July 1866. Chronological List lists 1st U.S. Cavalry Co. I.
[39] *Annual Report of Secretary of War (1866)*, 39.

(0132) Action, Crazy Woman's Fork, Dakota Territory (July 21, 1866)[40]
— Captain Thomas B. Burrowes (18th U.S. Infantry)
— 18th U.S. Infantry, 2nd Battalion Detachment Co. G
— **2 KILLED**[41]
— 1st Lieutenant Napoleon H. Daniels (18th U.S. Infantry)

— Private Terrence Callery (Co. G 18th U.S. Infantry)

(0133) Action, east of Owen's Lake, California (July 29, 1866)[42]
— Corporal F.R. Neale (1st U.S. Cavalry)
— 1st U.S. Cavalry Detachment Co. D
— **1 WOUNDED**[43]
— Enlisted Man (1st U.S. Cavalry)

(0134) Action, near Camp Cady, California (July 29, 1866)[44]
— 1st Lieutenant James R. Hardenbergh (9th U.S. Infantry)
— 9th U.S. Infantry Detachment Co. D
— **3 KILLED**[45]
— Corporal John Jones (Co. D 9th U.S. Infantry)
— Private Philip Atkins (Co. D 9th U.S. Infantry)
— Private Carl Schmidt (Co. D 9th U.S. Infantry)

— **1 WOUNDED**[46]
— Enlisted Man (9th U.S. Infantry)

(0135) Action, near Fort Rice, Dakota Territory (July 31, 1866)[47]
— 1st Lieutenant James M. Marshall (13th U.S. Infantry)
— 13th U.S. Infantry, 3rd Battalion Detachments Co. B, E, F, G, and H
— **1 KILLED**[48]
— Private George W. Batrick (13th U.S. Infantry)

(0136) Action, Grape Vine Spring, Skull Valley, Arizona Territory (August 13, 1866)[49]
— 2nd Lieutenant Oscar Hutton (1st Arizona Infantry)
— 14th U.S. Infantry, 1st Battalion Co. B
— 1st Arizona Infantry Co. F
— **1 KILLED**[50]
— Enlisted Man

[40] Indians. Chronological List, 24; Heitman (Volume 2), 426; Brown, *Fort Phil Kearny*, 85-90; Hagan, *Exactly in the Right Place*, 28-31; Hebard and Brininstool, *Bozeman Trail (Volume 2)*, 90-92; Johnson, *Bloody Bozeman*, 206-209; McDermott, *Red Clouds War (Volume 1)*, 100-104; Monnett, *Where a Hundred Soldiers*, 59-63. Heitman lists 20 July 1866.
[41] 18th U.S. Infantry 2nd Battalion Annual Return 1866; Register of Deaths Regular Army, 1860-1889 (Volume 1).
[42] Indians. Chronological List, 24; Heitman (Volume 2), 426.
[43] Chronological List, 24.
[44] Indians. *Annual Report of Commissioner of Indian Affairs (1866)*, 102; Chronological List, 24; Heitman (Volume 2), 426.
[45] 9th U.S. Infantry Regimental Return August 1866.
[46] 9th U.S. Infantry Regimental Return August 1866.
[47] Indians. Chronological List, 24; Heitman (Volume 2), 426. Chronological List lists 13th U.S. Infantry Detachments.
[48] 13th U.S. Infantry Regimental Return July 1866.
[49] Indians. Chronological List, 24; Heitman (Volume 2), 426; Alexander, *Arizona Frontier Military Place Names*, 64-65, 110; Farish, *History of Arizona (Volume 4)*, 114. Heitman lists 14th U.S. Infantry, 1st Battalion Co. B.
[50] Chronological List, 24.

(0137) Skirmish, West Fork of Salt River, Arizona Territory (August 17, 1866)[51]
   — 2nd Lieutenant Oscar Hutton (1st Arizona Infantry)
      — 14th U.S. Infantry, 1st Battalion Co. B
      — 1st Arizona Infantry Co. F

(0138) Skirmish, near San Francisco Mountains, Arizona Territory (August 24, 1866)[52]
   — 2nd Lieutenant Oscar Hutton (1st Arizona Infantry)
      — 1st Arizona Infantry Co. F

(0139) Skirmish, South Fork of Owyhee River, Idaho Territory (August 26, 1866)[53]
   — Captain James C. Hunt (1st U.S. Cavalry)
      — 1st U.S. Cavalry Co. M
      — 1st Oregon Cavalry Co. B

(0140) Citizens, near Fort Mohave, Arizona Territory (September 1866)[54]
   — (6) Citizens Killed

(0141) Operations, near Fort Phil Kearny, Dakota Territory (September 10 to 16, 1866)[55]
   — Captain William Fetterman (18th U.S. Infantry)
      — 18th U.S. Infantry, 2nd Battalion Co. A, C, E and H
— 2 KILLED[56]
      — Private Orlando Gilchrist (18th U.S. Infantry) — d. 09-10-1866
      — Private Peter Johnson (18th U.S. Infantry) — d. 09-16-1866

— 2 WOUNDED[57]
      — Private John Donovan (Co. A 18th U.S. Infantry) — w. 09-13-1866
        — *arrow wound, slight wound*
      — Private Henry Rineau (Co. H 18th U.S. Infantry)
        — *arrow wound, severe wound*

(0142) Skirmish, near Camp Watson, Oregon (September 14, 1866)[58]
   — Captain Eugene M. Baker (1st U.S. Cavalry)
      — 1st U.S. Cavalry Co. I

(0143) Action, near Fort C.F. Smith, Montana Territory (September 20, 1866)[59]
   — Captain Nathaniel C. Kinney (18th U.S. Infantry)
      — 18th U.S. Infantry, 2nd Battalion Co. D and G
— 2 KILLED[60]
      — Corporal Alvah H. Staples (Co. D 18th U.S. Infantry)
      — Private Thomas Fitzpatrick (Co. D 18th U.S. Infantry)

[51] Indians. Chronological List, 24; Heitman (Volume 2), 426. Heitman lists 14th U.S. Infantry, 1st Battalion Co. B.
[52] Indians. Chronological List, 24; Alexander, *Arizona Frontier Military Place Names*, 105.
[53] Indians. Chronological List, 24; Heitman (Volume 2), 426; Michno, *Deadliest Indian War*, 166. Heitman lists 1st U.S. Cavalry Co. M.
[54] Indians. Killed were six miners. *Annual Report of Commissioner of Indian Affairs (1867)*, 160.
[55] Indians. Chronological List, 24; Heitman (Volume 2), 426; Brown, *Plainsmen of the Yellowstone*, 159-160; Carrington, *Absaraka*, 127; Hebard and Brininstool, *Bozeman Trail (Volume 1)*, 282; McDermott, *Red Clouds War (Volume 1)*, 134-136; Monnett, *Where a Hundred Soldiers Were Killed*, 73-75.
[56] 18th U.S. Infantry, 2nd Battalion Annual Return 1866.
[57] 18th U.S. Infantry, 2nd Battalion Annual Return 1866.
[58] Indians. Chronological List, 24; Heitman (Volume 2), 426; Michno, *Deadliest Indian War*, 172.
[59] Indians. Chronological List, 24; Heitman (Volume 2), 426; Hagan, *Exactly in the Right Place*, 61; McDermott, *Red Clouds War (Volume 1)*, 131-132.
[60] 18th U.S. Infantry, 2nd Battalion Annual Return 1866; Register of Deaths Regular Army, 1860-1889 (Volume 1); Otis, *Report of Surgical Cases*, 151.

(0144) Action, Tongue River, Dakota Territory (September 21, 1866)[61]
— Captain Nathaniel C. Kinney (18th U.S. Infantry)
— 18th U.S. Infantry, 2nd Battalion Co. D and G
— **1 KILLED**[62]
— Private Charles Hackett (Co. D 18th U.S. Infantry) — d. 10-04-1866

(0145) Action, Dunder and Blitzen Creek, Idaho Territory (September 28, 1866)[63]
— Captain James C. Hunt (1st U.S. Cavalry)
— 1st U.S. Cavalry Detachment Co. M
— **1 WOUNDED**[64]
— Corporal Cooke (Co. M 1st U.S. Cavalry)

(0146) Action, La Bonte Creek, Montana Territory (September 28, 1866)[65]
— Major Charles E. Norris (2nd U.S. Cavalry)
— 2nd U.S. Cavalry Co. E
— **1 WOUNDED**[66]
— Enlisted Man (2nd U.S. Cavalry)

(0147) Action, near Fort Phil Kearny, Dakota Territory (September 29, 1866)[67]
— Captain William Fetterman (18th U.S. Infantry)
— 18th U.S. Infantry, 2nd Battalion Co. A, C, E and H
— **1 KILLED**[68]
— Private Patrick D. Smith (Co. H 18th U.S. Infantry)

(0148) Action, near Fort Phil Kearny, Dakota Territory (October 3, 1866)[69]
— Colonel Henry B. Carrington (18th U.S. Infantry)
— 18th U.S. Infantry, 2nd Battalion Detachment
— **2 KILLED**[70]
— Private John Wasser (Co. A 18th U.S. Infantry)
— Private Christian Oberly (Co. A 18th U.S. Infantry)

(0149) Skirmish, Cedar Valley, Arizona Territory (October 3, 1866)[71]
— Captain George B. Sanford (1st U.S. Cavalry)
— 1st U.S. Cavalry Co. E, Detachment Co. C
— 14th U.S. Infantry, 1st Battalion Detachments Co. B, D and F

"The success obtained by [Captain George B. Sanford] is most opportune. It disproves the assertion made, and which was fast being credited in all quarters, that the regular army, however gallant and

[61] Indians. Chronological List, 24; Heitman (Volume 2), 426; Hagan, *Exactly in the Right Place*, 63-65; McDermott, *Red Clouds War (Volume 1)*, 157.
[62] 18th U.S. Infantry, 2nd Battalion Annual Return 1866.
[63] Indians. *Annual Report of Commissioner of Indian Affairs (1867)*, 98; Chronological List, 24; Heitman (Volume 2), 426.
[64] Michno, *Deadliest Indian War*, 174.
[65] Indians. Chronological List, 24; Heitman (Volume 2), 426.
[66] Chronological List, 24.
[67] Indians. Chronological List, 24; Heitman (Volume 2), 427; Brown, *Fort Phil Kearny*, 124-125; Brown, *Plainsmen of the Yellowstone*, 160; Carrington, *Absaraka*, 128, 159; Goodrich, *Scalp Dance*, 24; McDermott, *Red Clouds War (Volume 1)*, 146-147. Heitman lists 27th U.S. Infantry Co. A, C, E, H.
[68] 18th U.S. Infantry, 2nd Battalion Annual Return 1866; Register of Deaths Regular Army, 1860-1889 (Volume 1); Otis, *Report of Surgical Cases*, 146.
[69] Indians. Fort Phil Kearny Post Return October 1866; Brown, *Fort Phil Kearny*, 131-132; McDermott, *Red Clouds War (Volume 1)*, 153.
[70] 18th U.S. Infantry 2nd Battalion Annual Return 1866.
[71] Indians. *Annual Report of Secretary of War (1867)*, 116, 133, 135-136, 477; Chronological List, 24; Heitman (Volume 2), 427. Chronological List and Heitman both list 1st U.S. Cavalry Detachments Co. C, E; 14th U.S. Infantry, 1st Battalion Co. B, D, F.

effective in civilized warfare, was unequal to the duty of irregular Indian hostilities... It shows that, whenever intelligent officers apply themselves to learn the particular kind of warfare required to ensure success in the work entrusted them, the men will soon be found equal to the emergency, and, when skillfully directed and gallantly led, they will faithfully and gallantly follow!"

— Edward R. Platt, U.S. Army[72]

(0150) Action, near Trinidad, Colorado Territory (October 3, 1866)[73]
— Major Andrew J. Alexander (8th U.S. Cavalry)
— 3rd U.S. Cavalry Co. G
— Detachment of Volunteers
— **1 KILLED**[74]
— Private Lewis Brodson/ Bruxson (Co. G 3rd U.S. Cavalry)

— **3 WOUNDED**[75]
— Private John Cooley (Co. G 3rd U.S. Cavalry)
— *arrow wound, left side*
— Private William Livingston (Co. G 3rd U.S. Cavalry)
— *arrow wound, right chest*
— Private Charles Willis (Co. G 3rd U.S. Cavalry)
— *gunshot wound, right knee*

"The success which attended [Major Andrew J. Alexander's] operations against these Indians illustrates the fact that promptness to determine, bravery in the encounter, and vigor in the pursuit, in war, insure success; whereas a more timid policy might invite disaffection which would require large forces and extended operations to suppress... Indian wars are not to be desired by us. They retard the progress of a country, and impoverish the public purse; but when they do occur, it is believed that such vigorous action... tends to prevent the spread of disaffection, and furnishes the best security against the recurrence of such wars."

— Chauncey McKeever, U.S. Army[76]

(0151) Skirmish, Long Valley, Nevada (October 3, 1866)[77]
— 1st Lieutenant John F. Small (1st U.S. Cavalry)
— 1st U.S. Cavalry Co. A

(0152) Skirmish, Fort Klamath, near Sprague River, Oregon (October 5, 1866)[78]
— 1st Lieutenant Harrison B. Oatman (1st Oregon Infantry)

[72] General Orders No. 40, Captain Edward R. Platt, Acting Assistant Adjutant General, Headquarters Department of California, San Francisco, California, 1 November 1866. *Annual Report of Secretary of War (1867)*, 116.
[73] Indians. *Annual Report of Secretary of War (1867)*, 478; Chronological List, 24; Heitman (Volume 2), 427. Heitman lists 3rd U.S. Cavalry Co. G.
[74] 3rd U.S. Cavalry Regimental Return October 1866.
[75] Otis, *Report of Surgical Cases*, 79-80, 152, 157.
[76] General Orders No. 31, Chauncey McKeever, Assistant Adjutant General, Headquarters Department of the Missouri, Fort Leavenworth, Kansas, December 12, 1866. *Annual Report of Secretary of War (1867)*, 478.
[77] Indians. Chronological List, 24; Heitman (Volume 2), 427; Michno, *Deadliest Indian War*, 176; Rathbun, *Nevada Military Place Names*, 89. Heitman lists 1st U.S. Cavalry Detachment Co. A.
[78] Indians. *Annual Report of Secretary of War (1867)*, 76, 79; Chronological List, 24; Michno, *Deadliest Indian War*, 176. Chronological List lists 1st Oregon Infantry Co. I

— 1st Oregon Infantry Detachment Co. I
— Detachment of Indian Scouts

(0153) Action, Harney Lake Valley, Oregon (October 14, 1866)[79]
— Captain Eugene M. Baker (1st U.S. Cavalry)
— 1st U.S. Cavalry Co. I
— Detachment of Indian Scouts
— **1 WOUNDED**[80]
— Enlisted Man (1st U.S. Cavalry)

(0154) Action, Fort Klamath, Oregon (October 15, 1866)[81]
— 1st Lieutenant Harrison B. Oatman (1st Oregon Infantry)
— 1st Oregon Infantry Detachment Co. I
— Detachment of Indian Scouts
— **2 WOUNDED**[82]
— Enlisted Man (1st Oregon Infantry)

— Indian Scout

(0155) Action, near Pryor's Gap, Dakota Territory (October 19, 1866)[83]
— 1st Lieutenant James H. Bradley (18th U.S. Infantry)
— 18th U.S. Infantry Detachment
— **1 KILLED**[84]
— Guide James Brannon (Citizen)

— **1 WOUNDED**[85]
— Private John Brooks (Co. H 18th U.S. Infantry)

(0156) Action, North Fork of Platte River, near Fort Sedgwick, Colorado Territory (October 23, 1866)[86]
— 2nd Lieutenant George A. Armes (10th U.S. Cavalry)
— 2nd U.S. Cavalry Detachment Co. M
— **2 WOUNDED**[87]
— Enlisted Man (2nd U.S. Cavalry)
— Enlisted Man (2nd U.S. Cavalry)

"Thus, [2nd Lieutenant George A. Armes] has set a fine example to the department of overcoming difficulties that would have discouraged and stopped many without loss of credit; of bold determination to succeed, and of striking without stopping to count his enemies. And he has presented to the profession perhaps the greatest cavalry feat heretofore recorded."
— Henry G. Litchfield, U.S. Army[88]

[79] Indians. *Annual Report of Secretary of War (1867)*, 76, 80; Chronological List, 25; Heitman (Volume 2), 427; Michno, *Deadliest Indian War*, 177. Chronological List and Heitman both list 1st U.S. Cavalry Co. I
[80] "one Corporal received two arrow wounds". Camp Watson Post Return October 1866.
[81] Indians. *Annual Report of Secretary of War (1867)*, 76, 79; Chronological List, 25. Chronological List lists 1st Oregon Infantry Co. I.
[82] *Annual Report of Secretary of War (1867)*, 76.
[83] Indians. Fort Phil Kearny Post Return October 1866; Heitman (Volume 2), 427; Hagan, *Exactly in the Right Place*, 58-59. Heitman lists 27th U.S. Infantry Detachments Co. A, C, E, H.
[84] Fort Phil Kearny Post Return October 1866.
[85] Fort Phil Kearny Post Return October 1866.
[86] Indians. *Annual Report of Secretary of War (1867)*, 478; Chronological List, 25; Heitman (Volume 2), 427; Armes, *Ups and Downs*, 186-191; Rodenbough, *From Everglade to Canyon*, 435; Williams, *Fort Sedgwick*, 65-67. Chronological List lists 2nd U.S. Cavalry Co. M.
[87] Chronological List, 25.
[88] General Orders No. 20, Henry G. Litchfield, Aide-de-Camp, A.A.A.G, Headquarters Department of the Platte, Omaha, Nebraska, 12 November 1866. *Annual Report of Secretary of War (1867)*, 478.

(0157) Action, near Lake Albert, Oregon (October 26, 1866)[89]
— 1st Lieutenant John F. Small (1st U.S. Cavalry)
— 1st U.S. Cavalry Detachment Co. A
— 1st Oregon Infantry Detachment Co. I
— Detachment of Indian Scouts
— **3 WOUNDED**[90]
— Private John Sargent (Co. I 1st Oregon Infantry)

— Enlisted Man

— Indian Scout

"[1st Lieutenant Harrison B. Oatman] commanded the line on the left with commendable skill and energy, and the troops acquitted themselves throughout the engagement in the most soldierly manner. I gave particular instructions that no woman or children should be killed during the fight or afterwards, which I am happy to say was strictly observed."
— John F. Small, U.S. Army[91]

(0158) Skirmish, Malheur Country, Oregon (October 30, 1866)[92]
— Captain Richard F. O'Beirne (32nd U.S. Infantry)
— 23rd U.S. Infantry Co. E

(0159) Skirmish, Trout Creek Canyon, Oregon (November 1, 1866)[93]
— Captain John H. Walker (23rd U.S. Infantry)
— 1st U.S. Cavalry Detachment Co. H
— 23rd U.S. Infantry Detachment Co. C

(0160) Skirmish, Sierra Ancha, Arizona Territory (November 17, 1866)[94]
— Captain George B. Sanford (1st U.S. Cavalry)
— 1st U.S. Cavalry Co. E
— Detachment of Indian Scouts

"To [1st Lieutenant Camillio C.C. Carr] and the enlisted men concerned in this campaign, I am exceedingly indebted for the activity and energy they displayed. The conduct of one and all was gallant in the extreme. Their success in the previous expedition had given them confidence in themselves, and every man exerted himself to the utmost to make the campaign a success. The long preserved reputation of the 1st U.S. Cavalry will never suffer in the hands of these men."
— George B. Sanford, U.S. Army[95]

[89] Indians. *Annual Report of Secretary of War (1867)*, 80, 129, 140-141, 481-482, 484; Chronological List, 25; Heitman (Volume 2), 427; Michno, *Deadliest Indian War*, 178-179. Chronological List lists 1st U.S. Cavalry Co. A; 1st Oregon Infantry Detachment. Heitman lists 1st U.S. Cavalry Detachment Co. A.

[90] *Annual Report of Secretary of War (1867)*, 141; Michno, *Deadliest Indian War*, 179.

[91] Official Report of 1st Lieutenant John F. Small, Camp Bidwell, California, 30 October 1866. *Annual Report of Secretary of War (1867)*, 141.

[92] Indians. *Annual Report of Secretary of War (1867)*, 76, 80-81; *Annual Report of Secretary of War (1868)*, 770; Chronological List, 25; Michno, *Deadliest Indian War*, 181-182. Chronological List and Heitman both list 23rd U.S. Infantry Detachment Co. E.

[93] Indians. *Annual Report of Secretary of War (1867)*, 80, 481; Chronological List, 25; Heitman (Volume 2), 427; Michno, *Deadliest Indian War*, 181-182. Heitman lists 31 October 1866. Chronological List lists 23rd U.S. Infantry Co. C.

[94] Indians. *Annual Report of Secretary of War (1867)*, 117-119, 133, 138-139, 479-480; Chronological List, 25; Heitman (Volume 2), 427; Farish, *History of Arizona (Volume 5)*, 196-202. Chronological List and Heitman both list 1st U.S. Cavalry Co. E.

[95] Official Report of Captain George B. Sanford, Headquarters Fort McDowell, Arizona Territory, 20 November 1866. *Annual Report of Secretary of War (1867)*, 119.

(0161) Citizens, Bell's Ranch, near Prescott, Arizona Territory (November 18, 1866)[96]
— (2) Citizens Killed

(0162) Operations, John Day's River, Oregon (November 18, 1866)[97]
— 1st Lieutenant John Barry (1st U.S. Cavalry)
— 1st U.S. Cavalry Detachment Co. I

(0163) Skirmish, near Camp Watson, Oregon (December 3, 1866)[98]
— Sergeant Thomas W. Connor (1st U.S. Cavalry)
— 1st U.S. Cavalry Detachment Co. I

(0164) Skirmish, Surprise Valley, California (December 5, 1866)[99]
— Sergeant J.T. Buckley (1st U.S. Cavalry)
— 1st U.S. Cavalry Detachment Co. A

(0165) Action, Goose Creek, Dakota Territory (December 6, 1866)[100]
— 2nd Lieutenant Horatio S. Bingham (2nd U.S. Cavalry)
— 2nd U.S. Cavalry Co. C
— 18th U.S. Infantry, 2nd Battalion Detachments Co. A, C, E and H
— **2 KILLED**[101]
— 2nd Lieutenant Horatio S. Bingham (2nd U.S. Cavalry)

— Sergeant George R. Bowers (Co. E 18th U.S. Infantry)

— **2 WOUNDED**[102]
— Sergeant George Aldrich (Co. C 2nd U.S. Cavalry)
— *arrow wound, back*
— Private John Donovan (Co. A 18th U.S. Infantry)
— *gunshot wound, back*

(0166) Citizens, near Camp Wallen, Arizona Territory (December 9, 1866)[103]
— (2) Citizens Killed

(0167) Action, Grief Hill, Arizona Territory (December 11, 1866)[104]
— Captain George M. Downey (32nd U.S. Infantry)
— 14th U.S. Infantry, 1st Battalion Detachment Co. C
— **1 KILLED**[105]
— Musician Louis Franklin (Co. C 14th U.S. Infantry)

(0168) Skirmish, Pinal Mountains, near Camp Wallen, Arizona Territory (December 14, 1866)[106]
— 1st Lieutenant William H. Winters (1st U.S. Cavalry)

[96] Indians. Killed were Indian Agent George W. Leihy and his clerk H.C. Everets. *Annual Report of Commissioner of Indian Affairs (1867)*, 154, 167-168; Farish, *History of Arizona (Volume 3)*, 296-297; Farish, *History of Arizona (Volume 4)*, 137-138.

[97] Indians. *Annual Report of Secretary of War (1867)*, 77, 80; Chronological List, 25; Heitman (Volume 2), 427; Michno, *Deadliest Indian War*, 185.

[98] Indians. *Annual Report of Secretary of War (1867)*, 77, 80, 482; *Annual Report of Secretary of War (1868)*, 482, 770; Chronological List, 25; Heitman (Volume 2), 427; Michno, *Deadliest Indian War*, 186-187.

[99] Indians. *Annual Report of Secretary of War (1867)*, 129, 484; Chronological List, 25; Heitman (Volume 2), 427; Michno, *Deadliest Indian War*, 187.

[100] Indians. Chronological List, 25; Heitman (Volume 2), 427; Brown, *Fort Phil Kearny*, 159-164; Carrington, *Absaraka*, 194-197; Hebard and Brininstool, *Bozeman Trail (Volume 1)*, 299-302; Hebard and Brininstool, *Bozeman Trail (Volume 2)*, 99-100; Johnson, *Bloody Bozeman*, 232-233; McDermott, *Red Clouds War (Volume 1)*, 184-196; Monnett, *Where a Hundred Soldiers*, 106-116; Smith, *Give Me Eighty Men*, 87-93; Vaughn, *Indian Fights*, 32-42. Heitman lists 2nd U.S. Cavalry Co C; 27th U.S. Infantry Detachments Co. A, C, E, H.

[101] 18th U.S. Infantry 2nd Battalion Annual Return 1866; Register of Deaths Regular Army, 1860-1889 (Volume 1).

[102] 18th U.S. Infantry, 2nd Battalion Annual Return 1866; Otis, *Report of Surgical Cases*, 38, 156.

[103] Indians. Killed were two men named Eduartz and Shurtliff. Shurtliff was a deserter, 1st U.S. Cavalry Co. G, and was reportedly on his way to turn himself in. *Annual Report of Secretary of War (1867)*, 141-142.

— 1st U.S. Cavalry Detachment Co. G
— 14th U.S. Infantry, 3rd Battalion Detachment Co. E

(0169) Engagement, near Fort Phil Kearny, Dakota Territory (December 21, 1866)[107]
— Captain William J. Fetterman (18th U.S. Infantry)
— 2nd U.S. Cavalry Detachment Co. C
— 18th U.S. Infantry, 2nd Battalion Detachments Co. A, C, E and H
— **81 KILLED**[108]
— Captain William J. Fetterman (18th U.S. Infantry)
— Captain Frederick H. Brown (18th U.S. Infantry)
— 2nd Lieutenant George W. Grummond (18th U.S. Infantry)

— Sergeant James Baker (Co. C 2nd U.S. Cavalry)
— Corporal Thomas F. Herrigan (Co. C 2nd U.S. Cavalry)
— Corporal James Kelly (Co. C 2nd U.S. Cavalry)
— Artificer John McCarty (Co. C 2nd U.S. Cavalry)
— Bugler Adolph Metzger (Co. C 2nd U.S. Cavalry)
— Private Thomas Amberson (Co. C 2nd U.S. Cavalry)
— Private Thomas Broglin (Co. C 2nd U.S. Cavalry)
— Private William L. Bugbee (Co. C 2nd U.S. Cavalry)
— Private Patrick Clancy (Co. C 2nd U.S. Cavalry)
— Private William L. Cornog (Co. C 2nd U.S. Cavalry)
— Private Charles Cuddy (Co. C 2nd U.S. Cavalry)
— Private Robert Daniel (Co. C 2nd U.S. Cavalry)
— Private Harvey S. Deming (Co. C 2nd U.S. Cavalry)
— Private Hugh B. Doran (Co. C 2nd U.S. Cavalry)
— Private Andrew M. Fitzgerald (Co. C 2nd U.S. Cavalry)
— Private Nathan Foreman (Co. C 2nd U.S. Cavalry)
— Private John Gitter (Co. C 2nd U.S. Cavalry)
— Private Daniel Green (Co. C 2nd U.S. Cavalry)
— Private Charles Gamford (Co. C 2nd U.S. Cavalry)
— Private Ferdinand Houser (Co. C 2nd U.S. Cavalry)
— Private Frank Jones (Co. C 2nd U.S. Cavalry)
— Private James P. McGuire (Co. C 2nd U.S. Cavalry)
— Private John McColly (Co. C 2nd U.S. Cavalry)
— Private George W. Nugent (Co. C 2nd U.S. Cavalry)
— Private Franklin Payne (Co. C 2nd U.S. Cavalry)
— Private James Ryan (Co. C 2nd U.S. Cavalry)
— Private Oliver Williams (Co. C 2nd U.S. Cavalry)

— First Sergeant August Lang (Co. A 18th U.S. Infantry)
— First Sergeant Hugh Murphy (Co. A 18th U.S. Infantry)

---

[104] Indians. Chronological List, 25; Heitman (Volume 2), 427.
[105] 14th U.S. Infantry Regimental Return December 1866; Register of Deaths Regular Army, 1860-1889 (Volume 1).
[106] Indians. *Annual Report of Secretary of War (1867)*, 129, 141-144, 484; Chronological List, 25; Heitman (Volume 2), 427. Chronological List lists 1st U.S. Cavalry Co G; 14th U.S. Infantry Co E. Heitman lists 1st U.S. Cavalry Detachment Co. G; 32nd U.S. Infantry Detachment Co. E.
[107] Indians. *Annual Report of Secretary of War (1867)*, 31-32; Chronological List, 25; Heitman (Volume 2), 427; Brown, *Fort Phil Kearny*, 173-183; Carrington, *Absaraka*, 200-210; Hebard and Brininstool, *Bozeman Trail (Volume 1)*, 305-323; Hebard and Brininstool, *Bozeman Trail (Volume 2)*, 100-102; Johnson, *Bloody Bozeman*, 233-235; McDermott, *Red Clouds War (Volume 1)*, 212-229; Monnett, *Where a Hundred Soldiers*, 119-151; Smith, *Give Me Eighty Men*, 94-122; Vaughn, *Indian Fights*, 45-71. Chronological List and Heitman both list 2nd U.S. Cavalry Co. C; 27th U.S. Infantry Co. A, C, E and H.
[108] Register of Deaths Regular Army, 1860-1889 (Volume 1); Hebard and Brininstool, *Bozeman Trail (Volume 1)*, 320-323. "List of officers and men taken from United States Senate Executive Documents, 1886-7, Volume I, Executive Document No. 97, 49th Congress, 2nd Session."

— Corporal William Dute (Co. A 18th U.S. Infantry)
— Corporal Robert Lennon (Co. A 18th U.S. Infantry)
— Private Frederick Ackerman (Co. A 18th U.S. Infantry)
— Private William Betzler (Co. A 18th U.S. Infantry)
— Private Thomas Burke (Co. A 18th U.S. Infantry)
— Private Henry Buchanan (Co. A 18th U.S. Infantry)
— Private Maximilian Dihring (Co. A 18th U.S. Infantry)
— Private George E.R. Goodall (Co. A 18th U.S. Infantry)
— Private Francis S. Gordon (Co. A 18th U.S. Infantry)
— Private Michael Harten (Co. A 18th U.S. Infantry)
— Private Martin Kelly (Co. A 18th U.S. Infantry)
— Private Patrick Shannon (Co. A 18th U.S. Infantry)
— Private Charles N. Taylor (Co. A 18th U.S. Infantry)
— Private Joseph D. Thomas (Co. A 18th U.S. Infantry)
— Private David Thorrey (Co. A 18th U.S. Infantry)
— Private John Timson (Co. A 18th U.S. Infantry)
— Private Albert H. Walters (Co. A 18th U.S. Infantry)
— Private John M. Weaver (Co. A 18th U.S. Infantry)
— Private John Woodruff (Co. A 18th U.S. Infantry)

— Sergeant Francis Raymond (Co. C 18th U.S. Infantry)
— Sergeant Patrick Rooney (Co. C 18th U.S. Infantry)
— Corporal Gustave A. Bauer (Co. C 18th U.S. Infantry)
— Corporal Patrick Gallagher (Co. C 18th U.S. Infantry)
— Private Henry E. Aarons (Co. C 18th U.S. Infantry)
— Private Michael O'Garra (Co. C 18th U.S. Infantry)
— Private Jacob Rosenburg (Co. C 18th U.S. Infantry)
— Private Patrick Smith (Co. C 18th U.S. Infantry)
— Private Frank P. Sullivan (Co. C 18th U.S. Infantry)

— Sergeant William Morgan (Co. E 18th U.S. Infantry)
— Corporal John Quinn (Co. E 18th U.S. Infantry)
— Private George W. Burrell (Co. E 18th U.S. Infantry)
— Private Timothy Cullinane (Co. E 18th U.S. Infantry)
— Private John Maher (Co. E 18th U.S. Infantry)
— Private George N. Waterbury (Co. E 18th U.S. Infantry)

— First Sergeant Alexander Smith (Co. H 18th U.S. Infantry)
— Sergeant Ephraim C. Bissel (Co. H 18th U.S. Infantry)
— Corporal Frank Karston (Co. H 18th U.S. Infantry)
— Corporal George Phillips (Co. H 18th U.S. Infantry)
— Corporal Michael Sharkey (Co. H 18th U.S. Infantry)
— Private George Davis (Co. H 18th U.S. Infantry)
— Private Perry F. Doland (Co. H 18th U.S. Infantry)
— Private Asa H. Griffin (Co. H 18th U.S. Infantry)
— Private James Kean (Co. H 18th U.S. Infantry)
— Private Herman Keil (Co. H 18th U.S. Infantry)
— Private Michael Kinney (Co. H 18th U.S. Infantry)
— Private Delos Reed (Co. H 18th U.S. Infantry)

— Private Thomas M. Madden (18th U.S. Infantry)

— Isaac Fisher (Citizen)
— James S. Wheatley (Citizen)

"It is a matter of gratitude that the bodies of all who fell… were recovered, were suitably cared for and buried by their friends. That they fought bravely, and to the last, need not be said. The officers who fell had served well before, and were ever eager to strike a foe when opportunity offered. Among the non-commissioned officers who fell there were many who were the pride of the garrison. Some were veterans of many fights… and could be daunted by no danger."

— Henry B. Carrington, U.S. Army[109]

(0170) Skirmish, Fort Buford, Dakota Territory (December 24 and 25, 1866)[110]
— Captain William G. Rankin (31st U.S. Infantry)
— 13th U.S. Infantry, 3rd Battalion Co. C

(0171) Skirmish, Mud Creek, near Fort Clark, Texas (December 24, 1866)[111]
— Captain John A. Wilcox (4th U.S. Cavalry)
— 4th U.S. Cavalry Detachment Co. C

(0172) Action, Owyhee Creek, Oregon (December 26, 1866)[112]
— Lt. Colonel George Crook (23rd U.S. Infantry)
— 1st U.S. Cavalry Co. F
— Detachment of Indian Scouts
— **1 KILLED**[113]
— Sergeant Lawrence O'Toole (Co. F 1st U.S. Cavalry) — d. 12-28-1866

— *Captain David Perry (1st U.S. Cavalry) brevet promotion to Lt. Colonel for gallantry in an engagement with a large band of Indians (Owyhee River, Idaho, December 26, 1866).*

— *Captain Eugene M. Baker (1st U.S. Cavalry) brevet promotion to Colonel for zeal and energy while in command of troops against hostile Indians (1866, 1867 and 1868).*

— *Captain John J. Coppinger (23rd U.S. Infantry) brevet promotion to Colonel for zeal and energy while in command of troops operating against hostile Indians (1866, 1867 and 1868).*

TOTAL KILLED 1866 — 7/106/0/3 (Officers, Enlisted Men, Indian Scouts, Citizens)

[109] General Order No. 1, Colonel Henry B. Carrington, Fort Phil Kearny, Dakota Territory, 1 January 1867. Hebard and Brininstool, *Bozeman Trail (Volume 1)*, 320.
[110] Indians. *Annual Report of Secretary of War (1867)*, 32; Chronological List, 25; Heitman (Volume 2), 427. Heitman lists 31st U.S. Infantry Co. C.
[111] Indians. Chronological List, 25; Heitman (Volume 2), 427; Smith, *Old Army in Texas*. 147.
[112] Indians. *Annual Report of Secretary of War (1867)*, 77, 81; Chronological List, 25; Heitman (Volume 2), 427; McDermott, *Forlorn Hope*, 57; Michno, *Deadliest Indian War*, 194-195. Chronological List lists 1st U.S. Cavalry Co. F. Heitman lists 1st U.S. Cavalry Detachment Co. F.
[113] 1st U.S. Cavalry Regimental Return December 1866; *Annual Report of Secretary of War (1867)*, 77.

1867

"The whole of this region, embracing more than half of our national limits, has been and still is occupied by aboriginal Indians, whose right, in some manner or shape, has been recognized, and treaties made, for which, I believe, we are solemnly bound... Nevertheless and not withstanding those treaties, constant and unceasing conflicts have existed and continue to exist between the Indians and our people on the frontier and in the distant settlements... All these people appeal to the military for help and protection, while our hands are tied in a measure by our inability to reach the real cause of these conflicts, and by being forced to confine our efforts to meet the scattered and endless attacks and collisions of the two hostile races."

— William T. Sherman, U.S. Army[1]

---

[1] Official Report of Lieutenant General William T. Sherman, Headquarters Military Division of the Missouri, St. Louis, Missouri, 1 July 1867. *Annual Report of Secretary of War (1867)*, 65.

(0173) Action, near Fort Stanton, New Mexico Territory (January 1, 1867)[2]
— Sergeant W. Brewster (3rd U.S. Cavalry)
— 3rd U.S. Cavalry Detachment Co. H
— **1 WOUNDED**[3]
— Enlisted Man (3rd U.S. Cavalry)

(0174) Citizens, Clear Creek, Montague County, Texas (January 5 and 6, 1867)[4]
— (7) Citizens Killed

(0175) Action, Crooked River, Oregon (January 6, 1867)[5]
— Interpreter John Darragh (Citizen)
— Interpreter William C. McKay (Citizen)
— Detachment of Indian Scouts
— **1 WOUNDED**[6]
— Indian Scout
— *severe wound*

(0176) Skirmish, Owyhee River, Idaho Territory (January 8, 1867)[7]
— 1st Lieutenant Moses Harris (1st U.S. Cavalry)
— 1st U.S. Cavalry Detachment Co. M
— Detachment of Indian Scouts

(0177) Skirmish, Malheur River, Oregon (January 9, 1867)[8]
— Lt. Colonel George Crook (23rd U.S. Infantry)
— 1st U.S. Cavalry Co. F
— Detachment of Indian Scouts

(0178) Action, Eden Valley, Nevada (January 18, 1867)[9]
— 2nd Lieutenant John Lafferty (8th U.S. Cavalry)
— 8th U.S. Cavalry Detachment Co. A
— **1 WOUNDED**[10]
— Sergeant John Kelly (Co. A 8th U.S. Cavalry)
— *arrow wound, hand*

(0179) Skirmish, Nueces River, Texas (January 19, 1867)[11]
— Sergeant John Griffin (4th U.S. Cavalry)
— 4th U.S. Cavalry Detachment Co. C

(0180) Action, Owyhee River or Stein's Mountain, Oregon (January 29, 1867)[12]
— Lt. Colonel George Crook (23rd U.S. Infantry)
— 1st U.S. Cavalry Co. M
— Detachment of Indian Scouts

[2] Indians. Chronological List, 25; Heitman (Volume 2), 427 .
[3] Chronological List, 25.
[4] Indians. Killed were four men, named Leatherwood, Parkhill, Mirvusco and Fitzpatrick; a fifth unnamed man; a woman named Fitzpatrick and a child named Gegog. *Annual Report of Secretary of War (1868)*, 204, 210-211.
[5] Indians. *Annual Report of Secretary of War (1867)*, 77, 81; *Annual Report of Secretary of War (1868)*, 770; Chronological List, 25; Heitman (Volume 2), 427; Michno, *Deadliest Indian War*, 200-201.
[6] *Annual Report of Secretary of War (1867)*, 77; *Annual Report of Secretary of War (1868)*, 770.
[7] Indians. Chronological List, 25; Heitman (Volume 2), 427; Michno, *Deadliest Indian War*, 197-198.
[8] Indians. *Annual Report of Secretary of War (1867)*, 81; *Annual Report of Secretary of War (1868)*, 770; Chronological List, 25; Heitman (Volume 2), 427; Michno, *Deadliest Indian War*, 196-197. Chronological List and Heitman both list 1st U.S. Cavalry Co. F.
[9] Indians. *Annual Report of Secretary of War (1867)*, 130, 133, 145, 418, 484; Chronological List, 26; Heitman (Volume 2), 427; Michno, *Deadliest Indian War*, 208-209; Rathbun, *Nevada Military Place Names*, 60-61, 127. Chronological List lists 8th U.S. Cavalry Co. A.
[10] *Annual Report of Secretary of War (1867)*, 130.
[11] Indians. *Annual Report of Secretary of War (1867)*, 482-483; Chronological List, 26; Heitman (Volume 2), 427; Smith, *Old Army in Texas*, 147.
[12] Indians. *Annual Report of Secretary of War (1867)*, 77, 81; *Annual Report of Secretary of War (1868)*, 770; Chronological List, 26; Heitman (Volume 2), 427; Michno, *Deadliest Indian War*, 202-204. Chronological List and Heitman both list 1st U.S. Cavalry Co. M.

— **1 KILLED**[13]
— Rufus Hanson (Citizen)

— **4 WOUNDED**[14]
— Enlisted Man (1st U.S. Cavalry)
— *arrow wound, slight wound*
— Enlisted Man (1st U.S. Cavalry)
— *arrow wound, slight wound*
— Enlisted Man (1st U.S. Cavalry)
— *arrow wound, slight wound*

— John Manning (Citizen)

— *Captain James G. Hunt (1st U.S. Cavalry) brevet promotion to Lt. Colonel for gallantry in an engagement with a band of Indians (Stein's Mountains, Oregon, January 29, 1867).*

(0181) Skirmish, near Camp McDowell, Arizona Territory (January 29, 1867)[15]
— Captain George B. Sanford (1st U.S. Cavalry)
— 1st U.S. Cavalry Co. E

(0182) Action, Vicksburg Mines, Nevada (February 7, 1867)[16]
— 2nd Lieutenant George F. Foote (9th U.S. Infantry)
— 1st U.S. Cavalry Co. B
— **1 WOUNDED**[17]
— Private William Hill (Co. B 1st U.S. Cavalry)
— *severe wound*

(0183) Skirmish, Black Slate Mountains, Nevada (February 15, 1867)[18]
— 2nd Lieutenant John Lafferty (8th U.S. Cavalry)
— 8th U.S. Cavalry Detachment Co. A

— *1st Lieutenant John Lafferty (8th U.S. Cavalry) brevet promotion to Captain for gallant service in actions against Indians (Black Slate Mountains, Nevada, February 15, 1867 and Chiricahua Pass, Arizona, October 20, 1869, where he was severely wounded).*

(0184) Skirmish, Surprise Valley, California (February 16, 1867)[19]
— Captain Samuel Munson (9th U.S. Infantry)
— 1st U.S. Cavalry Detachment Co. A
— 9th U.S. Infantry Detachment Co. C

(0185) Skirmish, near Warm Springs, Idaho Territory (February 22, 1867)[20]
— Lt. Colonel George Crook (23rd U.S. Infantry)

---

[13] *Annual Report of Commissioner of Indian Affairs (1867)*, 101.
[14] 1st U.S. Cavalry Regimental Return January 1867; Michno, *Deadliest Indian* War, 203.
[15] Indians. Chronological List, 26; Heitman (Volume 2), 427.
[16] Indians. Chronological List, 26; Heitman (Volume 2), 427; Michno, *Deadliest Indian War*, 209; Rathbun, *Nevada Military Place Names*, 149.
[17] Michno, *Deadliest Indian War*, 209.
[18] Indians. *Annual Report of Secretary of War (1867)*, 131, 133, 147, 486; Chronological List, 26; Heitman (Volume 2), 427; Michno, *Deadliest Indian War*, 209-210; Rathbun, *Nevada Military Place Names*, 31-32, 127-128. Chronological List lists 8th U.S. Cavalry Co. A.
[19] Indians. *Annual Report of Secretary of War (1867)*, 130, 148-149, 484-485; Chronological List, 26; Heitman (Volume 2), 427; Michno, *Deadliest Indian War*, 210. Chronological List lists 1st U.S. Cavalry Co. A; 9th U.S. Infantry Co. C
[20] Indians. *Annual Report of Secretary of War (1867)*, 77; Chronological List, 26; Heitman (Volume 2), 427. Chronological List and Heitman both list 16 February 1867. Chronological List and Heitman both list 1st U.S. Cavalry Co. M.

— 1ˢᵗ U.S. Cavalry Co. H and M

(0186) Action, Meadow Valley, Arizona Territory (February 23, 1867)[21]
— Captain George B. Sanford (1ˢᵗ U.S. Cavalry)
— 1ˢᵗ U.S. Cavalry Co. E
— 1 KILLED[22]
— Packer (Citizen)

— 1 WOUNDED[23]
— Corporal Duncan (Co. E 1ˢᵗ U.S. Cavalry)
— *gunshot wound, leg*

(0187) Action, near Fort Reno, Dakota Territory (February 27, 1867)[24]
— UNKNOWN
— 27ᵗʰ U.S. Infantry Detachments Co. B and I
— 3 KILLED[25]
— Sergeant Samuel McClure (Co. I 27ᵗʰ U.S. Infantry)
— Private Patrick Mahan (Co. B 27ᵗʰ U.S. Infantry)
— Private James Riley (Co. I 27ᵗʰ U.S. Infantry)

— *Sergeant George Grant (Co. E 18ᵗʰ U.S. Infantry) received MOH: Bravery, energy, and perseverance, involving much suffering and privation through attacks by hostile Indians, deep snows, etc, while voluntarily carrying dispatches (Fort Phil Kearny to Fort C.F. Smith, Dakota Territory, February, 1867).*

(0188) Citizens, Date Creek, Arizona Territory (March 2, 1867)[26]
— (3) Citizens Killed

(0189) Skirmish, Arab Canyon, Coso Mountains, California (March 11, 1867)[27]
— 1ˢᵗ Sergeant F.R. Neale (1ˢᵗ U.S. Cavalry)
— 1ˢᵗ U.S. Cavalry Detachment Co. D

(0190) Action, Pecos River, Texas (March 12, 1867)[28]
— Captain John A. Wilcox (4ᵗʰ U.S. Cavalry)
— 4ᵗʰ U.S. Cavalry Detachment Co. C
— 2 KILLED[29]
— Private John McGregor (Co. C 4ᵗʰ U.S. Cavalry)

— Guide Severino Patino (Citizen)

— 2 WOUNDED[30]
— Enlisted Man (4ᵗʰ U.S. Cavalry)

[21] Indians. Chronological List, 26; Heitman (Volume 2), 427; Alexander, *Arizona Frontier Military Place Names*, 85-86; Altshuler, *Chains of Command*, 87.
[22] Altshuler, *Chains of Command*, 87.
[23] 1ˢᵗ U.S. Cavalry Regimental Return February 1867; Alexander, *Arizona Frontier Military Place Names*, 85.
[24] Indians. Chronological List, 26; Heitman (Volume 2), 427; McChristian, *Fort Laramie*, 290; McDermott, *Red Clouds War (Volume 2)*, 328. Chronological List lists "hunting party from fort".
[25] Register of Deaths Regular Army, 1860-1889 (Volume 1).
[26] Indians. Killed were two teamsters and a third man. *Annual Report of Secretary of War (1867)*, 108; Heitman (Volume 2), 427; Farish, *History of Arizona (Volume 5)*, 242-243.
[27] Indians. *Annual Report of Secretary of War (1867)*, 130, 485; Chronological List, 26; Heitman (Volume 2), 427.
[28] Indians. Chronological List, 26; Heitman (Volume 2), 427; Smith, *Old Army in Texas*, 147-148; Williams, *Texas' Last Frontier*, 69.
[29] 4ᵗʰ U.S. Cavalry Regimental Return March 1867.
[30] 4ᵗʰ U.S. Cavalry Regimental Return March 1867.

— Enlisted Man (4th U.S. Cavalry)

(0191) Citizens, near Snake River, Oregon (March 25, 1867)[31]
— (2) Citizens Killed

(0192) Skirmish, Murderer's Creek, Oregon (March 28, 1867)[32]
— 1st Lieutenant Charles B. Western (14th U.S. Infantry)
— 8th U.S. Cavalry Detachment Co. F

(0193) Skirmish, Black Mountains, Arizona Territory (April 10, 1867)[33]
— Captain James M. Williams (8th U.S. Cavalry)
— 8th U.S. Cavalry Detachments Co. B and I

(0194) Action, near Fort Lyon, Colorado Territory (April 15, 1867)[34]
— 2nd Lieutenant Matthew Berry (7th U.S. Cavalry)
— 7th U.S. Cavalry Detachment Co. C
— **1 WOUNDED**[35]
— Enlisted Man (7th U.S. Cavalry)

(0195) Skirmish, Black Mountains, Arizona Territory (April 16, 1867)[36]
— Captain James M. Williams (8th U.S. Cavalry)
— 8th U.S. Cavalry Co. I, Detachment Co. B

— *Captain James M. Williams (8th U.S. Cavalry) brevet promotion to Major for conspicuous gallantry displayed in engagements with Indians (Verde, Arizona, April 16 and 17, 1867; Yampai Valley, Arizona, June 14, 1867 and Music Mountain, Arizona, July 9, 1867).*

(0196) Action, Rio Verde, Arizona Territory (April 18, 1867)[37]
— Captain James M. Williams (8th U.S. Cavalry)
— 8th U.S. Cavalry Co. I, Detachment Co. B
— **1 KILLED**[38]
— Saddler George W. Drummond (Co. B 8th U.S. Cavalry)

— **1 WOUNDED**[39]
— Private Dollinger/ Dollemeyer (8th U.S. Cavalry)

(0197) Action, Cimarron Crossing, Kansas (April 19, 1867)[40]
— 2nd Lieutenant Matthew Berry (7th U.S. Cavalry)
— 7th U.S. Cavalry Detachments Co. B and C
— **1 WOUNDED**[41]
— Enlisted Man (7th U.S. Cavalry)

[31] Indians. Killed were stagecoach driver William Younger and a passenger named Ullman. *Annual Report of Commissioner of Indian Affairs (1867)*, 101.
[32] Indians. *Annual Report of Secretary of War (1867)*, 77, 81; *Annual Report of Secretary of War (1868)*, 770; Chronological List, 26; Heitman (Volume 2), 427; Michno, *Deadliest Indian War*, 222.
[33] Indians. Chronological List, 26; Heitman (Volume 2), 427; Alexander, *Arizona Frontier Military Place Names*, 15-16; Altshuler, *Chains of Command*, 112; Thrapp, *Conquest of Apacheria*, 57.
[34] Indians. Chronological List, 26; Barnitz, *Life in Custer's Cavalry*, 44.
[35] Chronological List, 26.
[36] Indians. *Annual Report of Secretary of War (1867)*, 130-131, 150-152, 485; Chronological List, 26; Heitman (Volume 2), 427; Altshuler, *Chains of Command*, 112; Thrapp, *Conquest of Apacheria*, 57. Chronological List and Heitman both list 8th U.S. Cavalry Co. B, I.
[37] Indians. *Annual Report of Secretary of War (1867)*, 131, 133, 152-153, 485; Chronological List, 26; Heitman (Volume 2), 427; Altshuler, *Chains of Command*, 112; Thrapp, *Conquest of Apacheria*, 58. Chronological List and Heitman both list 8th U.S. Cavalry Co. B, I.
[38] *Annual Report of Secretary of War (1867)*, 131.
[39] *Annual Report of Secretary of War (1867)*, 131, 152, 485.
[40] Indians. *Annual Report of Secretary of War (1867)*, 46; Chronological List, 26; Heitman (Volume 2), 428; Chalfant, *Hancock's War*, 219-221; Strate, *Sentinel to the Cimarron*, 42.
[41] Chronological List, 26.

(0198) Skirmish, near Fort Mojave, Arizona Territory (April 24, 1867)[42]
— Captain Samuel B.M. Young (8th U.S. Cavalry)
— 8th U.S. Cavalry Detachments Co. B and K
— 14th U.S. Infantry Co. E

(0199) Action, Fort Reno, Dakota Territory (April 26, 1867)[43]
— UNKNOWN
— 27th U.S. Infantry Co. I
— **1 KILLED**[44]
— Private Charles Ernsberger (Co. I 27th U.S. Infantry)

(0200) Skirmish, Silvie's Creek, near Lake Harney, Oregon (April 27, 1867)[45]
— 1st Lieutenant Charles B. Western (14th U.S. Infantry)
— 8th U.S. Cavalry Detachment Co. F

(0201) Action, Laparelle Creek, Dakota Territory (May 1, 1867)[46]
— Corporal A. Dolfer (2nd U.S. Cavalry)
— 2nd U.S. Cavalry Detachment Co. E
— **1 KILLED**[47]
— Private Ralston Baker (Co. E 2nd U.S. Cavalry)

(0202) Skirmish, near Camp Watson, Oregon Territory (May 5, 1867)[48]
— Sergeant J.H. Jones (1st U.S. Cavalry)
— 1st U.S. Cavalry Detachment Co. I

(0203) Skirmish, Four Peaks, Mazatzal Mountains, Arizona Territory (May 6, 1867)[49]
— UNKNOWN
— 14th U.S. Infantry Detachment Co. D

(0204) Action, Four Peaks, Mazatzal Mountains, Arizona Territory (May 6, 1867)[50]
— Captain Joseph H. Van Derslice (14th U.S. Infantry)
— 14th U.S. Infantry Detachments Co. B, D and F
— 32nd U.S. Infantry Detachments Co. A and B
— **1 WOUNDED**[51]
— Sergeant Scarfe (Co. A 32nd U.S. Infantry)
— *right arm, severe wound*

(0205) Action, near Bridger's Ferry, Dakota Territory (May 23, 1867)[52]
— UNKNOWN
— 2nd U.S. Cavalry Detachment Co. E
— **2 KILLED**[53]

[42] Indians. Chronological List, 27; Heitman (Volume 2), 428. Heitman lists 8th U.S. Cavalry Detachments Co. B, K; 14th U.S. Infantry Detachment Co. E.
[43] Indians. Chronological List, 27; Heitman (Volume 2), 428. Heitman lists 27th U.S. Infantry Detachment Co. I.
[44] 27th U.S. Infantry Annual Report 1867.
[45] Indians. *Annual Report of Secretary of War (1867)*, 78, 81; *Annual Report of Secretary of War (1868)*, 770-771; Chronological List, 27; Heitman (Volume 2), 428; Michno, *Deadliest Indian War*, 222-223.
[46] Indians. Chronological List, 27; Heitman (Volume 2), 428; McDermott, *Red Clouds War (Volume 2)*, 329.
[47] Register of Deaths Regular Army, 1860-1889 (Volume 1).
[48] Indians. Chronological List, 27; Heitman (Volume 2), 428; Michno, *Deadliest Indian War*, 225.
[49] Indians. *Annual Report of Secretary of War (1867)*, 133, 157-158; Chronological List, 27; Heitman (Volume 2), 428. Chronological List lists 14th U.S. Infantry Detachments Co. B, D, F.
[50] Indians. *Annual Report of Secretary of War (1867)*, 133, 157-158; Chronological List, 27; Heitman (Volume 2), 428. Chronological List lists 1st Lieutenant Richard C. Dubois (14th U.S. Infantry) C/O. Chronological List lists 14th U.S. Infantry Detachments Co. B, D, F; 32nd U.S. Infantry Co. A, B. Heitman lists 14th U.S. Infantry Detachment Co. D; 32nd U.S. Infantry Detachment Co. A.
[51] *Annual Report of Secretary of War (1867)*, 157.
[52] Indians. Chronological List, 27; Heitman (Volume 2), 428. Heitman lists 2nd U.S. Cavalry Co. E.
[53] 2nd U.S. Cavalry Regimental Return May 1867.

— Private Thomas Jordan (Co. E 2nd U.S. Cavalry)
— Private Patrick Killiher/ Killigher (Co. E 2nd U.S. Cavalry)

(0206) Action, Big Timbers, Kansas (May 23, 1867)[54]
— UNKNOWN
    — 3rd U.S. Infantry Detachment Co. E
— 1 WOUNDED[55]
    — Enlisted Man (3rd U.S. Infantry)

(0207) Skirmish, Pond Creek Station, Kansas (May 27, 1867)[56]
— Captain Myles W. Keogh (7th U.S. Cavalry)
    — 7th U.S. Cavalry Co. I

(0208) Action, near Fort Reno, Dakota Territory (May 30, 1867)[57]
— UNKNOWN
    — 27th U.S. Infantry Detachment Co. F
— 1 KILLED[58]
    — Private Cornelius Slagle (Co. F 27th U.S. Infantry)

(0209) Action, Beale Station, Arizona Territory (May 30, 1867)[59]
— Corporal J. Brown (14th U.S. Infantry)
    — 14th U.S. Infantry Detachment Co. E
— 1 KILLED[60]
    — (1) Citizen — d. 5-31-1867

(0210) Skirmish, near Beale Station, Arizona Territory (May 30, 1867)[61]
— 2nd Lieutenant Jonathan D. Stevenson (8th U.S. Cavalry)
    — 8th U.S. Cavalry Detachment Co. K

(0211) Action, Bluff Ranch, near Fort Aubrey, Kansas (May 31, 1867)[62]
— UNKNOWN
    — 37th U.S. Infantry Detachment Co. I
— 2 KILLED[63]
    — Private John Ferguson (Co. I 37th U.S. Infantry)
    — Private Jeremiah Rogers (Co. I 37th U.S. Infantry)

(0212) Action, Fairview, Colorado Territory (June 1, 1867)[64]
— Captain William H. Powell (4th U.S. Infantry)
    — 4th U.S. Infantry Co. G
— 1 KILLED[65]
    — Enlisted Man (4th U.S. Infantry)

[54] Indians. *Annual Report of Secretary of War (1867)*, 46; Chronological List, 27; Chalfant, *Hancock's War*, 302. Chronological List lists "stage escort".
[55] *Annual Report of Secretary of War (1867)*, 46.
[56] Indians. *Annual Report of Secretary of War (1867)*, 46; Chronological List, 27; Heitman (Volume 2), 428; Monnett, *Battle of Beecher Island*, 82.
[57] Indians. Chronological List, 27; Heitman (Volume 2), 428; Hagan, *Exactly in the Right Place*, 96-97.
[58] Register of Deaths Regular Army, 1860-1889 (Volume 1).
[59] Indians. *Annual Report of Secretary of War (1867)*, 159; Chronological List, 27; Heitman (Volume 2), 428; Altshuler, *Chains of Command*, 99; Thrapp, *Conquest of Apacheria*, 41.
[60] *Annual Report of Secretary of War (1867)*, 159.
[61] Indians. *Annual Report of Secretary of War (1867)*, 133, 159; Chronological List, 27; Heitman (Volume 2), 428; Altshuler, *Chains of Command*, 99-100; Thrapp, *Conquest of Apacheria*, 41. Chronological List lists 8th U.S. Cavalry Co. K.
[62] Indians. Chronological List, 27; Heitman (Volume 2), 428.
[63] Register of Deaths Regular Army, 1860-1889 (Volume 1); 37th U.S. Infantry Regimental Return June 1867.
[64] Indians. Chronological List, 27; Heitman (Volume 2), 428. Heitman lists 2 June 1867.
[65] Chronological List, 27.

(0213) Action, Cimarron Crossing, Kansas (June 5, 1867)[66]
    — UNKNOWN
        — 37th U.S. Infantry Detachment Co. I
    — **1 KILLED**[67]
        — Private Thomas Lennon (Co. I 37th U.S. Infantry)

(0214) Skirmish, Chalk Bluffs, Kansas (June 8, 1867)[68]
    — 1st Lieutenant Henry J. Nowlan (7th U.S. Cavalry)
        — 7th U.S. Cavalry Detachment Co. F

(0215) Action, near Big Timbers, Kansas (June 11, 1867)[69]
    — 1st Lieutenant James M. Bell (7th U.S. Cavalry)
        — 7th U.S. Cavalry Detachment Co. I
        — 3rd U.S. Infantry Detachment Co. E
    — **1 KILLED**[70]
        — Private Jacob S. Miller (Co. E 3rd U.S. Infantry)

(0216) Action, near Fort Dodge, Kansas (June 12, 1867)[71]
    — 1st Lieutenant Stanley A. Brown (3rd U.S. Infantry)
        — 7th U.S. Cavalry Co. B
    — **1 KILLED**[72]
        — Private James Spillman (Co. B 7th U.S. Cavalry) — d. 6-13-1867

(0217) Action, near Fort Phil Kearny, Dakota Territory (June 12, 1867)[73]
    — Captain David S. Gordon (2nd U.S. Cavalry)
        — 2nd U.S. Cavalry Co. D
    — **1 KILLED**[74]
        — Bugler Edwin L. Train (Co. D 2nd U.S. Cavalry)

(0218) Action, near Grinnell Springs, Kansas (June 14, 1867)[75]
    — UNKNOWN
        — 37th U.S. Infantry Detachment Co. H
    — **1 KILLED**[76]
        — Private Caspar Burkel (Co. H 37th U.S. Infantry)

(0219) Skirmish, Yampai Valley, north of Peacock Springs, Arizona Territory (June 14, 1867)[77]
    — Captain James M. Williams (8th U.S. Cavalry)
        — 8th U.S. Cavalry Co. I

    — *Captain James M. Williams (8th U.S. Cavalry) brevet promotion to Major for conspicuous gallantry displayed in engagements with Indians (Verde, Arizona, April 16 and 17, 1867; Yampai Valley, Arizona, June 14, 1867 and Music Mountain, Arizona, July 9, 1867).*

---

[66] Indians. Heitman (Volume 2), 428.
[67] 37th U.S. Infantry Regimental Return June 1867.
[68] Indians. Chronological List, 27; Heitman (Volume 2), 428.
[69] Indians. Chronological List, 27; Heitman (Volume 2), 428; Chalfant, *Hancock's War*, 304; Chandler, *Of Garryowen in Glory*, 7; Monnett, *Battle of Beecher Island*, 82.
[70] Register of Deaths Regular Army, 1860-1889 (Volume 1); 3rd U.S. Infantry Regimental Return June 1867.
[71] Indians. Chronological List, 27; Heitman (Volume 2), 428; Chandler, *Of Garryowen in Glory*, 6; Strate, *Sentinel to the Cimarron*, 44.
[72] Register of Deaths Regular Army, 1860-1889 (Volume 1); Otis, *Report of Surgical Cases*, 146. Register of Deaths lists Private Joseph Wise alias Private James Spillman.
[73] Indians. Chronological List, 27; Heitman (Volume 2), 428.
[74] Register of Deaths Regular Army, 1860-1889 (Volume 1); Otis, *Report of Surgical Cases*, 153.
[75] Indians. *Annual Report of Secretary of War (1867)*, 46; Chronological List, 27; Heitman (Volume 2), 428.
[76] 37th U.S. Infantry Regimental Return June 1867.
[77] Indians. *Annual Report of Secretary of War (1867)*, 132, 159-160, 488; Chronological List, 27; Heitman (Volume 2), 428; Altshuler, *Chains of Command*, 117; Thrapp, *Conquest of Apacheria*, 58.

(0220) Action, Big Timbers, Kansas (June 15, 1867)[78]
    — UNKNOWN
        — 3rd U.S. Infantry Co. E
    — **3 KILLED**[79]
        — Private Edwar McNally (Co. E 3rd U.S. Infantry)
        — Private Joseph Waldruff (Co. E 3rd U.S. Infantry)

        — (1) Citizen

    — **3 WOUNDED**[80]
        — Enlisted Man (3rd U.S. Infantry)

        — (2) Citizens

(0221) Skirmish, Gallinas Mountains, New Mexico Territory (June 16, 1867)[81]
    — Sergeant R. Harrington (3rd U.S. Cavalry)
        — 3rd U.S. Cavalry Detachment Co. H

(0222) Skirmish, near Stein's Mountain, Oregon (June 20, 1867)[82]
    — Archie McIntosh (Chief Scout)
        — Detachment of Indian Scouts

(0223) Skirmish, Foot of Black Hills, Union Pacific Railroad, Nebraska (June 20, 1867)[83]
    — Major Frank North (Chief Scout)
        — Detachment of Indian Scouts

(0224) Action, near Fort Wallace, Kansas (June 21, 1867)[84]
    — 1st Lieutenant James M. Bell (7th U.S. Cavalry)
        — 7th U.S. Cavalry Detachments Co. G and I
    — **2 KILLED**[85]
        — Sergeant William H. Dummel (Co. G 7th U.S. Cavalry)
        — Private Frederick A. Bacon (Co. I 7th U.S. Cavalry)

    — **2 WOUNDED**[86]
        — Enlisted Man (7th U.S. Cavalry)
        — Enlisted Man (7th U.S. Cavalry)

(0225) Skirmish, near Calabases, Arizona Territory (June 21, 1867)[87]
    — 2nd Lieutenant Edward J. Harrington (1st U.S. Cavalry)
        — 1st U.S. Cavalry Detachment Co. G
        — 32nd U.S. Infantry Detachment Co. E

[78] Indians. Chronological List, 27; Heitman (Volume 2), 428; Chalfant, *Hancock's War*, 304; Goodrich, *Scalp Dance*, 62; Monnett, *Battle of Beecher Island*, 82. Heitman lists 3rd U.S. Infantry Detachment Co. E.
[79] Register of Deaths Regular Army, 1860-1889 (Volume 1); 3rd U.S. Infantry Regimental Return June 1867.
[80] Chronological List, 27.
[81] Indians. *Annual Report of Secretary of War (1867)*, 46; Chronological List, 27; Heitman (Volume 2), 428.
[82] Indians. *Annual Report of Secretary of War (1867)*, 78; *Annual Report of Secretary of War (1868)*, 771; Chronological List, 27; Heitman (Volume 2), 428; Michno, *Deadliest Indian War*, 226. Chronological List and Heitman both list 19 June 1867.
[83] Indians. Chronological List, 27; Heitman (Volume 2), 428.
[84] Indians. *Annual Report of Secretary of War (1867)*, 46; Chronological List, 27; Heitman (Volume 2), 428; Barnitz, *Life in Custer's Cavalry*, 63-64; Chandler, *Of Garryowen in Glory*, 425; Monnett, *Battle of Beecher Island*, 82. Heitman lists 7th U.S. Cavalry Detachments Co. G, I; 37th U.S. Infantry Detachment Co. D.
[85] Register of Deaths Regular Army, 1860-1889 (Volume 1).
[86] Chronological List, 27.
[87] Indians. *Annual Report of Secretary of War (1867)*, 132-133, 161-162, 488; Chronological List, 28; Heitman (Volume 2), 428. Chronological List lists 1st U.S. Cavalry Detachment Co. G; 32nd U.S. Infantry Co. E.

(0226) Action, Goose Creek Station, Colorado Territory (June 22, 1867)[88]
　　— Sergeant J.C. McDonald (37th U.S. Infantry)
　　　　— 37th U.S. Infantry Detachment Co. D
　— **2 WOUNDED**[89]
　　　　— Enlisted Man (37th U.S. Infantry)
　　　　— Enlisted Man (37th U.S. Infantry)

(0227) Skirmish, near Fort Wallace, Kansas (June 22, 1867)[90]
　　— 1st Lieutenant Henry J. Nowlan (7th U.S. Cavalry)
　　　　— 7th U.S. Cavalry Detachment Co. F

(0228) Action, North Fork of Republican River, Kansas (June 24, 1867)[91]
　　— Lt. Colonel George A. Custer (7th U.S. Cavalry)
　　　　— 7th U.S. Cavalry Co. A, E, H, K and M
　— **1 WOUNDED**[92]
　　　　— Enlisted Man (7th U.S. Cavalry)

(0229) Skirmish, North Fork of Republican River, Kansas (June 24, 1867)[93]
　　— Captain Louis M. Hamilton (7th U.S. Cavalry)
　　　　— 7th U.S. Cavalry Detachment Co. A

(0230) Skirmish, Wilson's Creek, Kansas (June 26, 1867)[94]
　　— Corporal D. Turner (38th U.S. Infantry)
　　　　— 38th U.S. Infantry Detachment Co. K

(0231) Action, near Fort Wallace, Kansas (June 26, 1867)[95]
　　— Captain Albert Barnitz (7th U.S. Cavalry)
　　　　— 7th U.S. Cavalry Co. G, Detachment Co. I
　— **6 KILLED**[96]
　　　　— Private John Welsh/Welch (Co. E 7th U.S. Cavalry)

　　　　— Sergeant Frederick Wyllyams (Co. G 7th U.S. Cavalry)
　　　　— Corporal James Douglass (Co. G 7th U.S. Cavalry)
　　　　— Bugler Charles Clarke (Co. G 7th U.S. Cavalry)
　　　　— Private Frank Reahme (Co. G 7th U.S. Cavalry)
　　　　— Private Nathan Trial (Co. G 7th U.S. Cavalry)

　— **6 WOUNDED**[97]
　　　　— Corporal James K. Ludlow (Co. G 7th U.S. Cavalry)
　　　　　　— *gunshot wound, abdomen, severe wound*
　　　　— Private Peter Britton (Co. G 7th U.S. Cavalry)
　　　　　　— *severe wound*

---

[88] Indians. *Annual Report of Secretary of War (1867)*, 46; Chronological List, 28; Heitman (Volume 2), 428. Chronological List lists 37th U.S. Infantry Detachment.

[89] *Annual Report of Secretary of War (1867)*, 46.

[90] Indians. Chronological List, 28; Heitman (Volume 2), 428.

[91] Indians. Chronological List, 28; Heitman (Volume 2), 428; Chalfant, *Hancock's War*, 343-344; Chandler, *Of Garryowen in Glory*, 4; Kennedy, *On the Plains*, 118; Monnett, *Battle of Beecher Isla*nd, 77; White, "Hancock and Custer Expeditions of 1867," *Journal of the West* 5 (July 1966): 355-378.

[92] Chronological List, 28.

[93] Indians. Chronological List, 28; Heitman (Volume 2), 428; Chalfant, *Hancock's War*, 348-351; Chandler, *Of Garryowen in Glory*, 4; Kennedy, *On the Plains*, 119; Monnett, *Battle of Beecher Island*, 77; White, "Hancock and Custer Expeditions of 1867," *Journal of the West* 5 (July 1966): 355-378.

[94] Indians. Chronological List, 28; Heitman (Volume 2), 428.

[95] Indians. *Annual Report of Secretary of War (1867)*, 46; Chronological List, 28; Heitman (Volume 2), 428; Barnitz, *Life in Custer's Cavalry*, 69-78; Chalfant, *Hancock's War*, 366-373; Kennedy, *On the Plains*, 120; Monnett, *Battle of Beecher Island*, 82-85; Nye, *Carbine and Lance*, 44-45.

[96] Official Report of Captain Albert Barnitz (7th U.S. Cavalry), near Fort Wallace, Kansas, 28 June 1867. Barnitz, *Life in Custer's Cavalry*, 74-78.

[97] Official Report of Captain Albert Barnitz (7th U.S. Cavalry), near Fort Wallace, Kansas, 28 June 1867. Barnitz, *Life in Custer's Cavalry*, 74-78.

— Private John Hummel (Co. G 7th U.S. Cavalry)
   — *gunshot wound, abdomen, lance wound, side, severe wounds*

— Corporal John Rivers (Co. I 7th U.S. Cavalry)
   — *slight wound*
— Private Hugh Riley (Co. I 7th U.S. Cavalry)
   — *severe wound*
— Private Thomas Townley (Co. I 7th U.S. Cavalry)
   — *slight wound*

(0232) Action, South Fork of Republican River, Kansas (June 26, 1867)[98]
   — 1st Lieutenant Samuel M. Robbins (7th U.S. Cavalry)
      — 7th U.S. Cavalry Detachment Co. D
   — **2 WOUNDED**[99]
      — Enlisted Man (7th U.S. Cavalry)
         — *slight wound*
      — Enlisted Man (7th U.S. Cavalry)
         — *slight wound*

(0233) Skirmish, near Fort Wallace, Kansas (June 27, 1867)[100]
   — 1st Lieutenant Henry J. Nowlan (7th U.S. Cavalry)
      — 7th U.S. Cavalry Co. F

(0234) Skirmish, near Fort Phil Kearny, Dakota Territory (June 30, 1867)[101]
   — Captain William P. McCleery (18th U.S. Infantry)
      — 18th U.S. Infantry Co. C

(0235) Engagement, Beaver Creek, Kansas (July 2, 1867)[102]
   — 2nd Lieutenant Lyman S. Kidder (2nd U.S. Cavalry)
      — 2nd U.S. Cavalry Detachment Co. M
   — **11 KILLED**[103]
      — 2nd Lieutenant Lyman S. Kidder (Co. M 2nd U.S. Cavalry)

   — Sergeant Oscar Close (Co. M 2nd U.S. Cavalry)
   — Corporal Charles H. Haynes (Co. M 2nd U.S. Cavalry)
   — Private Michael Connell (Co. M 2nd U.S. Cavalry)
   — Private Roger Curry (Co. M 2nd U.S. Cavalry)
   — Private William Floyed (Co. M 2nd U.S. Cavalry)
   — Private Michael Groman (Co. M 2nd U.S. Cavalry)
   — Private Michael Haley (Co. M 2nd U.S. Cavalry)
   — Private William J. Humphries (Co. M 2nd U.S. Cavalry)
   — Private Michael Lawler (Co. M 2nd U.S. Cavalry)

[98] Indians. *Annual Report of Secretary of War (1867)*, 486; Chronological List, 28; Heitman (Volume 2), 428; Chalfant, *Hancock's War*, 353-357; Kennedy, *On the Plains*, 120-121; Leckie, *Military Conquest of the Southern Plains*, 52-53; White, "Hancock and Custer Expeditions of 1867," *Journal of the West* 5 (July 1966): 355-378.
[99] *Annual Report of Secretary of War (1867)*, 486.
[100] Chronological List, 28; Heitman (Volume 2), 428; Chandler, *Of Garryowen in Glory*, 425; Monnett, *Battle of Beecher Island*, 85. Heitman lists 26 to 28 June 1867.
[101] Indians. Chronological List, 28; Heitman (Volume 2), 428.
[102] Indians. *Annual Report of Secretary of War (1867)*, 35; Chronological List, 29; Heitman (Volume 2), 429; Johnson, *Dispatch to Custer*, 32-35; Kennedy, *On the Plains*, 123-124; Monnett, *Battle of Beecher Island*, 78-80. Chronological List and Heitman both list 22 July 1867.
[103] Register of Deaths Regular Army, 1860-1889 (Volume 2); Johnson, *Dispatch to Custer*, 88-89.

— Private Charles Teltow (Co. M 2nd U.S. Cavalry)

— Red Bead (Indian Scout)

"We can picture what determination, what bravery, what heroism must have inspired this devoted little band of martyrs when surrounded and assailed by a vastly overwhelming force of bloodthirsty, merciless and unrestrained barbarians, and that they manfully struggled to the last, equally void of fear or hope."

— George A. Custer, U.S. Army[104]

(0236) Action, near Goose Creek, Colorado Territory (July 3, 1867)[105]
— UNKNOWN
— 3rd U.S. Infantry Detachments
— 1 WOUNDED[106]
— Private M. Hays (Co. E 3rd U.S. Infantry)

(0237) Skirmish, between Dunder and Blitzen Creek, Oregon (July 5, 1867)[107]
— Lt. Colonel George Crook (23rd U.S. Infantry)
— 1st U.S. Cavalry Co. F and M
— Detachment of Indian Scouts

(0238) Action, Beale's Springs, Arizona Territory (July 7, 1867)[108]
— UNKNOWN
— 8th U.S. Cavalry Detachment Co. K
— 1 KILLED[109]
— Private George Wilson (Co. K 8th U.S. Cavalry)

(0239) Skirmish, near Malheur River, Oregon (July 7, 1867)[110]
— Captain Eugene M. Baker (1st U.S. Cavalry)
— 1st U.S. Cavalry Detachment Co. I

(0240) Action, near Truxton Springs, Arizona Territory (July 9, 1867)[111]
— Colonel John I. Gregg (8th U.S. Cavalry)
— 8th U.S. Cavalry Co. B and I
— 2 WOUNDED[112]
— Captain James M. Williams (8th U.S. Cavalry)
— *arrow wounds, back, severe wound*

— Private Morgan (Co. I 8th U.S. Cavalry)
— *gunshot wound, thigh*

[104] Lt. Colonel George A. Custer (7th U.S. Cavalry) to Judge Kidder, 2nd Lieutenant Lyman Kidder's (2nd U.S. Cavalry) father, August 23, 1867. Barnett, *Touched by Fire*, 1.
[105] Indians. Chronological List, 28; Heitman (Volume 2), 428. Heitman lists 1 July 1867. Heitman lists 7th U.S. Cavalry Detachment Co. I; 3rd U.S. Infantry Detachment Co. E.
[106] 3rd U.S. Infantry Regimental Return July 1867.
[107] Indians. *Annual Report of Secretary of War (1867)*, 78, 82; Chronological List, 28.
[108] Indians. Chronological List, 28; Heitman (Volume 2), 428; Altshuler, *Chains of Command*, 101-102.
[109] 8th U.S. Cavalry Regimental Return July 1867.
[110] Indians. *Annual Report of Secretary of War (1868)*, 771; Chronological List, 28; Heitman (Volume 2), 428; Michno, *Deadliest Indian War*, 227. Chronological List and Heitman both list 8 July 1867. Chronological List and Heitman both list 1st U.S. Cavalry Co. I
[111] Indians. *Annual Report of Secretary of War (1867)*, 132, 133, 488; Chronological List, 28; Heitman (Volume 2), 428; Alexander, *Arizona Frontier Military Place Names*, 119; Altshuler, *Chains of Command*, 102-103; Thrapp, *Conquest of Apacheria*, 58-59.
[112] *Annual Report of Secretary of War (1867)*, 488.

— Captain James M. Williams (8th U.S. Cavalry) brevet promotion to Major for conspicuous gallantry displayed in engagements with Indians (Verde, Arizona, April 16 and 17, 1867; Yampai Valley, Arizona, June 14, 1867 and Music Mountain, Arizona, July 9, 1867).

(0241) Action, near Fort Sumner, New Mexico Territory (July 9, 1867) [113]
— 1st Lieutenant Charles E. Porter (5th U.S. Infantry)
— 3rd U.S. Cavalry Detachments Co. G and I
— **5 KILLED** [114]
— Private John Lee (Co. G 3rd U.S. Cavalry)
— Private James Cook (Co. I 3rd U.S. Cavalry)
— Private John Devine (Co. I 3rd U.S. Cavalry)
— Private William Kerr (Co. I 3rd U.S. Cavalry)
— Private Edward White (Co. I 3rd U.S. Cavalry)

— **3 WOUNDED** [115]
— Private Joseph A. Ankle (Co. I 3rd U.S. Infantry)
— arrow wound, right shoulder
— Private Robert Clinton (Co. I 3rd U.S. Infantry)
— arrow wound, back
— Private William Wagele (Co. I 3rd U.S. Infantry)
— arrow wound, right chest

(0242) Operations, South Fork of Malheur River, Oregon (July 13, 1867) [116]
— 1st Lieutenant Greenleaf A. Goodale (23rd U.S. Infantry)
— 23rd U.S. Infantry Detachment Co. K
— Detachment of Indian Scouts
— **1 KILLED** [117]
— Squalth (Indian Scout)

(0243) Action, Downer's Station, Kansas (July 17, 1867) [118]
— Sergeant James Connelly (7th U.S. Cavalry)
— 7th U.S. Cavalry Detachments Co. H and K
— **1 KILLED** [119]
— Private Harvey Alexander (Co. H 7th U.S. Cavalry)

— **1 WOUNDED** [120]
— Enlisted Man (7th U.S. Cavalry)

(0244) Skirmish, Malheur Country, Oregon (July 19, 1867) [121]
— Captain Eugene M. Baker (1st U.S. Cavalry)
— 1st U.S. Cavalry Co. I

[113] Indians. Chronological List, 28; Heitman (Volume 2), 428; Moore, *Chiefs, Agents & Soldiers*, 14-16.
[114] Reports of Diseases and Individual Cases, F 380; Register of Deaths Regular Army, 1860-1889 (Volume 2).
[115] Reports of Diseases and Individual Cases, F 380; Otis, *Report of Surgical Cases*, 157, 159.
[116] Indians. *Annual Report of Secretary of War (1867)*, 82; *Annual Report of Secretary of War (1868)*, 771; Chronological List, 28; Heitman (Volume 2), 429; Michno, *Deadliest Indian War*, 230.
[117] Michno, *Deadliest Indian War*, 230.
[118] Indians. Heitman (Volume 2), 429; Chalfant, *Hancock's War*, 415-417; Kennedy, *On the Plains*, 125-126; Monnett, *Battle of Beecher Island*, 80.
[119] 7th U.S. Cavalry Regimental Returns July and August 1867.
[120] 7th U.S. Cavalry Regimental Returns July and August 1867.
[121] Indians. Chronological, List, 28; Heitman (Volume 2), 429; Michno, *Deadliest Indian War*, 227.

(0245) Skirmish, Buffalo Springs, Texas (July 21, 1867)[122]
—1st Lieutenant Tullius C. Tupper (6th U.S. Cavalry)
— 6th U.S. Cavalry Detachments Co. A and E

(0246) Skirmish, between Camp C.F. Smith and Camp Harney, Oregon (July 27, 1867)[123]
— Lt. Colonel George Crook (23rd U.S. Infantry)
— 1st U.S. Cavalry Detachments Co. F, H and M
— Detachment of Indian Scouts

(0247) Action, Willows, Arizona Territory (July 29, 1867)[124]
— UNKNOWN
— 8th U.S. Cavalry Detachment Co. A
— **1 KILLED**[125]
— Sergeant C.C. Miller (Co. K 8th U.S. Cavalry)

(0248) Action, near Fort Hays, Kansas (July 29, 1867)[126]
— UNKNOWN
— 38th U.S. Infantry Detachment Co. G
— **1 KILLED**[127]
— Sergeant William Stewart (Co. C 38th U.S. Infantry)

(0249) Action, near Fort C.F. Smith, Montana Territory (August 1, 1867)[128]
— 2nd Lieutenant Sigismund Sternberg (27th U.S. Infantry)
— 27th U.S. Infantry Detachments Co. D, E, G, H and I
— **3 KILLED**[129]
— 2nd Lieutenant Sigismund Sternberg (27th U.S. Infantry)

— Private Thomas Navin (Co. H 27th U.S. Infantry)

— John G. Hollister (Citizen) — d. 08-02-1867

— **3 WOUNDED**[130]
— Sergeant James Norton (Co. I 27th US Infantry)
— *gunshot wound, left shoulder, severe wound*
— Private Francis M. Law (Co. E 27th US Infantry)
— *gunshot wound, knee, severe wound*
— Private Henry C. Vinson (Co. G 27th US Infantry)
— *gunshot wounds, both legs, right leg, fracture, severe wounds*

[122] Indians. Chronological, List, 28; Heitman (Volume 2), 429; Carter, *From Yorktown to Santiago*, 137-138, 277; Hamilton, *Sentinel of the Southern Plains*, 22-24; McConnell, *Five Years a Cavalryman*, 95-99; Smith, *Old Army in Texas*, 148.
[123] Indians. *Annual Report of Secretary of War (1868)*, 771; Chronological List, 29; Heitman (Volume 2), 429; Michno, *Deadliest Indian War*, 234-235. Chronological List lists 1st U.S. Cavalry Detachments Co. F, H, M. Heitman lists 1st U.S. Cavalry Co. F, M; Detachment of Indian Scouts.
[124] Indians. Chronological List, 29; Heitman (Volume 2), 429. Heitman lists 8th U.S. Cavalry Detachment Co. K.
[125] Fort Mojave Post Return August 1867.
[126] Indians. Heitman (Volume 2), 428.
[127] Register of Deaths Regular Army, 1860-1889 (Volume 2).
[128] Indians. Chronological List, 29; Heitman (Volume 2), 429; *Brown, Plainsmen of the Yellowstone*, 174-175; Gray, *Custer's Last Campaign*, 68-71; Hagan, *Exactly in the Right Place*, 115-124; Hebard and Brininstool, *Bozeman Trail (Volume 2)*, 159-170; Johnson, *Bloody Bozeman*, 275-280; McDermott, *Red Clouds War (Volume 2)*, 384-402; Vaughn, *Indian Fights*, 91-116, 236-239. Chronological List lists 27th U.S. Infantry Detachment.
[129] Official Report of Captain Thomas B. Burrowes (27th U.S. Infantry), Ft. C.F. Smith, 3 August 1867. Vaughn, *Indian Fights*, 237.
[130] Official Report of Captain Thomas B. Burrowes (27th U.S. Infantry), Ft. C.F. Smith, 3 August 1867. Vaughn, *Indian Fights*, 237.

"All agree in this that the men behaved exceedingly well, that they were calm and deliberate, seldom wasting a shot although their commanding officer, [2nd Lieutenant Sigismund Sternberg], was killed at the first onset and [Sergeant James Norton], the second in command, placed "hors de combat" shortly after."
— Thomas B. Burrowes, U.S. Army[131]

(0250) Action, Saline River, Kansas (August 2, 1867)[132]
— Captain George A. Armes (10th U.S. Cavalry)
— 10th U.S. Cavalry Co. F
— **1 KILLED**[133]
— Sergeant William Christy (Co. F 10th U.S. Cavalry)

— **1 WOUNDED**[134]
— Captain George A. Armes (10th U.S. Cavalry)
— *gunshot wound, hip*

(0251) Action, near Fort Phil Kearny, Dakota Territory (August 2, 1867)[135]
— Captain James Powell (27th U.S. Infantry)
— 27th U.S. Infantry Detachment Co. C
— **6 KILLED**[136]
— 1st Lieutenant John C. Jenness (Co. C 27th U.S. Infantry)

— Private Thomas C. Doyle (Co. C 27th U.S. Infantry)
— Private Henry Haggerty (Co. C 27th U.S. Infantry)
— Private George W. Haines (Co. C 27th U.S. Infantry)
— Private Horace Kittridge (Co. C 27th U.S. Infantry)
— Private Hermana Song (Co. C 27th U.S. Infantry)

— **2 WOUNDED**[137]
— Private Nelson V. Deming (Co. C 27th U.S. Infantry)
— *shoulder*
— Private John L. Somers (Co. C 27th U.S. Infantry)
— *thigh*

— *Captain James Powell (27th U.S. Infantry) brevet promotion to Lt. Colonel for gallant conduct in fight with Indians (Near Fort Phil Kearny, Dakota, August 2, 1867).*

"[1st Lieutenant John C. Jenness], a most excellent young officer, fell while affording to his men a fine example of coolness and daring in the performance of his duty, His loss is regretted by his command, by whom he was greatly esteemed and loved."

[131] Official Report of Captain Thomas B. Burrowes (27th U.S. Infantry), Ft. C.F. Smith, 3 August 1867. Vaughn, *Indian Fights*, 237.
[132] Indians. *Annual Report of Secretary of War (1867)*, 46; Chronological List 29; Heitman (Volume 2), 429; Armes, *Ups and Downs*, 236-241; Burton, *Black, Buckskin and Blue*, 178; Monnett, *Battle of Beecher Island*, 86; White, "Warpaths on the Southern Plains," *Journal of the West* 4 (October 1965): 491-499.
[133] 10th U.S. Cavalry Regimental Return August 1867.
[134] 10th U.S. Cavalry Regimental Return August 1867.
[135] Indians. *Annual Report of Secretary of War (1867)*, 486-487; Chronological List, 29; Heitman (Volume 2), 429; Brown, *Plainsmen of the Yellowstone*, 175-176; Chalfant, *Hancock's War*, 441-444; Hebard and Brininstool, *Bozeman Trail (Volume 2)*, 39-87; Johnson, *Bloody Bozeman*, 280-285; Keenan, *Wagon Box Fight*, 17-46; McDermott, *Red Clouds War (Volume 2)*, 411-433. Chronological List and Heitman both list 27th U.S. Infantry Co. A, C, F.
[136] Official Report of Captain James Powell (27th U.S. Infantry), Fort Phil Kearny, Dakota Territory, 4 August 1867. Keenan, *Wagon Box Fight*, 60-62.
[137] Official Report of Captain James Powell (27th U.S. Infantry), Fort Phil Kearny, Dakota Territory, 4 August 1867. Keenan, *Wagon Box Fight*, 60-62.

"[Captain James Powell], by his coolness and firmness in this most creditable affair, has shown what a few determined men can effect with good arms and strong hearts, even with such temporary defensive arrangements as are almost always at hand, and that it is always safer, leaving out the questions duty and professional honor, to stand and fight Indians than to retreat from them."
— Henry G. Litchfield, U.S. Army[138]

(0252) Action, Fort Stevenson, Dakota Territory (August 8, 1867)[139]
    — Captain Albert M. Powell (31st U.S. Infantry)
        — 31st Infantry Detachments Co. H and I
    — **1 KILLED**[140]
        — John F. Gould (Citizen)

(0253) Skirmish, O'Connor's Springs, Dakota Territory (August 13, 1867)[141]
    — Captain Henry B. Freeman (27th U.S. Infantry)
        — 27th U.S. Infantry Co. A and B
    — **3 WOUNDED**[142]
        — Private John Johnson (Co. A 27th U.S. Infantry)
           — *severe wound*
        — Private Winfield Seaman (Co. B 27th U.S. Infantry)
           — *severe wound*
        — Private Florival Smith (Co. B 27th U.S. Infantry)
           — *severe wound*

(0254) Skirmish, near Fort Reno, Dakota Territory (August 14, 1867)[143]
    — 1st Lieutenant Frederick F. Whitehead (18th U.S. Infantry)
        — 18th U.S. Infantry Detachment Co. G

(0255) Action, Chalk Springs, Dakota Territory (August 14, 1867)[144]
    — UNKNOWN
        — 27th U.S. Infantry Co. E
    — **1 KILLED**[145]
        — Corporal Franklin Roberts (Co. E 27th U.S. Infantry)

(0256) Citizens, near Fort Reno, Dakota Territory (August 16, 1867)[146]
    — (2) Citizens Killed

(0257) Skirmish, near Plum Creek Station, Nebraska Territory (August 17, 1867)[147]
    — Captain James Murie (Chief Scout)
        — Detachment of Indian Scouts

---

[138] General Orders No. 39, Henry G. Litchfield, A.A.A.G., Headquarters Department of the Platte, Omaha, Nebraska, 27 August 1867. *Annual Report of Secretary of War (1867)*, 487.
[139] Indians. *Annual Report of Secretary of War (1867)*, 52; Chronological List, 29; Heitman (Volume 2), 429. Chronological List lists 31st U.S. Infantry.
[140] Register of Deaths Regular Army, 1860-1889 (Volume 2); Fort Stevenson Cemetery Records.
[141] Indians. Chronological List, 29; Heitman (Volume 2), 429; Hagan, *Exactly in the Right Place*, 128. Heitman lists 27th U.S. Infantry Co. B, Detachment Co. A.
[142] 27th U.S. Infantry Annual Report 1867.
[143] Indians, Chronological List, 29; Heitman (Volume 2), 429.
[144] Indians. Chronological List, 29; Heitman (Volume 2), 429; Hagan, *Exactly in the Right Place*, 128. Heitman lists 27th U.S. Infantry Detachment Co. E.
[145] 27th U.S. Infantry Annual Report 1867.
[146] Indians. Killed in separate attacks were herders Peter Smith and John Canine. Canine was wounded and died the next day. Chronological List, 29; Heitman (Volume 2), 429; Hagan, *Exactly in the Right Place*, 128-129.
[147] Indians. *Annual Report of Secretary of War (1867)*, 487; Chronological List 29; Heitman (Volume 2), 429; Grinnell, *Two Great Scouts*, 145-146; Monnett, *Battle of Beecher Island*, 96-97; Paul, *Nebraska Indian Wars Reader*, 78.

"On the approach of [Captain James Murie] with the Pawnee Company the Indians advanced coolly to meet him thinking his company white men, as soon as they were near enough to recognize the Pawnee they broke in every direction with wild cried of "Pawnee, Pawnee!" The fight was a complete success. Captain Murie… and all the Scouts deserve the greatest credit."
— Richard I. Dodge, U.S. Army[148]

(0258) Engagement, Prairie Dog Creek, Kansas (August 21 and 22, 1867)[149]
— Captain George A. Armes (10th U.S. Cavalry)
— 10th U.S. Cavalry Co. F
— 18th Kansas Volunteer Cavalry Co. B and C
— **3 KILLED**[150]
— Private Thomas Smith (Co. F 10th U.S. Cavalry)
— Private Thomas Anderson (Co. B 18th Kansas Volunteer Cavalry)
— Private J.D. Masterson (Co. C 18th Kansas Volunteer Cavalry)

— **23 WOUNDED**[151]
— Captain George B. Jenness (Co. C 18th Kansas Volunteer Cavalry)
— *gunshot wound, left leg, slight wound*

— Sergeant William Johnson (Co. F 10th U.S. Cavalry)
— *gunshot wound, left thigh*
— Sergeant Jacob Thronton (Co. F 10th U.S. Cavalry)
— *gunshot wound, right leg, fracture, severe wound*
— Corporal Thomas Sheppard (Co. F 10th U.S. Cavalry)
— *gunshot wound, neck*
— Private James Anderson (Co. F 10th U.S. Cavalry)
— *gunshot wound, left thigh*
— Private James Brown (Co. F 10th U.S. Cavalry)
— *gunshot wound, right thigh*
— Private Nick Cosby/ Crosby (Co. F 10th U.S. Cavalry)
— *gunshot wound, left thigh*
— Private Charles Gartrill (Co. F 10th U.S. Cavalry)
— *gunshot wound, scalp*
— Private Isaac Marshall (Co. F 10th U.S. Cavalry)
— *gunshot wound, right leg, slight wound*
— Private Charles Murray (Co. F 10th U.S. Cavalry)
— *arrow wound, left leg*
— Private John Robinson (Co. F 10th U.S. Cavalry)
— *gunshot wound, left leg*
— Private William Turner (Co. F 10th U.S. Cavalry)
— *gunshot wound, right shoulder*

[148] Official Report of Major Richard I. Dodge (12th U.S. Infantry), Plum Creek, 19 August 1867. Paul, *Nebraska Indian Wars Reader*, 78.
[149] Indians. *Annual Report of Secretary of War (1867)*, 46; Chronological List, 29; Heitman (Volume 2), 429; Armes, *Ups and Downs*, 243-249; Barnitz, *Life in Custer's Cavalry*, 99-100; Burton, *Black, Buckskin and Blue*, 178-179; Chalfant, *Hancock's* War, 456-463; Crawford, *Kansas in the Sixties*, 261-262; Leckie, *Buffalo Soldiers*, 23-25; Monnett, *Battle of Beecher Island*, 86-90; White, "Warpaths on the Southern Plains," *Journal of the West* 4 (October 1965): 491-499. Chronological List lists 10th U.S. Cavalry Co. F; 18th Kansas Infantry Detachment. Heitman lists 10th U.S. Cavalry Co. F.
150 Reports of Diseases and Individual Cases, F 378; Register of Deaths Regular Army, 1860-1889 (Volume 2).
151 Reports of Diseases and Individual Cases, F 378.

— Sergeant Philip J. Lannigan/ Fannagan (Co. B 18th Kansas Volunteer Cavalry)
— *gunshot wound, left forearm*
— Private Tamberlane Forrester (Co. B 18th Kansas Volunteer Cavalry)
— *gunshot wound, left thigh*
— Private Joseph Gordon (Co. B 18th Kansas Volunteer Cavalry)
— *gunshot wound, left thigh*
— Private Joseph Hays (Co. B 18th Kansas Volunteer Cavalry)
— *gunshot wound, left shoulder, slight wound*
— Private William Hilly/ Hillory (Co. B 18th Kansas Volunteer Cavalry)
— *gunshot wound, left leg*

— Sergeant G.W. Carpenter (Co. C 18th Kansas Volunteer Cavalry)
— *gunshot wound, right leg*
— Sergeant J.H. Springer (Co. C 18th Kansas Volunteer Cavalry)
— *gunshot wound, right shoulder*
— Corporal James H. Towell (Co. C 18th Kansas Volunteer Cavalry)
— *gunshot wounds, both thighs, left shoulder*
— Private George A. Campbell (Co. C 18th Kansas Volunteer Cavalry)
— *gunshot wound, right shoulder, slight wound*
— Private William Southerland (Co. C 18th Kansas Volunteer Cavalry)
— *gunshot wound, right arm*

— Scout A.J. Plyley (Citizen)
— *gunshot wound, left leg*

(0259) Action, Mountain Pass, near Fort Chadbourne, Texas (August 22, 1867)[152]
— Sergeant B. Jenkins (4th U.S. Cavalry)
— 4th U.S. Cavalry Detachments Co. D, G and H
— **2 KILLED**[153]
— Private John Maroney (Co. D 4th U.S. Cavalry)
— Private Daniel Wurm (Co. H 4th U.S. Cavalry)

(0260) Action, Surprise Valley, near Warner's Lake, California (August 22, 1867)[154]
— Archie McIntosh (Chief Scout)
— Detachment of Indian Scouts
— **1 KILLED**[155]
— Coppinger (Indian Scout)

— **1 WOUNDED**[156]
— Indian Scout

[152] Indians. Chronological List, 29; Heitman (Volume 2), 429; Smith, *Old Army in Texas*, 148; Williams, *Texas' Last Frontier*, 87.
[153] 4th U.S. Cavalry Regimental Return August 1867.
[154] Indians. *Annual Report of Secretary of War (1868)*, 69; Chronological List, 29; Heitman (Volume 2), 429; Michno, *Deadliest Indian War*, 243-245.
[155] *Annual Report of Secretary of War (1868)*, 69; Michno, *Deadliest Indian War*, 243.
[156] *Annual Report of Secretary of War (1868)*, 69.

(0261) Action, near Fort Concho, Texas (August 23, 1867)[157]
— UNKNOWN
— 4th U.S. Cavalry Co. A
— **1 KILLED**[158]
— Private Hugh Collins (Co. A 4th U.S. Cavalry)

(0262) Citizens, near Camp Goodwin, Arizona Territory (August 28, 1867)[159]

(0263) Action, near Fort Belknap, Texas (August 30, 1867)[160]
— 1st Lieutenant Gustavus Schreyer (6th U.S. Cavalry)
— 6th U.S. Cavalry Co. F
— **2 WOUNDED**[161]
— Corporal Thomas O'Brien (Co. F 6th U.S. Cavalry)
— *arrow wound, chest*
— Private William Rosback (Co. F 6th U.S. Cavalry)
— *arrow wounds, scalp, leg*

(0264) Skirmish, near Silver River, Oregon (September 6, 1867)[162]
— 1st Lieutenant John F. Small (1st U.S. Cavalry)
— 1st U.S. Cavalry Co. A
— Detachment of Indian Scouts

(0265) Action, Silver River, Oregon (September 9, 1867)[163]
— 1st Lieutenant John F. Small (1st U.S. Cavalry)
— 1st U.S. Cavalry Co. A
— Detachment of Indian Scouts
— **3 WOUNDED**[164]
— Private Simon Askins (Co. A 1st U.S. Cavalry)
— *arrow wounds, neck, leg*
— Private Allen Boyd (Co. A 1st U.S. Cavalry)
— *arrow wound, thigh*

— Yekermsak (Indian Scout)
— *arrow wound, arm*

— *1st Lieutenant John F. Small (1st U.S. Cavalry) brevet promotion to Captain for gallantry in charging a band of Indians, killing and capturing more of the enemy than he had men (Silver Lake, Oregon, September 9, 1867).*

(0266) Skirmish, Live Oak Creek, Texas (September 10, 1867)[165]
— 1st Lieutenant Neil J. McCafferty (4th U.S. Cavalry)
— 4th U.S. Cavalry Detachment Co. K

[157] Indians. Chronological List, 29; Heitman (Volume 2), 429; Smith, *Old Army in Texas*, 148. Heitman lists 4th U.S. Cavalry Detachment Co. A.
[158] 4th U.S. Cavalry Regimental Return August 1867.
[159] Indians. Killed was a herder. Chronological List, 29.
[160] Indians. Chronological List, 29; Heitman (Volume 2), 429; Carter, *From Yorktown to Santiago*, 138, 277; Smith, *Old Army in Texas*, 148.
[161] Otis, *Report of Surgical Cases*, 149, 158.
[162] Indians. *Annual Report of Secretary of War (1868)*, 69; Chronological List, 29; Heitman (Volume 2), 429; Michno, *Deadliest Indian War*, 245-246. Chronological List and Heitman both list 1st U.S. Cavalry Co. A.
[163] Indians. *Annual Report of Secretary of War (1868)*, 69, 771; Chronological List, 29; Heitman (Volume 2), 429; Michno, *Deadliest Indian War*, 246-247. Chronological List and Heitman both list 8 September 1867. Chronological List and Heitman both list 1st U.S. Cavalry Co. A.
[164] Michno, *Deadliest Indian War*, 247.
[165] Indians. Chronological List, 29; Heitman (Volume 2), 429; Smith, *Fort Inge*, 15; Williams, *Texas' Last Frontier*, 87-88.

(0267) Action, Saline River, Kansas (September 16, 1867)[166]
— Sergeant C.H. Davis (10th U.S. Cavalry)
— 10th U.S. Cavalry Detachment Co. G
— **2 KILLED**[167]
— Thomas Parks (Citizen)
— Charles Saffel (Citizen)

— **1 WOUNDED**[168]
— Private John Randall (Co. G 10th U.S. Cavalry)

(0268) Skirmish, near Fort Inge, Texas (September 16, 1867)[169]
— 1st Lieutenant Neil J. McCafferty (4th U.S. Cavalry)
— 4th U.S. Cavalry Detachment Co. K

(0269) Action, Walker's Creek, near Fort Harker, Kansas (September 19, 1867)[170]
— 1st Lieutenant Mason Carter (5th U.S. Infantry)
— 5th U.S. Infantry Detachment Co. K
— **1 KILLED**[171]
— Enlisted Man (5th U.S. Infantry)

— **3 WOUNDED**[172]
— Enlisted Man (5th U.S. Infantry)
— Enlisted Man (5th U.S. Infantry)
— Enlisted Man (5th U.S. Infantry)

— *1st Lieutenant Mason Carter (5th U.S. Infantry) brevet promotion to Captain for gallant and meritorious service in an affair with Indians (In route from Fort Hayes to Fort Harker, Kansas).*

(0270) Skirmish, near Devil's River, Texas (September 20, 1867)[173]
— 1st Lieutenant David A. Irwin (4th U.S. Cavalry)
— 4th U.S. Cavalry Detachment Co. C

(0271) Action, Arkansas River, nine miles west of Cimarron Crossing, Kansas (September 23, 1867)[174]
— Captain David H. Brotherton (5th U.S. Infantry)
— 5th U.S. Infantry Co. K
— **1 KILLED**[175]
— Wagoner Christopher Hoggando (Co. K 5th U.S. Infantry)

— **1 WOUNDED**[176]
— 1st Lieutenant Ephraim Williams (5th U.S. Infantry)
— *gunshot wound, left thigh, fracture, amputation*

[166] Indians. Chronological List 29; Heitman (Volume 2), 429; Burton, *Black, Buckskin and Blue*, 179; Crawford, *Kansas in the Sixties*, 270; Leckie, *Buffalo Soldiers*, 25; Monnett, *Battle of Beecher Island*, 100.
[167] Cashin, *Under Fire with the 10th U.S. Cavalry*, 28-30; Monnett, *Battle of Beecher Island*, 100.
[168] Leckie, *Buffalo Soldiers*, 26.
[169] Indians. Chronological List, 29; Heitman (Volume 2), 429; Smith, *Fort Inge*, 156.
[170] Indians. *Annual Report of Secretary of War (1867)*, 46; Chronological List, 29; Heitman (Volume 2), 429. Chronological List lists 5th U.S. Infantry Detachment.
[171] *Annual Report of Secretary of War (1867)*, 46.
[172] *Annual Report of Secretary of War (1867)*, 46.
[173] Indians. Chronological List, 29; Heitman (Volume 2), 429; Smith, *Old Army in Texas*, 148.
[174] Indians. Chronological List, 30; Heitman (Volume 2), 429; Crawford, *Kansas in the Sixties*, 270; Strate, *Sentinel to the Cimarron*, 46.
[175] Register of Deaths Regular Army, 1860-1889 (Volume 2); 5th U.S. Infantry Regimental Return September 1867.
[176] Otis, *Report of Surgical Cases*, 213.

— *1st Lieutenant Ephraim Williams (5th U.S. Infantry) brevet promotion to Captain for coolness, gallantry and good conduct in action with Cheyenne Indians (Pawnee Fork, Kansas, September 23, 1867).*

(0272) Skirmish, Nine Mile Ridge, Kansas (September 24, 1867)[177]
— UNKNOWN
— 37th U.S. Infantry Detachment Co. I
— **1 WOUNDED**[178]
— Private Thomas Nolan (Co. I 37th U.S. Infantry)
— *gunshot wound, left shoulder*

(0273) Engagement, Infernal Caverns, near Pitt River, California (September 26 and 27, 1867)[179]
— Lt. Colonel George Crook (23rd U.S. Infantry)
— 1st U.S. Cavalry Co. H
— 23rd U.S. Infantry Co. D
— Detachment of Indian Scouts
— **7 KILLED**[180]
— 1st Lieutenant John Madigan (1st U.S. Cavalry) — d. 9-27-1867

— First Sergeant Charles Brashet (Co. H 1st U.S. Cavalry)
— Sergeant Michael Meara (Co. H 1st U.S. Cavalry)
— Private Bryan Carry (Co. H 1st U.S. Cavalry)
— Private James Lyons (Co. H 1st U.S. Cavalry)
— Private Willoughby Swayer (Co. H 1st U.S. Cavalry)

— Private John Braus (Co. D 23rd U.S. Infantry)

— **12 WOUNDED**[181]
— Private William Enson (Co. H 1st U.S. Cavalry)
— Private Emile Fischer (Co. H 1st U.S. Cavalry)
— Private Cornelius Glancy (Co. H 1st U.S. Cavalry)
— Private James Shay (Co. H 1st U.S. Cavalry)

— Corporal Thomas Fogarty (Co. D 23rd U.S. Infantry)
— Corporal Edward Furman (Co. D 23rd U.S. infantry)
— Corporal Peter McCause (Co. D 23rd U.S. Infantry)
— Private John Barbers (Co. D 23rd U.S. Infantry)
— Private Joseph Emblem (Co. D 23rd U.S. Infantry)
— Private Jerry Kingsfor (Co. D 23rd U.S. Infantry)
— Private Patrick Maguire (Co. D 23rd U.S. infantry)

— Lorenzo Trainer (Citizen)

[177] Indians. Chronological List, 30; Heitman (Volume 2), 429.
[178] Otis, *Report of Surgical Cases*, 59.
[179] Indians. *Annual Report of Secretary of War (1868)*, 69, 771-772; Chronological List, 30; Heitman (Volume 2), 429; Michno, *Deadliest Indian War*, 254-268. Chronological List and Heitman both list 26 to 28 September 1867.
[180] Reports of Diseases and Individual Cases, F 379; Register of Deaths Regular Army, 1860-1889 (Volume 2).
[181] Reports of Diseases and Individual Cases, F 379.

— 1st *Lieutenant Richard I. Eskridge (14th U.S. Infantry) brevet promotion to Captain for conspicuous gallantry in charging a large band of Indians, strongly fortified (Infernal Caverns, Pitt River, California, September 26, 1867).*

— 1st *Lieutenant John Madigan (1st U.S. Cavalry) brevet promotion to Captain for conspicuous gallantry in charging a large band of Indians, strongly fortified (Infernal Caverns, Pitt River, California, September 27, 1867, where he was killed).*

— 1st *Lieutenant William R. Parnell (1st U.S. Cavalry) brevet promotion to Lt. Colonel for conspicuous gallantry in charging a large body of Indians, strongly fortified (Infernal Caverns, Pitt River, California, September 26, 1867).*

"About twenty rods north of the main stream and thirty below the junction of the South Fork, [1st Lieutenant John Madigan] of Company H, 1st U.S. Cavalry, was buried with extra ceremony, of the kind… His friendship was of the genuine sort, and possessing a droll originality and humor, his presence at the campfire had become almost indispensable with Crook's officers, and no one could regret his taking off in the prime of life than the Colonel himself. Alas, poor Madigan!"
— Editor, *Owyhee Avalanche*, Citizen[182]

(0274) Action, Pretty Encampment, near Fort Garland, Colorado Territory (September 29, 1867)[183]
    — UNKNOWN
        — 37th U.S. Infantry Co. G
    — **2 KILLED**[184]
        — Private Joseph Drouch (Co. G 37th U.S. Infantry)
        — Private Edward Lewis (Co. G 37th U.S. Infantry)

(0275) Action, near Fort Dodge, Kansas (September 29, 1867)[185]
    — UNKNOWN
        — 37th U.S. Infantry Detachment
    — **1 KILLED**[186]
        — Private Smith (Co. I 37th U.S. Infantry)

    — **2 WOUNDED**[187]
        — Sergeant William Gleason (Co. I 37th U.S. Infantry)
            — *gunshot wounds, right knee, left leg, scalp*
        — Private Thomas Gavin (Co. I 37th U.S. Infantry)
            — *gunshot wound, left arm*

(0276) Action, Howard's Well, Texas (October 1, 1867)[188]
    — Corporal Emanuel Wright (9th U.S. Cavalry)
        — 9th U.S. Cavalry Detachment Co. D

---

[182] *Owyhee Avalanche*, 2 November 1867. Cozzens, *Eyewitnesses to the Indian Wars (Volume 2)*, 76.
[183] Indians. Chronological List, 30; Heitman (Volume 2), 429. Heitman lists 37th U.S. Infantry Detachment Co. G.
[184] 37th U.S. Infantry Regimental Return October 1867.
[185] Bandits. Fort Dodge Post Return September 1867.
[186] Fort Dodge Post Return September 1867.
[187] Otis, *Report of Surgical Cases*, 68, 83.
[188] Indians. Chronological List, 30; Heitman (Volume 2), 429; Leckie, *Buffalo Soldiers*, 87; Smith, *Old Army in Texas*, 148; Uglow, *Standing in the Gap*, 27.

— 2 KILLED[189]
— Corporal Emanuel Wright (Co. D 9th U.S. Cavalry)
— Private E.T. Jones (Co. D 9th U.S. Cavalry)

(0277) Action, near Camp Logan, Oregon (October 4, 1867)[190]
— 1st Lieutenant James Pike (1st U.S. Cavalry)
— 8th U.S. Cavalry Detachment Co. F
— 1 KILLED[191]
— 1st Lieutenant James Pike (1st U.S. Cavalry) — d. 10-14-1867

(0278) Skirmish, Trout Creek, Arizona Territory (October 6, 1867)[192]
— 1st Lieutenant Almond B. Wells (8th U.S. Cavalry)
— 8th U.S. Cavalry Co. L

(0279) Action, near Fort Stevenson, Dakota Territory (October 10, 1867)[193]
— UNKNOWN
— 31st U.S. Infantry Detachment Co. H
— 1 WOUNDED[194]
— Private William Imbler (Co. H 31st U.S. Infantry)
— *arrow wounds, left shoulder, right forearm, left elbow*

(0280) Skirmish, near Camp Lincoln, Arizona Territory (October 10, 1867)[195]
— Captain David Krause (14th U.S. Infantry)
— 14th U.S. Infantry Detachments Co. C and G

(0281) Skirmish, Deep Creek, Texas (October 17, 1867)[196]
— Sergeant W.A.F. Ahrberg (6th U.S. Cavalry)
— 6th U.S. Cavalry Detachments Co. F, I, K and L
— Detachment of Indian Scouts

(0282) Action, Sierra Diablo, New Mexico Territory (October 18, 1867)[197]
— Captain Francis H. Wilson (3rd U.S. Cavalry)
— 3rd U.S. Cavalry Co. D and K
— 1 KILLED[198]
— Private William Carty (Co. D 3rd U.S. Cavalry)

— 5 WOUNDED[199]
— Private Frank Burr (Co. D 3rd U.S. Cavalry)
— *arrow wound, right forearm, slight wound*
— Private James Daly (Co. D 3rd U.S. Cavalry)
— *arrow wound, right thigh, slight wound*

---

[189] Leckie, *Buffalo Soldiers*, 84-85.
[190] Indians. *Annual Report of Secretary of War (1868)*, 69, 771; Chronological List, 30; Heitman (Volume 2), 429; Michno, *Deadliest Indian War*, 272. Heitman lists 8th U.S. Cavalry Detachment Co. E.
[191] Either during the fight while clearing a jammed rifle or after the fight while disposing of Indian contraband, 1st Lieutenant James Pike (1st U.S. Cavalry) was accidentally wounded, a gunshot wound to the thigh. He died of infection on 14 October 1867. *Annual Report of Secretary of War (1868)*, 771.
[192] Indians. Chronological List, 30; Heitman (Volume 2), 429; Thrapp, *Conquest of Apacheria*, 46.
[193] Indians. *Annual Report of Secretary of War (1868)*, 34-35; Chronological List, 30; Heitman (Volume 2), 429.
[194] Otis, *Report of Surgical Cases*, 145.
[195] Indians. Chronological List, 30; Heitman (Volume 2), 429; Altshuler, *Chains of Command*, 124.
[196] Indians. *Annual Report of Secretary of War (1868)*, 712, 772; Chronological List, 30; Heitman (Volume 2), 429; Carter, *From Yorktown to Santiago*, 138, 277; Rister, *Fort Griffin*, 73; Smith, *Old Army in Texas*, 148; Uglow, *Standing in the Gap*, 106. Chronological List and Heitman both list 6th U.S. Cavalry Detachments Co. F, I, K, L.
[197] Indians. Chronological List, 30; Heitman (Volume 2), 429.
[198] Reports of Diseases and Individual Cases, F 382; Register of Deaths Regular Army, 1860-1889 (Volume 2).
[199] Reports of Diseases and Individual Cases, F 382; Otis, *Report of Surgical Cases*, 82, 157-159.

— Private Clarence G. Morrell (Co. D 3rd U.S. Cavalry)
— *arrow wound, right side, severe wound*
— Private Josephus Shaw (Co. D 3rd U.S. Cavalry)
— *arrow wound, right leg, severe wound*
— Private Francis Stalls (Co. D 3rd U.S. Cavalry)
— *arrow wound, right breast, slight wound*

(0283) Skirmish, Crazy Woman's Fork, Dakota Territory (October 20, 1867)[200]
— Captain Henry E. Noyes (2nd U.S. Cavalry)
— 2nd U.S. Cavalry Detachment

(0284) Skirmish, Truxell Springs, Arizona Territory (October 25, 1867)[201]
— 1st Lieutenant Almond B. Wells (8th U.S. Cavalry)
— 8th U.S. Cavalry Co. L

(0285) Skirmish, Shell Creek, Dakota Territory (October 26, 1867)[202]
— Captain David S. Gordon (2nd U.S. Cavalry)
— 2nd U.S. Cavalry Co. D

(0286) Skirmish, near Camp Winfield Scott, Nevada (October 26, 1867)[203]
— Captain John P. Baker (1st U.S. Cavalry)
— 1st U.S. Cavalry Co. L
— 8th U.S. Cavalry Co. A

(0287) Skirmish, Willow Grove, Arizona Territory (November 3, 1867)[204]
— 2nd Lieutenant Patrick Hasson (14th U.S. Infantry)
— 1st U.S. Cavalry Detachment Co. E

(0288) Action, Goose Creek, Dakota Territory (November 4, 1867)[205]
— 2nd Lieutenant Edmund R.P. Shurly (27th U.S. Infantry)
— 27th U.S. Infantry Detachments Co. D, E, G, H and I
— **3 KILLED**[206]
— Private Peter Donnelly (Co. H 27th U.S. Infantry) — d. 11-06-1867
— Private Joseph McKeever (Co. E 27th U.S. Infantry) — d. 11-08-1867
— Private Harold Partenheimer (Co. G 27th U.S. Infantry)

— **3 WOUNDED**[207]
— 2nd Lieutenant Edmund R.P. Shurly (27th U.S. Infantry)
— *gunshot wound, left foot, severe wound*

[200] Indians. *Annual Report of Secretary of War (1868)*, 30; Chronological List, 30; Heitman (Volume 2), 429; McDermott, *Red Cloud's War (Volume 2)*, 462. Neither Chronological List nor Heitman lists units involved.
[201] Indians. Chronological List, 30; Heitman (Volume 2), 429; Thrapp, *Conquest of Apacheria*, 48.
[202] Indians. Chronological List, 30; Heitman (Volume 2), 429; Rodenbough, *From Everglade to Canyon*, 435.
[203] Indians. Chronological List, 30; Heitman (Volume 2), 430; Michno, *Deadliest Indian War*, 283.
[204] Indians. Chronological List, 30; Heitman (Volume 2), 430. Chronological List lists 1st U.S. Cavalry Detachment Co. E. Heitman lists 1st U.S. Cavalry Detachment Co. E; 8th U.S. Cavalry Detachment Co. L.
[205] Indians. *Annual Report of Secretary of War (1868)*, 28-30; Chronological List, 30; Heitman (Volume 2), 430; Hagan, *Exactly in the Right Place*, 163-166; McDermott, *Red Cloud's War (Volume 2)*, 464-466.
[206] Official Report of 2nd Lieutenant Edmund R.P. Shurley (27th U.S. Infantry), Fort Phil Kearny, Dakota Territory, 10 November 1867; Register of Deaths Regular Army, 1860-1889 (Volume 2); Otis, *Report of Surgical Cases*, 32, 210.
[207] Official Report of 2nd Lieutenant Edmund R.P. Shurley (27th U.S. Infantry), Fort Phil Kearny, Dakota Territory, 10 November 1867.

— Corporal Gordon Fitzgerald (Co. I 27th U.S. Infantry)
— *hand, fracture, severe wound*

— William Freeland (Citizen)
— *gunshot wound, thigh*

— *2nd Lieutenant Edmund R.P. Shurly (27th U.S. Infantry) brevet promotion to Captain for gallant service in the successful defense of a Government supply train against a large force of Indians (Near Goose Creek, Dakota, November 4, 1867, where he was severely wounded).*

(0289) Action, near Camp Bowie, Arizona Territory (November 5, 1867)[208]
— **2 KILLED**[209]
— 1st Lieutenant John C. Carroll (32nd U.S. Infantry)

— John Slater (Citizen)

(0290) Action, near Fort Buford, Dakota Territory (November 6, 1867)[210]
— **UNKNOWN**
— 31st U.S. Infantry Detachment Co. C
— **1 KILLED**[211]
— Private Cornelius Coughlan (Co. C 31st U.S. Infantry)

— **1 WOUNDED**[212]
— Corporal Edward Monaghan (Co. C 31st U.S. Infantry)
— *arrow wound, right shoulder*

(0291) Skirmish, Toll Gate, Arizona Territory (November 7, 1867)[213]
— 1st Lieutenant Almond B. Wells (8th U.S. Cavalry)
— 8th U.S. Cavalry Co. L

(0292) Action, near Willows, Arizona Territory (November 7, 1867)[214]
— 2nd Lieutenant Patrick Hasson (14th U.S. Infantry)
— 1st U.S. Cavalry Detachment Co. E
— 8th U.S. Cavalry Detachment Co. L
— **1 KILLED**[215]
— Private George Duggan (Co. K 8th U.S. Cavalry) — d. 12-17-1867

— **4 WOUNDED**[216]
— Private John Ahern (Co. L 8th U.S. Cavalry)
— *arrow wounds, back, left shoulder*
— Private John Craig (Co. L 8th U.S. Cavalry)
— *arrow wound, left hand*

---

[208] Indians. Chronological List, 31; Heitman (Volume 2), 430; Alexander, *Arizona Frontier Military Place Names*, 29; McChristian, *Fort Bowie*, 97-98.
[209] Reports of Diseases and Individual Cases, F 381; Fort Bowie Post Return November 1867; Register of Deaths Regular Army, 1860-1889 (Volume 2)
[210] Indians. *Annual Report of Secretary of War (1868)*, 35; Heitman (Volume 2), 430.
[211] Register of Deaths Regular Army 1860-1889 (Volume 2).
[212] Otis, *Report of Surgical Cases*, 155.
[213] Indians. Chronological List, 31; Heitman (Volume 2), 430.
[214] Indians. Chronological List, 31; Heitman (Volume 2), 430; Thrapp, *Conquest of Apacheria*, 41-43. Heitman lists 8 November 1867. Chronological List lists 1st U.S. Cavalry Co. E; 8th U.S. Cavalry Detachment.
[215] Reports of Diseases and Individual Cases, F 399.
[216] Reports of Diseases and Individual Cases, F 399; Otis, *Report of Surgical Cases*, 156-158. Chronological List lists 2nd Lieutenant Patrick Hasson (14th U.S. Infantry) as WIA. His name does not appear on F 399.

— Private George Johnson (Co. L 8th U.S. Cavalry)
— *arrow wound, chest*
— Private Edward Malone (Co. L 8th U.S. Cavalry)
— *arrow wound, hip*

— *2nd Lieutenant Patrick Hasson (14th U.S. Infantry) brevet promotion to 1st Lieutenant for gallant service in action against Indians (Near Willows, Arizona, November 8, 1867, where he was severely wounded).*

"It gives us unbounded pleasure to announce to our readers, and the balance of mankind, that [2nd Lieutenant Patrick Hasson], of the 14th U.S. Infantry, has made a brilliant and successful raid against the [Hualapais]...."
— Editor, *Arizona Miner*, Citizen[217]

(0293) Action, Aqua Frio Springs, Arizona Territory (November 13, 1867)[218]
— 1st Lieutenant Oscar I. Converse (14th U.S. Infantry)
— 14th U.S. Infantry Detachment Co. C
— **4 WOUNDED**[219]
— 1st Lieutenant Oscar I. Converse (14th U.S. Infantry)

— Private James Burridge (Co. C 14th U.S. Infantry)
— *arrow wound, forearm*
— Private William Drum (Co. C 14th U.S. Infantry)
— *arrow wounds, face, left side*
— Private William Hardwick (Co. C 14th U.S. Infantry)
— *arrow wounds, left thigh, right arm*

(0294) Skirmish, near Tonto Creek, Arizona Territory (November 14 and 15, 1867)[220]
— UNKNOWN
— Detachment of Indian Scouts

(0295) Action, near Fort Mason, Texas (November 14, 1867)[221]
— Major John A. Thompson (7th U.S. Cavalry)
— 4th U.S. Cavalry Detachment
— **2 KILLED**[222]
— Major John A. Thompson (4th U.S. Cavalry)

— Sergeant John McDougall (Co. H 4th U.S. Cavalry)

---

[217] *Arizona Miner*, 16 November 1867. Thrapp, *Conquest of Apacheria*, 43.
[218] Indians. Chronological List, 31; Heitman (Volume 2), 430; Alexander, *Arizona Military Place Names*, 1. Chronological List lists this fight twice, once on 11 November 1867 and again on 13 November 1867.
[219] 14th U.S. Infantry Regimental Return November 1867; Orton, *Report of Surgical Cases*, 148, 155-156.
[220] Indians. Chronological List, 31; Heitman (Volume 2), 430.
[221] Bandits. Otis, *Report of Surgical Cases*, 23, 54; Smallwood, *Feud that Wasn't*, 32-33.
[222] Register of Deaths Regular Army, 1860-1889 (Volume 2); Otis, *Report of Surgical Cases*, 23, 54.

"[Major John A. Thompson] was universally esteemed... his many noble qualities winning him a large circle of friends who, with his inconsolable family, and the Army which loses one of its most valuable officers, will ever deplore his irreparable loss."

— John A. Hulse, U.S. Army[223]

(0296) Action, near Fort Sumner, New Mexico Territory (November 17, 1867)[224]
> — UNKNOWN
>> — 37th U.S. Infantry Co. F
> **— 1 KILLED[225]**
>> — Private Thomas Hedgecock (Co. E 37th U.S. Infantry)

(0297) Skirmish, near Fort Selden, New Mexico Territory (November 20, 1867)[226]
> — 2nd Lieutenant Oscar Elting (3rd U.S. Cavalry)
>> — 3rd U.S. Cavalry Co. K

(0298) Skirmish, De Schmidt Lake, Dakota Territory (November 22, 1867)[227]
> — Captain David S. Gordon (2nd U.S. Cavalry)
>> — 2nd U.S. Cavalry Co. D

(0299) Skirmish, Shell Creek, Dakota Territory (November 29, 1867)[228]
> — Captain David S. Gordon (2nd U.S. Cavalry)
>> — 2nd U.S. Cavalry Co. D

(0300) Action, Crazy Woman's Creek, Dakota Territory (December 2, 1867)[229]
> — Sergeant G. Gillaspy (18th U.S. Infantry)
>> — 18th U.S. Infantry Detachment Co. C
> **— 1 KILLED[230]**
>> — Private Albert H. Edwards (Co. C 18th U.S. Infantry)

> **— 7 WOUNDED[231]**
>> — Private Gottlieb Harr (Co. C 18th U.S. Infantry)
>>> — *arrow wound, left thigh, slight wound*
>> — Corporal George Wermer (Co. E 18th U.S. Infantry)
>>> — *gunshot wound, groin, slight wound*
>> — Private William Burton (Co. E 18th U.S. Infantry)
>>> — *gunshot wound, right arm, fracture, severe wound*

>> — William Caldwell (Citizen)
>>> — *gunshot wound, fracture, severe wound*

[223] Acting Assistant Surgeon John A. Hulse to Colonel John Thompson, father of Major John A. Thompson (4th U.S. Cavalry), Fort Mason, Texas, 11 November 1867.
[224] Indians. Chronological List, 31; Heitman (Volume 2), 430. Heitman lists 37th U.S. Infantry Detachment Co. E.
[225] Reports of Diseases and Individual Cases, F 383.
[226] Indians. Chronological List, 31; Heitman (Volume 2), 430; Billington, *New Mexico's Buffalo Soldiers*, 8.
[227] Indians. Chronological List, 31; Rodenbough, *From Everglade to Canyon*, 435.
[228] Indians. Chronological List, 31; Heitman (Volume 2), 430.
[229] Indians. *Annual Report of Secretary of War (1868)*, 30; Chronological List, 31; Heitman (Volume 2), 430.
[230] Reports of Diseases and Individual Cases, F 384.
[231] Reports of Diseases and Individual Cases, F 384; Otis, *Report of Surgical Cases*, 157, 224.

— William Fee (Citizen)
    — *arrow wound, right side, slight wound*
— John Fry (Citizen)
    — *gunshot wound, left leg, fracture, severe wound*
— John Navity (Citizen)
    — *gunshot wound, right arm, fracture, severe wound*

(0301) Action, Eagle Springs, Texas (December 5, 1867)[232]
— UNKNOWN
    — 9th U.S. Cavalry Detachment Co. F
— **1 KILLED**[233]
    — Private Nathan Johnson (Co. F 9th U.S. Cavalry)

(0302) Skirmish, Owyhee River, Oregon (December 11, 1867)[234]
— Interpreter David C. Pickett (Citizen)
    — Detachment of Indian Scouts

(0303) Citizens, near Fort Phil Kearny, Dakota Territory (December 14, 1867)[235]

(0304) Skirmish, near Camp Wallen, Arizona Territory (December 19, 1867)[236]
— 1st Lieutenant William H. Winters (1st U.S. Cavalry)
    — 1st U.S. Cavalry Detachment Co. G

(0305) Action, near Fort Lancaster, Texas (December 26, 1867)[237]
— Captain William T. Frohock (9th U.S. Cavalry)
    — 9th U.S. Cavalry Detachment Co. K
— **3 KILLED**[238]
    — Private Edward Boyer (Co. K 9th U.S. Cavalry)
    — Private William Sharpe (Co. K 9th U.S. Cavalry)
    — Private Anderson Trimble (Co. K 9th U.S. Cavalry)

— *Captain Eugene M. Baker (1st U.S. Cavalry) brevet promotion to Colonel for zeal and energy while in command of troops against hostile Indians (1866, 1867 and 1868).*

— *Captain John J. Coppinger (23rd U.S. Infantry) brevet promotion to Colonel for zeal and energy while in command of troops operating against hostile Indians (1866, 1867 and 1868).*

TOTAL KILLED 1867 — 6/84/3/10 (OFFICERS, ENLISTED MEN, INDIAN SCOUTS, CITIZENS)

[232] Indians. Chronological List, 31; Heitman (Volume 2), 430; Leckie, *Buffalo Soldiers*, 87; Smith, *Old Army in Texas*, 149; Wooster, *Frontier Crossroads*, 92.
[233] Register of Deaths Regular Army, 1860-1889 (Volume 2); 9th U.S. Cavalry Regimental Return December 1867.
[234] Indians. *Annual Report of Secretary of War (1868)*, 70; Chronological List, 31; Heitman (Volume 2), 430; Michno, *Deadliest Indian War*, 286-287. Chronological List and Heitman both list 12 December 1867.
[235] Indians. Chronological List, 31; Heitman (Volume 2), 430.
[236] Indians. Chronological List, 31; Heitman (Volume 2), 430.
[237] Indians. Chronological List, 31; Heitman (Volume 2), 430; Burton, *Black, Buckskin and Blue*,149-154; Leckie, *Buffalo Soldiers*, 87; Smith, *Old Army in Texas*, 149; Uglow, *Standing in the Gap*, 26-27; Williams, *Texas' Last Frontier*, 89.
[238] 9th U.S. Cavalry Regimental Return December 1867.

1868

"The co-ordinate departments of our government likewise continue to extend the surveys of public land westward, and grant patents to occupants; to locate and build railroads; to establish mail routes, with the necessary stations and relays of horses, as though that region of the country were in profound peace, and all danger of occupation and transit had passed away. Over all of these matters the military authorities have no control, yet their public nature implies public protection, and we are daily and hourly called upon for guards and escorts, and are left in the breach to catch all the kicks and cuffs of a war of races, without the privilege of advising or being consulted beforehand."

— William T. Sherman, U.S. Army[1]

---

[1] Official Report of Lieutenant General William T. Sherman, Headquarters Military Division of the Missouri, St. Louis, Missouri, 1 November 1868. *Annual Report of Secretary of War (1868)*, 1.

(0306) Citizens, Northern Texas (January 1868)[2]
— (25) Citizens Killed

(0307) Skirmish, near Owyhee River, Oregon (January 4, 1868)[3]
— Interpreter David C. Pickett (Citizen)
— 1st U.S. Cavalry Detachment Co. M
— Detachment of Indian Scouts

(0308) Action, Difficult Canyon, Arizona Territory (January 14, 1868)[4]
— Captain Samuel B.M. Young (8th U.S. Cavalry)
— 8th U.S. Cavalry Co. K
— **2 WOUNDED**[5]
— Private Robert McClusky (Co. K 8th U.S. Cavalry)
— *gunshot wound, left thigh, severe wound*
— Private Charles Dunn (Co. K 8th U.S. Cavalry)
— *gunshot wound, back, slight wound*

"They [the Hualapais Indians] fought desperately, being armed with about forty breech loading and about twenty muzzle loading arms, and had it not been a complete surprise, it is my opinion that not one of my party would ever have returned alive from that canyon... Too much cannot be said in commendation of those fourteen men. Braver or more daring men never slung a carbine."
— Samuel B.M. Young, U.S. Army[6]

(0309) Action, Beale Springs, Arizona Territory (January 14, 1868)[7]
— 1st Lieutenant Jonathan D. Stevenson (8th U.S. Cavalry)
— 8th U.S. Cavalry Co. K
— **1 WOUNDED**[8]
— 1st Lieutenant Jonathan D. Stevenson (Co. K 8th U.S. Cavalry)
— *gunshot wound, right and left thighs, genitalia, severe wounds*

— *Corporal Heinrich Bertram (Co. B 8th U.S. Cavalry) received MOH: Bravery in scouts and actions against Indians (Arizona, 1868).*

— *Private James Brophy (Co. B 8th U.S. Cavalry) received MOH: Bravery in scouts and actions against Indians (Arizona, 1868).*

— *Farrier Patrick J. Burke (Co. B 8th U.S. Cavalry) received MOH: Bravery in scouts and actions against Indians (Arizona, 1868).*

[2] Indians. *Annual Report of Secretary of War (1868)*, 210-211; *Annual Report of Secretary of War (1869)*, 55; Record of Engagements, 13.
[3] Indians. *Annual Report of Secretary of War (1868)*, 70; Chronological List, 31; Heitman (Volume 2), 430; Michno, *Deadliest Indian War*, 287-289.
[4] Indians. Chronological List, 31; Heitman (Volume 2), 430; Alexander, *Arizona Frontier Military Place Names*, 49-50; Altshuler, *Chains of Command*, 136; Thrapp, *Conquest of Apacheria*, 48-50.
[5] Reports of Diseases and Individual Cases, F 401.
[6] Captain Samuel B.M. Young (5th U.S. Cavalry) to Price, 20 January 1868. Altshuler, *Chains of Command*, 136.
[7] Indians. Chronological List, 31; Heitman (Volume 2), 430; Altshuler, *Chains of Command*, 136; Thrapp, *Conquest of Apacheria*, 48-50.
[8] Reports of Diseases and Individual Cases, F 401.

— *Sergeant Francis C. Green (Co. K 8th U.S. Cavalry) received MOH: Bravery in action (Arizona, 1868 and 1869).*

— *Corporal Jacob Gunther (Co. E 8th U.S. Cavalry) received MOH: Bravery in scouts and actions against Indians (Arizona, 1868 to 1869).*

— *Corporal David A. Matthews (Co. E 8th U.S. Cavalry) received MOH: Bravery in scouts and actions against Indians (Arizona, 1868 and 1869).*

— *First Sergeant James McNally (Co. E 8th U.S. Cavalry) received MOH: Bravery in scouts and actions against Indians (Arizona, 1868 and 1869).*

— *Sergeant John Moriarity (Co. E 8th U.S. Cavalry) received MOH: Bravery in scouts and actions against Indians (Arizona, 1868 and 1869).*

— *Private Samuel Richman (Co. E 8th U.S. Cavalry) received MOH: Bravery in action with Indians (Arizona, 1868 and 1869).*

— *Private Otto Smith (Co. K 8th U.S. Cavalry) received MOH: Bravery in scouts and actions against the Indians (Arizona, 1868 and 1869).*

— *Corporal Wilbur N. Taylor (Co. K 8th U.S. Cavalry) received MOH: Bravery in action with Indians (Arizona, 1868 and 1869).*

(0310) Skirmish, Malheur River, Oregon (January 16, 1868)[9]
— Captain Abraham Bassford (8th U.S. Cavalry)
— 8th U.S. Cavalry Co. D

(0311) Citizens, Legion Valley, Llano County, Texas (February 5, 1868)[10]
— (5) Citizens Killed

— *Sergeant James Fegan (Co. H 3rd U.S. Infantry) received MOH: While in charge of a powder train en route from Fort Harker to Fort Dodge, Kansas, was attacked by a party of desperadoes, who attempted to rescue a deserter in his charge and to fire the train. Sergeant Fegan, singlehanded, repelled the attacking party, wounding two of them, and brought his train through in safety (Plum Creek, Kansas, March 1868).*

(0312) Action, Paint Creek, Texas (March 6, 1868)[11]
— Captain Adna R. Chafee (6th U.S. Cavalry)
— 6th U.S. Cavalry Co. F and I
— Detachment of Indian Scouts
— **3 WOUNDED**[12]

---

[9] Indians. Chronological List, 31; Heitman (Volume 2), 430. Heitman lists 16 February 1868.

[10] Indians. Killed were Fielty Johnson, Nancy Johnson, Samantha Johnson, Rebecca Johnson and Amanda Townsend. Malinda Caudle and Temple Friend were kidnapped and eventually recovered. *Annual Report of Secretary of War (1869)*, 55; *Record of Engagements*, 13; Michno, *Fate Worse Than Death*, 386-395; Wilbarger, *Indian Depredations in Texas*, 633-637.

[11] Indians. *Annual Report of Secretary of War (1868)*, 713-714, 774; Chronological List, 31; Heitman (Volume 2), 430; Carter, *From Yorktown to Santiago*, 138-140, 277; Cashion, *Texas Frontier*, 106; Rister, *Fort Griffin*, 74-75; Smith, *Old Army in Texas*, 149. Chronological List and Heitman both list 6th U.S. Cavalry Co. F, I, K.

[12] Reports of Diseases and Individual Cases, F 403; Otis, *Report of Surgical Cases*, 157-158.

— Private James Ryan (Co. F 6th U.S. Cavalry)
    — *arrow wound, face, slight wound*
— Private John F. Butler (Co. I 6th U.S. Cavalry)
    — *arrow wound, forearm, slight wound*
— Private Charles Hoffman (Co. I 6th U.S. Cavalry)
    — *arrow wound, left thigh, severe wound*

    — *Captain Adna R. Chaffee (6th U.S. Cavalry) brevet promotion to Major for gallant and effective service in an engagement with Comanche Indians (Paint Creek, Texas, March 7, 1868).*

"The Commanding Officer takes pleasure in openly announcing to the troops of his command, the complete success of the detachment that left this post on the sixth instant, under the command of [Captain Adna R. Chaffee], 6th U.S. Cavalry. This short and decisive campaign has resulted in the… total breaking up of an Indian camp which had for a long time been a scourge to the people of the frontier."
— Samuel D. Sturgis, U.S. Army[13]

(0313) Skirmish, Headwaters of Colorado River, Texas (March 10, 1868)[14]
— Sergeant Charles Gale (4th U.S. Cavalry)
    — 4th U.S. Cavalry Detachment Co. D

(0314) Citizens, near Tularosa, New Mexico Territory (March 11, 1868)[15]
— (13) Citizens Killed

(0315) Action, Dunder and Blitzen Creek, Oregon (March 14, 1868)[16]
— Lt. Colonel George Crook (23rd U.S. Infantry)
    — 1st U.S. Cavalry Co. H
    — 8th U.S. Cavalry Co. C
    — 23rd U.S. Infantry Co. D
    — Detachment of Indian Scouts
— **4 WOUNDED**[17]
    — Sergeant Francis Rigby (Co. H 1st U.S. Cavalry)
       — *arrow wound, forearm, slight wound*

    — Ba-yan-za (Indian Scout)
       — *arrow wound, arm, slight wound*
    — Big Mac (Indian Scout)
       — *arrow wound, arm, slight wound*
    — Owine (Indian Scout)
       — *arrow wound, arm, slight wound*

---

[13] General Order No. 19, Lt. Colonel Samuel D. Sturgis, Headquarters, Fort Griffin, Texas, 10 March 1868. Carter, *From Yorktown to Santiago*, 139-140.
[14] Indians. *Annual Report of Secretary of War (1868)*, 713, 774; Chronological List, 31; Heitman (Volume 2), 430; Smith, *Old Army in Texas*, 149.
[15] Indians. Killed were eleven men and two women, kidnapped was one child. Chronological List, 31; Heitman (Volume 2), 430; Record of Engagements, 7.
[16] Indians. *Annual Report of Secretary of War (1868)*, 70; Chronological List, 32; Heitman (Volume 2), 430; Michno, *Deadliest Indian War*, 301-302. Chronological List and Heitman both list 1st U.S. Cavalry Co. H; 8th U.S. Cavalry Co. C; 23rd U.S. Infantry Co. D.
[17] Reports of Diseases and Individual Cases, F 404; Otis, *Report of Surgical Cases*, 157, 158. Chronological List lists 1st Lieutenant William R. Parnell (1st U.S. Cavalry) as WIA. His name does not appear on F 404.

(0316) Action, near Saw Mill, Fort Fetterman, Dakota Territory (March 18, 1868)[18]
    — UNKNOWN
        — 18th U.S. Infantry Detachment Co. K
    — 1 KILLED[19]
        — Private Thomas Bourke (Co. K 18th U.S. Infantry)

(0317) Citizens, Horseshoe and Twin Springs Ranches, Dakota Territory (March 20, 1868)[20]
    — (3) Citizens Killed

(0318) Action, near Camp Willow Grove, Arizona Territory (March 21, 1868)[21]
    — Corporal David Troy (14th U.S. Infantry)
        — 14th U.S. Infantry Detachment Co. E
    — 2 KILLED[22]
        — Corporal David Troy (Co. E 14th U.S. Infantry)
        — Private Bernard Flood (Co. E 14th U.S. Infantry)

    — 1 WOUNDED[23]
        — Mail Carrier Charles Spencer (Citizen)
          — *gunshot wound, thigh*

(0319) Citizens, Bluff Creek, Kansas (March 25, 1868)[24]

(0320) Action, Cottonwood Springs, Arizona Territory (March 25, 1868)[25]
    — Captain Guido Ilges (14th U.S. Infantry)
        — 14th U.S. Infantry Detachment Co. B
    — 1 WOUNDED[26]
        — Private Logan (Co. B 14th U.S. Infantry)

(0321) Action, Owyhee River, Oregon (March 26, 1868)[27]
    — Sergeant John New (8th U.S. Cavalry)
        — 8th U.S. Cavalry Detachment Co. D
    — 1 KILLED[28]
        — Teamster William Harris (Citizen)

(0322) Skirmish, Pinal Mountains, Arizona Territory (April 1, 1868)[29]
    — 1st Lieutenant William H. Winters (1st U.S. Cavalry)
        — 1st U.S. Cavalry Co. G

(0323) Citizens, Rock Creek, Wyoming Territory (April 3, 1868)[30]

(0324) Skirmish, Malheur River, Oregon (April 5, 1868)[31]
    — Captain David Perry (1st U.S. Cavalry)

[18] Indians. *Annual Report of Secretary of War (1868)*, 30; Chronological List, 32; Heitman (Volume 2), 430; Hagan, *Exactly in the Right Place*, 199; Lindmier, *Drybone*, 53.
[19] Fort Fetterman Post Return March 1868.
[20] Indians. *Annual Report of Secretary of War (1868)*, 28, 30; McChristian, *Fort Laramie*, 304.
[21] Indians. Chronological List, 32; Heitman (Volume 2), 430; Farish, *History of Arizona (Volume 5)*, 302-304; Thrapp, *Conquest of Apacheria*, 44-45.
[22] Register of Deaths Regular Army, 1860-1889 (Volume 2); 14th U.S. Infantry Regimental Return March 1868.
[23] Thrapp, *Conquest of Apacheria*, 44-45.
[24] Indians. Chronological List, 32; Record of Engagements, 7.
[25] Indians. Chronological List, 32; Heitman (Volume 2), 430.
[26] Rodenbough, *Army of the United States*, 608.
[27] Indians. Chronological List, 32; Heitman (Volume 2), 430; Michno, *Deadliest Indian War*, 307.
[28] Michno, *Deadliest Indian War*, 307.
[29] Indians. Chronological List, 32; Heitman (Volume 2), 430; Altshuler, *Chains of Command*, 142.
[30] Indians. *Annual Report of Secretary of War (1868)*, 31; Chronological List, 32; Heitman (Volume 2), 430.
[31] Indians. *Annual Report of Secretary of War (1868)*, 70-71; Chronological List, 32; Heitman (Volume 2), 430; Michno, *Deadliest Indian War*, 308-309. Heitman lists 1st U.S. Cavalry Co. F; 8th U.S. Cavalry Co. C; Detachment of Indian Scouts.

— 1st U.S. Cavalry Co. F
— 8th U.S. Cavalry Co. C
— 23rd U.S. Infantry Detachment Co. K
— Detachment of Indian Scouts

— Captain William Kelly (8th U.S. Cavalry) brevet promotion to Major for gallantry in an engagement with a large band of Indians (Malheur River, Oregon, April 5, 1868).

— Captain David Perry (1st U.S. Cavalry) brevet promotion to Colonel for gallantry in an engagement with a large band of Indians (Malheur River, Oregon, April 5, 1868).

— 2nd Lieutenant Alexander H. Stanton (1st U.S. Cavalry) brevet promotion to Captain for gallantry in an engagement with a large band of Indians (Malheur River, Oregon, April 5, 1868).

(0325) Skirmish, Camp Three Forks, Owyhee River, Idaho Territory (April 17, 1868)[32]
— Captain George K. Brady (23rd U.S. Infantry)
— 23rd U.S. Infantry Co. E

(0326) Action, Nesmith's Mills, near Tularosa, New Mexico Territory (April 17, 1868)[33]
— Sergeant Edward Glass (3rd U.S. Cavalry)
— 3rd U.S. Cavalry Detachment Co. H
— Detachment of Volunteers
— 6 WOUNDED[34]
— Enlisted Man (3rd U.S. Cavalry)

— (5) Citizens

" The major general commanding the department is pleased to notice the gallant and meritorious conduct displayed by Sergeant Edward Glass (3rd U.S. Cavalry), and four enlisted men… in resisting and repelling an attack made upon them by a body of Indians numbering about 200… The persistent energy of Sergeant Glass in returning and renewing the fight, after having twice been driven by his position by superior numbers, resulting in the final defeat of the Indians… was very credible, and is warmly commended."
— Chauncey McKeever, U.S. Army[35]

(0327) Citizens, Upper Yellowstone River, Montana Territory (April 21, 1868)[36]
— (1) Citizen Killed

(0328) Skirmish, near Camp Grant, Arizona Territory (April 21, 1868)[37]
— 1st Lieutenant Edmond G. Fechet (8th U.S. Cavalry)
— 8th U.S. Cavalry Co. I

---

[32] Indians. Chronological List, 32; Heitman (Volume 2), 430; Michno, *Deadliest Indian War*, 309.

[33] Indians. *Annual Report of Secretary of War (1868)*, 772; Chronological List, 32; Heitman (Volume 2), 430; Record of Engagements, 7.

[34] Chronological List, 32.

[35] General Orders No. 16, Chauncey McKeever, Assistant Adjutant General, Headquarters Department of the Missouri, Fort Leavenworth, Kansas, May 20, 1868. *Annual Report of Secretary of War (1868)*, 772-773.

[36] Indians. *Annual Report of Secretary of War (1868)*, 35; Chronological List, 32; Heitman (Volume 2), 430; Rockwell, *U.S. Army in Frontier Montana*, 150-151.

[37] Indians. Chronological List, 32; Heitman (Volume 2), 430.

(0329) Citizens, near Fort McPherson, Nebraska (April 22, 1868)[38]
— (5) Citizens Killed

(0330) Citizens, near Fort Ellis, Montana Territory (April 23, 1868)[39]
— (1) Citizen Killed

(0331) Skirmish, near Camp Harney, Oregon (April 23, 1868)[40]
— Archie McIntosh (Chief Scout)
— Detachment of Indian Scouts

(0332) Action, near Camp Winfield Scott, Paradise Valley, Nevada (April 29, 1868)[41]
— 2nd Lieutenant Pendleton Hunter (8th U.S. Cavalry)
— 8th U.S. Cavalry Detachment Co. A
— 1 KILLED[42]
— Private Thomas Ward (Co. A 8th U.S. Cavalry) — d. 5-02-1868

— 2 WOUNDED[43]
— 2nd Lieutenant Pendleton Hunter (8th U.S. Cavalry)
— *gunshot wounds, right buttocks, right forearm*

— Sergeant John Kelly (Co. A 8th U.S. Cavalry) — d. 09-28-1868
— *gunshot wounds, chest, left lung, right thigh*

— *Private James C. Reed (Co. A 8th U.S. Cavalry) received MOH: Defended his position with three others against a party of seventeen hostile Indians under heavy fire at close quarters, the entire party except himself being severely wounded (Arizona, April 29, 1868).*

"The general commanding the department takes pleasure in commending [2nd Lieutenant Pendleton Hunter], Sergeant John Kelly and Privates Thomas Ward and James C. Reed... for coolness and gallantry under trying circumstances in a recent Indian fight near Camp Winfield Scott, Nevada, in which Lieutenant Hunter, although badly wounded in several places, with Private Reed, kept at bay for several hours, seventeen Indian, and protected their wounded comrades until assistance arrived."
— John P. Sherburne, U.S. Army[44]

(0333) Action, south of Otseos Lodge, Warner Mountains, Oregon (April 29, 1868)[45]
— 1st Lieutenant Azor H. Nickerson (23rd U.S. Infantry)
— 23rd U.S. Infantry Detachment Co. D
— 1 KILLED[46]
— Private Charles A. Fonda (Co. D 23rd U.S. Infantry) — d. 4-30-1868

— 1 WOUNDED[47]

---

[38] Indians. Killed were five herders. *Annual Report of Secretary of War (1868)*, 31; Chronological List, 32; Heitman (Volume 2), 430.

[39] Indians. Killed was herder Nate Crabtree. *Annual Report of Secretary of War (1868)*, 35; Chronological List, 32; Heitman (Volume 2), 431; Otis, *Report of Surgical Cases*, 145; Rockwell, *U.S. Army in Frontier Montana*, 151. Chronological List lists 28 May 1868.

[40] Indians. Chronological List, 32; Heitman (Volume 2), 431; Michno, *Deadliest Indian War*, 310.

[41] Indians. *Annual Report of Secretary of War (1868)*, 773; Chronological List, 33; Heitman (Volume 2), 431; Michno, *Deadliest Indian War*, 310-313; Rathbun, *Nevada Military Place Names*, 129-130. Chronological List and Heitman both list Arizona Territory.

[42] Register of Deaths Regular Army, 1860-1889 (Volume 2).

[43] Otis, *Report of Surgical Cases*, 31, 57.

[44] General Orders No. 28, Major John P. Sherburne, Assistant Adjutant General, Headquarters Department of California, San Francisco, California, 20 May 1868. *Annual Report of Secretary of War (1868)*, 773.

[45] Indians. Chronological List, 33; Heitman (Volume 2), 431; Michno, *Deadliest Indian War*, 313-315.

[46] Reports of Diseases and Individual Cases, F 406; Register of Deaths Regular Army 1860-1889 (Volume 2); Otis, *Report of Surgical Cases*, 206.

[47] Reports of Diseases and Individual Cases, F 406; Otis, *Report of Surgical Cases*, 237-238.

— Private Alonzo Youngman (Co. D 23rd U.S. Infantry)
— *gunshot wound, wrist, severe wound*

(0334) Action, Hoag's Bluff, Warner Valley, Oregon (May 1, 1868)[48]
— Captain Samuel Munson (9th U.S. Infantry)
— 8th U.S. Cavalry Detachment Co. G
— 9th U.S. Infantry Co. C
— **1 KILLED**[49]
— Guide Daniel Hoag (Citizen)

— **2 WOUNDED**[50]
— 2nd Lieutenant Hayden Delany (9th U.S. Infantry)
— *gunshot wound, forearm, severe wound*

— Private Charles Armstedt/ Arnshedt (Co. G 8th U.S. Cavalry)
— *gunshot wound, thigh, severe wound*

— *2nd Lieutenant Hayden Delany (9th U.S. Infantry) brevet promotion to 1st Lieutenant for gallant and meritorious service in action with the Paiute Indians (Warner Valley, Oregon, May 1, 1868).*

(0335) Action, near Camp Crittenden, Arizona Territory (May 1, 1868)[51]
— Captain Harrison Moulton (1st U.S. Cavalry)
— 1st U.S. Cavalry Co. C
— **1 WOUNDED**[52]
— Enlisted Man (Co. C 1st U.S. Cavalry)

(0336) Skirmish, San Pedro River, Arizona Territory (May 1, 1868)[53]
— 1st Lieutenant CaMillo C.C. Carr (1st U.S. Cavalry)
— 1st U.S. Cavalry Co. E

(0337) Skirmish, Gila River, near Camp Grant, Arizona Territory (May 1, 1868)[54]
— 1st Lieutenant Edmond G. Fechet (8th U.S. Cavalry)
— 8th U.S. Cavalry Co. I

(0338) Citizens, near Fort Buford, Dakota Territory (May 13, 1868)[55]
— (2) Citizens Killed

(0339) Citizens, between Fort Stevenson and Fort Totten, Dakota Territory (May 15, 1868)[56]
— (2) Citizens Killed

(0340) Skirmish, Rio Salinas, Arizona Territory (May 18, 1868)[57]
— 1st Lieutenant Robert Carrick (8th U.S. Cavalry)

---

[48] Indians. Chronological List, 33; Heitman (Volume 2), 431; Michno, *Deadliest Indian War*, 316-317.
[49] Michno, *Deadliest Indian War*, 316-317.
[50] Reports of Diseases and Individual Cases, F 405.
[51] Indians. Chronological List, 33; Heitman (Volume 2), 431.
[52] Chronological List, 33.
[53] Indians. Chronological List, 33; Heitman (Volume 2), 431.
[54] Indians. Chronological List, 33; Heitman (Volume 2), 431.
[55] Indians. *Annual Report of Secretary of War (1868)*, 35; Chronological List, 33; Heitman (Volume 2), 431.
[56] Indians. Killed were two mail carriers, McDonald and Rolette. *Annual Report of Secretary of War (1868)*, 35; Chronological List, 33; Heitman (Volume 2), 431.
[57] Indians. Chronological List, 33; Heitman (Volume 2), 431.

— 8th U.S. Cavalry Co. B and L

(0341) Skirmish, Mouth of Musselshell River, Dakota Territory (May 19, 1868)[58]
  — Captain Robert Nugent (13th U.S. Infantry)
    — 13th U.S. Infantry Co. E, Detachments Co. B and H

(0342) Citizens, near Camp Reeve, Montana Territory (May 24, 1868)[59]
  — (2) Citizens Killed

(0343) Action, Mouth of Musselshell River, Dakota Territory (May 24, 1868)[60]
  — 1st Lieutenant Andrew N. Canfield (13th U.S. Infantry)
    — 13th U.S. Infantry Co. E, Detachments Co. B and H
— 2 KILLED[61]
  — Private Constand Queswelle (Co. B 13th U.S. Infantry)
  — Private James N. Cook (Co. B 13th U.S. Infantry)

(0344) Skirmish, near Yellowstone River, Montana Territory (May 24, 1868)[62]
  — Sergeant James Keating (13th U.S. Infantry)
    — 13th U.S. Infantry Detachment Co. F
  — Detachment of Volunteers

(0345) Action, Apache Pass, Arizona Territory (May 26, 1868)[63]
  — UNKNOWN
    — 32nd U.S. Infantry Detachment
— 4 KILLED[64]
  — Private George Knowles (Co. D 32nd U.S. Infantry)
  — Private Robert King (Co. D 32nd U.S. Infantry)

  — Teamster John Brownley (Citizen)
  — Driver Charles Hadsell (Citizen)

(0346) Skirmish, near Owyhee River, Idaho Territory (May 29, 1868)[65]
  — Sergeant Henry Miller (1st U.S. Cavalry)
    — 1st U.S. Cavalry Detachment Co. M
  — Detachment of Indian Scouts

(0347) Action, Tonto Basin, San Carlos Trail, Arizona Territory (May 30, 1868)[66]
  — Lt. Colonel Thomas C. Devin (8th U.S. Cavalry)
    — 8th U.S. Cavalry Co. B and L
— 1 KILLED[67]
  — (1) Citizen

[58] Indians. Chronological List, 33; Heitman (Volume 2), 431.
[59] Indians. *Annual Report of Secretary of War (1868)*, 35.
[60] Indians. Chronological List, 33; Heitman (Volume 2), 431. Heitman lists 13th U.S. Infantry Detachments Co. B, F, H.
[61] Register of Deaths Regular Army, 1860-1889 (Volume 2); 13th U.S. Infantry Regimental Return May 1868; Otis, *Report of Surgical Cases*, 145.
[62] Indians. *Annual Report of Secretary of War (1868)*, 35; Chronological List, 33; Heitman (Volume 2), 431; Rockwell, *U.S. Army in Frontier Montana*, 151. Chronological List lists 13th U.S. Infantry Detachment Co. F.
[63] Indians. McChristian, *Fort Bowie*, 101-102.
[64] Register of Deaths Regular Army, 1860-1889 (Volume 2); Camp Bowie Cemetery Records.
[65] Indians. *Annual Report of Secretary of War (1868)*, 71; Chronological List, 33; Heitman (Volume 2), 431; Michno, *Deadliest Indian War*, 323-324.
[66] Indians. Chronological List, 33; Heitman (Volume 2), 431.
[67] Chronological List, 33.

— **1 WOUNDED**[68]
    — Enlisted Man (8th U.S. Cavalry)

    — *Private Edgar R. Aston (Co. L 8th U.S. Cavalry) received MOH: With two other men he volunteered to search for a wagon passage out of a 4,000-foot valley wherein an infantry column was immobile. This small group passed six miles among hostile Apache terrain finding the sought passage. On their return trip down the canyon they were attacked by Apaches who were successfully held at bay (San Carlos, Arizona, May 30, 1868).*

    — *Private William G. Cubberly (Co. L 8th U.S. Cavalry) received MOH: With two other men he volunteered to search for a wagon passage out of a 4,000-foot valley wherein an infantry column was immobile. This small group passed six miles among hostile Apache terrain finding the sought passage. On their return trip down the canyon they were attacked by Apaches who were successfully held at bay (San Carlos, Arizona, May 30, 1868).*

(0348) Action, Castle Rock, near North Fork of Malheur River, Oregon (May 31, 1868)[69]
    — 2nd Lieutenant Alexander H. Stanton (1st U.S. Cavalry)
        — 1st U.S. Cavalry Detachment Co. F
        — Detachment of Indian Scouts
— **1 WOUNDED**[70]
        — Sergeant W.W. McCullough (Co. F 1st U.S. Cavalry)
            — *gunshot wound, right chest*

(0349) Operations, Apache Springs, New Mexico Territory (June 8 to 13, 1868)[71]
    — 1st Lieutenant Deane Monahan (3rd U.S. Cavalry)
        — 3rd U.S. Cavalry Detachments Co. G and I

(0350) Skirmish, Snake Canyon, Idaho Territory (June 9, 1868)[72]
    — Corporal J. Moan (23rd U.S. Infantry)
        — 23rd U.S. Infantry Detachment Co. H
        — Detachment of Indian Scouts

(0351) Skirmish, Twenty-Five Yard Creek, Montana Territory (June 13, 1868)[73]
    — Captain Joseph L. Horr (13th U.S. Infantry)
        — 13th U.S. Infantry Detachment Co. F

(0352) Action, Toddy Mountain, Arizona Territory (June 16, 1868)[74]
    — Sergeant Joseph Lemon (1st U.S. Cavalry)
        — 1st U.S. Cavalry Detachment Co. E
— **4 KILLED**[75]
        — Sergeant Jospeh Lemon (Co. E 1st U.S. Cavalry)
        — Private Benson H. Merrill (Co. E 1st U.S. Cavalry)

---

[68] Chronological List, 33.
[69] Indians. *Annual Report of Secretary of War (1868)*, 71; Chronological List, 33; Heitman (Volume 2), 431; Michno, *Deadliest Indian War*, 324-325. Chronological List lists 1st U.S. Cavalry Detachment Co. F. Heitman lists 1st U.S. Cavalry Detachment Co. E.
[70] Otis, *Report of Surgical Cases*, 39.
[71] Indians. Chronological List, 33; Heitman (Volume 2), 431; Record of Engagements, 7; Moore, *Chiefs, Agents and Soldiers*, 30.
[72] Indians. Chronological List, 33; Heitman (Volume 2), 431; Michno, *Deadliest Indian War*, 326.
[73] Indians. Chronological List, 33; Heitman (Volume 2), 431. Chronological List lists 13th U.S. Infantry Detachment.
[74] Indians. Chronological List, 33; Heitman (Volume 2), 431; Alexander, *Arizona Frontier Military Place Names*, 57-58; Thrapp, *Conquest of Apacheria*, 56-57.
[75] Register of Deaths Regular Army, 1860-1889 (Volume 2).

— Private James Murphy (Co. E 1st U.S. Cavalry)
— Private John Murphy (Co. E 1st U.S. Cavalry)

— 1 WOUNDED[76]
— Private Theeley (Co. E 1st U.S. Cavalry)

(0353) Skirmish, near Battle Creek, Idaho Territory (June 24, 1868)[77]
— Captain Joseph J. Coppinger (23rd U.S. Infantry)
— 23rd U.S. Infantry Co. A
— Detachment of Indian Scouts

(0354) Citizens, near Brazos River, Texas (July 1868)[78]
— (4) Citizens Killed

(0355) Skirmish, between Verde River and Salt River, Arizona Territory (July 8, 1868)[79]
— 1st Lieutenant CaMillo C.C. Carr (1st U.S. Cavalry)
— 1st U.S. Cavalry Detachment Co. E
— 8th U.S. Cavalry Co. I

(0356) Citizens, near Niobrara River, Nebraska (July 11, 1868)[80]
— (1) Citizen Killed

(0357) Action, near Fort Reno, Dakota Territory (July 19, 1868)[81]
— 2nd Lieutenant Edmund R.P. Shurly (27th U.S. Infantry)
— 2nd U.S. Cavalry Detachment Co. A
— 27th U.S. Infantry Co. B and F
— 1 KILLED[82]
— Private George Peach (Co. A 2nd U.S. Cavalry)

— 1 WOUNDED[83]
— Private Joseph Miller (Co. A 2nd U.S. Cavalry)
— *arrow wound, shoulder*

(0358) Action, near Camp Crittenden, Arizona Territory (July 22, 1868)[84]
— UNKNOWN
— 1st U.S. Cavalry Detachment Co. K
— 1 KILLED[85]
— Farrier John White (Co. K 1st U.S. Cavalry)

(0359) Skirmish, Big Salmon River, Idaho Territory (July 23, 1868)[86]
— Captain James B. Sinclair (23rd U.S. Infantry)

---

[76] Thrapp, *Conquest of Apacheria*, 56-57.
[77] Indians. *Annual Report of Secretary of War (1868)*, 71; Chronological List, 33; Heitman (Volume 2), 431; Michno, *Deadliest Indian War*, 326. Heitman lists 23rd U.S. Infantry Co. A.
[78] Indians. *Annual Report of Secretary of War (1869)*, 55.
[79] Indians. *Annual Report of Secretary of War (1868)*, 35; Chronological List, 33; Heitman (Volume 2), 431; Thrapp, *Conquest of Apacheria*, 59-60. Chronological List lists 1st U.S. Cavalry Detachment Co. E; 8th U.S. Cavalry Detachment Co. I.
[80] Indians. *Annual Report of Secretary of War (1868)*, 35; Chronological List, 33.
[81] Indians. *Annual Report of Secretary of War (1868)*, 31; Chronological List, 33; Heitman (Volume 2), 431; Hagan, *Exactly in the Right Place*, 229-231; McDermott, *Red Cloud's War (Volume 2)*, 521; Rodenbough, *From Everglade to Canyon*, 435. Chronological List lists 2nd U.S. Cavalry Detachment Co. A; 27th U.S. Infantry Detachments.
[82] 2nd U.S. Cavalry Regimental Return July 1868; Register of Deaths Regular Army, 1860-1889 (Volume 3)
[83] Otis, *Report of Surgical Cases*, 158.
[84] Indians. Heitman (Volume 2), 431.
[85] 1st U.S. Cavalry Regimental Return July 1868.
[86] Indians. *Annual Report of Secretary of War (1868)*, 71; Chronological List, 34; Heitman (Volume 2), 431; Michno, *Deadliest Indian War*, 333-334. Chronological List and Heitman both list 25 July 1868.

— 23rd U.S. Infantry Detachment Co. H
— Detachment of Indian Scouts

(0360) Skirmish, Juniper Canyon, Idaho Territory (July 26, 1868)[87]
— 1st Lieutenant George M. Taylor (23rd U.S. Infantry)
— 23rd U.S. Infantry Detachment Co. E

(0361) Skirmish, near Old Camp Sully, Dakota Territory (July 28, 1868)[88]
— 2nd Lieutenant Cornelius C. Cusick (31st U.S. Infantry)
— 31st U.S. Infantry Detachments Co. B, C and E

(0362) Action, Tonto Valley, near Camp Reno, Arizona Territory (July 30, 1868)[89]
— 2nd Lieutenant William F. Denney (31st U.S. Infantry)
— 31st U.S. Infantry Detachment Co. A
— **1 WOUNDED**[90]
— Enlisted Man (31st U.S. Infantry)

(0363) Skirmish, Cimarron River, Kansas (August 2, 1868)[91]
— Captain Robert M. West (7th U.S. Cavalry)
— 7th U.S. Cavalry Co. K

(0364) Skirmish, Fort Quitman, Texas (August 6, 1868)[92]
— UNKNOWN
— 9th U.S. Cavalry Co. H

(0365) Operations, Juniper Mountains, Idaho Territory (August 8 to September 5, 1868)[93]
— Sergeant T. Slatter (23rd U.S. Infantry)
— 23rd U.S. Infantry Detachment Co. A
— Detachment of Indian Scouts

(0366) Citizens, Saline River, Kansas (August 10, 1868)[94]
— (2) Citizens Killed

(0367) Citizens, Solomon River, Kansas (August 12, 1868)[95]
— (17) Citizens Killed

(0368) Citizens, Republican River, Kansas (August 12, 1868)[96]
— (2) Citizens Killed

(0369) Skirmish, Saline River, Kansas (August 12, 868)[97]
— Captain Frederick W. Benteen (7th U.S. Cavalry)
— 7th U.S. Cavalry Detachment Co. H

---

[87] Indians. *Annual Report of Secretary of War (1868)*, 71; Chronological List, 34; Heitman (Volume 2), 431; Michno, *Deadliest Indian War*, 334-335.
[88] Indians. Chronological List, 34; Heitman (Volume 2), 431. Chronological List lists 31st U.S. Infantry Detachment.
[89] Indians. Chronological List, 34; Heitman (Volume 2), 431.
[90] Chronological List, 34.
[91] Indians. Chronological List, 34; Heitman (Volume 2), 431.
[92] Indians. Chronological List, 34.
[93] Indians. Chronological List, 34; Heitman (Volume 2), 431; Michno, *Deadliest Indian War*, 335.
[94] Indians. *Annual Report of Secretary of War (1868)*, 3, 11, 13; *Annual Report of Secretary of War (1869)*, 53; Chronological List, 34; Record of Engagements, 7; Broome, *Dog Soldier Justice*, 7-33; Chalfant, *Cheyennes at Dark Water Creek*, 4-5.
[95] Indians. *Annual Report of Secretary of War (1868)*, 3, 11, 13; *Annual Report of Secretary of War (1869)*, 53; Chronological List, 34; Record of Engagements, 8; Broome, *Dog Soldier Justice*, 7-33; Chalfant, *Cheyennes at Dark Water Creek*, 4-5; Monnett, *Battle of Beecher Island*, 57-59.
[96] Indians. *Annual Report of Secretary of War (1868)*, 3, 11, 13; *Annual Report of Secretary of War (1869)*, 53; Chronological List, 34; Record of Engagements, 8; Broome, *Dog Soldier Justice*, 7-33; Chalfant, *Cheyennes at Dark Water Creek*, 4-5; Monnett, *Battle of Beecher Island*, 57-59.
[97] Indians. *Annual Report of Secretary of War (1868)*, 11; Chronological List, 34; Record of Engagements, 8; Leckie, *Military Conquest of the Southern Plains*, 71-72.

(0370) Skirmish, Walnut Grove, Arizona Territory (August 13, 1868)[98]
    — 1st Lieutenant Almond B. Wells (8th U.S. Cavalry)
        — 8th U.S. Cavalry Co. L

(0371) Skirmish, Saline River, Kansas (August 13, 1868)[99]
    — Captain Frederick W. Benteen (7th U.S. Cavalry)
        — 7th U.S. Cavalry Detachments Co. H and M

    — *Captain Frederick W. Benteen (7th U.S. Cavalry) brevet promotion to Colonel for gallant and meritorious conduct in an engagement with hostile Indians (Saline River, Kansas, August 13, 1868).*

(0372) Citizens, Granny Creek, Republican River, Kansas (August 14, 1868)[100]
    — (1) Citizen Killed

(0373) Action, near Sulphur Springs, Texas (August 14, 1868)[101]
    — UNKNOWN
        — 6th U.S. Cavalry Detachment Co. H
    — 1 KILLED[102]
        — First Sergeant Edward Creery (Co. H 6th U.S. Cavalry)
        — Private John Miller (Co. H 6th U.S. Cavalry) — d. 8-15-1868

(0374) Citizens, Twin Butte Creek, Kansas (August 19, 1868)[103]
    — (3) Citizens Killed

(0375) Citizens, Comstock's Ranch, Kansas (August 20, 1868)[104]
    — (2) Citizens Killed

(0376) Action, Fort Buford, Dakota Territory (August 20, 1868)[105]
    — Captain Charles J. Dickey (31st U.S. Infantry)
        — 31st U.S. Infantry Co. B, C, E and G
    — 3 KILLED[106]
        — Private George Beals (Co. E 31st U.S. Infantry)
        — Private Henry Henderson (Co. G 31st U.S. Infantry)
        — Private Max Liehman (Co. G 31st U.S. Infantry)

    — 3 WOUNDED[107]
        — Private James W. Cooper (Co. E 31st U.S. Infantry)
            — *arrow wound, abdomen, severe wound*
        — Private Michael Zuck (Co. E 31st U.S. Infantry)
            — *arrow wound. hip, slight wound*

[98] Indians. Chronological List, 34; Heitman (Volume 2), 431.

[99] Indians. *Annual Report of Secretary of War (1868)*, 11; Chronological List, 34; Heitman (Volume 2), 431. Chronological List lists 7th U.S. Cavalry Detachment Co. H.

[100] Indians. *Annual Report of Secretary of War (1869)*, 53; Chronological List, 34; Record of Engagements, 8; Broome, *Dog Soldier Justice*, 7-33.

[101] Bandits. Reports of Diseases and Individual Cases, F 407.

[102] Reports of Diseases and Individual Cases, F 407; Register of Deaths Regular Army, 1860-1889 (Volume 3); Otis, *Report of Surgical Cases*, 10.

[103] Indians. Killed were John McNeil, Andrew Pratt and Isaac Burwick. *Annual Report of Secretary of War (1868)*, 13; *Annual Report of Secretary of War (1869)*, 53; Chronological List, 34; Record of Engagements, 9; Greene, *Washita*, 51.

[104] Indians. *Annual Report of Secretary of War (1868)*, 11, 13; Chronological List, 34.

[105] Indians. *Annual Report of Secretary of War (1868)*, 35-36; Chronological List, 34; Heitman (Volume 2), 431. Chronological List lists 31st U.S. Infantry Co. B, E, G.

[106] Reports of Diseases and Individual Cases, F 408; Register of Deaths Regular Army, 1860-1889 (Volume 3); Fort Buford Post Return August 1868.

[107] Reports of Diseases and Individual Cases, F 408; Otis, *Report of Surgical Cases*, 154, 159. Chronological List lists 2nd Lieutenant Cornelius C. Cusick (31st U.S. Infantry) as WIA. His name does not appear on F 408.

— Private Henry Stackford (Co. G 31st U.S. Infantry)
— *arrow wound, left arm, slight wound*

(0377) Skirmish, Santa Maria River, Arizona Territory (August 22, 1868) [108]
— 2nd Lieutenant Rufus Somerby (8th U.S. Cavalry)
— 8th U.S. Cavalry Co. B

— *Private Thomas Carroll (Co. L 8th U.S. Cavalry) received MOH: Bravery in scouts and actions against Indians (Arizona, August to October, 1868).*

— *Private George Carter (Co. B 8th U.S. Cavalry) received MOH: Bravery in scouts and actions against Indians (Arizona, August to October, 1868).*

— *Private Charles Crandall (Co. B 8th U.S. Cavalry) received MOH: Bravery in scouts and actions against Indians (Arizona, August to October, 1868).*

— *Private Charles Daily (Co. B 8th U.S. Cavalry) received MOH: Bravery in scouts and actions against Indians (Arizona, August to October, 1868).*

— *Blacksmith William Dougherty (Co. B 8th U.S. Cavalry) received MOH: Bravery in scouts and actions against Indians (Arizona, August to October, 1868).*

— *Corporal James Dowling (Co. B 8th U.S. Cavalry) received MOH: Bravery in scouts and actions against Indians (Arizona, August to October, 1868).*

— *Sergeant Henry Falcott (Co. L 8th U.S. Cavalry) received MOH: Bravery in scouts and actions against Indians (Arizona, August to October, 1868).*

— *Private Daniel Farren (Co. B 8th U.S. Cavalry) received MOH: Bravery in scouts and actions against Indians (Arizona, August to October, 1868).*

— *Private William H. Folly (Co. B 8th U.S. Cavalry) received MOH: Bravery in scouts and actions against Indians (Arizona, August to October, 1868).*

— *Private Nicholas Foran (Co. L 8th U.S. Cavalry) received MOH: Bravery in scouts and actions against Indians (Arizona, August to October, 1868).*

— *Private Charles Gardner (Co. B 8th U.S. Cavalry) received MOH: Bravery in scouts and actions against Indians (Arizona, August to October, 1868).*

[108] Indians. Chronological List, 34; Heitman (Volume 2), 431.

— Private *Thomas H. Gay (Co. B 8th U.S. Cavalry) received MOH: Bravery in scouts and actions against Indians (Arizona, August to October, 1868).*

— *Sergeant Patrick Golden (Co. B 8th U.S. Cavalry) received MOH: Bravery in scouts and actions against Indians (Arizona, August to October, 1868).*

— *Private John Hall (Co. B 8th U.S. Cavalry) received MOH: Bravery in scouts and actions against Indians (Arizona, August to October, 1868).*

— *Private Clamor Heise (Co. B 8th U.S. Cavalry) received MOH: Bravery in scouts and actions against Indians (Arizona, August to October, 1868).*

— *Private Thomas P. Higgins (Co. B 8th U.S. Cavalry) received MOH: Bravery in scouts and actions against Indians (Arizona, August to October, 1868).*

— *Private John Keenan (Co. B 8th U.S. Cavalry) received MOH: Bravery in scouts and actions against Indians (Arizona, August to October, 1868).*

— *Private Albert Knaak (Co. B 8th U.S. Cavalry) received MOH: Bravery in scouts and actions against Indians (Arizona, August to October, 1868).*

— *Private James Lawrence (Co. B 8th U.S. Cavalry) received MOH: Bravery in scouts and actions against Indians (Arizona, August to October, 1868).*

— *Bugler Thomas Little (Co. B 8th U.S. Cavalry) received MOH: Bravery in scouts and actions against Indians (Arizona, August to October, 1868).*

— *Private Bernard McBride (Co. B 8th U.S. Cavalry) received MOH: Bravery in scouts and actions against Indians (Arizona, August to October, 1868).*

— *Corporal James McDonald (Co. B 8th U.S. Cavalry) received MOH: Bravery in scouts and actions against Indians (Arizona, August to October, 1868).*

— *Private Daniel McKinley (Co. B 8th U.S. Cavalry) received MOH: Bravery in scouts and actions against Indians (Arizona, August to October, 1868).*

— *Private Charles H. McVeagh (Co. B 8th U.S. Cavalry) received MOH: Bravery in scouts and actions against Indians (Arizona, August to October, 1868).*

— *Private George W. Miller (Co. B 8th U.S. Cavalry) received MOH: Bravery in scouts and actions against Indians (Arizona, August to October, 1868).*

— *Sergeant John O'Callaghan (Co. B 8th U.S. Cavalry) received MOH: Bravery in scouts and actions against Indians (Arizona, August to October, 1868).*

— *Private Michael O'Regan (Co. B 8th U.S. Cavalry) received MOH: Bravery in scouts and actions against Indians (Arizona, August to October, 1868).*

— *Sergeant Lewis Phife (Co. B 8th U.S. Cavalry) received MOH: Bravery in scouts and actions against Indians (Arizona, August to October, 1868).*

— *Private William Shaffer (Co. B 8th U.S. Cavalry) received MOH: Bravery in scouts and actions against Indians (Arizona, August to October, 1868).*

— *Private Benoni Strivson (Co. B 8th U.S. Cavalry) received MOH: Bravery in scouts and actions against Indians (Arizona, August to October, 1868).*

— *Corporal John A. Sutherland (Co. L 8th U.S. Cavalry) received MOH: Bravery in scouts and actions against Indians (August to October, 1868).*

— *Private Andrew J. Weaher (Co. B 8th U.S. Cavalry) received MOH: Bravery in scouts and actions against Indians (Arizona, August to October, 1868).*

— *Private Joseph Witcome (Co. B 8th U.S. Cavalry) received MOH: Bravery in scouts and actions against Indians (Arizona, August to October, 1868).*

— *Sergeant George G. Wortman (Co. B 8th U.S. Cavalry) received MOH: Bravery in scouts and actions against Indians (Arizona, August to October, 1868).*

(0378) Citizens, North Texas (August 23, 1868)[109]
    — (8) Citizens Killed

(0379) Citizens, between Pond Creek Station, Kansas and Lake Station, Colorado Territory (August 23, 1868)[110]
    — (1) Citizen Killed

(0380) Action, near Fort Totten, Dakota Territory (August 23, 1868)[111]
    — UNKNOWN
        — 31st U.S. Infantry Detachments Co. A, B and K
    — **3 KILLED**[112]
        — Sergeant James Devoe (Co. K 31st U.S. Infantry)
        — Private Michael Hiffin (Co. A 31st U.S. Infantry)
        — Private Lewis Martin (Co. A 31st U.S. Infantry)

(0381) Citizens, near Fort Dodge, Kansas (August 25, 1868)[113]
    — (1) Citizen Killed

(0382) Citizens, between Fort Lyon, Colorado Territory and Fort Sheridan, Kansas (August 27, 1868)[114]
    — (1) Citizen Killed

(0383) Action, near Big Spring Station, Kansas (August 27, 1868)[115]
    — UNKNOWN
        — Detachment of Scouts
    — **1 KILLED**[116]
        — Scout William Comstock (Citizen)

    — **1 WOUNDED**[117]

[109] Indians, *Annual Report of Secretary of War (1869)*, 53; Record of Engagements, 9.
[110] Indians. Killed was William McCarty. *Annual Report of Secretary of War (1868)*, 13; *Annual Report of Secretary of War (1869)*, 53; Chronological List, 35; Record of Engagements, 9; Leckie, *Military Conquest of the Southern Plains*, 74.
[111] Indians. *Annual Report of Secretary of War (1868)*, 36; Chronological List, 35; Heitman (Volume 2), 431. Heitman lists 31st U.S. Infantry Detachments Co. A, D, K.
[112] Register of Deaths Regular Army, 1860-1889 (Volume 3).
[113] Indians. Chronological List, 35; Record of Engagements, 9.
[114] Indians. Killed was a man named Woodworth. *Annual Report of Secretary of War (1868)*, 13; *Annual Report of Secretary of War (1869)*, 53; Chronological List, 35; Record of Engagements, 9.
[115] Indians. *Annual Report of Secretary of War (1869)*, 53; Monnett, *Battle of Beecher Island*, 113-114.
[116] *Annual Report of Secretary of War (1869)*, 53.
[117] Monnett, *Battle of Beecher Island*, 113-114.

— Scout Abner "Sharp" Grover (Citizen)
— *gunshot wound, back*

(0384) Skirmish, Hatchett Mountains, New Mexico Territory (August 27, 1868)[118]
— Captain Alexander Moore (38th U.S. Infantry)
— 38th U.S. Infantry Co. F

(0385) Citizens, near Kiowa Station, Kansas (August 28, 1868)[119]
— (3) Citizens Killed

(0386) Skirmish, near Platte River, Nebraska (August 28, 1868)[120]
— Captain Charles E. Morse (26th U.S. Infantry)
— Detachment of Indian Scouts

(0387) Skirmish, Republican River, Nebraska (August 30, 1868)[121]
— UNKNOWN
— Detachment of Indian Scouts

(0388) Citizens, Lake Station, Colorado Territory (September 1, 1868)[122]
— (2) Citizens Killed

(0389) Citizens, Reed's Springs, Colorado Territory (September 1, 1868)[123]
— (3) Citizens Killed

(0390) Citizens, near Spanish Fort, Texas (September 1, 1868)[124]
— (9) Citizens Killed

(0391) Action, near Sulphur Springs, Texas (September 2, 1868)[125]
— UNKNOWN
— 6th U.S. Cavalry Detachment Co. H
— **1 WOUNDED**[126]
— Bugler Michael Connelly (Co. H 6th U.S. Cavalry)
— *gunshot wound, thigh, slight wound*

(0392) Action, Little Coon Creek, Kansas (September 2, 1868)[127]
— Corporal James Goodwin (7th U.S. Cavalry)
— 7th U.S. Cavalry Detachment Co. B
— 3rd U.S. Infantry Detachments Co. A and F
— **3 WOUNDED**[128]
— Private James Goodwin (Co. B 7th U.S. Cavalry)
— *gunshot wound, shoulder*

[118] Indians. *Annual Report of Secretary of War (1868)*, 774; *Annual Report of Secretary of War (1869)*, 52; Chronological List, 35; Heitman (Volume 2), 431.
[119] Indians. *Annual Report of Secretary of War (1868)*, 13; *Annual Report of Secretary of War (1869)*, 53; Chronological List, 35; Record of Engagements, 9.
[120] Indians. Chronological List, 35; Heitman (Volume 2), 432.
[121] Indians. Chronological List, 35; Heitman (Volume 2), 432.
[122] Indians. Killed and scalped were a woman and child. *Annual Report of Secretary of War (1868)*, 14; *Annual Report of Secretary of War (1869)*, 53; Record of Engagements, 10.
[123] Indians. *Annual Report of Secretary of War (1868)*, 15; *Annual Report of Secretary of War (1869)*, 53; Chronological List, 35; Record of Engagements, 10.
[124] Indians. *Annual Report of Secretary of War (1869)*, 53; Chronological List, 35; Record of Engagements, 10; Leckie, *Military Conquest of the Southern Plains*, 117-118.
[125] Bandits. Reports of Diseases and Individual Cases, F 409.
[126] Reports of Diseases and Individual Cases, F 409.
[127] Indians. *Annual Report of Secretary of War (1868)*, 14, 774; *Annual Report of Secretary of War (1869)*, 52; Chronological List, 35; Heitman (Volume 2), 432; Strate, *Sentinel to the Cimarron*, 76-78; White, "General Sully's Expedition to the Northern Canadian," *Journal of the West* 11 (January 1972): 85-91. Chronological List lists 7th U.S. Cavalry Detachments; 3rd U.S. Infantry Detachments. Heitman lists 7th U.S. Cavalry Detachment Co. B; 3rd U.S. Infantry Co. A, F.
[128] Otis, *Report of Surgical Cases*, 27; Strate, *Sentinel to the Cimarron*, 77.

— Private John O'Donnell (Co. A 3rd U.S. Infantry)
    — *gunshot wounds, thigh, neck, face*
— Private Charles Faxton
    — *gunshot wounds, arm, buttocks*

— *Corporal Leander Herron (Co. A 3rd U.S. Infantry) received MOH: While detailed as a mail courier from Fort Dodge, voluntarily went to the assistance of a party of four enlisted men, who were attacked by about fifty Indians at some distance from the fort and remained with them into the until the party was relieved (Near Fort Dodge, Kansas, September 2, 1868).*

"So let's give three cheers for our comrades,
That gallant and brave little band,
Who, against odds, would never surrender
But bravely by their arms did stand."
— Frederick Haxby, Citizen[129]

(0393) Citizens, Hugo Springs Station, Colorado Territory (September 3, 1868)[130]

(0394) Citizens, Colorado City Station, Colorado Territory (September 3, 1868)[131]
    — (4) Citizens Killed

(0395) Skirmish, Tonto Creek, Arizona Territory (September 4, 1868)[132]
    — Major Andrew J. Alexander (8th U.S. Cavalry)
        — 1st U.S. Cavalry Co. E
        — 8th U.S. Cavalry Co. I
        — Detachment of Indian Scouts

(0396) Citizens, Willow Springs Station, Colorado Territory (September 5, 1868)[133]

(0397) Citizens, Colorado Territory (September 6 and 7, 1868)[134]
    — (25) Citizens Killed

(0398) Citizens, Turkey Creek, Kansas (September 8, 1868)[135]

(0399) Citizens, near Sheridan, Kansas (September 8, 1868)[136]
    — (2) Citizens Killed

(0400) Citizens, Cimarron Crossing, Kansas (September 8, 1868)[137]
    — (17) Citizens Killed

[129] Englishman Lord Frederick Haxby was visiting Fort Dodge when the wounded arrived. He memorialized their stand in a hastily written short ballad entitled "The Battle of Little Coon Creek", which he mailed to several Eastern newspapers. Strate, *Sentinel to the Cimarron*, 77-78.
[130] Indians. *Annual Report of Secretary of War (1868)*, 14; Chronological List, 35.
[131] Indians . *Annual Report of Secretary of War (1868)*, 14; *Annual Report of Secretary of War (1869)*, 53; Chronological List, 35.
[132] Indians. Chronological List, 35; Heitman (Volume 2), 432. Heitman lists 4 to 6 September 1868.
[133] Indians. *Annual Report of Secretary of War (1868)*, 14; *Annual Report of Secretary of War (1869)*, 53; Chronological List, 35.
[134] Indians. *Annual Report of Secretary of War (1869)*, 53; Chronological List, 35.
[135] Indians. *Annual Report of Secretary of War (1868)*, 14; *Annual Report of Secretary of War (1869)*, 53; Chronological List, 35.
[136] Indians. Chronological List, 35.
[137] Indians. *Annual Report of Secretary of War (1868)*, 14-15; *Annual Report of Secretary of War (1869)*, 53; Chronological List, 35.

(0401) Citizens, between Fort Wallace and Sheridan, Kansas (September 9, 1868)[138]
— (6) Citizens Killed

(0402) Skirmish, Tonto Plateau, Arizona Territory (September 9, 1868)[139]
— 2nd Lieutenant Rufus Somerby (8th U.S. Cavalry)
— 8th U.S. Cavalry Co. B

(0403) Citizens, near Lake Station, Colorado Territory (September 10, 1868)[140]

(0404) Action, Rule Creek or Purgatory River, Colorado Territory (September 10, 1868)[141]
— Captain William H. Penrose (3rd U.S. Infantry)
— 7th U.S. Cavalry Co. L
— **2 KILLED**[142]
— Private Phillip Sheridan (Co. L 7th U.S. Cavalry)
— Private Henry Rickie (Co. L 7th U.S. Cavalry)

— **1 WOUNDED**[143]
— Private Edward Myers (Co. L 7th U.S. Cavalry)
— *gunshot wound, left hand, slight wound*

(0405) Skirmish, Lower Aqua Fria, Arizona Territory (September 10, 1868)[144]
— 2nd Lieutenant Rufus Somerby (8th U.S. Cavalry)
— 8th U.S. Cavalry Co. B

(0406) Skirmish, Rio Verde, Arizona Territory (September 11, 1868)[145]
— 2nd Lieutenant Rufus Somerby (8th U.S. Cavalry)
— 8th U.S. Cavalry Co. B

— *2nd Lieutenant Rufus Somerby (8th U.S. Cavalry) brevet promotion to 1st Lieutenant for gallant conduct in engagements with Apache Indians (August 30 to September 12, 1868).*

(0407) Action, near North Fork, Canadian River, Indian Territory (September 11, 1868)[146]
— Lt. Colonel Alfred Sully (3rd U.S. Infantry)
— 7th U.S. Cavalry Co. A, B, C, D, E, F, G, I and K
— 3rd U.S. Infantry Co. F
— **1 KILLED**[147]
— Private James Curran (Co. F 3rd U.S. Infantry)

— **3 WOUNDED**[148]

[138] Indians. *Annual Report of Secretary of War (1868)*, 15; Chronological List, 35.
[139] Indians. Chronological List, 35; Heitman (Volume 2), 432. Heitman lists 8th U.S. Cavalry Detachment Co. B.
[140] Indians. *Annual Report of Secretary of War (1869)*, 53; Chronological List, 35.
[141] Indians. *Annual Report of Secretary of War (1868)*, 15, 774; *Annual Report of Secretary of War (1869)*, 52; Chronological List, 35; Heitman (Volume 2), 432.
[142] Reports of Diseases and Individual Cases, F 418; Register of Deaths Regular Army, 1860-1889 (Volume 3).
[143] Reports of Diseases and Individual Cases, F 418.
[144] Indians. Chronological List, 36; Heitman (Volume 2), 432; Alexander, *Arizona Military Place Names*, 1. Heitman lists 8th U.S. Cavalry Detachment Co. B.
[145] Indians. Chronological List, 36; Heitman (Volume 2), 432. Heitman lists 8th U.S. Cavalry Detachment Co. B.
[146] Indians. *Annual Report of Secretary of War (1868)*, 18; *Annual Report of Secretary of War (1869)*, 52; Chronological List, 36; Heitman (Volume 2), 432; Record of Engagements, 11; Barnitz, *Life in Custer's Cavalry*, 186, 189; Carriker, *Fort Supply, Indian Territory*, 10-12; Hoig, *Tribal Wars of the Southern Plains*, 245-248; White, "General Sully's Expedition to the Northern Canadian," *Journal of the West* 11 (January 1972): 85-91. Chronological List and Heitman both list a single event, 11 to 15 September 1868.
[147] Reports of Diseases and Individual Cases, F 412.
[148] Reports of Diseases and Individual Cases, F 412.
[149] Indians. *Annual Report of Secretary of War (1868)*, 18; *Annual Report of Secretary of War (1869)*, 52; Chronological List, 36; Heitman (Volume 2), 432; Record of Engagements, 11; Barnitz, *Life in Custer's Cavalry*, 186-187, 190; Carriker, *Fort Supply, Indian Territory*, 10-12; Hoig, *Tribal Wars of the Southern*

— Sergeant William H. Welsh (Co. I 7th U.S. Cavalry)
— *gunshot wound, right arm, slight wound*
— Private Alexander Kennedy (Co. F 7th U.S. Cavalry)
— *gunshot wound, side, severe wound*
— Bugler John Punk (Co. F 7th U.S. Cavalry)
— *gunshot wound, left hand, slight wound*

(0408) Action, near Canadian River, Indian Territory (September 12, 1868)[149]
— Lt. Colonel Alfred Sully (3rd U.S. Infantry)
— 7th U.S. Cavalry Co. A, B, C, D, E, F, G, I and K
— 3rd U.S. Infantry Co. F
— **1 WOUNDED**[150]
— Private Herman Teves (Co. G 7th U.S. Cavalry)
— *gunshot wound, left leg, slight wound*

(0409) Skirmish, near Fort Reynolds, Colorado Territory (September 12, 1868)[151]
— Colonel William A. Nichols (Assistant Adjutant General)
— UNKNOWN

(0410) Action, Dragoon Fork, Verde River, Arizona Territory (September 13, 1868)[152]
— 2nd Lieutenant Rufus Somerby (8th U.S. Cavalry)
— 8th U.S. Cavalry Co. B
— **1 WOUNDED**[153]
— Private Charles Gardner (Co. B 8th U.S. Cavalry)

(0411) Action, Sand Hills, Indian Territory (September 13, 1868)[154]
— Lt. Colonel Alfred Sully (3rd U.S. Infantry)
— 7th U.S. Cavalry Co. A, B, C, D, E, F, G, I and K
— 3rd U.S. Infantry Co. F
— **1 KILLED**[155]
— Private Cyrus Corbett (Co. F 7th U.S. Cavalry)

(0412) Action Canadian River, Indian Territory (September 14, 1868)[156]
— Lt. Colonel Alfred Sully (3rd U.S. Infantry)
— 7th U.S. Cavalry Co. A, B, C, D, E, F, G, I and K
— 3rd U.S. Infantry Co. F
— **1 KILLED**[157]
— Private Charles Kreiger (Co. I 7th U.S. Cavalry) – d. 9-15-1868

Plains, 245-248; White, "General Sully's Expedition to the Northern Canadian," *Journal of the West* 11 (January 1972): 85-91. Chronological List and Heitman both list a single event, 11 to 15 September 11 1868.
[150] Reports of Diseases and Individual Cases, F 413.
[151] Indians. *Annual Report of Secretary of War (1868)*, 15; Chronological List, 36; Heitman (Volume 2), 432. Chronological List lists "guard", Heitman lists "escort".
[152] Indians. Chronological List, 36; Heitman (Volume 2), 432. Heitman lists 8th U.S. Cavalry Detachment Co. B.
[153] Rodenbough, *Army of the United States*, 271.
[154] Indians. *Annual Report of Secretary of War (1868)*, 18; *Annual Report of Secretary of War (1869)*, 52; Chronological List, 36; Heitman (Volume 2), 432; Record of Engagements, 11; Barnitz, *Life in Custer's Cavalry*, 187, 189-190; Carriker, *Fort Supply, Indian Territory*, 10-12; Hoig, *Tribal Wars of the Southern Plains*, 245-248; White, "General Sully's Expedition to the Northern Canadian," *Journal of the West* 11 (January 1972): 85-91. Chronological List and Heitman both list a single event, 11 to 15 September 1868.
[155] Reports of Diseases and Individual Cases, F 414; Register of Deaths Regular Army, 1860-1889 (Volume 3).
[156] Indians. *Annual Report of Secretary of War (1868)*, 18; *Annual Report of Secretary of War (1869)*, 52; Chronological List, 36; Heitman (Volume 2), 432; Record of Engagements, 11; Barnitz, *Life in Custer's Cavalry*, 187, 190; Carriker, *Fort Supply, Indian Territory*, 10-12; Hoig, *Tribal Wars of the Southern Plains*, 245-248; White, "General Sully's Expedition to the Northern Canadian," *Journal of the West* 11 (January 1972): 85-91. Chronological List and Heitman both list a single event, 11 to 15 September 1868.
[157] Reports of Diseases and Individual Cases, F 415; Register of Deaths Regular Army, 1860-1889 (Volume 3).

— **1 WOUNDED**[158]
> — Private Edwin Connor (Co. E 7th U.S. Cavalry)
>> — *gunshot wound, right ankle, slight wound*

(0413) Action, Horse Head Hills, Texas (September 14, 1868)[159]
> — 1st Lieutenant Patrick Cusack (9th U.S. Cavalry)
>> — 9th U.S. Cavalry Detachments Co. C, F and K
> — Detachment of Volunteers
— **3 WOUNDED**[160]
> — Private Lewis White (Co. C 9th U.S. Cavalry)
>> — *arrow wound, thorax, slight wound*
> — Private Gilbert Colyer (Co. F 9th U.S. Cavalry)
>> — *lance wound, thorax, severe wound*
> — Private John Foster (Co. K 9th U.S. Cavalry)
>> — *lance wound, right gluteal region, slight wound*

— *1st Lieutenant Patrick Cusack (9th U.S. Cavalry) brevet promotion to Captain for conspicuous gallantry in engagement with Indians (Horse Head Hills, Texas, September 14, 1868).*

(0414) Action, Big Sandy Creek, Colorado Territory (September 15, 1868)[161]
> — Captain George W. Graham (10th U.S. Cavalry)
>> — 10th U.S. Cavalry Co. I
— **1 WOUNDED**[162]
> — Enlisted Man (10th U.S. Cavalry)

— *Captain George W. Graham (2nd U.S. Cavalry) brevet promotion to Major for gallant and meritorious service at the affair with Indians (Big Sandy Creek, Colorado, September 15, 1868).*

(0415) Citizens, Ellis Station, Kansas (September 17, 1868)[163]
> — (1) Citizen Killed

(0416) Citizens, near Fort Bascom, New Mexico Territory (September 17, 1868)[164]
> — (1) Citizen Killed

(0417) Engagement, Arickaree Fork of Republican River, Kansas (September 17 to 25, 1868)[165]
> — Major George A. Forsyth (9th U.S. Cavalry)
>> — Detachment of Scouts
— **6 KILLED**[166]
> — 1st Lieutenant Frederick H. Beecher (3rd U.S. Infantry)

> — Scout George W. Culver (Citizen)
> — Scout Louis Farley (Citizen) — d. 9-25-1868

[158] Reports of Diseases and Individual Cases, F 415.
[159] Indians. *Annual Report of Secretary of War (1868)*, 716, 774; Chronological List, 36; Heitman (Volume 2), 432; Burton, *Black, Buckskin and Blue*, 154; Smith, *Old Army in Texas*, 149, Williams, *Texas' Last Frontier*, 102-103; Wooster, *Frontier Crossroads*, 94. Chronological List and Heitman both list 9th U.S. Cavalry Co. C, F, K.
[160] Reports of Diseases and Individual Cases, F 410; Otis, *Report of Surgical Cases*, 102, 159.
[161] Indians. *Annual Report of Secretary of War (1868)*, 18, 773; *Annual Report of Secretary of War (1869)*, 52; Chronological List, 36; Heitman (Volume 2), 432; Burton, *Black, Buckskin and Blue*, 180, 209-210; Leckie, *Buffalo Soldiers*, 33.
[162] *Annual Report of Secretary of War (1869)*, 52.
[163] Indians. *Annual Report of Secretary of War (1868)*, 15; *Annual Report of Secretary of War (1869)*, 54; Chronological List, 36.
[164] Indians. *Annual Report of Secretary of War (1869)*, 54; Chronological List, 36.
[165] Indians. *Annual Report of Secretary of War (1868)*, 18, 773; *Annual Report of Secretary of War (1869)*, 52; Chronological List, 36; Heitman (Volume 2), 432; Barnitz, *Life in Custer's Cavalry*, 196-197; Crawford, *Kansas in the Sixties*, 293-296; Dixon, *Hero of Beecher Island*, 76-87; Miles, *Personal Recollections*, 145-150; Monnett, *Battle of Beecher Island*, 131-162, White, "Battle of Beecher Island," *Journal of the West* 5 (January 1966): 6-18. Chronological List and Heitman both list Detachment of Indian Scouts
[166] Reports of Diseases and Individual Cases, F 411; Register of Deaths Regular Army, 1860-1889 (Volume 3); Otis, *Report of Surgical Cases*, 206.

— Scout Thomas O'Donnell (Citizen) — d. 11-18-1868
— Scout William Wilson (Citizen)

— Acting Assistant Surgeon John H. Moore (Citizen) — d. 9-18-1868

— **15 WOUNDED**[167]
— Major George A. Forsyth (9th U.S. Cavalry)
— *gunshot wounds, right thigh, left leg, fracture, severe wound*

— Scout Walter Armstrong (Citizen)
— *gunshot wound, back, severe wound*
— Scout George B. Clark (Citizen)
— *gunshot wound, right leg, severe wound*
— Scout Harry Davenport (Citizen)
— *gunshot wound, left thigh, severe wound*
— Scout Thadeus K. Davis (Citizen)
— *gunshot wound, right arm, severe wound*
— Scout Bernard Day (Citizen)
— *gunshot wound, right hand, slight wound*
— Scout Hudson Farley (Citizen)
— *gunshot wound, left shoulder*
— Scout Richard Gantt (Citizen)
— *gunshot wounds, right shoulder, left thigh, severe wounds*
— Scout John Haley (Citizen)
— *gunshot wound, left hip, slight wound*
— Scout Frank Harrington (Citizen)
— *gunshot and arrow wounds, forehead, severe wounds*
— Scout William H.H. McCall (Citizen)
— *gunshot wound, neck, severe wound*
— Scout Louis A. McLaughlin (Citizen)
— *gunshot wound, left breast, slight wound*
— Scout Howard Morton (Citizen)
— *gunshot wound, left eye, severe wound*
— Scout Henry H. Tucker (Citizen)
— *gunshot wound, left arm, severe wound*
— Scout Fletcher Violott (Citizen)
— *gunshot wound, left knee, slight wound*

— *Captain Henry C. Bankhead (5th U.S. Infantry) brevet promotion to Brigadier General for prompt, energetic and meritorious service rendered by him during the campaign against hostile Indians and especially during the relief of Colonel Forsyth's beleaguered party on the Republican River (September, 1868).*

---

[167] Reports of Diseases and Individual Cases, F 411; Otis, *Report of Surgical Cases*, 60, 80.

— *Captain Louis Carpenter (10th U.S. Cavalry) received MOH: Was gallant and meritorious throughout the campaigns, especially in the combat of October 15 and in the forced march on September 23, 24 and 25 to the relief of Forsyth's scouts, who were known to be in danger of annihilation by largely superior forces of Indians (Indian Campaigns, Kansas and Colorado, September to October, 1868).*

— *Major George A. Forsyth (3rd U.S. Infantry) brevet promotion to Brigadier General for gallant conduct and meritorious service in an engagement with hostile Indians (Arickaree Fork of Republican River, Kansas, September 17 to 20, 1868).*

"Let me say here, that I had many fights with the Indians for ten years after the Beecher fight, and I never saw anything to equal it. I say it was the greatest fight that was ever fought by any soldiers of the regular army at any time, not excepting the Custer fight or the massacre at Fort Phil Kearny, and I say further that in all the fights we had with the Indians, I mean the regular army, we never killed as many Indians. I saw Lone Wolf, who was in the Beecher fight, and he told us that they lost 400 killed and fatally wounded."

— Ruben Waller, U.S. Army[168]

(0418) Action, Saline River, Kansas (September 17, 1868)[169]
— Captain William H. Penrose (3rd U.S. Infantry)
— 7th U.S. Cavalry Detachment Co. L
— **3 WOUNDED**[170]
— Enlisted Man (7th U.S. Cavalry)
— Enlisted Man (7th U.S. Cavalry)
— Enlisted Man (7th U.S. Cavalry)

(0419) Action, Travis County, Texas (September 22, 1868)[171]
— 1st Lieutenant Henry S. Howe (17th U.S. Infantry)
— 6th U.S. Cavalry Detachment
— **2 KILLED**[172]
— Private Bernard Curry (Co. B 6th U.S. Cavalry)
— Private Daniel O'Connor (Co. B 6th U.S. Cavalry)

(0420) Action, near Fort Rice, Dakota Territory (September 26, 1868)[173]
— UNKNOWN
— 22nd U.S. Infantry Co. A, B, H and I
— **1 KILLED**[174]
— Private John T. Vane (Co. I 22nd U.S. Infantry)

(0421) Citizens, Sharp's Creek, Kansas (September 29, 1868)[175]
— (1) Citizen Killed

(0422) Action, between Fort Larned and Fort Dodge, Kansas (October 2, 1868)[176]
— UNKNOWN

---

[168] Private Reuben Waller (10th U.S. Cavalry) rode with Captain Louis Carpenter (10th U.S. Cavalry)in relief of the Forsyth scouts on 25 September 1868. His remarks were made "years later". Burton, *Black, Buckskin and Blue*, 212-213.
[169] Indians. *Annual Report of Secretary of War (1868)*, 18; Chronological List, 36. Chronological List lists 7th U.S. Cavalry Detachment.
[170] *Annual Report of Secretary of War (1868)*, 18.
[171] Bandits. *Annual Report of Secretary of War (1868)*, 716.
[172] *Annual Report of Secretary of War (1868)*, 716; Otis, *Report of Surgical Cases*, 44, 52.
[173] Indians. Chronological List, 36; Heitman (Volume 2), 432. Heitman lists 22nd U.S. Infantry Detachments Co. A, B, I, K.
[174] Register of Deaths Regular Army, 1860-1889 (Volume 3).
[175] Indians. Killed was Mr. Basset. His wife and child were kidnapped. *Annual Report of Secretary of War (1869)*, 54; Chronological List, 36; Record of Engagements, 12.
[176] Indians. *Annual Report of Secretary of War (1868)*, 15; *Annual Report of Secretary of War (1869)*, 54; Chronological List, 36; Heitman (Volume 2), 432. Heitman lists 1 October 1868.

— 3rd U.S. Infantry Co. E
— **3 KILLED**[177]
    — (3) Citizens Killed

— **3 WOUNDED**[178]
    — (3) Citizens

(0423) Citizens, near Fort Zarah, Kansas (October 2, 1868)[179]
    — (1) Citizen Killed

(0424) Skirmish, Fort Zarah, Kansas (October 2, 1868)[180]
    — 1st Lieutenant August Kaiser (3rd U.S. Infantry)
        — 3rd U.S. Infantry Co. D

(0425) Action, near Fort Wallace, Kansas (October 2, 1868)[181]
    — UNKNOWN
        — 7th U.S. Cavalry Detachment Co. E
    — **1 KILLED**[182]
        — Private William Johnston (Co. E 7th U.S. Cavalry)

(0426) Action, Miembres Mountains, New Mexico Territory (October 3, 1868)[183]
    — Sergeant Charles Brown (3rd U.S. Cavalry)
        — 3rd U.S. Cavalry Detachment Co. E
    — **1 WOUNDED**[184]
        — Private James Francis (Co. A 38th U.S. Infantry)

(0427) Citizens, near Fort Dodge, Kansas (October 4, 1868)[185]
    — (2) Citizens Killed

(0428) Citizens, Sand Creek, Colorado Territory (October 6, 1868)[186]
    — (2) Citizens Killed

(0429) Citizens, Purgatory Creek, Colorado Territory (October 7, 1868)[187]
    — (1) Citizen Killed

(0430) Skirmish, Salt River and Cherry Creek, Arizona Territory (October 9, 1868)[188]
    — Major Andrew J. Alexander (8th U.S. Cavalry)
        — 1st U.S. Cavalry Co. E
        — 8th U.S. Cavalry Co. I
        — 14th U.S. Infantry Co. F
        — 32nd U.S. Infantry Co. A
        — Detachment of Indian Scouts

[177] Chronological List, 36.
[178] Chronological List, 36.
[179] Indians. Killed was a teamster. *Annual Report of Secretary of War (1868)*, 15; *Annual Report of Secretary of War (1869)*, 54; Chronological List, 36.
[180] Indians. *Annual Report of Secretary of War (1868)*, 15; *Annual Report of Secretary of War (1869)*, 54; Chronological List, 36; Heitman (Volume 2), 432. Heitman lists 1 October 1868.
[181] Indians. Reports of Diseases and Individual Cases, F 416; Otis, *Report of Surgical Cases*, 8.
[182] Reports of Diseases and Individual Cases, F 416; Register of Deaths Regular Army, 1860-1889 (Volume 3); Otis, *Report of Surgical Cases*, 8.
[183] Indians. Chronological List, 36; Heitman (Volume 2), 432. Heitman lists 1 October 1868.
[184] Fort Bayard Post Return October 1868.
[185] Indians. *Annual Report of Secretary of War (1868)*, 15; *Annual Report of Secretary of War (1869)*, 54; Chronological List, 37.
[186] Indians. Kidnapped and eventually killed were Clara and Willi Blinn. *Annual Report of Secretary of War (1868)*, 15; *Annual Report of Secretary of War (1869)*, 54; Chronological List, 37; Michno, *Fate Worse than Death*, 151-156; Monnett, *Battle of Beecher Island*, 60-61. Chronological List lists 14 October 1868.
[187] Indians. *Annual Report of Secretary of War (1868)*, 15; *Annual Report of Secretary of War (1869)*, 54; Chronological List, 37.
[188] Indians. Chronological List, 37; Heitman (Volume 2), 432.

(0431) Citizens, Fort Zarah, Kansas (October 10, 1868)[189]

(0432) Citizens, Ellsworth, Kansas (October 12, 1868)[190]
— (1) Citizen Killed

(0433) Skirmish, Big Bend of Arkansas River, Kansas (October 12, 1868)[191]
— Major Joel H. Elliott (7th U.S. Cavalry)
— 7th U.S. Cavalry Co. H, K and M

(0434) Operations, White Woman's Fork, near Republican River, Kansas (October 13 to 30, 1868)[192]
— Captain Edward Ball (2nd U.S. Cavalry)
— 2nd U.S. Cavalry Co. H

(0435) Citizens, Prairie Dog Creek, Kansas (October 14, 1868)[193]
— (1) Citizen Killed

(0436) Action, Prairie Dog Creek, Kansas (October 14, 1868)[194]
— Major William B. Royall (5th U.S. Cavalry)
— 5th U.S. Cavalry Co. L
— **1 KILLED**[195]
— Private Bernard Cusick (Co. L 5th U.S. Cavalry)

— **1 WOUNDED**[196]
— Private Jacob H. Weaver (Co. L 5th U.S. Cavalry)

(0437) Action, Beaver Creek, Kansas (October 18, 1868)[197]
— Captain Louis H. Carpenter (10th U.S. Cavalry)
— 10th U.S. Cavalry Co. H and I
— **3 WOUNDED**[198]
— Enlisted Man (10th U.S. Cavalry)
— Enlisted Man (10th U.S. Cavalry)
— Enlisted Man (10th U.S. Cavalry)

— Captain Louis Carpenter (10th U.S. Cavalry) received MOH: Was gallant and meritorious throughout the campaigns, especially in the combat of October 15 and in the forced march on September 23, 24 and 25 to the relief of Forsyth's scouts, who were known to be in danger of annihilation by largely superior forces of Indians (Indian Campaigns, Kansas and Colorado, September to October, 1868).

— Captain Louis H. Hamilton (10th U.S. Cavalry) brevet promotion to Colonel for gallant and meritorious service in the engagement with Indians (Beaver Creek, Kansas, October 18, 1868).

[189] Indians. *Annual Report of Secretary of War (1868)*, 15; *Annual Report of Secretary of War (1869)*, 54; Chronological List, 37.
[190] Indians. *Annual Report of Secretary of War (1868)*, 15; Chronological List, 37.
[191] Indians. Chronological List, 37; Heitman (Volume 2), 432.
[192] Indians. Chronological List, 37; Heitman (Volume 2), 432.
[193] Indians. *Annual Report of Secretary of War (1869)*, 54.
[194] Indians. *Annual Report of Secretary of War (1868)*, 16; Chronological List, 37; Heitman (Volume 2), 432; Chalfant, *Cheyennes at Dark Water Creek*, 9; Monnett, *Battle of Beecher Island*, 184; Price, *Across the Continent*, 132, 657.
[195] Register of Deaths Regular Army, 1860-1889 (Volume 3).
[196] Price, *Across the Continent*, 672.
[197] Indians. *Annual Report of Secretary of War (1868)*, 16, 20, 775; *Annual Report of Secretary of War (1869)*, 52; Chronological List, 37; Heitman (Volume 2), 432; Burton, *Black, Buckskin and Blue*, 180; Chalfant, *Cheyennes at Dark Water Creek*, 9-10; King, *War Eagle*, 82-84; Leckie, *Buffalo Soldiers*, 37-38; Monnett, *Battle of Beecher Island*, 184-185. Chronological List lists 10th U.S. Cavalry Co. H, I, M.
[198] Chronological List, 37.

— *2nd Lieutenant Louis H. Orleman (10th U.S. Cavalry) brevet promotion to 1st Lieutenant for gallant service in actions against Indians (Beaver Creek, Kansas, October 18, 1868 and the Wichita Agency, Indian Territory, August 22, 1874).*

(0438) Action, Dragoon Fork of Verde River, Arizona Territory (October 19, 1868)[199]
    — 2nd Lieutenant Rufus Somerby (8th U.S. Cavalry)
        — 8th U.S. Cavalry Co. B
— **1 WOUNDED**[200]
    — Private Charles Gardner (Co. B 8th U.S. Cavalry)
        — *severe wound*

— *2nd Lieutenant Rufus Somerby (8th U.S. Cavalry) brevet promotion to Captain for gallant and effective service in actions with Apache Indians (October 7 to 23, 1868).*

(0439) Action, between Fort Verde and Fort Whipple, Arizona Territory (October 21, 1868)[201]
    — UNKNOWN
        — 8th U.S. Cavalry Detachment Co. L
        — 14th U.S. Infantry Detachment Co. G
— **1 KILLED**[202]
    — Private Robert Nix (Co. G 14th U.S. Infantry)

— *Private John Kay (Co. L 8th U.S. Cavalry) received MOH: Brought a comrade, severely wounded, from under the fire of a large party of the enemy (Arizona, October 21, 1868).*

(0440) Citizens, Fort Zarah, Kansas (October 23, 1868)[203]
    — (2) Citizens Killed

(0441) Action, Beaver Creek and Prairie Dog Creek, Kansas (October 25 and 26, 1868)[204]
    — Major Eugene A. Carr (5th U.S. Cavalry)
        — 5th U.S. Cavalry Co. A, B, F, H, I, L and M
        — Detachment of Indian Scouts
— **1 WOUNDED**[205]
    — Private William Frederick (Co. M 5th U.S. Cavalry)

— *2nd Lieutenant William C. Forbush (5th U.S. Cavalry) brevet promotion to 1st Lieutenant for gallant service in action against Indians (Beaver Creek, Kansas, October 25 and 26, 1868).*

— *1st Lieutenant Edward M. Hayes (5th U.S. Cavalry) brevet promotion to Captain for gallant service in action against Indians (Beaver Creek, Kansas, October 25 and 26, 1868).*

[199] Indians. *Annual Report of Secretary of War (1869)*, 127; Chronological List, 37; Heitman (Volume 2), 432.
[200] *Annual Report of Secretary of War (1869)*, 127.
[201] Indians. Chronological List, 37; Heitman (Volume 2), 432.
[202] Register of Deaths Regular Army, 1860-1889 (Volume 3); Otis, *Report of Surgical Cases*, 145.
[203] Indians. *Annual Report of Secretary of War (1869)*, 54; Chronological List, 37.
[204] Indians. *Annual Report of Secretary of War (1869)*, 52; Chronological List, 37; Heitman (Volume 2), 432; King, *War Eagle*, 86; Monnett, *Battle of Beecher Island*, 185; Price, *Across the Continent*, 132, 658.
[205] Price, *Across the Continent*, 237.

"We have… no pleasures in killing the poor miserable savages, but desire, in common with the whole Army, by performance of our duty, to deliver the settlers from the dangers to which they are exposed."
— Eugene A. Carr, U.S. Army[206]

(0442) Citizens, Central City, New Mexico Territory (October 26, 1868)[207]
— (3) Citizens Killed

(0443) Action, near Belton, Texas (October 29, 1868)[208]
    — UNKNOWN
        — UNKNOWN
    — **1 KILLED**[209]
        — Private John Eberhardt (Co. A 17th U.S. Infantry)

(0444) Citizens, Grinnell Station, Kansas (October 30, 1868)[210]

(0445) Action, between Wickenberg and Prescott, Arizona Territory (November 2, 1868)[211]
    — UNKNOWN
        — 14th U.S. Infantry Detachment Co. H
    — **1 KILLED**[212]
        — Private Jerome Boothe (Co. H 14th U.S. Infantry)

(0446) Skirmish, Big Coon Creek, Kansas (November 3, 1868)[213]
    — Captain Frederick W. Benteen (7th U.S. Cavalry)
        — 7th U.S. Cavalry Detachment Recruits

(0447) Citizens, near Coon Creek, Kansas (November 7, 1868)[214]

(0448) Skirmish, Willow Grove, Arizona Territory (November 7 to 15, 1868)[215]
    — Major William R. Price (8th U.S. Cavalry)
        — 8th U.S. Cavalry Detachments Co. E and K

(0449) Operations, Tonto Plateau, near Squaw Peak, Arizona Territory (November 11, 1868)[216]
    — 1st Lieutenant Almond B. Wells (8th U.S. Cavalry)
        — 8th U.S. Cavalry Detachments Co. B and L
    — **2 WOUNDED**[217]
        — Private E.R. Aston (Co. L 8th U.S. Cavalry)
        — Private William Cubberly (Co. L 8th U.S. Cavalry)

— Saddler Julius H. Stickoffer (Co. L 8th U.S. Cavalry) received MOH: Gallantry in action (Cienega Springs, Arizona, November 11, 1868).

[206] Major Eugene A. Carr (5th U.S. Cavalry) to Charles D. Ruggles, 20 July 1869. King, *War Eagle*, 118, 282.
[207] Indians. Chronological List, 37; Heitman (Volume 2), 432.
[208] Bandits. Otis, *Report of Surgical Cases*, 86.
[209] Registers of Deaths Regular Army, 1860-1889 (Volume 3); Otis, *Report of Surgical Cases*, 86.
[210] Indians. *Annual Report of Secretary of War (1869)*, 54; Chronological List, 37.
[211] Indians. Chronological List, 37; Heitman (Volume 2), 432.
[212] Register of Deaths Regular Army, 1860-1889 (Volume 3).
[213] Indians. Chronological List, 37; Heitman (Volume 2), 432.
[214] Indians. *Annual Report of Secretary of War (1869)*, 54; Chronological List, 37.
[215] Indians. Chronological List, 37; Heitman (Volume 2), 432.
[216] Indians. Chronological List, 37; Heitman (Volume 2), 432. Heitman lists 9 to 11 November 1868.
[217] Rodenbough, *Army of the United States*, 271, 279.

(0450) Action, near Fort Hays, Kansas (November 18, 1868)[218]
— UNKNOWN
— Detachment of Indian Scouts
— **2 KILLED**[219]
— Indian Scout
— Indian Scout

(0451) Citizens, near Fort Dodge, Kansas (November 19, 1868)[220]
— (1) Citizen Killed

(0452) Citizens, Little Coon Creek, Kansas (November 19, 1868)[221]
— (1) Citizen Killed

(0453) Action, near Farmersville, Collin County, Texas (November 19, 1868)[222]
— Sergeant Walsh (6th U.S. Cavalry)
— 6th U.S. Cavalry Detachment Co. A
— **1 KILLED**[223]
— Private John Hoffman (Co. A 6th U.S. Cavalry) — d. 11-20-1868

— **1 WOUNDED**[224]
— Private Anthony Albert (Co. A 6th U.S. Cavalry)
— *gunshot wounds, arm, leg, hand, slight wounds*

(0454) Skirmish, near Fort Dodge, Kansas (November 19, 1868)[225]
— Sergeant John Wilson (10th U.S. Cavalry)
— 10th U.S. Cavalry Detachment Co. A

(0455) Action, near Fort Dodge, Kansas (November 19, 1868)[226]
— 2nd Lieutenant Quintin Campbell (5th U.S. Infantry)
— 3rd U.S. Infantry Co. A and H
— 5th U.S. Infantry Detachment Co. E
— **3 WOUNDED**[227]
— Enlisted Man
— Enlisted Man
— Enlisted Man

(0456) Action, Mulberry Creek, near Fort Dodge, Kansas (November 20, 1868)[228]
— UNKNOWN
— Detachment of Scouts
— **2 KILLED**[229]

[218] Indians. Chronological List, 37; Heitman (Volume 2), 432. Chronological List lists "detachment of scouts".
[219] Chronological List, 37.
[220] Indians. *Annual Report of Secretary of War (1869)*, 54; Chronological List, 37.
[221] Indians. *Annual Report of Secretary of War (1869)*, 54; Chronological List, 38.
[222] Bandits. Reports of Diseases and Individual Cases, F 420.
[223] Reports of Diseases and Individual Cases, F 420; Register of Deaths Regular Army, 1860-1889 (Volume 3); Otis, *Report of Surgical Cases*, 43.
[224] Reports of Diseases and Individual Cases, F 420; Otis, *Report of Surgical Cases*, 69.
[225] Indians. Chronological List, 38; Heitman (Volume 2), 432; Leckie, *Buffalo Soldiers*, 41. Heitman lists 10th U.S. Cavalry Detachment Co. A; 3rd U.S. Infantry Co. A, H; 5th U.S. Infantry Detachment Co. E.
[226] Indians. Chronological List, 38; Heitman (Volume 2), 432. Heitman lists 10th U.S. Cavalry Detachment Co. A; 3rd U.S. Infantry Co. A, H; 5th U.S. Infantry Detachment Co. E.
[227] Chronological List, 38.
[228] Indians. *Annual Report of Secretary of War (1869)*, 54-55; Chronological List, 38; Heitman (Volume 2), 432; Carriker, *Fort Supply, Indian Territory*, 19-20. Heitman lists Detachment of Indian Scouts.
[229] *Annual Report of Secretary of War (1869)*, 54-55.

— Scout Bill Davis (Citizen)
— Scout Nate Marshall (Citizen)

(0457) Skirmish, southeast of Bill Williams Mountains, Arizona Territory (November 23, 1868)[230]
— Captain Henry P. Wade (8th U.S. Cavalry)
— 8th U.S. Cavalry Co. B

(0458) Operations, near Camp McDowell, Arizona Territory (November 25 to December 2, 1868)[231]
— Major Andrew J. Alexander (8th U.S. Cavalry)
— 1st U.S. Cavalry Co. E
— 8th U.S. Cavalry Co. I
— 32nd U.S. Infantry Co. A
— Detachment of Indian Scouts
— **1 WOUNDED**[232]
— Indian Scout

(0459) Engagement, Washita River, near Antelope Hills, Indian Territory (November 27, 1868)[233]
— Lt. Colonel George A. Custer (7th U.S. Cavalry)
— 7th U.S. Cavalry Co. A, B, C, D, E, F, G, H, I, K and M
— **21 KILLED**[234]
— Major Joel H. Elliot (7th U.S. Cavalry)
— Captain Louis M. Hamilton (7th U.S. Cavalry)
— Sergeant-Major Walter Kennedy (7th U.S. Cavalry)

— Private Charles Cuddy (Co. B 7th U.S. Cavalry)
— Corporal Harry Mercer (Co. E 7th U.S. Cavalry)
— Private Thomas Christie (Co. E 7th U.S. Cavalry)
— Private John McClernan (Co. E 7th U.S. Cavalry)

— Corporal William Carrick (Co. H 7th U.S. Cavalry)
— Private Eugene Clover (Co. H 7th U.S. Cavalry)
— Private John George (Co. H 7th U.S. Cavalry)
— Private Benjamin McCasey (Co. H 7th U.S. Cavalry) — d. 11-30-1868
— Private William Milligan (Co. H 7th U.S. Cavalry)

— Corporal James F. Williams (Co. I 7th U.S. Cavalry)
— Private Thomas Downey (Co. I 7th U.S. Cavalry)

— Sergeant Erwin Vanousky (Co. M 7th U.S. Cavalry)
— Farrier Thomas Fitzpatrick (Co. M 7th U.S. Cavalry)
— Private Ferdinand Lineback (Co. M 7th U.S. Cavalry)
— Private Carson D.J. Myers (Co. M 7th U.S. Cavalry)

---

[230] Indians. Chronological List, 38; Heitman (Volume 2), 432.

[231] Indians. Chronological List, 38; Heitman (Volume 2), 432. Chronological List and Heitman both list 1st U.S. Cavalry Co. E; 8th U.S. Cavalry Co. I; 32nd U.S. Infantry Co. A.

[232] Chronological List, 38.

[233] Indians. *Annual Report of Secretary of War (1869)*, 46-47, 52; Chronological List, 38; Heitman (Volume 2), 432; Barnitz, *Life in Custer's Cavalry*, 219-229; Greene, *Washita*; Hardorff, *Washita Memories*; Leckie, *Military Conquest of the Southern Plains*, 97-105; Nye, *Carbine and Lance*, 60-70. Chronological List lists 7th U.S. Cavalry.

[234] Reports of Diseases and Individual Cases, F 421; Register of Deaths Regular Army, 1860-1889 (Volume 3); Otis, *Report of Surgical Cases*, 151.

— Private John Myers (Co. M 7ᵗʰ U.S. Cavalry)

— Private Cal Sharpe (Co. M 7ᵗʰ U.S. Cavalry)
— Private Frederick Stocabus (Co. M 7ᵗʰ U.S. Cavalry)

— **14 WOUNDED**[235]
    — Captain Albert Barnitz (7ᵗʰ U.S. Cavalry)
      — *gunshot wound, abdomen, severe wound*
    — 1ˢᵗ Lieutenant Thomas W. Custer (7ᵗʰ U.S. Cavalry)
      — *gunshot wound, right hand, slight wound*
    — 2ⁿᵈ Lieutenant Thomas J. March (7ᵗʰ U.S. Cavalry)
      — *arrow wound, left hand, slight wound*

    — Corporal William Eastwood (Co. A 7ᵗʰ U.S. Cavalry)
      — *gunshot wound, right elbow, severe wound*
    — Private Mortier Gale (Co. A 7ᵗʰ U.S. Cavalry)
      — *gunshot wound, right arm, slight wound*
    — Private Augustus Delaney (Co. B 7ᵗʰ U.S. Cavalry)
      — *gunshot wound, thorax, severe wound*
    — Private George Zimmer (Co. D 7ᵗʰ U.S. Cavalry)
      — *gunshot wound, left arm, fracture, severe wound*
    — Private Frederick Klink (Co. E 7ᵗʰ U.S. Cavalry)
      — *gunshot wound, left arm, slight wound*

    — Private William Brown (Co. F 7ᵗʰ U.S. Cavalry)
      — *gunshot wound, left arm, slight wound*
    — Saddler August Martin (Co. G 7ᵗʰ U.S. Cavalry)
      — *gunshot wound, right arm, fracture, severe wound*
    — Private Daniel Morrison (Co. G 7ᵗʰ U.S. Cavalry)
      — *arrow wound, right temple, slight wound*

    — Private Hugh Morgan (Co. I 7ᵗʰ U.S. Cavalry)
      — *gunshot wound, right arm, severe wound*
    — Private Conrad Strahle (Co. I 7ᵗʰ U.S. Cavalry)
      — *gunshot wound, left ankle, flesh wound*
    — Bugler John Murphy (Co. M 7ᵗʰ U.S. Cavalry)
      — *arrow wound, thorax, severe wound*

— Captain Albert Barnitz (7ᵗʰ U.S. Cavalry) brevet promotion to Colonel for distinguished gallantry in the battle of the Washita (Washita River, Indian Territory, November 27, 1868, in which engagement he was severely wounded).

[235] Reports of Diseases and Individual Cases, F 421; Otis, *Report of Surgical Cases*, 151, 158, 250-251.

— *Captain Louis M. Hamilton (7ᵗʰ U.S. Cavalry) brevet promotion to Major for gallant and meritorious service in engagements with Indians, particularly in the battle with Cheyenne on the Washita (Washita River, Indian Territory, November 27, 1868, where he was killed gallantly leading his command).*

"I cannot sufficiently commend the admirable conduct of the officers and men... This command has marched five days amidst terrible snowstorms and over a rough country covered by more than twelve inches of snow… They have endured every privation and fought with unsurpassed gallantry against a powerful and well armed foe… Every officer, man, scout and Indian guide did their full duty. I only regret the loss of the gallant spirits who fell in the "battle of the Washita." Those whose loss we are called upon to deplore were among our bravest and best."

— George A. Custer, U.S. Army[236]

(0460) Action, near Canadian River, Texas (December 2, 1868)[237]
     — UNKNOWN
        — UNKNOWN
   — **1 WOUNDED**[238]
        — Private Samuel Brown (Co. F 10ᵗʰ U.S. Cavalry) — d. 12-04-1868
        — *arrow wound, abdomen, severe wound*

(0461) Skirmish, Walker Springs, Arizona Territory (December 10, 1868)[239]
     — Major William R. Price (8ᵗʰ U.S. Cavalry)
        — 8ᵗʰ U.S. Cavalry Co. E and K

— *Major William R. Price (8ᵗʰ U.S. Cavalry) brevet promotion to Colonel for gallant and meritorious service in engagements with Indians (Walker Springs, Arizona, December 10 and 13, 1868).*

(0462) Action, Willow Grove, Arizona Territory (December 11, 1868)[240]
     — Major William R. Price (8ᵗʰ U.S. Cavalry)
        — 8ᵗʰ U.S. Cavalry Co. K
   — **1 KILLED**[241]
        — Sergeant Curtis C. Miller (Co. K 8ᵗʰ U.S. Cavalry)

(0463) Skirmish, Walker Springs, Arizona Territory (December 13, 1868)[242]
     — Major William R. Price (8ᵗʰ U.S. Cavalry)
        — 8ᵗʰ U.S. Cavalry Co. E and K

[236] Official Report of Lt. Colonel George A. Custer (7ᵗʰ U.S. Cavalry), Headquarters 7ᵗʰ United States Cavalry, In the Field, on the Washita River, 28 November 1868. Hardorff, *Washita Memories*, 65.
[237] Indians. Otis, *Report of Surgical Cases*, 153.
[238] Register of Deaths Regular Army, 1860-1889 (Volume 3); Otis, *Report of Surgical Cases*, 153.
[239] Indians. Chronological List, 38; Heitman (Volume 2), 432.
[240] Indians. Chronological List, 38; Heitman (Volume 2), 432.
[241] Rodenbough, *Army of the United States*, 278.
[242] Indians. Chronological List, 38; Heitman (Volume 2), 432.

— Major William R. Price (8th U.S. Cavalry) brevet promotion to Colonel for gallant and meritorious service in engagements with Indians (Walker Springs, Arizona, December 10 and 13, 1868).

(0464) Action, Wichita Mountains, North Fork of Red River, Indian Territory (December 25, 1868)[243]
> — Major Andrew W. Evans (3rd U.S. Cavalry)
>> — 3rd U.S. Cavalry Co. A, C, D, F, G and I
>> — 37th U.S. Infantry Co. F and I

— 1 KILLED[244]
>> — Private George Van Plyf (Co. F 37th U.S. Infantry) — d. 12-30-1868

— 1 WOUNDED[245]
>> — Private John Hickey (Co. A 3rd U.S. Cavalry)
>>> *— gunshot wound, right leg, slight wound*

— Major Andrew W. Evans (3rd U.S. Cavalry) brevet promotion to Colonel for gallant and meritorious service resulting in the capture and destruction of a Comanche Indian village (Western base of the Wichita Mountains, December 25, 1868).

— Captain Eugene M. Baker (1st U.S. Cavalry) brevet promotion to Colonel for zeal and energy while in command of troops against hostile Indians (1866, 1867 and 1868).

— Captain John J. Coppinger (23rd U.S. Infantry) brevet promotion to Colonel for zeal and energy while in command of troops operating against hostile Indians (1866, 1867 and 1868).

TOTAL KILLED 1868 — 3/56/14/13 (OFFICERS, ENLISTED MEN, INDIAN SCOUTS, CITIZENS)

[243] Indians. *Annual Report of Secretary of War (1869)*, 49-52; Chronological List, 38; Heitman (Volume 2), 432; Carriker, *Fort Supply, Indian Territory*, 27-28; Leckie, *Military Conquest of the Southern Plains*, 114-117; Nye, *Carbine and Lance*, 78-83.
[244] Reports of Diseases and Individual Cases, F 422; Register of Deaths Regular Army, 1860-1889 (Volume 3).
[245] Reports of Diseases and Individual Cases, F 422.

1869

"While the nation at large is at peace, a state of quasi war has existed and continues to exist, over one half its extent, and the troops therein are exposed to labors, marches, fights and dangers that amount to war… I hope the officers and men composing the Army will receive the assurance of the country, to which they are fairly entitled, that their services are appreciated."

— William T. Sherman, U.S. Army[1]

---

[1] Official Report of the General William T. Sherman, Headquarters of the Army, Washington, D.C., 20 November 1869. *Annual Report of Secretary of War (1869)*, 24.

(0465) Action, Sitka, Department of Alaska (January 1 and 2, 1869)[2]
— UNKNOWN
    — 2nd U.S. Artillery Detachment
— **1 WOUNDED**[3]
    — Enlisted Man (2nd U.S. Artillery)

(0466) Citizens, Lake Station, Colorado Territory (January 8, 1869)[4]
— (2) Citizens Killed

(0467) Operations, Bill Williams Mountains, Arizona Territory (January 8 to 15, 1869)[5]
— Major David R. Clendenin (8th U.S. Cavalry)
    — 8th U.S. Cavalry Co. B and L

(0468) Skirmish, Mount Turnbull, Arizona Territory (January 13, 1869)[6]
— 1st Lieutenant William H. Winters (1st U.S. Cavalry)
    — 1st U.S. Cavalry Detachment Co. G
    — 32nd U.S. Infantry Detachments Co. F and G

(0469) Action, Kirkland's Creek, Juniper Mountains, Arizona Territory (January 25, 1869)[7]
— Captain Samuel B.M. Young (8th U.S. Cavalry)
    — 8th U.S. Cavalry Co. E and K
— **1 WOUNDED**[8]
    — Corporal Kenny Parker (Co. K 8th U.S. Cavalry) — d. 1-30-1869

(0470) Action, Solomon River, Kansas (January 28, 1869)[9]
— UNKNOWN
    — 7th U.S. Cavalry Detachment
— **2 WOUNDED**[10]
    — Enlisted Men (7th U.S. Cavalry)
    — Enlisted Men (7th U.S. Cavalry)

(0471) Action, Mulberry Creek, Kansas (January 29, 1869)[11]
— Captain Edward Byrne (10th U.S. Cavalry)
    — 9th U.S. Cavalry Detachments Co. C, G, H and K
— **2 WOUNDED**[12]
    — Enlisted Men (9th U.S. Cavalry)
    — Enlisted Men (9th U.S. Cavalry)

(0472) Citizens, Saline River, Kansas (January 30, 1869)[13]
— (2) Citizens Killed

[2] Indians. *Annual Report of Commissioner of Indian Affairs (1869)*, 554, 572-573, 586-587, 589.
[3] *Annual Report of Commissioner of Indian Affairs (1869)*, 554, 572-573, 586-587, 589.
[4] Indians. *Annual Report of Secretary of War (1869)*, 54; Chronological List, 38.
[5] Indians. Chronological List, 38; Heitman (Volume 2), 433.
[6] Indians. Chronological List, 38; Heitman (Volume 2), 433. Chronological List lists 1st U.S. Cavalry Detachment Co. G; 32nd U.S. Infantry Detachment.
[7] Indians. Chronological List, 39; Heitman (Volume 2), 433.
[8] Reports of Diseases and Individual Cases, F 423; Register of Deaths Regular Army, 1860-1889 (Volume 3).
[9] Indians. Chronological List, 39; Record of Engagements, 19.
[10] Chronological List, 39.
[11] Indians. *Annual Report of Secretary of War (1869)*, 52; Chronological List, 39; Heitman (Volume 2), 433; Record of Engagements, 19; Burton, *Black, Buckskin and Blue*, 180-181; Leckie, *Buffalo Soldiers*, 41. Chronological List lists "detachment of cavalry recruits".
[12] Chronological List, 39.
[13] Indians. *Annual Report of Secretary of War (1869)*, 54; Chronological List, 39.

(0473) Skirmish, Arivaypa Mountains, Arizona Territory (February 4, 1869) [14]
— Captain Reuben F. Bernard (1st U.S. Cavalry)
— 1st U.S. Cavalry Detachments Co. G and K
— Detachment of Indian Scouts

(0474) Skirmish, Black Mesa, Arizona Territory (February 5, 1869) [15]
— UNKNOWN
— 8th U.S. Cavalry Co. L

— *Captain Henry Inman (Assistant Quartermaster) brevet promotion to Lt. Colonel for meritorious service during the campaign against Indians (February 11, 1869).*

(0475) Action, near Camp Grant, Arizona Territory (February 27, 1869) [16]
— UNKNOWN
— 14th U.S. Infantry Detachment Co. B
— **2 KILLED** [17]
— (2) Citizens

— **1 WOUNDED** [18]
— Enlisted Men (14th U.S. Infantry)

(0476) Skirmish, Oak Grove, Arizona Territory (March 3, 1869) [19]
— UNKNOWN
— 32nd U.S. Infantry Detachment Co. F

(0477) Skirmish, Fort Harker, Kansas (March 9, 1869) [20]
— UNKNOWN
— 7th U.S. Cavalry Co. A, B, C, D, E, F, G, H, I, K and M

(0478) Citizens, Shields River, Montana Territory (March 12, 1869) [21]
— (4) Citizens Killed

(0479) Skirmish, Shields River, Montana Territory (March 13, 1869) [22]
— Captain Emory W. Clift (3rd U.S. Infantry)
— 13th U.S. Infantry Detachments Co. D, F and G

(0480) Action, Fort Randall, Dakota Territory (March 16, 1869) [23]
— UNKNOWN
— 22nd U.S. Infantry Detachments Co. C and F
— **1 KILLED** [24]
— Wagoner Elias A. Prall (Co. F 22nd U.S. Infantry)

[14] Indians. Chronological List, 39; Heitman (Volume 2), 433; McChristian, *Fort Bowie*, 109-110; Russell, *One Hundred and Three Fights*, 63-66. Chronological List lists 1st U.S. Cavalry Detachments Co. G, K; Detachment of Scouts.
[15] Indians. Chronological List, 39; Heitman (Volume 2), 433. Heitman lists 8th U.S. Cavalry Detachment Co. L.
[16] Indians. Chronological List, 39; Heitman (Volume 2), 433.
[17] Camp Grant Post Return February 1869.
[18] Camp Grant Post Return February 1869.
[19] Indians. Chronological List, 39; Heitman (Volume 2), 433.
[20] Indians. Chronological List, 39; Heitman (Volume 2), 433; Record of Engagements, 19. Heitman lists 13 March 1869.
[21] Indians. Fort Ellis Post Return March 1869; Rockwell, *U.S. Army in Frontier Montana*, 157-158.
[22] Indians. Chronological List, 39; Heitman (Volume 2), 433; Rockwell, *U.S. Army in Frontier Montana*, 157-158. Chronological List combines the two entries at Shields River, Montana Territory on 12 and 13 March 1869.
[23] Indians. Chronological List, 39; Heitman (Volume 2), 433. Chronological List lists 22nd U.S. Infantry Co. C, F.
[24] Fort Randall Post Return March 1869.

(0481) Skirmish, near Fort Bayard, New Mexico Territory (March 17, 1869)[25]
    — Captain Henry C. Corbin (38th U.S. Infantry)
       — 38th U.S. Infantry Co. C

(0482) Skirmish, near Camp Goodwin, Arizona Territory (March 17 to 30, 1869)[26]
    — Captain Frank W. Perry (32nd U.S. Infantry)
       — 32nd U.S. Infantry Detachments Co. B, F and G

(0483) Skirmish, near Fort Steele, Wyoming Territory (March 22, 1869)[27]
    — 2nd Lieutenant Robert H. Young (30th U.S. Infantry)
       — 30th U.S. Infantry Detachments Co. A, B, F, H and K

    — *1st Lieutenant James H. Spencer (30th U.S. Infantry) brevet promotion to Captain for gallant service in action against Indians (Near Fort Fred Steele, Wyoming, March 22, 1869).*

    — *2nd Lieutenant Robert H. Young (30th U.S. Infantry) brevet promotion to 1st Lieutenant for gallant service in action against Indians (Fort Fred Steel, Wyoming, March 22, 1869).*

(0484) Action, near Camp Grant, Arizona Territory (March 23, 1869)[28]
    — UNKNOWN
       — 32nd U.S. Infantry Detachment Co. E
  — **1 KILLED**[29]
       — Rodgers (Citizen)

  — **2 WOUNDED**[30]
       — Private Sherman (Co. E 32nd U.S. Infantry)
         — *severe wound*
       — Private Keiser (Co. E 32nd U.S. Infantry)
         — *severe wound*

(0485) Action, near Larabee Creek, Humboldt County, California (March 29, 1869)[31]
    — UNKNOWN
       — 9th U.S. Infantry Detachment
  — **1 KILLED**[32]
       — Private Edward Brooks (Co. K 9th U.S. Infantry)

(0486) Action, near La Bonte Creek, Wyoming Territory (April 6, 1869)[33]
    — Sergeant Robert Rae (4th U.S. Infantry)
       — 4th U.S. Infantry Detachment Co. A
  — **2 KILLED**[34]
       — Sergeant Robert Rae (Co. A 4th U.S. Infantry)
       — Private Russell B. Emery (Co. A 4th U.S. Infantry)

[25] Indians. *Annual Report of Secretary of War (1869)*, 52; Chronological List, 39; Record of Engagements, 19. Heitman lists 26 March 1869.
[26] Indians. Chronological List, 39; Heitman (Volume 2), 433.
[27] Indians. Chronological List, 39; Heitman (Volume 2), 433.
[28] Indians. Chronological List, 39; Heitman (Volume 2), 433.
[29] Fort Lowell Post Return March 1869.
[30] Fort Lowell Post Return March 1869.
[31] Bandits. Reports of Diseases and Individual Cases, F 512.
[32] Reports of Diseases and Individual Cases, F 512; Register of Deaths Regular Army, 1860-1889 (Volume 3).
[33] Indians. Chronological List, 39; Heitman (Volume 2), 433; Lindmier, *Drybone*, 69-70; McChristian, *Fort Laramie*, 314.
[34] 4th U.S. Infantry Regimental Returns April and May 1869.

(0487) Action, Musselshell River, Montana Territory (April 7, 1869)[35]
— Captain Emory W. Clift (13th U.S. Infantry)
— 13th U.S. Infantry Detachments Co. D, F and G
— **1 KILLED**[36]
— Private Terrence Conry (13th U.S. Infantry)

— **4 WOUNDED**[37]
— Private Michael Fitzgerald (Co. F 13th U.S. Infantry)
— *gunshot wound, ankle, fracture, severe wound*
— Private George W. Cruson (Co. G 13th U.S. Infantry)
— *gunshot wound, elbow, fracture, severe wound*

— (2) Citizens

(0488) Action, Cienega, Arizona Territory (April 14, 1869)[38]
— UNKNOWN
— 32nd U.S. Infantry Detachment Co. E
— **2 WOUNDED**[39]
— Private Phillip Noll (Co. E 32nd U.S. Infantry)
— Private William Smith (Co. E 32nd U.S. Infantry)

(0489) Action, near Camp Crittenden, Arizona Territory (April 20, 1869)[40]
— UNKNOWN
— 32nd U.S. Infantry Detachment Co. H
— **1 KILLED**[41]
— Private William Burgess (Co. H 32nd U.S. Infantry)

— **1 WOUNDED**[42]
— Private James F. Tompkins (Co. K 32nd U.S. Infantry)
— *arrow wound, left thigh*

(0490) Skirmish, Sangre Canyon, New Mexico Territory (April 22, 1869)[43]
— UNKNOWN
— 3rd U.S. Cavalry Co. A, F and H
— 37th U.S. Infantry Co. I

(0491) Action, near Fort Bliss, Texas (April 23, 1869)[44]
— **1 KILLED**[45]
— 2nd Lieutenant Bernard Herkness (35th U.S. Infantry)

---

[35] Indians. Chronological List, 39; Heitman (Volume 2), 433; Record of Engagements, 19; Rockwell, *U.S. Army in Frontier Montana*, 159-160.
[36] Reports of Diseases and Individual Cases, F 426; Register of Deaths Regular Army, 1860-1889 (Volume 3).
[37] Reports of Diseases and Individual Cases, F 426.
[38] Indians. Chronological List, 39; Heitman (Volume 2), 433.
[39] 32nd U.S. Infantry Regimental Return April 1869
[40] Indians. Chronological List, 39; Heitman (Volume 2), 433; Otis, *Report of Surgical Cases*, 156.
[41] Register of Deaths Regular Army, 1860-1889 (Volume 3); 32nd U.S. Infantry Regimental Return April 1869; Camp Crittenden Post Return April 1869.
[42] Camp Crittenden Post Return April 1869; Otis, *Report of Surgical Cases*, 156.
[43] Indians. *Annual Report of Secretary of War (1869)*, 52; Chronological List, 39; Heitman (Volume 2), 433; Record of Engagements , 19; Randall, *Only the Echoes*, 48. Chronological List lists "cavalry scouting party".
[44] Deserters. Fort Bliss Post Return April 1869; Heitman (Volume 1), 525.
[45] Register of Deaths Regular Army, 1860-1889 (Volume 3); Fort Bliss Texas Post Return April 1869.

(0492) Skirmish, Turnbull Mountain, Arizona Territory (April 29, 1869)[46]
— Major John Green (1st U.S. Cavalry)
— 1st U.S. Cavalry Detachments Co. C, G and K
— 14th U.S. Infantry Co. B
— 32nd U.S. Infantry Co. I
— Detachment of Indian Scouts

— *Major John Green (1st U.S. Cavalry) brevet promotion to Colonel for gallant service in actions against Indians (Turnbull Mountains, Arizona, April 29, 1869).*

(0493) Operations, Val de Chino Valley, Arizona Territory (May 2 to 9, 1869)[47]
— 2nd Lieutenant Ambrose B. Curtiss (8th U.S. Cavalry)
— 8th U.S. Cavalry Detachment Co. L

(0494) Action, Grief Hill, near Camp Verde, Arizona Territory (May 6, 1869)[48]
— Sergeant Charles McVeagh (8th U.S. Cavalry)
— 8th U.S. Cavalry Detachment Co. B
— 14th U.S. Infantry Detachment Co. C
— **1 KILLED**[49]
— Private Joseph Clark (Co. C 14th U.S. Infantry) — d. 5-07-1869

— **4 WOUNDED**[50]
— Sergeant Charles McVeagh (Co. B 8th U.S. Cavalry)
— Private Patrick Daley (Co. B 8th U.S. Cavalry)
— *gunshot wound, upper left arm, fracture, amputation*
— Private Joseph Whitcomb (Co. B 8th U.S. Cavalry)
— *gunshot wound, left forearm, fracture*
— Private James O'Hara (Co. C 14th U.S. Infantry)

(0495) Action, San Augustine Pass, New Mexico Territory (May 7, 1869)[51]
— Corporal Charles Younge (3rd U.S. Cavalry)
— 3rd U.S. Cavalry Detachment Co. K
— **1 KILLED**[52]
— Corporal Charles Younge (Co. K 3rd U.S. Cavalry)

— **2 WOUNDED**[53]
— Private John Stewart (Co. K 3rd U.S. Cavalry)
— *gunshot wound, thigh*

— (1) Citizen
— *slight wound*

[46] Indians. Chronological List, 39; Heitman (Volume 2), 433; Alexander, *Arizona Frontier Military Place Names*, 122-123. Heitman lists 1st U.S. Cavalry Detachments Co. C, G, K; 14th U.S. Infantry Co. B; 32nd U.S. Infantry Detachment Co. I; Detachment of Indian Scouts.
[47] Indians. Chronological List, 39; Heitman (Volume 2), 433.
[48] Indians. Chronological List, 39; Heitman (Volume 2), 433. Chronological List lists 8th U.S. Cavalry Detachment Co. B; 14th U.S. Infantry Co. C.
[49] Register of Deaths Regular Army, 1860-1889 (Volume 3); Camp Verde Post Return May 1869.
[50] Camp Verde Post Return May 1869; Otis, *Report of Surgical Cases*, 64, 181.
[51] Indians. *Annual Report of Secretary of War (1869)*, 52; Chronological List, 40; Heitman (Volume 2), 433; Rathbun, *New Mexico Frontier Military Place Names*, 152.
[52] Fort Selden Post Return May 1869.
[53] Fort Selden Post Return May 1869.

(0496) Skirmish, Paint Creek, near Double Mountain Fork, Texas (May 7, 1869)[54]
— Captain George W. Smith (35th U.S. Infantry)
— 35th U.S. Infantry Detachments Co. E and F
— Detachment of Indian Scouts

— *Assistant Surgeon Henry McElderry brevet promotion to Major for meritorious service in action against Indians (Double Mountain Fork of Brazos River, Texas, May 7, 1869) and for gallant service in action against Indians (Lava Beds, California, January 17, 1873).*

(0497) Action, Fort Hays, Kansas (May 10, 1869)[55]
— UNKNOWN
— 5th U.S. Infantry Detachments Co. E and G
— **1 KILLED**[56]
— Enlisted Man (5th U.S. Infantry)

(0498) Action, Beaver Creek or Elephant Rock, Kansas (May 13, 1869)[57]
— Major Eugene A. Carr (5th U.S. Cavalry)
— 5th U.S. Cavalry Co. A, B, F, H, I, L and M
— **4 KILLED**[58]
— Sergeant John Ford (Co. B 5th U.S. Cavalry)
— Sergeant John A.C. Stone (Co. B 5th U.S. Cavalry)
— Sergeant Charles Alcorn (Co. B 5th U.S. Cavalry)
— Private John Meyer (Co. A 5th U.S. Cavalry)

—**2 WOUNDED**[59]
— Private Michael Young (Co. H 5th U.S. Cavalry)
— *gunshot wound, right shoulder, slight wound*
— Private George Russell (Co. M 5th U.S. Cavalry)
— *gunshot wound, head, slight wound*

(0499) Action, near Fort Lowell, Arizona Territory (May 15, 1869)[60]
— UNKNOWN
— 1st U.S. Cavalry Detachment Co. G
— **1 WOUNDED**[61]
— Private Metcalf (Co. G 1st U.S. Cavalry)
— *severe wound*

(0500) Action, Spring Creek, Nebraska (May 16, 1869)[62]
— Major Eugene A. Carr (5th U.S. Cavalry)
— 5th U.S. Cavalry Co. A, B, F, H, I, L and M
— **3 WOUNDED**[63]

[54] Indians. Chronological List, 40; Heitman (Volume 2), 433; Smith, *Old Army in Texas*, 149. Chronological List lists 35th U.S. Infantry Detachment.
[55] Indians. Chronological List, 40; Heitman (Volume 2), 433; Record of Engagements, 19. Chronological List lists "attack of Indian prisoners on the guard".
[56] Chronological List, 40.
[57] Indians. *Annual Report of Secretary of War (1869)*, 50; Chronological List, 40; Heitman (Volume 2), 433; Record of Engagements, 20; Chalfant, *Cheyennes at Dark Water Creek*, 17-18; King, *War Eagle*, 96-97; Leckie, *Military Conquest of the Southern Plains*, 127-128; Monnett, *Battle of Beecher Island*, 187; Price, *Across the Continent*, 134, 658; White, "Indian Raids on the Kansas Frontier, 1869," *Kansas Historical Quarterly* 38 (Winter 1972): 369-388.
[58] Reports of Diseases and Individual Cases, F 428; Register of Deaths Regular Army, 1860-1889 (Volume 3); Otis, *Report of Surgical Cases*, 159.
[59] Reports of Diseases and Individual Cases, F 428.
[60] Indians. Chronological List, 40; Heitman (Volume 2), 433. Heitman lists 11 May 1869.
[61] Fort Lowell Post Return May 1869.
[62] Indians. Chronological List, 40; Heitman (Volume 2), 433; Record of Engagements, 20; Chalfant, *Cheyennes at Dark Water Creek*, 17-18; King, *War Eagle*, 98-99; Leckie, *Military Conquest of the Southern Plains*, 128; Price, *Across the Continent*, 135, 658.
[63] Chronological List, 40.

— Enlisted Man (5th U.S. Cavalry)
— Enlisted Man (5th U.S. Cavalry)
— Enlisted Man (5th U.S. Cavalry)

— *1st Lieutenant John B. Babcock (5th U.S. Cavalry) received MOH: While serving with a scouting column, this officer's troop was attacked by a vastly superior force of Indians. Advancing to high ground, he dismounted his men, remaining mounted himself to encourage them, and there fought the Indians until relieved, his horse being wounded (Spring Creek, Nebraska, May 16, 1869).*

(0501) Operations, Black Range Mountains, New Mexico Territory (May 18 to 26, 1869)[64]
— Major Henry C. Merriam (24th U.S. Infantry)
— 3rd U.S. Cavalry Detachment Co. B

(0502) Citizens, Fort Bayard, New Mexico Territory (May 18, 1869)[65]

(0503) Skirmish, near Fort Fred Steele, Wyoming Territory (May 21, 1869)[66]
— 1st Lieutenant James H. Spencer (4th U.S. Infantry)
— 4th U.S. Infantry Co. B and H

(0504) Operations, near Mineral Springs, Arizona Territory (May 22 to 28, 1869)[67]
— Captain Isaac R. Dunkelberger (1st U.S. Cavalry)
— 1st U.S. Cavalry Co. K
— 32nd U.S. Infantry Co. I
— Detachment of Indian Scouts

(0505) Citizens, Jewell County, Kansas (May 25, 1869)[68]
— (6) Citizens Killed

(0506) Citizens, near Sheridan, Kansas (May 26, 1869)[69]

(0507) Citizens, Fossil Creek Station, Kansas (May 29, 1869)[70]
— (2) Citizens Killed

(0508) Citizens, Salt Creek, Kansas (May 30, 1869)[71]
— (1) Citizen Killed

(0509) Citizens, near Fort Hays, Kansas (May 30, 1869)[72]

(0510) Operations, near Camp Toll Gate, Arizona Territory (May 30 to June 3, 1869)[73]
— Major William R. Price (8th U.S. Cavalry)
— 8th U.S. Cavalry Detachments Co. E, F and K

[64] Indians. *Annual Report of Secretary of War (1869)*, 52; Chronological List, 40; Heitman (Volume 2), 433; Record of Engagements, 20.
[65] Indians. Chronological List, 40.
[66] Indians. Chronological List, 40; Heitman (Volume 2), 433.
[67] Indians. Chronological List, 40; Heitman (Volume 2), 433. Heitman lists 1st U.S. Cavalry Co. K; 32nd U.S. Infantry Detachment Co. I; Detachment of Indian Scouts.
[68] Indians. Chronological List, 40; Record of Engagements, 20; Chalfant, *Cheyennes at Dark Water Creek*, 19-20.
[69] Indians. Chronological List, 40; Record of Engagements, 20; Chalfant, *Cheyennes at Dark Water Creek*, 19-20.
[70] Indians. Killed were railroad workers Alexander McKeever and John Lynch. Chronological List, 40; Record of Engagements, 20-21; Broome, *Dog Soldier Justice*, 82; Chalfant, *Cheyennes at Dark Water Creek*, 19-20; Monnett, *Battle of Beecher Island*, 100; White, "Indian Raids on the Kansas Frontier, 1869," *Kansas Historical Quarterly* 38 (Winter 1972): 369-388.
[71] Indians. Chronological List, 40; Record of Engagements, 21; Chalfant, *Cheyennes at Dark Water Creek*, 19-20.
[72] Indians. Chronological List, 40; Record of Engagements, 21; Chalfant, *Cheyennes at Dark Water Creek*, 19-20.
[73] Indians. Chronological List, 40; Heitman (Volume 2), 433.

(0511) Skirmish, Rose Creek, Kansas (May 31, 1869)[74]
    — UNKNOWN
        — 7th U.S. Cavalry Detachment Co. G
    — **2 WOUNDED**[75]
        — Enlisted Man (7th U.S. Cavalry)
        — Enlisted Man (7th U.S. Cavalry)

(0512) Citizens, Solomon River, Kansas (June 1, 1869)[76]
    — (13) Citizens Killed

(0513) Action, Solomon River, Kansas (June 1, 1869)[77]
    — UNKNOWN
        — 7th U.S. Cavalry Detachment Co. G
    — **1 WOUNDED**[78]
        — Enlisted Man (7th U.S. Cavalry)

(0514) Action, Rio Pinto River, Pinal Mountains, Arizona Territory (June 3 and 4, 1869)[79]
    — Captain George B. Sanford (1st U.S. Cavalry)
        — 1st U.S. Cavalry Co. E
        — 8th U.S. Cavalry Co. C
        — 14th U.S. Infantry Detachment Co. F
    — **1 WOUNDED**[80]
        — Enlisted Man

    — *Bugler George Gates (Co. F 8th U.S. Cavalry) received MOH: Killed an Indian warrior and captured his arms (Picacho Mountains, Arizona, June 4, 1869).*

    — *Private Joseph Watson (Co. F 8th U.S. Cavalry) received MOH: Killed an Indian warrior and captured his arms (Picacho Mountains, Arizona, June 4, 1869).*

(0515) Action, Pecos River, Texas (June 7, 1869)[81]
    — Colonel Ranald S. Mackenzie (41st U.S. Infantry)
        — 9th U.S. Cavalry Detachments Co. G, L and M
    — **1 KILLED**[82]
        — Private Edward Williams (Co. L 9th U.S. Cavalry)

    — *Captain John M. Bacon (9th U.S. Cavalry) brevet promotion to Lt. Colonel for gallant service in action against Indians (Pecos River, Texas, June 7, 1869 and near the headwaters of the Brazos River, Texas, October 28 and 29, 1869).*[83]

---

[74] Indians. Chronological List, 40; Heitman (Volume 2), 433; Record of Engagements, 21.
[75] Chronological List, 40.
[76] Indians. Chronological List, 40; Record of Engagements, 21; Chalfant, *Cheyennes at Dark Water Creek*, 19-20.
[77] Indians. Chronological List, 40; Heitman (Volume 2), 433; Record of Engagements, 21.
[78] Chronological List, 40.
[79] Indians. Chronological List, 41; Heitman (Volume 2), 433. Chronological List lists 1st U.S. Cavalry Co. E; 8th U.S. Cavalry Co. C; 14th U.S. Infantry Detachment.
[80] Chronological List, 41.
[81] Indians. Chronological List, 41; Heitman (Volume 2), 433; Smith, *Old Army in Texas*, 149; Williams, *Texas' Last Frontier*, 115.
[82] Drowned "while in pursuit of Indians" 8 June 1869. 9th U.S. Cavalry Regimental Return June 1869.
[83] Heitman lists the brevet as being for action against Indians on the Pecos River, 7 June 1867. There was no action involving the 9th U.S. Cavalry on the Pecos in 1867.

— *1st Lieutenant Byron Dawson (9th U.S. Cavalry) brevet promotion to Captain for gallant service in actions against Indians (Pecos River, Texas, June 7, 1869 and Brazos River, Texas, October 28 and 29, 1869).*

— *Captain Edward M. Heyl (9th U.S. Cavalry) brevet promotion to Major for gallant service in actions against Indians (Pecos River, Texas, June 7, 1869, the Salt Fork of the Brazos River, Texas, September 16, 1869 and the South Fork of the Stano River, Texas, September 24, 1869, where he was severely wounded).*

(0516) Skirmish, Solomon River, Kansas (June 11, 1869)[84]
— Captain William M. Graham (1st U.S. Artillery)
— 1st U.S. Artillery Co. A

(0517) Action, near Toll Gate, Arizona Territory (June 16, 1869)[85]
— 2nd Lieutenant Aaron B. Jerome (8th U.S. Cavalry)
— 8th U.S. Cavalry Detachments Co. E and F
— **1 KILLED**[86]
— Private Nathan Eberhard (Co. E 8th U.S. Cavalry)

— **1 WOUNDED**[87]
— Enlisted Man (8th U.S. Cavalry)

(0518) Skirmish, Fort Wallace, Kansas (June 19, 1869)[88]
— UNKNOWN
— 5th U.S. Infantry Detachments Co. B, C and D

(0519) Action, near Sheridan, Kansas (June 19, 1869)[89]
— UNKNOWN
— 7th U.S. Cavalry Detachment Co. E
— **2 WOUNDED**[90]
— Enlisted Man (7th U.S. Cavalry)
— Enlisted Man (7th U.S. cavalry)

(0520) Operations, Red Rock Country, Arizona Territory (June 19 to July 5, 1869)[91]
— 2nd Lieutenant Ambrose B. Curtiss (8th U.S. Cavalry)
— 8th U.S. Cavalry Co. L

(0521) Skirmish, Santa Maria River, near Toll Gate, Arizona Territory (June 26, 1869)[92]
— Major William R. Price (8th U.S. Cavalry)
— 8th U.S. Cavalry Co. F

— *Private Albert Sale (Co. F 8th U.S. Cavalry) received MOH: Gallantry in killing an Indian warrior and capturing pony and effects (Santa Maria River, Arizona, June 29, 1869).*

[84] Indians. Chronological List, 41; Heitman (Volume 2), 433; Record of Engagements, 21. Heitman lists 1st U.S. Artillery Co. K.
[85] Indians. Chronological List, 41; Heitman (Volume 2), 433.
[86] 8th U.S. Cavalry Regimental Return June 1869.
[87] Chronological List, 41.
[88] Indians. Chronological List, 41; Heitman (Volume 2), 433; Record of Engagements, 21. Chronological List lists "garrison troops".
[89] Indians. Chronological List, 41; Heitman (Volume 2), 433; Record of Engagements, 21. Chronological List lists 7th U.S. Cavalry Detachment.
[90] Chronological List, 41.
[91] Indians. Chronological List, 41; Heitman (Volume 2), 433.
[92] Indians. Chronological List, 41; Heitman (Volume 2), 434.

(0522) Skirmish, Great Mouth Canyon, Arizona Territory (June 27, 1869)[93]
    — Captain Samuel B.M. Young (8th U.S. Cavalry)
        — 8th U.S. Cavalry Co. K

(0523) Skirmish, Burro Mountains, New Mexico Territory (June 30, 1869)[94]
    — Captain Reuben F. Bernard (1st U.S. Cavalry)
        — 1st U.S. Cavalry Co. G

(0524) Skirmish, Hell Canyon, Arizona Territory (July 3, 1869)[95]
    — 2nd Lieutenant Ambrose B. Curtiss (8th U.S. Cavalry)
        — 8th U.S. Cavalry Co. L

    — First Sergeant Sanford Bradbury (Co. L 8th U.S. Cavalry) received MOH: Conspicuous gallantry in action (Hell Canyon, Arizona, July 3, 1869).

    — Corporal Paul Haupt (Co. L 8th U.S. Cavalry) received MOH: Gallantry in action (Hell Canyon, Arizona, July 3, 1869).

    — Corporal John J. Mitchell (Co. L 8th U.S. Cavalry) received MOH: Gallantry in action (Hell Canyon, Arizona, July 3, 1869).

(0525) Skirmish, Frenchman's Fork, Nebraska (July 6, 1869)[96]
    — 1st Lieutenant George F. Price (5th U.S. Cavalry)
        — 5th U.S. Cavalry Co. A

(0526) Action, Hac-qua-Hallawater, Arizona Territory (July 6, 1869)[97]
    — 1st Lieutenant William McCleave (8th U.S. Cavalry)
        — 1st U.S. Cavalry Detachment Co. E
        — 8th U.S. Cavalry Detachment Co. C
    — **1 KILLED**[98]
        — Private James Howell (Co. C 8th U.S. Cavalry) — d. 8-03-1869

(0527) Skirmish, near Republican River, Kansas (July 8, 1869)[99]
    — Corporal John Kyle (5th U.S. Cavalry)
        — 5th U.S. Cavalry Detachment Co. M

    — Corporal John Kyle (Co. M 5th U.S. Cavalry) received MOH: This soldier and two others were attacked by eight Indians, but beat them off and badly wounded two of them (Republican River, Kansas, July 8, 1869).

(0528) Action, Republican River, Kansas (July 8, 1869)[100]
    — Major Eugene A. Carr (5th U.S. Cavalry)

[93] Indians. Chronological List, 41; Heitman (Volume 2), 434.
[94] Indians. *Annual Report of Secretary of War (1869)*, 52; Chronological List, 41; Heitman (Volume 2), 434; Russell, *One Hundred and Three Fights*, 71.
[95] Indians. Chronological List, 41; Heitman (Volume 2), 434.
[96] Indians. Chronological List, 41; Heitman (Volume 2), 434. Heitman lists 5 July 1869. Heitman lists 5th U.S. Cavalry Co. A, E, M; Detachment of Indian Scouts.
[97] Indians. Chronological List, 41; Heitman (Volume 2), 434; Alexander, *Arizona Frontier Military Place Names*, 67.
[98] Reports of Diseases and Individual Cases, F 429; Otis, *Report of Surgical Cases*, 11-12.
[99] Indians. Chronological List, 41; Heitman (Volume 2), 434; Record of Engagements, 22; King, *War Eagle*, 110; Paul, *Nebraska Indian Wars Reader*, 49; Price, *Across the Continent*, 136.
[100] Indians. *Annual Report of Secretary of War (1869)*, 68; Chronological List, 41; Heitman (Volume 2), 434; Record of Engagements, 22; Chalfant, *Cheyennes at Dark Water Creek*, 22; Grinnell, *Two Great Scouts*, 191; King, *War Eagle*, 110; Leckie, *Military Conquest of the Southern Plains*, 129-132; Paul, *Nebraska Indian Wars Reader*, 50; Price, *Across the Continent*, 136; Van de Logt, *War Party in Blue*, 126. Chronological List lists "night attack on General Carr's camp".

— 5th U.S. Cavalry Co. A, C, D, E, G, H and M
— Detachment of Indian Scouts
— **1 WOUNDED**[101]
— Sergeant Co-Rux-Te-Chod-Ish, aka Mad Bear (Indian Scout)
— *gunshot wound, serious wound*

— *Sergeant Co-Rux-Te-Chod-Ish, aka Mad Bear (Indian Scout, U.S. Army) received MOH: Ran out from the command in pursuit of a dismounted Indian, was shot down and badly wounded by a bullet from his own command (Republican River, Kansas, July 8, 1869).*

(0529) Citizens, New Mexico Territory (July 10 to 17, 1869)[102]
— (10) Citizens Killed

(0530) Action, Summit Springs, Colorado Territory (July 11, 1869)[103]
— Major Eugene A. Carr (5th U.S. Cavalry)
— 5th U.S. Cavalry Detachments Co. A, C, D, E, G, H and M
— Detachment of Indian Scouts
— **1 WOUNDED**[104]
— Enlisted Man (5th U.S. Cavalry)

— *Captain Samuel S. Sumner (5th U.S. Cavalry) brevet promotion to Lt. Colonel for gallant service in action against Indians (Summit Springs, Colorado, July 11, 1869).*

"Resolved, by the Legislature of the State of Nebraska, that the thanks of the people of Nebraska be, and are hereby tendered, to [Brevet Major-General Eugene A. Carr] and the officers and soldiers under his command, of the Fifth United States Cavalry, for their courage and their perseverance in their campaign against the hostile Indians on the frontier of this state, in July, 1869; driving the enemy from our borders and achieving a victory at Summit Springs, Colorado Territory, by which the people of the State were freed from the merciless savages."

"Second. Resolved that the thanks of this body and the people of the State of Nebraska are hereby tendered to Major Frank North and the officers and soldiers under his command, of the Pawnee Scouts, for the heroic manner in which they assisted in driving hostile Indians from our frontier settlements." [105]

(0531) Operations, White Mountains, near Camp Grant, Arizona Territory (July 13 to August 19, 1869)[106]
— Major John Green (1st U.S. Cavalry)
— 1st U.S. Cavalry Detachments Co. K and L
—32nd U.S. Infantry Detachments Co. B, F and I
— Detachment of Indian Scouts

(0532) Citizens, near Fort Benton, Montana Territory (July 17, 1869)[107]
— (2) Citizens Killed

[101] Paul, *Nebraska Indian Wars Reader*, 50.
[102] Indians. Chronological List, 41; Record of Engagements, 22-23.
[103] Indians. *Annual Report of Secretary of War (1869)*, 68; Chronological List, 41; Heitman (Volume 2), 434; Record of Engagements, 22; Broome, "Death at Summit Springs," *Wild West* (October 2003): 39-45, 72; Chalfant, *Cheyennes at Dark Water Creek*, 23-24; Filipiak, "Battle of Summit Springs," *Colorado Magazine* 41 (Fall 1964): 350-352; Grinnell, *Two Great Scouts*, 195-204; King, *War Eagle*, 111-116; Monnett, *Battle of Beecher Island*, 189-191; Paul, *Nebraska Indian Wars Reader*, 52-62; Price, *Across the Continent*, 137-140; Van de Logt, *War Party in Blue*, 127-132.
[104] Chronological List, 41.
[105] Grinnell, *Two Great Scouts*.
[106] Indians. *Annual Report of Commissioner of Indian Affairs (1869)*, 102-103; Chronological List, 41; Heitman (Volume 2), 434. Chronological List and Heitman both list 1st U.S. Cavalry Detachments Co. K, L; 32nd U.S. Infantry Detachments Co. B, F, I.
[107] Indians. Killed were two herders. *Annual Report of Commissioner of Indian Affairs (1869)*, 300-301.

(0533) Action, North Platte, Nebraska (July 22 and 23, 1869)[108]
— 1st Lieutenant John A. Wanless (2nd U.S. Cavalry)
— 2nd U.S. Cavalry Co. K
— **1 WOUNDED**[109]
— Enlisted Man (2nd U.S. Cavalry)

(0534) Skirmish, Fort Stevenson, Dakota Territory (August 3, 1869)[110]
— Captain Samuel A. Wainwright (22nd U.S. Infantry)
— 22nd U.S. Infantry Co. E and F
— Detachment of Indian Scouts

(0535) Skirmish, Fort Stevenson, Dakota Territory (August 5, 1869)[111]
— 1st Lieutenant Foster E. Parsons (22nd U.S. Infantry)
— 22nd U.S. Infantry Detachment
— Detachment of Indian Scouts

(0536) Citizens, Fort Buford, Dakota Territory (August 10, 1869)[112]
— (4) Citizens Killed

(0537) Skirmish, near San Augustine Pass, New Mexico Territory (August 15, 1869)[113]
— Captain Frank Stanwood (3rd U.S. Cavalry)
— 3rd U.S. Cavalry Co. F and H

(0538) Citizens, near Helena, Montana Territory (August 19, 1869)[114]
— (1) Citizen Killed

(0539) Action, Eagle Creek, Montana Territory (August 19, 1869)[115]
— UNKNOWN
— 13th U.S. Infantry Detachment Co. B
— **1 KILLED**[116]
— (1) Citizen

— **1 WOUNDED**[117]
— (1) Citizen

(0540) Skirmish, Santa Maria River, Arizona Territory (August 25, 1869)[118]
— 2nd Lieutenant Rufus Somerby (8th U.S. Cavalry)
— 8th U.S. Cavalry Co. B

---

[108] Indians. Chronological List, 41; Heitman (Volume 2), 434; Rodenbough, *From Everglade to Canyon*, 435.
[109] Chronological List, 41.
[110] Indians. Heitman (Volume 2), 434; Record of Engagements, 23. Heitman lists 22nd U.S. Infantry Co. E, F; Detachment of Indian Scouts.
[111] Indians. Chronological List, 41. Chronological List lists "garrison of post and detachment of [Indian] scouts".
[112] Indians. Killed were Peter S. Dugan, Adam Jones, Joseph Araldo and James H. MacLane. Chronological List, 42; Fort Buford Cemetery Records.
[113] Indians. Chronological List, 42; Heitman (Volume 2), 434; Record of Engagements, 23; Randall, *Only the Echoes*, 49.
[114] Indians. Killed was a man named Malcolm Clark. Chronological List, 42; Record of Engagements, 23; Rockwell, *U.S. Army in Frontier Montana*, 170-174.
[115] Indians. Chronological List, 42; Heitman (Volume 2), 434; Record of Engagements, 23. Chronological List lists "train from Camp Cook, Montana".
[116] Chronological List, 42.
[117] Chronological List, 42.
[118] Indians. Chronological List, 42; Heitman (Volume 2), 434.

(0541) Skirmish, Tonto Station, near Toll Gate, Arizona Territory (August 25, 1869)[119]
— 1st Lieutenant Robert Carrick (8th U.S. Cavalry)
— 8th U.S. Cavalry Co. E, F and K

— Corporal Michael Corcoran (Co. E 8th U.S. Cavalry) received MOH: Gallantry in action (Aqua Fria River, Arizona, August 25, 1869).

— Sergeant Cornelius Donavan (Co. E 8th U.S. Cavalry) received MOH: Gallantry in action (Aqua Fria River, Arizona, August 25, 1869).

— Private Frank Hamilton (Co. E 8th U.S. Cavalry) received MOH: Gallantry in action (Aqua Fria River, Arizona, August 25, 1869).

— Private Herbert Mahers (Co. F 8th U.S. Cavalry) received MOH: Gallantry in action (Seneca Mountain, Arizona, August 25, 1869).

— Private John Moran (Co. F 8th U.S. Cavalry) received MOH: Gallantry in action (Seneca Mountain, Arizona, August 25, 1869).

— Corporal Philip Murphy (Co. F 8th U.S. Cavalry) received MOH: Gallantry in action (Seneca Mountain, Arizona, August 25, 1869).

— Corporal Thomas Murphy (Co. F 8th U.S. Cavalry) received MOH: Gallantry in action (Seneca Mountain, Arizona, August 25, 1869).

(0542) Action, Tonto Plateau, near Camp Toll Gate, Arizona Territory (August 26, 1869)[120]
— 1st Lieutenant Robert Carrick (8th U.S. Cavalry)
— 8th U.S. Cavalry Co. E, F and K
— **1 KILLED**[121]
— Enlisted Man (8th U.S. Cavalry)

— Corporal Edward Stanley (Co. F 8th U.S. Cavalry) received MOH: Gallantry in action (Seneca Mountain, Arizona, August 26, 1869).

(0543) Action, near Camp Date Creek, Arizona Territory (September 5, 1869)[122]
— 2nd Lieutenant Rufus Somerby (8th U.S. Cavalry)
— 8th U.S. Cavalry Co. B
— 12th U.S. Infantry Detachment Co. F
— **1 KILLED**[123]
— Private Joseph Whitcomb (Co. B 8th U.S. Cavalry) — d. 10-07-1869.

[119] Indians. Chronological List, 42; Heitman (Volume 2), 434.
[120] Indians. Chronological List, 42; Heitman (Volume 2), 434.
[121] Chronological List, 42.
[122] Indians. Chronological List, 42; Heitman (Volume 2), 434.
[123] 8th U.S. Cavalry Regimental Return October 1869.

(0544) Citizens, near Vulture City, Arizona Territory (September 7, 1869)[124]
— (3) Citizens Killed

(0545) Action, Laramie Peak, Wyoming Territory (September 12, 1869)[125]
— 2nd Lieutenant Theodore E. True (4th U.S. Infantry)
— 4th U.S. Infantry Detachments Co. D and G
— **1 KILLED**[126]
— Private Peter Worrick (Co. G 4th U.S. Infantry)

— **1 WOUNDED**[127]
— Private Joseph Apgar (Co. D 4th U.S. Infantry)

(0546) Action, Little Wind River, Wyoming Territory (September 14, 1869)[128]
— **1 KILLED**[129]
— Private John Holt (Co. K 7th U.S. Infantry)

(0547) Action, Popo Agie River, Wyoming Territory (September 14, 1869)[130]
— 1st Lieutenant Charles B. Stambaugh (2nd U.S. Cavalry)
— 2nd U.S. Cavalry Co. D
— **2 WOUNDED**[131]
— Enlisted Man (2nd U.S. Cavalry)
— Enlisted Man (2nd U.S. Cavalry)

(0548) Action, near Whiskey Gap, Wyoming Territory (September 15, 1869)[132]
— 1st Lieutenant James H. Spencer (4th U.S. Infantry)
— 4th U.S. Infantry Detachment Co. B
— 7th U.S. Infantry Detachments Co. B, D, F and I
— **1 KILLED**[133]
— Private Charles Barry (Co. B 7th U.S. Infantry)

(0549) Action, Salt Fork of Brazos River, Texas (September 16, 1869)[134]
— Captain Henry Carroll (9th U.S. Cavalry)
— 9th U.S. Cavalry Co. B, E, F and M
— 41st U.S. Infantry Detachment
— **3 WOUNDED**[135]
— Enlisted Man
— Enlisted Man
— Enlisted Man

— *1st Lieutenant George E. Albee (41st U.S. Infantry) brevet promotion to Captain for gallant service in actions against Indians (Brazos River, Texas, September 16, 1869 and October 28 and 29, 1869).*

---

[124] Indians. *Annual Report of Secretary of War (1869)*, 133.
[125] Indians. Chronological List, 42; Heitman (Volume 2), 434; Record of Engagements, 24.
[126] 4th U.S. Infantry Regimental Return September 1879; Fort Laramie Cemetery Records.
[127] 4th U.S. Infantry Regimental Return September 1879.
[128] Indians. Chronological List, 42; Heitman (Volume 2), 434; Record of Engagements, 24.
[129] Chronological List, 42.
[130] Indians. *Annual Report of Commissioner of Indian Affairs (1869)*, 275; Chronological List, 42; Heitman (Volume 2), 434; Record of Engagements, 24; Rodenbough, *From Everglade to Canyon*, 435.
[131] Chronological List, 42.
[132] Indians. Chronological List, 42; Record of Engagements, 24. Chronological List lists 4th U.S. Infantry Detachments; 7th U.S. Infantry Detachments.
[133] Register of Deaths Regular Army, 1860-1889 (Volume 4).
[134] Indians. Chronological List, 42; Heitman (Volume 2), 434; Leckie, *Buffalo Soldiers*, 90-91; Neal, *Valor Across the Lone Star*, 39-42; Smith, *Old Army in Texas*, 149; Williams, *Texas' Last Frontier*, 118. Heitman lists 9th U.S. Cavalry Co. B, E, F, M.
[135] Chronological List, 42.

— *Captain Henry Carroll (9ᵗʰ U.S. Cavalry) brevet promotion to Major for gallant service in actions against Indians (Main Fork of Brazos River, Texas, September 16, 1869 and San Andreas Mountains, New Mexico, April 7, 1880, where he was severely wounded).*

— *Captain Edward M. Heyl (9ᵗʰ U.S. Cavalry) brevet promotion to Major for gallant service in actions against Indians (Pecos River, Texas, June 7, 1869, the Salt Fork of the Brazos River, Texas, September 16, 1869 and the South Fork of the Stano River, Texas, September 24, 1869, where he was severely wounded).*

(0550) Citizens, Point of Rocks, Wyoming Territory (September 17, 1869)[136]
— (1) Citizen killed

(0551) Citizens, Twin Creek, Wyoming Territory (September 17, 1869)[137]

(0552) Action, Brazos River, Texas (September 20 and 21, 1869)[138]
— Captain Henry Carroll (9ᵗʰ U.S. Cavalry)
    — 9ᵗʰ U.S. Cavalry Detachments Co. B and E
— **1 WOUNDED**[139]
    — Enlisted Man (9ᵗʰ U.S. Cavalry)

(0553) Skirmish, Red Creek, Arizona Territory (September 23, 1869)[140]
— 1ˢᵗ Lieutenant Thomas W. Gibson (8ᵗʰ U.S. Cavalry)
    — 8ᵗʰ U.S. Cavalry Co. D and L

— *Corporal George Ferrari (Co. D 8ᵗʰ U.S. Cavalry) received MOH: Gallantry in action (Red Creek, Arizona, September 23, 1869).*

— *Sergeant Charles D. Harris (Co. D 8ᵗʰ U.S. Cavalry) received MOH: Gallantry in action (Red Creek, Arizona, September 23, 1869).*

— *Private John Walker (Co. D 8ᵗʰ U.S. Cavalry) received MOH: Gallantry in action with Indians (Red Creek, Arizona, September 23, 1869).*

(0554) Citizens, near Fort Bayard, New Mexico Territory (September 24, 1869)[141]

(0555) Skirmish, Prairie Dog Creek, Kansas (September 26, 1869)[142]
— Lt. Colonel Thomas Duncan (5ᵗʰ U.S. Cavalry)
    — 2ⁿᵈ U.S. Cavalry Co. B, C and M
    — 5ᵗʰ U.S. Cavalry Co. B, C, F, L and M

(0556) Action, Dragoon Springs, Arizona Territory (October 5, 1869)[143]
— UNKNOWN
    — 21ˢᵗ U.S. Infantry Detachment Co. D

[136] Indians. Chronological List, 42; Record of Engagements, 24.
[137] Indians. Chronological List, 42; Record of Engagements, 24. Chronological List lists "mail escort".
[138] Indians. Chronological List, 42; Heitman (Volume 2), 434; Smith, *Old Army in Texas*, 150.
[139] Chronological List, 42.
[140] Indians. Chronological List, 43; Heitman (Volume 2), 434.
[141] Indians. Chronological List, 43; Record of Engagements, 24.
[142] Indians. *Annual Report of Secretary of War (1869)*, 72; Chronological List, 43; Heitman (Volume 2), 434; Record of Engagements, 24; Fisher, "Royall and Duncan Pursuits," *Nebraska History* 50 (Fall 1969): 300-301; Paul, *Nebraska Indian Wars Reader*, 81-82; Price, *Across the Continent*, 141-142, 658. Heitman lists 2ⁿᵈ U.S. Cavalry Co. C, D, M; 5ᵗʰ U.S. Cavalry Co. B, E, F, L, M; Detachment of Indian Scouts.
[143] Indians. Chronological List, 43; Heitman (Volume 2), 434; Altshuler, *Chains of Command*, 173; McChristian, *Fort Bowie*, 112; Sweeney, *Cochise*, 268.

— **6 KILLED**[144]
— Private Michael Blake (Co. D 21st U.S. Infantry)
— Private William A. Gates (Co. D 21st U.S. Infantry)
— Private Shellberger (Co. D 21st U.S. Infantry)
— Private John Slocum (Co. D 21st U.S. Infantry)

— Driver Kaler (Citizen)
— John Finkel Stone (Citizen)

(0557) Action, Chiricahua Pass, Arizona Territory (October 8, 1869)[145]
— 1st Lieutenant William H. Winters (1st U.S. Cavalry)
— 1st U.S. Cavalry Co. G
— **2 WOUNDED**[146]
— Private James Summer (Co. G 1st U.S. Cavalry)
— *gunshot wound, shoulder, arm*
— Enlisted Man (1st U.S. Cavalry)

(0558) Skirmish, Red Rock, Arizona Territory (October 12, 1869)[147]
— UNKNOWN
— 8th U.S. Cavalry Co. L

— *Private David Goodman (Co. L 8th U.S. Cavalry) received MOH: Bravery in action (Lyry Creek, Arizona, October 14, 1869).*

— *Private John F. Rowalt (Co. L 8th U.S. Cavalry) received MOH: Gallantry in action with Indians (Lyry Creek, Arizona, October 14, 1869).*

— *Private John Raerick (Co. L 8th U.S. Cavalry) received MOH: Gallantry in action with Indians (Lyry Creek, Arizona, October 14, 1869).*

(0559) Action, Chiricahua Mountains, Arizona Territory (October 20, 1869)[148]
— Captain Reuben F. Bernard (1st U.S. Cavalry)
— 1st U.S. Cavalry Co. G
— 8th U.S. Cavalry Co. G
— **2 KILLED**[149]
— Private Thomas Collins (Co. G 1st U.S. Cavalry)
— Sergeant Stephen S. Fuller (Co. G 8th U.S. Cavalry)

— **2 WOUNDED**[150]
— 1st Lieutenant John Lafferty (8th U.S. Cavalry)
— *gunshot wound, jaw, fracture, severe wound*

---

[144] 21st U.S. Infantry Regimental Return October 1869; Sweeney, *Cochise*, 268.
[145] Indians. Chronological List, 43; Heitman (Volume 2), 434; Altshuler, *Chains of Command*, 173; McChristian, *Fort Bowie*, 113; Sweeney, *Cochise*, 270-272.
[146] Otis, *Report of Surgical Cases*, 61.
[147] Indians. Chronological List, 43; Heitman (Volume 2), 434.
[148] Indians. Chronological List, 43; Altshuler, *Chains of Command*, 174-175; McChristian, *Fort Bowie*, 114-115; Russell, *One Hundred and Three Fights*, 72-76.
[149] 1st U.S. Cavalry Regimental Return October 1869; 8th U.S. Cavalry Regimental Return October 1869.
[150] 8th U.S. Cavalry Regimental Return October 1869; McChristian, *Fort Bowie*, 114-115, 308; Russell, *One Hundred and Three Fights*, 72, 76.

— Private Edwin Elwood (Co. G 8th U.S. Cavalry)
— *gunshot wound, right breast, severe wound*

— *Captain Reuben F. Bernard (1st U.S. Cavalry) brevet promotion to Brigadier General for gallant service in action against Indians (Chiricahua Mountains, Arizona, October 20, 1869) and in actions against Indians (Silver River, Oregon, June 28, 1878 and Birch Creek, Oregon, July 8, 1878).*

— *Corporal Charles H. Dickens (Co. G 8th U.S. Cavalry) received MOH: Gallantry in action (Chiricahua Mountains, Arizona, October 20, 1869).*

— *Private John L. Donahue (Co. G 8th U.S. Cavalry) received MOH: Gallantry in action (Chiricahua Mountains, Arizona, October 20, 1869).*

— *Private Edwin L. Elwood (Co. G 8th U.S. Cavalry) received MOH: Gallantry in action (Chiricahua Mountains, Arizona, October 20, 1869).*

— *Private John Georgian (Co. G 8th U.S. Cavalry) received MOH: Bravery in action (Chiricahua Mountains, Arizona, October 20, 1869).*

— *Blacksmith Mosher A. Harding (Co. G 8th U.S. Cavalry) received MOH: Gallantry in action (Chiricahua Mountains, Arizona, October 20, 1869).*

— *Sergeant Frederick Jarvis (Co. G 1st U.S. Cavalry) received MOH: Gallantry in action (Chiricahua Mountains, Arizona, October 20, 1869).*

— *Trumpeter Bartholomew T. Keenan (Co. G 1st U.S. Cavalry) received MOH: Gallantry in action (Chiricahua Mountains, Arizona, October 20, 1869).*

— *Private Charles Kelley (Co. G 1st U.S. Cavalry) received MOH: Gallantry in action (Chiricahua Mountains, Arizona, October 20, 1869).*

— *1st Lieutenant John Lafferty (8th U.S. Cavalry) brevet promotion to Captain for gallant service in actions against Indians (Black Slate Mountains, Nevada, February 15, 1867 and Chiricahua Pass, Arizona, October 20, 1869, where he was severely wounded).*

— *Corporal Nicholas Meaher (Co. G 1st U.S. Cavalry) received MOH: Gallantry in action (Chiricahua Mountains, Arizona, October 20, 1869).*

— *Private Edward Murphy (Co. G 1st U.S. Cavalry) received MOH: Gallantry in action (Chiricahua Mountains, Arizona, October 20, 1869).*

— *First Sergeant Francis Oliver (Co. G 1st U.S. Cavalry) received MOH: Bravery in action (Chiricahua Mountains, Arizona, October 20, 1869).*

— *Private Edward Pengally (Co. B 8th U.S. Cavalry) received MOH: Gallantry in action (Chiricahua Mountains, Arizona, October 20, 1869).*

— *Corporal Thomas Powers (Co. G 1st U.S. Cavalry) received MOH: Gallantry in action (Chiricahua Mountains, Arizona, October 20, 1869).*

— *Private James Russell (Co. G 1st U.S. Cavalry) received MOH: Gallantry in action with Indians (Chiricahua Mountains, Arizona, October 20, 1869).*

— *Private Charles Schroeter (Co. G 1st U.S. Cavalry) received MOH: Gallantry in action (Chiricahua Mountains, Arizona, October 20, 1869).*

— *Private Robert B. Scott (Co. G 8th U.S. Cavalry) received MOH: Gallantry in action (Chiricahua Mountains, Arizona, October 20, 1869).*

— *Sergeant Andrew J. Smith (Co. G 8th U.S. Cavalry) received MOH: Gallantry in action (Chiricahua Mountains, Arizona, October 20, 1869).*

— *Private Theodore F. Smith (Co. G 1st U.S. Cavalry) received MOH: Gallantry in action (Chiricahua Mountains, Arizona, October 20, 1869).*

— *Private Thomas Smith (Co. G 1st U.S. Cavalry) received MOH: Gallantry in action (Chiricahua Mountains, Arizona, October 20, 1869).*

— *Private Thomas J. Smith (Co. G 1st U.S. Cavalry) received MOH: Gallantry in action (Chiricahua Mountains, Arizona, October 20, 1869).*

— *Private William Smith (Co. G 1st U.S. Cavalry) received MOH: Gallantry in action (Chiricahua Mountains, Arizona, October 20, 1869).*

— *Private William H. Smith (Co. G 1st U.S. Cavalry) received MOH: Gallantry in action (Chiricahua Mountains, Arizona, October 20, 1869).*

— *Private Orizoba Spence (Co. G 1st U.S. Cavalry) received MOH: Gallantry in action (Chiricahua Mountains, Arizona, October 20, 1869).*

— *Private George Springer (Co. G 1st U.S. Cavalry) received MOH: Gallantry in action (Chiricahua Mountains, Arizona, October 20, 1869).*

— *Saddler Christian Steiner (Co. G 8th U.S. Cavalry) received MOH: Gallantry in action (Chiricahua Mountains, Arizona, October 20, 1869).*

— *Private Thomas Sullivan (Co. G 1st U.S. Cavalry) received MOH: Gallantry in action (Chiricahua Mountains, Arizona, October 20, 1869).*

— *Private James Sumner (Co. G 1st U.S. Cavalry) received MOH: Gallantry in action (Chiricahua Mountains, Arizona, October 20, 1869).*

— *Sergeant John Thompson (Co. G 1st U.S. Cavalry) received MOH: Bravery in action with Indians (Chiricahua Mountains, Arizona, October 20, 1869).*

— *Private John Tracy (Co. G 8th U.S. Cavalry) received MOH: Bravery in action with Indians (Chiricahua Mountains, Arizona, October 20, 1869).*

— *Private Charles H. Ward (Co. G 1st U.S. Cavalry) received MOH: Gallantry in action with Indians (Chiricahua Mountains, Arizona, October 20, 1869).*

— *Private Enoch R. Weiss (Co. G 1st U.S. Cavalry) received MOH: Gallantry in action with Indians (Chiricahua Mountains, Arizona, October 20, 1869).*

(0560) Skirmish, Chiricahua Mountains, Arizona Territory (October 27, 1869)[151]
— Captain Reuben F. Bernard (1st U.S. Cavalry)
   — 1st U.S. Cavalry Co. G
   — 8th U.S. Cavalry Co. G

— *Private John Carr (Co. G 8th U.S. Cavalry) received MOH: Gallantry in action (Chiricahua Mountains, Arizona, October 27, 1869).*

(0561) Action, Headwaters of Brazos River, Texas (October 28 and 29, 1869)[152]
— Captain John M. Bacon (9th U.S. Cavalry)
— 4th U.S. Cavalry Co. D and F
— 9th U.S. Cavalry Co. B, E, F, G, L and M
— 24th U.S. Infantry Detachment
— Detachment of Indian Scouts
— **8 WOUNDED**[153]
— Enlisted Man
— Enlisted Man
— Enlisted Man
— Enlisted Man
— Enlisted Man
— Enlisted Man
— Enlisted Man
— Enlisted Man

— *1st Lieutenant George E. Albee (41st U.S. Infantry) brevet promotion to Captain for gallant service in actions against Indians (Brazos River, Texas, September 16, 1869 and October 28 and 29, 1869).*

— *1st Lieutenant George E. Albee (41st U.S. Infantry) received MOH: Attacked with two men a force of eleven Indians, drove them from the hills, and reconnoitered the country beyond (Brazos River, Texas, October 28, 1869).*

— *Captain John M. Bacon (9th U.S. Cavalry) brevet promotion to Lt. Colonel for gallant service in actions against Indians (Pecos River, Texas, June 7, 1869 and near the headwaters of the Brazos River, Texas, October 28 and 29, 1869).*[154]

— *1st Lieutenant Peter M. Boehm (4th U.S. Cavalry) brevet promotion to Captain for gallant service in action against Indians (Brazos River, Texas, October 28 and 29, 1869), special gallantry in action (Brazos River Texas, October 10, 1871) and gallant conduct in action against Indians (Red River, Texas, September 29, 1872).*

— *1st Lieutenant Byron Dawson (9th U.S. Cavalry) brevet promotion to Captain for gallant service in actions against Indians (Pecos River, Texas, June 7, 1869 and Brazos River, Texas, October 28 and 29, 1869).*

(0562) Skirmish, Chiricahua Mountains, Arizona Territory (October 31, 1869)[155]
— Captain Reuben F. Bernard (1st U.S. Cavalry)
— 1st U.S. Cavalry Co. G
— 8th U.S. Cavalry Co. G

(0563) Skirmish, Garde, Arizona Territory (November 6, 1869)[156]

[151] Indians. Chronological List, 50; Heitman (Volume 2), 434; McChristian, *Fort Bowie*, 115-116; Russell, *One Hundred and Three Fights*, 77. Heitman lists 29 October 1869.
[152] Indians. Chronological List, 43; Heitman (Volume 2), 434; Burton, *Black, Buckskin and Blue*, 154; Leckie, *Buffalo Soldiers*, 92; Neal, *Valor Across the Lone Star*, 44-46; Smith, *Old Army in Texas*, 150; Williams, *Texas' Last Frontier*, 119. Heitman lists 4th U.S. Cavalry Detachments Co. D, F; 9th U.S. Cavalry Co. B, E, F, G, L, M; Detachment of Indian Scouts.
[153] Chronological List, 43.
[154] Heitman lists the brevet as being for action against Indians on the Pecos River, 7 June 1867. There was no action involving the 9th U.S. Cavalry on the Pecos in 1867.
[155] Indians. Chronological List, 43; Heitman (Volume 2), 434; McChristian, *Fort Bowie*, 117; Russell, *One Hundred and Three Fights*, 77-78.
[156] Indians. Chronological List, 43; Heitman (Volume 2), 434.

— 1st Lieutenant Jonathan D. Stevenson (8th U.S. Cavalry)
— 8th U.S. Cavalry Co. K

(0564) Action, between Fort Laramie and Fort Fetterman, Wyoming Territory (November 6, 1869) [157]
— Captain James Egan (2nd U.S. Cavalry)
— 2nd U.S. Cavalry Co. K
— **2 KILLED** [158]
— Private John A. McAllister (Co. K 2nd U.S. Cavalry)
— Private George M. Kenna (Co. K 2nd U.S. Cavalry)

(0565) Skirmish, Tompkins Valley, Arizona Territory (November 10, 1869) [159]
— UNKNOWN
— 8th U.S. Cavalry Co. L

(0566) Operations, Santa Maria River, Arizona Territory (November 16 to 28, 1869) [160]
— Captain Charles Hobart (8th U.S. Cavalry)
— 8th U.S. Cavalry Detachments Co. D and L

— *Sergeant John Crist (Co. L 8th U.S. Cavalry) received MOH: Gallantry in action (Arizona, November 26, 1869).*

(0567) Action, Guadaloupe Mountains, New Mexico Territory (November 18, 1869) [161]
— 1st Lieutenant Howard B. Cushing (3rd U.S. Cavalry)
— 3rd U.S. Cavalry Detachment Co. F
— **2 WOUNDED** [162]
— Corporal St. Clair (Co. F 3rd U.S. Cavalry)
— *arrow wound, face, slight wound*
— Private Thomas Hansington (Co. F 3rd U.S. Cavalry)
— *gunshot wound, left leg*

(0568) Action, Headwaters of Llano River, Texas (November 24, 1869) [163]
— Captain Edward M. Heyl (9th U.S. Cavalry)
— 9th U.S. Cavalry Detachments Co. F and M
— **1 WOUNDED** [164]
— Captain Edward M. Heyl (9th U.S. Cavalry)
— *arrow wound, back*

(0569) Action, near Horseshoe Creek, Wyoming Territory (December 1, 1869) [165]
— Sergeant Conrad Bahr (4th U.S. Infantry)
— 4th U.S. Infantry Detachments Co. A, D, E, F, G and K

[157] Indians. Heitman (Volume 2), 434; Lindmier, *Drybone*, 70.
[158] Fort Fetterman Cemetery Records.
[159] Indians. Chronological List, 43; Heitman (Volume 2), 434. Heitman lists 8th U.S. Cavalry Detachment Co. L.
[160] Indians. Chronological List, 43; Heitman (Volume 2), 434.
[161] Indians. Chronological List, 43; Heitman (Volume 2), 434; Record of Engagements, 25; Randall, *Only the Echoes*, 49. Heitman lists 3rd U.S. Cavalry Co. F.
[162] Fort Stanton Post Return November 1869.
[163] Indians. Chronological List, 43; Heitman (Volume 2), 434; Smith, *Old Army in Texas*, 150; Williams, *Texas' Last Frontier*, 120.
[164] Otis, *Report of Surgical Cases*, 155.
[165] Indians. Chronological List, 43; Heitman (Volume 2), 434; Record of Engagements, 25; Lindmier, *Drybone*, 70. Chronological List lists 4th U.S. Infantry Detachment.

— **1 KILLED**[166]
— Private Jonathan J. Johnson (Co. E 4th U.S. Infantry) — d. 12-02-1869

— **2 WOUNDED**[167]
— Private Hubert Erne (Co. D 4th U.S. Infantry)
— *gunshot wound, left hip, fracture, severe wound*
— Corporal August Wernicke (Co. K 4th U.S. Infantry)
— *slight wound*

(0570) Action, Mount Buford or Chilson's Creek, Arizona Territory (December 10, 1869)[168]
— Captain George B. Sanford (1st U.S. Cavalry)
— 1st U.S. Cavalry Co. E
— 8th U.S. Cavalry Co. A
— **1 KILLED**[169]
— Private Joseph Darragh (Co. E 1st U.S. Cavalry) — d. 12-11-1869

(0571) Skirmish, Johnson's Mail Station, Texas (December 25, 1869)[170]
— UNKNOWN
— 9th U.S. Cavalry Detachment Co. E

(0572) Action, Fort Wrangel, Department of Alaska (December 26, 1869)[171]
— 1st Lieutenant William Borrowe (2nd U.S. Artillery)
— 2nd U.S. Artillery Co. I
— **1 WOUNDED**[172]
— (1) Citizen

(0573) Action, Sanguinara Canyon, Guadalupe Mountains, Texas (December 26, 1869)[173]
— 1st Lieutenant Howard B. Cushing (3rd U.S. Cavalry)
— 3rd U.S. Cavalry Co. F
— **1 WOUNDED**[174]
— 2nd Lieutenant Franklin Yeaton (3rd U.S. Cavalry)
— *gunshot wound, left wrist, right chest*

(0574) Skirmish, Delaware Creek, Guadalupe Mountains, Texas (December 30, 1869)[175]
— 1st Lieutenant Howard B. Cushing (3rd U.S. Cavalry)
— 3rd U.S. Cavalry Co. F

TOTAL KILLED 1869 — 1/24/0/5 (Officers, Enlisted Men, Indian Scouts, Citizens)

[166] 4th U.S. Infantry Regimental Return December 1869; Otis, *Report of Surgical Cases*, 30.
[167] 4th U.S. Infantry Regimental Return December 1869; Otis, *Report of Surgical Cases*, 230-232.
[168] Indians. Chronological List, 43; Heitman (Volume 2), 434.
[169] Register of Deaths Regular Army, 1860-1889 (Volume 4); Otis, *Report of Surgical Cases*, 50.
[170] Indians. Chronological List, 43; Heitman (Volume 2), 434; Burton, *Black, Buckskin and Blue*, 154; Smith, *Old Army in Texas*, 150; Williams, *Texas' Last Frontier*, 120.
[171] Indians. Chronological List, 44; Heitman (Volume 2), 435.
[172] Chronological List, 44.
[173] Indians. Chronological List, 43; Heitman (Volume 2), 435; Record of Engagements, 25; Randall, *Only the Echoes*, 49-50; Rathbun, *New Mexico Frontier Military Place Names*, 81-82; Smith, *Old Army in Texas*, 150.
[174] Otis, *Report of Surgical Cases*, 25.
[175] Indians. Chronological List, 44; Heitman (Volume 2), 435; Record of Engagements, 25; Randall, *Only the Echoes*, 50; Rathbun, *New Mexico Frontier Military Place Names*, 82; Smith, *Old Army in Texas*, 150.

1870

"To lay out a reservation for Indians in the very region they have always occupied, and every path in which is known to them, and from which they have always made their raids upon settlements, is simply to furnish them with what alone they have needed in the past to secure success in their hostile expeditions, or security to themselves, in case of failure... a depot of supplies furnished by the Government and... a place of safety where they are protected by an agent of the Government from the consequences of any crimes they chose to commit."

— John Pope, U.S. Army[1]

---

[1] Official Report of General John Pope, Headquarters Department of the Missouri, Fort Leavenworth, Kansas, 31 October 1870. *Annual Report of Secretary of War (1870)*, 18.

(0575) Operations, Rio Grande and Pecos Rivers, Texas (January 3 to February 6, 1870)[2]
— Captain John M. Bacon (9th U.S. Cavalry)
— 9th U.S. Cavalry Co. G
— 24th U.S. Infantry Detachments Co. K and L

(0576) Skirmish, Guadaloupe Mountains, Texas (January 6, 1870)[3]
— UNKNOWN
— 9th U.S. Cavalry Co. H

(0577) Skirmish, Lower Pecos River, Texas (January 11, 1870)[4]
— 1st Lieutenant Charles Parker (9th U.S. Cavalry)
— 9th U.S. Cavalry Co. L

(0578) Action, Delaware Creek, Guadaloupe Mountains, Texas (January 20, 1870)[5]
— Captain Francis S. Dodge (9th U.S. Cavalry)
— 9th U.S. Cavalry Detachments Co. C, D, I and K
— **2 WOUNDED**[6]
— Enlisted Man (9th U.S. Cavalry)
— Enlisted Man (9th U.S. Cavalry)

(0579) Action, Marias River, Montana Territory (January 23, 1870)[7]
— Major Eugene M. Baker (2nd U.S. Cavalry)
— 2nd U.S. Cavalry Co. F, G, H and L
— 13th U.S. Infantry Co. A, Detachments Co. F, I and K
— **1 KILLED**[8]
— Private Walter McKay (Co. L 2nd U.S. Cavalry)

"As much obloquy was heaped upon Major Baker, his officers and men… I think it only justice to him and his command that the truth should be fully made known to the public. Recollecting the season of the year in which the expedition was made, the terrible cold through which it marched day after day, and the spirit with which the troops engaged an enemy whom they deemed as strong as themselves, I think the command is entitled to the special commendation of the military authorities and the hearty thanks of the nation."
— Winfield S. Hancock, U.S. Army[9]

(0580) Skirmish, Dragoon Mountains, Arizona Territory (January 28, 1870)[10]
— Captain Reuben F. Bernard (1st U.S. Cavalry)
— 1st U.S. Cavalry Co. G
— 8th U.S. Cavalry Detachment Co. G

(0581) Action, near Fort McKavett, Texas (February 2, 1870)[11]
— UNKNOWN

[2] Indians. Chronological List, 44; Heitman (Volume 2), 435; Williams, *Texas' Last Frontier*, 121. Heitman lists 9th U.S. Cavalry Co. G, Detachment Co. L; 24th U.S. Infantry Detachments Co. K, L.
[3] Indians. Chronological List, 44; Heitman (Volume 2), 435. Heitman lists 6 January to 10 February 1870. Heitman lists 9th U.S. Cavalry Detachments Co. H, L.
[4] Indians. Chronological List, 44.
[5] Indians. Chronological List, 44; Heitman (Volume 2), 435; Leckie, *Buffalo Soldiers*, 92-93; Smith, *Old Army in Texas*, 150; Williams, *Texas' Last Frontier*, 122; Wooster, *Frontier Crossroads*, 94.
[6] Chronological List, 44.
[7] Indians. *Annual Report of Secretary of War (1870)*, 29-30; Chronological List, 44; Heitman (Volume 2), 435; Record of Engagements, 26; Ege, *Tell Baker to Strike Them Hard*, 41-45; Rockwell, *U.S. Army in Frontier Montana*, 201-203, 207-209, 211-214; Rodenbough, *From Everglade to Canyon*, 435. Chronological List and Heitman both list 2nd U.S. Cavalry Co. F, G, H, L; 13th U.S. Infantry Co. A, F, I, K.
[8] Reports of Diseases and Individual Cases, F 424; Register of Deaths Regular Army, 1860-1889 (Volume 4).
[9] Official Report of Major General Winfield S. Hancock, Headquarters Department of the Dakota, St. Paul, Minnesota, 1 November 1870. *Annual Report of Secretary of War (1870)*, 30.
[10] Indians. Chronological List, 44; Heitman (Volume 2), 435; McChristian, *Fort Bowie*, 118; Russell, *One Hundred and Three Fights*, 79.
[11] Bandits. 9th U.S. Cavalry Regimental Return February 1870; Otis, *Report of Surgical Cases*, 35, 46.

— UNKNOWN
— **2 KILLED**[12]
— Corporal Albert Marshall (Co. F 9th U.S. Cavalry)
— Private Charles Murray (Co. F 9th U.S. Cavalry)

(0582) Action, Reno Road, near Camp McDowell, Arizona Territory (March 9, 1870)[13]
— Sergeant Francis Brannon (8th U.S. Cavalry)
— 8th U.S. Cavalry Detachment Co. I
— **1 KILLED**[14]
— Private Conrad Tragesor (Co. I 8th U.S. Cavalry) — d. 3-10-1870

— **1 WOUNDED**[15]
— Paymaster's Clerk Vedder (Citizen)
— *slight wound*

(0583) Skirmish, near Sol's Wash, Arizona Territory (March 15 and 16, 1870)[16]
— 1st Lieutenant John F. Cluley (21st U.S. Infantry)
— 21st U.S. Infantry Detachment Co. H

(0584) Citizens, Headwaters of Sweetwater River, Wyoming Territory (April 2, 1870)[17]
— (6) Citizens Killed

(0585) Skirmish, San Martine Springs, Texas (April 3, 1870)[18]
— UNKNOWN
— 9th U.S. Cavalry Detachment Co. H

(0586) Skirmish, North Hubbard Creek, Texas (April 3, 1870)[19]
— Captain Wirt Davis (4th U.S. Cavalry)
— 4th U.S. Cavalry Detachment Co. F

(0587) Citizens, Bluff Creek, Kansas (April 6, 1870)[20]

(0588) Skirmish, near Clear Creek, Texas (April 6, 1870)[21]
— 2nd Lieutenant William R. Harmon (10th U.S. Cavalry)
— 10th U.S. Cavalry Detachment Co. M

(0589) Skirmish, Crow Springs, Texas (April 25, 1870)[22]
— Major Albert P. Morrow (9th U.S. Cavalry)
— 9th U.S. Cavalry Detachments Co. C and K

(0590) Skirmish, Pinal Mountains, near San Carlos, Arizona Territory (April 30, 1870)[23]
— Captain George B. Sanford (1st U.S. Cavalry)

[12] Register of Deaths Regular Army, 1860-1889 (Volume 4); 9th U.S. Cavalry Regimental Return February 1870.
[13] Indians. Chronological List, 44; Heitman (Volume 2), 435.
[14] Register of Deaths Regular Army, 1860-1889 (Volume 4); Camp McDowell Post Return March 1870.
[15] Camp McDowell Post Return March 1870.
[16] Indians. Chronological List, 44; Heitman (Volume 2), 435.
[17] Indians. Killed were six miners. *Annual Report of Secretary of War (1870)*, 31; Chronological List, 44.
[18] Indians. Chronological List, 44; Heitman (Volume 2), 435; Smith, *Old Army in Texas*, 151.
[19] Indians. Chronological List, 44; Heitman (Volume 2), 435; Smith, *Old Army in Texas*, 151.
[20] Indians. Chronological List, 44; Record of Engagements, 26. Chronological List lists "train escort".
[21] Indians. Chronological List, 44; Heitman (Volume 2), 435; Smith, *Old Army in Texas*, 151.
[22] Indians. Chronological List, 45; Heitman (Volume 2), 435; Burton, *Black, Buckskin and Blue*, 154; Smith, *Old Army in Texas*, 151; Williams, *Texas' Last Frontier*, 123.
[23] Indians. Chronological List, 45; Heitman (Volume 2), 435. Heitman lists 1st U.S. Cavalry Detachment Co. E; 3rd U.S. Cavalry Co. B; 21st U.S. Infantry Detachment Co. A.

— 1st U.S. Cavalry Detachment Co. E
— 3rd U.S. Cavalry Detachment Co. B
— 21st U.S. Infantry Detachment

(0591) Action, Miner's Delight, near Twin Creek, Wyoming Territory (May 4, 1870)[24]
— Captain David S. Gordon (2nd U.S. Cavalry)
— 2nd U.S. Cavalry Co. D
— 1 KILLED[25]
— 1st Lieutenant Charles B. Stambaugh (Co. D 2nd U.S. Cavalry)

— 1 WOUNDED[26]
— Sergeant Alexander Brown (Co. D 2nd U.S. Cavalry)
— *gunshot wound, jaw, fracture, severe wound*

— *Captain David S. Gordon (2nd U.S. Cavalry) brevet promotion to Lt. Colonel for gallant action against Indians (Miner's Delight, Wyoming. May 4, 1870).*

"[1st Lieutenant Charles B. Stambaugh] was a mere boy in years, noble and generous, brave as a lion, and as an officer and gentleman the peer of the highest. His death is a sore loss to us."
— Editor, *Lancaster Gazette*, Citizen[27]

(0592) Action, Mount Adams, Texas (May 14, 1870)[28]
— 2nd Lieutenant William Russell, Jr. (4th U.S. Cavalry)
— 4th U.S. Cavalry Detachment Co. M
— 1 KILLED[29]
— 2nd Lieutenant William Russell, Jr. (4th U.S. Cavalry) — d. 5-15-1870

— 2 WOUNDED[30]
— Private Robert Powers (Co. M 4th U.S. Cavalry)
— *gunshot wound, abdomen, slight wound*
— Private Thomas Riley (Co. M 4th U.S. Cavalry)
— *gunshot wound, abdomen, slight wound*

"*Whereas, on last Saturday at noon, within twelve miles of this place, [2nd Lieutenant William Russell], of the United States Army, fell by the hands of a savage in his defense of our homes against the brutal savages who infest our frontier. In his death a gallant and brave soldier died; and may his name ever remain dear to us....*"
— Editor, *Daily State Journal*, Citizen[31]

(0593) Citizens, Kansas Pacific Railroad, Kansas (May 16, 1870)[32]
— (10) Citizens Killed

[24] Indians. *Annual Report of Secretary of War (1870)*, 31-32; Chronological List, 45; Heitman (Volume 2), 435; Record of Engagements, 27; Rodenbough, *From Everglade to Canyon*, 435.
[25] *Annual Report of Secretary of War (1870)*, 31-32.
[26] *Annual Report of Secretary of War (1870)*, 31-32; Otis, *Report of Surgical Cases*, 18.
[27] *Lancaster (Ohio) Gazette*, 19 May 1870.
[28] Indians. Chronological List, 45; Heitman (Volume 2), 435; Smith, *Old Army in Texas*, 151.
[29] Reports of Diseases and Individual Cases, F 425; Register of Deaths Regular Army, 1860-1889 (Volume 4); Otis, *Report of Surgical Cases*, 51.
[30] Reports of Diseases and Individual Cases, F 425.
[31] *Daily State (Texas) Journal*, 22 May 1870.
[32] Indians. Killed were ten railroad workers. *Annual Report of Secretary of War (1870)*, 6-7; Chronological List, 45; Record of Engagements, 27.

(0594) Action, Spring Creek or Little Blue, Nebraska (May 17, 1870)[33]
— Sergeant Patrick A. Leonard (2nd U.S. Cavalry)
— 2nd U.S. Cavalry Detachment Co. C
— 1 WOUNDED[34]
— Private Thomas Hubbard (Co. C 2nd U.S. Cavalry)
— *gunshot wound, left forearm, fracture*

— *Private Heth Canfield (Co. C 2nd U.S. Cavalry) received MOH: Gallantry in action (Little Blue, Nebraska, May 17, 1870).*

— *Private Michael Himmelsback (Co. C 2nd U.S. Cavalry) received MOH: Gallantry in action (Little Blue, Nebraska, May 17, 1870).*

— *Private Thomas Hubbard (Co. C 2nd U.S. Cavalry) received MOH: Gallantry in action (Little Blue, Nebraska, May 17, 1870).*

— *Sergeant Patrick Leonard (Co. C 2nd U.S. Cavalry) received MOH: Gallantry in action (Little Blue, Nebraska, May 17, 1870).*

— *Private George W. Thompson (Co. C 2nd U.S. Cavalry) received MOH: Gallantry in action (Little Blue, Nebraska, May 17, 1870).*

(0595) Skirmish, Kickapoo Springs, Texas (May 19 and 20, 1870)[35]
— Sergeant Emanuel Stance (9th U.S. Cavalry)
— 9th U.S. Cavalry Detachment Co. F

— *Sergeant Emanuel Stance (Co. F 9th U.S. Cavalry) received MOH: Gallantry on scout after Indians (Kickapoo Springs, Texas, May 20, 1870).*

"The gallantry displayed by [Sergeant Emanuel Stance] and his party as well as good judgment used on both occasions deserves much praise. As this is the fourth and fifth encounter that Sergeant Stance has had with Indians in the past two years, on all of which occasions he has been mentioned for good behavior by his Commanding Officer, it is a pleasure to commend him to higher authority."
— Henry Carroll, U.S. Army[36]

(0596) Skirmish, Tonto Valley, Arizona Territory (May 25, 1870)[37]
— Captain George B. Sanford (1st U.S. Cavalry)
— 1st U.S. Cavalry Co. E
— 3rd U.S. Cavalry Co. E

[33] Indians. Chronological List, 45; Heitman (Volume 2), 435; Record of Engagements, 27; Paul, *Nebraska Indian Wars Reader*, 219-220.
[34] Otis, *Report of Surgical Cases*, 63.
[35] Indians. Chronological List, 45; Heitman (Volume 2), 435; Burton, *Black, Buckskin and Blue*, 154; Leckie, *Buffalo Soldiers*, 96-97; Neal, *Valor Across the Lone Star*, 53-56; Smith, *Old Army in Texas*, 151; Williams, *Texas' Last Frontier*, 124-125.
[36] Neal, *Valor Across the Lone Star*, 56-57.
[37] Indians. Chronological List, 45; Heitman (Volume 2), 435; Alexander, *Arizona Frontier Military Place Names*, 118-119.

(0597) Citizens, near Camp Supply, Indian Territory (May 28, 1870)[38]
— (2) Citizens Killed

(0598) Operations, near Camp Apache, Arizona Territory (May 29 to June 26, 1870)[39]
— Captain William Hawley (3rd U.S. Cavalry)
— 3rd U.S. Cavalry Detachment Co. A

(0599) Action, Bass Canyon, Texas (May 29, 1870)[40]
— 1st Lieutenant Ira W. Trask (9th U.S. Cavalry)
— 9th U.S. Cavalry Co. I
— **1 KILLED**[41]
— Private William Magruder (Co. I 9th U.S. Cavalry)

(0600) Action, Holiday Creek, Texas (May 30, 1870)[42]
— 1st Lieutenant Isaac N. Walter (6th U.S. Cavalry)
— 6th U.S. Cavalry Detachments Co. C and D
— **1 KILLED**[43]
— Private Harry Kennard (Co. C 6th U.S. Cavalry)

— **2 WOUNDED**[44]
— Ben Dawdrick (Citizen)
— Joseph Taylor (Citizen)

(0601) Action, Bear Creek Station, Kansas (May 31, 1870)[45]
— Sergeant James Murray (3rd U.S. Infantry)
— 3rd U.S. Infantry Detachments Co. B and F
— **2 KILLED**[46]
— Private John Connerlin (Co. B 3rd U.S. Infantry)
— Private Augustine Buck (Co. F 3rd U.S. Infantry)

— **1 WOUNDED**[47]
— Sergeant James Murray (Co. B 3rd U.S. Infantry)
— *arrow wounds, 2 right arm, 2 left arm, right arm pit, right chest, left temple*

(0602) Skirmish, Solomon River, Kansas (June 1, 1870)[48]
— UNKNOWN
— 7th U.S. Cavalry Co. M

(0603) Action, near Copper Canyon, Arizona Territory (June 2, 1870)[49]
— UNKNOWN
— 21st U.S. Infantry Detachment Co. C
— **1 KILLED**[50]

---

[38] Indians. In separate fights killed were two teamsters. Chronological List, 45; Record of Engagements, 27; Carriker, *Fort Supply, Indian Territory*, 48-49.
[39] Indians. Chronological List, 45; Heitman (Volume 2), 435. Chronological List lists 3rd U.S. Cavalry Detachment.
[40] Indians. Chronological List, 45; Heitman (Volume 2), 435; Smith, *Old Army in Texas*, 151. Heitman lists 9th U.S. Cavalry Co. K.
[41] 9th U.S. Cavalry Regimental Return June 1870.
[42] Indians. Chronological List, 45; Heitman (Volume 2), 435; Carter, *From Yorktown to Santiago*, 140-141, 277; Hamilton, *Sentinel of the Southern Plains*, 54; Neal, *Valor Across the Lone Star*, 60; Smith, *Old Army in Texas*, 151. Chronological List lists 6th U.S. Cavalry Detachment.
[43] 6th U.S. Cavalry Regimental Return June 1870; Register of Deaths Regular Army, 1860-1889 (Volume 4).
[44] Hamilton, *Sentinel of the Southern Plains*, 54.
[45] Indians. Chronological List, 45; Heitman (Volume 2), 435; Record of Engagements, 27; Carriker, *Fort Supply, Indian Territory*, 49-50. Chronological List lists "3rd U.S. Infantry Detachment (mail guard)".
[46] 3rd U.S. Infantry Regimental Return June 1870.
[47] Otis, *Report of Surgical Cases*, 156.
[48] Indians. Chronological List, 45; Heitman (Volume 2), 435; Record of Engagements, 27. Chronological List lists " troop of 7th U.S. Cavalry".
[49] Indians. Chronological List, 45; Heitman (Volume 2), 435; Alexander, *Arizona Frontier Military Place Names*, 42. Chronological List lists "24th U.S. Infantry Detachments (post guard)".
[50] Register of Deaths Regular Army, 1860-1889 (Volume 4); Camp Verde Post Return June 1870.

— Corporal James Wright (Co. C 21st U.S. Infantry)

(0604) Skirmish, near Fort Whipple, Arizona Territory (June 3, 1870)[51]
  — 2nd Lieutenant John C. Graham (3rd U.S. Cavalry)
    — 3rd U.S. Cavalry Detachment Co. M

(0605) Skirmish, Apache Mountains, Arizona Territory (June 5, 1870)[52]
  — 1st Lieutenant Howard B. Cushing (3rd U.S. Cavalry)
    — 1st U.S. Cavalry Detachment Co. K
    — 3rd U.S. Cavalry Detachments Co. B and F

(0606) Skirmish, Black Canyon, Arizona Territory (June 5, 1870)[53]
  — 2nd Lieutenant John C. Graham (3rd U.S. Cavalry)
    — 3rd U.S. Cavalry Detachment Co. M

(0607) Skirmish, Red Willow Creek, Nebraska (June 8, 1870)[54]
  — 2nd Lieutenant Earl D. Thomas (5th U.S. Cavalry)
    — 5th U.S. Cavalry Co. I

  — *2nd Lieutenant Earl D. Thomas (5th U.S. Cavalry) brevet promotion to 1st Lieutenant for gallant service in action against Indians (Near Fort McPherson, Nebraska, June 8, 1870).*

(0608) Action, between Fort Dodge, Kansas and Camp Supply, Indian Territory (June 8, 1870)[55]
  — 1st Lieutenant John A. Bodamer (10th U.S. Cavalry)
    — 10th U.S. Cavalry Detachments Co. F and H
  — **2 WOUNDED**[56]
    — Corporal Freeman (10th U.S. Cavalry)
      — *slight wound*
    — Private Winchester (10th U.S. Cavalry)
      — *slight wound*

(0609) Skirmish, Snake Creek, Indian Territory (June 10, 1870)[57]
  — Captain Louis H. Carpenter (10th U.S. Cavalry)
    — 10th U.S. Cavalry Co. H

(0610) Skirmish, Camp Supply, Indian Territory (June 11, 1870)[58]
  — Lt. Colonel Anderson D. Nelson (3rd U.S. Infantry)
    — 10th U.S. Cavalry Co. A, F, H, I and K
    — 3rd U.S. Infantry Co. B, E and F

(0611) Action, Fort Buford, Dakota Territory (June 13, 1870)[59]
  — Lt. Colonel Henry A. Morrow (13th U.S. Infantry)

[51] Indians. Chronological List, 45; Heitman (Volume 2), 435.
[52] Indians. Chronological List, 45; Heitman (Volume 2), 435; Alexander, *Arizona Military Place Names*, 6; Randall, *Only the Echoes*, 51-52; Thrapp, *Conquest of Apacheria*, 66-67.
[53] Indians. Chronological List, 45; Heitman (Volume 2), 435.
[54] Indians. Chronological List, 46; Heitman (Volume 2), 435; Record of Engagements, 28; Price, *Across the Continent*, 142-143, 658.
[55] Indians. Chronological List, 45; Record of Engagements, 28; Heitman (Volume 2), 435; Carriker, *Fort Supply, Indian Territory*, 51-52; Leckie, *Military Conquest of the Southern Plains*, 139. Heitman lists 9 June 1870. Chronological List lists 10th U.S. Cavalry Detachment.
[56] 10th U.S. Cavalry Regimental Return June 1870.
[57] Indians. Chronological List, 45; Heitman (Volume 2), 435.
[58] Indians. Chronological List, 45; Heitman (Volume 2), 435; Record of Engagements, 28; Carriker, *Fort Supply, Indian Territory*, 52-53; Leckie, *Buffalo Soldiers*, 54.
[59] Indians. Chronological List, 46; Heitman (Volume 2), 435.

— 13th U.S. Infantry Co. C, E and H
— **4 WOUNDED**[60]
— (4) Citizens

(0612) Skirmish, Grinnell Station, Kansas (June 13, 1870)[61]
— UNKNOWN
— 7th U.S. Cavalry Detachment Co. M

(0613) Citizens, near Fort Bascom, New Mexico Territory (June 15, 1870)[62]
— (1) Citizen Killed

(0614) Skirmish, East Branch of Rio Verde, Arizona Territory (June 15, 1870)[63]
— Captain Alexander Sutorious (3rd U.S. Cavalry)
— 3rd U.S. Cavalry Co. E

(0615) Citizens, Mulberry Creek, Kansas (June 16, 1870)[64]
— (3) Citizens Killed

(0616) Skirmish, North Platte, Nebraska (June 18, 1870)[65]
— Captain Elijah R. Wells (2nd U.S. Cavalry)
— 2nd U.S. Cavalry Co. E

(0617) Citizens, near Carson, Colorado Territory (June 21, 1870)[66]
— (5) Citizens Killed

(0618) Action, White Mountains, Arizona Territory (June 24, 1870)[67]
— Captain William Hawley (3rd U.S. Cavalry)
— 3rd U.S. Cavalry Detachments Co. A, C, L and M
— **3 WOUNDED**[68]
— Sergeant John F. Hilmer (Co. L 3rd U.S. Cavalry)
— *arrow wound, right arm*
— Trumpeter James Marshall (Co. A 3rd U.S. Cavalry)
— *arrow wound, right hip*
— Private George Silence (Co. A 3rd U.S. Cavalry)
— *arrow wound, left shoulder*

(0619) Skirmish, Medicine Bow Station, Wyoming Territory (June 25, 1870)[69]
— 1st Lieutenant Christopher T. Hall (2nd U.S. Cavalry)
— 2nd U.S. Cavalry Co. I

(0620) Action, Pine Grove Meadow, Wyoming Territory (June 27, 1870)[70]
— 2nd Lieutenant Robert H. Young (4th U.S. Infantry)

[60] Fort Buford Post Return June 1870.
[61] Indians. Chronological List, 46; Heitman (Volume 2), 435; Record of Engagements, 28. Chronological List lists "detachment of cavalry".
[62] Indians. Chronological List, 46; Record of Engagements, 28.
[63] Indians. Chronological List, 46; Heitman (Volume 2), 435.
[64] Indians. Killed were three wood cutters. Chronological List, 46; Record of Engagements, 28; Carriker, *Fort Supply, Indian Territory*, 53; Leckie, *Military Conquest*, 139-140.
[65] Indians. Chronological List, 46; Heitman (Volume 2), 435.
[66] Indians. Killed were five teamsters. Chronological List, 46; Record of Engagements, 28.
[67] Indians. Chronological List, 46; Heitman (Volume 2), 435.
[68] Otis, *Report of Surgical Cases*, 157-158.
[69] Indians. Chronological List, 46; Heitman (Volume 2), 435; Record of Engagements, 28; Rodenbough, *From Everglade to Canyon*, 435. Heitman lists 2nd U.S. Cavalry Detachment Co. I.
[70] Indians. Chronological List, 46; Heitman (Volume 2), 435; Record of Engagements, 28.

— 2nd U.S. Cavalry Detachment Co. A
— **1 WOUNDED**[71]
— Enlisted Man (2nd U.S. Cavalry)

(0621) Skirmish, Calamus River, Nebraska (June 27, 1870)[72]
— 2nd Lieutenant Edward C. Bartlett (2nd U.S. Cavalry)
— 2nd U.S. Cavalry Detachment Co. K

(0622) Action, near North Fork, Little Wichita River, Texas (July 12, 1870)[73]
— Captain Curwen B. McLellan (6th U.S. Cavalry)
— 6th U.S. Cavalry Detachments Co. A, C, D, H, K and L
— **2 KILLED**[74]
— Corporal John J. Given (Co. K 6th U.S. Cavalry)
— Private George Blum (Co. K 6th U.S. Cavalry)

— **9 WOUNDED**[75]
— Sergeant William Winterbottom (Co. A 6th U.S. Cavalry)
— *gunshot wound, back, slight wound*
— Private William B. Gallagher (Co. A 6th U.S. Cavalry)
— *gunshot wound, left arm, severe wound*
— Private Samuel Wagoner (Co. A 6th U.S. Cavalry)
— *gunshot wound, left shoulder, slight wound*

— Corporal John Connor (Co. H 6th U.S. Cavalry)
— *gunshot wound, forehead, slight wound*
— Private Benjamin Amery (Co. H 6th U.S. Cavalry)
— *gunshot wound, right shoulder, slight wound*
— Private Albert Ford (Co. H 6th U.S. Cavalry)
— *gunshot wound, left shoulder, severe wound*
— Private Gaston Smith (Co. H 6th U.S. Cavalry)
— *gunshot wound, right leg, slight wound*
— Private Robert Stuart (Co. H 6th U.S. Cavalry)
— *gunshot wound, right forearm, slight wound*

— Acting Assistant Surgeon G.W. Hatch (Citizen)
— *gunshot wound, left foot, slight wound*

— *Corporal John Connor (Co. H 6th U.S. Cavalry) received MOH: Gallantry in action (Wichita River, Texas, July 12, 1870).*

— *Sergeant George H. Eldridge (Co. C 6th U.S. Cavalry) received MOH: Gallantry in action (Wichita River, Texas, July 12, 1870).*

[71] Chronological List, 46.
[72] Indians. Chronological List, 46; Heitman (Volume 2), 435.
[73] Indians. Chronological List, 46; Heitman (Volume 2), 435; Carter, *From Yorktown to Santiago*, 141-146, 277; Carter, *On the Border with Mackenzie*, 77-78; Hamilton, *Sentinel of the Southern Plains*, 55-58; Leckie, *Military Conquest of the Southern Plains*, 140-141; McConnell, *Five Years a Cavalryman*, 216-218; Neal, *Valor Across the Lone Star*, 61-72; Nye, *Carbine and Lance*, 113; Smith, *Old Army in Texas*, 151-152.
[74] Reports of Diseases and Individual Cases, F 430; Register of Deaths Regular Army, 1860-1889 (Volume 4).
[75] Reports of Diseases and Individual Cases, F 430; Otis, *Report of Surgical Cases*, 6, 39, 59, 60, 69, 84.

— *Corporal John J. Given (Co. K 6th U.S. Cavalry) received MOH: Bravery in action (Wichita River, Texas, July 12, 1870).*

— *Sergeant Thomas Kerrigan (Co. H 6th U.S. Cavalry) received MOH: Gallantry in action (Wichita River, Texas, July 12, 1870).*

— *First Sergeant John Kirk (Co. L 6th U.S. Cavalry) received MOH: Gallantry in action (Wichita River, Texas, July 12, 1870).*

— *Sergeant John May (Co. L 6th U.S. Cavalry) received MOH: Gallantry in action (Wichita River, Texas, July 12, 1870).*

— *Private Solon D. Neal (Co. L 6th U.S. Cavalry) received MOH: Gallantry in action (Wichita River, Texas, July 12, 1870).*

— *Farrier Samuel Porter (Co. L 6th U.S. Cavalry) received MOH: Gallantry in action (Wichita River, Texas, July 12, 1870).*

— *Corporal Charles E. Smith (Co. H 6th U.S. Cavalry) received MOH: Gallantry in action (Wichita River, Texas, July 12, 1870).*

— *First Sergeant Alonzo Stokes (Co. H 6th U.S. Cavalry) received MOH: Gallantry in action (Wichita River, Texas, July 12, 1870).*

— *Corporal James C. Watson (Co. I 6th U.S. Cavalry) received MOH: Gallantry in action (Wichita River, Texas, July 12, 1870).*

— *Bugler Claron A. Windus (Co. L 6th U.S. Cavalry) received MOH: Gallantry in action (Wichita River, Texas, July 12, 1870).*

— *Sergeant William Winterbottom (Co. A 6th U.S. Cavalry) received MOH: Gallantry in action (Wichita River, Texas, July 12, 1870).*

"I regret that I cannot claim a victory, but at the same time will state that it was one of the most important engagements that ever took place in Northern Texas, and taking all into consideration, I regard the expedition a perfect success. I found Indians in force and fought them with my small command for four and a half hours, and taught them a lesson which they will not soon forget. In conclusion I extend to the entire command my heartfelt thanks for the gallant manner in which they behaved..."

— Curwen B. McLellan, U.S. Army[76]

[76] Official Report of Captain Curwen B. McLellan (6th U.S. Cavalry), Fort Richardson, Texas, 16 July 1870. Carter, *From Yorktown to Santiago*, 141-146.

(0623) Skirmish, near Mount Paso, Texas (July 14, 1870)[77]
    — Captain Wirt Davis (4th U.S. Cavalry)
        — 4th U.S. Cavalry Detachments Co. D and F

(0624) Action, Fort Leavenworth, Kansas (July 22, 1870)[78]
    — **1 KILLED**[79]
        — Captain David H. Buel (Ordnance Department)

"As an officer [Captain David H. Buel] was distinguished for his bravery, ranking high in his class. During the war he sustained himself with great credit and filled the highest positions with ability. As a man he was marked for his upright, dignified bearing and was deservedly popular with his fellow officers."
        — Editor, *Leavenworth Times*, Citizen[80]

(0625) Skirmish, Pinal Mountains, Arizona Territory (July 25, 1870)[81]
    — 1st Lieutenant Howard B. Cushing (3rd U.S. Cavalry)
    — 3rd U.S. Cavalry Co. F

(0626) Action, Skirmish Canyon, Apache Mountains, Arizona Territory (August 1, 1870)[82]
    — 1st Lieutenant Howard B. Cushing (3rd U.S. Cavalry)
        — 1st U.S. Cavalry Co. K
        — 3rd U.S. Cavalry Co. F
    — **1 KILLED**[83]
        — Private Joseph Graff (Co. K 1st U.S. Cavalry)

(0627) Skirmish, Staked Plains, New Mexico Territory (August 10, 1870)[84]
    — 2nd Lieutenant Harrison S. Weeks (8th U.S. Cavalry)
        — 8th U.S. Cavalry Co. D

(0628) Action, Mescal Ranch, Arizona Territory (August 18, 1870)[85]
    — UNKNOWN
        — 21st U.S. Infantry Detachment Co. D
    — **3 KILLED**[86]
        — Private Lawrence Moore (Co. D 21st U.S. Infantry)
        — Private Washington Peabody (Co. D 21st U.S. Infantry)

        — (1) Citizens

(0629) Skirmish, near Camp McDowell, Arizona Territory (August 22, 1870)[87]
    — Captain George B. Sanford (1st U.S. Cavalry)
        — 1st U.S. Cavalry Detachment Co. E

---

[77] Indians. Chronological List, 46; Heitman (Volume 2), 435; Rister, *Fort Griffin*, 76; Smith, *Old Army in Texas*, 152-153.
[78] Deserter. Heitman (Volume 1), 259; Otis, *Report of Surgical Cases*, 36.
[79] Otis, *Report of Surgical Cases*, 36.
[80] *Leavenworth (Kansas) Times*, 27 July 1870.
[81] Indians. Chronological List, 46; Heitman (Volume 2), 436; Randall, *Only the Echoes*, 52.
[82] Indians. Chronological List, 46; Heitman (Volume 2), 436; Randall, *Only the Echoes*, 52-53; Thrapp, *Conquest of Apacheria*, 69-70.
[83] 1st U.S. Cavalry Regimental Return August 1866; Register of Deaths Regular Army, 1860-1889 (Volume 4).
[84] Indians. Chronological List, 46; Heitman (Volume 2), 436.
[85] Indians. Chronological List, 46; Heitman (Volume 2), 436; McChristian, *Fort Bowie*, 123.
[86] Fort Bowie Post Return August 1870.
[87] Indians. Chronological List, 46; Heitman (Volume 2), 436.

(0630) Action, near Fort Concho, Texas (September 30, 1870)[88]
— UNKNOWN
— 4th U.S. Cavalry Detachment Co. E
— **1 KILLED**[89]
— Private Martin Wurmser (Co. E 4th US Cavalry)

(0631) Skirmish, Yellowstone River, Dakota Territory (October 1, 1870)[90]
— 2nd Lieutenant William H. Nelson (7th U.S. Infantry)
— Detachment of Indian Scouts

(0632) Skirmish, near Little Wichita River, Texas (October 5, 1870)[91]
— Captain William A. Rafferty (6th U.S. Cavalry)
— 6th U.S. Cavalry Co. M
— Detachment of Indian Scouts

— *Private James Anderson (Co. M 6th U.S. Cavalry) received MOH: Gallantry during the pursuit and fight with Indians (Wichita River, Texas, October 5, 1870).*

— *Corporal Samuel Bowden (Co. M 6th U.S. Cavalry) received MOH: Gallantry in pursuit of and fight with Indians (Wichita River, Texas, October 5, 1870).*

— *Guide James B. Doshier (Citizen) received MOH: Gallantry in action and on the march (Holiday Creek, Texas, October 5, 1870).*[92]

— *Corporal Daniel Keating (Co. M 6th U.S. Cavalry) received MOH: Gallantry in action and in pursuit of Indians (Wichita River, Texas, October 5, 1870).*

— *Captain William A. Rafferty (6th U.S. Cavalry) brevet promotion to Major for gallant service in actions against Indians (Little Wichita River, Texas, October 5, 1870 and Hatchet Mountain, New Mexico, April 28, 1882).*

— *Sergeant Michael Welch (Co. M 6th U.S. Cavalry) received MOH: Gallantry in action (Wichita River, Texas, October 5, 1870).*

— *Private Benjamin Wilson (Co. M 6th U.S. Cavalry) received MOH: Gallantry in action (Wichita River, Texas, October 5, 1870).*

(0633) Skirmish, Looking Glass Creek or Shell Creek, Nebraska (October 6, 1870)[93]
— Captain James Egan (2nd U.S. Cavalry)
— 2nd U.S. Cavalry Co. K

[88] Indians. Chronological List, 47; Heitman (Volume 2), 436; Nye, *Carbine and Lance*, 118-119; Smith, *Old Army in Texas*, 152; Williams, *Texas' Last Frontier*, 139.
[89] Otis, *Report of Surgical Cases*, 150.
[90] Indians. Chronological List, 47; Heitman (Volume 2), 436.
[91] Indians. Chronological List, 47; Heitman (Volume 2), 436; Carter, *From Yorktown to Santiago*, 148-149, 277; Hamilton, *Sentinel of the Southern Plains*, 60; McConnell, *Five Years a Cavalryman*, 220; Neal, *Valor Across the Lone Star*, 80-82; Nye, *Carbine and Lance*, 119; Smith, *Old Army in Texas*, 152
[92] In 1916, the general review of all Medals of Honor deemed 900 unwarranted. This recipient was one of them. In June 1989, the U.S. Army Board of Correction of Records restored the medal to this recipient.
[93] Indians. Chronological List, 47; Heitman (Volume 2), 436; Record of Engagements, 29.

(0634) Action, Pinal Mountains, Arizona Territory (October 6, 1870)[94]
— 1st Lieutenant Howard B. Cushing (3rd U.S. Cavalry)
— 3rd U.S. Cavalry Co. F
— **2 WOUNDED**[95]
— Private Andrew Smith (Co. F 3rd U.S. Cavalry)
— *gunshot wound, right side, slight wound*
— Private Louis Shire (Co. F 3rd U.S. Cavalry)
— *gunshot wound, left leg, fracture, amputation, severe wound*

(0635) Skirmish, near Little Wichita River, Texas (October 6, 1870)[96]
— Captain Tullius C. Tupper (6th U.S. Cavalry)
— 6th U.S. Cavalry Co. G

(0636) Skirmish, Guadaloupe Mountains, New Mexico Territory (October 16, 1870)[97]
— Captain William McCleave (8th U.S. Cavalry)
— 8th U.S. Cavalry Co. A and B

(0637) Action, Pinal Mountains, Arizona Territory (October 29, 1870)[98]
— Captain Harrison Moulton (1st U.S. Cavalry)
— 1st U.S. Cavalry Co. C
— **2 WOUNDED**[99]
— Private William Harland (Co. C 1st U.S. Cavalry)
— Private William Middleton (Co. C 1st U.S. Cavalry)

(0638) Citizens, near Carson, Colorado Territory (November 10, 1870)[100]

(0639) Skirmish, near Fort Richardson, Texas (November 14, 1870)[101]
— Captain Adna R. Chaffee (6th U.S. Cavalry)
— 6th U.S. Cavalry Detachment Co. I

(0640) Citizens, Lowell Station, Kansas (November 18, 1870)[102]
— (1) Citizen Killed

(0641) Skirmish, Turnbull Mountains, Arizona Territory (December 14, 1870)[103]
— 1st Lieutenant Howard B. Cushing (3rd U.S. Cavalry)
— 3rd U.S. Cavalry Co. F

— *Corporal Julius Schou (Co. I 22nd U.S. Infantry) received MOH: Carried dispatches to Fort Buford (Sioux Campaign, 1870).*

TOTAL KILLED 1870 — 3/14/0/1 (OFFICERS, ENLISTED MEN, INDIAN SCOUTS, CITIZENS)

---

[94] Indians. Chronological List, 47; Heitman (Volume 2), 436; Randall, *Only the Echoes*, 57; Thrapp, *Conquest of Apacheria*, 69-70.
[95] Otis, *Report of Surgical Cases*, 204; Randall, *Only the Echoes*, 57.
[96] Indians. Chronological List, 47; Heitman (Volume 2), 436; Carter, *From Yorktown to Santiago*, 150-152, 277; Smith, *Old Army in Texas*, 152.
[97] Indians. Chronological List, 47; Heitman (Volume 2), 436; Record of Engagements, 29. Heitman lists 8th U.S. Cavalry Co. B.
[98] Indians. Chronological List, 47; Heitman (Volume 2), 436.
[99] Camp McDowell Post Return November 1870.
[100] Indians. Chronological List, 47; Record of Engagements, 29.
[101] Indians. Chronological List, 47; Heitman (Volume 2), 436; Carter, *From Yorktown to Santiago*, 152-153, 277; Hamilton, *Sentinel of the Southern Plains*, 60; Smith, *Old Army in Texas*, 152.
[102] Indians. Chronological List, 47; Heitman (Volume 2), 436; Record of Engagements, 29.
[103] Indians. Chronological List, 47; Heitman (Volume 2), 436; Randall, *Only the Echoes*, 58.

1871

"The general condition of affairs... has been peaceful during the past year. This condition has not, however, diminished the activity of our small force, which has been constantly engaged in protecting our exposed frontier settlements; the different lines of commercial travel and telegraph lines, in furnishing escorts for surveying parties, for railroad and scientific purposes, and in guarding Indian agents on reservations, and in aiding in the police and management of such reservations."

— Phillip H. Sheridan, U.S. Army[1]

[1] Official Report of Lieutenant General Phillip H. Sheridan, Military Division of the Missouri. *Annual Report of Secretary of War (1871)*, 24.

(0642) Skirmish, near Gila River, Arizona Territory (January 1, 1871)[2]
   — Captain Reuben F. Bernard (1st U.S. Cavalry)
      — 1st U.S. Cavalry Detachment Co. G
      — 3rd U.S. Cavalry Detachment Co. H

(0643) Action, Cienega, near Camp Verde, Arizona Territory (January 7, 1871)[3]
   — 1st Lieutenant George W. Cradlebaugh (3rd U.S. Cavalry)
      — 3rd U.S. Cavalry Detachments Co. A, E and G
  — **1 WOUNDED**[4]
      — Acting Assistant Surgeon A.G. Steigers (Citizen)
        — *gunshot wound, left arm*

(0644) Skirmish, Mazatzal Mountains, Arizona Territory (January 9, 1871)[5]
   — Captain William Hawley (3rd U.S. Cavalry)
      — 3rd U.S. Cavalry Detachments Co. A, E and G

(0645) Skirmish, Chiricahua Mountains, Arizona Territory (February 12, 1871)[6]
   — Captain William Kelly (8th U.S. Cavalry)
      — 8th U.S. Cavalry Co. C

(0646) Skirmish, Sierra Galiero, Arizona Territory (February 13, 1871)[7]
   — 1st Lieutenant Howard B. Cushing (3rd U.S. Cavalry)
      — 3rd U.S. Cavalry Co. F

(0647) Skirmish, Arivaypa Mountains, Arizona Territory (February 14, 1871)[8]
   — 1st Lieutenant Howard B. Cushing (3rd U.S. Cavalry)
      — 3rd U.S. Cavalry Co. F

(0648) Citizens, near Grinnell, Kansas (February 26, 1871)[9]

(0649) Skirmish, Paloncillo Mountains, Arizona Territory (March 21, 1871)[10]
   — Captain Gerald Russell (3rd U.S. Cavalry)
      — 3rd U.S. Cavalry Detachment Co. K

(0650) Action, Gila River, near Gila Mountains, Arizona Territory (March 28, 1871)[11]
   — Captain Gerald Russell (3rd U.S. Cavalry)
      — 3rd U.S. Cavalry Detachment Co. K
  — **1 WOUNDED**[12]
      — Enlisted Man (3rd U.S. Cavalry)

[2] Indians. Chronological List, 47; Heitman (Volume 2), 436; McChristian, *Fort Bowie*, 125; Russell, *One Hundred and Three Fights*, 79-80. Chronological List lists 1st U.S. Cavalry Detachment; 3rd U.S. Cavalry Detachment.
[3] Indians. Chronological List, 47; Heitman (Volume 2), 436; Alexander, *Arizona Frontier Military Place Names*, 36.
[4] Camp Verde Post Return January 1871.
[5] Indians. Chronological List, 47; Heitman (Volume 2), 436.
[6] Indians. *Annual Report of Secretary of War (1871)*, 44; Chronological List, 47; Heitman (Volume 2), 436; Alexander, *Arizona Frontier Military Place Names*, 34. Heitman lists 8th U.S. Cavalry Detachment Co. C
[7] Indians. Chronological List, 47; Heitman (Volume 2), 436; Randall, *Only the Echoes*, 58-59.
[8] Indians. Chronological List, 47; Randall, *Only the Echoes*, 59.
[9] Indians. Chronological List, 47.
[10] Indians. Chronological List, 47; Heitman (Volume 2), 436; Alexander, *Arizona Frontier Military Place Names*, 95; McChristian, *Fort Bowie*, 125.
[11] Indians. Chronological List, 47; Heitman (Volume 2), 436; McChristian, *Fort Bowie*, 125.
[12] "one private wounded". 3rd U.S. Cavalry Regimental Return April 1871.

(0651) Operations, near Camp Date Creek, Arizona Territory (April 1 to 3, 1871)[13]
    — 1st Lieutenant James A. Haughey (21st U.S. Infantry)
        — 3rd U.S. Cavalry Detachment Co. B

(0652) Skirmish, Sierra Aniba, Arizona Territory (April 4, 1871)[14]
    — 1st Lieutenant Howard B. Cushing (3rd U.S. Cavalry)
        — 3rd U.S. Cavalry Co. F

(0653) Skirmish, Apache Mountains, Arizona Territory (April 11, 1871)[15]
    — 1st Lieutenant Howard B. Cushing (3rd U.S. Cavalry)
        — 3rd U.S. Cavalry Co. F

(0654) Skirmish, Apache Mountains, Arizona Territory (April 12, 1871)[16]
    — 1st Lieutenant Howard B. Cushing (3rd U.S. Cavalry)
        — 3rd U.S. Cavalry Co. F

(0655) Skirmish, Dragoon Mountains, Arizona Territory (April 16, 1871)[17]
    — Captain Gerald Russell (3rd U.S. Cavalry)
        — 3rd U.S. Cavalry Detachment Co. K

(0656) Skirmish, Fort Sill, Indian Territory (April 27, 1871)[18]
    — 1st Lieutenant Samuel L. Woodward (10th U.S. Cavalry)
        — 10th U.S. Cavalry Detachment Co. E

(0657) Citizens, Colorado Territory (April 30, 1871)[19]
    — (20) Citizens Killed

(0658) Citizens, near Cimarron, New Mexico Territory (May 3, 1871)[20]
    — (3) Citizens Killed

(0659) Action, Whetstone Mountains, Arizona Territory (May 5, 1871)[21]
    — 1st Lieutenant Howard B. Cushing (3rd U.S. Cavalry)
        — 3rd U.S. Cavalry Detachment Co. F
    — **3 KILLED**[22]
        — 1st Lieutenant Howard B. Cushing (3rd U.S. Cavalry)

        — Private Martin Green (Co. F 3rd U.S. Cavalry)

        — Packer William H. Simpson (Citizen)

---

[13] Indians. Chronological List, 48; Heitman (Volume 2), 436.
[14] Indians. Chronological List, 48; Heitman (Volume 2), 436; Randall, *Only the Echoes*, 60.
[15] Indians. Chronological List, 48; Heitman (Volume 2), 436; Randall, *Only the Echoes*, 60.
[16] Indians. Chronological List, 48; Heitman (Volume 2), 436; Randall, *Only the Echoes*, 60.
[17] Indians. Chronological List, 48; Heitman (Volume 2), 436.
[18] Indians. Chronological List, 48; Heitman (Volume 2), 436.
[19] Indians. Chronological List, 48.
[20] Indians. Chronological List, 48.
[21] Indians. Chronological List, 48; Heitman (Volume 2), 436; Alexander, *Arizona Military Place Names*, 12-13; Randall, *Only the Echoes*, 62-70; Roberts, *Once They Moved Like the Wind*, 60-61; Thrapp, *Conquest of Apacheria*, 72-78.
[22] 3rd U.S. Cavalry Regimental Return May 1871; Randall, *Only the Echoes*, 68.

— **1 WOUNDED**[23]
    — Private George Pierce (Co. F 3rd U.S. Cavalry)

— *Private Hermann Fichter (Co. F 3rd U.S. Cavalry) received MOH: Gallantry in action (Whetstone Mountains, Arizona, May 5, 1871).*

    — *Private John Kilmartin (Co. F 3rd U.S. Cavalry) received MOH: Gallantry in action (Whetstone Mountains, Arizona, May 5, 1871).*

    — *Private Daniel H. Miller (Co. F 3rd U.S. Cavalry) received MOH: Gallantry in action (Whetstone Mountains, Arizona, May 5, 1871).*

    — *Sergeant John Mott (Co. F 3rd U.S. Cavalry) received MOH: Gallantry in action (Whetstone Mountains, Arizona, May 5, 1871).*

    — *Private John P. Yount (Co. F 3rd U.S. Cavalry) received MOH: Gallantry in action with Indians (Whetstone Mountains, Arizona Territory, May 5, 1871).*

"There is not a hostile tribe in Arizona or New Mexico that will not celebrate the killing of [1st Lieutenant Howard B. Cushing] as a great triumph. He was a beau sabreur, an unrelenting fighter, and although the Indians have 'got him' at last, he sent before him a long procession of them to open his path to that undiscovered country...."
    — Sylvester Mowry, Citizen[24]

(0660) Skirmish, near Red River, Texas (May 12, 1871)[25]
    — UNKNOWN
        — 10th U.S. Cavalry Detachment Co. L

(0661) Action, Fort Sill, Indian Territory (May 17, 1871)[26]
    — UNKNOWN
        — 10th U.S. Cavalry Co. B, D, E and H
    — **1 WOUNDED**[27]
        — Enlisted Man (10th U.S. Cavalry)

    (0662) Citizens, near Red River, Texas (May 18, 1871)[28]
        — (7) Citizens Killed

(0663) Action, Brazos and Big Wishita Divide, Texas (May 20, 1871)[29]
    — 1st Lieutenant Peter M. Boehm (4th U.S. Cavalry)
        — 4th U.S. Cavalry Co. A
    — **1 WOUNDED**[30]
        — Enlisted Man (4th U.S. Cavalry)

[23] Randall, *Only the Echoes*, 68.
[24] Sylvester Mowry, a noted Arizona pioneer, wrote this letter to the *New York Herald* on 15 May 1871. Thrapp, *Conquest of Apacheria*, 77.
[25] Indians. Chronological List, 48; Heitman (Volume 2), 436; Smith, *Old Army In Texas*, 152. Chronological List lists "troops from Fort Sill".
[26] Indians. *Annual Report of Secretary of War (1871)*, 65; Chronological List, 48; Heitman (Volume 2), 436. Chronological List lists "troops from post".
[27] Chronological List, 48.
[28] Indians. Killed were teamsters Nathan Long, James Elliott, Samuel Elliott, M.J. Baxter, Jesse Bowman, John Mullins, and James Williams. *Annual Report of Secretary of War (1871)*, 65; Chronological List, 48; Record of Engagements, 30; Carter, *On the Border with Mackenzie*, 80-82; Hamilton, *Sentinel of the Southern Plains*, 79-81; Leckie, *Military Conquest of the Southern Plains*, 148; Nye, *Carbine and Lance*, 124-131; Uglow, *Standing in the Gap*, 87. Chronological List lists 12 May 1871.
[29] Indians. Chronological List, 48; Heitman (Volume 2), 436; Hamilton, *Sentinel of the Southern Plains*, 83; Leckie, *Military Conquest of the Southern Plains*, 149; Robinson, *Bad Hand*, 81; Smith, *Old Army in Texas*, 152-153; Wallace, *Ranald S. Mackenzie*, 33-34.
[30] Chronological List, 48.

(0664) Action, near Camp Melvin Station, Texas (May 21, 1871)[31]
    — Sergeant J. Walker (25th U.S. Infantry)
        — 25th U.S. Infantry Detachment Co. K
    — **2 WOUNDED**[32]
        — Enlisted Man (25th U.S. Infantry)
        — Enlisted Man (25th U.S. Infantry)

(0665) Skirmish, Birdwood Creek, Nebraska (May 24, 1871)[33]
    — 1st Lieutenant Edward M. Hayes (5th U.S. Cavalry)
        — 5th U.S. Cavalry Detachments Co. G, H, I and L

(0666) Skirmish, Canadian Mountains, Texas (May 28, 1871)[34]
    — Captain James F. Randlett (8th U.S. Cavalry)
        — 8th U.S. Cavalry Co. D

(0667) Skirmish, Kiowa Springs, New Mexico Territory (May 29, 1871)[35]
    — 1st Lieutenant Andrew P. Caraher (8th U.S. Cavalry)
        — 8th U.S. Cavalry Co. F

(0668) Skirmish, Huachuca Mountains, Arizona Territory (June 1, 1871)[36]
    — Captain Alexander Moore (3rd U.S. Cavalry)
        — 3rd U.S. Cavalry Co. F

(0669) Skirmish, East Fork of Verde River, Mazatzal Mountains and Wild Rye Creek, Arizona Territory (June 8 and 9, 1871)[37]
    — 2nd Lieutenant Charles Morton (3rd U.S. Cavalry)
        — 3rd U.S. Cavalry Detachments Co. A, E and G

    — *2nd Lieutenant Charles Morton (3rd U.S. Cavalry) brevet promotion to 1st Lieutenant for gallant service in action against Indians (Tonto Country, June 5, 1871).*

(0670) Skirmish, Huachuca Mountains, Arizona Territory (June 10, 1871)[38]
    — Captain Alexander Moore (3rd U.S. Cavalry)
        — 3rd U.S. Cavalry Co. F

(0671) Skirmish, Camp Brown, Wyoming Territory (June 26, 1871)[39]
    — Sergeant N.F. Cheeney (2nd U.S. Cavalry)
        — 2nd U.S. Cavalry Detachment Co. B
        — 13th U.S. Infantry Detachment Co. A

(0672) Citizens, near Pawnee Fork, Kansas (June 28, 1871)[40]

---

[31] Indians. Chronological List, 48; Heitman (Volume 2), 436; Smith, *Old Army in Texas*, 153.
[32] Chronological List, 48.
[33] Indians. Chronological List, 48; Heitman (Volume 2), 436.
[34] Indians. Chronological List, 48; Heitman (Volume 2), 436; Smith, *Old Army in Texas*, 153.
[35] Indians. Chronological List, 48; Heitman (Volume 2), 436; Rathbun, *New Mexico Frontier Military Place Names*, 96-97.
[36] Indians. Chronological List, 48; Heitman (Volume 2), 436.
[37] Indians. Chronological List, 49; Heitman (Volume 2), 436.
[38] Indians. Chronological List, 49; Heitman (Volume 2), 436.
[39] Indians. Chronological List, 49; Heitman (Volume 2), 436.
[40] Indians. Chronological List, 49.

(0673) Skirmish, Staked Plains, Texas (June 30, 1871)[41]
— Lt. Colonel William R. Shafter (24th U.S. Infantry)
— 9th U.S. Cavalry Detachment Co. I

(0674) Operations, between Fort Apache and Fort McDowell, Arizona Territory (July 1871)[42]
— Captain Guy V. Henry (3rd U.S. Cavalry)
— UNKNOWN

(0675) Skirmish, Fort Larned, Kansas (July 2, 1871)[43]
— UNKNOWN
— 3rd U.S. Infantry Co. C and E

(0676) Skirmish, Bandaro Pass, Texas (July 4, 1871)[44]
— Sergeant D. Harrington (4th U.S. Cavalry)
— 4th U.S. Cavalry Detachment Co. M

(0677) Action, Cienega de Los Pinos, Arizona Territory (July 13, 1871)[45]
— Captain Harry M. Smith (21st U.S. Infantry)
— 21st U.S. Infantry Co. G
— **1 KILLED**[46]
— Private Charles W. Harris (Co. G 21st U.S. Infantry)

— **3 WOUNDED**[47]
— Private Joseph Bossard (Co. G 21st U.S. Infantry)
— Private Jeremiah Hennesy (Co. G 21st U.S. Infantry)
— Private John Williams (Co. G 21st U.S. Infantry)

(0678) Skirmish, Double Mountain, Fork of Brazos River, Texas (July 15, 1871)[48]
— 1st Lieutenant William C. Hemphill (4th U.S. Cavalry)
— 4th U.S. Cavalry Detachment Co. G

(0679) Citizens, near Camp Bowie, Arizona Territory (July 19, 1871)[49]
— (2) Citizens Killed

(0680) Action, Bear Springs, near Camp Bowie, Arizona Territory (July 19, 1871)[50]
— 1st Lieutenant George A. Drew (3rd U.S. Cavalry)
— 3rd U.S. Cavalry Detachment Co. K
— **1 WOUNDED**[51]
— First Sergeant John F. Farley (Co. K 3rd U.S. Cavalry)
— *gunshot wound, hip*

---

[41] Indians. Chronological List, 49; Heitman (Volume 2), 436; Leckie, *Buffalo Soldiers*, 98-99; Smith, *Old Army in Texas*, 153; Wooster, *Frontier Crossroads*, 96-97. Heitman lists 9th U.S. Cavalry Detachment Co. I.

[42] Indians. *Annual Report of Secretary of War (1871)*, 78; Chronological List, 49; Thrapp, *Conquest of Apacheria*, 100-101.

[43] Indians. Chronological List, 49; Heitman (Volume 2), 436. Chronological List lists "garrison of post".

[44] Indians. Chronological List, 49; Heitman (Volume 2), 436; Smith, *Old Army in Texas*, 153.

[45] Indians. Chronological List, 49; Heitman (Volume 2), 436; McChristian, *Fort Bowie*, 133.

[46] 21st U.S. Infantry Regimental Return July 1971.

[47] 21st U.S. Infantry Regimental Return July 1971.

[48] Indians. Chronological List, 49; Heitman (Volume 2), 436; Smith, *Old Army in Texas*, 153.

[49] Indians. Killed were a butcher and another man. Chronological List, 49; McChristian, *Fort Bowie*, 133-134. Chronological List combines the events at Camp Bowie on 19 July 1871.

[50] Indians. Chronological List, 49; Heitman (Volume 2), 437, McChristian, *Fort Bowie*, 133-134. Chronological List combines the events at Camp Bowie on 19 July 1871.

[51] Camp Bowie Post Return July 1871.

(0681) Action, Headwaters of Concho River, Texas (July 22, 1871)[52]
— UNKNOWN
— 9th U.S. Cavalry Detachment Co. F
— **1 WOUNDED**[53]
— Enlisted Man (9th U.S. Cavalry)

(0682) Skirmish, near Fort McKavett, Texas (July 31, 1871)[54]
— Captain Frederick M. Crandal (24th U.S. Infantry)
— 9th U.S. Cavalry Detachment Co. M
— 24th U.S. Infantry Detachment Co. A

(0683) Citizens, near Fort Stanton, New Mexico Territory (August 18, 1871)[55]
— (1) Citizen Killed

(0684) Skirmish, Arivaypa Canyon, Arizona Territory (August 25, 1871)[56]
— Captain Frank Stanwood (3rd U.S. Cavalry)
— 3rd U.S. Cavalry Co. H

(0685) Skirmish, near Fort McKavett, Texas (September 1, 1871)[57]
— Captain John W. Clous (24th U.S. Infantry)
— 9th U.S. Cavalry Detachment Co. M
— 24th U.S. Infantry Detachment Co. E

(0686) Citizens, Chino Valley, Arizona Territory (September 5, 1871)[58]
— (1) Citizen Killed

(0687) Citizens, near Tucson, Arizona Territory (September 13, 1871)[59]
— (2) Citizens Killed

(0688) Action, Foster Springs, Indian Territory (September 19, 1871)[60]
— Captain John B. Van de Wiele (10th U.S. Cavalry)
— 10th U.S. Cavalry Detachment Co. B
— **1 KILLED**[61]
— Bugler Larkin Foster (Co. B 10th U.S. Cavalry)

(0689) Citizens, Fort Sill, Indian Territory (September 22, 1871)[62]
— (2) Citizens Killed

(0690) Action, Freshwater Fork of Brazos River, Texas (October 11, 1871)[63]
— Colonel Ranald S. Mackenzie (4th U.S. Cavalry)
— 4th U.S. Cavalry Co A, F, G, H and K
— **1 KILLED**[64]

[52] Indians. Chronological List, 49; Heitman (Volume 2), 437; Smith, *Old Army in Texas*, 153.
[53] Chronological List, 49.
[54] Indians. Chronological List, 49; Smith, *Old Army in Texas*, 153.
[55] Indians. Chronological List, 49.
[56] Indians. Chronological List, 49; Heitman (Volume 2), 437. Heitman lists 3rd U.S. Cavalry Co. D, H; Detachment Co. F.
[57] Indians. Chronological List, 49; Heitman (Volume 2), 437; Leckie, *Buffalo Soldiers*, 99; Smith, *Old Army in Texas*, 153. Chronological List lists 9th U.S. Cavalry Detachment; 24th U.S. Infantry Detachment.
[58] Indians. Killed was a herder by the name of Gabriel. *Annual Report of Secretary of War (1872)*, 79; Chronological List, 49; Heitman (Volume 2), 437.
[59] Indians. Killed in separate attacks were a mail rider and a herder. *Annual Report of Secretary of War (1872)*, 79; Chronological List, 49.
[60] Indians. Chronological List, 49; Heitman (Volume 2), 437; Leckie, *Buffalo Soldiers*, 66; Nye, *Carbine and Lance*, 150.
[61] Register of Deaths Regular Army, 1860-1889 (Volume 4).
[62] Indians. Killed were herders Patrick O'Neal and John Johnson. Chronological List, 49; Leckie, *Buffalo Soldiers*, 66; Nye, *Carbine and Lance*, 150.
[63] Indians. Chronological List, 49; Heitman (Volume 2), 437; Carter, *On the Border with Mackenzie*, 165-183; Hamilton, *Sentinel of the Southern Plains*, 111-115; Gwynne, *Empire of the Summer Moon*, 9-11, 242-244; Leckie, *Military Conquest of the Southern Plains*, 159; Neal, *Valor Across the Lone Star*, 88-96; Neeley, *Last Comanche Chief*, 113-116; Robinson, *Bad Hand*, 100-102; Wallace, *Ranald S. Mackenzie*, 46-51. Chronological List lists 4th U.S. Cavalry.
[64] Register of Deaths Regular Army, 1860-1889 (Volume 4); 4th U.S. Cavalry Regimental Return October 1871.

— Private Seander Gregg (Co. G 4ᵗʰ U.S. Cavalry)

— 2 WOUNDED[65]
    — Private Melville (Co. G 4ᵗʰ U.S. Cavalry)
      — *gunshot wound, arm*
    — Private Downey (Co. G 4ᵗʰ U.S. Cavalry)
      — *gunshot wound, hand*

    — *1ˢᵗ Lieutenant Peter M. Boehm (4ᵗʰ U.S. Cavalry) brevet promotion to Captain for gallant service in actions against Indians (Brazos River, Texas, October 28 and 29, 1869), special gallantry in action (Brazos River Texas, October 10, 1871) and gallant conduct in action against Indians (Red River, Texas, September 29, 1872).*

    — *2ⁿᵈ Lieutenant Robert G. Carter (4ᵗʰ U.S. Cavalry) brevet promotion to 1ˢᵗ Lieutenant for especially gallant conduct in action against Indians (Brazos River, Texas, October 10, 1871).*

    — *2ⁿᵈ Lieutenant Robert G. Carter (4ᵗʰ U.S. Cavalry) received MOH: Held the left of the line with a few men during the charge of a large body of Indians, after the right of the line had retreated, and by delivering a rapid fire succeeded in checking the enemy until other troops came to the rescue (Brazos River, Texas, October 10, 1871).*

(0691) Citizens, Cienega Sauz, Arizona Territory (October 14, 1871)[66]
    — (1) Citizen Killed

(0692) Action, Freshwater Fork of Brazos River, Texas (October 19, 1871)[67]
    — Colonel Ranald S. Mackenzie (4ᵗʰ U.S. Cavalry)
      — 4ᵗʰ U.S. Cavalry
— 2 WOUNDED[68]
    — Colonel Ranald S. Mackenzie (4ᵗʰ U.S. Cavalry)
      — *arrow wound, right thigh*

    — Farrier Stiegel (4ᵗʰ U.S. Cavalry)
      — *gunshot wound, abdomen*

[65] Carter, *On the Border with Mackenzie*, 175-178.
[66] Indians. Killed was Richard Barnes. *Annual Report of Secretary of War (1872)*, 79; Chronological List, 49.
[67] Indians. Chronological List, 49; Heitman (Volume 2), 437; Carter, *On the Border with Mackenzie*, 196-201; Gwynne, *Empire of the Summer Moon*, 248-249; Neal, *Valor Across the Lone Star*, 97; Neeley, *Last Comanche Chief*, 118-121; Robinson, *Bad Hand*, 105-106; Wallace, *Ranald S. Mackenzie*, 54-55; Smith, *Old Army in Texas*, 154. Chronological List lists 4ᵗʰ U.S. Cavalry.
[68] Carter, *On the Border with Mackenzie*, 198-201.

(0693) Action, Horseshoe Canyon, Arizona Territory (October 24, 1871)[69]
    — Captain Gerald Russell (3rd U.S. Cavalry)
        — 3rd U.S. Cavalry Co. K
  — **1 KILLED**[70]
        — R. H. Whitney (Citizen)

  — **1 WOUNDED**[71]
        — Private Blockhaus (Co. K 3rd U.S. Cavalry)
            — *left shoulder, severe wound*

(0694) Citizens, near Wickenburg, Arizona Territory (November 5, 1871)[72]
    — (6) Citizens Killed

    — *Sergeant Major Frederick W. Gerber (U.S. Engineers) received MOH: Distinguished gallantry in many actions and in recognition of long, faithful and meritorious services covering a period of thirty-two years (1839-1971).*

— *Chiquito (Indian Scout) received MOH: Gallant conduct during campaigns and engagements with Apaches (Winter of 1871 to 1873).*

    — *Jim (Indian Scout) received MOH: Gallant conduct during campaigns and engagements with Apaches (Winter of 1871 to 1873).*

TOTAL KILLED 1871 — 1/4/0/2 (Officers, Enlisted Men, Indian Scouts, Citizens)

---

[69] Indians. Chronological List, 49; Heitman (Volume 2), 437; McChristian, *Fort Bowie*, 137.
[70] Camp Bowie Post Return October 1871.
[71] Camp Bowie Post Return October 1871.
[72] Indians. Killed were stagecoach driver John Lauz, Frederick W. Loring, R.M. Hamel, W.G. Salmon, C.S. Adams and Frederick W. Shoholen. *Annual Report of Secretary of War (1872)*, 79; Chronological List, 50; Alexander, *Arizona Frontier Military Place Names*, 90-91; Altshuler, *Chains of Command*, 205-206; Thrapp, *Al Sieber*, 92.

1872

"I fully endorse the efforts now being made to civilize and Christianize the wild Indians, and think that the reservation system and the policy of the government toward the wild tribes is the most liberal and humane that has ever been adopted by any governments towards savage people; and so far as the military is concerned, every effort will be made to carry out its intentions. The principal error that I discover in it successful management is that, while efforts are being made to teach the Indian what is right, and to induce him to do right, sufficient importance has not been given to teaching him what is wrong."

— Philip H. Sheridan, U.S. Army[1]

---

[1] Official Report of Lieutenant General Phillip H. Sheridan, 12 October 1872. *Annual Report of Secretary of War (1872)*, 35.

(0695) Citizens, Apache Pass, Arizona Territory (January 20, 1872)[2]
— (3) Citizens Killed

(0696) Skirmish, North Concho River, Texas (February 9, 1872)[3]
— Captain Joseph Rendlebrock (4th U.S. Cavalry)
— 4th U.S. Cavalry Detachment Co. B

(0697) Citizens, Cullumber's Station, Arizona Territory (February 22, 1872)[4]
— (2) Citizens Killed

(0698) Citizens, Camp Bowie, Arizona Territory (February 26, 1872)[5]
— (1) Citizen Killed

(0699) Citizens, near Camp Verde, Arizona Territory (March 17, 1872)[6]
— (1) Citizen Killed

(0700) Citizens, near Camp Verde, Arizona Territory (March 24, 1872)[7]
— (1) Citizen Killed

(0701) Skirmish, near Fort Concho, Texas (March 28, 1872)[8]
— Sergeant William Wilson (4th U.S. Cavalry)
— 4th U.S. Cavalry Detachment Co. I

— *Sergeant William Wilson (Co. I 4th U.S. Cavalry) received MOH: In pursuit of a band of cattle thieves from New Mexico Territory (Colorado Valley, Texas, March 28, 1872).*

(0702) Citizens, Mint Valley, Arizona Territory (April 17, 1872)[9]
— (1) Citizen Killed

(0703) Action, near Camp Apache, Arizona Territory (April 17, 1872)[10]
— UNKNOWN
— 21st U.S. Infantry Detachment Co. D
— 1 KILLED[11]
— Private William Irwin (Co. D 21st U.S. Infantry)

(0704) Citizens, near Wormser, Arizona Territory (April 20, 1872)[12]
— (2) Citizens Killed

(0705) Action, near Howard's Well, Texas (April 20, 1872)[13]
— Captain Michael Cooney (9th U.S. Cavalry)
— 9th U.S. Cavalry Co. A and H
— 1 KILLED[14]

---

[2] Indians. Killed were mail carriers A.J. Bice, John Petty and John Donovan. *Annual Report of Secretary of War (1872)*, 79; McChristian, *Fort Bowie*, 139.
[3] Indians. Chronological List, 50; Heitman (Volume 2), 437; Record of Engagements, 32; Smith, *Old Army in Texas*, 154.
[4] Indians. Killed were S.T. Cullember and Thomas Harris. *Annual Report of Secretary of War (1872)*, 80; Chronological List, 50.
[5] Indians. Killed was herder John McWilliams. *Annual Report of Secretary of War (1872)*, 80; Chronological List, 50; McChristian, *Fort Bowie*, 140.
[6] Indians. Killed was Eudilleso Rebas. *Annual Report of Secretary of War (1872)*, 80; Chronological List, 50.
[7] Indians. Killed was a man named Rivas. *Annual Report of Secretary of War (1872)*, 80.
[8] Bandits. *Annual Report of Secretary of War (1872)*,55-56; Chronological List, 50; Heitman (Volume 2), 437; Record of Engagements, 32; Hamilton, *Sentinel of the Southern Plains*, 126; Leckie, *Military Conquest of the Southern Plains*, 167-168; Neal, *Valor Across the Lone Star*, 105-107. Chronological List and Heitman both list 27 and 28 March 1872.
[9] Indians. Killed was Osborn P. Clack. *Annual Report of Secretary of War (1872)*, 80; Chronological List, 50.
[10] Indians. *Annual Report of Secretary of War (1872)*, 80; Chronological List, 50; Heitman (Volume 2), 437.
[11] *Annual Report of Secretary of War (1872)*, 80.
[12] Indians. Killed were George W. Smith and Joseph Ackerman. *Annual Report of Secretary of War (1872)*, 80; Chronological List, 50.
[13] Indians. Chronological List, 50; Heitman (Volume 2), 437; Record of Engagements, 32; Hamilton, *Sentinel of the Southern Plains*, 125; Leckie, *Buffalo Soldiers*, 103-104; Nye, *Carbine and Lance*, 152-153; Uglow, *Standing in the Gap*, 39; Williams, *Texas' Last Frontier*, 156.
[14] Register of Deaths Regular Army, 1860-1889 (Volume 4); 9th U.S. Cavalry Regimental Return April 1872.

— 1ˢᵗ Lieutenant Frederick R. Vincent (9ᵗʰ U.S. Cavalry)

(0706) Skirmish, Tierra Amarilla, New Mexico Territory (April 25, 1872)[15]
— UNKNOWN
— 8ᵗʰ U.S. Cavalry Detachment Co. K

(0707) Citizens, near Camp Crittenden, Arizona Territory (April 26, 1872)[16]
— (1) Citizen Killed

(0708) Skirmish, South Fork of Loupe River, Nebraska (April 26, 1872)[17]
— Captain Charles Meinhold (3ʳᵈ U.S. Cavalry)
— 3ʳᵈ U.S. Cavalry Co. B

— *Scout William F. Cody (Civilian) received MOH: Gallantry in action (Platte River, Nebraska, April 26, 1872).*[18]

— *Sergeant John H. Foley (Co. B 3ʳᵈ U.S. Cavalry) received MOH: Gallantry in action (Loupe Fork, Platte River, Nebraska, April 26, 1872).*

— *Private William H. Strayer (Co. B 3ʳᵈ U.S. Cavalry) received MOH: Gallantry in action (Loupe Fork, Platte River, Nebraska, April 26, 1872).*

— *First Sergeant Leroy H. Vokes (Co. B 3ʳᵈ U.S. Cavalry) received MOH: Gallantry in action (Loupe Fork, Platte River, Nebraska, April 26, 1872).*

(0709) Citizens, Sonoita Valley, Arizona Territory (April 27, 1872)[19]
— (2) Citizens Killed

(0710) Action, near La Bonte Creek, Wyoming Territory (May 2, 1872)[20]
— Sergeant James A. Mularky (14ᵗʰ U.S. Infantry)
— 14ᵗʰ U.S. Infantry Detachments Co. D, E, F and G
— **1 KILLED**[21]
— Sergeant James A. Mularky (Co. E 14ᵗʰ U.S. Infantry)

(0711) Citizens, between Tucson and Camp Bowie, Arizona Territory (May 4, 1872)[22]
— (1) Citizen Killed

(0712) Skirmish, near Camp Hualapais, Arizona Territory (May 5, 1872)[23]
— First Sergeant Rudolph Stauffer (5ᵗʰ U.S. Cavalry)
— 5ᵗʰ U.S. Cavalry Detachment Co. K

[15] Indians. Chronological List, 50; Heitman (Volume 2), 437.
[16] Indians. *Annual Report of Secretary of War (1872)*, 80; Chronological List, 50.
[17] Indians. Chronological List, 50; Heitman (Volume 2), 437; Record of Engagements, 32; Paul, *Nebraska Indian Wars Reader, 220.*
[18] In 1916, the general review of all Medals of Honor deemed 900 unwarranted. This recipient was one of them. In June 1989, the U.S. Army Board of Correction of Records restored the medal to this recipient.
[19] Indians. Killed were Mr. Whitehead and a herder. *Annual Report of Secretary of War (1872)*, 80; Chronological List, 50.
[20] Indians. Chronological List, 50; Heitman (Volume 2), 437; Lindmier, *Drybone,* 71-72. Chronological List lists 14ᵗʰ U.S. Infantry Detachment.
[21] Register of Deaths Regular Army, 1860-1889 (Volume 4).
[22] Indians. Killed was Henry Abrahams. *Annual Report of Secretary of War (1872)*, 80; Chronological List, 51.
[23] Indians. Chronological List, 51; Heitman (Volume 2), 437. Heitman lists 6 May 1872.

— *First Sergeant Rudolph Stauffer (Co. K 5th U.S. Cavalry) received MOH: Gallantry on scouts after Indians (Camp Hualapais, Arizona, 1872).*

(0713) Action, Tierra Amarillo, New Mexico Territory (May 6, 1872)[24]
— 1st Lieutenant Jonathan D. Stevenson (8th U.S. Cavalry)
— 8th U.S. Cavalry Detachments Co. E and K
— **1 KILLED**[25]
— Enlisted Man (8th U.S. Cavalry)

— **1 WOUNDED**[26]
— Enlisted Man (8th U.S. Cavalry)

(0714) Citizens, near Camp Verde, Arizona Territory (May 10, 1872)[27]
— (3) Citizens Killed

(0715) Action, between Big and Little Washita River, Texas (May 12, 1872)[28]
— Captain John A. Wilcox (4th U.S. Cavalry)
— 4th U.S. Cavalry Detachment Co. C
— **1 WOUNDED**[29]
— Enlisted Man (4th U.S. Cavalry)

(0716) Citizens, twenty-five miles from Fort Belknap, Texas (May 19, 1872)[30]
— (1) Citizen Killed

(0717) Action, near Camp Hualapai, Arizona Territory (May 19, 1872)[31]
— First Sergeant Rudolph Stauffer (5th U.S. Cavalry)
— 5th U.S. Cavalry Detachment Co. K
— **2 WOUNDED**[32]
— Private Charles H. Waitz (Co. K 5th U.S. Cavalry)
— Private Charles F. Coe (Co. K 5th U.S. Cavalry)

(0718) Skirmish, La Pendencia River, Texas (May 20, 1872)[33]
— 2nd Lieutenant Gustavus Valois (9th U.S. Cavalry)
— 9th U.S. Cavalry Detachment Co. C
— 24th U.S. Infantry Detachment Co. K
— Detachment of Indian Scouts

(0719) Citizens, near Prescott, Arizona Territory (May 22, 1872)[34]
— (1) Citizen Killed

[24] Indians. *Annual Report of Commissioner of Indian Affairs (1872)*, 308; Chronological List, 51; Heitman (Volume 2), 437; Record of Engagements, 32.
[25] Chronological List, 51.
[26] Chronological List, 51.
[27] Indians. *Annual Report of Secretary of War (1872)*, 80; Chronological List, 51.
[28] Indians. Chronological List, 51; Heitman (Volume 2), 437; Record of Engagements, 32. Chronological List lists 4th U.S. Cavalry Detachment.
[29] Chronological List, 51.
[30] Indians. Chronological List, 51; Record of Engagements, 32; Hamilton, *Sentinel of the Southern Plains*, 125; Leckie, *Military Conquest of the Southern Plains*, 162. Nye, *Carbine and Lance*, 153.
[31] Indians. Chronological List, 51; Heitman (Volume 2), 437; Thrapp, *Conquest of Apacheria*, 114.
[32] Price, *Across the Continent*, 674.
[33] Indians. Chronological List, 51; Heitman (Volume 2), 437; Record of Engagements, 32; Smith, *Old Army in Texas*, 155; Williams, *Texas' Last Frontier*, 160. Chronological List lists 9th U.S. Cavalry Detachment; Detachment of Indian Scouts.
[34] Indians. Killed was Theodore Putz. *Annual Report of Secretary of War (1872)*, 80; Chronological List, 51; Thrapp, *Conquest of Apacheria*, 114.

(0720) Citizens, Sonoita Valley, Arizona Territory (May 22, 1872)[35]
— (1) Citizen Killed

(0721) Action, between Fort Dodge, Kansas and Fort Supply, Indian Territory (May 22, 1872)[36]
— UNKNOWN
— 6th U.S. Cavalry Detachment Co. E
— **2 KILLED**[37]
— Private Alexander Christopher (Co. E 6th U.S. Cavalry)
— Private Henry Wussman (Co. E 6th U.S. Cavalry) — d. 6-01-1872

(0722) Skirmish, Sycamore Canyon, Arizona Territory (May 23, 1872)[38]
— 1st Lieutenant William H. Boyle (21st U.S. Infantry)
— 1st U.S. Cavalry Detachment Co. A

— *First Sergeant Richard Barrett (Co. A 1st U.S. Cavalry) received MOH: Conspicuous gallantry in a charge upon the Tonto Apaches (Sycamore Canyon, Arizona (May 23, 1872).*

(0723) Action, Lost Creek, Texas (May 24, 1872)[39]
— Captain Edward M. Heyl (4th U.S. Cavalry)
— 4th U.S. Cavalry Detachments Co. A and K
— **1 KILLED**[40]
— Private B. Henchey (Co. K 4th U.S. Cavalry)

(0724) Citizens, Sonoita Valley Arizona Territory (June 7, 1872)[41]
— (1) Citizen Killed

(0725) Citizens, near Clear Fork of Brazos River, Texas (June 9, 1872)[42]
— (3) Citizens Killed

(0726) Skirmish, Bill William's Mountain, Arizona Territory (June 10, 1872)[43]
— 2nd Lieutenant Thomas Garvey (1st U.S. Cavalry)
— 1st U.S. Cavalry Detachment Co. A

(0727) Citizens, San Juan River, New Mexico Territory (June 11, 1872)[44]
— (1) Citizen Killed

(0728) Citizens, near Prescott, Arizona Territory (June 13, 1872)[45]
— (1) Citizen Killed

(0729) Skirmish, Ponca Agency, Dakota Territory (June 14, 1872)[46]
— 2nd Lieutenant Oskaloosa M. Smith (22nd U.S. Infantry)
— 22nd U.S. Infantry Detachments Co. B, D, G, H and K

---

[35] Indians. Killed was Florence Cosgrove. *Annual Report of Secretary of War (1872)*, 80; Chronological List, 51.
[36] Indians. Chronological List, 51; Heitman (Volume 2), 437; Record of Engagements, 32; Carriker, *Fort Supply, Indian Territory*, 67; Carter, *From Yorktown to Santiago*, 277. Chronological List lists "6th U.S. Cavalry courier".
[37] Register of Deaths Regular Army, 1860-1889 (Volume 4).
[38] Indians. Chronological List, 51; Heitman (Volume 2), 437.
[39] Indians. Chronological List, 51; Heitman (Volume 2), 437; Record of Engagements, 32; Hamilton, *Sentinel of the Southern Plains*, 125-126; Smith, *Old Army in Texas*, 155; Williams, *Texas' Last Frontier*, 160.
[40] 4th U.S. Cavalry Regimental Return May 1872.
[41] Indians. *Report of Secretary of War (1872)*, 80.
[42] Indians. Killed were Abel Lee, his wife, and daughter Frances. His daughters, Susanna and Millie, and son John were all kidnapped. They were all eventually recovered. *Annual Report of Commissioner of Indian Affairs (1872)*, 247-248; Hamilton, *Sentinel of the Southern Plains*, 125; Leckie, *Military Conquest of the Southern Plains*, 162-163; Michno, *Fate Worse Than Death*, 438-442; Nye, *Carbine and Lance*, 154.
[43] Indians. Chronological List, 51; Heitman (Volume 2), 437; Alexander, *Arizona Military Place Names*, 15; Thrapp, *Conquest of Apacheria*, 115.
[44] Indians. Killed was Indian Agent James H. Miller. *Annual Report of Commissioner of Indian Affairs (1872)*, 296.
[45] Indians. Killed was Adam Riesbeck. *Annual Report of Secretary of War (1872)*, 80; Chronological List, 51.
[46] Indians. Chronological List, 51; Heitman (Volume 2), 437.

(0730) Citizens, Granite Mountains, Arizona Territory (June 15, 1872)[47]

(0731) Skirmish, Johnson's Mail Station, Granite Mountains, Texas (June 15, 1872)[48]
— Corporal Hickey (11th U.S. Infantry)
— 11th U.S. Infantry Detachment Co. H

(0732) Citizens, Sonoita Valley, Arizona Territory (June 24, 1872)[49]
— (1) Citizen Killed

(0733) Skirmish, Deep River, Indian Territory (July 12, 1872)[50]
— Captain Nicholas Nolan (10th U.S. Cavalry)
— 10th U.S. Cavalry Co. A and L

(0734) Action, Canyon of Whetstone Mountains, Arizona Territory (July 13, 1872)[51]
— 2nd Lieutenant William P. Hall (5th U.S. Cavalry)
— 5th U.S. Cavalry Detachment Co. F
— **2 WOUNDED**[52]
— First Sergeant Denis Leonard (Co. F 5th U.S. Cavalry)
— Private William Porter (Co. F 5th U.S. Cavalry)

— Private Michael Glynn (Co. F 5th U.S. Cavalry) received MOH: Drove off, single-handedly, eight hostile Indians, killing and wounding five (Whetstone Mountains, Arizona, July 13, 1872).

— First Sergeant Henry Newman (Co. F 5th U.S. Cavalry) received MOH: He and two companions covered the withdrawal of wounded comrades from the fire of an Apache band well concealed among rocks (Whetstone Mountains, Arizona, July 13, 1872).

— Private John Nihill (Co. F 5th U.S. Cavalry) received MOH: Fought and defeated four hostile Apaches located between him and his comrades (Whetstone Mountains, Arizona, July 13, 1872).

— Private John Nihill (Co. F 5th U.S. Cavalry) received Certificate of Merit: For gallantry in action with Indians (Whetstone Mountains, Arizona, July 13, 1872).

(0735) Skirmish, Otter Creek, Indian Territory (July 22, 1872)[53]
— Captain Nicholas Nolan (10th U.S. Cavalry)
— 10th U.S. Cavalry Co. A and L

(0736) Operations, First Yellowstone Expedition (July 26 to October 15, 1872)[54]
— Colonel David S. Stanley (22nd Infantry)
— 8th U.S. Infantry Co. A, B, C, F, H and K
— 17th U.S. Infantry Co. A, C and F

[47] Indians. *Annual Report of Secretary of War (1872)*, 80; Chronological List, 51.
[48] Indians. Chronological List, 51; Heitman (Volume 2), 437; Record of Engagements, 32-33; Smith, *Old Army in Texas*, 155; Williams, *Texas' Last Frontier*, 160.
[49] Indians. Killed was Adolphus Brown. *Annual Report of Secretary of War (1872)*, 80.
[50] Indians. Chronological List, 51; Heitman (Volume 2), 437; Leckie, *Military Conquest of the Southern Plains*, 164.
[51] Indians. Chronological List, 51; Heitman (Volume 2), 437; Alexander, *Arizona Frontier Military Place Names*, 127.
[52] Price, *Across the Continent*, 674.
[53] Indians. Chronological List, 51; Heitman (Volume 2), 437.
[54] Indians. *Annual Report of Secretary of War (1872)*, 40; Chronological List, 51; Heitman (Volume 2), 437; Lubetkin, *Jay Cooke's Gamble*, 114-161.

— 22nd U.S. Infantry Co. D, F and G
— Detachment of Indian Scouts
— **3 KILLED**[55]
— 1st Lieutenant Eben Crosby (17th U.S. Infantry) — d. 10-03-1872
— 1st Lieutenant Lewis D. Adair (22nd U.S. Infantry) — d. 10-05-1872

— Stephen Harris (Citizen) — d. 10-04-1872

(0737) Skirmish, Mount Graham, Arizona Territory (July 27, 1872)[56]
— 1st Lieutenant William Stephenson (8th U.S. Cavalry)
— 8th U.S. Cavalry Co. A

(0738) Skirmish, Central Mail Station, Texas (July 28, 1872)[57]
— Sergeant J. Walker (25th U.S. Infantry)
— 25th U.S. Infantry Detachment Co. K

(0739) Skirmish, near Fort Griffin, Texas (August 5, 1872)[58]
— UNKNOWN
— 11th U.S. Infantry Detachment

— *Private Franklin M. McDonald (Co. G 11th U.S. Infantry) received MOH: Gallantry in defeating Indians who attacked the mail (Near Fort Griffin, Texas, August 5, 1872).*

(0740) Skirmish, Chiricahua Mountains, Arizona Territory (August 6, 1872)[59]
— 1st Lieutenant William Stephenson (8th U.S. Cavalry)
— 8th U.S. Cavalry Co. A

(0741) Action, near Prior's Fork, Montana Territory (August 14, 1872)[60]
— Major Eugene M. Baker (2nd U.S. Cavalry)
— 2nd U.S. Cavalry Co. F, G, H and L
— 7th U.S. Infantry Co. C, E, G and I
— **2 KILLED**[61]
— Sergeant James McClarren (Co. C 7th U.S. Infantry)

— William Francis (Citizen) — d. 08-17-1872

— **3 WOUNDED**[62]
— Private Abel Cox (Co. F 2nd U.S. Cavalry)
— *gunshot wound, abdomen, severe wound*
— Private John Ward (Co. L 2nd U.S. Cavalry)
— *gunshot wound, severe wound*

[55] Lubetkin, *Jay Cooke's Gamble*, 155-156.
[56] Indians. Chronological List, 51; Heitman (Volume 2), 437.
[57] Indians. Chronological List, 51; Heitman (Volume 2), 437; Nankivell, *Buffalo Soldier Regiment*, 23; Williams, *Texas' Last Frontier*, 162.
[58] Indians. Neal, *Valor Across the Lone Star*, 111-123.
[59] Indians. Chronological List, 52.
[60] Indians. *Annual Report of Secretary of War (1872)*, 40; Chronological List, 52; Heitman (Volume 2), 437; Record of Engagements, 33; Bradley, *March of the Montana Column*, 59-63; Brown, *Plainsmen of the Yellowstone*, 200-201; Gray, *Custer's Last Campaign*, 93-94; Lubetkin, *Jay Cooke's Gamble*, 138-140; Robertson, "We Are Going to Have a Big Sioux War," *Montana, the Magazine of Western History* 34 (January 1984): 2-15; Rockwell, *U.S. Army in Frontier Montana*, 246-249; Rodenbough, *From Everglade to Canyon*, 435. Heitman lists 4 August 1874.
[61] Reports of Diseases and Individual Cases, F 436; Bradley, *March of the Montana Column*, 63.
[62] Reports of Diseases and Individual Cases, F 436.

— Private Thomas O'Malley (Co. E 7th U.S. Infantry)
— *gunshot wound, thigh, severe wound*

(0742) Action, Palo Duro Creek, New Mexico Territory (August 15, 1872)[63]
— Captain William McCleave (8th U.S. Cavalry)
— 8th U.S. Cavalry Co. B
— **1 WOUNDED**[64]
— Enlisted Man (8th U.S. Cavalry)

(0743) Action, near Fort McKeen, Dakota Territory (August 26, 1872)[65]
— UNKNOWN
— 6th U.S. Infantry Detachments Co. B and C
— Detachment of Indian Scouts
— **2 KILLED**[66]
— Spotted Eagle (Indian Scout)
— Amongst (Indian Scout)

(0744) Citizens, Santa Cruz River, Arizona Territory (August 27, 1872)[67]
— (4) Citizens Killed

(0745) Action, Davidson's Canyon, Arizona Territory (August 27, 1872)[68]
— 2nd Lieutenant Reid T. Stewart (5th U.S. Cavalry)
— Sergeant James Brown (5th U.S. Cavalry)
— 5th U.S. Cavalry Detachment Co. F
— **2 KILLED**[69]
— 2nd Lieutenant Reid T. Stewart (5th U.S. Cavalry)

— Corporal Joseph Black (Co. F 5th U.S. Cavalry)

— *Sergeant James Brown (Co. F 5th U.S. Cavalry) received MOH: In command of a detachment of four men defeated a superior force (Davidson Canyon, Arizona, August 27, 1872).*

(0746) Citizens, near Camp Mojave, Arizona Territory (September 4, 1872)[70]
— (1) Citizen Killed

(0747) Action, Camp Date Creek, Arizona Territory (September 8, 1872)[71]
— 1st Lieutenant William J. Volkmar (5th U.S. Cavalry)
— 5th U.S. Cavalry Co. E
— **1 WOUNDED**[72]
—Sergeant Frank E. Hill (Co. E 5th U.S. Cavalry)
— *gunshot wound, thorax, severe wound*

---

[63] Indians. Chronological List, 52; Heitman (Volume 2), 437; Record of Engagements, 33.
[64] Chronological List, 52.
[65] Indians. Chronological List, 52; Heitman (Volume 2), 437; Record of Engagements, 33. Chronological List lists 6th U.S. Infantry Detachments; Detachment of Indian Scouts.
[66] Reports of Diseases and Individual Cases, F 437.
[67] Indians. *Annual Report of Secretary of War (1872)*, 80; Chronological List, 52; Thrapp, *Conquest of Apacheria*, 116.
[68] Indians. *Annual Report of Secretary of War (1872)*, 80; Chronological List, 52; Heitman (Volume 2), 438; Alexander, *Arizona Frontier Military Place Names*, 47; Thrapp, *Conquest of Apacheria*, 115-116. Chronological List lists 2nd Lieutenant Reid T. Stewart (5th U.S. Cavalry) C/O.
[69] *Annual Report of Secretary of War (1872)*, 80.
[70] Indians. Killed was W.V. Goodrich. *Annual Report of Secretary of War (1872)*, 80; Chronological List, 52.
[71] Indians. Reports of Diseases and Individual Cases, F 438; Heitman (Volume 2), 438; Alexander, *Arizona Frontier Military Place Names*, 46-47, 91; Altshuler, *Chains of Command*, 216.
[72] Reports of Diseases and Individual Cases, F 438.

— *Sergeant Frank E. Hill (Co. E 5ᵗʰ U.S. Cavalry) received MOH: Secured the person of a hostile Apache Chief, although while holding the chief he was severely wounded in the back by another Indian (Date Creek, Arizona, September 8, 1872).*

(0748) Operations, between Beaver Creek and Sweet Water River, Wyoming Territory (September 10 to 13, 1872)[73]
— 1ˢᵗ Lieutenant Randolph Norwood (2ⁿᵈ U.S. Cavalry)
— 2ⁿᵈ U.S. Cavalry Co. B

(0749) Citizens, Crow Agency, Montana Territory (September 21, 1872)[74]
— (4) Citizens Killed

(0750) Action, Muchos Canyon, Santa Maria River, Arizona Territory (September 25, 1872)[75]
— Captain Julius W. Mason (5ᵗʰ U.S. Cavalry)
— 5ᵗʰ U.S. Cavalry Co. B, C and K
— Detachment of Indian Scouts
— **1 WOUNDED**[76]
— Hama-Hu-Mah (Indian Scout)
— *gunshot wound, neck, slight wound*

— *Captain Emil Adam (5ᵗʰ U.S. Cavalry) brevet promotion to Major for gallant service in action against Indians (Muchos Canyon, Arizona, September 25, 1872).*

— *2ⁿᵈ Lieutenant Francis Michler (5ᵗʰ U.S. Cavalry) brevet promotion to 1ˢᵗ Lieutenant for gallant service in actions against Indians (Muchos Canyon, Arizona, September 25, 1872 and Tonto Creek, Arizona, January 22, 1873).*

— *Captain Robert H. Montgomery (5ᵗʰ U.S. Cavalry) brevet promotion to Major for gallant service in action against Indians (Muchos Canyon, Arizona, September 25, 1872) and during a scout made by him (Tonto Basin, Arizona, November and December, 1874).*

— *2ⁿᵈ Lieutenant Walter S. Schuyler (5ᵗʰ U.S. Cavalry) brevet promotion to 1ˢᵗ Lieutenant for gallant service in actions against Indians (Muchos Canyon, Arizona, September 25, 1872; Lost River, Arizona, June 26, 1873; Salt River, Arizona, Arizona, April 28, 1874 and Red Rock Country, Arizona, May 14, 1874).*

(0751) Action, North Fork of Red River, Texas (September 29, 1872)[77]
— Colonel Ranald S. Mackenzie (4ᵗʰ U.S. Cavalry)
— 4ᵗʰ U.S. Cavalry Co. A, D, F, I and L
— Detachment of Indian Scouts
— **2 KILLED**[78]
— Private John Doral/ Dorcas/ Dorst (Co. F 4ᵗʰ U.S. Cavalry)
— Private John Kelly (Co. F 4ᵗʰ U.S. Cavalry)

---

[73] Indians. Chronological List, 52; Heitman (Volume 2), 438; Record of Engagements, 33.
[74] Indians. Killed were a man named Frost, two Crow women and a child. *Annual Report of Commissioner of Indian Affairs (1872)*, 274.
[75] Indians. *Annual Report of Commissioner of Indian Affairs (1872)*, 94; Chronological List, 52; Heitman (Volume 2), 438; Alexander, *Arizona Frontier Military Place Names*, 90-91; Altshuler, *Chains of Command*, 216-217; Thrapp, *Conquest of Apacheria*, 113-114. Chronological List lists 5ᵗʰ U.S. Cavalry Co. B, C, K.
[76] Reports of Diseases and Individual Cases, F 439.
[77] Indians. *Annual Report of Commissioner of Indian Affairs (1872)*, 93-94; Chronological List, 52; Heitman (Volume 2), 438; Record of Engagements, 33; Carter, *On the Border with Mackenzie*, 376-383; Hamilton, *Sentinel of the Southern Plains*, 132-133; Leckie, *Military Conquest of the Southern Plains*, 169-172; Neal, *Valor Across the Lone Star*, 128-136; Nye, *Carbine and Lance*, 161-163; Gwynne, *Empire of the Summer Moon*, 254-256; Robinson, *Bad Hand*, 119-121; Wallace, *Ranald S. Mackenzie*, 77-89.
[78] Reports of Diseases and Individual Cases, F 440.

— **2 WOUNDED**[79]
— Corporal Henry A. McMasters (Co. A 4th U.S. Cavalry)
— *gunshot wounds, left arm, chest, severe wounds*
— Private William Rankin (Co. F 4th U.S. Cavalry)
— *gunshot wound, abdomen, slight wound*

— *1st Lieutenant Peter M. Boehm (4th U.S. Cavalry) brevet promotion to Captain for gallant service in actions against Indians (Brazos River, Texas, October 28 and 29, 1869), special gallantry in action (Brazos River Texas, October 10, 1871) and gallant conduct in action against Indians (Red River, Texas, September 29, 1872).*

— *Private Edward Branagan (Co. F 4th U.S. Cavalry) received MOH: Gallantry in action (Red River, Texas, September 29, 1872).*

— *Captain Wirt Davis (4th U.S. Cavalry) brevet promotion to Lt. Colonel for gallant service in actions against Indians (North Fork of Red River, Texas, September 29, 1872 and Big Horn Mountains, Montana, November 25, 1876).*

— *Sergeant William Foster (Co. F 4th U.S. Cavalry) received MOH: Gallantry in action (Red River, Texas, September 29, 1872).*

— *Farrier David Larkin (Co. F 4th U.S. Cavalry) received MOH: Gallantry in action (Red River, Texas. September 29, 1872).*

— *Major Alfred E. Latimer (4th U.S. Cavalry) brevet promotion to Lt. Colonel for gallant service in action against Indians (North Fork of Red River, Texas, September 29, 1872).*

— *Corporal Henry A. McMasters (Co. A 4th U.S. Cavalry) received MOH: Gallantry in action (Red River, Texas, September 29, 1872).*

— *First Sergeant William McNamara (Co. F 4th U.S. Cavalry) received MOH: Gallantry in action (Red River, Texas, September 29, 1872).*

— *Corporal William O'Neill (Co. I 4th U.S. Cavalry) received MOH: Bravery in action (Red River, Texas, September 29, 1872).*

— *Blacksmith James Pratt (Co. I 4th U.S. Cavalry) received MOH: Gallantry in action (Red River, Texas, September 29, 1872).*

— *Private William Rankin (Co. F 4th U.S. Cavalry) received MOH: Gallantry in action with Indians (Red River, Texas, September 29, 1872).*

---

[79] Reports of Diseases and Individual Cases, F 440.

— *Sergeant William Wilson (Co. I 4th U.S. Cavalry) received MOH: Distinguished conduct in action with Indians (Red River, Texas, September 29, 1872).*

(0752) Skirmish, Squaw Peak, Arizona Territory (September 30, 1872)[80]
    — 1st Lieutenant Max Wesendorf (1st U.S. Cavalry)
        — 1st U.S. Cavalry Detachment Co. A

    — *1st Lieutenant Max Wesendorf (1st U.S. Cavalry) brevet promotion to Captain for gallant service in action against Indians (Squaw Peak, Arizona, September 30, 1872).*

(0753) Action, near Camp Crittenden, Arizona Territory (September 30, 1872)[81]
    — Sergeant George Stewart (5th U.S. Cavalry)
        — 5th U.S. Cavalry Co. F
  — **4 KILLED**[82]
    — Sergeant George Stewart (Co. F 5th U.S. Cavalry)
    — Private Andrew Carr (Co. F 5th U.S. Cavalry)
    — Private William Nation (Co. F 5th U.S. Cavalry)
    — Private John Walsh (Co. F 5th U.S. Cavalry)

(0754) Action, Fort McKeen, Dakota Territory (October 2, 1872)[83]
    — Lt. Colonel Daniel Huston, jr. (6th U.S. Infantry)
        — 6th U.S. Infantry Co. C
        — Detachment of Indian Scouts
  — **3 KILLED**[84]
    — Red Bear (Indian Scout)
    — Chief Youngman (Indian Scout)
    — Crow's Tail (Indian Scout)

  — **1 WOUNDED**[85]
    — Bear in the Bush (Indian Scout)

(0755) Action, near Fort McKeen, Dakota Territory (October 14, 1872)[86]
    — Lt. Colonel William P. Carlin (17th U.S. Infantry)
        — 6th U.S. Infantry Co. C
        — 17th U.S. Infantry Co. H
        — Detachment of Indian Scouts
  — **2 KILLED**[87]
    — (2) Citizens

(0756) Operations, near Santa Maria Mountains or Sycamore Creek, Arizona Territory (October 25 to November 3, 1872)[88]
    — Captain Julius W. Mason (5th U.S. Cavalry)

---

[80] Indians. *Annual Report of Commissioner of Indian Affairs (1872)*, 94; Chronological List, 52; Heitman (Volume 2), 438.
[81] Indians. Chronological List, 52; Heitman (Volume 2), 438; Thrapp, *Conquest of Apacheria*, 117-118. Heitman lists 5th U.S. Cavalry Detachment Co. F.
[82] 5th U.S. Cavalry Regimental Return September 1872.
[83] Indians. Chronological List, 52; Heitman (Volume 2), 438; Record of Engagements, 33; Lubetkin, *Jay Cooke's Gamble*, 159-160. Heitman lists 6th U.S. Infantry Co. B, C; Detachment of Indian Scouts.
[84] Register of Deaths Regular Army, 1860-1889 (Volume 5); Fort McKeen/Fort Lincoln Cemetery Records.
[85] Reports of Diseases and Individual Cases, F 441.
[86] Indians. Chronological List, 52; Heitman (Volume 2), 438; Record of Engagements, 34. Heitman lists 6th U.S. Infantry Co. B, C; 17th U.S. Infantry Co. H; Detachment of Indian Scouts.
[87] Chronological List, 52.
[88] Indians. Chronological List, 52; Heitman (Volume 2), 438. Chronological List and Heitman both list 5th U.S. Cavalry Co. B, C, K.

— 5th U.S. Cavalry Co. B, C and K
— Detachment of Indian Scouts
— **1 KILLED**[89]
— Keh-An-Tah (Indian Scout)

— **1 WOUNDED**[90]
— Qual-Ten-E-Quam-Yah (Indian Scout)
— *gunshot wound, head, slight wound*

(0757) Action, Red Rocks or Hell Canyon, Arizona Territory (November 25, 1872)[91]
— Captain Emil Adam (5th U.S. Cavalry)
— 5th U.S. Cavalry Co. C
— Detachment of Indian Scouts
— **1 KILLED**[92]
— Indian Scout

— **1 WOUNDED**[93]
— Sergeant Michael Madigan (Co. C 5th U.S. Cavalry)

(0758) Action, near Lost River, Oregon (November 29, 1872)[94]
— Captain James Jackson (1st U.S. Cavalry)
— 1st U.S. Cavalry Co. B
— **2 KILLED**[95]
— Private Daniel Gallagher (Co. B 1st U.S. Cavalry) — d. 12-12-1872
— Private James Harris (Co. B 1st U.S. Cavalry)

— **6 WOUNDED**[96]
— Corporal Alfred W. Challinor (Co. B 1st U.S. Cavalry)
— *gunshot wound, slight wound*
— Corporal Thomas Fitzgerald (Co. B 1st U.S. Cavalry)
— *gunshot wound, hip, severe wound*
— Private John Doyle (Co. B 1st U.S. Cavalry)
— *gunshot wound, thigh, slight wound*
— Private Frank Kasshafer (Co. B 1st U.S. Cavalry)
— *gunshot and arrow wounds, thigh, severe wounds*
— Private Edward Kenshaw (Co. B 1st U.S. Cavalry)
— *gunshot wound, face, slight wound*
— Private James D. Totten (Co. B 1st U.S. Cavalry)
— *gunshot wound, left hand, slight wound*

[89] Reports of Diseases and Individual Cases, F 443.
[90] Reports of Diseases and Individual Cases, F 443.
[91] Indians. Chronological List, 52; Heitman (Volume 2), 438; Alexander, *Arizona Frontier Military Place Names*, 69; Thrapp, *Conquest of Apacheria*, 121.
[92] 5th U.S. Cavalry Regimental Return November 1873.
[93] 5th U.S. Cavalry Regimental Return November 1873.
[94] Indians. *Annual Report of Commissioner of Indian Affairs (1873)*, 80-81; Chronological List, 52; Heitman (Volume 2), 438; Dillon, *Burnt Out Fires*, 127-140; Murray, *Modocs and Their War*, 82-90; Thompson, *Modoc War*, 14-18.
[95] Reports of Diseases and Individual Cases, F 435.
[96] Reports of Diseases and Individual Cases, F 435.

— *2nd Lieutenant Frazier A. Bouetelle (1st U.S. Cavalry) brevet promotion to 1st Lieutenant for gallantry in action against Indians (Lost River, Oregon, November 29, 1872) and conspicuous gallantry during the whole Modoc War.*

— *Captain James Jackson (1st U.S. Cavalry) brevet promotion to Lt. Colonel for gallant and meritorious service in action against Indians (Modoc War, especially in the action on Lost River, Oregon, November 29, 1872) and gallant service in action against Indians (Clearwater, Idaho, July 12, 1877).*

(0759) Action, near Lost River, Oregon (November 29, 1872)[97]
    — Oliver Applegate (Citizen)
        — Detachment of Oregon Volunteers
  — **2 KILLED**[98]
        — Jack Thurber (Citizen)
        — William Nus (Citizen)

  — **1 WOUNDED**[99]
        — Joe Penning (Citizen)

(0760) Skirmish, Red Rock Country, Arizona Territory (December 7 and 8, 1872)[100]
    — 1st Lieutenant William F. Rice (23rd U.S. Infantry)
        — 5th U.S. Cavalry Detachment Co. K
    — 23rd U.S. Infantry Detachment Co. G
        — Detachment of Indian Scouts

(0761) Skirmish, Bad Rock Mountains, north of Old Fort Reno, Arizona Territory (December 11, 1872)[101]
    — 1st Lieutenant Thomas Garvey (1st U.S. Cavalry)
        — 1st U.S. Cavalry Detachments Co. L and M
        — 23rd U.S. Infantry Detachment Co. I
        — Detachment of Indian Scouts

(0762) Skirmish, Mazatzal Mountains, north of Old Fort Reno, Arizona Territory (December 13, 1872)[102]
    — 1st Lieutenant William C. Manning (23rd U.S. Infantry)
        — 1st U.S. Cavalry Detachments Co. L and M
        — 23rd U.S. Infantry Detachment Co. I
        — Detachment of Indian Scouts

— *2nd Lieutenant Peter S. Bomus (1st U.S. Cavalry) brevet promotion to 1st Lieutenant for gallant service in action against Indians (Mazatzal Mountains, Arizona, December 13, 1872).*

---

[97] Indians. *Annual Report of Commissioner of Indian Affairs (1873)*, 80-81; Dillon, *Burnt Out Fires*, 131-133; Murray, *Modocs and Their War*, 82-90; Nelson, *Fighting for Paradise*, 177-179; Thompson, *Modoc War*, 18-20.
[98] Dillon, *Burnt Out Fires*, 132; Murray, *Modocs and Their War*, 88-89; Thompson, *Modoc War*, 19-20.
[99] Dillon, *Burnt Out Fires*, 132; Murray, *Modocs and Their War*, 89; Thompson, *Modoc War*, 19-20.
[100] Indians. Chronological List, 53; Heitman (Volume 2), 438; Thrapp, *Conquest of Apacheria*, 122-123. Heitman lists 5th U.S. Cavalry Co. K; 23rd U.S. Infantry Detachment Co. G; Detachment of Indian Scouts.
[101] Indians. Chronological List, 53; Heitman (Volume 2), 438; Alexander, *Arizona Military Place Names*, 9; Thrapp, *Conquest of Apacheria*, 124.
[102] Indians. Chronological List, 53; Heitman (Volume 2), 438; Thrapp, *Conquest of Apacheria*, 124.

— *1st Lieutenant William C. Manning (23rd U.S. Infantry) brevet promotion to Captain for gallant service in action against Indians (Mazatzal Mountains, Arizona, December 13, 1872).*

(0763) Skirmish, Indian Run, near Verde River, Arizona Territory (December 14, 1872)[103]
     — Captain George F. Price (5th U.S. Cavalry)
         — 5th U.S. Cavalry Co. E

(0764) Action, Red Rocks, Arizona Territory (December 15, 1872)[104]
     — 2nd Lieutenant Frank Michler (5th U.S. Cavalry)
         — 5th U.S. Cavalry Co. K
         — Detachment of Indian Scouts
   — **1 KILLED**[105]
         — Hat-Ta-Hu-Mah (Indian Scout)

   — **1 WOUNDED**[106]
         — Che-Set-Ak-Ab (Indian Scout)
            — *gunshot wound, head, slight wound*

(0765) Action, near Land's Ranch, Tule Lake, California (December 21, 1872)[107]
     — Captain Reuben F. Bernard (1st U.S. Cavalry)
         — 1st U.S. Cavalry Co. G
   — **2 KILLED**[108]
         — Private Sidney A. Smith (Co. G 1st U.S. Cavalry)
         — Private William Donahue (Co. G 1st U.S. Cavalry) — d. 12-22-1872

(0766) Action, Salt River Canyon, Arizona Territory (December 28, 1872)[109]
     — Captain William H. Brown (5th U.S. Cavalry)
         — 5th U.S. Cavalry Co. G, L and M
         — Detachment of Indian Scouts
   — **1 KILLED**[110]
         — Indian Scout

   — **1 WOUNDED**[111]
         — Indian Scout

— *2nd Lieutenant John G. Bourke (3rd U.S. Cavalry) brevet promotion to Captain for gallant service in actions against Indians (Caves, Arizona, December 28, 1872).*

— *Captain Alfred B. Taylor (5th U.S. Cavalry) brevet promotion to Major for gallant service in actions against Indians (Caves, Arizona, December 28, 1872).*

[103] Indians. Chronological List, 53; Heitman (Volume 2), 438; Thrapp, *Conquest of Apacheria*, 122-123.
[104] Indians. Reports of Diseases and Individual Cases, F 444.
[105] Reports of Diseases and Individual Cases, F 444.
[106] Reports of Diseases and Individual Cases, F 444.
[107] Indians. Chronological List, 53; Heitman (Volume 2), 438; Dillon, *Burnt Out Fires*, 164-165; Murray, *Modocs and Their War*, 107-108; Russell, *One Hundred Three Fights*, 97; Thompson, *Modoc War*, 29-30. Chronological List lists 2 December 1872.
[108] Reports of Diseases and Individual Cases, F 431.
[109] Indians. Chronological List, 53; Heitman (Volume 2), 438; Alexander, *Arizona Military Place Names*, 4; King, *War Eagle*, 133-134; Lockwood, *Apache Indians*, 196-199; Thrapp, *Conquest of Apacheria*, 127-130.
[110] "one Pima killed and one wounded". Camp McDowell Post Return December 1872.
[111] "one Pima killed and one wounded". Camp McDowell Post Return December 1872.

— *1ˢᵗ Lieutenant Earl D. Thomas (5ᵗʰ U.S. Cavalry) brevet promotion to Captain for gallant service in action against Indians (Caves, Arizona, December 28, 1872) and distinguished service in the campaign against Indians (Arizona, 1874).*

(0767) Skirmish, Mouth of Baby Canyon, Arizona Territory (December 30, 1872)[112]
   — Sergeant W. L. Day (5ᵗʰ U.S. Cavalry)
      — 5ᵗʰ U.S. Cavalry Detachment Co. E

— *First Sergeant William L. Day (Co. E 5ᵗʰ U.S. Cavalry) received MOH: Gallant conduct during campaigns and engagements with Apaches (Arizona, 1872 to 1873).*

— *Kelsay (Indian Scout) received MOH: Gallant conduct during campaigns and engagements with Apaches (Arizona, Winter of 1872 to 1873).*

— *Machol (Indian Scout) received MOH: Gallant conduct during campaign and engagements with Apaches (Arizona, 1872 to 1873).*

— *Nannasaddie (Indian Scout) received MOH: Gallant conduct during campaigns and engagements with Apaches (Arizona, 1872 to 1873).*

— *Nantaje (Indian Scout) received MOH: Gallant conduct during campaigns and engagements with Apaches (Arizona, 1872 to 1873).*

— *Sergeant Rudolph Von Medem (Co. A 5ᵗʰ U.S. Cavalry) received MOH: Gallantry in actions and campaigns (Arizona, 1872 to 1873).*

— *First Sergeant James H. Turpin (Co. L 5ᵗʰ U.S. Cavalry) received MOH: Gallantry in action with Apaches (Arizona, 1872 to 1874).*

— *Alchesay (Indian Scout) received MOH: Gallant conduct during campaigns and engagements with Apaches (Winter of 1872 to 1873).*

— *Sergeant James E. Bailey (Co. E 5ᵗʰ U.S. Cavalry) received MOH: Gallant conduct during campaigns and engagements with Apaches (Winter of 1872 to 1873).*

— *First Sergeant Clay Beauford (Co. B 5ᵗʰ U.S. Cavalry) received MOH: Gallant conduct during the campaigns and engagements with Apaches (Winter of 1872 to 1873).*

— *First Sergeant James Blair (Co. I 1ˢᵗ U.S. Cavalry) received MOH: Gallant conduct during campaigns and engagements with Apaches (Winter of 1872 to 1873).*

---

[112] Indians. Chronological List, 53; Heitman (Volume 2), 438; Alexander, *Arizona Military Place Names*, 8-9; Thrapp, *Conquest of Apacheria*, 132.

— *Blanquet (Indian Scout) received MOH: Gallant conduct during the campaigns and engagements with Apaches (Winter of 1872 to 1873).*

— *Elsatsoosu (Indian Scout) received MOH: Gallant conduct during campaigns and engagements with Apaches (Winter of 1872 to 1873).*

— *Sergeant Lehmann Hinemann (Co. L 1ˢᵗ U.S. Cavalry) received MOH: Gallant conduct during campaigns and engagements with Apaches (Winter of 1872 to 1873).*

— *Private James W. Huff (Co. I 1ˢᵗ U.S. Cavalry) received MOH: Gallant conduct during campaigns and engagements with Apache (Winter of 1872 to 1873).*

— *Sergeant Henry J. Hyde (Co. M 1ˢᵗ U.S. Cavalry) received MOH: Gallant conduct during campaigns and engagements with Apaches (Winter of 1872 to 1873).*

— *Kosoha (Indian Scout) received MOH: Gallant conduct during campaigns and engagements with Apaches (Winter of 1872 to 1873).*

— *Private Moses Orr (Co. A 1ˢᵗ U.S. Cavalry) received MOH: Gallant conduct during campaigns and engagements with Apaches (Winter of 1872 to 1873).*

— *Sergeant William Osborne (Co. M 1ˢᵗ U.S. Cavalry) received MOH: Gallant conduct during campaigns and engagements with Apaches (Winter of 1872 to 1873).*

TOTAL KILLED 1872 — 4/14/9/5

1873

"To give protection to the citizens of the frontier against these Indians and to guard the long line of our Mexican border against robberies by Mexicn citizens and Indians living in Mexico; to explore unknown territory and furnish escorts to surveying parties for scientific purposes and for projected railraods; to assist and guard the railways already built and other commerical lines of travel; to aid in the enforcement of civil law in remote places; and to do generally all that is constantly requeired of our Army in the way of helping and urging forward civilization upon the border, and at the same time to protect the Indians in the rights and immunities guaranteed them under existing treaties, has been the work of the troops... for the past year, and that work has beem successfully accomplished."

— Philiip H. Sheridan, U.S. Army[1]

---

[1] Official Report of Lieutenant General Phillip H. Sheridan, Military Division of the Missouri, 27 October 1873. *Annual Report of Secretary of War (1873)*, 40.

(0768) Action, Clear Creek Canyon, Arizona Territory (January 2, 1873)[2]
— 1st Lieutenant William F. Rice (23rd U.S. Infantry)
— 5th U.S. Cavalry Detachment Co. K
— 23rd U.S. Infantry Co. G
— Detachment of Indian Scouts
— **1 WOUNDED**[3]
— Private John Baker (Co. K 5th U.S. Cavalry)
— *gunshot wound, head*

— *Private James Lenihan (Co. K 5th U.S. Cavalry) received MOH: Gallantry in action (Clear Creek, Arizona, January 2, 1873).*

(0769) Action, Tule Lake, California (January 12, 1873)[4]
— Captain Reuben F. Bernard (1st U.S. Cavalry)
— 1st U.S. Cavalry Co. G
— **1 WOUNDED**[5]
— Private Warren Jefferson (Co. G 1st U.S. Cavalry)
— *thigh*

(0770) Skirmish, Superstitious Mountains, Arizona Territory (January 16, 1873)[6]
— Captain William H. Brown (5th U.S. Cavalry)
— 5th U.S. Cavalry Co. B, C, G, H, L and M

— *Captain John M. Hamilton (5th U.S. Cavalry) brevet promotion to Major for gallant service in action against Tonto Apache Indians in connection with the closing campaigns against these Indians (Tortilla Mountains, Arizona, January 16, 1873).*

(0771) Engagement, Modoc Caves in Lava Beds, near Tule Lake, California (January 17, 1873)[7]
— Lt. Colonel Frank Wheaton (21st U.S. Infantry)
— 1st U.S. Cavalry Co. B, F and G
— 21st U.S. Infantry Co. B and C, Detachment Co. F
— Detachment of California Volunteers
— Detachment of Oregon Volunteers
— **11 KILLED**[8]
— 1st Lieutenant George Roberts (Fairchild's Detachment California Volunteers)
— d. 2-09-1873

[2] Indians. Chronological List, 53; Heitman (Volume 2), 438; Price, *Across the Continent*, 659. Heitman lists 5th U.S. Cavalry Detachment Co. K; 23rd U.S. Infantry Detachment Co. G.
[3] Reports of Diseases and Individual Cases, F 446.
[4] Indians. Chronological List, 53; Heitman (Volume 2), 438; Dillon, *Burnt Out Fires*, 168.
[5] 1st U.S. Cavalry Regimental Return January 1873.
[6] Indians. Chronological List, 53; Heitman (Volume 2), 438; Thrapp, *Conquest of Apacheria*, 131-132.
[7] Indians. Chronological List, 53; Heitman (Volume 2), 438; Dillon, *Burnt Out Fires*, 170-179; Murray, *Modocs and Their War*, 114-126; Russell, *One Hundred and Three Fights*, 101-103; Thompson, *Modoc War*, 33-44.
[8] Reports of Diseases and Individual Cases, F 432.

— Private George Hollas (Co. F 1st U.S. Cavalry)
— Private Charles W. Lavelle (Co. G 1st U.S. Cavalry)
— Private Patrick Maher (1st U.S. Cavalry) — d. 1-22-1873

— Private Carl Glaeman (Co. B 21st U.S. Infantry)
— Private James Munroe (Co. B 21st U.S. Infantry)
— Private John Branner (Co. C 21st U.S. Infantry)
— Private John Benson (Co. F 21st U.S. Infantry)
— Private Robert Long (Co. F 21st U.S. Infantry)

— Private John Brown (1st Regiment Oregon Volunteers)
— Private Frank Trimble (1st Regiment Oregon Volunteers)

— 21 WOUNDED[9]

— Captain David Perry (Co. F 1st U.S. Cavalry)
    — *gunshot wound, left arm, slight wound*
— 2nd Lieutenant John G. Kyle (Co. G 1st U.S. Cavalry)
    — *gunshot wound, left arm, slight wound*

— Sergeant William Connally (Co. B 1st U.S. Cavalry)
    — *gunshot wound, right thigh, slight wound*
— Private Frank McBride (Co. B 1st U.S. Cavalry)
    — *gunshot wound, right thigh, slight wound*

— Corporal Julius Eisenman (Co. F 1st U.S. Cavalry)
    — *gunshot wound, left arm, slight wound*
— Private Patrick Doyle (Co. F 1st U.S. Cavalry)
    — *gunshot wound, right arm, fracture, severe wound*
— Private Otis Gutermuth (Co. F 1st U.S. Cavalry)
    — *gunshot wound, side, severe wound*

— Sergeant Gerhardt Licht (Co. G 1st U.S. Cavalry)
    — *gunshot wound, right leg, severe wound*
— Private John Anderson (Co. G 1st U.S. Cavalry)
    — *gunshot wound, left arm, slight wound*
— Private Frederick Cutter (Co. G 1st U.S. Cavalry)
    — *gunshot wound, slight wound*

---

[9] Reports of Diseases and Individual Cases, F 432.
[10] Indians. Chronological List, 53; Heitman (Volume 2), 438; Price, *Across the Continent*, 659; Thrapp, *Conquest of Apacheria*, 132-133. Heitman lists 5th U.S. Cavalry Detachment Co. E

— Private Warner Jefferson (Co. G 1st U.S. Cavalry)
    — *gunshot wound, left thigh, slight wound*
— Private William Warren (Co. G 1st U.S. Cavalry)
    — *gunshot would, face, slight wound*

— Sergeant Josiah S. Brown (Co. B 21st U.S. Infantry)
    — *gunshot wound, left arm, slight wound*
— Private Ole Anderson (Co. B 21st U.S. Infantry)
    — *gunshot wound, right thigh, severe wound*
— Private Isaac Miller (Co. C 21st U.S. Infantry)
    — *gunshot wound, left elbow, fracture, severe wound*
— Private Simeon Olsen (Co. C 21st U.S. Infantry)
    — *gunshot wound, right arm, severe wound*
— Private James Murphy (Co. C 21st U.S. Infantry)
    — *gunshot wound, right hand, fracture*
— Private Samuel P. Jones (Co. F 21st U.S. Infantry)
    — *gunshot wound, right hand, slight wound*

— Private Nathaniel Beswick (Fairchild's Detachment California Volunteers)
    — *gunshot wound, left thigh, slight wound*
— Private W.J. Small (Fairchild's Detachment California Volunteers)
    — *gunshot wound, shoulder, severe wound*
— Private Jeremiah Crooks (Fairchild's Detachment California Volunteers)
    — *gunshot wounds, left thigh, right hand, severe wounds*

— *Captain George H. Burton (21st U.S. Infantry) brevet promotion to Major for gallant service in actions against Indians (Lava Beds, California, January 17, 1873 and Clearwater, Idaho, July 11 and 12, 1877).*

— *Major John Green (1st U.S. Cavalry) brevet promotion to Brigadier General for gallant service in actions against Indians (Lava Beds, California, January 17, 1873 and in several actions during the Modoc War).*

— *Major John Green (1st U.S. Cavalry) received MOH: In order to reassure his command, this officer, in the most fearless manner and exposed to very great danger, walked in front of the line, the command, thus encouraged, advanced over the lava upon the Indians who were concealed among the rocks (Lava Beds, California, January 17, 1873).*

— *Assistant Surgeon Henry McElderry brevet promotion to Major for meritorious service in action against Indians (Double Mountain Fork of Brazos River, Texas, May 7, 1869) and for gallant service in action against Indians (Lava Beds, California, January 17, 1873).*

— *John O. Skinner (Contract Surgeon, U.S. Army) received MOH: Rescued a wounded soldier who lay under a close and heavy fire during the assault on the Modoc stronghold after two soldiers had unsuccessfully attempted to make the rescue and both had been wounded in doing so (Lava Beds, California, January 17, 1873).*

(0772) Skirmish, East Fork of Verde River, Arizona Territory (January 19, 1873)[10]
    — First Sergeant William L. Day (5th U.S. Cavalry)
        — Detachment of Scouts

(0773) Skirmish, Lower Miembres, New Mexico Territory (January 20, 1873)[11]
— 1st Lieutenant Jonathan D. Stevenson (8th U.S. Cavalry)
— 8th U.S. Cavalry Co. I

(0774) Action, Tonto Creek, Arizona Territory (January 22, 1873)[12]
— 2nd Lieutenant Francis Michler (5th U.S. Cavalry)
— 5th U.S. Cavalry Co. K
— **1 KILLED**[13]
— Private George Hooker (Co. K 5th U.S. Cavalry)

— Private George Hooker (Co. K 5th U.S. Cavalry) received MOH: Gallantry in action in which he was killed (Tonto Creek, Arizona, January 22, 1873).

— 2nd Lieutenant Francis Michler (5th U.S. Cavalry) brevet promotion to 1st Lieutenant for gallant service in actions against Indians (Muchos Canyon, Arizona, September 25, 1872 and Tonto Creek, Arizona, January 22, 1873).

"Private George Hooker was foremost of the party that came up on one side of the Rancheria. I regret his loss exceedingly, as [Hooker] was an excellent soldier, brave and trustworthy. I cannot speak too highly of the conduct of the men, especially in the fight. Their behavior throughout is deserving of the highest commendation."
— Francis Michler, U.S. Army[14]

(0775) Skirmish, Hell Canyon, Arizona Territory (February 6, 1873)[15]
— Captain Thomas McGregor (1st U.S. Cavalry)
— 1st U.S. Cavalry Detachment Co. A

(0776) Skirmish, near Fossil Creek, Arizona Territory (February 20, 1873)[16]
— Captain CaMillo C.C. Carr (1st U.S. Cavalry)
— 1st U.S. Cavalry Co. I

(0777) Skirmish, Angostura, New Mexico Territory (February 26, 1873)[17]
— Sergeant J.F. Rowalt (8th U.S. Cavalry)
—8th U.S. Cavalry Co. L

(0778) Citizens, near Camp Supply, Indian Territory (March 18, 1873)[18]
— (4) Citizens Killed

[11] Indians. Chronological List, 53; Heitman (Volume 2), 438.
[12] Indians. Chronological List, 53; Heitman (Volume 2), 438; Price, *Across the Continent*, 659; Thrapp, *Conquest of Apacheria*, 133.
[13] 5th U.S. Cavalry Regimental Return January 1873.
[14] Official Report of 2nd Lieutenant Francis Michler (5th U.S. Cavalry), 7 February 1873. Price, *Across the Continent*, 675.
[15] Indians. Chronological List, 53; Heitman (Volume 2), 438; Thrapp, *Conquest of Apacheria*, 133.
[16] Indians. Chronological List, 53; Heitman (Volume 2), 438.
[17] Indians. Chronological List, 53; Heitman (Volume 2), 438.
[18] Indians. Killed were Chief Surveyor A.N. Deming and three others. *Annual Report of Commissioner of Indian Affairs (1873)*, 221; Hoig, *Tribal Wars of the Southern Plains*, 18, 291; Leckie, *Buffalo Soldiers*, 73.

(0779) Skirmish, Mazatzal Mountains, Arizona Territory (March 19, 1873)[19]
— 2nd Lieutenant Francis Michler (5th U.S. Cavalry)
— 5th U.S. Cavalry Co. K

(0780) Skirmish, near Turret Mountains, Arizona Territory (March 25, 1873)[20]
— First Sergeant James M. Hill (5th U.S. Cavalry)
— 5th U.S. Cavalry Detachment Co. A

— Sergeant Daniel Bishop (Co. A 5th U.S. Cavalry) received MOH: Gallantry in engagements (Turret Mountain, Arizona, March 25, 1873).

— First Sergeant James M. Hill (Co. A 5th U.S. Cavalry) received MOH: Gallantry in action (Turret Mountain, Arizona, March 25, 1873).

— Private Eben Stanley (Co. A 5th U.S. Cavalry) received MOH: Gallantry in action (Turret Mountain, Arizona, March 25 and 27, 1873).

(0781) Skirmish, Turret Mountains, Arizona Territory (March 27, 1873)[21]
— Captain George M. Randall (23rd U.S. Infantry)
— 5th U.S. Cavalry Detachment Co. A
— 23rd U.S. Infantry Detachment Co. I
— Detachment of Indian Scouts

— First Sergeant William Allen (Co. I 23rd U.S. Infantry) received MOH: Gallantry in action (Turret Mountain, Arizona, March 27, 1873).

— Captain George M. Randall (23rd U.S. Infantry) brevet promotion to Lt. Colonel for gallant service in actions against Indians (Turret Mountains, Arizona, March 27, 1873 and Diamond Butte, Arizona, April 22, 1873).

(0782) Action, near Lava Beds, California (April 11, 1873)[22]
— Brigadier General Edward R.S. Canby (Commander Department of Columbia)
— Peace Delegation to Modoc Indians
— **2 KILLED**[23]
— Brigadier General Edward R.S. Canby (Commander Department of Columbia)
— Reverend Eleasar Thomas (Citizen)

---

[19] Indians. Chronological List, 53; Heitman (Volume 2), 438; Price, *Across the Continent*, 659; Thrapp, *Conquest of Apacheria*, 135.
[20] Indians. Chronological List, 53; Heitman (Volume 2), 438; Price, *Across the Continent*, 660; Thrapp, *Conquest of Apacheria*, 137.
[21] Indians. Chronological List, 54; Heitman (Volume 2), 438; Alexander, *Arizona Frontier Military Place Names*, 123-125; Thrapp, *Conquest of Apacheria*, 135-137.
[22] Indians. *Annual Report of Commissioner of Indian Affairs (1873)*, 16-17; 74-78; Chronological List, 54; Heitman (Volume 2), 438; Dillon, *Burnt Out Fires*, 230-232, 236-240; Heyman, *Prudent Soldier*, 375-377; Miles, *Personal Recollections*, 152-155; Murray, *Modocs and Their War*, 180-192; Russell, *One Hundred and Three Fights*, 108; Thompson, *Modoc War*, 59-65. Chronological List and Heitman both list a single entry 11 to 20 April 1873.
[23] Dillon, *Burnt Out Fires*, 237-238; Murray, *Modocs and Their War*, 189-190.

— **1 WOUNDED**[24]
　　— Superintendant Alfred B. Meacham (Citizen)
　　　　— *gunshot wounds, head, face, right arm; knife wound, head*

"Though dead, the record of [General Edward Canby's] fame is resplendent with noble deeds well done, and no name on our Army Register stands fairer or higher for the personal qualities that command the universal respect, honor, affection and love of his countrymen. General Canby leaves to his country a heart-broken widow...."
　　　　　　— William D. Whipple, U.S. Army[25]

"What we reverence after all, is character - broad, strong, noble character. We have ready applause for brilliant deeds, and are no slow to admire genius; and yet the thing which most commands our profound and abiding reverence in not the flash of some brilliant achievement, but the steady, strong, broad progress of noble character. And this is the kind of power with which the memory of General Canby comes to us today. He was great in war and good, and equally so in peace."
　　　　　　— J.H. Bayliss, Citizen[26]

(0783) Engagement, Lava Beds, California (April 11, 15 to 17, 1873)[27]
　　— Colonel Alvan C. Gillem (1st U.S. Cavalry)
　　　　— 1st U.S. Cavalry Co. B, F, G, H and K
　　　　— 12th U.S. Infantry Co. E and G
　　　　— 21st U.S. Infantry Co. B, C and I
　　　　— 4th U.S. Artillery Co. A, B, E, G, H and K
　　　　— Detachment of Indian Scouts
　— **8 KILLED**[28]
　　　　— 1st Lieutenant William L. Sherwood (21st U.S. Infantry) — d. 4-14-1873

　　　　— Bugler William W. Seales (Co. F 1st U.S. Cavalry) — d. 4-15-1873
　　　　— Private Charles Johnson (Co. K 1st U.S. Cavalry) — d. 4-13-1873
　　　　— Corporal Edward Drew (Co. G 12th U.S. Infantry) — d. 4-15-1873

　　　　— Sergeant Richard Morgan (Co. E 4th U.S. Artillery) — d. 4-17-1873
　　　　— Bugler William Smith (Co. M 4th U.S. Artillery) — d. 4-16-1873
　　　　— Private Henry C. Harmon (Co. E 4th U.S. Artillery) — d. 4-16-1873

　　　　— Eugene Hovey (Citizen)

　— **14 WOUNDED**[29]
　　　　— 1st Lieutenant Charles O. Eagan (12th U.S. Infantry)
　　　　　　— *gunshot wound, left thigh, slight wound*

[24] Dillon, *Burnt Out Fires*, 238-239; Murray, *Modocs and Their War*, 190-191.
[25] By Command of General William T. Sherman. Miles, *Personal Recollections*, 155.
[26] Reverend J. H. Bayliss' eulogy of General Edward Canby. *Indianapolis Sentinel*, 24 May 1873. Heyman, *Prudent Soldier*, 383.
[27] Indians. Chronological List, 54; Heitman (Volume 2), 438; Dillon, *Burnt Out Fires*, 233-236, 249-259; Murray, *Modocs and Their War*, 192-222; Russell, *One Hundred and Three Fights*, 106-109; Thompson, *Modoc War*, 61-78. Chronological List and Heitman both list a single entry, 11 to 20 April 1873. Heitman lists 1st U.S. Cavalry Co. B, F, G, H, K; 12th U.S. Infantry Co. E, G; 21st U.S. Infantry B, C, I, Detachment Co. F; 4th U.S. Artillery Co. A, E, K, M; Detachment of Indian Scouts.
[28] Reports of Diseases and Individual Cases, F 433; Register of Deaths Regular Army, 1860-1889 (Volume 5).
[29] Reports of Diseases and Individual Cases, F 433.

— Private John Jones (Co. F 1st U.S. Cavalry)
   — *gunshot wound, right hand, severe wound*
— Private Thomas Bernard (Co. K 1st U.S. Cavalry)
   — *gunshot wound, left shoulder, fracture, severe wound*
— Sergeant Herman Gude (Co. G 12th U.S. Infantry)
   — *gunshot wound, right leg, fracture, severe wound*
— Private Martin Connard (Co. G 12th U.S. Infantry)
   — *gunshot wound, right leg, slight wound*

— Private William Cunningham (Co. E 4th U.S. Artillery)
   — *gunshot wound, back, slight wound*
— Private Terrence McManus (Co. E 4th U.S. Artillery)
   — *gunshot wounds, left thigh, fracture, left hand, severe wound*
— Private Henry Meakins (Co. E 4th U.S. Artillery)
   — *gunshot wound, right leg, slight wound*

— Corporal Dennis Delaney (Co. K 4th U.S. Artillery)
   — *gunshot wound, left leg, slight wound*
— Corporal Edward Kilreck (Co. K 4th U.S. Artillery)
   — *gunshot wound, head, slight wound*
— Private Owen Dooley (Co. K 4th U.S. Artillery)
   — *gunshot wound, right arm, slight wound*
— Private Eugene O'Connor (Co. M 4th U.S. Artillery)
   — *gunshot wound, left leg, slight wound*

— Callus Bob (Indian Scout)
   — *gunshot wound, left leg, slight wound*
— Nez Perce Joe (Indian Scout)
   — *gunshot wound, right knee, slight wound*

— *1st Lieutenant Charles C. Cresson (1st U.S. Cavalry) brevet promotion to Lt. Colonel for gallant and meritorious serve in action against Indians (Lava Beds, California, April 17, 1873) and gallant service in action against Indians (Camas Meadows, Idaho, August 20, 1877).*

— *1st Lieutenant Charles P. Eagan (12th U.S. Infantry) brevet promotion to Captain for gallant service in action against Indians (Lava Beds, California, April 17, 1873, where he was wounded).*

— *1st Lieutenant Peter Leary Jr. (4th U.S. Artillery) brevet promotion to Captain for gallant and meritorious service in actions against Indians (Lava Bed, California, April 15 and 16, 1874).*

— *Major Edwin C. Mason (21st U.S. Infantry) brevet promotion to Brigadier General for gallant and meritorious service in actions against Indians (Lava Beds, California, April 17, 1873 and Clearwater, Idaho, July 11 and 12, 1877).*

— *Captain Marcus P. Miller (4th U.S. Artillery) brevet promotion to Colonel for gallant and meritorious service in action against Indians (Lava Beds, California, April 17, 1873) and special gallantry and military ability in actions against Indians (Clearwater, Idaho, July 11 and 12, 1877).*

— *2nd Lieutenant William H. Miller (1st U.S. Cavalry) brevet promotion to 1st Lieutenant for gallant service in action against Indians (Lava Beds, California, April 17, 1873) and gallant and meritorious conduct during the Modoc War.*

"The cruel and treacherous act that removed [1ˢᵗ Lieutenant William Sherwood] from us, deprived the service of a faithful, intelligent and gallant officer; society of an worthy, bright and honorable member; his comrades of a true, kindly and generous friend. Ever awake to the calls of duty, the dictates of courtesy and the impulses of kindness, by his conscientious character and attractive manners he earned the respect and affection of both his seniors and juniors, and his untimely decease is mourned by all."
— Edwin C. Mason, U.S. Army[30]

(0784) Action, Scorpion Point, near Tule Lake, California (April 20, 1873)[31]
— 1ˢᵗ Lieutenant Albion Howe (4ᵗʰ U.S. Artillery)
— 12ᵗʰ U.S. Infantry Detachment
— 4ᵗʰ U.S. Artillery Detachment
— **1 KILLED**[32]
— Private John Welsh (Co. G 12ᵗʰ U.S. Infantry)

— **1 WOUNDED**[33]
— Private Morris Darcey (Co. M 4ᵗʰ U.S. Artillery)
— *gunshot wound, left arm, fracture, severe wound*

(0785) Skirmish, near Canyon Creek, Arizona Territory (April 25, 1873)[34]
— Captain George M. Randall (23ʳᵈ U.S. Infantry)
— 1ˢᵗ U.S. Cavalry Detachments Co. L and M
— 23ʳᵈ U.S. Infantry Detachment Co. I

— *Captain George M. Randall (23ʳᵈ U.S. Infantry) brevet promotion to Lt. Colonel for gallant service in actions against Indians (Turret Mountains, Arizona, March 27, 1873 and Diamond Butte, Arizona, April 22, 1873).*

(0786) Engagement, Hardin Butte, Lava Beds, California (April 26, 1873)[35]
— Captain Evan Thomas (4ᵗʰ U.S. Artillery)
— 12ᵗʰ U.S. Infantry Co. E
— 4ᵗʰ U.S. Artillery Co. A and K
— **26 KILLED**[36]
— Captain Evan Thomas (4ᵗʰ U.S. Artillery)
— 1ˢᵗ Lieutenant Thomas F. Wright (12ᵗʰ U.S. Infantry)
— 1ˢᵗ Lieutenant Arthur Cranston (4ᵗʰ U.S. Artillery)
— 1ˢᵗ Lieutenant George M. Harris (4ᵗʰ U.S. Artillery) — d. 5-12-1873
— 1ˢᵗ Lieutenant Albion Howe (4ᵗʰ U.S. Artillery)

— First Sergeant Malachi Clinton (Co. E 12ᵗʰ U.S. Infantry) — d. 6-14-1873
— Corporal Julius St. Clair (Co. E 12ᵗʰ U.S. Infantry)
— Private Michael Flynn (Co. E 12ᵗʰ U.S. Infantry)
— Private William Boyle (Co. E 12ᵗʰ U.S. Infantry)

[30] The words of Major Edwin C. Mason (21ˢᵗ U.S. Infantry), delivered in a letter composed on April 14 and signed by thirteen other officers, were shared during 1ˢᵗ Lieutenant William Sherwood's (21ˢᵗ U.S. Infantry) funeral as conducted by Reverend Cheater of Buffalo, New York. *Buffalo (New York) Courier and Republic*, 17 May 1873.
[31] Indians. Chronological List, 54; Heitman (Volume 2), 438; Dillon, *Burnt Out Fires*, 265; Murray, *Modocs and Their War*, 220; Thompson, *Modoc War*, 81-82. Chronological List and Heitman both list a single entry, 11 to 20 April 1873. Heitman lists 1ˢᵗ U.S. Cavalry Co. B, F, G, H, K; 12ᵗʰ U.S. Infantry Co. E, G; 21ˢᵗ U.S. Infantry Co. B, C, I, Detachment Co. F; 4ᵗʰ U.S. Artillery Co. A, E, K, M; Detachment of Indian Scouts.
[32] Reports of Diseases and Individual Cases, F 433; Register of Deaths Regular Army, 1869-1889 (Volume 5).
[33] Reports of Diseases and Individual Cases, F 433.
[34] Indians. Chronological List, 54; Heitman (Volume 2), 438; Thrapp, *Conquest of Apacheria*, 142-143.
[35] Indians. Chronological List, 54; Heitman (Volume 2), 438; Dillon, *Burnt Out Fires*, 267-276; Murray, *Modocs and Their War*, 223-240; Russell, *One Hundred and Three Fights*, 109-110; Thompson, *Modoc War*, 83-91.
[36] Reports of Diseases and Individual Cases, F 433; Register of Deaths Regular Army, 1860-1889 (Volume 5).

— Private Frederick Geile (Co. E 12th U.S. Infantry)
— Private Thomas Howard (Co. E 12th U.S. Infantry)
— Private Bartell Nusbaum (Co. E 12th U.S. Infantry)
— Private William Denham (Co. E 12th U.S. Infantry) — d. 5-06-1873

— First Sergeant Robert S. Romer (Co. A 4th U.S. Artillery)
— Sergeant Herman Seelig (Co. A 4th U.S. Artillery)
— Corporal Lawrence Seelig (Co. A 4th U.S. Artillery)
— Artificer John Parker (Co. A 4th U.S. Artillery)
— Bugler Edward Moran (Co. A 4th U.S. Artillery)
— Private James E. Allin (Co. A 4th U.S. Artillery)
— Private Louis Bloom (Co. A 4th U.S. Artillery)
— Private John Collins (Co. A 4th U.S. Artillery)
— Private John Lynch (Co. A 4th U.S. Artillery)

— Private James Rose (Co. K 4th U.S. Artillery)
— Private Michael Wallace (Co. K 4th U.S. Artillery)
— Private John W. Ward (Co. K 4th U.S. Artillery)

— Packer Lewis Webber (Citizen)

— 17 WOUNDED[37]

— Private William Nolan (Co. G 1st U.S. Cavalry)
    — *gunshot wound, right arm, slight wound*
— Private Charles Kitchen (Co. K 1st U.S. Cavalry)
    — *gunshot wound, right arm, slight wound*

— Sergeant Martin Kennedy (Co. E 12th U.S. Infantry)
    — *gunshot wound, right elbow, fracture, severe wound*
— Private James Butler (Co. E 12th U.S. Infantry)
    — *gunshot wounds, right, left thigh, slight wound*
— Private Charles Guff (Co. E 12th U.S. Infantry)
    — *gunshot wound, left hand, fracture, severe wound*
— Private Matthew Murphy (Co. E 12th U.S. Infantry)
    — *gunshot wound, hand, slight wound*
— Private George Vandewater (Co. E 12th U.S. Infantry)
    — *gunshot wound, right hip, slight wound*

— Sergeant August Beck (Co. A 4th U.S. Artillery)
    — *gunshot wounds, right arm, mouth, slight wounds*
— Corporal James Noble (Co. A 4th U.S. Artillery)
    — *gunshot wound, neck, slight wound*

---

[37] Reports of Diseases and Individual Cases, F 433.

— Private Joseph Broderick (Co. A 4th U.S. Artillery)
 — *gunshot wound, left thigh, slight wound*
— Private James McMillan (Co. A 4th U.S. Artillery)
 — *gunshot wound, hand, slight wound*

— Private John Gifford (Co. K 4th U.S. Artillery)
 — *gunshot wounds, back, thigh, slight wounds*
— Private John Higgins (Co. K 4th U.S. Artillery)
 — *gunshot wounds, left leg, right shoulder, slight wounds*
— Private William McCoy (Co. K 4th U.S. Artillery)
 — *gunshot wound, right buttocks, slight wound*
— Private Joseph McLaughlin (Co. K 4th U.S. Artillery)
 — *gunshot wounds, right, left, foot, severe wounds*
— Private Francis Rolla (Co. K 4th U.S. Artillery)
 — *gunshot wound, left leg, slight wound*

— Acting Assistant Surgeon B.G. Semig (Citizen)
 — *gunshot wounds, right arm, left ankle, fracture, severe wounds*

"[1st Lieutenant Albion Howe] was a gallant and intelligent officer of artillery, a cultivated scholar of extensive acquirements and reading, and a refined and courteous gentleman. His loss to the military service is great, but to his friends, his comrades and family, is not to be measured by mere words."
— Editor, *Buffalo Courier and Republic*, Citizen[38]

(0787) Skirmish, Eagle Springs, Texas (April 27, 1873)[39]
 — Corporal E. Parker (25th U.S. Infantry)
  — 25th U.S. Infantry Detachment Co. B

(0788) Skirmish, Barilla Springs, Texas (May 1873)[40]
 — Sergeant W. Smith (25th U.S. Infantry)
  — 25th U.S. Infantry Detachment Co. D

(0789) Skirmish, Santa Maria River, Arizona Territory (May 6, 1873)[41]
 — Captain Thomas McGregor (2nd U.S. Cavalry)
  — 1st U.S. Cavalry Co. A

 — *Bugler Samuel Hoover (Co. A 1st U.S. Cavalry) received MOH: Gallantry in action, also services as trailer in May 1872 (Santa Maria Mountains, Arizona, May 6, 1873).*

[38] *Buffalo (New York) Courier and Republic*, 5 May 1873
[39] Indians. Chronological List, 54; Heitman (Volume 2), 438; Williams, *Texas' Last Frontier*, 167.
[40] Indians. Chronological List, 54.
[41] Indians. Chronological List, 54; Heitman (Volume 2), 439.
[42] Indians. Chronological List, 54; Heitman (Volume 2), 439; Dillon, *Burnt Out Fires*, 282; Murray, *Modocs and Their War*, 245-246; Thompson, *Modoc War*, 96. Heitman lists 21st U.S. Infantry Co. B.
[43] Reports of Diseases and Individual Cases, F 433.
[44] Indians. Chronological List, 54; Murray, *Modocs and Their War*, 244; Thompson, *Modoc War*, 97.

— *Captain Thomas McGregor (1st U.S. Cavalry) brevet promotion to Major for gallant service in action against Indians (Santa Maria Mountains, Arizona, May 6, 1873).*

(0790) Action, Scorpion Point, near Lava Beds, California (May 7, 1873)[42]
— Major Edwin C. Mason (21st U.S. Infantry)
     — 21st U.S. Infantry Co. B, C, and I, Detachment Co. F
— **2 WOUNDED**[43]
     — Private James Evans (Co. B 21st U.S. Infantry)
       — *gunshot wound, left thigh, slight wound*
     — Private John Bergwell (Co. I 21st U.S. Infantry)
       — *gunshot wound, left shoulder, slight wound*

(0791) Action, Lava Beds, California (May 7, 1873)[44]
— Captain Henry C. Hasbrouck (4th U.S. Artillery)
     — 1st U.S. Cavalry Co. B and G
     — 4th U.S. Artillery Co. B
— **1 WOUNDED**[45]
     — Private James Byrne (Co. G 1st U.S. Cavalry)
       — *gunshot wound, left hand, fracture, severe wound*

(0792) Skirmish, Fort Abraham Lincoln, Dakota Territory (May 7, 1873)[46]
— Lt. Colonel W.P. Carlin (17th U.S. Infantry)
     — 6th U.S. Infantry Co. B and C
     — 7th U.S. Infantry Co. H
     — Detachment of Indian Scouts

(0793) Action, Lake Soras, California (May 10, 1873)[47]
— Captain Henry C. Hasbrouck (4th U.S. Artillery)
     — 1st U.S. Cavalry Co. B and G
     — 4th U.S. Artillery Co. B
     — Detachment of Indian Scouts
— **6 KILLED**[48]
     — Corporal James Totten (Co. B 1st U.S. Cavalry)
     — Private Adolphus Fisher (Co. B 1st U.S. Cavalry)
     — Private Patrick McGrath (Co. B 1st U.S. Cavalry) — d. 05-24-1873

     — Sebastea (Indian Scout) — d. 5-11-1873
     — Peter (Indian Scout)
     — Wassamucka (Indian Scout)

[45] Reports of Diseases and Individual Cases, F 433.
[46] Indians. Chronological List, 54; Heitman (Volume 2), 439; Record of Engagements, 35; Hedren, *Fort Laramie in 1876*, 7.
[47] Indians. *Annual Report of Commissioner of Indian Affairs (1873)*, 320; Chronological List, 54; Heitman (Volume 2), 439; Dillon, *Burnt Out Fires*, 283-285; Murray, *Modocs and Their War*, 246-250; Russell, *One Hundred and Three Fights*, 110; Thompson, *Modoc War*, 97-99.
[48] Reports of Diseases and Individual Cases, F 433; Register of Deaths Regular Army, 1860-1889 (Volume 5).

— **7 WOUNDED**[49]
   — Corporal George Brown (Co. B 1st U.S. Cavalry)
      — *gunshot wound, left leg, slight wound*
   — Private Louis Dunbar (Co. B 1st U.S. Cavalry)
      — *gunshot wound, head, slight wound*
   — Private Peter Griffin (Co. B 1st U.S. Cavalry)
      — *gunshot wound, left hip, slight wound*
   — Private Samuel McGlew (Co. B 1st U.S. Cavalry)
      — *gunshot wound, right arm, slight wound*
   — Private Jesse Reeves (Co. B 1st U.S. Cavalry)
      — *gunshot wound, right arm, fracture, severe wound*
   — Private Michael Mahar (Co. G 1st U.S. Cavalry)
      — *gunshot wound, right hip, slight wound*

   — Postimine (Indian Scout)
      — *gunshot wound, right arm, slight wound*

— *Captain Henry C. Hasbrouck (4th U.S. Artillery) brevet promotion to Major for gallant service in action against Indians (Soras Lake, California, May 10, 1873)*

(0794) Skirmish, near Butte Creek, Oregon (May 17, 1873)[50]
   — Captain Henry C. Hasbrouck (4th U.S. Artillery)
      — 1st U.S. Cavalry Co. B and G
      — 4th U.S. Artillery Co. B
      — Detachment of Indian Scouts

(0795) Action, near Remolino, Coahuila, Mexico (May 18, 1873)[51]
   — Colonel Ranald S. Mackenzie (4th U.S. Cavalry)
      — 4th U.S. Cavalry A, B, C, E, I and M
      — Detachment of Indian Scouts
— **1 KILLED**[52]
   — Private Peter Carrigan (Co. I 4th U.S. Cavalry) — 5-23-1873

— **2 WOUNDED**[53]
   — Private Leonard Knippenberg (Co. E 4th U.S. Cavalry)
      — *gunshot wound, face, slight wound*

[49] Reports of Diseases and Individual Cases, F 433.
[50] Indians. Chronological List, 54; Heitman (Volume 2), 439; Murray, *Modocs and Their War*, 256-257; Thompson, *Modoc War*, 104-105.
[51] Indians. Chronological List, 55; Heitman (Volume 2), 439; Record of Engagements, 35; Carter, *On the Border with Mackenzie*, 438-449; Leckie, *Buffalos Soldiers*, 106-107; Mulroy, *Freedom on the Border*, 118-121; Robinson, *Bad Hand*, 138-141; Smith, *Old Army in Texas*, 156; Wallace, *Ranald S. Mackenzie*, 98-104.
[52] Reports of Diseases and Individual Cases, F 445.
[53] Reports of Diseases and Individual Cases, F 445.

— Private William Pair (Co. I 4th U.S. Cavalry)
— *gunshot wound, right arm, fracture, severe wound*

— *1st Lieutenant John L. Bullis (24th U.S. Infantry) brevet promotion to Captain for gallant service in actions against Indians (Remolino, Mexico, May 18, 1873 and Pecos River, Texas, April 26, 1875).*

— *2nd Lieutenant Robert G. Carter (4th U.S. Cavalry) brevet promotion to Captain for gallant service in action against Kickapoo Lipan and Mescalero Indians (Remolino, Mexico, May 18, 1873).*

"As a boy of seventeen, on the Gettysburg Campaign… I saw many charges of fifteen miles of country during that day, but I never saw such a magnificent charge as that made by those six troops of the 4th U.S. Cavalry on the morning of May 18, 1873 at Remolino, Mexico."
— Robert G. Carter, U.S. Army[54]

(0796) Surrender of 150 Indians, near Fairchild's Ranch, California (May 22, 1873)[55]

(0797) Action, San Carlos Agency, Arizona Territory (May 27, 1873)[56]
— **1 KILLED**[57]
— 1st Lieutenant Jacob Almy (5th U.S. Cavalry)

(0798) Surrender of 33 Indians, Langell's Valley, California (May 30, 1873)[58]

(0799) Surrender of 7 Indians, Willow Creek, California (June 1, 1873)[59]

— *1st Lieutenant Sydney W. Taylor (4th U.S. Artillery) brevet promotion to Captain for gallant and meritorious conduct in actions against Indians (Modoc War, 1873).*

(0800) Action, Fort Abraham Lincoln, Dakota Territory (June 15 to 17, 1873)[60]
— Lt. Colonel William P. Carlin (17th U.S. Infantry)
— 6th U.S. Infantry Co. B and C
— 8th U.S. Infantry Co. C
— 17th U.S. Infantry Co. H
— Detachment of Indian Scouts

[54] Carter, *On the Border with Mackenzie*, 440-441.
[55] Indians. Chronological List, 55; Murray, *Modocs and Their War*, 260; Thompson, *Modoc War*, 106-107.
[56] Indians. *Annual Report of Secretary of War (1874)*, 62; Chronological List, 55; Altshuler, *Chains of Command*, 225-226; Thrapp, *Conquest of Apacheria*, 153-154.
[57] 5th U.S. Cavalry Regimental Return May 1873.
[58] Indians. Chronological List, 55; Heitman (Volume 2), 439; Dillon, *Burnt Out Fires*, 296-297; Murray, *Modocs and Their War*, 268-269; Thompson, *Modoc War*, 112-113, 180.
[59] Indians. Chronological List, 55; Heitman (Volume 2), 439; Dillon, *Burnt Out Fires*, 299-300; Murray, *Modocs and Their War*, 269, Thompson, *Modoc War*, 114-115, 180.
[60] Indians. Chronological List, 55; Heitman (Volume 2), 439; Record of Engagements, 35; Hedren, *Fort Laramie in 1876*, 7. Chronological List lists 6th U.S. Infantry Co. B, C; 17th U.S. Infantry Co. H.

— **1 WOUNDED**[61]
    — Goose (Indian Scout)
        — *gunshot wound, thigh, slight wound*

(0801) Action, Forks of Tonto Creek, Arizona Territory (June 16, 1873)[62]
    — 1st Lieutenant John B. Babcock (5th U.S. Cavalry)
        — 5th U.S. Cavalry Detachment Co. C
        — Detachment of Indian Scouts
    — **1 KILLED**[63]
        — Indian Scout

    — *1st Lieutenant John B. Babcock (5th U.S. Cavalry) brevet Lt. Colonel for gallant service in action against Indians (Tonto Creek, Arizona, June 16, 1873 and Four Peaks, Arizona, January 16, 1874).*

    — *Sergeant Patrick Martin (Co. G 5th U.S. Cavalry) received MOH: Gallant services in operations of Captain James Burns, 5th U.S. Cavalry (Castle Dome and Santa Maria Mountains, Arizona June and July 1873).*

    — *2nd Lieutenant Walter S. Schuyler (5th U.S. Cavalry) brevet promotion to 1st Lieutenant for gallant service in actions against Indians (Muchos Canyon, Arizona, September 25, 1872; Lost River, Arizona, June 26, 1873; Salt River, Arizona, Arizona, April 28, 1874 and Red Rock Country, Arizona, May 14, 1874).*

(0802) Action, Canada Alamosa, New Mexico Territory (July 13, 1873)[64]
    — Captain George W. Chilson (8th U.S. Cavalry)
        — 8th U.S. Cavalry Co. C
    — **1 KILLED**[65]
        — Corporal Frank Bratling (Co. C 8th U.S. Cavalry)

    — *Corporal Frank Bratling (Co. C 8th U.S. Cavalry) received MOH: Services against hostile Indians (Near Fort Selden, New Mexico, July 8 to 11, 1873).*

    — *Sergeant Leonidas S. Lytle (Co. C 8th U.S. Cavalry) received MOH: Services against hostile Indians (Near Fort Selden, New Mexico, July 8 to 11, 1873).*

[61] Reports of Diseases and Individual Cases, F 447.
[62] Indians. Chronological List, 55; Heitman (Volume 2), 439; Price, *Across the Continent*, 660.
[63] "a loss of one Indian mortally wounded". Camp Apache Post Return June 1873.
[64] Indians. Chronological List, 55; Heitman (Volume 2), 439; Record of Engagements, 35; Rathbun, *New Mexico Frontier Military Place Names*, 4; Thrapp, *Victorio*, 160.
[65] 8th U.S. Cavalry Regimental Return July 1873.

— *First Sergeant James L. Morris (Co. C 8th U.S. Cavalry) received MOH: Services against hostile Indians (Near Fort Selden, New Mexico, July 8 to 11, 1873).*

— *Blacksmith John Sheerin (Co. C 8th U.S. Cavalry) received MOH: Services against hostile Indians (Near Fort Selden, New Mexico, July 8 to 11, 1873).*

— *Private Henry Wills (Co. C 8th U.S. Cavalry) received MOH: Service against hostile Indians (Near Fort Selden, New Mexico, July 8 to 11, 1873).*

(0803) Skirmish, Lipan Creek, Texas (July 14, 1873)[66]
— Captain Theodore J. Wint (4th U.S. Cavalry)
— 4th U.S. Cavalry Co. L

(0804) Action, Tongue River, Montana Territory (August 4, 1873)[67]
— Captain Myles Moylan (7th U.S. Cavalry)
— 7th U.S. Cavalry Co. A and B
— 1 WOUNDED[68]
— Private John B. Crowe (Co. A 7th U.S. Cavalry)
— *gunshot wound, left arm, slight wound*

(0805) Action, Tongue River, Montana Territory (August 4, 1873)[69]
— Lt. Colonel George A. Custer (7th U.S. Cavalry)
— 7th U.S. Cavalry Co. A, B, E, F, G, K, L and M
— 3 KILLED[70]
— Private John Ball (7th U.S. Cavalry)

— Veterinarian John Honsinger (Citizen)
— Sutler Augustus Baliran (Citizen)

(0806) Action, near Bighorn River, Second Yellowstone Expedition, Montana Territory (August 11, 1873)[71]
— Lt. Colonel George A. Custer (7th U.S. Cavalry)
— 7th U.S. Cavalry Co. A, B, E, F, G, K, L and M
— Detachment of Indian Scouts
— 1 KILLED[72]
— Private John H. Tuttle (Co. E 7th U.S. Cavalry)

[66] Indians. Chronological List, 55; Heitman (Volume 2), 439; Smith, *Old Army in Texas*, 156; Williams, *Texas' Last Frontier*, 171.
[67] Indians. Chronological List, 55; Heitman (Volume 2), 439; Record of Engagements, 36; Brown, *Plainsmen of the Yellowstone*, 205-206; Frost, *Custer's 7th*, 66-69; Lubetkin, *Jay Cooke's Gamble*, 241-252; Rockwell, *U.S. Army in Frontier Montana*, 259-261.
[68] Reports of Diseases and Individual Cases, F 448.
[69] Indians. Record of Engagements, 36; Brown, *Plainsmen of the Yellowstone*, 205-206; Frost, *Custer's 7th*, 66-69; Lubetkin, *Jay Cooke's Gamble*, 241-252; Rockwell, *U.S. Army in Frontier Montana*, 259-261.
[70] Official Report of Lt. Colonel George A. Custer (7th U.S. Cavalry), HQ Battalion 7th U.S. Cavalry, Pompey's Pillar, Yellowstone River, Montana Territory, 15 August 1873; 7th U.S. Cavalry Regimental Return August 1873; Rockwell, *U.S. Army in Frontier Montana*, 259-261.
[71] Indians. Chronological List, 55; Heitman (Volume 2), 439; Record of Engagements, 36; Brown, *Plainsmen of the Yellowstone*, 206-208; Lubetkin, *Jay Cooke's Gamble*, 253-263; Frost, *Custer's 7th*, 83-87; Rockwell, *U.S. Army in Frontier Montana*, 261-264. Chronological List lists 7th U.S. Cavalry Co. A, B, E, F, G, K, L, M.
[72] Register of Deaths Regular Army, 1860-1889 (Volume 5); 7th U.S. Cavalry Regimental Return August 1873.

— **3 WOUNDED**[73]
> — 2nd Lieutenant Charles Braden (7th U.S. Cavalry)
>> — *gunshot wound, thigh, fracture, severe wound*

> — Private John Sweeney (Co. F 7th U.S. Cavalry)
>> — *gunshot wound, right thigh, slight wound*
> — Private Englebert Saylor (Co. K 7th U.S. Cavalry)
>> — *gunshot wound, right arm, fracture, severe wound*

— 2nd Lieutenant Charles Braden (7th U.S. Cavalry) brevet promotion to 1st Lieutenant for gallant and meritorious service in action against Indians where he was severely wounded (Big Horn River, Montana, August 11, 1873).

— 2nd Lieutenant Charles Braden (7th U.S. Cavalry) received Distinguished Service Cross for extraordinary heroism: Braden, with twenty men, having been attacked by nearly two hundred Indians, although severely wounded in the encounter, by his personal gallantry and splendid leadership so inspired his small command as to enable it to repulse the attack by overwhelmingly superior numbers (Big Horn River, Montana, August 11, 1873)

— 1st Lieutenant Hiram H. Ketchum (22nd U.S. Infantry) brevet promotion to Captain for gallant service in action with Indians (Mouth of Bighorn River, Montana, August 11, 1873).

(0807) Skirmish, Barilla Springs, Texas (August 19, 1873)[74]
> — Corporal G. Collins (25th U.S. Infantry)
>> — 25th U.S. Infantry Detachment Co. E

(0808) Skirmish, near Pease River, Texas (August 31, 1873)[75]
> — Captain Theodore A. Baldwin (10th U.S. Cavalry)
>> — 10th U.S. Cavalry Co. E and I

(0809) Skirmish, Sierra San Mater, New Mexico Territory (September 1873)[76]
> — 1st Lieutenant Henry J. Farnsworth (8th U.S. Cavalry)
>> — 8th U.S. Cavalry Co. H

(0810) Citizens, San Carlos Agency, Arizona Territory (September 17, 1873)[77]
> — (1) Citizen Killed

(0811) Skirmish, near Fort Fetterman, Wyoming Territory (September 20, 1873)[78]
> — Captain James Egan (2nd U.S. Cavalry)

---

[73] Reports of Diseases and Individual Cases, F 449.
[74] Indians. Chronological List, 55.
[75] Indians. Chronological List, 55; Heitman (Volume 2), 439; Record of Engagements, 36; Smith, *Old Army in Texas*, 156.
[76] Indians. Chronological List, 55; Record of Engagements, 36.
[77] Indians. Killed was John M. Logan. *Annual Report of Commissioner of Indian Affairs (1874)*, 296.
[78] Indians. Chronological List, 55; Heitman (Volume 2), 439.

— 2nd U.S. Cavalry Co. K

(0812) Skirmish, Hardscrabble Creek or Mescal Range, Arizona Territory (September 23, 1873)[79]
 — 2nd Lieutenant Walter S. Schuyler (5th U.S. Cavalry)
  — 5th U.S. Cavalry Detachment Co. K
  — Detachment of Indian Scouts

(0813) Skirmish, Sierra Ancha, Arizona Territory (September 29, 1873)[80]
 — Captain William H. Brown (5th U.S. Cavalry)
  — 5th U.S. Cavalry Detachments Co. F, I and L
  — 23rd U.S. Infantry Detachment Co. H
  — Detachment of Indian Scouts

(0814) Skirmish, Central Mail Station, Texas (October 1, 1873)[81]
 — Sergeant Benjamin Mew (25th U.S. Infantry)
  — 25th U.S. Infantry Detachment Co. K

(0815) Skirmish, Guadaloupe Mountains, New Mexico Territory (October 1, 1873)[82]
 — Captain George W. Chilson (8th U.S. Cavalry)
  — 8th U.S. Cavalry Co. C

(0816) Skirmish, Chiricahua Mountains, Arizona Territory (October 8, 1873)[83]
 — Captain Almond B. Wells (8th U.S. Cavalry)
  — 8th U.S. Cavalry Co. A

(0817) Operations, Mazatzal Mountains, Sunflower Valley or Sycamore Springs, Arizona Territory (October 28 to 30, 1873)[84]
 — Captain William H. Brown (5th U.S. Cavalry)
  — 5th U.S. Cavalry Detachment Co. F and L
  — 23rd U.S. Infantry Detachment Co. H
  — Detachment of Indian Scouts

(0818) Skirmish, Pajarit Springs, New Mexico Territory (October 30, 1873)[85]
 — 1st Lieutenant Argalus G. Hennisee (8th U.S. Cavalry)
  — 8th U.S. Cavalry Co. D

(0819) Citizens, near Camp Supply, Indian Territory (December 1873)[86]
 — (1) Citizen Killed

---

[79] Indians. Chronological List, 55; Heitman (Volume 2), 439; Alexander, *Arizona Frontier Military Place Names*, 67.
[80] Indians. Chronological List, 55; Heitman (Volume 2), 439; Price, *Across the Continent*, 660.
[81] Indians. Chronological List, 55; Heitman (Volume 2), 439; Record of Engagements, 36; Smith, *Old Army in Texas*, 156; Williams, *Texas' Last Frontier*, 174.
[82] Indians. Chronological List, 55; Heitman (Volume 2), 439; Record of Engagements, 36; Mehren, "Scouting for Mescaleros: The Price Campaign of 1873", *Arizona and the West* 10 (Summer 1968): 171-190; Williams, *Texas' Last Frontier*, 175.
[83] Indians. Chronological List, 55; Heitman (Volume 2), 439.
[84] Indians. Chronological List, 55; Heitman (Volume 2), 439; Price, *Across the Continent*, 660.
[85] Indians. Chronological List, 55; Heitman (Volume 2), 439.
[86] Indians. Killed was Jacob Dittsey. *Annual Report of Commissioner of Indian Affairs (1874)*, xyz.

(0820) Skirmish, East Fork of Verde River, Arizona Territory (December 4, 1873)[87]
  — 2nd Lieutenant Walter S. Schuyler (5th U.S. Cavalry)
    — 5th U.S. Cavalry Co. K
    — Detachment of Indian Scouts

(0821) Skirmish, Elm Creek, Texas (December 5, 1873)[88]
  — 2nd Lieutenant Edward P. Turner (10th U.S. Cavalry)
    — 10th U.S. Cavalry Detachment Co. D

(0822) Operations, near San Carlos, Arizona Territory (December 8, 1873 to January 20, 1874)[89]
  — 1st Lieutenant William F. Rice (23rd U.S. Infantry)
    — 5th U.S. Cavalry Detachment Co. C
    — Detachment of Indian Scouts

(0823) Action, Kickapoo Springs, West Fork of Nueces River, Texas (December 10, 1873)[90]
  — 1st Lieutenant Charles L. Hudson (4th U.S. Cavalry)
    — 4th U.S. Cavalry Detachments Co. A, B, C and I
    — Detachment of Indian Scouts
  — **1 WOUNDED**[91]
    — Enlisted Man (4th U.S. Cavalry)
     — *slight wound*

(0824) Skirmish, near Ehrenberg, Arizona Territory (December 21, 1873)[92]
  — Captain James Burns (5th U.S. Cavalry)
    — 5th U.S. Cavalry Co. G

(0825) Skirmish, Cave Creek, Arizona Territory (December 23, 1873)[93]
  — 2nd Lieutenant Walter S. Schuyler (5th U.S. Cavalry)
    — 5th U.S. Cavalry Co. K
    — Detachment of Indian Scouts

(0826) Skirmish, Sunflower Valley, near Old Fort Reno, Arizona Territory (December 31, 1873)[94]
  — 1st Lieutenant John B. Babcock (5th U.S. Cavalry)
    — 5th U.S. Cavalry Co. B
    — Detachment of Indian Scouts

TOTAL KILLED 1873 — 9/44/3/5 (Officers, Enlisted Men, Indian Scouts, Citizens)

---

[87] Indians. Chronological List, 56; Heitman (Volume 2), 439; Thrapp, *Conquest of Apacheria*, 159.
[88] Bandits. Chronological List, 56; Heitman (Volume 2), 439; Record of Engagements, 37; Smith, *Old Army in Texas*, 156.
[89] Indians. Chronological List, 56; Heitman (Volume 2), 439.
[90] Indians. *Annual Report of Secretary of War (1874)*, 28; Chronological List, 56; Heitman (Volume 2), 439; Record of Engagements, 37; Hamilton, *Sentinel of the Southern Plains*, 143-144; Leckie, *Military Conquest of the Southern Plains*, 182-183; Nye, *Carbine and Lance*, 184; Gwynne, *Empire of the Summer Moon*, 263; Robinson, *Bad Hand*, 160; Wallace, *Ranald S. Mackenzie*, 118-119.
[91] "one private slightly wounded". Fort Clark Post Return December 1873.
[92] Indians. Chronological List, 56.
[93] Indians. Chronological List, 56; Heitman (Volume 2), 439; Thrapp, *Conquest of Apacheria*, 159.
[94] Indians. Chronological List, 56; Heitman (Volume 2), 439.

1874

"I enclose the reports of all these officers... demonstrating that the small Army of the United States, called a peace establishment, is the hardest worked body of men in this or any country. The discipline and behavior of the officers and men have been worthy of all praise; and, whether employed on the extreme and distant frontier, or in aiding the civil officers in the execution of civil process, have been a model for the imitation of all good men."
— William T. Sherman, U.S. Army[1]

---

[1] Official Report of General William T. Sherman, 25 October 1874. *Annual Report of Secretary of War (1874),* 5.

(0827) Skirmish, Wild Rye Creek, Arizona Territory (January 4, 1874)[2]
— 1st Lieutenant John B. Babcock (5th U.S. Cavalry)
— 5th U.S. Cavalry Co. B
— Detachment of Indian Scouts

(0828) Skirmish, Pleasant Valley, Headwaters of Cherry Creek, Arizona Territory (January 8, 1874)[3]
— 1st Lieutenant John B. Babcock (5th U.S. Cavalry)
— 5th U.S. Cavalry Co. B
— Detachment of Indian Scouts

— *1st Lieutenant John B. Babcock (5th U.S. Cavalry) brevet Lt. Colonel for gallant service in action against Indians (Tonto Creek, Arizona, June 16, 1873 and Four Peaks, Arizona, January 16, 1874).*

(0829) Skirmish, Canyon Creek, Arizona Territory (January 10, 1874)[4]
— 2nd Lieutenant Walter S. Schuyler (5th U.S. Cavalry)
— 5th U.S. Cavalry Co. K
— Detachment of Indian Scouts

(0830) Citizens, near San Carlos Agency, Arizona Territory (January 31, 1874)[5]
— (2) Citizens Killed

(0831) Skirmish, Home Creek, Texas (February 2, 1874)[6]
— Sergeant T. Allsup (10th U.S. Cavalry)
— 10th U.S. Cavalry Detachment Co. A

(0832) Citizens, near Old Camp Grant, Arizona Territory (February 3, 1874)[7]
— (5) Citizens Killed

(0833) Action, Double Mountain, Fork of the Brazos River, Texas (February 5, 1874)[8]
— Lt. Colonel George P. Buell (11th U.S. Infantry)
— 10th U.S. Cavalry Co. G, Detachment Co. D
— 11th U.S. Infantry Co. F, Detachments Co. A and G
— Detachment of Indian Scouts
— **1 WOUNDED**[9]
— Enlisted Man

(0834) Citizens, Red Cloud Agency, Dakota Territory (February 8, 1874)[10]
— (1) Citizen Killed

(0835) Action, Cottonwood Creek, near Laramie Peak, Wyoming Territory (February 9, 1874)[11]
— 2nd Lieutenant Levi H. Robinson (14th U.S. Infantry)

[2] Indians. Chronological List, 56; Heitman (Volume 2), 439.
[3] Indians. Chronological List, 56; Heitman (Volume 2), 439; Alexander, *Arizona Frontier Military Place Names*, 32.
[4] Indians. Chronological List, 56; Heitman (Volume 2), 439; Thrapp, *Conquest of Apacheria*, 159.
[5] Indians. Killed were two teamsters. *Annual Report of Secretary of War (1874)*, 62.
[6] Indians. Chronological List, 56; Heitman (Volume 2), 439; Hamilton, *Sentinel of the Southern Plains*, 144; Smith, *Old Army in Texas*, 157.
[7] Indians. Killed were two men, a woman and two children. *Annual Report of Secretary of War (1874)*, 62; Lockwood, *Apache Indians*, 207.
[8] Indians. *Annual Report of Secretary of War (1874)*, 28; Chronological List, 56; Heitman (Volume 2), 439; Record of Engagements, 39; Leckie, *Buffalo Soldiers*, 82; Gwynne, *Empire of the Summer Moon*, 263; Smith, *Old Army in Texas*, 157; Williams, *Texas' Last Frontier*, 175.
[9] Chronological List, 56.
[10] Indians. Killed was Frank D. Appleton. *Annual Report of Commissioner of Indian Affairs (1874)*, 251.
[11] Indians. *Annual Report of Secretary of War (1874)*, 25; Chronological List, 56; Heitman (Volume 2), 439; Record of Engagements, 39; Lindmier, *Drybone*, 72. Chronological List lists 2nd U.S. Cavalry Detachment; 14th U.S. Infantry Detachment.

— 2nd U.S. Cavalry Detachment Co. K
— 14th U.S. Infantry Detachment Co. A
— **2 KILLED**[12]
— 2nd Lieutenant Levi H. Robinson (14th U.S. Infantry)

— Corporal John G. Coleman (Co. K 2nd U.S. Cavalry)

(0836) Operations, Bill William's Mountains, Arizona Territory (February 20 to April 21, 1874)[13]
— 1st Lieutenant Earl D. Thomas (5th U.S. Cavalry)
— 5th U.S. Cavalry Detachment Co. G

(0837) Skirmish, Pinal Mountains, Arizona Territory (March 8, 1874)[14]
— Captain George M. Randall (23rd U.S. Cavalry)
— 5th U.S. Cavalry Detachments Co. B, F, H, I, L and M
— Detachment of Indian Scouts

— *Captain George M. Randall (23rd U.S. Infantry) brevet promotion to Colonel for gallant service in action against Indians (Pinal Mountains, Arizona, March 8, 1874) and distinguished service during the campaigns against Indians (Arizona, 1874).*

(0838) Action, Pinal Mountains, Arizona Territory (March 15, 1874)[15]
— Captain John M. Hamilton (5th U.S. Cavalry)
— 5th U.S. Cavalry Co. H, Detachments Co. F and M
— **1 WOUNDED**[16]
— Private Peter M. Blanchard (Co. M 5th U.S. Cavalry)

(0839) Citizens, Los Almos, Texas (March 16, 1874)[17]
— (1) Citizen Killed

(0840) Skirmish, Superstitious Mountains, Arizona Territory (March 25 and 26, 1874)[18]
— 2nd Lieutenant Walter S. Schuyler (5th U.S. Cavalry)
— 5th U.S. Cavalry Co. K

(0841) Skirmish, China Tree Creek, Texas (April 1874)[19]
— Captain Warren C. Beach (11th U.S. Infantry)
— 10th U.S. Cavalry Co. K
— 11th U.S. Infantry Co. D
— 25th U.S. Infantry Detachment Co. C

---

[12] Fort Laramie Post Return February 1874.
[13] Indians. Chronological List, 56; Heitman (Volume 2), 439.
[14] Indians. Chronological List, 56; Heitman (Volume 2), 439; Alexander, *Arizona Frontier Military Place Names*, 97; Thrapp, *Conquest of Apacheria*, 157-158.
[15] Indians. Chronological List, 57; Heitman (Volume 2), 439.
[16] "Private Peter M. Blanchard (Co. M 5th U.S. Cavalry) was wounded". Camp Grant Post Return March 1874.
[17] Bandits. Killed was Vidal Le Hallie. *Annual Report of Secretary of War (1875)*, 102.
[18] Indians. Chronological List, 57; Heitman (Volume 2), 440; Thrapp, *Al Sieber*, 138-142. Heitman lists 5th U.S. Cavalry Detachment Co. K.
[19] Indians. Chronological List, 57.

(0842) Skirmish, Pinal Creek, Arizona Territory (April 2, 1874)[20]
— 1st Lieutenant Alfred B. Bache (5th U.S. Cavalry)
— 5th U.S. Cavalry Co. F, L and M
— Detachment of Indian Scouts

— *Sergeant George Deary (Co. L 5th U.S. Cavalry) received MOH: Gallantry in action (Apache Creek, Arizona, April 2, 1874).*

"The command (5th U.S. Cavalry Co. F, L and M) behaved admirably. The men were marched over terrible country, and in many places our Indian Scouts were obliged to pull the men over the rocks by sheer force. Where all displayed so much eagerness it is impossible to distinguish any by name."
— Alfred B. Bache, U.S. Army[21]

(0843) Operations, Pinal Mountains, Arizona Territory (April 3 to 14, 1874)[22]
— Captain John M. Hamilton (5th U.S. Cavalry)
— 5th U.S. Cavalry Co. B, H and I
— Detachment of Indian Scouts

(0844) Skirmish, Bull Bear Creek, Indian Territory (April 11, 1874)[23]
— Captain Tullius C. Tupper (6th U.S. Cavalry)
— 6th U.S. Cavalry Detachment Co. G

(0845) Skirmish, near Fort Abraham Lincoln, Dakota Territory (April 23, 1874)[24]
— Lt. Colonel George A. Custer (7th U.S. Cavalry)
— 7th U.S. Cavalry Co. A, B, E, F, G and L

(0846) Skirmish, Arivaypa Mountains, Arizona Territory (April 28, 1874)[25]
— 2nd Lieutenant Walter S. Schuyler (5th U.S. Cavalry)
— 5th U.S. Cavalry Co. K

— *2nd Lieutenant Walter S. Schuyler (5th U.S. Cavalry) brevet promotion to 1st Lieutenant for gallant service in actions against Indians (Muchos Canyon, Arizona, September 25, 1872; Lost River, Arizona, June 26, 1873; Salt River, Arizona, Arizona, April 28, 1874 and Red Rock Country, Arizona, May 14, 1874).*

— *1st Lieutenant Earl D. Thomas (5th U.S. Cavalry) brevet promotion to Captain for gallant service in action against Indians (Caves, Arizona, December 12, 1872) and distinguished service in the campaign against Indians (Arizona, April, 1874).*

[20] Indians. Chronological List, 57; Heitman (Volume 2), 440; Thrapp, *Conquest of Apacheria*, 158-159.
[21] Official Report of 1st Lieutenant Alfred B. Bache (5th U.S. Cavalry), 2 April 1874. Price, *Across the Continent*, 677.
[22] Indians. Chronological List, 57; Heitman (Volume 2), 440.
[23] Indians. Chronological List, 57; Heitman (Volume 2), 440; Carter, *From Yorktown to Santiago*, 160-161, 277.
[24] Indians. Chronological List, 57.
[25] Indians. Chronological List, 57; Heitman (Volume 2), 440; Alexander, *Arizona Military Place Names*, 26-27; Thrapp, *Conquest of Apacheria*, 159. Heitman lists 5th U.S. Cavalry Detachment Co. K.

(0847) Skirmish, between Red River and Big Wichita River, Texas (May 2, 1874)[26]
— 2nd Lieutenant Quincy O. Gillmore (10th U.S. Cavalry)
— 10th U.S. Cavalry Detachment Co. K

(0848) Citizens, Peneschal Ranch, Hidalgo County, Texas (May 9, 1874)[27]
— (4) Citizens Killed

(0849) Skirmish, Tonto Creek, Arizona Territory (May 9, 1874)[28]
— 2nd Lieutenant Charles H. Heyl (23rd U.S. Infantry)
— 5th U.S. Cavalry Detachment Co. K
— Detachment of Indian Scouts

(0850) Skirmish, Four Peaks, Mazatzal Mountains, Arizona Territory (May 17 and 18, 1874)[29]
— 2nd Lieutenant Walter S. Schuyler (5th U.S. Cavalry)
— 5th U.S. Cavalry Co. K

— *2nd Lieutenant Walter S. Schuyler (5th U.S. Cavalry) brevet promotion to 1st Lieutenant for gallant service in actions against Indians (Muchos Canyon, Arizona, September 25, 1872; Lost River, Arizona, June 26, 1873; Salt River, Arizona, Arizona, April 28, 1874 and Red Rock Country, Arizona, May 14, 1874).*

(0851) Skirmish, Carrizo Mountains, Texas (May 18, 1874)[30]
— Captain Charles Bentzoni (25th U.S. Infantry)
— 25th U.S. Infantry Detachment Co. B

(0852) Citizens, Upper Arkansas Agency, Indian Territory (May 21, 1874)[31]
— (1) Citizen Killed

(0853) Operations, near Diamond Butte, Arizona Territory (May 21 to June 6, 1874)[32]
— 1st Lieutenant Charles King (5th U.S. Cavalry)
— 5th U.S. Cavalry Detachment Co. K

— *1st Lieutenant Charles King (5th U.S. Cavalry) brevet promotion to Captain for gallant and distinguished service in action against Indians (Near Diamond Butte, Arizona, May 21, 1874).*[33]

(0854) Action, Sierra Anchas Mountains, Arizona Territory (May 27, 1874)[34]
— 2nd Lieutenant Charles H. Heyl (23rd U.S. Infantry)
— 5th U.S. Cavalry Detachment Co. A
— Detachment of Indian Scouts
— **1 WOUNDED**[35]
— Indian Scout
— *arrow wound*

[26] Indians. *Annual Report of Secretary of War (1874)*, 28; Chronological List, 57; Heitman (Volume 2), 440; Record of Engagements, 39; Haley, *Buffalo War*, 187; Smith, *Old Army in Texas*, 157. Chronological List lists Big Wishita River, Texas.
[27] Bandits. Killed were John M. Fletcher, M. Morton, P.F.M. Cookley and H. Filger. *Annual Report of Secretary of War (1875)*, 101.
[28] Indians. Chronological List, 57; Heitman (Volume 2), 440.
[29] Indians. Chronological List, 57; Heitman (Volume 2), 440; Thrapp, *Conquest of Apacheria*, 159. Heitman lists 5th U.S. Cavalry Detachments Co. E, K.
[30] Indians. *Annual Report of Secretary of War (1874)*, 28; Chronological List, 57; Heitman (Volume 2), 440; Record of Engagements, 39; Smith, *Old Army in Texas*, 157.
[31] Indians. Killed was John F. Holloway. *Annual Report of Commissioner of Indian Affairs (1874)*, 233.
[32] Indians. Chronological List, 57; Heitman (Volume 2), 440; Russell, *Campaigning with King*, 44-45.
[33] 1st Lieutenant Charles King (5th U.S. Cavalry) declined his brevet promotion. *Army Register (1901)*, 378.
[34] Indians. Chronological List, 57; Heitman (Volume 2), 440.
[35] "one Indian Scout wounded by arrows". Camp Verde Post Return June 1874.

— *2nd Lieutenant Charles H. Heyl (23rd U.S. Infantry) brevet promotion to 1st Lieutenant for gallant service in action against Indians (South side of the Verde River, Arizona, May 24, 1874) and gallantry in action against Indians (Grace Creek, Nebraska, April 28, 1876).*

(0855) Skirmish, Pleasant Valley, Arizona Territory (June 8, 1874)[36]
     — 1st Lieutenant John B. Babcock (5th U.S. Cavalry)
         — 5th U.S. Cavalry Co. B
         — Detachment of Indian Scouts

(0856) Action, Buffalo Creek, Indian Territory (June 19, 1874)[37]
     — UNKNOWN
         — 6th U.S. Cavalry Detachment Co. K
         — 3rd U.S. Infantry Detachment Co. D
     — **1 WOUNDED**[38]
         — Enlisted Man

(0857) Action, Buffalo Creek, Indian Territory (June 21, 1874)[39]
     — Major Charles E. Compton (6th U.S. Cavalry)
         — 6th U.S. Cavalry Detachment Co. G
         — 3rd U.S. Infantry Detachment Co. A
     — **1 WOUNDED**[40]
         — Enlisted Man

(0858) Skirmish, near Bear Creek Redoubt, Kansas (June 24, 1874)[41]
     — Major Charles E. Compton (6th U.S. Cavalry)
         — 6th U.S. Cavalry Detachment Co. G
         — 3rd U.S. Infantry Detachment Co. A

(0859) Citizens, Adobe Walls, Texas (June 27, 1874)[42]
     — (4) Citizens Killed

(0860) Citizens, near King Fisher Ranch, Indian Territory (July 2, 1874)[43]
     — (1) Citizen Killed

(0861) Citizens, near Fort Rice, Dakota Territory (July 2, 1874)[44]
     — (1) Citizen Killed

(0862) Citizens, Turkey Creek, Indian Territory (July 4, 1874)[45]
     — (4) Citizens Killed

---

[36] Indians. Chronological List, 57; Heitman (Volume 2), 440.

[37] Indians. *Annual Report of Secretary of War (1874)*, 26, 30; Chronological List, 57; Heitman (Volume 2), 440; Carter, *From Yorktown to Santiago*, 161, 277; Haley, *Buffalo War*, 95-96; Leckie, *Military Conquest of the Southern Plains*, 190. Chronological List lists 6th U.S. Cavalry Detachments, 3rd U.S. Infantry Detachments.

[38] "the corporal in charge wounded". Camp Supply Post Return June 1874.

[39] Indians. *Annual Report of Secretary of War (1874)*, 26, 30; Chronological List, 57; Heitman (Volume 2), 440; Record of Engagements, 39-40; Carter, *From Yorktown to Santiago*, 161-162, 277; Haley, *Buffalo War*, 95-96; Leckie, *Military Conquest of the Southern Plains*, 189-190.

[40] "one man of the mail escort wounded". Camp Supply Post Return June 1874.

[41] Indians. *Annual Report of Secretary of War (1874)*, 26, 30; Chronological List, 57; Heitman (Volume 2), 440; Record of Engagements, 40; Carter, *From Yorktown to Santiago*, 162, 277; Haley, *Buffalo War*, 96; Leckie, *Military Conquest of the Southern Plains*, 189-190.

[42] Indians. Killed were Ike and Shorty Shadler, William Olds, and Billy Tyler. *Annual Report of Secretary of War (1874)*, 26, 30; Record of Engagements, 40; Haley, *Buffalo War*, 67-78; Leckie, *Military Conquest of the Southern Plains*, 190-194; Neeley, *Last Comanche Chief*, 86-101; Rister, *Fort Griffin*, 109-110; West, "Battle of Adobe Walls," *Panhandle-Plains Historical Review* 36 (1963): 18-26.

[43] Indians. Killed was William Watkins. *Annual Report of Commissioner of Indian Affairs (1874)*, 234.

[44] Indians. Killed was Joseph Putney. *Annual Report of Commissioner of Indian Affairs (1874)*, 234.

[45] Indians. Killed were head freighter Pat Hennesey, George Fand, Thomas Calloway, and Ed Cook. *Annual Report of Commissioner of Indian Affairs (1874)*, 32; Haley, *Buffalo War*, 97; Leckie, *Military Conquest of the Southern Plains*, 194; Nye, *Carbine and Lance*, 191.

(0863) Action, Bad Water Branch of Wind River of Snake Mountains or Owl Mountains, Wyoming Territory (July 4, 1874)[46]
— Captain Alfred E. Bates (2nd U.S. Cavalry)
— 2nd U.S. Cavalry Co. B
— Detachment of Indian Scouts
— **4 KILLED**[47]
— Private Peter Engall (Co. B 2nd U.S. Cavalry)
— Private James M. Walker (Co. B 2nd U.S. Cavalry)

— Pe-a-quite (Indian Scout)
— Indian Scout

— **5 WOUNDED**[48]
— 2nd Lieutenant Robert H. Young (4th U.S. Infantry)
— *gunshot wound, left leg, severe wound*

— Private Charles D. French (Co. B 2nd U.S. Cavalry)
— *gunshot wound, face severe wound*
— Private Wesley Gable (Co. B 2nd U.S. Cavalry)
— *gunshot wound, left arm, severe wound*
— Private George Pearson (Co. B 2nd U.S. Cavalry)
— *gunshot wound, left hand, severe wound*

— Acting Assistant Surgeon Thomas Maghee (Citizen)
— *gunshot wound, head, slight wound*

(0864) Operations, Crow Agency, Montana Territory (July 8 to 13, 1874)[49]
— Sergeant J. Mason (7th U.S. Infantry)
— 7th U.S. Infantry Detachment Co. A

(0865) Action, Rattlesnake Hills, Wyoming Territory (July 19, 1874)[50]
— Captain Alfred E. Bates (2nd U.S. Cavalry)
— 2nd U.S. Cavalry Co. B
— Detachment of Indian Scouts
— **1 WOUNDED**[51]
— Big Round Bone (Indian Scout)

(0866) Citizens, Shields River, near Fort Ellis, Montana Territory (July 26, 1874)[52]
— (1) Citizen Killed

[46] Indians. *Annual Report of Secretary of War (1874)*, 25, 32-33; *Annual Report of Secretary of War (1875)*, 321; Chronological List, 57; Heitman (Volume 2), 440; Record of Engagements, 40; Rodenbough, *From Everglade to Canyon*, 435.
[47] Register of Deaths Regular Army, 1860-1889 (Volume 5).
[48] Reports of Diseases and Individual Cases, F 450.
[49] Indians. Chronological List, 57; Heitman (Volume 2), 440.
[50] Indians. *Annual Report of Secretary of War (1875)*, 321; Chronological List, 57; Heitman (Volume 2), 440.
[51] Reports of Diseases and Individual Cases, F 451.
[52] Indians. *Annual Report of Secretary of War (1874)*, 39.

(0867) Skirmish, near San Carlos, Arizona Territory (August 15, 1874)[53]
— Desaline (Indian Scout)
— Detachment of Indian Scouts

(0868) Skirmish, Black Mesa, Arizona Territory (August 18, 1874)[54]
— Guide Corydon E. Cooley (Citizen)
— Detachment of Indian Scouts

(0869) Action, Adobe Walls, Texas (August 19, 1874)[55]
— 1st Lieutenant Frank D. Baldwin (5th U.S. Infantry)
— 6th U.S. Cavalry Detachment
— Detachment of Scouts
— Detachment of Indian Scouts
— **1 KILLED**[56]
— Scout George Huffman (Citizen)

(0870) Skirmish, North End of Sierra Ancha, Arizona Territory (August 22, 1874)[57]
— Guide Corydon E. Cooley (Citizen)
— Detachment of Indian Scouts

(0871) Citizens, near Wichita Agency, Indian Territory (August 22 and 23, 1874)[58]
— (4) Citizens Killed

(0872) Action, Wichita Agency, Indian Territory (August 22 and 23, 1874)[59]
— Lt. Colonel John W. Davidson (10th U.S. Cavalry)
— 10th U.S. Cavalry Co. C, E, H and L
— 25th U.S. Infantry Co. I
— **4 WOUNDED**[60]
— Sergeant Louis Mack (Co. H 10th U.S. Cavalry)
— *gunshot wound, right foot, slight wound*
— Sergeant Jospeh A. Blackburn (Co. L 10th U.S. Cavalry)
— *gunshot wound, right arm, slight wound*
— Saddler Adam Corke (Co. E 10th U.S. Cavalry)
— *gunshot wound, back, severe wound*
— Private Frederick Robinson (Co. I 25th U.S. Infantry)
— *gunshot wound, left wrist, slight wound*

— *2nd Lieutenant Louis H. Orleman (10th U.S. Cavalry) brevet promotion to 1st Lieutenant for gallant service in actions against Indians (Beaver Creek, Kansas, October 18, 1868 and the Wichita Agency, Indian Territory, August 22, 1874).*

[53] Indians. Chronological List, 57; Heitman (Volume 2), 440.
[54] Indians. Chronological List, 57; Heitman (Volume 2), 440; Alexander, *Arizona Military Place Names*, 15.
[55] Indians. *Annual Report of Secretary of War (1875)*, 78; Heitman (Volume 2), 440; Carter, *From Yorktown to Santiago*, 277; Leckie, *Military Conquest of the Southern Plains*, 209; Smith, *Old Army in Texas*, 157.
[56] Leckie, *Military Conquest of the Southern Plains*, 209.
[57] Indians. Chronological List, 57; Heitman (Volume 2), 440.
[58] Indians. *Annual Report of the Commissioner of Indian Affairs (1874)*, 221; Nye, *Carbine and Lance*, 209.
[59] Indians. *Annual Report of Secretary of War (1874)*, 41-42; *Annual Report of Secretary of War (1875)*, 321; Chronological List, 58; Heitman (Volume 2), 440; Record of Engagements, 40; Burton, *Black, Buckskin and Blue*, 182-186; Fowler, *Black Infantry in the West*, 30-32; Hamilton, *Sentinel of the Southern Plains*, 154-155; Leckie, *Buffalo Soldiers*, 120-125; Nye, *Carbine and Lance*, 206-210. Chronological List lists 10th U.S. Cavalry Co. E, H, L; 25th U.S. Infantry Co. I
[60] Reports of Diseases and Individual Cases, F 452.

(0873) Action, Mulberry Creek or Salt Fork of Red River, Texas (August 30, 1874)[61]
— Colonel Nelson A. Miles (5th U.S. Infantry)
— 6th U.S. Cavalry Co. A, D, F, G, H, I, L and M
— 5th U.S. Infantry Co. C, D, E and I
— Detachment of Indian Scouts
— **2 WOUNDED**[62]
— Sergeant Michael Bantley (Co. F 6th U.S. Cavalry)
— *gunshot wound, leg, fracture, severe wound*
— Private Frank Lewis (Co. G 6th U.S. Cavalry)
— *gunshot wound, leg, slight wound*

— *1st Lieutenant Frank D. Baldwin (5th U.S. Infantry) brevet promotion to Captain for gallant service in actions against Indians (Salt Fork of Red River, Texas, August 30, 1874 and McClellan Creek, Texas, November 8, 1874).*

— *Captain Adna R. Chaffee (6th U.S. Cavalry) brevet promotion to Lt. Colonel for gallant service in leading a cavalry charge over rough and precipitous bluffs held by Indians (Red River, Texas, August 30, 1874) and gallant service in action against Indians (Big Dry Wash, Arizona, July 17, 1882).*

— *Major Charles E. Compton (6th U.S. Cavalry) brevet promotion to Colonel for distinguished service in leading a cavalry battalion in a gallant and successful charge in action against Indians (Red River, Texas, August 30, 1874).*

— *Captain Curwen B. McClellan (6th U.S. Cavalry) brevet promotion to Lt. Colonel for gallant service in actions against Indians (Red River, Indian Territory, August 30, 1874 and Sand Andreas Mountains, New Mexico, April 7, 1880).*

— *Captain Tullius C. Tupper (6th U.S. Cavalry) brevet promotion to Lt. Colonel for gallant service in successfully leading a cavalry charge against Indians (Red River, Texas, August 30, 1874) and for gallant service in action against Indians (Las Animas Mountain, New Mexico, April 28, 1882).*

(0874) Action, Elm Fork of Red River, Texas (September 8, 1874)[63]
— 1st Lieutenant Frank D. Baldwin (5th U.S. Infantry)
— Detachment of Scouts
— **1 WOUNDED**[64]
—Enlisted Man

(0875) Action, Dry Fork of Wichita River, Texas (September 9 to 11, 1874)[65]
— Captain Wyllys Lyman (5th U.S. Infantry)
— 6th U.S. Cavalry Detachments Co. H and I
— 5th U.S. Infantry Co. I

[61] Indians. *Annual Report of Secretary of War (1874)*, 26; *Annual Report of Secretary of War (1875)*, 73, 78-79, 321; Chronological List, 58; Heitman (Volume 2), 440; Record of Engagements, 40; Carter, *From Yorktown to Santiago*, 163-165, 277; Cruse, *Battles of the Red River War*, 53-75; Hoig, *Tribal Wars of the Southern Plains*, 296-297; Leckie, *Buffalo Soldiers*, 126; Miles, *Personal Recollections*, 167-170; Gwynne, *Empire of the Summer Moon*, 276-277; Smith, *Old Army in Texas*, 158. Chronological List lists 6th U.S. Cavalry Co. A, D, F, G, H, I, L, M; 5th U.S. Infantry Co. C, D, E, L. Heitman lists 6th U.S. Cavalry Co. A, D, F, G, H, I, L, M; 5th U.S. Infantry Co. C, D, E, I.
[62] Reports of Diseases and Individual Cases, F 453.
[63] Indians. *Annual Report of Secretary of War (1875)*, 79; Heitman (Volume 2), 440; Haley, *Buffalo War*, 149-153. Heitman lists 7 September 1874. Heitman lists Detachment of Indian Scouts.
[64] *Annual Report of Secretary of War (1875)*, 79.
[65] Indians. *Annual Report of Secretary of War (1874)*, 26-27; *Annual Report of Secretary of War (1875)*, 73, 79, 86, 321; Chronological List, 58; Heitman (Volume 2), 440; Record of Engagements, 41; Archambeau, "Battle of Lyman's Wagon Train," *Panhandle-Plains Historical Review* 36 (1963): 89-101; Carter, *From Yorktown to Santiago*, 167-168, 278; Cruse, *Battles of the Red River War*, 76-86; Haley, *Buffalo War*, 155; Leckie, *Military Conquest of the Southern Plains*, 211-214; Miles, *Personal Recollections*, 172-173; Neal, *Valor Across the Lone Star*, 143-150; Nye, *Carbine and Lance*, 215-219. Chronological List and Heitman both list 9 September 1874.

— **1 KILLED**[66]
  — Sergeant William De Armond (Co. I 5th U.S. Infantry)

— **4 WOUNDED**[67]
  — 1st Lieutenant Granville Lewis (Co. I 5th U.S. Infantry)
   — *gunshot wound, knee, severe wound*

  — Sergeant John Singleton (Co. I 5th U.S. Infantry)
   — *gunshot wound, leg, slight wound*
  — Private D.R. Buck (Co. I 5th U.S. Infantry)
   — *gunshot wound, head, slight wound*

  — Wagonmaster James L. Sanford (Citizen)
   — *gunshot wound, hip, slight wound*

— *Sergeant William De Armond (Co. I 5th U.S. Infantry) received MOH: Gallantry in action (Upper Washita, Texas, September 9 to 11, 1874).*

— *Sergeant Fred S. Hay (Co. I 5th U.S. Infantry) received MOH: Gallantry in action (Upper Wichita, Texas, September 9, 1874).*

— *Corporal John James (5th U.S. Infantry) received MOH: Gallantry in action (Upper Wichita, Texas, September 9 to 11, 1874).*

— *Corporal John J.H. Kelly (Co. I 5th U.S. Cavalry) received MOH: Gallantry in action (Upper Wichita, Texas, September 9, 1874).*

— *Private Thomas Kelly (Co. I 5th U.S. Cavalry) received MOH: Gallantry in action (Upper Wichita, Texas, September 9, 1874).*

— *Sergeant George K. Kitchen (Co. H 6th U.S. Cavalry) received MOH: Gallantry in action (Upper Wichita, Texas, September 9, 1874).*

— *Sergeant John W. Knox (Co. I 5th U.S. Cavalry) received MOH: Gallantry in action (Upper Wichita, Texas, September 9, 1874).*

— *Sergeant William Koelpin (Co. I 5th U.S. Cavalry) received MOH: Gallantry in action (Upper Wichita, Texas, September 9, 1874).*

---

[66] Reports of Diseases and Individual Cases, F 454.
[67] Reports of Diseases and Individual Cases, F 454; Cruse, *Battles of the Red River War*, 77, 234.

— *1st Lieutenant Granville Lewis (5th U.S. Infantry) brevet promotion to Captain for gallant service in action against Indians (Upper Washita River, Texas, September 9, 1874, where he was severely wounded).*

— *Captain Wyllys Lyman (5th U.S. Infantry) brevet promotion to Lt. Colonel for gallant and meritorious service in action against Indians (Upper Washita River, Texas, September 9 to 11, 1874).*

— *First Sergeant John Mitchell (Co. I 5th U.S. Infantry) received MOH: Gallantry in engagement with Indians (Upper Washita, Texas, September 9 to 11, 1874).*

— *Corporal William W. Morris (Co. H 6th U.S. Cavalry) received MOH: Gallantry in engagement with Indians (Upper Washita, Texas, September 9 to 11, 1874).*

— *Sergeant Frederick S. Neilon (Co. A 6th U.S. Cavalry) received MOH: Gallantry in action (Upper Washita, Texas, September 9 to 11, 1874).*

— *Sergeant Josiah Pennsyl (Co. M 6th U.S. Cavalry) received MOH: Gallantry in action (Upper Washita, Texas, September 11, 1874).*

— *2nd Lieutenant Frank West (6th U.S. Cavalry) brevet promotion to 1st Lieutenant for gallant service in action against Indians (Washita River, Texas, September 9 to 11, 1874).*

(0876) Action, Sweetwater Creek, Texas (September 9, 1874)[68]
    — UNKNOWN
        — 6th U.S. Cavalry Detachment Co. H
  — **1 WOUNDED**[69]
        — Enlisted Man (6th U.S. Cavalry)

(0877) Skirmish, near Wichita River, Texas (September 11 and 12, 1874)[70]
    — Corporal Edward C. Sharpless (6th U.S. Cavalry)
        — 6th U.S. Cavalry Detachment Co. H

— *Corporal Edward C. Sharpless (Co. H 6th U.S. Cavalry) received MOH: While carrying dispatches was attacked by 125 hostile Indians, whom he and his comrades fought throughout the day (Wichita River, Texas, September 12, 1874).*

(0878) Action, Canadian River, Texas (September 12, 1874)[71]
    — Sergeant Zachariah T. Woodall (6th U.S. Cavalry)
        — 6th U.S. Cavalry Detachment

[68] Indians. Chronological List, 58; Heitman (Volume 2), 440; Carter, *From Yorktown to Santiago*, 277; Smith, *Old Army in Texas*, 158.
[69] Chronological List, 58.
[70] Indians. Chronological List, 58; Heitman (Volume 2), 440; Carter, *From Yorktown to Santiago*, 278.
[71] Indians. *Annual Report of Secretary of War (1875)*, 79; Chronological List, 58; Record of Engagements, 42; Carter, *From Yorktown to Santiago*, 165-167; Cruse, *Battles of the Red River War*, 87-94; Leckie, *Military Conquest of the Southern Plains*, 214-215; Miles, *Personal Recollections*, 173-174; Neal, *Valor Across the Lone Star*, 158-166; Nye, *Carbine and Lance*, 219; Smith, *Old Army in Texas*, 158. Chronological List lists 6th U.S. Cavalry Detachment.

— Detachment of Scouts
— **1 KILLED**[72]
— Private George W. Smith (Co. M 6th U.S. Cavalry) — d. 9-13-1874

— **3 WOUNDED**[73]
— Sergeant Zachariah T. Woodall (Co. I 6th U.S. Cavalry)
— *gunshot wound, severe wound*
— Private John Harrington (Co. H 6th U.S. Cavalry)
— *gunshot wound, severe wound*

— Scout Amos Chapman (Citizen)
— *gunshot wound, leg, fracture, severe wound*

— *Scout Amos Chapman (Civilian) received MOH: Gallantry in action (Washita River, Texas, September 12, 1874).*[74]

— *Scout William Dixon (Civilian) received MOH: Gallantry in action (Washita River, Texas, September 12, 1874).*[75]

— *Private John Harrington (Co. H 6th U.S. Cavalry) received MOH: While carrying dispatches was attacked by 125 hostile Indians, whom he and his comrades fought throughout the day. He was severely wounded in the hip and unable to move. He continued to fight, defending an exposed dying man (Washita River, Texas, September 12, 1874).*

— *Private John Harrington (Co. H 6th U.S. Cavalry) received Certificate of Merit: For gallantry in action, in carrying dispatches, he was attacked by 125 hostile Indians, whom he and his comrades fought throughout the day (Washita River, Texas, September 12, 1874).*

— *Private Peter Roth (Co. A 6th U.S. Cavalry) received MOH: While carrying dispatches was attacked by 125 hostile Indians, whom he and his comrades fought throughout the day (Washita River, Texas, September 12, 1874).*

— *Private George W. Smith (Co. M 6th U.S. Cavalry) received MOH: While carrying dispatches, was attacked by 125 hostile Indians, whom he and his comrades fought throughout the day. (Washita River, Texas, September 12, 1874).*

— *Sergeant Zachariah T. Woodall (Co. I 6th U.S. Cavalry) received MOH: While in command of men and carrying dispatches, was attacked by 125 Indians. He and his command fought throughout the day, he being severely wounded (Washita River, Texas, September 12, 1874).*

---

[72] Reports of Diseases and Individual Cases, F 454.
[73] Reports of Diseases and Individual Cases, F 454.
[74] In 1916, the general review of all Medals of Honor deemed 900 unwarranted. This recipient was one of them. In June 1989, the U.S. Army Board of Correction of Records restored the medal to this recipient.
[75] In 1916, the general review of all Medals of Honor deemed 900 unwarranted. This recipient was one of them. In June 1989, the U.S. Army Board of Correction of Records restored the medal to this recipient.

— *Sergeant Zachariah T. Woodall (Co. I 6th U.S. Cavalry) received Certificate of Merit: For gallantry in action against hostile Comanche, Cheyenne, and Kiowa Indians, while in command of a detachment of five men and carrying dispatches, he was attacked by 125 Indians, whom he and his command fought throughout the day, he being seriously wounded (Washita River, Texas, September 12, 1874).*

"The simple recital of their deeds and the mention of the odds against which they fought; how the wounded defended the dying, and the dying aided the wounded by exposure to fresh wounds after the power of action was gone; these alone present a scene of cool courage, heroism and self-sacrifice which duty, as well as inclination, prompts us to recognize, but which we cannot fitly honor."
— Nelson A. Miles, U.S. Army[76]

(0879) Skirmish, between Sweetwater Creek and Dry Fork of Wichita River, Texas (September 12, 1874)[77]
— Major William R. Price (8th U.S. Cavalry)
— 8th U.S. Cavalry Co. C, K and L

(0880) Action, Headwaters of Cave Creek, Arizona Territory (September 18, 1874)[78]
— Sergeant Alexander Garner (5th U.S. Cavalry)
— 5th U.S. Cavalry Detachment Co. K
— Detachment of Indian Scouts
— 1 KILLED[79]
—Indian Scout

— 1 WOUNDED[80]
— Indian Scout
— *gunshot wound, left forearm, fracture severe wound*

(0881) Action, Red River, near Tule Canyon or Palo Duro Canyon, Texas (September 26 to 28, 1874)[81]
— Colonel Ranald S. Mackenzie (4th U.S. Cavalry)
— 4th U.S. Cavalry Co. A, D, E, F, H, I and K
— 1 WOUNDED[82]
— Bugler Henry E. Hard (Co. L 4th U.S. Cavalry)
— *slight wound*

— *Private Gregory Mahoney (Co. E 4th U.S. Cavalry) received MOH: Gallantry in attack on a large party of Cheyenne (Red River, Texas, September 26 to 28, 1874).*

[76] Colonel Nelson A. Miles (5th U.S. Infantry) to Adjutant-General, 24 September 1874. Miles, *Personal Recollections*, 174.
[77] Indians. Chronological List, 58; Heitman (Volume 2), 440; Record of Engagements, 42; Cruse, *Battles of the Red River War*, 96-104; Haley, *Buffalo War*, 161-163; Leckie, *Buffalo Soldiers*, 126; Smith, *Old Army in Texas*, 158. Chronological List lists "Miles expedition".
[78] Indians. *Annual Report of Secretary of War (1875)*, 321; Chronological List, 58; Heitman (Volume 2), 440; Price, *Across the Continent*, 661; Thrapp, *Al Sieber*, 149-150. Chronological List and Heitman both list 17 September 1874.
[79] Reports of Diseases and Individual Cases, F 455. Form 55, the List of Wounded, identifies two Tonto scouts.
[80] Reports of Diseases and Individual Cases, F 455. Form 55 identifies two Tonto scouts.
[81] Indians. Chronological List, 58; Heitman (Volume 2), 440; Record of Engagements, 42; Carter, *On the Border with Mackenzie*, 485-494; Cruse, *Battles of the Red River War*, 105-113, 146; Gwynne, *War of the Summer Moon*, 277-283; Haley, *Buffalo War*, 176; Mulroy, *Freedom on the Border*, 122-124; Neal, *Valor Across the Lone Star*, 170-189; Nye, *Carbine and Lance*, 221-225; Robinson, *Bad Hand*, 171-178; Wallace, *Ranald S. Mackenzie*, 138-146. Heitman lists 4th U.S. Cavalry Co. A, D, E, F, H, I, K, L.
[82] "Henry E. Hard slightly wounded". 4th U.S. Cavalry Regimental Return September 1874.

— Private William McCabe (Co. E 4ᵗʰ U.S. Cavalry) received MOH: Gallantry in attack on large party of Cheyenne (Red River, Texas, September 26 to 28, 1874).

— Private Adam Paine (Indian Scout) received MOH: Rendered invaluable service to Colonel R.S. Mackenzie, 4ᵗʰ U.S. Cavalry, during this engagement (Canyon Blanco tributary of Red River, Texas, September 26 and 27, 1874).

— Corporal Edwin Phoenix received MOH: Gallantry in action (Red River, Texas, September 26 to 28, 1874).

— 1ˢᵗ Lieutenant William A. Thompson (4ᵗʰ U.S. Cavalry) brevet promotion to Captain for gallant service in actions against Indians (Canyon, near Red River, Texas, September 27 and 28, 1874 and Las Lagunas Quatro, Texas, November 5, 1874).

(0882) Skirmish, near Canadian River, Texas (October 1874)[83]
    — Captain Ambrose E. Hooker (9ᵗʰ U.S. Cavalry)
        — 9ᵗʰ U.S. Cavalry Co. E and K

(0883) Operations, near Fort Sill, Indian Territory (October 4 to 31, 1874)[84]
    — Captain Charles Parker (9ᵗʰ U.S. Cavalry)
        — 9ᵗʰ U.S. Cavalry Co. K

(0884) Skirmish, Salt Fork of Red River, Texas (October 9, 1874)[85]
    — Lt. Colonel George P. Buell (11ᵗʰ U.S. Infantry)
        — 11ᵗʰ U.S. Infantry Co. A, E, F, H and I
        — Detachment of Indian Scouts

(0885) Skirmish, near Gageby Creek, Indian Territory (October 13, 1874)[86]
    — Major William R. Price (8ᵗʰ U.S. Cavalry)
        — 8ᵗʰ U.S. Cavalry Co. H, K and L
        — Detachment of Indian Scouts

— 1ˢᵗ Lieutenant Henry W. Sprole (8ᵗʰ U.S. Cavalry) brevet promotion to Captain for gallant service in the pursuit of Indians (Washita River, Texas, October 14 and 15, 1874) and in action against Indians (Muster Creek, Texas, November 29, 1874).

(0886) Skirmish, near Washita River, Indian Territory (October 17, 1874)[87]
    — Captain Adna R. Chafee (6ᵗʰ U.S. Cavalry)
        — 8ᵗʰ U.S. Cavalry Co. C
        — 6ᵗʰ U.S. Cavalry Co. I
        — 5ᵗʰ U.S. Infantry Co. C

[83] Indians. Chronological List, 58; Record of Engagements, 43; Smith, *Old Army in Texas*, 159.
[84] Indians. Chronological List, 58; Heitman (Volume 2), 440. Heitman lists 4 October 1874.
[85] Indians. Chronological List, 58; Heitman (Volume 2), 440; Record of Engagements, 42; Cruse, *Battles of the Red River War*, 146; Haley, *Buffalo War*, 190; Leckie, *Military Conquest of the Southern Plains*, 224; Nye, *Carbine and Lance*, 225; Rister, *Fort Griffin*, 122.
[86] Indians. Chronological List, 58; Heitman (Volume 2), 441; Record of Engagements, 42; Haley, *Buffalo War*, 191; Nye, *Carbine and Lance*, 225. Chronological List lists 8ᵗʰ U.S. Cavalry Detachment; Detachment of Indian Scouts.
[87] Indians. *Annual Report of Secretary of War (1875)*, 80; Chronological List, 58; Heitman (Volume 2), 441; Record of Engagements, 42; Carter, *From Yorktown to Santiago*, 278; Haley, *Buffalo War*, 191; Nye, *Carbine and Lance*, 225. Chronological List and Heitman both list 6ᵗʰ U.S. Cavalry Co. I.

(0887) Skirmish, Old Pueblo Fork of Little Colorado River, Arizona Territory (October 23, 1874)[88]
— 1st Lieutenant Bernard Reilly, Jr. (5th U.S. Cavalry)
— 5th U.S. Cavalry Detachments Co. A and I
— Detachment of Indian Scouts

(0888) Operations, near Fort Sill, Indian Territory (October 28 to November 8, 1874)[89]
— Lt. Colonel John W. Davidson (10th U.S. Cavalry)
— 6th U.S. Cavalry Co. D
— 10th U.S. Cavalry Co. B, C, H, K, L and M
— 5th U.S. Infantry Co. D
— 11th U.S. Infantry D, E and I
— Detachment of Indian Scouts

(0889) Skirmish, Cave Creek, Arizona Territory (October 29, 1874)[90]
— Sergeant Rudolph Stauffer (5th U.S. Cavalry)
— 5th U.S. Cavalry Detachment Co. K

(0890) Citizens, near Upper Arkansas Indian Agency, Indian Territory (November 1874)[91]
— (2) Citizens Killed

(0891) Action, Sunset Pass, Little Colorado River, Arizona Territory (November 1, 1874)[92]
— 1st Lieutenant Charles King (5th U.S. Cavalry)
— 5th U.S. Cavalry Detachments Co. A and K
— **1 WOUNDED**[93]
— 1st Lieutenant Charles King (5th U.S. Cavalry)
— *gunshot wound, right arm, fracture, severe wound*

— *Sergeant Bernard Taylor (Co. A 5th U.S. Cavalry) received MOH: Bravery in rescuing 1st Lieutenant Charles King, 5th U.S. Cavalry from Indians (Sunset Pass, Arizona Territory, November 1, 1874).*

(0892) Skirmish, Las Lagunas, Quatro, Texas (November 3, 1874)[94]
— Colonel Ranald S. Mackenzie (4th U.S. Cavalry)
— 4th U.S. Cavalry Co. A, D, E, F, H, I, K and L

— *Farrier Ernest Veuve (Co. A 4th U.S. Cavalry) received MOH: Gallant manner in which he faced a desperate Indian (Staked Plains, Texas, November 3, 1874).*

(0893) Skirmish, near Laguna Tahoka, Texas (November 6, 1874)[95]
— 1st Lieutenant William A. Thompson (4th U.S. Cavalry)
— 4th U.S. Cavalry Co. A

[88] Indians. Chronological List, 59; Heitman (Volume 2), 441; Price, *Across the Continent*, 661. Heitman lists 5th U.S. Cavalry Detachment Co. I; Detachment of Indian Scouts.
[89] Indians. Chronological List, 59; Heitman (Volume 2), 441; Carter, *From Yorktown to Santiago*, 278; Hamilton, *Sentinel of the Southern Plains*, 156; Leckie, *Buffalo Soldiers*, 133; Nye, *Carbine and Lance*, 225-226.
[90] Indians. Chronological List, 59; Heitman (Volume 2), 441; Alexander, *Arizona Frontier Military Place Names*, 31; Price, *Across the Continent*, 661.
[91] Indians. Killed were hunters Charles M. Monohan and Edward O'Leary. *Annual Report of the Commissioner of Indian Affairs (1874)*, 233-234.
[92] Indians. *Annual Report of Secretary of War (1875)*, 321; Chronological List, 59; Heitman (Volume 2), 441; Alexander, *Arizona Frontier Military Place Names*, 114; Price, *Across the Continent*, 662; Russell, *Campaigning with King*, 47-52.
[93] Reports of Diseases and Individual Cases, F 456.
[94] Indians. Chronological List, 59; Heitman (Volume 2), 441; Record of Engagements, 43; Carter, *On the Border with Mackenzie*, 506; Haley, *Buffalo War*, 192; Neal, *Valor Across the Lone Star*, 191-203; Robinson, *Bad Hand*, 180-181; Wallace, *Ranald S. Mackenzie*, 155-156.
[95] Indians. Chronological List, 59; Heitman (Volume 2), 441; Carter, *On the Border with Mackenzie*, 506; Neal, *Valor Across the Lone Star*, 191-203; Rister, *Fort Griffin*, 119; Robinson, *Bad Hand*, 180-181; Smith, *Old Army in Texas*, 159; Wallace, *Ranald S. Mackenzie*, 155-156.

— *Corporal John W. Comfort (Co. A 4th U.S. Cavalry) received MOH: Ran down and killed an Indian (Staked Plains, Texas, November 5, 1874).*

— *1st Lieutenant William A. Thompson (4th U.S. Cavalry) brevet promotion to Captain for gallant service in actions against Indians (Canyon, near Red River, Texas, September 27 and 28, 1874 and Las Lagunas Quatro, Texas, November 5, 1874).*

(0894) Action, McClellan Creek, near North Fork of Red River, Texas (November 6, 1874)[96]
— 1st Lieutenant Henry J. Farnsworth (8th U.S. Cavalry)
   — 8th U.S. Cavalry Detachment Co. H
— 1 KILLED[97]
   — Private William Densham (Co. H 8th U.S. Cavalry)
   — Private Rufus Hibbard (Co. H 8th U.S Cavalry)

— 4 WOUNDED[98]
   — Blacksmith Henry Fields (Co. H 8th U.S. Cavalry)
      — *gunshot wounds, back, left elbow, slight wounds*
   — Bugler Herman Fehr (Co. H 8th U.S. Cavalry)
      — *gunshot wound, back, severe wound*
   — Corporal Thomas J. Thompson (Co. H 8th U.S. Cavalry)
      — *gunshot wound, back, severe wound*
   — Private George Robinson (Co. H 8th U.S. Cavalry)
      — *gunshot wound, right hand, slight wound*

(0895) Skirmish, near McClellan Creek, Texas (November 8, 1874)[99]
— 1st Lieutenant Frank D. Baldwin (5th U.S. Infantry)
   — 6th U.S. Cavalry Detachment Co. D
   — 5th U.S. Infantry Detachment Co. D

— *2nd Lieutenant Hobart K. Bailey (5th U.S. Infantry) brevet promotion to 1st Lieutenant for gallant service in action (McClellan Creek, Texas, November 8, 1874).*

— *1st Lieutenant Frank D. Baldwin (5th U.S. Infantry) brevet promotion to Captain for gallant service in actions against Indians (Salt Fork of Red River, Texas, August 30, 1874 and McClellan Creek, Texas, November 8, 1874).*

— *1st Lieutenant Frank D. Baldwin (5th U.S. Infantry) received MOH: Rescued, with 2 companies, two white girls by a voluntary attack upon Indians whose superior numbers and strong position would have warranted delay for reinforcements, but which delay would have permitted the Indians to escape and kill their captives (November 8, 1874).*

[96] Indians. *Annual Report of Secretary of War (1875)*, 80, 321; Chronological List, 59; Heitman (Volume 2), 441; Record of Engagements, 43; Cruse, *Battles of the Red River War*, 114-142; Haley, *Buffalo War*, 192; Leckie, *Buffalo Soldiers*, 133; Nye, *Carbine and Lance*, 226. Chronological List and Heitman both list 8th U.S. Cavalry Co. H.
[97] Reports of Diseases and Individual Cases, F 457; Register of Deaths Regular Army, 1860-1889 (Volume 6); 8th U.S. Cavalry Regimental Return November 1876. Private Rufus Hibbard is not listed on F457.
[98] Reports of Diseases and Individual Cases, F 457.
[99] Indians. *Annual Report of Secretary of War (1875)*, 80; Heitman (Volume 2), 441; Record of Engagements, 43; Carter, *From Yorktown to Santiago*, 169-170, 278; Haley, *Buffalo War*, 193; Hoig, *Fort Reno*, 31-32; Miles, *Personal Recollections*, 174-175; Neal, *Valor Across the Lone Star*, 210-214; Nye, *Carbine and Lance*, 226.

— *1st Lieutenant Gilbert E. Overton (6th U.S. Cavalry) brevet promotion to Captain for gallant service in leading a cavalry charge in action against Indians (McClellan Creek, Texas, November 8, 1874).*

(0896) Action, near Fort Dodge, Kansas (November 10, 1874)[100]
— 2nd Lieutenant Robert Hanna (6th U.S. Cavalry)
— 6th U.S. Cavalry Detachment Co. B
— **1 WOUNDED**[101]
— Private Alfred Skelton (Co. B 6th U.S. Cavalry)
— *gunshot wound, right hand, slight wound*

(0897) Citizens, Fort Peck Agency, Montana Territory (November 13, 1874)[102]
— (1) Citizen Killed

(0898) Citizens, near Central Station, Staked Plains, Texas (November 22, 1874)[103]
— (1) Citizen Killed

(0899) Skirmish, Snow Lake or Jarvis Pass, Arizona Territory (November 25, 1874)[104]
— 2nd Lieutenant George O. Eaton (5th U.S. Cavalry)
— 5th U.S. Cavalry Detachments Co. A and K

(0900) Citizens, near Sycamore Creek, Texas (November 27, 1874)[105]
— (1) Citizen Killed

(0901) Skirmish, near Muster Creek, Texas (November 29, 1874)[106]
— Captain Charles A. Hartwell (8th U.S. Cavalry)
— 8th U.S. Cavalry Co. C, H, K and L

— *1st Lieutenant Henry W. Sprole (8th U.S. Cavalry) brevet promotion to Captain for gallant service in the pursuit of Indians (Washita River, Texas, October 14 and 15, 1874) and in action against Indians (Muster Creek, Texas, November 29, 1874).*

(0902) Skirmish, Canyon Creek, Tonto Basin, Arizona Territory (December 1, 1874)[107]
— Captain Robert H. Montgomery (5th U.S. Cavalry)
— 5th U.S. Cavalry Detachment Co. B
— Detachment of Indian Scouts

— *Captain Robert H. Montgomery (5th U.S. Cavalry) brevet promotion to Major for gallant service in action against Indians (Muchos Canyon, Arizona, September 25, 1872) and during a scout made by him (Tonto Basin, Arizona, November and December, 1874).*

---

[100] Bandits. Heitman (Volume 2), 441; Carter, *From Yorktown to Santiago*, 172; Rodenbough, *Army of the United States*, 243-244.
[101] Fort Dodge Post Return November 1874.
[102] Indians. Killed was William Benoist. *Annual Report of Commissioner of Indian Affairs (1875)*, 310.
[103] Indians. Killed was an "unnamed Frenchman". *Annual Report of Secretary of War (1875)*, 99.
[104] Indians. Chronological List, 59; Heitman (Volume 2), 441; Price, *Across the Continent*, 662; Russell, *Campaigning with King*, 53.
[105] Indians. Killed was Juan Dias. *Annual Report of Secretary of War (1875)*, 99.
[106] Indians. *Annual Report of Secretary of War (1875)*, 81; Chronological List, 59; Heitman (Volume 2), 441; Record of Engagements, 43; Cruse, *Battles of the Red River War*, 146-147; Rodenbough, *Army of the United* States, 270, 272-273; Smith, *Old Army in Texas*, 160. Chronological List and Heitman both list 28 November 1874.
[107] Indians. Chronological List, 59; Heitman (Volume 2), 441; Price, *Across the Continent*, 662.

(0903) Skirmish, Gageby Creek, Indian Territory (December 2, 1874)[108]
　　— First Sergeant Dennis Ryan (6th U.S. Cavalry)
　　　　— 6th U.S. Cavalry Detachment Co. I

　　— First Sergeant Dennis Ryan (Co. I 6th U.S. Cavalry) received MOH: Courage while in command of a detachment (Gageby Creek, Indian Territory, December 2, 1874).

(0904) Skirmish, near Kingfisher Creek, Indian Territory (December 7, 1874)[109]
　　— Captain Alexander S.B. Keyes (10th U.S. Cavalry)
　　　　— 10th U.S. Cavalry Co. D, Detachment Co. M

(0905) Skirmish, Muchaquay Valley, Staked Plains, Texas (December 8, 1874)[110]
　　— 2nd Lieutenant Matthew Leeper (4th U.S. Cavalry)
　　　　— 4th U.S. Cavalry Co. I

　　— Private Frederick Bergerndahl (Band 4th U.S. Cavalry) received MOH: Gallantry in long chase after Indians (Staked Plains, Texas, December 8, 1874).

　　— Private John O'Sullivan (Co. I 4th U.S. Cavalry) received MOH: Gallantry in long chase after Indians (Stakes Plains, Texas, December 8, 1874).

　　— 1st Lieutenant Lewis Warrington (4th U.S. Cavalry) received MOH: Gallantry in combat with five Indians (Muchaquay Valley, Texas, December 8, 1874).

(0906) Skirmish, Standing Rock Agency, Dakota Territory (December 12, 1874)[111]
　　— Captain George W. Yates (7th U.S. Cavalry)
　　　　— 7th U.S. Cavalry Co. F and L

(0907) Skirmish, North Fork of Canadian River, Indian Territory (December 28, 1874)[112]
　　— Captain Alexander S.B. Keyes (10th U.S. Cavalry)
　　　　— 10th U.S. Cavalry Co. I and M

　　— Captain George M. Randall (23rd U.S. Infantry) brevet promotion to Colonel for gallant service in action against Indians (Pinal Mountains, Arizona, March 8, 1874) and distinguished service during the campaigns against Indians (Arizona, 1874).

TOTAL KILLED 1874 — 1/7/3/1 (Officers, Enlisted Men, Indian Scouts, Citizens)

---

[108] Indians. *Annual Report of Secretary of War (1875)*, 81; Chronological List, 59; Heitman (Volume 2), 441; Record of Engagements, 44; Carter, *From Yorktown to Santiago*, 172, 278; Cruse, *Battles of the Red River War*, 147; Haley, *Buffalo War*, 195; Leckie, *Military Conquest of the Southern Plains*, 228.
[109] Indians. Chronological List, 59; Record of Engagements, 44; Haley, *Buffalo War*, 195.
[110] Indians. Chronological List, 59; Heitman (Volume 2), 441; Carter, *On the Border with Mackenzie*, 516-518; Haley, *Buffalo War*, 197; Neal, *Valor Across the Lone Star*, 224-227; Smith, *Old Army in Texas*, 160; Wallace, *Ranald S. Mackenzie*, 162-163.
[111] Indians. Chronological List, 59; Heitman (Volume 2), 441.
[112] Indians. Chronological List, 59; Record of Engagements, 44; Haley, *Buffalo War*, 197; Leckie, *Buffalo Soldiers*, 134-135.

1875

"No class of citizens is more desirous of peace with the Indians that are officers of the Army. There is no glory to be won in savage warfare, and when to this feeling is added the conviction that the Indians have been driven to war by injustice and outrage, the indignation felt by honorable soldiers can easily be imagined. The present system places the question of war or peace in our remote Territories absolutely under the control of irresponsible civil agents, while the Army officers, who must fight the battles are powerless to avert the unnecessary evil."

— John M. Schofield, U.S. Army[1]

---

[1] Official Report of Major General John M. Schofield, Commander Military Division of Pacific, 20 September 1875. *Annual Report of Secretary of War (1875)*, 122.

(0908) Operations, near Camp Apache, Arizona Territory (January 2 to February 23, 1875)[2]
— Captain Frederick D. Ogilby (8th U.S. Infantry)
— 5th U.S. Cavalry Detachments Co. B and I
— Detachment of Indian Scouts

(0909) Operations, Hackberry Creek, Kansas (January 3 to 6, 1875)[3]
— 2nd Lieutenant Frank S. Hinkle (5th U.S. Infantry)
— 5th U.S. Infantry Detachment Co. F
— 19th U.S. Infantry Detachment Co. K

(0910) Skirmish, Camp Apache, Arizona Territory (January 9, 1875)[4]
— Captain William S. Worth (8th U.S. Infantry)
— 8th U.S. Infantry Co. K

(0911) Action, Solis Ranch, near Ringgold Barracks, Texas (January 26, 1875)[5]
— Sergeant Edmund Troutman (9th U.S. Cavalry)
— 9th U.S. Cavalry Detachment Co. G
— **2 KILLED**[6]
— Private Jerry Owsley (Co. G 9th U.S. Cavalry)
— Private Moses Turner (Co. G 9th U.S. Cavalry)

(0912) Citizens, Hidalgo County, Texas (February 27, 1875)[7]
— (2) Citizens Killed

(0913) Citizens, Tio Cuno Ranch, Texas (March 16, 1875)[8]
— (1) Citizen Killed

(0914) Citizens, near Edinburgh, Texas (March 23, 1875)[9]
— (1) Citizen Killed

[2] Indians. Chronological List, 59; Heitman (Volume 2), 441.
[3] Indians. Chronological List, 59; Heitman (Volume 2), 441.
[4] Indians. Chronological List, 59.
[5] Bandits. *Annual Report of Secretary of War (1875)*, 99; Heitman (Volume 2), 441; Record of Engagements, 46; Leckie, *Buffalo Soldiers*, 108-109; Smith, *Old Army in Texas*, 160.
[6] 9th U.S. Cavalry Regimental Return January 1875.
[7] Bandits. Killed were former Justice of the Peace Joseph F. Fulton and his clerk Manrico Villaneuna. *Annual Report of Secretary of War (1875)*, 100, 102.
[8] Bandits. Killed was George Hill. *Annual Report of Secretary of War (1875)*, 100, 102.
[9] Bandits. Killed was Alexander Morel. *Annual Report of Secretary of War (1875)*, 100, 102.
[10] Indians. *Annual Report of Secretary of War (1875)*, 75, 86-88, 321; Chronological List, 59; Heitman (Volume 2), 441; Record of Engagements, 46-47; Carter, *From Yorktown to Santiago*, 173, 278; Hoig, *Fort Reno*, 34-36; Leckie, *Buffalo Soldiers*, 136-138. Chronological List and Heitman both list 6th U.S. Cavalry Co. M; 10th U.S. Cavalry Co. D, M; 5th U.S. Infantry Detachment Co. H.

(0915) Action, Sand Hills, near Cheyenne Agency, Indian Territory (April 6, 1875) [10]
  — Lt. Colonel Thomas H. Neill (6th U.S. Cavalry)
     — 6th U.S. Cavalry Co. M
     — 10th U.S. Cavalry Co. D and M
  — 1 KILLED [11]
     — Private Clark Young (Co. M 10th U.S. Cavalry) — d. 4-12-1875

  — 14 WOUNDED [12]
     — Sergeant August Springer (Co. M 6th U.S. Cavalry)
       — gunshot wound, right thigh, slight wound
     — Private George Abbott (Co. M 6th U.S. Cavalry)
       — gunshot wounds, right shoulder, slight wound, left arm, fracture, severe wound
     — Private Eugene Evans (Co. M 6th U.S. Cavalry)
       — gunshot wound, right shoulder, slight wound
     — Private Henry Smeaton (Co. M 6th U.S. Cavalry)
       — gunshot wound, right foot, slight wound

     — Corporal Richard Lewis (Co. D 10th U.S. Cavalry)
       — gunshot wound, neck, slight wound
     — Private John Green (Co. D 10th U.S. Cavalry)
       — gunshot wound, left arm, slight wound
     — Private Robert Logan (Co. D 10th U.S. Cavalry)
       — arrow wound, back, slight wound
     — Private David Sattler (Co. D 10th U.S. Cavalry)
       — gunshot wounds, right thigh, abdomen, slight wounds
     — Private Jacob Slemp (Co. D 10th U.S. Cavalry)
       — gunshot wound, left thigh, slight wound
     — Private Benjamin Smith (Co. D 10th U.S. Cavalry)
       — gunshot wound, thigh, slight wound
     — Private Ephraim Smith (Co. D 10th U.S. Cavalry)
       — gunshot wound, right hand, fracture, severe wound
       — arrow wound, hand, slight wound
     — Private Samuel Vivins (Co. D 10th U.S. Cavalry)
       — gunshot wound, right hand, fracture, severe wound

     — Corporal Perry Hayman (Co. M 10th U.S. Cavalry)
       — gunshot wound, back, slight wound
     — Private George Berry (Co. M 10th U.S. Cavalry)
       — gunshot wound, right side, slight wound

[11] Reports of Diseases and Individual Cases, F 458.
[12] Reports of Diseases and Individual Cases, F 458.

"[Captain William A. Rafferty's] men (6ᵗʰ U.S. Cavalry Co. M) behaved very well, and worked their way up dismounted to within seventy-five yards of the crest of the sand-hill, when night set in; they did all men could do. [Captain Andrew S. Bennett's] men (5ᵗʰ U.S. Infantry Co. B) behaved admirably in all that was required of them."
— Thomas H. Neill, U.S. Army[13]

(0916) Action, North Fork of Sappa Creek, Kansas (April 23, 1875)[14]

— 2ⁿᵈ Lieutenant Austin Henely (6ᵗʰ U.S. Cavalry)
— 6ᵗʰ U.S. Cavalry Detachment Co. H
— 19ᵗʰ U.S. Infantry Detachment Co. K
— Detachment of Volunteers
— **2 KILLED**[15]
— Sergeant Theodore Papier (Co. H 6ᵗʰ U.S. Cavalry)
— Private Robert Theims (Co. H 6ᵗʰ U.S. Cavalry)

— *Private James F. Ayers (Co. H 6ᵗʰ U.S. Cavalry) received MOH: Rapid pursuit, gallantry, energy, and enterprise in an engagement with Indians (Sappa Creek, Kansas, April 23, 1875).*

— *Trumpeter Michael Dawson (Co. H 6ᵗʰ U.S. Cavalry) received MOH: Gallantry in action (Sappa Creek, Kansas, April 23, 1875).*

— *Private Peter W. Gardiner (Co. H 6ᵗʰ U.S. Cavalry) received MOH: With five other men he waded in mud and water up the creek to a position directly behind an entrenched Cheyenne position, who were using natural bank pits to good advantage against the main column. This surprise attack from the enemy rear broke their resistance (Sappa Creek, Kansas, April 23, 1875).*

— *Private Simpson Hornaday (Co. H 6ᵗʰ U.S. Cavalry) received MOH: With five other men he waded in mud and water up the creek to a position directly behind an entrenched Cheyenne position, who were using natural bank pits to good advantage against the main column. This surprise attack from the enemy rear broke their resistance (Sappa Creek, Kansas, April 23, 1875).*

— *Private James Lowthers (Co. H 6ᵗʰ U.S. Cavalry) received MOH: With five other men he waded in mud and water up the creek to a position directly behind an entrenched Cheyenne position,*

[13] Official Report of Lt. Colonel Thomas H. Neill (6ᵗʰ U.S. Cavalry), 7 April 1875. *Annual Report of Secretary of War (1875)*, 87.
[14] Indians. *Annual Report of Secretary of War (1875)*, 75, 88-94, 321; Chronological List, 59; Heitman (Volume 2), 441; Record of Engagements, 47; Carter, *From Yorktown to Santiago*, 173-174, 278; Chalfant, *Cheyennes at Dark Water Creek*, 112-135; Hoig, *Fort Reno*, 36; Leckie, *Buffalo Soldiers*, 138; Monnett, *Massacre at Cheyenne Hole*, 67-86. Chronological List and Heitman both list 6ᵗʰ U.S. Cavalry Detachment Co. H; 19ᵗʰ U.S. Infantry Detachment Co. K.
[15] Reports of Diseases and Individual Cases, F 459.

who were using natural bank pits to good advantage against the main column. This surprise attack from the enemy rear broke their resistance (Sappa Creek, Kansas, April 23, 1875).

— Sergeant Frederick Platten (Co. H 6th U.S. Cavalry) received MOH: With five other men he waded in mud and water up the creek to a position directly behind an entrenched Cheyenne position, who were using natural bank pits to good advantage against the main column. This surprise attack from the enemy rear broke their resistance (Sappa Creek, Kansas, April 23, 1875).

— Private Marcus M. Robbins (Co. H 6th U.S. Cavalry) received MOH: With five other men he waded in mud and water up the creek to a position directly behind an entrenched Cheyenne position, who were using natural bank pits to good advantage against the main column. This surprise attack from the enemy rear broke their resistance (Sappa Creek, Kansas, April 23, 1875).

— Sergeant Richard L. Tea (Co. H 6th U.S. Cavalry) received MOH: With five other men he waded in mud and water up the creek to a position directly behind an entrenched Cheyenne position, who were using natural bank pits to good advantage against the main column. This surprise attack from the enemy rear broke their resistance (Sappa Creek, Kansas, April 23, 1875).

"I cannot find words to express the courage, patience, endurance, and intelligence exhibited by all under my command. [2nd Lieutenant Christian C. Hewitt], although by his duties not required to be at the front, was under fire continuously, exhibited great courage, and performed important service. Dr. F.H. Atkins gave proof of the greatest courage and fortitude… he was cheerful and full of words of encouragement to us all, exhibiting the greatest nerve when the stoutest hearts despaired."
— Austin Henely, U.S. Army[16]

(0917) Skirmish, Eagle Nest, crossing Pecos River, Texas (April 25, 1875)[17]
— 1st Lieutenant John L. Bullis (24th U.S. Infantry)
— Detachment of Indian Scouts

— 1st Lieutenant John L. Bullis (24th U.S. Infantry) brevet promotion to Captain for gallant service in actions against Indians (Remolino, Mexico, May 18, 1873 and Pecos River, Texas, April 25, 1875).

— Private Pompey Factor (Indian Scout) received MOH: With three other men, he participated in a charge against twenty-five hostiles while on a scouting patrol (Pecos River, Texas, April 25, 1875).

[16] Official Report of 2nd Lieutenant Austin Henely (6th U.S. Cavalry), 26 April 1875. *Annual Report of Secretary of War (1875)*, 91.
[17] Indians. Chronological List, 59; Heitman (Volume 2), 441; Record of Engagements, 47; Burton, *Black, Buckskin and Blue*, 96-97; Mulroy, *Freedom on the Border*, 124-125; Neal, *Valor Across the Lone Star*, 233-237; Smith, *Old Army in Texas*, 160.

— *Trumpeter Isaac Payne (Indian Scout) received MOH: With three other men, he participated in a charge against twenty-five hostiles while on a scouting patrol (Pecos River, Texas, April 25, 1875).*

— *Sergeant John Ward (Indian Scout) received MOH: With three other men, he participated in a charge against twenty-five hostiles while on a scouting patrol (Pecos River, Texas, April 25, 1875).*

(0918) Skirmish, La Luz Canyon, New Mexico Territory (April 30, 1875)[18]
— Captain James F. Randlett (8th U.S. Cavalry)
— 8th U.S. Cavalry Co. D

(0919) Skirmish, Battle Point, Texas (May 5, 1875)[19]
— Sergeant John Marshall (10th U.S. Cavalry)
— 10th U.S. Cavalry Detachments Co. A, F, G, I and L
— Detachment of Indian Scouts

(0920) Skirmish, Hackberry Creek, Indian Territory (June 3, 1875)[20]
— 2nd Lieutenant John A. McKinney (4th U.S. Cavalry)
— 4th U.S. Cavalry Detachment Co. A

(0921) Citizens, near Fort Brown, Texas (June 7, 1875)[21]
— (1) Citizen Killed

(0922) Operations, Tonto Basin, Arizona Territory (June 27 to July 8, 1875)[22]
— Captain George M. Brayton (8th U.S. Infantry)
— 8th U.S. Infantry Co. A and B
— Detachment of Indian Scouts
— **1 WOUNDED**[23]
— Indian Scout

— *Captain George M. Brayton (8th U.S. Infantry) brevet promotion to Lt. Colonel for gallant service in actions against Indians in Arizona (June 25, 1875; July 4, 1875; January 10, 1877 and January 30, 1877).*

(0923) Skirmish, near Reynolds' Ranch, Texas (June 29, 1875)[24]
— 2nd Lieutenant John A. McKinney (4th U.S. Cavalry)

---

[18] Indians. Chronological List, 59; Heitman (Volume 2), 441.
[19] Indians. Chronological List, 60; Heitman (Volume 2), 441; Record of Engagements, 47; Leckie, *Buffalo Soldiers*, 143-144; Smith, *Old Army in Texas*, 160. Chronological List lists 10th U.S. Cavalry Detachments.
[20] Indians. Chronological List, 60; Heitman (Volume 2), 441; Record of Engagements, 47. Chronological List lists 4th U.S. Cavalry Detachments.
[21] Bandits. Killed was teacher William McMahon. *Annual Report of Secretary of War (1875)*, 100, 102, 106-108.
[22] Indians. Chronological List, 60; Heitman (Volume 2), 441; Thrapp, *Al Sieber*, 180 . Heitman lists 8th U.S. Infantry Detachment Co. A, B; Detachment of Indian Scouts.
[23] Fort Verde Post Return July 1875.
[24] Indians. Chronological List, 60; Heitman (Volume 2), 441; Smith, *Old Army in Texas*, 160.

— 4th U.S. Cavalry Co. A

(0924) Citizens, near Crow Agency, Montana Territory (July 1875)[25]
    — (1) Citizen Killed

(0925) Skirmish, Little Popo Agie River, Wyoming Territory (July 1, 1875)[26]
    — Corporal R.W. Payne (2nd U.S. Cavalry)
        — 2nd U.S. Cavalry Detachment Co. D

(0926) Citizens, near Crow Agency, Montana Territory (July 5, 1875)[27]
    — (1) Citizen Killed

(0927) Skirmish, Ponca Agency, Dakota Territory (July 6, 1875)[28]
    — Sergeant A.C. Danvers (1st U.S. Infantry)
        — 1st U.S. Infantry Detachment Co. G

(0928) Action, near Camp Lewis, Montana Territory (July 7, 1875)[29]
    — 1st Lieutenant George H. Wright (7th U.S. Infantry)
        — 7th U.S. Infantry Detachments Co. G and K
    — **3 KILLED**[30]
        — Private Stephen A. Harrison (7th U.S. Infantry)
        — Private George Laroren (7th U.S. Infantry)
        — Private George Weaver (7th U.S. Infantry)

(0929) Citizens, near Crow Agency, Montana Territory (August 1875)[31]
    — (1) Citizen Killed

(0930) Operations, North Platte River, north of Sidney, Nebraska (August 28 to September 2, 1875)[32]
    — 1st Lieutenant Emmet Crawford (3rd U.S. Cavalry)
        — 3rd U.S. Cavalry Detachment Co. G

(0931) Action, near Buffalo Station or Smoky Hill Station, Kansas (October 27, 1875)[33]
    — Captain John M. Hamilton (5th U.S. Cavalry)
        — 5th U.S. Cavalry Detachment Co. H
    — **1 WOUNDED**[34]

[25] Indians. Killed was herder Jose Trojio. *Annual Report of Commissioner of Indian Affairs (1875)*, 302.
[26] Indians. Chronological List, 60; Heitman (Volume 2), 441; Record of Engagements, 47.
[27] Indians. Killed was an Agency teamster. *Annual Report of Commissioner of Indian Affairs (1875)*, 302.
[28] Indians. *Annual Report of Secretary of War (1875)*, 65; Chronological List, 60; Heitman (Volume 2), 441.
[29] Indians. *Annual Report of Secretary of War (1875)*, 63; *Annual Report of Secretary of War (1876)*, 320; Chronological List, 60; Heitman (Volume 2), 441; Record of Engagements, 47.
[30] Reports of Diseases and Individual Cases, F 460.5.
[31] Indians. Killed was herder James Hilderbrand. *Annual Report of Commissioner of Indian Affairs (1875)*, 302-303.
[32] Indians. Chronological List, 60; Heitman (Volume 2), 441.
[33] Indians. *Annual Report of Secretary of War (1876)*, 320; Chronological List, 60; Heitman (Volume 2), 441; Record of Engagements, 48; Carriker, *Fort Supply, Indian Territory*, 109-110; King, *War Eagle*, 144-147.
[34] Reports of Diseases and Individual Cases, F 460.

— Private William Evans (Co. H 5th U.S. Cavalry)
— *gunshot wound, neck, severe wound*

(09932) Skirmish, near Pecos River, Texas (November 2, 1875)[35]
— 1st Lieutenant Andrew Geddes (25th U.S. Infantry)
— 10th U.S. Cavalry Co. G and L
— Detachment of Indian Scouts

(0933) Skirmish, near Antelope Station, Nebraska (November 20, 1875)[36]
— 1st Lieutenant Emmet Crawford (3rd U.S. Cavalry)
— 3rd U.S. Cavalry Detachment Co. G

TOTAL KILLED 1875 — 0/8/0/0 (OFFICERS, ENLISTED MEN, INDIAN SCOUTS, CITIZENS)

---

[35] Indians. Chronological List, 60; Heitman (Volume 2), 441; Record of Engagements, 48; Leckie, *Buffalo Soldiers*, 148-149; Smith, *Old Army in Texas*, 161; Williams, *Texas' Last Frontier*, 189-190.
[36] Indians. Chronological List, 60; Heitman (Volume 2), 441; Record of Engagements, 48.

1st Lieutenant Lewis D. Adair
(Photo from Author's Collection)

1st Lieutenant Frederick H. Beecher *(Photo Courtesy of Ruth Eifert)*

1st Lieutenant Jacob Almy

Captain Andrew S. Bennett *(Photo Courtesy of Prairie Home Cemetery, Waukesha, Wisconsin)*

2nd Lieutenant Jonathan W. Biddle *(Photo Courtesy of Laurel Hill Cemetery)*

2nd Lieutenant Horatio S. Bingham
(Photo Courtesy of Michael Olson)

Captain Frederick H. Brown *(Photo Courtesy of Michael Olson)*

1st Lieutenant James H.
Bradley *(Photo Courtesy
of Williams County
Public Library)*

Captain David H. Buell *(Photo from Author's Collection)*

1st Lieutenant James Calhoun *(Photo Courtesy of Paula Johnson)*

Brigadier General Richard R.S. Canby *(Photos Courtesy of Mary N. Davis and Mike Johnson)*

1st Lieutenant John C. Carroll

2nd Lieutenant Samuel A. Cherry *(Photo Courtesy of Robert Yoder)*

1st Lieutenant Edward W. Casey
(Photo Courtesy of Gwen Salsig)

(Photo Courtesy of Carla A. Boudreau)

Casey Lot North Kingston, Rhode Island

2nd Lieutenant Caspar W. Collins *(Photo from Author's Collection)*

Captain Emmett Crawford *(Photo from Author's Collection)*

1st Lieutenant Arthur Cranston

2nd Lieutenant John J. Crittenden
(Photo Courtesy of Michael Olson)

2nd Lieutenant Eben Crosby *(Photo Courtesy of Michael Olson)*

1st Lieutenant Howard B. Cushing

Lt. Colonel George A. Custer *(Photo Courtesy of Art Unger)*

Captain Thomas W. Custer *(Photo Courtesy of Paula Johnson)*

1st Lieutenant William L. English *(Photo Courtesy of Jim Pierson, Superintendant Diamond Grove Cemetery)*

Major Joel H. Elliot

Captain William J. Fetterman *(Photo Courtesy of Michael Olson)*

Captain William D. Fouts *(Photo Courtesy of Fort McPherson National Cemetery)*

2nd Lieutenant George W. Grummond
(Photo Courtesy of Jennifer Shafer)

2nd Lieutenant James H. French
(Photo Courtesy of Laurel Hill Cemetery)

Captain Owen Hale *(Photo Courtesy of Michael P. Barrett)*

2nd Lieutenant Henry M. Harrington
(Photo Courtesy of Jill Numbers)

Captain Louis
M. Hamilton
*(Photo Courtesy of
Poughkeepsie Rural
Cemetery)*

1st Lieutenant John C. Jenness
(Photo Courtesy of Michael Olson)

2nd Lieutenant Benjamin H. Hodgson
(Photo Courtesy of Laurel Hill Cemetery)

1st Lieutenant George M. Harris
(Photo Courtesy of Laurel Hill Cemetery)

1st Lieutenant Albion Howe *(Photo Courtesy of Forrest Lawn Cemetery, Buffalo, New York)*

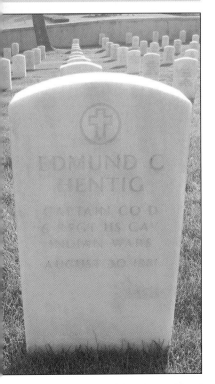

Captain Edmund C. Hentig *(Photo Antonio Alberto)*

Captain Myles W. Keogh *(Photo Courtesy of Fort Hill Cemetery Association)*

Lt. Colonel William H. Lewis
(Photo Courtesy of Washington County Historical Society)

Assistant Surgeon Thomas J.C. Maddox
(Photo Courtesy of Craig Camp)

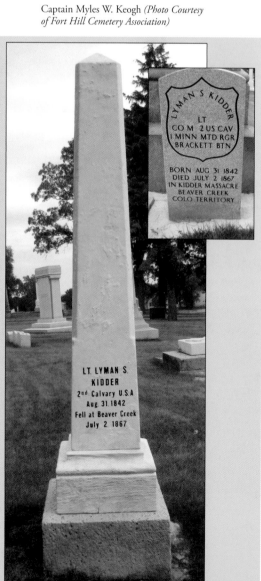

2ⁿᵈ Lieutenant Lyman S. Kidder

Captain William Logan *(Photo Courtesy of Michael Olson)*

1ˢᵗ Lieutenant James D. Mann *(Photo from Author's Collection)*

Assistant Surgeon George E. Lord *(Photo Courtesy of Michael Olson)*

Lt. Colonel Charles McDermitt

1st Lieutenant John A. McKinney
(Photo Courtesy of Elmwood Cemetery)

Captain James F. Millar

1st Lieutenant Donald McIntosh
(Photo from Author's Collection)

2nd Lieutenant Seward Mott

1st Lieutenant James Pike
(Photo Courtesy of Matthew W. Prull)

2nd Lieutenant William Russell Jr.

2nd Lieutenant Sevier M. Rains
(Photo Courtesy of Matthew W. Prull)

1st Lieutenant George Roberts

1st Lieutenant William L. Sherwood
(Photo Courtesy of Forrest Lawn Cemetery, Buffalo, New York)

1st Lieutenant James E. Porter
(Photo Courtesy of Erica Bracy)

1st Lieutenant Algernon E. Smith
(Photo Courtesy of Paula Johnson)

2nd Lieutenant James G. Sturgis
(Photo Courtesy of Michael Olson)

2nd Lieutenant George W. Smith
(Photo from Author's Collection)

Captain Evan Thomas
(Photo from Author's Collection)

2nd Lieutenant Sigismund Sternberg
(Photo Courtesy of Michael Olson)

2nd Lieutenant Reid T. Stewart

Major John A. Thompson

Major Thomas T. Thornburgh *(Photo from Author's Collection)*

1ˢᵗ Lieutenant William B. Weir *(Photo Courtesy of Art Unger)*

1ˢᵗ Lieutenant Benjamin S. Wilson *(Photo Courtesy of Richard Baldwin)*

1ˢᵗ Lieutenant Frederick R. Vincent *(Photo Courtesy of National Cemetery Administration)*

Captain Melville G. Wilkinson *(Photo Courtesy of Mark Lindahl)*

Captain George W.M. Yates *(Photo Courtesy of Paula Johnson)*

Captain George D. Wallace *(Photo Courtesy of John D. Macintosh)*

1876

"The harrowing sight of the dead bodies crowning the height on which Custer fell, and which will remain vividly in my memory until death, is too recent for me not to ask the good people of this country, whether a policy that sets opposing parties in the field, armed, clothed, equipped by one and the same government, should not be abolished."

— Marcus A. Reno, U.S. Army[1]

---

[1] Official Report of Major Marcus A. Reno (7th U.S. Cavalry), 5 July 1876. *Annual Report of Secretary of War (1876)*, 35.

(0934) Skirmish, Cimarron River, 125 miles east of Camp Supply, Indian Territory (January 22, 1876)[2]
— 2nd Lieutenant Hoel S. Bishop (5th U.S. Cavalry)
— 5th U.S. Cavalry Detachment Co. G

(0935) Skirmish, Camp Apache, Arizona Territory (January 31, 1876)[3]
— Captain Frederick D. Ogilby (8th U.S. Infantry)
— 6th U.S. Cavalry Co. A and D
— 8th U.S. Infantry Co. E and K
— Detachment of Indian Scouts

(0936) Skirmish, near Chevelon's Fork, Arizona Territory (February 1, 1876)[4]
— Captain Frederick D. Ogilby (8th U.S. Infantry)
— Detachment of Indian Scouts

(0937) Skirmish, Carrizo Mountains, Texas (February 18, 1876)[5]
— Captain Charles Bentzoni (25th U.S. Infantry)
— 25th U.S. Infantry Detachment Co. B

(0938) Operations, Fort Pease Trading Post, Montana Territory (February 22 to March 17, 1876)[6]
— Major James S. Brisbin (2nd U.S. Cavalry)
— 2nd U.S. Cavalry Co. F, G, H and L
— 7th U.S. Infantry Detachment Co. C
— Detachment of Volunteers
— **6 KILLED**[7]
— (6) Citizens

(0939) Action, Dry Forks of Powder River, Wyoming Territory (March 5, 1876)[8]
— Captain Edwin M. Coates (4th U.S. Infantry)
— 4th U.S. Infantry Co. C and I
— **1 WOUNDED**[9]
— Corporal James Slavey (Co. I 4th U.S. Infantry)
— *gunshot wound, right cheek, slight wound*

(0940) Action, Little Powder River, Montana Territory (March 17, 1876)[10]
— Colonel Joseph J. Reynolds (3rd U.S. Cavalry)
— 2nd U.S. Cavalry Co. A, B, E, I and K
— 3rd U.S. Cavalry Co. A, D, E, F and M
— **4 KILLED**[11]
— Private George Schneider (Co. K 2nd U.S. Cavalry)
— Private Peter Dowdy (Co. E 3rd U.S. Cavalry)
— Private Michael McCannon (Co. F 3rd U.S. Cavalry)

---

[2] Indians. Chronological List, 60; Heitman (Volume 2), 442; Record of Engagements, 49; Price, *Across the Continent*, 662.
[3] Indians. *Annual Report of Secretary of War (1876)*, 100; Chronological List, 60; Heitman (Volume 2), 442; Carter, *From Yorktown to Santiago*, 183. Chronological List and Heitman both list 9 January 1876.
[4] Indians. Chronological List, 60; Heitman (Volume 2), 442.
[5] Indians. Chronological List, 60; Heitman (Volume 2), 442; Nankivell, *Buffalo Soldier Regiment*, 27; Smith, *Old Army in Texas*, 161; Williams, *Texas' Last Frontier*, 198-199.
[6] Indians. *Annual Report of Secretary of War (1876)*, 458-459; Chronological List, 61; Record of Engagements, 49; Bradley, *March of the Montana Column*, 69-70; Brown, *Plainsmen of the Yellowstone*, 223-225; Gray, *Custer's Last Campaign*, 126-129; Hedren, *Great Sioux War Orders of Battle*, 77-78. Chronological List lists 6th U.S. Cavalry Co. F, G, H, L; 7th U.S. Infantry Detachment Co. C.
[7] Chronological List, 61.
[8] Indians. Chronological List, 61; Heitman (Volume 2), 442; Gray, *Centennial Campaign*, 49-50
[9] Reports of Diseases and Individual Cases, F 461.
[10] Indians. *Annual Report of Secretary of War (1876)*, 29, 320, 441; Chronological List, 61; Heitman (Volume 2), 442; Record of Engagements, 50-51; Brown, *Plainsmen of the Yellowstone*, 246-248; Gray, *Centennial Campaign*, 53-57; Hedren, *Great Sioux War Orders of Battle*, 78-81; Rockwell, *U.S. Army in Frontier Montana*, 303-306; Vaughn, *Reynolds Campaign on Powder River*, 68-136. Record of Engagements lists 2nd U.S. Cavalry Co. A, B, E, I, K; 3rd U.S. Cavalry Co. E, F, M, Detachment Co. A.
[11] Reports of Diseases and Individual Cases, F 461.

— Private Lorenzo E. Ayers (Co. M 3rd U.S. Cavalry)

— **5 WOUNDED**[12]
    — Corporal John Lang (Co. E 2nd U.S. Cavalry)
        — *gunshot wound, right ankle, severe wound*
    — Artificer Patrick Goings (Co. K 2nd U.S. Cavalry)
        — *gunshot wound, left shoulder, slight wound*
    — Private John Droege (Co. K 2nd U.S. Cavalry)
        — *gunshot wound, left arm, fracture, severe wound*
    — Private Edward Egan (Co. K 2nd U.S. Cavalry)
        — *gunshot wound, right side, severe wound*

    — Sergeant Charles Kaminski (Co. M 3rd U.S. Cavalry)
        — *gunshot wound, left knee, slight wound*

    — *1st Lieutenant John G. Bourke (3rd U.S. Cavalry) brevet promotion to Major for gallantry in an attack on Indians (Powder River, Montana, March 17, 1876) and in action against Indians (Rosebud Creek, Montana, June 17, 1876).*

    — *Hospital Steward William C. Bryan (U.S. Army) received MOH: Accompanied a detachment of cavalry in a charge on a village of hostile Indians and fought through the engagements, having his horse killed under him, He continued to fight on foot, under severe fire and without assistance conveyed two wounded comrades to places of safety, saving them from capture (Powder River, Montana, March 17, 1876).*

    — *Blacksmith Albert Glavinski (Co. M 3rd U.S. Cavalry) received MOH: During a retreat he selected exposed positions; he was part of the rear guard (Powder River, Montana, March 17, 1876).*

    — *Private Jeremiah Murphy (Co. M 3rd U.S. Cavalry) received MOH: Being the only member of his picket not disabled, he attempted to save a wounded comrade (Powder River, Montana, March 17, 1876).*

    — *Major Thadeus H. Stanton (Paymaster) brevet promotion to Lt. Colonel for gallant service in action against Indians under Crazy Horse (Powder River, Montana, March 17, 1876).*

(0941) Skirmish, Tonto Basin, Arizona Territory (March 27 and 28, 1876)[13]
    — Guide E. Stanley (Citizen)
        — Detachment of Indian Scouts

(0942) Action, Central Station, Texas (April 1876)[14]
    — Sergeant W. Smith (25th U.S. Infantry)
        — 25th U.S. Infantry Detachment Co. D
    — **1 KILLED**[15]

---

[12] Reports of Diseases and Individual Cases, F 461. Chronological List lists 1st Lieutenant William C. Rawolle (2nd U.S. Cavalry) as being WIA. His name does not appear on F 461.
[13] Indians. *Annual Report of Secretary of War (1876)*, 100; Chronological List, 61; Heitman (Volume 2), 442.
[14] Indians. Chronological List, 61.
[15] Chronological List, 61.

— (1) Citizen

(0943) Citizens, Sulphur Springs, Dragoon Mountains, New Mexico Territory (April 7, 1876)[16]

— (2) Citizens Killed

(0944) Citizens, near San Pedro River, Arizona Territory (April 8, 1876)[17]

— (1) Citizen Killed

(0945) Skirmish, San Jose Mountains, near Mexico line, Arizona Territory (April 10, 1876)[18]

— 2nd Lieutenant Austin Henely (6th U.S. Cavalry)

— 6th U.S. Cavalry Detachment Co. H

(0946) Skirmish, near Fort Sill, Indian Territory (April 13, 1876)[19]

— 1st Lieutenant Otho W. Budd (4th U.S. Cavalry)

— 4th U.S. Cavalry Detachment Co. I

(0947) Action, Grace Creek, Nebraska (April 28, 1876)[20]

— 2nd Lieutenant Charles H. Heyl (23rd U.S. Infantry)

— 23rd U.S. Infantry Detachment Co. A

— 1 KILLED[21]

— Sergeant William H. Dougherty (Co. A 23rd U.S. Infantry)

— 2nd Lieutenant Charles H. Heyl (23rd U.S. Infantry) brevet promotion to 1st Lieutenant for gallant service in action against Indians (South side of the Verde River, Arizona, May 24, 1874) and gallantry in action against Indians (Grace Creek, Nebraska, April 28, 1876).

— 2nd Lieutenant Charles H. Heyl (23rd U.S. Infantry) received MOH: Voluntarily, and with most conspicuous gallantry, charged with three men upon six Indians who were entrenched upon a hillside (Near Fort Hartsuff, Nebraska, April 28, 1876).

— Corporal Patrick Leonard (Co. A 23rd U.S. Infantry) received MOH: Gallantry in charge on hostile Sioux (Near Fort Hartsuff, Nebraska, April 28, 1876).

— Corporal Jeptha L. Lytton (Co. A 23rd U.S. Infantry) received MOH: Gallantry in charge on hostile Sioux (Near Fort Hartsuff, Nebraska, April 28, 1876).

(0948) Action, near Mouth of Big Horn River, Montana Territory (May 23, 1876)[22]

— UNKNOWN

— 2nd U.S. Cavalry Detachment Co. H

— 3 KILLED[23]

— Private Henry Raymeyer (Co. H 2nd U.S. Cavalry)

— Private Augustus Stoker (Co. H 2nd U.S. Cavalry)

[16] Indians. Killed were station agent Nicholas M. Rogers and his assistant, Orizoba O. Spence. *Annual Report of Secretary of War (1876)*, 76; Carter, *From Yorktown to Santiago*, 183-184; Lockwood, *Apache Indians*, 215; McChristian, *Fort Bowie*, 162; Sweeney, *Cochise to Geronimo*, 47-48; Thrapp, *Conquest of Apacheria*, 169-170. While serving with the 8th U.S. Cavalry on 20 October 1869, Private Orizoba Spence had received the Medal of Honor.

[17] Indians. Killed was a man named Lewis. *Annual Report of Commissioner of Indian Affairs (1876)*, xvii, 3, 10; Lockwood, *Apache Indians*, 215; Sweeney, *Cochise to Geronimo*, 49.

[18] Indians. *Annual Report of Secretary of War (1876)*, 98; Chronological List, 61; Heitman (Volume 2), 442; Carter, *From Yorktown to Santiago*, 184, 278; Lockwood, *Apache Indians*, 216; McChristian, *Fort Bowie*, 162; Sweeney, *Cochise to Geronimo*, 49-50.

[19] Indians. Chronological List, 61.

[20] Indians. *Annual Report of Secretary of War (1876)*, 331; Chronological List, 61; Heitman (Volume 2), 442; Record of Engagements, 51; Hedren, *Fort Laramie in 1876*, 86.

[21] Register of Deaths Regular Army, 1860-1889 (Volume 7).

[22] Indians. *Annual Report of Secretary of War (1876)*, 331, 472; Bradley, *March of the Montana Column*, 119-120; Gray, *Centennial Campaign*, 83; Overfield, *Little Big Horn*, 134; Rockwell, *U.S. Army in Frontier Montana*, 324.

[23] 2nd U.S. Cavalry Regimental Return May 1876; Gray, *Centennial Campaign*, 83.

— Teamster James Quinn (Citizen)

(0949) Action, Tongue River, Wyoming Territory (June 9, 1876)[24]
    — Lt. Colonel William B. Royall (3rd U.S. Cavalry) — Crooke's Expedition
        — 2nd U.S. Cavalry Co. A, B, D, E and I
        — 3rd U.S. Cavalry Co. A, B, C, D, E, F, G, I, L and M
        — 4th U.S. Infantry Co. D and F
        — 9th U.S. Infantry Co. C, G and H
  — **1 WOUNDED**[25]
        — Sergeant John C.A. Warfield (Co. F 3rd U.S. Cavalry)
           — *right arm, slight wound*

(0950) Engagement, Rosebud Creek, Montana Territory (June 17, 1876)[26]
    — Brigadier General George Crook
        — 2nd U.S. Cavalry Co. A, B, D, E and I
        — 3rd U.S. Cavalry Co. A, B, C, D, E, F, H, I, L and M
        — 4th U.S. Infantry Co. D and F
        — 9th U.S. Infantry Co. C, G and H
        — Detachment of Indian Scouts
  — **10 KILLED**[27]
        — Sergeant Daniel Marshall (Co. F 3rd U.S. Cavalry)
        — Private Gilbert Roe (Co. F 3rd U.S. Cavalry)
        — Private William W. Allen (Co. I 3rd U.S. Cavalry)
        — Private Eugene Flynn (Co. I 3rd U.S. Cavalry)

        — Sergeant Antoine Newkirken (Co. L 3rd U.S. Cavalry)
        — Private Richard Bennett (Co. L 3rd U.S. Cavalry)
        — Private Brooks Connor (Co. L 3rd U.S. Cavalry)
        — Private Allen J. Mitchell (Co. L 3rd U.S. Cavalry)
        — Private George Potts (Co. L 3rd U.S. Cavalry)

        — Indian Scout[28]

  — **26 WOUNDED**[29]
        — Captain Guy V. Henry (Co. D 3rd U.S. Cavalry)
           — *gunshot wound, jaw, fracture, severe wound*

        — Sergeant Patrick O'Donnell (Co. D 2nd U.S. Cavalry)
           — *gunshot wound, right arm, slight wound*
        — Corporal Thomas Meagher (Co. I 2nd U.S. Cavalry)
           — *gunshot wound, right forearm, severe wound*

[24] Indians. Chronological List, 61; Heitman (Volume 2), 442; Gray, *Centennial Campaign*, 115; McDermott, *General George Crook's 1876 Campaigns*, 25-27; Davenport, "Skirmish at the Tongue River Heights" in Greene, *Battles and Skirmishes*, 20-25; Mangum, *Battle of the Rosebud*, 38-40; Rockwell, *U.S. Army in Frontier Montana*, 331. Heitman lists 2nd U.S. Cavalry Co. D; 3rd U.S. Cavalry Co. A, B, C, D, E, F, G, I, L, M; 4th U.S. Infantry Co. D, F; 9th U.S. Infantry Co. C, G, H.

[25] Mangum, *Battle of the Rosebud*, 40, 120.

[26] Indians. *Annual Report of Secretary of War (1876)*, 30, 321, 442-443, 504-505; Chronological List, 61; Heitman (Volume 2), 442; Record of Engagements, 51-52; Brown, *Plainsmen of the Yellowstone*, 264-267; Gray, *Centennial Campaign*, 121-123; Mangum, *Battle of the Rosebud*, 54-88; Rockwell, *U.S. Army in Frontier Montana*, 334-338. Heitman lists 2nd U.S. Cavalry Co. A, B, D, E, I; 3rd U.S. Cavalry Co. A, B, C, D, E, F, G, I, L, M; 4th U.S. Infantry Co. D, F; 9th U.S. Infantry Co. C, G, H.

[27] Reports of Diseases and Individual Cases, F 462.

[28] The Indian Scout is only identified as a Snake Indian in F 462.

[29] Reports of Diseases and Individual Cases, F 462.

— Private Henry Steiner (Co. B 3rd U.S. Cavalry)
    — *gunshot wound, fracture of left shoulder, severe wound*
— Private Horace Harrold (Co. E 3rd U.S. Cavalry)
    — *gunshot wound, right shoulder and jaw, severe wound*
— Private William Featherly (Co. F 3rd U.S. Cavalry)
    — *gunshot wound, left arm, severe wound*
— Private Phineas Towne (Co. F 3rd U.S. Cavalry)
    — *gunshot wound, abdomen, severe wound*

— Sergeant Andrew Grosh (Co. I 3rd U.S. Cavalry)
    — *gunshot wound, chest and fracture of both arms, severe wound*
— Private John Loscoboski (Co. I 3rd U.S. Cavalry)
    — *gunshot wound, fracture of right elbow, severe wound*
— Private James O'Brien (Co. I 3rd U.S. Cavalry)
    — *gunshot wound, left forearm, severe wound*
— Private Francis Smith (Co. I 3rd U.S. Cavalry)
    — *gunshot wound, fracture of right leg, severe wound*
— Private Charles Stewart (Co. I 3rd U.S. Cavalry)
    — *gunshot wound, left wrist and arm, severe wound*

— Sergeant Samuel Cook (Co. L 3rd U.S. Cavalry)
    — *gunshot wound, left thigh, severe wound*
— Trumpeter William H. Edwards (Co. L 3rd U.S. Cavalry)
    — *gunshot wound, left thigh, severe wound*
— Private John Creamer (Co. L 3rd U.S. Cavalry)
    — *gunshot wound, fracture of shoulder, severe wound*
— Trumpeter Elmer A. Snow (Co. M 3rd U.S. Cavalry)
    — *gunshot wound, fracture of right wrist and arm, severe wound*

— Private James A. Devine (Co. D 4th U.S. Infantry)
    — *gunshot wound, head, severe wound*
— Private Richard Flynn (Co. D 4th U.S. Infantry)
    — *gunshot wound, left shoulder, slight wound*
— Private John H. Terry (Co. D 4th U.S. Infantry)
    — *gunshot wound, fracture of left leg, slight wound*

— (7) Indian Scouts[30]

— 1st Lieutenant John G. Bourke (3rd U.S. Cavalry) brevet promotion to Major for gallantry in an attack on Indians (Powder River, Montana, March 17, 1876) and in action against Indians (Rosebud Creek, Montana, June 17, 1876).

---

[30] F 462 lists seven Indian Scout (three Snake and four Crow) as WIA. Unfortunately their names are not given. Reports of Diseases and Individual Cases, F 462.

— *First Sergeant Michael McGann (Co. F 3rd U.S. Cavalry) received MOH: Gallantry in action (Rosebud Creek, Montana, June 17, 1876).*

— *Captain Guy V. Henry (3rd U.S. Cavalry) brevet promotion to Brigadier General for gallant and meritorious service in action against Indians (Rosebud Creek, Montana, June 17, 1876, where he was severely wounded).*

— *2nd Lieutenant Bainbridge Reynolds (3rd U.S. Cavalry) brevet promotion to 1st Lieutenant for gallant service in action against Indians (Rosebud Creek, Montana, June 17, 1876).*

— *First Sergeant Joseph Robinson (Co. D 3rd U.S. Cavalry) received MOH: Discharged his duties while in charge of the skirmish line under fire with judgment and great coolness and brought up the led horses at a critical moment (Rosebud Creek, Montana, June 17, 1876).*

— *Lt. Colonel William B. Royall (3rd U.S. Cavalry) brevet promotion to Brigadier General for gallant service in action against Indians (Rosebud Creek, Montana, June 17, 1876).*

— *First Sergeant John H. Shingle (Co. I 3rd U.S. Cavalry) received MOH: Gallantry in action (Rosebud Creek, Montana, June 17, 1876).*

— *Trumpeter Elmer A. Snow (Co. M 3rd U.S. Cavalry) received MOH: Bravery in action, wounded in both arms (Rosebud Creek, Montana, June 17, 1876).*

(0951) Skirmish, Elkhorn River, Nebraska (June 22, 1876)[31]
— Captain James Egan (2nd U.S. Cavalry)
    — 2nd U.S. Cavalry Co. K

(0952) Engagement, Little Big Horn River, Montana Territory (June 25 and 26, 1876)[32]
— Major Marcus A. Reno (7th U.S. Cavalry)
    — 7th U.S. Cavalry Co. A, B, D, G, H, K and M
    — Detachment of Indian Scouts
— **60 KILLED**[33]
    — 1st Lieutenant Donald McIntosh (Co. G 7th U.S. Cavalry)
    — 2nd Lieutenant Benjamin H. Hodgson (Co. B 7th U.S. Cavalry)

    — Corporal James Dalious (Co. A 7th U.S. Cavalry)
    — Corporal George H. King (Co. A 7th U.S. Cavalry) — d. 07-02-1876
    — Private John E. Armstrong (Co. A 7th U.S. Cavalry)
    — Private James Drinan (Co. A 7th U.S. Cavalry)
    — Private James McDonald (Co. A 7th U.S. Cavalry)
    — Private William Moodie (Co. A 7th U.S. Cavalry)

[31] Indians. Chronological List, 61; Heitman (Volume 2), 442.
[32] Indians. *Annual Report of Secretary of War (1876)*, 30-35, 321, 443-444, 476-480; Chronological List, 61; Heitman (Volume 2), 442; Record of Engagements, 53-58; Gray, *Custer's Last Campaign*, 287-332; Miles, *Personal Recollections*, 205-211, 286-293; Rockwell, *U.S. Army in Frontier Montana*, 347-355, 363-370. Chronological List lists 7th U.S. Cavalry Co. A, B, D, G, H, K, M.
[33] Nichols, *Men with Custer*, 374-391.

— Private Richard Rollins (Co. A 7th U.S. Cavalry)
— Private John Sullivan (Co. A 7th U.S. Cavalry)
— Private Thomas P. Sweetser (Co. A 7th U.S. Cavalry)

— Private Richard B. Dorn (Co. B 7th U.S. Cavalry)
— Private George B. Mask (Co. B 7th U.S. Cavalry)
— Private James C. Bennett (Co. C 7th U.S. Cavalry) — d. 07-05-1876

— Farrier Vincent Charley (Co. D 7th U.S. Cavalry)
— Private Patrick M. Golden (Co. D 7th U.S. Cavalry)
— Private Edward Housen (Co. D 7th U.S. Cavalry)

— Sergeant Edward Botzer (Co. G 7th U.S. Cavalry)
— Sergeant Martin Considine (Co. G 7th U.S. Cavalry)
— Corporal James Martin (Co. G 7th U.S. Cavalry)
— Corporal Otto Hagemann (Co. G 7th U.S. Cavalry)
— Trumpeter Henry Dose (Co. G 7th U.S. Cavalry)
— Farrier Benjamin O. Wells (Co. G 7th U.S. Cavalry)
— Saddler Crawford Selby (Co. G 7th U.S. Cavalry)
— Private John J. McGinniss (Co. G 7th U.S. Cavalry)
— Private Andrew J. Moore (Co. G 7th U.S. Cavalry)
— Private John Rapp (Co. G 7th U.S. Cavalry)
— Private Benjamin F. Rogers (Co. G 7th U.S. Cavalry)
— Private Henry Seafferman (Co. G 7th U.S. Cavalry)
— Private Edward Stanley (Co. G 7th U.S. Cavalry)

— Corporal George Lell (Co. H 7th U.S. Cavalry)
— Private William M. George (Co. H 7th U.S. Cavalry) — d. 07-03-1876
— Private Julien D. Jones (Co. H 7th U.S. Cavalry)
— Private Thomas Meador (Co. H 7th U.S. Cavalry)
— Private David Cooney (Co. I 7th U.S. Cavalry) — d. 07-20-1876

— First Sergeant DeWitt Winney (Co. K 7th U.S. Cavalry)
— Sergeant Robert H. Hughes (Co. K 7th U.S. Cavalry)
— Corporal John J. Callahan (Co. K 7th U.S. Cavalry)
— Trumpeter Julius Helmer (Co. K 7th U.S. Cavalry)
— Private Elihu F. Clear (Co. K 7th U.S. Cavalry)

— Sergeant Miles F. O'Harra (Co. M 7th U.S. Cavalry)
— Corporal Henry M. Cody (Co. M 7th U.S. Cavalry)
— Corporal Frederick Stressinger (Co. M 7th U.S. Cavalry)
— Private Frank Braun (Co. M 7th U.S. Cavalry) — d. 10-04-1876
— Private James H. Gebhart (Co. M 7th U.S. Cavalry)
— Private Henry Gordon (Co. M 7th U.S. Cavalry)
— Private Henry Klotzbucher (Co. M 7th U.S. Cavalry)
— Private George Lorentz (Co. M 7th U.S. Cavalry)
— Private William D. Meyer (Co. M 7th U.S. Cavalry)
— Private George E. Smith (Co. M 7th U.S. Cavalry)
— Private David Summers (Co. M 7th U.S. Cavalry)
— Private Henry J. Turley (Co. M 7th U.S. Cavalry)
— Private Henry C. Voight (Co. M 7th U.S. Cavalry)

— Bloody Knife (Indian Scout)
— Bob Tailed Bull (Indian Scout)
— Little Brave (Indian Scout)

— Guide Charles A. Reynolds (Citizen)
— Interpreter Isaiah Dorman (Citizen)
— Packer Frank C. Mann (Citizen)
— Acting Assistant Surgeon James M. DeWolf (Citizen)

— 62 WOUNDED[34]

— Captain Frederick W. Benteen (Co. H 7th U.S. Cavalry)
— 2nd Lieutenant Charles A. Varnum (Co. A 7th U.S. Cavalry)

— First Sergeant William Heyn (Co. A 7th U.S. Cavalry)
— Private Jacob Deihle (Co. A 7th U.S. Cavalry)
— Private Samuel J. Foster (Co. A 7th U.S. Cavalry)
— Private Frederick Holmstead (Co. A 7th U.S. Cavalry)
— Private Francis M. Reeves (Co. A 7th U.S. Cavalry)
— Private Elijah T. Strode (Co. A 7th U.S. Cavalry)

— Sergeant Benjamin C. Criswell (Co. B 7th U.S. Cavalry)
— Sergeant Thomas Murray (Co. B 7th U.S. Cavalry)
— Corporal Charles Cunningham (Co. B 7th U.S. Cavalry)
— Corporal William M. Smith (Co. B 7th U.S. Cavalry)
— Private James Pym (Co. B 7th U.S. Cavalry)

— Private John B. McGuire, Jr. (Co. C 7th U.S. Cavalry)
— Private Peter Thompson (Co. C 7th U.S. Cavalry)
— Private Alfred Whitaker (Co. C 7th U.S. Cavalry)

— Private Jacob Hetler (Co. D 7th U.S. Cavalry)
— Private Joseph Kretchmer (Co. D 7th U.S. Cavalry)
— Private Patrick McDonnell (Co. D 7th U.S. Cavalry)

— Sergeant James T. Riley (Co. E 7th U.S. Cavalry)
— Saddler William M. Shields (Co. E 7th U.S. Cavalry)

— Private James P. Boyle (Co. G 7th U.S. Cavalry)
— Private Charles W. Campbell (Co. G 7th U.S. Cavalry)
— Private John Hackett (Co. G 7th U.S. Cavalry)
— Private John McVay (Co. G 7th U.S. Cavalry)
— Private John Morrison (Co. G 7th U.S. Cavalry)
— Private Henry Petring (Co. G 7th U.S. Cavalry)

— First Sergeant Joseph McCurry (Co. H 7th U.S. Cavalry)
— Sergeant Patrick Connelly (Co. H 7th U.S. Cavalry)

[34] Nichols, *Men with Custer*, 1-367, 374-391.

— Sergeant Thomas McLaughlin (Co. H 7th U.S. Cavalry)
— Sergeant John Pahl (Co. H 7th U.S. Cavalry)
— Corporal Alexander B. Bishop (Co. H 7th U.S. Cavalry)
— Trumpeter William Ramell (Co. H 7th U.S. Cavalry)
— Saddler Otto Voit (Co. H 7th U.S. Cavalry)
— Private P. Henry Bishley (Co. H 7th U.S. Cavalry)
— Private Charles H. Bishop (Co. H 7th U.S. Cavalry)
— Private Henry Black (Co. H 7th U.S. Cavalry)
— Private John Cooper (Co. H 7th U.S. Cavalry)
— Private William Farley (Co. H 7th U.S. Cavalry)
— Private Thomas Hughes (Co. H 7th U.S. Cavalry)
— Private Jan Moller (Co. H 7th U.S. Cavalry)
— Private John Phillips (Co. H 7th U.S. Cavalry)
— Private Samuel Severs (Co. H 7th U.S. Cavalry)
— Private William C. Williams (Co. H 7th U.S. Cavalry)
— Private Charles Windolph (Co. H 7th U.S. Cavalry)

— Saddler Michael P. Madden (Co. K 7th U.S. Cavalry)
— Private Patrick Corcoran (Co. K 7th U.S. Cavalry)
— Private Max Mielke (Co. K 7th U.S. Cavalry)
— Private Jasper Marshall (Co. L 7th U.S. Cavalry)

— Sergeant Patrick Carey (Co. M 7th U.S. Cavalry)
— Sergeant Henry C. Weihe (Co. M 7th U.S. Cavalry)
— Private James W. Darcy (Co. M 7th U.S. Cavalry)
— Private John H. Meier (Co. M 7th U.S. Cavalry)
— Private William E. Morris (Co. M 7th U.S. Cavalry)
— Private Daniel J. Newell (Co. M 7th U.S. Cavalry)
— Private Edward D. Pigford (Co. M 7th U.S. Cavalry)
— Private Roman Rutten (Co. M 7th U.S. Cavalry)
— Private Thomas B. Varner (Co. M 7th U.S. Cavalry)
— Private Charles T, Wiedman (Co. M 7th U.S. Cavalry)

— Goose (Indian Scout)
— White Swan (Indian Scout)

— Chief Packer John C. Wagoner (Citizen)

— *Private Neil Bancroft (Co. A 7th U.S. Cavalry) received MOH: Brought water for the wounded under a most galling fire (Little Big Horn, Montana, June 25 and 26, 1876).*

— *Captain Frederick W. Benteen (7th U.S. Cavalry) brevet promotion to Brigadier General for gallant service in action against Indian (Little Big Horn, Montana, June 25 and 26, 1876) and in action against Indians (Canyon Creek, Montana, September 13, 1877).*

— *Private Abram B. Brant (Co. D 7th U.S. Cavalry) received MOH: Brought water for the wounded under a most galling fire (Little Big Horn, June 25, 1876).*

— *Private Thomas J. Callen (Co. B 7th U.S. Cavalry) received MOH: Volunteered and succeeded in obtaining water for the wounded of the command; also displayed conspicuously good conduct in assisting to drive away the Indians (Little Big Horn, Montana, June 25 and 26, 1876).*

— *Sergeant Benjamin C. Criswell (Co. B 7th U.S. Cavalry) received MOH: Rescued the body of 2nd Lieutenant Benjamin H. Hodgson from within the enemy's lines, brought up ammunition and encouraged the men in the most exposed positions under heavy fire (Little Big Horn, June 25, 1876).*

— *Corporal Charles Cunningham (Co. B 7ᵗʰ U.S. Cavalry) received MOH: Declined to leave the line when wounded in the neck during heavy fire and fought bravely all next day (Little Big Horn, Montana, June 25, 1876).*

— *Private Frederick Deetline (Co. D 7ᵗʰ U.S. Cavalry) received MOH: Voluntarily brought water to the wounded under fire (Little Big Horn, Montana, June 25, 1876).*

— *Sergeant George Geiger (Co. H 7ᵗʰ U.S. Cavalry) received MOH: With three comrades during the entire engagement courageously held a position that secured water for the command (Little Big Horn, Montana, June 25, 1876).*

— *Private Theodore W. Goldin (Co. G 7ᵗʰ U.S. Cavalry) received MOH: One of a party of volunteers who, under a heavy fire from the Indians, went for and brought water to the wounded (Little Big Horn, Montana, June 26, 1876).*

— *Sergeant Richard P. Hanley (Co. C 7ᵗʰ U.S. Cavalry) received MOH: Recaptured, single-handedly, and without orders, within the enemy's lines and under a galling fire lasting some twenty minutes, a stampeded pack mule loaded with ammunition (Little Big Horn, Montana, June 25, 1876).*

— *Private David W. Harris (Co. A 7ᵗʰ U.S. Cavalry) received MOH: Brought water to the wounded, at great danger to his life, under a most galling fire from the enemy (Little Big Horn, Montana, June 25, 1876).*

— *Private William M. Harris (Co. D 7ᵗʰ U.S. Cavalry) received MOH: Voluntarily brought water to the wounded under fire of the enemy (Little Big Horn, Montana, June 25, 1876).*

— *Private Henry Holden (Co. D 7ᵗʰ U.S. Cavalry) received MOH: Brought up ammunition under a galling fire from the enemy (Little Big Horn, Montana, June 25, 1876).*

— *Sergeant Rufus D. Hutchinson (Co. B 7ᵗʰ U.S. Cavalry) received MOH: Guarded and carried the wounded, brought water to the same, and posted and directed the men in his charge under galling fire from the enemy (Little Big Horn, Montana, June 25, 1876).*

— *Blacksmith Henry W.B. Mechlin (Co. H 7ᵗʰ U.S. Cavalry) received MOH: With three comrades during the entire engagement courageously held a position that secured water for the command (Little Big Horn, Montana, June 25, 1876).*

— *Sergeant Thomas Murray (Co. B 7ᵗʰ U.S. Cavalry) received MOH: Brought up the pack train and on the second day the rations, under a heavy fire from the enemy (Little Big Horn, Montana).*

— *Private James Pym (Co. B 7ᵗʰ U.S. Cavalry) received MOH: Voluntarily went for water and secured the same under heavy fire (Little Big Horn, Montana, June 25, 1876).*

— *Sergeant Stanislaus Roy (Co. A 7ᵗʰ U.S. Cavalry) received MOH: Brought water to the wounded at great danger to life and under a most galling fire of the enemy (Little Big Horn, Montana, June 25, 1876).*

— *Private George D. Scott (Co. D 7ᵗʰ U.S. Cavalry) received MOH: Voluntarily brought water to the wounded under fire (Little Big Horn, Montana, June 25 and 26, 1876).*

— *Private Thomas W. Stivers (Co. D 7ᵗʰ U.S. Cavalry) received MOH: Voluntarily brought water to the wounded under fire (Little Big Horn, Montana, June 25 and 26, 1876).*

— *Private Peter Thompson (Co. C 7ᵗʰ U.S. Cavalry) received MOH: After having voluntarily brought water to the wounded, in which effort he was shot through the head, he made two successful trips for the same purpose, not withstanding remonstrances of his sergeant (Little Big Horn, Montana, June 25, 1876).*

— Private Frank Tolan (Co. D 7th U.S. Cavalry) received MOH: Voluntarily brought water to the wounded under fire (Little Big Horn, Montana, June 25, 1876).

— Saddler Otto Voit (Co. H 7th U.S. Cavalry) received MOH: Volunteered with George Geiger, Charles Windolph, and Henry Mechlin to hold an exposed position, standing erect on the brow of the hill facing the Little Big Horn River. They fired constantly in this manner for more than twenty minutes diverting fire and attention from another group filling canteens of water that were desperately needed. (Little Big Horn, Montana, June 25, 1876).

— Private Charles H. Welch (Co. D 7th U.S. Cavalry) received MOH: Voluntarily brought water to the wounded under fire (Little Big Horn, Montana, June 25 and 26, 1876).

— Private Charles Windolph (Co. H 7th U.S. Cavalry) received MOH: With three comrades, during the entire engagement, courageously held a position that secured water for the command. (Little Big Horn, Montana, June 25 and 26, 1876).

(0953) Engagement, Little Big Horn River, Montana Territory (June 25, 1876)[35]
— Lt. Colonel George A. Custer (7th U.S. Cavalry)
— 7th U.S. Cavalry Co. C, E, F, I and L
— **208 KILLED**[36]
— Lt. Colonel George A. Custer (F&S 7th U.S. Cavalry)
— 1st Lieutenant William W. Cooke (F&S 7th U.S. Cavalry)
— Assistant Surgeon George E. Lord (F&S 7th U.S. Cavalry)
— Sergeant Major William H. Sharrow (F&S 7th U.S. Cavalry)
— Chief Trumpeter Henry Voss (F&S 7th U.S. Cavalry)

— Captain Thomas W. Custer (Co. C 7th U.S. Cavalry)
— 2nd Lieutenant Henry M. Harrington (Co. C 7th U.S. Cavalry)
— First Sergeant L. Edwin Bobo (Co. C 7th U.S. Cavalry)
— Sergeant Jeremiah Finley (Co. C 7th U.S. Cavalry)
— Sergeant George A. Finckle (Co. C 7th U.S. Cavalry)
— Corporal Henry E. French (Co. C 7th U.S. Cavalry)
— Corporal John Foley (Co. C 7th U.S. Cavalry)
— Corporal Daniel Ryan (Co. C 7th U.S. Cavalry)
— Trumpeter Thomas J. Bucknell (Co. C 7th U.S. Cavalry)
— Trumpeter William Kramer (Co. C 7th U.S. Cavalry)
— Blacksmith John King (Co. C 7th U.S. Cavalry)
— Saddler George Howell (Co. C 7th U.S. Cavalry)
— Private Fred E. Allan (Co. C 7th U.S. Cavalry)
— Private John Brightfield (Co. C 7th U.S. Cavalry)
— Private Christopher Criddle (Co. C 7th U.S. Cavalry)
— Private George Eiseman (Co. C 7th U.S. Cavalry)

[35] Indians. *Annual Report of Secretary of War (1876)*, 30-35, 321, 443-444, 476-479; Chronological List, 61; Heitman (Volume 2), 442; Record of Engagements, 53-58; Gray, *Centennial Campaign*, 176-178; Gray, *Custer's Last Campaign*, 333-399; Miles, *Personal Recollections*, 205-211, 286-293; Rockwell, *U.S. Army in Frontier Montana*, 356-362.
[36] Nichols, *Men with Custer*, 374-391.
[37] Listed on battle monument as J.S. Hiley. Nichols, *Men with Custer*, 105.

— Private Gustave Engle (Co. C 7th U.S. Cavalry)
— Private James Farrand (Co. C 7th U.S. Cavalry)
— Private Patrick Griffen (Co. C 7th U.S. Cavalry)
— Private James Hathersall (Co. C 7th U.S. Cavalry)
— Private John Lewis (Co. C 7th U.S. Cavalry)
— Private August Meyer (Co. C 7th U.S. Cavalry)
— Private Frederick Meier (Co. C 7th U.S. Cavalry)
— Private Edgar Phillips (Co. C 7th U.S. Cavalry)
— Private John Rauter (Co. C 7th U.S. Cavalry)
— Private Edward Rix (Co. C 7th U.S. Cavalry)
— Private James H. Russell (Co. C 7th U.S. Cavalry)
— Private Ludwick St. John (Co. C 7th U.S. Cavalry)
— Private Samuel S. Shade (Co. C 7th U.S. Cavalry)
— Private Jeremiah Shea (Co. C 7th U.S. Cavalry)
— Private Nathan Short (Co. C 7th U.S. Cavalry)
— Private Alpheus Stuart (Co. C 7th U.S. Cavalry)
— Private Ygnatz Stungewitz (Co. C 7th U.S. Cavalry)
— Private John Thadus (Co. C 7th U.S. Cavalry)
— Private Garret Van Allen (Co. C 7th U.S. Cavalry)
— Private Oscar T. Warner (Co. C 7th U.S. Cavalry)
— Private Willis B. Wright (Co. C 7th U.S. Cavalry)
— Private Henry Wyman (Co. C 7th U.S. Cavalry)

— 1st Lieutenant Algernon E. Smith (Co. E 7th U.S. Cavalry)
— 2nd Lieutenant James G. Sturgis (Co. E 7th U.S. Cavalry)
— First Sergeant Frederick Hohmeyer (Co. E 7th U.S. Cavalry)
— Sergeant John S. Ogden (Co. E 7th U.S. Cavalry)
— Sergeant William B. James (Co. E 7th U.S. Cavalry)
— Corporal Thomas P. Eagan (Co. E 7th U.S. Cavalry)
— Corporal Henry S. Mason (Co. E 7th U.S. Cavalry)
— Corporal George C. Brown (Co. E 7th U.S. Cavalry)
— Corporal Albert H. Meyer (Co. E 7th U.S. Cavalry)
— Trumpeter Thomas McElroy (Co. E 7th U.S. Cavalry)
— Trumpeter George A. Moonie (Co. E 7th U.S. Cavalry)
— Private William H. Baker (Co. E 7th U.S. Cavalry)
— Private Robert Barth (Co. E 7th U.S. Cavalry)
— Private Owen Boyle (Co. E 7th U.S. Cavalry)
— Private James Brogan (Co. E 7th U.S. Cavalry)
— Private Edward Connor (Co. E 7th U.S. Cavalry)
— Private John Darris (Co. E 7th U.S. Cavalry)
— Private William Davis (Co. E 7th U.S. Cavalry)
— Private Richard Farrell (Co. E 7th U.S. Cavalry)
— Private John S.S. Forbes (Co. E 7th U.S. Cavalry)[37]
— Private John Heim (Co. E 7th U.S. Cavalry)
— Private John Henderson (Co. E 7th U.S. Cavalry)
— Private Sykes Henderson (Co. E 7th U.S. Cavalry)
— Private William Huber (Co. E 7th U.S. Cavalry)
— Private Andy Knecht (Co. E 7th U.S. Cavalry)
— Private Herod T. Liddiard (Co. E 7th U.S. Cavalry)
— Private Patrick E. O'Conner (Co. E 7th U.S. Cavalry)
— Private William H. Rees (Co. E 7th U.S. Cavalry)
— Private Edward Rood (Co. E 7th U.S. Cavalry)
— Private Henry Schele (Co. E 7th U.S. Cavalry)
— Private William Smallwood (Co. E 7th U.S. Cavalry)

— Private Albert A. Smith (Co. E 7th U.S. Cavalry)
— Private James Smith (1st) (Co. E 7th U.S. Cavalry)
— Private James Smith (2nd) (Co. E 7th U.S. Cavalry)
— Private Benjamin F. Stafford (Co. E 7th U.S. Cavalry)
— Private Alexander Stella (Co. E 7th U.S. Cavalry)
— Private William A. Torrey (Co. E 7th U.S. Cavalry)
— Private Cornelius Van Sant (Co. E 7th U.S. Cavalry)
— Private George Walker (Co. E 7th U.S. Cavalry)

— Captain George W.M. Yates (Co. F 7th U.S. Cavalry)
— 2nd Lieutenant William V.W. Reily (Co. F 7th U.S. Cavalry)
— First Sergeant Michael Kenney (Co. F 7th U.S. Cavalry)
— Sergeant John H. Groesbeck (Co. F 7th U.S. Cavalry)[38]
— Sergeant Frederick Nursey (Co. F 7th U.S. Cavalry)
— Sergeant John R. Wilkinson (Co. F 7th U.S. Cavalry)
— Corporal Charles Coleman (Co. F 7th U.S. Cavalry)
— Corporal William Teeman (Co. F 7th U.S. Cavalry)
— Corporal John Briody (Co. F 7th U.S. Cavalry)
— Blacksmith James R. Manning (Co. F 7th U.S. Cavalry)
— Farrier Benjamin Brandon (Co. F 7th U.S. Cavalry)
— Trumpeter Thomas N. Way (Co. F 7th U.S. Cavalry)
— Private Thomas Atcheson (Co. F 7th U.S. Cavalry)
— Private William Brady (Co. F 7th U.S. Cavalry)
— Private Benjamin F. Brown (Co. F 7th U.S. Cavalry)
— Private William Brown (Co. F 7th U.S. Cavalry)
— Private Patrick Bruce (Co. F 7th U.S. Cavalry)
— Private Lucien Burnham (Co. F 7th U.S. Cavalry)
— Private James Carney (Co. F 7th U.S. Cavalry)
— Private Armantheus D. Cather (Co. F 7th U.S. Cavalry)
— Private Anton Dohman (Co. F 7th U.S. Cavalry)
— Private Timothy Donnelly (Co. F 7th U.S. Cavalry)
— Private William Gardner (Co. F 7th U.S. Cavalry)
— Private George W. Hammon (Co. F 7th U.S. Cavalry)
— Private Gustav Klein (Co. F 7th U.S. Cavalry)
— Private John P. Kelly (Co. F 7th U.S. Cavalry)
— Private Herman Knauth (Co. F 7th U.S. Cavalry)
— Private William H. Lerock (Co. F 7th U.S. Cavalry)
— Private Werner L. Liemann (Co. F 7th U.S. Cavalry)
— Private William A. Lossee (Co. F 7th U.S. Cavalry)
— Private Christian Madsen (Co. F 7th U.S. Cavalry)
— Private Francis E. Milton (Co. F 7th U.S. Cavalry)
— Private Joseph Monroe (Co. F 7th U.S. Cavalry)

[38] Listed on battle monument as John Vickory. Nichols, *Men with Custer*, 130.

— Private Sebastian Omling (Co. F 7th U.S. Cavalry)
— Private Patrick Rudden (Co. F 7th U.S. Cavalry)
— Private Richard D. Saunders (Co. F 7th U.S. Cavalry)
— Private Francis W. Sicfous (Co. F 7th U.S. Cavalry)
— Private George A. Warren (Co. F 7th U.S. Cavalry)

— Captain Myles W. Keogh (Co. I 7th U.S. Cavalry)
— 1st Lieutenant James E. Porter (Co. I 7th U.S. Cavalry)
— First Sergeant Frank E. Varden (Co. I 7th U.S. Cavalry)
— Sergeant James Bustard (Co. I 7th U.S. Cavalry)
— Corporal John Wild (Co. I 7th U.S. Cavalry)
— Corporal George C. Morris (Co. I 7th U.S. Cavalry)
— Corporal Samuel F. Staples (Co. I 7th U.S. Cavalry)
— Trumpeter John McGucker (Co. I 7th U.S. Cavalry)
— Trumpeter John W. Patton (Co. I 7th U.S. Cavalry)
— Blacksmith Henry A. Bailey (Co. I 7th U.S. Cavalry)
— Private John D. Barry (Co. I 7th U.S. Cavalry)
— Private Joseph F. Broadhurst (Co. I 7th U.S. Cavalry)
— Private Thomas Connors (Co. I 7th U.S. Cavalry)
— Private Thomas P. Downing (Co. I 7th U.S. Cavalry)
— Private Edward Driscoll (Co. I 7th U.S. Cavalry)
— Private David C. Gillette (Co. I 7th U.S. Cavalry)
— Private George H. Gross (Co. I 7th U.S. Cavalry)
— Private Adam Hetesimer (Co. I 7th U.S. Cavalry)
— Private Edward P. Holcomb (Co. I 7th U.S. Cavalry)
— Private Marion E. Horn (Co. I 7th U.S. Cavalry)
— Private Patrick Kelly (Co. I 7th U.S. Cavalry)
— Private Frederick Lehmann (Co. I 7th U.S. Cavalry)
— Private Henry Lehman (Co. I 7th U.S. Cavalry)
— Private Edward W. Lloyd (Co. I 7th U.S. Cavalry)
— Private Archibald McIlhargey (Co. I 7th U.S. Cavalry)
— Private John E. Mitchell (Co. I 7th U.S. Cavalry)
— Private Jacob Noshing (Co. I 7th U.S. Cavalry)
— Private John O'Bryan (Co. I 7th U.S. Cavalry)
— Private George Post (Co. I 7th U.S. Cavalry)
— Private John Parker (Co. I 7th U.S. Cavalry)
— Private Felix Pitter (Co. I 7th U.S. Cavalry)
— Private James Quinn (Co. I 7th U.S. Cavalry)
— Private William Reed (Co. I 7th U.S. Cavalry)
— Private John Rossbury (Co. I 7th U.S. Cavalry)
— Private Darwin L. Symms (Co. I 7th U.S. Cavalry)
— Private James E. Troy (Co. I 7th U.S. Cavalry)
— Private Charles Van Bramer (Co. I 7th U.S. Cavalry)
— Private William B. Whaley (Co. I 7th U.S. Cavalry)

— 1st Lieutenant James Calhoun (Co. L 7th U.S. Cavalry)
— 2nd Lieutenant John J. Crittenden (Co. L 7th U.S. Cavalry)
— First Sergeant James Butler (Co. L 7th U.S. Cavalry)
— Sergeant William Cashan (Co. L 7th U.S. Cavalry)
— Sergeant Amos B. Warren (Co. L 7th U.S. Cavalry)
— Corporal William H. Harrison (Co. L 7th U.S. Cavalry)
— Corporal John Seiler (Co. L 7th U.S. Cavalry)
— Corporal William H. Gilbert (Co. L 7th U.S. Cavalry)
— Trumpeter Frederick Walsh (Co. L 7th U.S. Cavalry)
— Blacksmith Charles Siemon (Co. L 7th U.S. Cavalry)
— Farrier William H. Heath (Co. L 7th U.S. Cavalry)
— Saddler Charles Perkins (Co. L 7th U.S. Cavalry)

— Private George E. Adams (Co. L 7th U.S. Cavalry)
— Private William Andrews (Co. L 7th U.S. Cavalry)
— Private Anthony Assadaly (Co. L 7th U.S. Cavalry)
— Private Elmer Babcock (Co. L 7th U.S. Cavalry)
— Private Ami Cheever (Co. L 7th U.S. Cavalry)
— Private William B. Crisfield (Co. L 7th U.S. Cavalry)
— Private John L. Crowley (Co. L 7th U.S. Cavalry)[39]
— Private William Dye (Co. L 7th U.S. Cavalry)
— Private John Duggan (Co. L 7th U.S. Cavalry)
— Private James J. Galvan (Co. L 7th U.S. Cavalry)
— Private Charles Graham (Co. L 7th U.S. Cavalry)
— Private Henry Hamilton (Co. L 7th U.S. Cavalry)
— Private Weston Harrington (Co. L 7th U.S. Cavalry)
— Private Louis Hauggi (Co. L 7th U.S. Cavalry)
— Private Francis T. Hughes (Co. L 7th U.S. Cavalry)
— Private Thomas G. Kavanagh (Co. L 7th U.S. Cavalry)
— Private Louis Lobering (Co. L 7th U.S. Cavalry)
— Private Charles McCarthy (Co. L 7th U.S. Cavalry)
— Private Peter McGue (Co. L 7th U.S. Cavalry)
— Private Bartholomew Mahoney (Co. L 7th U.S. Cavalry)
— Private Thomas E. Maxwell (Co. L 7th U.S. Cavalry)
— Private John Miller (Co. L 7th U.S. Cavalry)
— Private David J. O'Connell (Co. L 7th U.S. Cavalry)
— Private Oscar F. Pardee (Co. L 7th U.S. Cavalry)[40]
— Private Christian Reibold (Co. L 7th U.S. Cavalry)
— Private Henry Roberts (Co. L 7th U.S. Cavalry)
— Private Walter B. Rogers (Co. L 7th U.S. Cavalry)
— Private Charles Schmidt (Co. L 7th U.S. Cavalry)
— Private Charles Scott (Co. L 7th U.S. Cavalry)
— Private Bent Siemonson (Co. L 7th U.S. Cavalry)
— Private Andrew Snow (Co. L 7th U.S. Cavalry)
— Private Byron L. Tarbox (Co. L 7th U.S. Cavalry)
— Private Edward D. Tessier (Co. L 7th U.S. Cavalry)
— Private Thomas S. Tweed (Co. L 7th U.S. Cavalry)
— Private Johann M. Vetter (Co. L 7th U.S. Cavalry)

— Interpreter Mitch Bouyer (Citizen)
— Guide Boston Custer (Citizen)
— Correspondent Marcus H. Kellogg (Citizen)
— Harry A. Reed (Citizen)

---

[39] Listed on battle monument as John Duggan. Nichols, *Men with Custer*, 70.
[40] Listed on battle monument as John Burke. Nichols, *Men with Custer*, 257.

"As the lips of Custer and those who died with him are forever sealed... it is but charity to withhold any severe criticism upon so gallant and distinguished officer... It is one of the saddest and greatest sacrifices that was ever made by heroic men on any battlefield. No man of military knowledge in riding over this field now, and examining the position that Custer quickly took upon that crest commanding the valley, could fail to recognize the military ability of that commander; and those graves remain as monuments to the fortitude of the men who stood their ground."

— Nelson A. Miles, U.S. Army[41]

(0954) Skirmish, Headwaters of Tongue River, Montana Territory (July 7, 1876)[42]
— 2nd Lieutenant Frederick W. Sibley (2nd U.S. Cavalry)
— 2nd U.S. Cavalry Detachments Co. A, B, D and I

— *2nd Lieutenant Frederick W. Sibley (2nd U.S. Cavalry) brevet promotion to 1st Lieutenant for gallant service in action against Indians (Little Big Horn River, Montana, July 7, 1876).*

— *Private George Watts (Co. I 2nd U.S. Cavalry) received Certificate of Merit: For distinguished conduct during the Sioux campaign, in his efforts, at the risk of his life, to prevent the men of the detachment from needlessly expending their limited ammunition while being pursued by an overwhelming force of hostile Indians (Montana, July 6 to 9, 1876).*

— *Private James Bell (Co. E 7th U.S. Infantry) received MOH: Carried dispatches to General Crook at the imminent risk of his life (Big Horn, Montana, July 9, 1876).*

— *Private James Bell (Co. E 7th U.S. Infantry) received Certificate of Merit: For gallantry in voluntarily carrying dispatches from General Terry, then on the Big Horn River, to General Crook, on the headwaters of the Powder River, through a country infested with hostile Sioux Indians, after scouts had abandoned the attempt as helpless (Montana, July 9, 1876).*

— *Private William Evans (Co. E 7th U.S. Infantry) received MOH: Carried dispatches to General Crook through a country occupied by Sioux (Big Horn River, Montana, July 9, 1876).*

— *Private Benjamin F. Stewart (Co. E 7th U.S. Infantry) received MOH: Carried dispatches to General Crook at imminent risk to his life (Big Horn River, Montana, July 9, 1876).*

(0955) Citizens, near Camp Bowie, Arizona Territory (July 14, 1876)[43]
— (2) Citizens Killed

(0956) Skirmish, near Hat Creek or Indian Creek, Wyoming Territory (July 17, 1876)[44]
— Colonel Wesley Merritt (5th U.S. Cavalry)
— 5th U.S. Cavalry Co. A, B, D, G, I, K and M

[41] Miles, *Personal Recollections*, 290.
[42] Indians. Chronological List, 61; Heitman (Volume 2), 442; Record of Engagements, 59; Gray, *Centennial Campaign*, 199-200.
[43] Indians. Killed were miners, men named Todenworth and either Keho or Cadotte. *Annual Report of Secretary of War (1876)*, 99; *Annual Report of Secretary of War (1877)*, 135.
[44] Indians. Chronological List, 62; Heitman (Volume 2), 442; Record of Engagements, 59; Hedren, *Fort Laramie in 1876*, 133-134; King, *War Eagle*, 160-162; Russell, *Campaigning with King*, 64-68.

(0957) Action, Mouth of Powder River, Montana Territory (July 29, 1876)[45]
— Lt. Colonel Elwell S. Otis (22nd U.S. Infantry)
— 22nd U.S. Infantry Co. E, F, G, H, I and K
— **1 WOUNDED**[46]
— Private John Donahoe (Co. G 22nd U.S. Infantry)
— *gunshot wound, scrotum, slight wound*

(0958) Skirmish, near Saragossa, Coahuila, Mexico (July 30, 1876)[47]
— 1st Lieutenant John L. Bullis (24th U.S. Infantry)
— 10th U.S. Cavalry Detachment Co. B
— Detachment of Indian Scouts

— *1st Lieutenant John L. Bullis (24th U.S. Infantry) brevet promotion to Major for gallant service in actions against Indians (Saragossa, Mexico, July 30, 1876 and Sierra Burras Mountains, Coahuila, Mexico, May 3, 1881).*

(0959) Skirmish, Red Canyon, Montana Territory (August 1, 1876)[48]
— Captain William S. Collier (4th U.S. Infantry)
— 4th U.S. Infantry Co. K

(0960) Action, near Mouth of Rosebud Creek, Montana Territory (August 2, 1876)[49]
— Major Orlando H. Moore (6th U.S. Infantry)
— 6th U.S. Infantry Co. D and I
— 17th U.S. Infantry Co. C
— **1 KILLED**[50]
— Scout Wesley Brockmeyer (Citizen)

(0961) Action, Red Rock Country, Arizona Territory (August 15, 1876)[51]
— Captain Charles Porter (8th U.S. Infantry)
— 6th U.S. Cavalry Detachment Co. E
— Detachment of Indian Scouts
— **1 WOUNDED**[52]
— No. 17 (Indian Scout)
— *gunshot wound, shoulder, slight wound*

— *Captain Charles Porter (8th U.S. Infantry) brevet promotion to Major for gallant service in actions against Indians (Arizona, August 15, 1876; January 1, 1878 and April 3, 1878).*

(0962) Action, near Mouth of Yellowstone River, Montana Territory (August 23, 1876)[53]
— 1st Lieutenant Nelson Bronson (6th U.S. Infantry)
— 6th U.S. Infantry Co. G

---

[45] Indians. *Annual Report of Secretary of War (1877)*, 358; Chronological List, 62; Heitman (Volume 2), 442; Greene, *Yellowstone Command*, 32.
[46] Reports of Diseases and Individual Cases, F 465.
[47] Indians. Chronological List, 62; Heitman (Volume 2), 442; Record of Engagements, 59; Burton, *Black, Buckskin and Blue*, 187; Leckie, *Buffalo Soldiers*, 152; Mulroy, *Freedom on the Border*, 126-127; Williams, *Texas' Last Frontier*, 201-202.
[48] Indians. Chronological List, 62; Heitman (Volume 2), 442; Hedren, *Fort Laramie in 1876*, 139-140.
[49] Indians. *Annual Report of Secretary of War (1876)*, 480-481; Chronological List, 62; Record of Engagements, 60; Gray, *Centennial Campaign*, 210-211; Greene, *Yellowstone Command*, 34-35; Moore, "Skirmish at Powder River, August 2, 1876" in Greene, *Battles and Skirmishes*, 92-95. Chronological List lists 6th U.S. Infantry 2 Co's; 17th U.S. Infantry 1 Co.
[50] Greene, *Yellowstone Command*, 35.
[51] Indians. *Annual Report of Secretary of War (1876)*, 100; *Annual Report of Secretary of War (1877)*, 134-135, 358; Chronological List, 62; Heitman (Volume 2), 442; Carter, *From Yorktown to Santiago*, 278; Thrapp, *Al Sieber*, 183.
[52] Reports of Diseases and Individual Cases, F 466.
[53] Indians. Chronological List, 62; Heitman (Volume 2), 442; Record of Engagements, 60; Gray, *Centennial Campaign*, 231-232; Greene, *Yellowstone Command*, 53.

— 1 KILLED[54]
   — Private Dennis Shields (Co. G 6th U.S. Infantry)

(0963) Engagement, Slim Buttes, Dakota Territory (September 9, 1876)[55]
   — Brigadier General George Crook
   — Captain Anson Mills (3rd U.S. Cavalry)
      — 2nd U.S. Cavalry Co. A, B, D, E and I
      — 3rd U.S. Cavalry Co. A, B, C, D, E, F, G, I, L and M
      — 5th U.S. Cavalry Co. A, B, C, D, E, F, G, I, K and M
      — 4th U.S. Infantry Co. D, F and G
      — 9th U.S. Infantry Co. C, G and H
      — 14th U.S. Infantry Co. B, C, F and I
— 3 KILLED[56]
      — Private John Wenzel (Co. A 3rd U.S. Cavalry)
      — Private Edward Kennedy (Co. C 5th U.S. Cavalry)

      — Scout Jonathan White — aka Buffalo Chips (Citizen)

— 14 WOUNDED[57]
      — 1st Lieutenant Adolphus H. Von Leuttwitz (Co. E 3rd U.S. Cavalry)
         — *gunshot wound, right knee, fracture, amputation at thigh, severe wound*

      — Private J. Stevenson (Co. I 2nd U.S. Cavalry)
         — *gunshot wound, left foot, fracture, severe wound*
      — Private William Dubois (Co. C 3rd U.S. Cavalry)
         — *gunshot wound, left side of head, severe wound*
      — Private August Dorn (Co. D 3rd U.S. Cavalry)
         — *gunshot wound, right side of face over eye, severe wound*
      — Private Charles Foster (Co. D 3rd U.S. Cavalry)
         — *gunshot wound, right thigh and left hand, severe wound*

      — Sergeant Edward Glass (Co. E 3rd U.S. Cavalry)
         — *gunshot wound, right forearm, severe wound*
      — Private Edward McKiernan (Co. E 3rd U.S. Cavalry)
         — *gunshot wound, right thigh, severe wound*
      — Sergeant John A. Kirkwood (Co. M 3rd U.S. Cavalry)
         — *gunshot wound, left side, severe wound*

      — Private George Cloutier (Co. D 5th U.S. Cavalry)
         — *gunshot wound, right gluteal region, severe wound*

[54] Gray, *Centennial Campaign*, 232.
[55] Indians. *Annual Report of Secretary of War (1876)*, 37, 446, 505-507; *Annual Report of Secretary of War (1877)*, 358; Chronological List, 62; Heitman (Volume 2), 442; Record of Engagements, 60-61; Gray, *Centennial Campaign*, 246-251; Greene, *Slim Buttes*, 59-96; King, *War Eagle*, 177-179. Chronological List lists 2nd U.S. Cavalry Co. A, B, D, E, I; 3rd U.S. Cavalry; 5th U.S. Cavalry; 4th U.S. Infantry Co. D, F, G; 9th U.S. Infantry Co. C, G, H; 14th U.S. Infantry Co. B, C, F, I.
[56] Reports of Diseases and Individual Cases, F 467; Register of Deaths Regular Army, 1860-1889 (Volume 7); 5th U.S. Cavalry Regimental Return September 1876.
[57] Reports of Diseases and Individual Cases, F 467.

— Private Daniel Ford (Co. F 5th U.S. Cavalry)
— *gunshot wound, right hip, slight wound*
— Private Michael H. Donnally (Co. F 5th U.S. Cavalry)
— *gunshot wound, right thigh, severe wound*
— Sergeant Lucifer Schreiber (Co. K 5th U.S. Cavalry)
— *gunshot wound, right thigh, severe wound*
— Private William Madden (Co. M 5th U.S. Cavalry)
— *gunshot wound, right leg, slight wound*

— Private Robert Fitzhenry (Co. H 9th U.S. Infantry)
— *gunshot wound, left thigh, severe wound*

— *Private William B. Dubois (Co. C 3rd U.S. Cavalry) received Certificate of Merit: For gallantry in action with Indians, though severely wounded, he refused to be carried from the field, saying the men were needed to fight (Slim Buttes, Dakota, September 9, 1876).*

— *Private John Hale (Co. G 3rd U.S. Cavalry) received Certificate of Merit: For gallant and heroic conduct in action against hostile Sioux Indians, while charging with a small detachment upon a large body of the enemy who had attempted to regain their village, he had become separated from his command, and singularly charged into the midst of the Indians and was severely wounded (Slim Buttes, Dakota, September 9, 1876).*

— *Sergeant John A. Kirkwood (Co. M 3rd U.S. Cavalry) received MOH: Bravely endeavored to dislodge some Sioux Indians secreted in a ravine (Slim Buttes, Dakota, September 9, 1876).*

— *Private Edward McKiernan (Co. E 3rd U.S. Cavalry) received Certificate of Merit: For gallantry in action with Indians, though severely wounded and unable to stand up, he called for a carbine and continued the fight (Slim Buttes, Dakota, September 9, 1876).*

— *Captain Anson Mills (3rd U.S. Cavalry) brevet promotion to Colonel for gallant service in action against Indians (Slim Buttes, Dakota, September 9, 1876).*

— *Private James Quinn (Co. E 3rd U.S. Cavalry) received Certificate of Merit: For gallantry in action with Indians, in building breastworks under a heavy fire, and also in a charge on the village (Slim Buttes, Dakota, September 9, 1876).*

— *Private Robert Smith (Co. M 3rd U.S. Infantry) received MOH: Special bravery in endeavoring to dislodge Indians secreted in a ravine (Slim Buttes, Dakota, September 9, 1876).*

— *Private John A. Taylor (Co. G 3rd U.S. Cavalry) received Certificate of Merit: For gallantry in action with Indians, in charging with a small detachment into the center of the enemy, under a heavy fire and bringing out the ponies at the risk of his life (Slim Buttes, Dakota, September 9, 1876).*

(0964) Action, Owl Creek, Belle Fourche River, Dakota Territory (September 14, 1876)[58]
— UNKNOWN
— 5th U.S. Cavalry Detachment
— **1 KILLED**[59]
— Private Cyrus B. Milner (Co. A 5th U.S. Cavalry)

(0965) Action, Florida Mountains, New Mexico Territory (September 15, 1876)[60]
    — Captain Henry Carroll (9th U.S. Cavalry)
        — 9th U.S. Cavalry Detachment Co. F
    — **1 WOUNDED**[61]
        — Private Harrison Bland (Co. F 9th U.S. Cavalry)
            — *gunshot wound, right arm, slight wound*

(0966) Skirmish, caves east of Camp Verde, Arizona Territory (September 18, 1876)[62]
    — Guide Al Sieber (Citizen)
        — Detachment of Indian Scouts

(0967) Skirmish, Tonto Basin, Arizona Territory (October 4, 1876)[63]
    — Captain Charles Porter (8th U.S. Infantry)
        — 6th U.S. Cavalry Detachment Co. E
        — Detachment of Indian Scouts

(0968) Citizens, Eagle Springs, Texas (October 9, 1876)[64]
    — (1) Citizen Killed

(0969) Skirmish, Spring Creek, Montana Territory (October 11, 1876)[65]
    — Captain Charles W. Miner (22nd U.S. Infantry)
        — 17th U.S. Infantry Co. C
        — 22nd U.S. Infantry Co. G, H and K

"The men and officers did all of them exceedingly well, and it is due to them that the train came off as well as it did. The wagon-masters were the only men that I had available as scouts, and were invaluable to me in that capacity in looking over the country in my front."
          — Charles W. Miner, U.S. Army[66]

(0970) Action, Richard Creek, Wyoming Territory (October 14, 1876)[67]
    — Sergeant Joseph Parker (2nd U.S. Cavalry)
        — 2nd U.S. Cavalry Detachment Co. K
    — **1 KILLED**[68]
        — Private Warren C. Tasker (Co. K 2nd U.S. Cavalry)

[58] Indians. *Annual Report of Secretary of War (1876)*, 512; Chronological List, 62; Heitman (Volume 2), 442; Record of Engagements, 61; Greene, *Slim Buttes*, 103.
[59] *Annual Report of Secretary of War (1876)*, 512; 5th U.S. Cavalry Regimental Return September 1876.
[60] Indians. *Annual Report of Secretary of War (1877)*, 358; Chronological List, 62; Heitman (Volume 2), 442; Record of Engagements, 61; Billington, *New Mexico's Buffalo Soldiers*, 48; Sweeney, *Cochise to Geronimo*, 71; Thrapp, *Victorio*, 182-183. Chronological List lists 9th U.S. Cavalry Co. F.
[61] Reports of Diseases and Individual Cases, F 471.
[62] Indians. *Annual Report of Secretary of War (1877)*, 135; Chronological List, 62; Heitman (Volume 2), 442; Thrapp, *Al Sieber*, 184.
[63] Indians. *Annual Report of Secretary of War (1877)*, 135; Chronological List, 62; Heitman (Volume 2), 442; Carter, *From Yorktown to Santiago*, 278; Thrapp, *Al Sieber*, 184. Chronological List lists 6th U.S. Cavalry Detachments; Detachment of Indian Scouts.
[64] Indians. Killed was Juan Marengo. Chronological List, 62; Record of Engagements, 75.
[65] Indians. *Annual Report of Secretary of War (1877)*, 488-490; Chronological List, 62; Heitman (Volume 2), 442; Record of Engagements, 61; Smith and Sharpe, "Spring Creek Encounters" in Greene, *Battles and Skirmishes*, 116-131; Greene, *Yellowstone Command*, 81-83; Hedren, *Great Sioux War Orders of Battle*, 127-128. Chronological List lists 15th U.S. Infantry Co. C 22nd U.S. Infantry Co. G, H, K.
[66] *Annual Report of Secretary of War (1876)*, 486-487.
[67] Indians. Chronological List, 62; Heitman (Volume 2), 442; Record of Engagements, 63; Hedren, *Fort Laramie in 1876*, 183.
[68] Register of Deaths Regular Army, 1860-1889 (Volume 7); 2nd U.S. Cavalry Regimental Return October 1876.

(0971) Action, Clear Creek, Montana Territory (October 15 and 16, 1876)[69]
   — Lt. Colonel Elwell S. Otis (22nd U.S. Infantry)
      — 17th U.S. Infantry Co. C and G
      — 22nd U.S. Infantry Co. G and H, Detachments Co. K
   — **3 WOUNDED**[70]
      — Private Francis Marrggie (Co. G 17th U.S. Infantry)
         — gunshot wound, leg, slight wound
      — Sergeant Robert Anderson (Co. G 22nd U.S. Infantry)
         — gunshot wound, leg, slight wound
      — Private John Donahue (Co. G 22nd U.S. Infantry)
         — gunshot wound, knee, slight wound

— 1st Lieutenant William Conway (22nd U.S. Infantry) brevet promotion to Captain for gallant service in action against Indians (Clear Creek, Montana, October 15 and 16, 1876).

— Captain Mott Hooton (22nd U.S. Infantry) brevet promotion to Major for service in action against Indians (Clear Creek, Montana, October 15 and 16, 1876).

— 2nd Lieutenant William H. Kell (22nd U.S. Infantry) brevet promotion to 1st Lieutenant for gallant service in action against Indians (Clear Creek, Montana, October 15 and 16, 1876).

— 1st Lieutenant Benjamin C. Lockwood (22nd U.S. Infantry) brevet promotion to Captain for gallant service in action against Indians (Spring Creek, Montana, October 15 and 16, 1876).

— Private John Moloney (Co. I 22nd U.S. Infantry) received Certificate of Merit: For gallantry in action with Indians, in voluntarily carrying dispatches from Glendive, then surrounded by hostile Indians, to Fort Buford, and successfully scouting in advance of the wagon train in route to the Tongue River, the train being surrounded by a large force of Indians (Glendive Creek, Montana, October 14 and 15, 1876).

— Captain Charles W. Miner (22nd U.S. Infantry) brevet promotion to Major for gallant service in action against Indians (Spring Creek, Montana, October 15 and 16, 1876).

— 2nd Lieutenant James Nickerson (17th U.S. Infantry) brevet promotion to 1st Lieutenant for gallant service in action against Indians. (Spring Creek, Montana, October 15 and 16, 1876).[71]

— 2nd Lieutenant Alfred C. Sharpe (22nd U.S. Cavalry) brevet promotion to 1st Lieutenant for gallant service in action against Indians (Spring Creek, Montana, October 15 and 16, 1876).

— 1st Lieutenant Oskaloosa M. Smith (22nd U.S. Infantry) brevet promotion to Captain for gallant service in action against Indians (Spring Creek, Montana, October 15 and 16, 1876).

[69] Indians. *Annual Report of Secretary of War (1876)*, 485; *Annual Report of Secretary of War (1877)*, 358-359, 490-492; Chronological List, 63; Heitman (Volume 2), 442; Record of Engagements, 61-62; Smith and Sharpe, "Spring Creek Encounters" in Greene, *Battles and Skirmishes*, 116-131; Greene, *Yellowstone Command*, 85-90; Hedren, *Great Sioux War Orders of Battle*, 127-128. Chronological List lists 15 October 1876. Chronological List lists 22nd U.S. Infantry Co. G, H, Detachments Co. I, K; 17th U.S. Infantry Co. C, G.
[70] Reports of Diseases and Individual Cases, F 471.
[71] 2nd Lieutenant James Nickerson (17th U.S. Infantry) declined his brevet promotion. *Army Register (1901)*, 359.

"I cannot speak too highly of the conduct of both officers and men. The officers obeyed instructions with alacrity and executed their orders with great efficiency. They fought the enemy twelve hours, and fired during that time upward of seven thousand rounds of ammunition. They defeated a strong enemy, estimated by many at from seven to eight hundred, which had defiantly placed himself across our trail with the deliberate purpose of capturing the train and gave him a lesson which he will heed and never forget."
— Elwell S. Otis, U.S. Army[72]

(0972) Action, Big Dry River or Clear Creek, Montana Territory (October 21, 1876)[73]
    — Colonel Nelson A. Miles (5th U.S. Infantry)
        — 5th U.S. Infantry Co. A, B, C, D, E, F, G, H, I and K
    — **2 WOUNDED**[74]
        — Sergeant Robert McPhelan (Co. E 5th U.S. Infantry)
            — *gunshot wound, thigh, slight wound*
        — Private John Geyer (Co. I 5th U.S. Infantry)
            — *gunshot wound, thigh, slight wound*

    — *Musician John Baker (Co. D 5th U.S. Infantry) received MOH: Gallantry in engagements (Montana, October 1876 to 1877).*

    — *Private Richard Burke (Co. G 5th U.S. Infantry) received MOH: Gallantry in engagements (Montana, October 1876 to January 1877).*

    — *Sergeant Denis Byrne (Co. G 5th U.S. Infantry) received MOH: Gallantry in engagements (Montana, October 1876 to January 1877).*

    — *Private Joseph A. Cable (Co. I 5th U.S. Infantry) received MOH: Gallantry in action (Montana, October 1876 to January 1877).*

    — *Private James S. Calvert (Co. C 5th U.S. Cavalry) received MOH: Gallantry in action (Montana, October 1876 to January 1877).*

    — *Sergeant Aquilla Coonrod (Co. C 5th U.S. Infantry) received MOH: Gallantry in action (Montana, October 1876 to January 1877).*

    — *Private John S. Donelly (Co. G 5th U.S. Infantry) received MOH: Gallantry in action (Montana, October 1876 to January 1877).*

    — *Private Christopher Freemeyer (Co. D 5th U.S. Infantry) received MOH: Gallantry in action (Montana, October 21, 1876 to January 8, 1877).*

[72] *Annual Report of Secretary of War (1877)*, 491-492.
[73] Indians. *Annual Report of Secretary of War (1876)*, 38, 446, 470, 482-485; *Annual Report of Secretary of War (1877)*, 358, 493, 541; Chronological List, 63; Heitman (Volume 2), 442; Record of Engagements, 62-63; Greene, *Yellowstone Command*, 92-104; Hedren, *Great Sioux War Orders of Battle*, 130-132; Miles, *Personal Recollections*, 225-228. Chronological List lists 5th U.S. Infantry.
[74] Reports of Diseases and Individual Cases, F 472.

— Corporal John Hall (Co. B 5th U.S. Infantry) received MOH: Gallantry in action (Montana, October 1876 to January 1877).

— First Sergeant Henry Hogan (Co. G 5th U.S. Infantry) received MOH: Gallantry in action (October 1876 to January 8, 1877).

— Corporal David Holland (Co. A 5th U.S. Infantry) received MOH: Gallantry in action (Montana, October 1876 to January 1877).

— Private Fred O. Hunt (Co. A 5th U.S. Infantry) received MOH: Gallantry in action (October 1876 to January 8, 1877).

— Corporal Edward Johnston (Co. C 5th U.S. Infantry) received MOH: Gallantry in action (Montana, October 1876 to January 8, 1877).

— Private Phillip Kennedy (Co. C 5th U.S. Infantry) received MOH: Gallantry in action (Montana, October 21, 1876 to January 8, 1877).

— First Sergeant Wendelin Kreher (Co. C 5th U.S. Infantry) received MOH: Gallantry in action (Montana, October 21, 1876 to January 8, 1877).

— Private Bernard McCann (Co. F 22nd U.S. Infantry) received MOH: Gallantry in action (Montana, October 21, 1876 to January 8, 1877).

— Private Michael McCormick (Co. G 5th U.S. Infantry) received MOH: Gallantry in action (Montana, October 21, 1876 to January 8, 1877).

— Private Owen McGar (Co. C 5th U.S. Infantry) received MOH: Gallantry in action (Montana, October 21, 1876 to January 8, 1877).

— Sergeant Michael McLoughlin (Co. A 5th U.S. Infantry) received MOH: Gallantry in action (Montana, October 21, 1876 to January 8, 1877).

— Private John McHugh (Co. A 5th U.S. Infantry) received MOH: Gallantry in action (Montana, October 21, 1876 to January 8, 1877).

— Sergeant Robert McPhelan (Co. E 5th U.S. Cavalry) received MOH: Gallantry in action (Montana, October 21, 1876 to January 8, 1877).

— Corporal George Miller (Co. H 5th U.S. Infantry) received MOH: Gallantry in action (Montana, October 21, 1876 to January 8, 1877).

— Private Charles H. Montrose (Co. I 5th U.S. Infantry) received MOH: Gallantry in action (Montana, October 21, 1876 to January 8, 1877).

— First Sergeant David Roche (Co. A 5th U.S. Infantry) received MOH: Gallantry in action (Montana, October 21, 1876 to January 8, 1877).

— Private Henry Rodenburg (Co. A 5th U.S. Infantry) received MOH: Gallantry in action (Montana, October 21, 1876 to January 8, 1877).

— Private Edward Rooney (Co. D 5th U.S. Infantry) received MOH: Gallantry in action (Montana, October 21, 1876 to January 8, 1877).

— Private David Ryan (Co. G 5th U.S. Infantry) received MOH: Gallantry in action (Montana, October 21, 1876 to January 8, 1877).

— *Private Charles Sheppard (Co. A 5th U.S. Infantry) received MOH: Bravery in actions with Sioux (Montana, October 21, 1876 to January 8, 1877).*

— *Sergeant William Wallace (Co. C 5th U.S. Infantry) received MOH: Gallantry in action (Montana, October 21, 1876 to January 8, 1877).*

— *Private Patton G. Whitehead (Co. C 5th U.S. Infantry) received MOH: Gallantry in action (Montana, October 21, 1876 to January 8, 1877).*

— *Corporal Charles Wilson (Co. H 5th U.S. Infantry) received MOH: Gallantry in action (Montana, October 21, 1876 to January 8, 1877).*

(0973) Surrender of 400 Indians, near Camp Robinson, Nebraska (October 23, 1876)[75]

(0974) Surrender of 2,000 Indians, Big Dry River, Montana Territory (October 27, 1876)[76]

(0975) Action, Bates Creek, near North Fork of Powder River, Wyoming Territory (November 25, 1876)[77]
— Colonel Ranald S. Mackenzie (4th U.S. Cavalry)
     — 2nd U.S. Cavalry Co. K
     — 3rd U.S. Cavalry Co. H and K
     — 4th U.S. Cavalry Co. B, D, E, F, I and M
     — 5th U.S. Cavalry Co. H and L
     — Detachment of Indian Scouts
— **7 KILLED**[78]
     — 1st Lieutenant John A. McKinney (Co. M 4th U.S. Cavalry)

     — Corporal Patrick F. Ryan (Co. D 4th U.S. Cavalry)
     — Private James Baird (Co. D 4th U.S. Cavalry)
     — Private Alexander Keller (Co. E 4th U.S. Cavalry)
     — Private John Sullivan (Co. H 4th U.S. Cavalry)

     — Private Joseph Mengia (Co. H 5th U.S. Cavalry)
     — Private Alexander McFarland (Co. L 5th U.S. Cavalry) — d. 11-28-1876

— **26 WOUNDED**[79]
     — Sergeant Daniel Cunningham (Co. H 3rd U.S. Cavalry)
         — *gunshot wound, foot, fracture, severe wound*
     — Private Henry Holden (Co. H 3rd U.S. Cavalry)
         — *gunshot wound, thorax, severe wound*

[75] Indians. Chronological List, 63; Heitman (Volume 2), 443; Record of Engagements, 64; Bellas. "Crook-Mackenzie Campaigns" in Greene, *Battles and Skirmishes*, 169-171; Grinnell, *Two Great Scouts*, 253-255; Hedren, *Fort Laramie in 1876*, 185; Robinson, *Bad Hand*, 203-206.

[76] Indians. *Annual Report of Secretary of War (1876)*, 446; Chronological List, 63; Heitman (Volume 2), 442; Record of Engagements, 63.

[77] Indians. *Annual Report of Secretary of War (1877)*, 359; Chronological List, 63; Heitman (Volume 2), 443; Record of Engagements, 64-65; Bourke, *Mackenzie's Last Event*, 29-42; Grinnell, *Two Great Scouts*, 265-273; Hedren, *Great Sioux War Orders of Battle*, 141-147; Hoig, *Perilous Pursuit*, 11-17; Niderost, "Cheyenne Fall: The Battle of Red Fork," *Wild West* (October 2011): 26-33; Robinson, *Bad Hand*, 215-222; Smith, *Sagebrush Soldier*, 71-88, 95-96. Chronological List lists November 25 and 25, 1876. Chronological List lists 2nd U.S. Cavalry Co. K; 3rd U.S. Cavalry Co. H, K; 4th U.S. Cavalry Co. B, D, E, F, I, M; 5th U.S. Cavalry Co. H, L.

[78] Reports of Diseases and Individual Cases, F 474; Register of Deaths Regular Army, 1860-1889 (Volume 7).

[79] Reports of Diseases and Individual Cases, F 474.

— Private J.E. Talmadge (Co. H 3rd U.S. Cavalry)
    — *gunshot wound, back, slight wound*

— Private Eugene Hall (Co. B 4th U.S. Cavalry)
    — *gunshot wound, hand, slight wound*
— Private G.H.M. Replogle (Co. B 4th U.S. Cavalry)
    — *gunshot wound, hip, slight wound*
— Private William B. Smith (Co. B 4th U.S. Cavalry)
    — *thorax, severe wound*
— Private Edward Fitzgerald (Co. D 4th U.S. Cavalry)
    — *gunshot wound, slight wound*
— Private E.L. Buck (Co. E 4th U.S. Cavalry)
    — *gunshot wound, thigh, severe wound*

— Private Henry Bennett (Co. F 4th U.S. Cavalry)
    — *sprain, slight wound*
— Private Charles Lewis (Co. F 4th U.S. Cavalry)
    — *gunshot wound, thigh, slight wound*
— Private August Stick (Co. E 4th U.S. Cavalry)
    — *gunshot wound, thigh, severe wound*
— Private Charles Thompson (Co. F 4th U.S. Cavalry)
    — *shoulder, slight wound*

— Corporal William H. Poole (Co. I 4th U.S. Cavalry)
    — *gunshot wound, hand, slight wound*
— Corporal Jacob Schaufler (Co. I 4th U.S. Cavalry)
    — *gunshot wound, left arm, fracture, severe wound*
— Private William Harrison (Co. I 4th U.S. Cavalry)
    — *gunshot wound, foot, fracture, severe wound*
— Private George Kenney (Co. I 4th U.S. Cavalry)
    — *gunshot wound, neck, severe wound*
— Private Daniel Stevens (Co. I 4th U.S. Cavalry)
    — *gunshot wound, thorax, severe wound*

— Sergeant Thomas H. Forsyth (Co. M 4th U.S. Cavalry)
    — *gunshot wound, head, slight wound*
— Corporal William Lynn (Co. M 4th U.S. Cavalry)
    — *gunshot wound, thigh, fracture, severe wound*
— Private E.W. Iveson (Co. M 4th U.S. Cavalry)
    — *gunshot wound, abdomen, slight wound*
— Private Isaac Maguire (Co. M 4th U.S. Cavalry)
    — *gunshot wound, thigh, severe wound*
— Private James McMahon (Co. M 4th U.S. Cavalry)
    — *gunshot wounds, arm, slight wound, thorax, severe wound*
— Private Patrick Reardon (Co. M 4th U.S. Cavalry)
    — *gunshot wound, arm, slight wound*

— Private Charles Folsom (Co. H 5th U.S. Cavalry)
    — *gunshot wound, thigh, fracture, severe wound*
— Private George H. Stickney (Co. H 5th U.S. Cavalry)
    — *gunshot wound, thorax, slight wound*

— Anzi (Indian Scout)
    — *gunshot wound, abdomen, severe wound*

— Captain Wirt Davis (4ᵗʰ U.S. Cavalry) brevet promotion to Lt. Colonel for gallant service in actions against Indians (North Fork of Red River, Texas, September 29, 1872 and Big Horn Mountains, Wyoming, November 25, 1876).

— 2ⁿᵈ Lieutenant Hayden De Lany (9ᵗʰ U.S. Infantry) brevet promotion to Captain for gallant service in action against Indians (Big Horn Mountains, Wyoming, November 25, 1876).

— First Sergeant Thomas H. Forsyth (Co. M 4ᵗʰ U.S. Cavalry) received MOH: Though dangerously wounded, he maintained his ground with a small party against a largely superior force after his commanding officer had been shot down during a sudden attack and rescued that officer and a comrade from the enemy (Big Horn Mountains, Wyoming, November 25, 1876).

— Private Thomas Ryan (Co. M 4ᵗʰ U.S. Cavalry) received Certificate of Merit" For gallantry in action with Indians, in maintaining his stand with but two comrades, one of them disabled, against superior numbers, and rallying the troops in time to rescue the body of his commanding officer (Big Horn Mountains, Wyoming, November 25, 1876).

— 1ˢᵗ Lieutenant Walter S. Schuyler (5ᵗʰ U.S. Cavalry) brevet promotion to Captain for gallantry in action against Indians (Big Horn Mountains, Wyoming, November 25, 1876).

(0976) Skirmish, Bark Creek, Montana Territory (December 7, 1876)[80]
—1ˢᵗ Lieutenant Frank D. Baldwin (5ᵗʰ U.S. Infantry)
     — 5ᵗʰ U.S. Infantry Co. G, H and I

(0977) Skirmish, near Headwaters of Red Water Creek, Montana Territory (December 18, 1876)[81]
     — 1ˢᵗ Lieutenant Frank D. Baldwin (5ᵗʰ U.S. Infantry)
     — 5ᵗʰ U.S. Infantry Co. G, H and I

— 1ˢᵗ Lieutenant Frank D. Baldwin (5ᵗʰ U.S. Infantry) brevet promotion to Major for gallant and successful attack on Sitting Bulls camp of Indians (Red Water Creek, Montana, December 18, 1876) and conspicuous gallantry in action against Indians (Wolf Mountains, Montana, January 8, 1877),

TOTAL KILLED 1876 — 15/270/4/17 (OFFICERS, ENLISTED MEN, INDIAN SCOUTS, CITIZENS)

[80] Indians. *Annual Report of Secretary of War (1877)*, 493-494; Chronological List, 63; Heitman (Volume 2), 443; Record of Engagements, 65; Baldwin, "Fights at Bark Creek and Ash Creek" in Greene, *Battles and Skirmishes*, 157-166; Greene, *Yellowstone Command*, 136-138.
[81] Indians. *Annual Report of Secretary of War (1877)*, 493-494; Chronological List, 63; Heitman (Volume 2), 443; Record of Engagements, 65; "Fights at Bark Creek and Ash Creek" by Frank D. Baldwin in Greene, *Battles and Skirmishes*, 157-166; Greene, *Yellowstone Command*, 140-143.

1877

"What is more to be deplored, much loss of life has resulted from the necessity of engaging strong forces of Indian with detachments of troops generally inferior in point of numbers. An Army of respectable strength is of inestimable value as a means of preventing war. This is especially true of Indian war. The savages are well informed as to the strength of our frontier posts, and they are more influenced by an exhibition of force than by anything else."

— George W. McCrary, Citizen[1]

---

[1] Official Report of Secretary of War George W. McCrary, 19 November 1877.
Annual Report of Secretary of War (1877), v.

(0978) Action, Valley of Tongue River, Wyoming Territory (January 3, 1877)[2]
    — Colonel Nelson A. Miles (5th U.S. Infantry)
        — 5th U.S. Infantry Co. A, C, D, E and K
        — 22nd U.S. Infantry Co. E and F
  — **1 KILLED**[3]
        — Private William Batty (Co. C 5th U.S. Infantry)

(0979) Engagement, Wolf Mountains, Montana Territory (January 8, 1877)[4]
    — Colonel Nelson A. Miles (5th U.S. Infantry)
        — 5th U.S. Infantry Co. A, C, D, E, and K
        — 22nd U.S. Infantry Co. E and F
  — **2 KILLED**[5]
        — Corporal Augustus Rathman (Co. A 5th U.S. Infantry)
        — Private Bernard McCann (Co. F 22nd U.S. Infantry) — d. 01-12-1877

  — **2 WOUNDED**[6]
        — Private Henry Rodenburgh (Co. A 5th U.S. Infantry)
           — *gunshot wound, face, severe wound*
        — Private George Danka (Co. H 5th U.S. Infantry)
           — *gunshot wound, chest, slight wound*

      — *1st Lieutenant Frank D. Baldwin (5th U.S. Infantry) brevet promotion to Major for gallant and successful attack on Sitting Bulls camp of Indians (Red Water Creek, Montana, December 18, 1876) and conspicuous gallantry in action against Indians (Wolf Mountains, Montana, January 8, 1877),*

      — *Captain Edmond Butler (5th U.S. Infantry) brevet promotion to Major for conspicuous gallantry in leading his command in a successful charge against a superior number of Indians, strongly posted (Wolf Mountain, Montana, January 8, 1877).*

      — *Captain Edmond Butler (5th U.S. Infantry) received MOH: Most distinguished gallantry in action with hostile Indians (Wolf Mountain, Montana, January 8, 1877).*

      — *Captain James S. Casey (5th U.S. Infantry) brevet promotion to Lt. Colonel for conspicuous gallantry in leading his command in a successful charge against a superior number of Indians strongly posted (Wolf Mountain, Montana, January 8, 1877).*

      — *Captain James S. Casey (5th U.S. Infantry) received MOH: Led his command in a successful charge against superior numbers of the enemy strongly posted (Wolf Mountain, Montana, January 8, 1877).*

      — *Captain Ezra P. Ewers (5th U.S. Infantry) brevet promotion to Major for gallant service in action against Indians under Crazy Horse (Tongue River, Montana, January 8, 1877).*

---

[2] Indians. *Annual Report of Secretary of War (1877)*, 359, 494-496; Record of Engagements, 66; Greene, *Yellowstone Command*, 162.
[3] Reports of Diseases and Individual Cases, F 476; Register of Deaths Regular Army, 1860-1889 (Volume 7).
[4] Indians. *Annual Report of Secretary of War (1877)*, 359, 494-496; Chronological List, 63; Heitman (Volume 2), 443; Record of Engagements, 66; Greene, *Yellowstone Command*, 165-176; Hedren, *Great Sioux War Orders of Battle*, 147-149; Miles, *Personal Recollections*, 236-239. Chronological List lists 5th U.S. Infantry Co. A, C, D, E, K, Detachments Co. B, H; 22nd U.S. Infantry Co. E, F.
[5] Reports of Diseases and Individual Cases, F 476; Register of Deaths Regular Army, 1860-1889 (Volume 7).
[6] Reports of Diseases and Individual Cases, F 476.

— *1ˢᵗ Lieutenant Robert McDonald (5ᵗʰ U.S. Infantry) received MOH: Led his command in a successful charge against superior numbers of hostile Indians, strongly posted (Wolf Mountain, Montana, January 8, 1877).*

— *1ˢᵗ Lieutenant Robert McDonald (5ᵗʰ U.S. Infantry) brevet promotion to Captain for conspicuous gallantry in leading his command in a successful charge against Indians strongly posted (Wolf Mountains, Montana, January 8, 1877).*[7]

(0980) Action, Leidendorf Range of Mountains, New Mexico Territory (January 9, 1877)[8]
— 2ⁿᵈ Lieutenant John A. Rucker (6ᵗʰ U.S. Cavalry)
    — 6ᵗʰ U.S. Cavalry Detachments Co. H and L
    — Detachment of Indian Scouts
— **1 WOUNDED**[9]
    — Es-Kin-E-Car (Indian Scout)
        — *gunshot wound, right side, severe wound*

(0981) Operations, Tonto Basin, Arizona Territory (January 10 to February 4, 1877)[10]
— Captain George M. Brayton (8ᵗʰ U.S. Infantry)
    — 6ᵗʰ U.S. Cavalry Detachments Co. E
    — Detachment of Indian Scouts

— *Captain George M. Brayton (8ᵗʰ U.S. Infantry) brevet promotion to Lt. Colonel for gallant service in actions against Indians (Arizona, June 25, 1875; July 4, 1875; January 10, 1877 and January 30, 1877).*

(0982) Action, Elkhorn Creek, Wyoming Territory (January 12, 1877)[11]
— Corporal Charles A. Bessey (3ʳᵈ U.S. Cavalry)
    — 3ʳᵈ U.S. Cavalry Detachment Co. A
— **3 WOUNDED**[12]
    — Corporal Charles A. Bessey (Co. A 3ʳᵈ U.S. Cavalry)
        — *severe wound*
    — Private William Featherall (Co. A 3ʳᵈ U.S. Cavalry)
        — *severe wound*
    — Private James Taggert (Co. A 3ʳᵈ U.S. Cavalry)
        — *slight wound*

— *Corporal Charles A. Bessey (Co. A 3ʳᵈ U.S. Cavalry) received MOH: While scouting with four men and attacked in ambush by fourteen Indians, he held his ground, two of his men being wounded, until he himself was wounded in the side, and then went to the assistance of his wounded comrades (Elkhorn Creek, Wyoming, January 13, 1877).*

[7] 1ˢᵗ Lieutenant Robert McDonald (5ᵗʰ U.S. Infantry) declined his brevet promotion. *Army Register (1901)*, 379.
[8] Indians. *Annual Report of Secretary of War (1877)*, 135, 359; Chronological List, 63; Heitman (Volume 2), 443; Record of Engagements, 66; Carter, *From Yorktown to Santiago*, 188-189, 278; Rathbun, *New Mexico Frontier Military Place Names*, 6; Sweeney, *Cochise to Geronimo*, 76-78; Thrapp, *Victorio*, 184.
[9] Reports of Diseases and Individual Cases, F 475.
[10] Indians. *Annual Report of Secretary of War (1877)*, 135; Chronological List, 63; Heitman (Volume 2), 443; Carter, *From Yorktown to Santiago*, 188, 278; Thrapp, *Conquest of Apacheria*, 176. Chronological List lists 9 January to 5 February 1877.
[11] Indians. Chronological List, 63; Heitman (Volume 2), 443; Record of Engagements, 67; Hedren, *Fort Laramie in 1876*, 218-219.
[12] 3ʳᵈ U.S. Cavalry Regimental Return January 1877.

— *Private Maurice Bresnahan (Co. A 3rd U.S. Cavalry) received Certificate of Merit: For gallant conduct in action in bravely defending himself against an attack by a superior force of hostile Indians, and thus saving his detachment from being massacred (Elkhorn Creek, Wyoming, January 13, 1877).*

— *Private James Taggert (Co. A 3rd U.S. Cavalry) received Certificate of Merit: For gallant conduct in action in bravely defending himself against an attack by a superior force of hostile Indians, and thus saving his detachment from being massacred (Elkhorn Creek, Wyoming, January 13, 1877).*

(0983) Skirmish, Bluff Station, Wyoming Territory (January 20 to 22, 1877)[13]
— Major Andrew W. Evans (3rd U.S. Cavalry)
    — 3rd U.S. Cavalry Co. B and D

— *Sergeant William B. Lewis (Co. B 3rd U.S. Cavalry) received MOH: Bravery in skirmish (Bluff Station, Wyoming, January 20 to 22, 1877).*

(0984) Skirmish, Florida Mountains, New Mexico Territory (January 23, 1877)[14]
— 2nd Lieutenant Henry H. Wright (9th U.S. Cavalry)
    — 9th U.S. Cavalry Detachment Co. C

— *Corporal Clinton Greaves (Co. C 9th U.S. Cavalry) received MOH: While part of a small detachment to persuade a band of renegade Apache Indians to surrender, his group was surrounded. Corporal Greaves, in the center of the savage hand-to-hand fighting, managed to shoot and bash a gap through the swarming Apaches, permitting his companions to break free (Florida Mountains, New Mexico, January 24, 1877).*

— *2nd Lieutenant Henry H. Wright (9th U.S. Cavalry) brevet promotion to 1st Lieutenant for gallant service in actions against Indians (Florida Mountains, New Mexico, January 24, 1877; Sacramento Mountains, New Mexico, July 29, 1878 and Miembres Mountains, New Mexico, May 29, 1879).*

(0985) Skirmish, Siena Boca Grande, Mexico (January 28, 1877)[15]
— Captain Charles D. Beyer (9th U.S. Cavalry)
    — 9th U.S. Cavalry Detachment Co. C

(0986) Citizens, Staked Plains, Texas (February 22, 1877)[16]
— (1) Citizen Killed

(0987) Skirmish, Deadwood, Dakota Territory (February 23, 1877)[17]
— 2nd Lieutenant Joseph F. Cummings (3rd U.S. Cavalry)
    — 3rd U.S. Cavalry Co. C

[13] Indians.
[14] Indians. Chronological List, 63; Heitman (Volume 2), 443; Billington, *New Mexico's Buffalo Soldiers*, 50-51; Burton, *Black, Buckskin and Blue*, 157; Leckie, *Buffalo Soldiers*, 181; Rathbun, *New Mexico Frontier Military Place Names*, 15-17; Thrapp, *Conquest of Apacheria*, 176.
[15] Indians. Chronological List, 63; Heitman (Volume 2), 443; Billington, *New Mexico's Buffalo Soldiers*, 51-52; Leckie, *Buffalo Soldiers*, 182; Thrapp, *Conquest of Apacheria*, 176.
[16] Indians. Killed was buffalo hunter Marshall Sewell. Chronological List, 63; Record of Engagements, 75; Rister, *Fort Griffin*, 179-180.
[17] Indians. Chronological List, 63; Heitman (Volume 2), 443; Record of Engagements, 67.

(0988) Citizens, near Fort Davis, Texas (March 7, 1877)[18]
— (2) Citizens Killed

(0989) Surrender of 2,300 Indians, Red Cloud Agency and Spotted Tail Agency, Montana Territory (April and May 1877)[19]

(0990) Skirmish, Rio Grande, near Devil's River, Texas (April 1, 1877)[20]
— 1st Lieutenant John L. Bullis (24th U.S. Infantry)
— Detachment of Indian Scouts

(0991) Citizens, Fort Clark, Texas (April 20 to 22, 1877)[21]
— (3) Citizens Killed

(0992) Action, Lake Quemado, Texas (May 4, 1877)[22]
— Captain Phillip L. Lee (10th U.S. Cavalry)
— 10th U.S. Cavalry Co. G
— Detachment of Indian Scouts
— **1 KILLED**[23]
— First Sergeant Charles Butler (Co. G 10th U.S. Cavalry)

(0993) Engagement, Little Muddy Creek, Montana Territory (May 7, 1877)[24]
— Colonel Nelson A. Miles (5th U.S. Infantry)
— 2nd U.S. Cavalry Co. F, G, H and K
— 5th U.S. Infantry B and H
— 22nd U.S. Infantry E, F, G and H
— **4 KILLED**[25]
— Private Frank Glockowsky (Co. F 2nd U.S. Cavalry)
— Private Charles Martindale (Co. F 2nd U.S. Cavalry)
— Private Peter Louys (Co. H 2nd U.S. Cavalry)
— Private Charles Shrenger (Co. H 2nd U.S. Cavalry)

— **10 WOUNDED**[26]
— 2nd Lieutenant Alfred M. Fuller (Co. F 2nd U.S. Cavalry)
— *gunshot wound, shoulder, severe wound*

— Private Patrick Flynn (Co. F 2nd U.S. Cavalry)
— *gunshot wound, right arm, fracture, severe wound*
— Private Samuel Freier (Co. F 2nd U.S. Cavalry)
— *gunshot wound, right arm, slight wound*
— Private Thomas Jones (Co. F 2nd U.S. Cavalry)
— *gunshot wound, head, slight wound*

[18] Indians. Killed were Deroteo Cardinas and John Williams. Chronological List, 63; Record of Engagements, 75; Thrapp, *Conquest of Apacheria*, 176.
[19] Indians. Chronological List, 63; Record of Engagements, 67.
[20] Indians. Chronological List, 63; Heitman (Volume 2), 443; Smith, *Old Army in Texas*, 161.
[21] Indians. Chronological List, 63; Record of Engagements, 75.
[22] Indians. *Annual Report of Secretary of War (1877)*, 359; Chronological List, 63; Heitman (Volume 2), 443; Record of Engagements, 67; Cashion, *Texas Frontier*, 181; Leckie, *Buffalo Soldiers*, 158; Rister, *Fort Griffin*, 187-188; Smith, *Old Army in Texas*, 161.
[23] Reports of Diseases and Individual Cases, F Miscellaneous; Register of Deaths Regular Army, 1860-1889 (Volume 7); 10th U.S. Cavalry Regimental Return May 1877.
[24] Indians. *Annual Report of Commissioner of Indian Affairs (1877)*, 14-17; Chronological List, 64; Heitman (Volume 2), 443; Record of Engagements, 68; Brown, *Plainsmen of the Yellowstone*, 308-309; Greene, *Yellowstone Command*, 203-213; Miles, *Personal Recollections*, 249-252; Zimmer, *Frontier Soldier*, 45-51. Heitman lists 2nd U.S. Cavalry Co. F, G, H, L; 5th U.S. Infantry Co. B, H; 22nd U.S. Infantry Co. E, F, G, H.
[25] Reports of Diseases and Individual Cases, F 477; Register of Deaths Regular Army, 1860-1889 (Volume 7).
[26] Reports of Diseases and Individual Cases, F 477.
[27] Indians. Killed was mail carrier Frank Taite. *Annual Report of Secretary of War (1877)*, 137; McChristian, *Fort Bowie*, 166-167.
[28] Indians. Chronological List, 64; Heitman (Volume 2), 443; Carter, *From Yorktown to Santiago*, 278; Thrapp, *Conquest of Apacheria*, 176.

— Private William Osmer (Co. F 2nd U.S. Cavalry)
— *gunshot wound, hand, slight wound*

— Private Andrew Jeffers (Co. G 2nd U.S. Cavalry)
— *gunshot wound, forehead, slight wound*
— Private Patrick Ryan (Co. G 2nd U.S. Cavalry)
— *gunshot wound, arm, slight wound*
— Private Thomas Gillmore (Co. H 2nd U.S. Cavalry)
— *gunshot wound, neck, slight wound*

— Private William Leonard (Co. L 2nd U.S. Cavalry)
— *gunshot wound, face, chin, slight wound*
— Private Frederick Wilkes (Co. L 2nd U.S. Cavalry)
— *gunshot wound, hand, slight wound*

— *2nd Lieutenant Edward W. Casey (22nd U.S. Infantry) brevet promotion to 1st Lieutenant for gallant service in action against Indians (Muddy Creek, Montana, May 7, 1877).*

— *2nd Lieutenant Alfred M. Fuller (2nd U.S. Cavalry) brevet promotion to 1st Lieutenant for gallant service in action against Indians (Rosebud, Montana, May 7, 1877, where he was wounded).*

— *Corporal Harry Garland (Co. L 2nd U.S. Cavalry) received MOH: Gallantry in action with hostile Sioux, at Little Muddy Creek, Montana; having been wounded in the hip so as to be unable to stand, at Camas Meadows, Idaho, he still continued to direct the men under his charge until the enemy withdrew (Little Muddy Creek, Montana, May 7, 1877).*

— *Farrier William H. Jones (Co. L 2nd U.S. Cavalry) received MOH: Gallantry in attack against hostile Sioux Indians (Muddy Creek, Montana, May 7, 1877) and in the engagement with the Nez Perce Indians in which he sustained a painful knee wound (Camas Meadows, Idaho, August 20, 1877).*

— *Private William Leonard (Co. L 2nd U.S. Cavalry) received MOH: Bravery in action (Muddy Creek, Montana, May 7, 1877).*

— *Captain Randolph Norwood (2nd U.S. Cavalry) brevet promotion to Major for gallantry in action against Indians (Rosebud, Montana, May 7, 1877) and gallant service in action against Indians (Camas Meadows, Idaho, August 20, 1877).*

— *Private Samuel D. Phillips (Co. H 2nd U.S. Cavalry) received MOH: Gallantry in action (Muddy Creek, Montana, May 7, 1877).*

— *Captain James N. Wheelan (2nd U.S. Cavalry) brevet promotion to Major for gallant service in action against Indians (Rosebud, Montana, May 7, 1877).*

— *First Sergeant Henry Wilkens (Co. L 2nd U.S. Cavalry) received MOH: Bravery in action with Indians (Little Muddy Creek, Montana Territory, May 7, 1877 and Camas Meadows, Idaho Territory, August 20, 1877).*

(0994) Citizens, near Camp Bowie, Arizona Territory (May 29, 1877)[27]
— (1) Citizen Killed

(0995) Skirmish, near Camp Bowie, Arizona Territory (May 29, 1877)[28]
— 1st Lieutenant Frank West (6th U.S. Cavalry)
— 6th U.S. Cavalry Co. H and L

(0996) Citizens, near Fort Davis, Texas (May 30, 1877)[29]
— (1) Citizen Killed

(0997) Citizens, Salmon River, near Carver Creek, Idaho Territory (June 13, 1877)[30]
— (1) Citizens Killed

(0998) Citizens, near John Day Creek, Idaho Territory (June 14, 1877)[31]
— (3) Citizens Killed

(0999) Citizens, near White Bird Creek, Idaho Territory (June 14, 1877)[32]
— (3) Citizens Killed

(1000) Citizens, near Grangeville, Idaho Territory (June 14, 1877)[33]
— (5) Citizens Killed

(1001) Citizens, near White Bird Creek, Idaho Territory (June 15, 1877)[34]
— (2) Citizens Killed

(1002) Citizen, near Salmon River, Idaho Territory (June 16, 1877)[35]
— (1) Citizen Killed

(1003) Citizen, near Mount Idaho, Idaho Territory (June 16, 1877)[36]
— (1) Citizen Killed

(1004) Action, Tongue River, Montana Territory (June 17, 1877)[37]
— UNKNOWN
    — 5th U.S. Infantry Detachment
— **1 WOUNDED**[38]
    — Private Perry West (Co. H 5th U.S. Infantry)

(1005) Engagement, White Bird Canyon, Idaho Territory (June 17, 1877)[39]
— Captain David Perry (1st U.S. Cavalry)
    — 1st U.S. Cavalry Co. F and H
    — Detachment of Volunteers
— **34 KILLED**[40]
    — 1st Lieutenant Edward R. Theller (Co. G 21st U.S. Infantry)

    — Sergeant Patrick H. Gunn (Co. F 1st U.S. Cavalry)
    — Sergeant Thomas Ryan (Co. F 1st U.S. Cavalry)
    — Corporal Jonathan Thompson (Co. F 1st U.S. Cavalry)
    — Trumpeter John Jones (Co. F 1st U.S. Cavalry)
    — Private Charles Armstrong (Co. F 1st U.S. Cavalry)

[29] Indians. Killed was Bescento Acosta. Chronological List, 64; Record of Engagements, 75.
[30] Indians. Killed was Richard Devine. *Annual Report of Commissioner of Indian Affairs (1877)*, 9-13; Arnold, *Indian Wars of Idaho*, 149; Brown, *Flight of the Nez Perce*, 102; Greene, *Nez Perce Summer*, 31; McDermott, *Forlorn Hope*, 5-7.
[31] Indians. Killed were Jurden H. Elfers, Henry B. Beckrodge and Robert Bland. *Annual Report of Commissioner of Indian Affairs (1877)*, 9-13; Arnold, *Indian Wars of Idaho*, 149; Brown, *Flight of the Nez Perce*, 102-103; Greene, *Nez Perce Summer*, 31; McDermott, *Forlorn Hope*, 7-8.
[32] Indians. Killed were Samuel Benedict, August Bacon and James Baker. *Annual Report of Commissioner of Indian Affairs (1877)*, 9-13; Brown, *Flight of the Nez Perce*, 103-105; Greene, *Nez Perce Summer*, 31; McDermott, *Forlorn Hope*, 16-18.
[33] Indians. Killed were Benjamin B. Norton, Lew Day, John Chamberlin and his daughter, Hattie Chamberlin. Joe Moore later died of his wounds. *Annual Report of Commissioner of Indian Affairs (1877)*, 9-13; Arnold, *Indian Wars of Idaho*, 155-161; Greene, *Nez Perce Summer*, 32; McDermott, *Forlorn Hope*, 30-32, 160.
[34] Indians. Killed were William Osborne and Harry Mason. *Annual Report of Commissioner of Indian Affairs (1877)*, 9-13; Greene, *Nez Perce Summer*, 31-32; McDermott, *Forlorn Hope*, 21-22.
[35] Indians. Killed was Frank Chodoze. *Annual Report of Commissioner of Indian Affairs (1877)*, 9-13; Greene, *Nez Perce Summer*, 32.
[36] Indians. Killed was Charles Horton. *Annual Report of Commissioner of Indian Affairs (1877)*, 9-13; Green, *Nez Perce Summer*, 32; McDermott, *Forlorn Hope*, 33.
[37] Indians. *Annual Report of Secretary of War (1877)*, 359; Greene, *Yellowstone Command*, 220-221; Zimmer, *Frontier Soldiers*, 63.
[38] Reports of Diseases and Individual Cases, F 470.

— Private Joseph Blaine (Co. F 1st U.S. Cavalry)
— Private Frank E. Burch (Co. F 1st U.S. Cavalry)
— Private John C. Colbert (Co. F 1st U.S. Cavalry)
— Private Patrick Connolly (Co. F 1st U.S. Cavalry)
— Private Lawrence K. Dauch (Co. F 1st U.S. Cavalry)
— Private Jonathan H. Doune (Co. F 1st U.S. Cavalry)
— Private William L. Hurlbert (Co. F 1st U.S. Cavalry)
— Private James S. Lewis (Co. F 1st U.S. Cavalry)
— Private William Lisbon (Co. F 1st U.S. Cavalry)
— Private James M. Martin (Co. F 1st U.S. Cavalry)
— Private John R. Mosforth (Co. F 1st U.S. Cavalry)
— Private David Quinlan (Co. F 1st U.S. Cavalry)
— Private Peter Schulein (Co. F 1st U.S. Cavalry)
— Private Andrew Shaw (Co. F 1st U.S. Cavalry)
— Private Charles Sullivan (Co. F 1st U.S. Cavalry)

— Corporal Remon D. Lee (Co. H 1st U.S. Cavalry)
— Corporal Michael Curran (Co. H 1st U.S. Cavalry)
— Trumpeter Frank A. Marshall (Co. H 1st U.S. Cavalry)
— Saddler John Galvin (Co. H 1st U.S. Cavalry)
— Private Adalaska B. Crawford (Co. H 1st U.S. Cavalry)
— Private Valentine Edwards (Co. H 1st U.S. Cavalry)
— Private Lawrence Kavanaugh (Co. H 1st U.S. Cavalry)
— Private James E. Morrisey (Co. H 1st U.S. Cavalry)
— Private John J. Murphy (Co. H 1st U.S. Cavalry)
— Private Olaf Nielson (Co. H 1st U.S. Cavalry)
— Private John Shay (Co. H 1st U.S. Cavalry)
— Private John Simpson (Co. H 1st U.S. Cavalry)
— Private Albert Wesner (Co. H 1st U.S. Cavalry)

— 2 WOUNDED[41]

— Private Thomas McLaughlin (Co. F 1st U.S. Cavalry)
— *gunshot wound, right forearm, slight wound*
— Private Joseph Kelly (Co. H 1st U.S. Cavalry)
— *gunshot wound, left thigh, slight wound*

— *First Sergeant Michael McCarthy (Co. H 1st U.S. Cavalry) received MOH: Was detailed with six men to hold a commanding position, and held it with great gallantry until the troops fell back. He then fought his way through the Indians, rejoined a portion of his command, and continued the fight in retreat. He had two horses shot from under him, and was captured, but escaped and reported for duty after three days hiding and wandering in the mountains (White Bird Canyon, Idaho, June 1877 to January 1878).*

[39] Indians. *Annual Report of Secretary of War (1877)*, 131-132, 359; Chronological List, 64; Heitman (Volume 2), 443; Arnold, *Indian Wars of Idaho*, 117-119; Brown, *Flight of the Nez Perce*, 130-141; Greene, *Nez Perce Summer*, 34-48; McDermott, *Forlorn Hope*, 83-111. Chronological List lists 1st U.S. Cavalry Co. F, H.
[40] Reports of Diseases and Individual Cases, F 469; Register of Deaths Regular Army, 1860-1889 (Volume 7).
[41] Reports of Diseases and Individual Cases, F 469.

— 1ˢᵗ Lieutenant William R. Parnell (1ˢᵗ U.S. Cavalry) brevet promotion to Colonel for gallant service in action against Indians (White Bird Canyon, Idaho, June 17, 1877).

— 1ˢᵗ Lieutenant William R. Parnell (1ˢᵗ U.S. Cavalry) received MOH: With a few men, in the face of heavy fire from pursuing Indians and at imminent peril, returned and rescued a soldier whose horse had been killed and who had been left behind in the retreat (White Bird Canyon, Idaho, June 17, 1877).

(1006) Skirmish, near Whitebird River, Idaho Territory (June 28, 1877)[42]
 — Brigadier General Oliver O. Howard (Commander Department of Columbia)
  — 1ˢᵗ U.S. Cavalry Co. F and H
  — 21ˢᵗ U.S. Infantry Co. C
  — 4ᵗʰ U.S. Artillery Co. A, D, G and M

(1007) Skirmish, Looking Glass's Camp, near Clear Creek, Idaho Territory (July 1, 1877)[43]
 — Captain Stephen G. Whipple (1ˢᵗ U.S. Cavalry)
  — 1ˢᵗ U.S. Cavalry Co. E and L

(1008) Engagement, Cottonwood Ranch, near Craig's Mountain, Idaho Territory (July 3, 1877)[44]
 — 2ⁿᵈ Lieutenant Sevier M. Rains (1ˢᵗ U.S. Cavalry)
  — 1ˢᵗ U.S. Cavalry Detachments Co. E and L
 — **13 KILLED**[45]
  — 2ⁿᵈ Lieutenant Sevier M. Rains (Co. L 1ˢᵗ U.S. Cavalry)

  — Sergeant Charles Lampman (Co. E 1ˢᵗ U.S. Cavalry)
  — Private John Burk (Co. E 1ˢᵗ U.S. Cavalry)
  — Private Patrick Quinn (Co. E 1ˢᵗ U.S. Cavalry)
  — Private William Roach (Co. E 1ˢᵗ U.S. Cavalry)
  — Private Samuel Ryan (Co. E 1ˢᵗ U.S. Cavalry)

  — Private David Carroll (Co. L 1ˢᵗ U.S. Cavalry)
  — Private George H. Dinterman (Co. L 1ˢᵗ U.S. Cavalry)
  — Private Frederick Meyer (Co. L 1ˢᵗ U.S. Cavalry)
  — Private Franklin Moody (Co. L 1ˢᵗ U.S. Cavalry)
  — Private Otto H. Ricter (Co. L 1ˢᵗ U.S. Cavalry)

  — Scout William Foster (Citizen)
  — Scout Charles Blewett (Citizen)

(1009) Skirmish, Cottonwood Ranch, near Clearwater River, Idaho Territory (July 4, 1877)[46]
 — Captain David Perry (1ˢᵗ U.S. Cavalry)
  — 1ˢᵗ U.S. Cavalry Co. E, F and L

---

[42] Indians. Chronological List, 64; Brown, *Flight of the Nez Perce*, 162; Greene, *Nez Perce Summer*, 46.

[43] Indians. Chronological List, 64; Heitman (Volume 2), 443; Brown, *Flight of the Nez Perce*, 167-169; Greene, *Nez Perce Summer*, 51-57. Chronological List lists single entry 1 to 3 July 1877.

[44] Indians. *Annual Report of Secretary of War (1877)*, 427-428; Chronological List, 64; Heitman (Volume 2), 443; Arnold, *Indian Wars of Idaho*, 162-165; Brown, *Flight of the Nez Perce*, 173-175; Greene, *Nez Perce Summer*, 62-63. Chronological List lists single entry 1 to 3 July 1877.

[45] Reports of Diseases and Individual Cases, F 478; Register of Deaths Regular Army, 1860-1889 (Volume 8); *Annual Report of Secretary of War (1877)*, 132.

[46] Indians. Chronological List, 64; Heitman (Volume 2), 443; Brown, *Flight of the Nez Perce*, 175-177; Greene, *Nez Perce Summer*, 67-70. Chronological List lists single entry 4 and 5 July 1877. Heitman lists single entry 3 to 5 July 1877.

— Detachment of Volunteers

— *1st Lieutenant Frederick H.E. Ebstein (21st U.S. Infantry) brevet promotion to Captain for gallant service in actions against Indians (Cottonwood Ranch, Idaho, July 4, 1877; Camas Meadows, Idaho, August 20, 1877 and the Umatilla Agency, Oregon, July 13, 1878).*

(1010) Action, near Cottonwood Ranch, Idaho Territory (July 5, 1877)[47]
— "Captain" Darius B. Randall (Citizen)
— Detachment of Volunteers
— **3 KILLED**[48]
— Benjamin Evans (Citizen)
— D.H. Hauser (Citizen) — d. 7-17-1877
— Darius B. Randall (Citizen)

— **2 WOUNDED**[49]
— Charles Johnson (Citizen)
— Alonzo B. Leland (Citizen)

(1011) Engagement, South Fork of Clearwater River, Idaho Territory (July 11 and 12, 1877)[50]
— Brigadier General Oliver O. Howard (Commander Department of Columbia)
— 1st U.S. Cavalry Co. B, E, F, H and L
— 21st U.S. Infantry Co. A, B, C, D, E, H and I
— 4th U.S. Artillery Co. A, D, E and G
— **15 KILLED**[51]
— Private Frederick Gandmeyer (Co. E 1st U.S. Cavalry)
— Private Juan Plater (Co. E 1st U.S. Cavalry)
— Private Mayer Cohen (Co. H 1st U.S. Cavalry)
— Private Edward Wykoff (Co. B 21st U.S. Infantry)
— Private William Hutchinson (Co. C 21st U.S. Infantry)
— Private David W. McAnally (Co. E 21st U.S. Infantry)

— Musician John G. Hineman (Co. I 21st U.S. Infantry) — d. 07-13-1877
— Corporal Charles Carlin (Co. I 21st U.S. Infantry) — d. 07-13-1877
— Corporal Patrick Doyle (Co. I 21st U.S. Infantry)
— Private Charles Clark (Co. I 21st U.S. Infantry)
— Private Elson Compton (Co. I 21st U.S. Infantry) — d. 07-12-1877

— Sergeant James A. Workman (Co. A 4th U.S. Artillery)
— Corporal Charles Marquardt (Co. A 4th U.S. Artillery)
— Private Frederick Montaudon (Co. E 4th U.S. Artillery)
— Private Charles E. Simonds (Co. G 4th U.S. Artillery) — d. 07-12-1877

[47] Indians. Chronological List, 64; Arnold, *Indian Wars of Idaho*, 121-125; Brown, *Flight of the Nez Perce*, 177-181; Greene, *Nez Perce Summer*, 70-71. Chronological List lists single entry 4 and 5 July 1877. Heitman lists single entry 3 to 5 July 1877.
[48] Brown, *Flight of the Nez Perce*, 180; Greene, *Nez Perce Summer*, 361.
[49] Greene, *Nez Perce Summer*, 361.
[50] Indians. *Annual Report of Secretary of War (1878)*, 428; Chronological List, 64; Arnold, *Indian Wars of Idaho*, 126-128; Brown, *Flight of the Nez Perce*, 187-198; Greene, *Nez Perce Summer*, 77-96.
[51] Reports of Diseases and Individual Cases, F 479; Register of Deaths Regular Army, 1860-1889 (Volume 8).

— 25 WOUNDED[52]

— Captain Eugene A. Bancroft (Co. A 4th U.S. Artillery)
— *gunshot wound, left shoulder and thorax, severe wound*
— 2nd Lieutenant Charles A. Williams (Co. C 21st U.S. Infantry)
— *gunshot wounds, right forearm, right thigh, severe wound, slight wound*

— Sergeant Richard Hanson (Co. E 1st U.S. Cavalry)
— *gunshot wound, right leg, slight wound*
— Sergeant Bernard Simpson (Co. L 1st U.S. Cavalry)
— *gunshot wound, left leg, severe wound*
— Bugler Joseph Held (Co. H 1st U.S. Cavalry)
— *gunshot wound, left foot, slight wound*
— Private Fritz Heber (Co. M 1st U.S. Cavalry)
— *gunshot wounds, right arm and right leg, slight wounds*
— Private Samuel Ferguson (Co. E 1st U.S. Cavalry)
— *gunshot wound, left thigh, slight wound*

— First Sergeant Henry V. Richet (Co. C 21st U.S. Infantry)
—*gunshot wound, left thorax, severe wound*
— First Sergeant William Kenkle (Co. I 21st U.S. Infantry)
— *gunshot wound, thorax, slight wound*
— Sergeant Abraham Repert (Co. I 21st U.S. Infantry)
— *gunshot wound, left buttock, severe wound*
— Corporal Thomas Connelly (Co. H 21st U.S. Infantry)
— *gunshot wound, back, slight wound*
— Corporal Peter Murphy (Co. I 21st U.S. Infantry)
— *gunshot wounds, right arm and thorax, slight wounds*
— Private Levi Shaffner (Co. I 21st U.S. Infantry)
— *gunshot wounds, right thigh, left thigh and left leg, slight wounds*
— Private William Buckow (Co. B 21st U.S. Infantry)
— *gunshot wound, right thigh, amputated, severe wound*
— Private Daniel McGrath (Co. H 21st U.S. Infantry)
— *gunshot wound, left arm, severe wound*
— Private William Garvin (Co. I 21st U.S. Infantry)
— *gunshot wound, scalp wound, slight wound*
— Private Francis Winters (Co. B 21st U.S. Infantry)
— *gunshot wound, left thigh, slight wound, slight wound*
— Private Gottlich Wickerle (Co. I 21st U.S. Infantry)
— *gunshot wound, both buttocks, severe wound*
— Private Frederick Schickler (Co. H 21st U.S. Infantry)
— *gunshot wounds, right arm, left thigh and right hand, slight wounds*
— Private William Barton (Co. B 21st U.S. Infantry)

[52] Reports of Diseases and Individual Cases, F 479.

— gunshot wound, left shoulder, slight wound

— Sergeant Peter Blumenberg (Co. E 4th U.S. Artillery)
— gunshot wound, thorax, slight wound
— Corporal Ephraim Hess (Co. A 4th U.S. Artillery)
— gunshot wound, left arm, fracture of humerus, severe wound
— Corporal Thomas Burns (Co. E 4th U.S. Artillery)
— gunshot wound, left foot, slight wound
— Corporal Eugene McFilmore (Co. E 4th U.S. Artillery)
— gunshot wound, left arm, fracture of humerus, severe wound
— Private George Graham (Co. E 4th U.S. Artillery)
— gunshot wounds, back and jaw, slight wounds

— Major Charles T. Alexander (Surgeon) brevet promotion to Colonel for gallant service in action against Indians (Clearwater, Idaho, July 11 and 12, 1877).

— Captain Lawrence S. Babbitt (Ordnance Department) brevet promotion to Major for gallant service in action against Indians (Clearwater, Idaho, July 11 and 12, 1877).

— 2nd Lieutenant Harry L. Bailey (21st U.S. Infantry) brevet promotion to 1st Lieutenant for gallant service in actions against Indians (Clearwater, Idaho, July 11 and 12, 1877).

— Captain Eugene A. Bancroft (4th U.S. Artillery) brevet promotion to Major for gallant service in action against Indians, where he as severely wounded (Clearwater, Idaho, July 11 and 12, 1877).

— Captain George H. Burton (21st U.S. Infantry) brevet promotion to Major for gallant service in actions against Indians (Lava Beds, California, January 17, 1873 and Clearwater, Idaho, July 11 and 12, 1877).

— 2nd Lieutenant Joseph W. Duncan (21st U.S. Infantry) brevet promotion to 1st Lieutenant for gallant service in action against Indians (Clearwater, Idaho, July 11 and 12, 1877).

— 2nd Lieutenant Francis E. Eltonhead (21st U.S. Infantry) brevet promotion to 1st Lieutenant for distinguished service and conspicuous gallantry in action against Indians (Clearwater, Idaho, July 11 and 12, 1877).

— 1st Lieutenant Robert H. Fletcher (21st U.S. Infantry) brevet promotion to Captain for gallant service in actions against Indians (Clearwater, Idaho, July 11 and 12, 1877 and Canyon Creek, Montana, September 13, 1877).

— Private William Garvean (Co. I 21st U.S. Infantry) received Certificate of Merit: For most conspicuous and extraordinary gallantry in action against hostile Nez Perce Indians, crawling several times beyond the line to procure ammunition from an exposed position while wounded (Clearwater, Idaho, July 11, 1877).

— Assistant Surgeon William R. Hall brevet promotion to Captain for gallant service in action against Indians in attending to his professional duties under fire (Clearwater, Idaho, July 11 and 12, 1877).

— 1st Lieutenant James A. Haughey (21st U.S. Infantry) brevet promotion to Captain for gallant service in action against Indians (Clearwater, Idaho, July 11 and 12, 1877).

— 1st Lieutenant Charles F. Humphrey (4th U.S. Artillery) brevet promotion to Captain for gallant service in action against Indians (Clearwater, Idaho, July 11, 1877).

— *1ˢᵗ Lieutenant Charles F. Humphrey (4ᵗʰ U.S. Artillery) received MOH: Voluntarily and successfully conducted, in the face of a withering fire, a party which recovered possession of an abandoned howitzer and two Gatling guns lying between the lines a few yards from the Indians(Clearwater, Idaho, July 11, 1877).*

— *Captain James Jackson (1ˢᵗ U.S. Cavalry) brevet promotion to Lt. Colonel for gallant and meritorious service in action against Indians (Modoc War, especially in the action on Lost River, Oregon, November 29, 1872) and gallant service in action against Indians (Clearwater, Idaho, July 12, 1877).*

— *Captain Stephen P. Jocelyn (21ˢᵗ U.S. Infantry) brevet promotion to Major for conspicuous gallantry in action against Indians (Clearwater, Idaho, July 11 and 12, 1877).*

— *Private William S. LeMay (Co. E 4ᵗʰ U.S. Artillery) received Certificate of Merit: For gallantry in action while the piece he was serving was closely pressed by the Indians, within twenty yards of the muzzle, four of the gun detachment being killed or wounded, he was the only cannoneer who made the effort to load and fire; lying on his back between the wheels, he loaded the piece several times at great risk, and thus assisted in driving back the enemy and saving the gun (Clearwater, Idaho, July 11, 1877).*

— *Major Edwin C. Mason (21ˢᵗ U.S. Infantry) brevet promotion to Brigadier General for gallant and meritorious service in actions against Indians (Lava Beds, California, April 17, 1873 and Clearwater, Idaho, July 11 and 12, 1877).*

— *Captain Evan Miles (21ˢᵗ U.S. Infantry) brevet promotion to Major for gallant service in actions against Indians (Clearwater, Idaho, July 11 and 12, 1877 and the Umatilla Agency, Oregon, July 13, 1878).*

— *Captain Marcus P. Miller (4ᵗʰ U.S. Artillery) brevet promotion to Colonel for gallant and meritorious service in action against Indians (Lava Beds, California, April 17, 1873) and special gallantry and military ability in actions against Indians (Clearwater, Idaho, July 11 and 12, 1877).*

— *Captain Arthur Morris (4ᵗʰ U.S. Artillery) brevet promotion to Major for gallant service in action against Indians (Clearwater, Idaho, July 11 and 12, 1877).*

— *Captain Robert Pollock (21ˢᵗ U.S. Infantry) brevet promotion to Major for marked bravery and gallant service in actions against Indians (Clearwater, Idaho, July 11 and 12, 1877).*

— *Major George M. Sternberg (Surgeon) brevet promotion to Lt. Colonel for gallant service in performance of his professional duty under fire in action against Indians (Clearwater, Idaho, July 12, 1877).*

— *Captain William F. Stewart (4ᵗʰ U.S. Artillery) brevet promotion to Major for gallant service in action against Indians (Clearwater, Idaho, July 11 and 12, 1877).*

— *Private Paul Tschan (Co. D 21ˢᵗ U.S. Infantry) received Certificate of Merit: For gallant and meritorious conduct in action against hostile Nez Perce Indians, in a successful attempt to obtain water from a spring ½ mile from the line and under fire from the enemy (a soldier who made a previous attempt having been killed), and thus securing water for his comrades who had been without it for twenty hours (Clearwater, Idaho, July 11 and 12, 1877).*

— *Captain Stephen G. Whipple (1ˢᵗ U.S. Cavalry) brevet promotion to Major for gallant service in action against Indians (Clearwater, Idaho, July 11 and 12, 1877).*

— *1ˢᵗ Lieutenant Melville C. Wilkinson (3ʳᵈ U.S. Infantry) brevet promotion to Major for gallant service in actions against Indians (Clearwater, Idaho, July 11 and 12, 1877 and Kamiah, Idaho, July 13, 1877).*

— *2ⁿᵈ Lieutenant Charles A. Williams (21ˢᵗ U.S. Infantry) brevet promotion to 1ˢᵗ Lieutenant for gallant service in action against Indians (Clearwater, Idaho, July 11, 1877, where he was severely wounded).*

(1012) Action, Kamiah, Idaho Territory (July 13, 1877)[53]

— Brigadier General Oliver O. Howard (Commander Department of Columbia)

---

[53] Indians. Chronological List, 64; Arnold, *Indian Wars of Idaho*, 128; Brown, *Flight of the Nez Perce*, 200; Greene, *Nez Perce Summer*, 98.

— 1st U.S. Cavalry Co. B, F, H and L
— 21st U.S. Infantry Co. A, B, C, D, E, H and I
— 4th U.S. Artillery Co. A, D, E and G
— **1 WOUNDED**[54]
— Corporal William Mulcahy (Co. A 4th U.S. Artillery)
— *gunshot wound, forehead, severe wound*

— *1st Lieutenant Melville C. Wilkinson (3rd U.S. Infantry) brevet promotion to Major for gallant service in actions against Indians (Clearwater, Idaho, July 11 and 12, 1877 and Kamiah, Idaho, July 13, 1877).*

"The Indians had been well led and well fought. They had defeated two companies in pitched battle. They had eluded the pursuit and had crossed the Salmon... They had finally been forced to concentrate, it is true, and had been brought to battle. But, in battle with regular troops, they had held out for nearly two days before they were beaten... The result would necessitate a long and tedious chase."
— Oliver O. Howard, U.S. Army[55]

(1013) Action, Weippe Prairie, Oro Fino Creek, Idaho Territory (July 17, 1877)[56]
— Major Edwin C. Mason (21st U.S. Infantry)
— 1st U.S. Cavalry Detachments Co. B, E, H and L
— Detachment of Indian Scouts
— Detachment of Volunteers
— **2 KILLED**[57]
— John Levi - aka Sheared Wolf (Indian Scout)
— Abraham Brooks (Indian Scout)

— **1 WOUNDED**[58]
— James Reuben (Indian Scout)
— *gunshot wound, right arm*

(1014) Skirmish, Belle Fourche, Dakota Territory (July 21, 1877)[59]
— 2nd Lieutenant Henry R, Lemly (3rd U.S. Cavalry)
— 3rd U.S. Cavalry Detachments Co. A, D, E, F and G

(1015) Citizens, near El Muerto, Texas (August 1, 1877)[60]
— (2) Citizens Killed

(1016) Engagement, near Big Hole Basin, Montana Territory (August 9 and 10, 1877)[61]
— Colonel John Gibbon (7th U.S. Infantry)
— 2nd U.S. Cavalry Detachments Co. B and E
— 7th U.S. Infantry Co. A, D, F, G, I and K

[54] *Annual Report of Secretary of War (1877)*, 133.

[55] Arnold, *Indian Wars of Idaho*, 128-129.

[56] Indians. Chronological List, 65; Heitman (Volume 2), 443; Brown, *Flight of the Nez Perce*, 203-204; Greene, *Nez Perce Summer*, 101-102. Chronological List lists 1st U.S. Cavalry Detachments; Detachment of Indian Scouts; Detachment of Volunteers.

[57] Greene, *Nez Perce Summer*, 364.

[58] Greene, *Nez Perce Summer*, 364.

[59] Indians. Chronological List, 65; Heitman (Volume 2), 443.

[60] Indians. Killed in separate attacks were stagecoach driver Henry Dill and Sandy Ball. *Annual Report of Secretary of War (1878)*, 82; Chronological List, 64; Record of Engagements, 75; Wooster, *Frontier Crossroads*, 99.

[61] Indians. *Annual Report of Secretary of War (1877)*, 501-505, 556-557; *Annual Report of Secretary of War (1878)*, 428; Chronological List, 65; Heitman (Volume 2), 443; Record of Engagements, 70-71; Haines, *Battle of the Big Hole*, 51-100; Arnold, *Indian Wars of Idaho*, 134-137; Brown, *Flight of the Nez Perce*, 246-267; Greene, *Nez Perce Summer*, 129-138. Heitman lists 2nd U.S. Cavalry Co. L; 7th U.S. Infantry Co. A, D, F, G, I, K, Detachments Co. B, E.

— Detachment of Volunteers
— **31 KILLED**[62]
   — Captain William Logan (Co. A 7th U.S. Infantry)
   — 1st Lieutenant James H. Bradley (Co. B 7th U.S. Infantry)
   — 1st Lieutenant William L. English (Co. I 7th U.S. Infantry) — d. 09-19-1877

   — Sergeant Edward Page (Co. L 2nd U.S. Cavalry)
   — Private John B. Smith (Co. A 7th U.S. Infantry)

   — Corporal Isaac Eisenhartt (Co. D 7th U.S. Infantry)
   — Corporal William H. Payne (Co. D 7th U.S. Infantry)
   — Musician Michael Gallagher (Co. D 7th U.S. Infantry)
   — Private Matthew Butterby (Co. E 7th U.S. Infantry)

   — Sergeant William W. Watson (Co. F 7th U.S. Infantry) — d. 08-29-1877
   — Private James Maginnis (Co. F 7th U.S. Infantry)
   — Private William D. Pomeroy (Co. F 7th U.S. Infantry)

   — First Sergeant Robert L. Edgeworth (Co. G 7th U.S. Infantry)
   — Sergeant William H. Martin (Co. G 7th U.S. Infantry)
   — Corporal Dominick O'Connor (Co. G 7th U.S. Infantry)
   — Corporal Robert E. Dale (Co. G 7th U.S. Infantry)
   — Private Gottileb Mautz (Co. G 7th U.S. Infantry)
   — Private F. Jonathan O'Brien (Co. G 7th U.S. Infantry)

   — Private McKenzie L. Drake (Co. H 7th U.S. Infantry)
   — Sergeant Michael Hogan (Co. I 7th U.S. Infantry)
   — Corporal Daniel McCafferey (Co. I 7th U.S. Infantry)
   — Private Herman Broetz (Co. I 7th U.S. Infantry)

   — First Sergeant Frederick J. Stortz (Co. K 7th U.S. Infantry)
   — Musician Thomas P. Stinebaker (Co. K 7th U.S. Infantry)
   — Private Jonathan Klein (Co. K 7th U.S. Infantry)

   — John Armstrong (Citizen)
   — Henry S. Bostwick (Citizen)
   — L.C. Elliot (Citizen)
   — Alvin Lockwood (Citizen)
   — Campbell Mitchell (Citizen)
   — David Morrow (Citizen)

---

[62] Reports of Diseases and Individual Cases, F 481; Register of Deaths Regular Army, 1860-1889 (Volume 8); *Army and Navy Journal* (Volume 15), 86.

— 36 WOUNDED[63]
- Colonel John Gibbon (F&S 7th U.S. Infantry)
  - *gunshot wound, leg, severe wound*
- Captain Constant Williams (Co. F 7th U.S. Infantry)
  - *gunshot wounds, scalp, slight wound, right side, severe wound*
- 1st Lieutenant Charles A. Coolidge (Co. A 7th U.S. Infantry)
  - *gunshot wounds, thigh, right hand*
- 1st Lieutenant Charles A. Woodruff (Co. K 7th U.S. Infantry)
  - *gunshot wounds, leg, thigh foot, severe wounds*

- Private Charles Alberts (Co. A 7th U.S. Infantry)
  - *gunshot wound, left breast, severe wound*
- Private Lorenzo D. Brown (Co. A 7th U.S. Infantry)
  - *gunshot wound, right shoulder, severe wound*
- Private James C. Lehmer (Co. A 7th U.S. Infantry)
  - *gunshot wound, right leg, severe wound*
- Private George Leher (Co. A 7th U.S. Infantry)
  - *gunshot wound, scalp, slight wound*

- Sergeant James Bell (Co. D 7th U.S. Infantry)
  - *gunshot wound, right shoulder, severe wound*
- Sergeant Patrick C. Daly (Co. D 7th U.S. Infantry)
  - *gunshot wound, forehead, slight wound*
- Sergeant William Wright (Co. E 7th U.S. Infantry)
  - *gunshot wound, scalp, slight wound*
- Corporal John Murphy (Co. D 7th U.S. Infantry)
  - *gunshot wound, right hip, severe wound*
- Musician Timothy Cronan (Co. D 7th U.S. Infantry)
  - *gunshot wounds, right shoulder, chest, severe wounds*
- Private James Keys (Co. D 7th U.S. Infantry)
  - *gunshot wound, right foot, severe wound*

- Corporal Christian Luttman (Co. F 7th U.S. Infantry)
  - *gunshot wounds, left and right legs*
- Musician John Erickson (Co. F 7th U.S. Infantry)
  - *gunshot wound, left arm*
- Private Charles B. Gould (Co. F 7th U.S. Infantry)
  - *gunshot wound, left side, severe wound*
- Private Edward D. Hunter (Co. F 7th U.S. Infantry)
  - *gunshot wound, right hand, severe wound*
- Private George Maurer/Morrow (Co. F 7th U.S. Infantry)
  - *gunshot wound, left and right cheeks, severe wound*

---

[63] Reports of Diseases and Individual Cases, F 481; *Army and Navy Journal* (Volume 15), 86, 116.
[64] 1st Lieutenant Joshua W. Jacobs (7th U.S. Infantry) declined his brevet promotion. *Army Register (1901)*, 350.

— Sergeant Robert Bentsinger (Co. G 7th U.S. Infantry)
— *gunshot wound, right breast, severe wound*
— Sergeant John W.H. Frederick (Co. G 7th U.S. Infantry)
— *gunshot wound, left shoulder, slight wound*
— Private George Banghart (Co. G 7th U.S. Infantry)
— *gunshot wounds, right shoulder, thigh, wrist, severe wounds*
— Private James Burk (Co. G 7th U.S. Infantry)
— *gunshot wound, right breast, severe wound*
— Private John J. Connor (Co. G 7th U.S. Infantry)
— *gunshot wound, right eye, slight wound*

— Sergeant Howard Clark (Co. I 7th U.S. Infantry)
— Corporal Richard N. Cunliffe (Co. I 7th U.S. Infantry)
— *gunshot wounds, shoulder, arm, slight wounds*
— Private Joseph Devoss (Co. I 7th U.S. Infantry)
— *gunshot wounds, ankle, leg, heel, slight wounds*
— Private Patrick Fallon (Co. I 7th U.S. Infantry)
— *gunshot wounds, hip, leg, severe wound*
— Private William Thompson (Co. I 7th U.S. Infantry)
— *gunshot wound, left shoulder, slight wound*

— Private Mathew Devine (Co. K 7th U.S. Infantry)
— *gunshot wound, left forearm, severe wound*
— Private Davis Heaton (Co. K 7th U.S. Infantry)
— *gunshot wounds, wrist, severe wound*
— Private Philo O. Hurlburt (Co. K 7th U.S. Infantry)
— *gunshot wound, left shoulder, slight wound*

— Jacob Baker (Citizen)
— Myron Lockwood (Citizen)
— Otto Lyford (Citizen)
— William Ryan (Citizen)

— *Sergeant James Bell (Co. E 7th U.S. Infantry) received Certificate of Merit: For conspicuous gallantry in action against hostile Nez Perce Indians (Big Hole, Montana, August 9, 1877).*

— *Private Lorenzo D. Brown (Co. A 7th U.S. Infantry) received MOH: After having been severely wounded in right shoulder, continued to do duty in a most courageous manner (Big Hole, Montana, August 9, 1877).*

— *Private Thomas Bundy (Co. F 7th U.S. Infantry) received Certificate of Merit: For distinguished service in the campaign against hostile Nez Perce Indians, performing a dangerous journey to Cow Island on foot and within sight of several hundred hostiles and thus securing reinforcements (Big Hole, Montana, August 9, 1877).*

— *Private Wilfred Clark (Co. L 2nd U.S. Cavalry) received MOH: Conspicuous gallantry, especially skilled as sharpshooter (Big Hole, Montana, August 9, 1877; Camas Meadows, Idaho, August 20, 1877).*

— *Captain Richard Comba (7th U.S. Infantry) brevet promotion to Lt. Colonel for gallant service in action against Indians (Big Hole Montana, August 9, 1877).*

— *Captain Charles A. Coolidge (7th U.S. Infantry) brevet promotion to Major for gallant service in action against Indians (Big Hole, Montana, August 9, 1877) where he as wounded three times.*

— *First Sergeant William D. Edwards (Co. F 7th U.S. Infantry) received MOH: Bravery in action (Big Hole, Montana, August 9, 1877).*

— *2nd Lieutenant Edward E. Hardin (7th U.S. Infantry) brevet promotion to 1st Lieutenant for gallant service in action against Indians (Big Hole, Montana, August 9, 1877).*

— *1st Lieutenant Allan H. Jackson (7th U.S. Infantry) brevet promotion to Lt. Colonel for gallant service in action against Indians (Big Hole, Montana, August 9, 1877).*

— *1st Lieutenant Joshua W. Jacobs (7th U.S. Infantry) brevet promotion to Captain for gallant and meritorious services in action against Indians (Big Hole, Montana, August 9, 1877) preceded by important and hazardous service in a reconnaissance which led to the action (Big Hole, Montana, August 8, 1877).*[64]

— *Private Oliver Johnson (Co. F 7th U.S. Infantry) received Certificate of Merit: For gallant conduct in throwing up a breastwork under fire of the enemy, and by his good example, bringing others to the same labor, in action against hostile Indians (Big Hole, Montana, August 9, 1877).*

— *Musician John McLennon (Co. A 7th U.S. Infantry) received MOH: Gallantry in action (Big Hole, Montana, August 9, 1877).*

— *Sergeant Patrick Rogan (Co. A 7th U.S. Infantry) received MOH: Verified and reported the company while subjected to a galling fire from the enemy (Big Hole, Montana Territory, August 9, 1877).*

— *Captain James M.J. Sanno (7th U.S. Infantry) brevet promotion to Major for gallant service in action against Indians (Big Hole, Montana, August 9, 1877).*

— *2nd Lieutenant John T. Van Orsdale (7th U.S. Infantry) brevet promotion to 1st Lieutenant for gallant service in action against Indians (Big Hole, Montana, August 9, 1877).*

— *Captain Constant Williams (7th U.S. Infantry) brevet promotion to Major for gallant service in action against Indians (Big Hole, Montana, August 9, 1877, where he was twice wounded).*

— *Sergeant Milden H. Wilson (Co. I 7th U.S. Infantry) received MOH: Gallantry in forming company from line of skirmishers and deploying again under a galling fire, and in carrying dispatches at the imminent risk of his life (Big Hole, Montana Territory, August 9, 1877).*

— *2nd Lieutenant Francis Woodbridge (7th U.S. Infantry) brevet promotion to 1st Lieutenant for gallant service in action against Indians (Big Hole, Montana, August 9, 1877).*

— *1st Lieutenant Charles A. Woodruff (7th U.S. Infantry) brevet promotion to Captain for gallant service in action against Indians (Big Hole, Montana, August 9, 1877, where he was three times wounded).*

(1017) Action, Camas Meadows, Idaho Territory (August 20, 1877)[65]
— Major George B. Sanford (1st U.S. Cavalry)
    — 1st U.S. Cavalry Co. B, C, I and K

[65] Indians. *Annual Report of Secretary of War (1877)*, 506; *Annual Report of Secretary of War (1878)*, 428-429; Chronological List, 65; Heitman (Volume 2), 443; Record of Engagements, 71; Arnold, *Indian Wars of Idaho*, 138-139; Brown, *Flight of the Nez Perce*, 286-297; Greene, *Nez Perce Summer*, 151-162. Chronological List lists 1st U.S. Cavalry Co. B, I, K; 2nd U.S. Cavalry Co. L.

— 2nd U.S. Cavalry Co. L
— 8th U.S. Infantry Co. H
— 4th U.S. Artillery Detachment Co. E

— **3 KILLED**[66]
— Trumpeter Bernard A. Brooks (Co. B 1st U.S. Cavalry)
— Farrier Samuel A. Glass (Co. L 2nd U.S. Cavalry) — d. 08-24-1877
— Private Harry Trevor (Co. L 2nd U.S. Cavalry) — d. 10-04-1877

— **6 WOUNDED**[67]
— 1st Lieutenant Henry M. Benson (Co. L 7th U.S. Infantry)[68]
— *gunshot wound, hip, severe wound*

— Farrier James King (Co. I 1st U.S. Cavalry)
— *gunshot wound, left forearm, severe wound*
— First Sergeant Henry Wilkins (Co. L 2nd U.S. Cavalry)
— *gunshot wound, head, slight wound*
— Corporal Harry Garland (Co. L 2nd U.S. Cavalry)
— *gunshot wound, left iliac region, fracture, severe wound*
— Private Wilfred Clark (Co. L 2nd U.S. Cavalry)
— *gunshot wound, left shoulder, slight wound*
— Private William H. Jones (Co. L 2nd U.S. Cavalry)
— *gunshot wound, over right patella, slight wound*

— *1st Lieutenant Henry M. Benson (7th U.S. Infantry) brevet promotion to Captain for gallant service in action against Indians, where he was severely wounded (Camas Meadows, Idaho, August 20, 1877).*

— *Captain Camillo C. Carr (1st U.S. Cavalry) brevet promotion to Major for gallant service in action against Indians (Camas Meadows, Idaho, August 20, 1877).*

— *Private Wilfred Clark (Co. L 2nd U.S. Cavalry) received MOH: Conspicuous gallantry, especially skilled as sharpshooter (Big Hole, Montana, August 9, 1877; Camas Meadows, Idaho, August 20, 1877).*

— *1st Lieutenant Charles C. Cresson (1st U.S. Cavalry) brevet promotion to Lt. Colonel for gallant and meritorious serve in action against Indians (Lava Beds, California, April 17, 1873) and gallant service in action against Indians (Camas Meadows, Idaho, August 20, 1877).*

— *1st Lieutenant Frederick H.E. Ebstein (21st U.S. Infantry) brevet promotion to Captain for gallant service in actions against Indians (Cottonwood Ranch, Idaho, July 4, 1877; Camas Meadows, Idaho, August 20, 1877 and the Umatilla Agency, Oregon, July 13, 1878).*

— *Corporal Harry Garland (Co. L 2nd U.S. Cavalry) received MOH: Gallantry in action with hostile Sioux, at Little Muddy Creek, Montana; having been wounded in the hip so as to be unable to stand, at Camas*

---

[66] Reports of Diseases and Individual Cases, F 482; Register of Deaths Regular Army, 1860-1889 (Volume 8).
[67] Reports of Diseases and Individual Cases, F 482.
[68] 1st Lieutenant Henry M. Benson (Co. L 7th U.S. Infantry) was attached to Co. L 2nd U.S. Infantry. Reports of Diseases and Individual Cases, F 482.

Meadows, Idaho, he still continued to direct the men under his charge until the enemy withdrew (Little Muddy Creek, Montana, May 7, 1877; Camas Meadows, Idaho, August 20, 1877).

— *2ⁿᵈ Lieutenant Guy Howard (21ˢᵗ U.S. Infantry) brevet promotion to 1ˢᵗ Lieutenant for gallant service in action against Indians (Camas Meadows, Idaho, August 20, 1877).*

— *Captain James Jackson (1ˢᵗ U.S. Cavalry) received MOH: Dismounted from his horse in the face of a heavy fire from pursuing Indians, and with the assistance of one or two of the men of his command secured to a place of safety the body of his trumpeter, who had been shot and killed (Camas Meadows, Idaho, August 20, 1877).*

— *Farrier William H. Jones (Co. L 2ⁿᵈ U.S. Cavalry) received MOH: Gallantry in attack against hostile Sioux Indians (Muddy Creek, Montana, May 7, 1877) and in the engagement with the Nez Perce Indians in which he sustained a painful knee wound (Camas Meadows, Idaho, August 20, 1877).*

— *Captain Randolph Norwood (2ⁿᵈ U.S. Cavalry) brevet promotion to Major for gallantry in action against Indians (Rosebud, Montana, May 7, 1877) and gallant service in action against Indians (Camas Meadows, Idaho, August 20, 1877).*

(1018) Skirmish, near Black Rock, Arizona Territory (August 29, 1877)[69]
— 1ˢᵗ Lieutenant Gilbert E. Overton (6ᵗʰ U.S. Cavalry)
— 6ᵗʰ U.S. Cavalry Detachment Co. F

(1019) Citizens, New Mexico Territory (September 1877)[70]
— (8) Citizens Killed

(1020) Operations, near San Francisco River and Mogollon Mountains, New Mexico Territory (September 8 to 10, 1877)[71]
— Captain Tullius C. Tupper (6ᵗʰ U.S. Cavalry)
— 6ᵗʰ U.S. Cavalry Detachments Co. B and M
— Detachment of Indian Scouts

(1021) Engagement, Canyon Creek, Montana Territory (September 13, 1877)[72]
— Colonel Samuel D. Sturgis (7ᵗʰ U.S. Cavalry)
— 1ˢᵗ U.S. Cavalry Co. K, Detachments Co. C and I
— 7ᵗʰ U.S. Cavalry Co. F, G, H, I, L and M
— **4 KILLED**[73]
— Blacksmith Edson F. Archer (Co. L 7ᵗʰ U.S. Cavalry) — d. 9-14-1877
— Private James Lawler (Co. G 7ᵗʰ U.S. Cavalry) — d. 9-18-1877
— Private Nathan T. Brown (Co. L 7ᵗʰ U.S. Cavalry)
— Private Frank J. Gosslin (Co. M 7ᵗʰ U.S. Cavalry)

[69] Indians. Chronological List, 65; Heitman (Volume 2), 443; Carter, *From Yorktown to Santiago*, 278; Thrapp, *Conquest of Apacheria*, 176.
[70] Indians. *Annual Report of Commissioner of Indian Affairs (1879)*, xxxix.
[71] Indians. Chronological List, 65; Heitman (Volume 2), 443; Carter, *From Yorktown to Santiago*, 191-192, 278; Rathbun, *New Mexico Frontier Military Place Names*, 154; Sweeney, *Cochise to Geronimo*, 94, 97. Chronological List lists 6ᵗʰ U.S. Cavalry Detachment Co. B, H, L, M; Detachment of Indian Scouts.
[72] Indians. *Annual Report of Secretary of War (1877)*, 634; *Annual Report of Secretary of War (1878)*, 429; Chronological List, 65; Heitman (Volume 2), 443; Record of Engagements, 72; Arnold, *Indian Wars of Idaho*, 140-141; Greene, *Nez Perce Summer*, 216-226. Heitman lists 1ˢᵗ U.S. Cavalry Co. K, Detachments Co. C, I; 7ᵗʰ U.S. Cavalry Co. F, G, H, I, L, M; 4ᵗʰ U.S. Artillery Detachment Co. E.
[73] Reports of Diseases and Individual Cases, F 483; Register of Deaths Regular Army, 1860-1889 (Volume 8).

— **7 WOUNDED**[74]
 — Sergeant Edward Deverine (Co. F 7th U.S. Cavalry)
  — *gunshot wound, left arm, slight wound*
 — Private George A. Campfield (Co. F 7th U.S. Cavalry)
  — *gunshot wound, left shoulder, severe wound*
 — Private William Young (Co. G 7th U.S. Cavalry)
  — *gunshot wound, both hips, severe wound*

 — Private E. P. Crombie (Co. I 7th U.S. Cavalry)
  — *gunshot wound, left shoulder, severe wound*
 — Private Levi Weigel (Co. L 7th U.S. Cavalry)
  — *gunshot wounds, leg, fracture, severe wound, shoulder, slight wound*
 — Private Albert B. Fowler (Co. L 7th U.S. Cavalry)
  — *gunshot wound, left leg, slight wound*
 — Private Jacob P. Watson (Co. M 7th U.S. Cavalry)
  — *gunshot wound, left ankle, severe wound*

— *Captain James M. Bell (7th U.S. Cavalry) brevet promotion to Lt. Colonel for gallant service in action against Indians (Canyon Creek, Montana, September 13, 1877).*

— *Captain Charles Bendire (7th U.S. Cavalry) brevet promotion to Major for gallant service in action against Indians (Canyon Creek, Montana, September 13, 1877).*

— *Captain Frederick W. Benteen (7th U.S. Cavalry) brevet promotion to Brigadier General for gallant service in action against Indian (Little Big Horn, Montana, June 25 and 26, 1876) and in action against Indians (Canyon Creek, Montana, September 13, 1877).*

— *1st Lieutenant Robert H. Fletcher (21st U.S. Infantry) brevet promotion to Captain for gallant service in actions against Indians (Clearwater, Idaho, July 11 and 12, 1877 and Canyon Creek, Montana, September 13, 1877).*

— *1st Lieutenant Ezra B. Fuller (7th U.S. Cavalry) brevet promotion to 1st Lieutenant for gallant service in action against Indians (Canyon Creek, Montana, September 13, 1877).*

— *Major Lewis Merrill (7th U.S. Cavalry) brevet promotion to Brigadier General for gallant service in action against Indians (Canyon Creek, Montana, September 13, 1877)*

— *Captain Henry J. Nowlan (7th U.S. Cavalry) brevet promotion to Major for gallant service in action against Indians (Canyon Creek, Montana, September 13, 1877).*

— *2nd Lieutenant Henry J. Slocum (2nd U.S. Cavalry) brevet promotion to 1st Lieutenant for gallant service in action against Indians (Canyon Creek, Montana, September 13, 1877).*

---

[74] Reports of Diseases and Individual Cases, F 483.

— 1st Lieutenant John W. Wilkinson (7th U.S. Cavalry) brevet promotion to Captain for gallant service in action against Indians (Canyon Creek, Montana, September 13, 1877).

(1022) Action, Cow Island, Montana Territory (September 23, 1877)[75]
  — Sergeant William Molchart (7th U.S. Infantry)
    — 7th U.S. Infantry Detachment Co. B
    — Detachment of Volunteers
 — 1 KILLED[76]
    — Private Byron Martin (Co. B 7th U.S. Infantry)

 — 2 WOUNDED[77]
    — E.W. Bookwater (Citizen)
      — hand and side
    — George Trauman (Citizen)
      — right shoulder

(1023) Action, near Cow Creek Canyon, Montana Territory (September 25, 1877)[78]
  — Major Guido Ilges (7th U.S. Infantry)
    — Detachment of Volunteers
 — 1 KILLED[79]
    — Edmund Bradley (Citizen)

(1024) Skirmish, near Saragosa, Mexico (September 26, 1877)[80]
    — 1st Lieutenant John L. Bullis (24th U.S. Infantry)
    — 8th U.S. Cavalry Detachments Co. A and F
    — 10th U.S. Cavalry Detachment Co. C
    — Detachment of Indian Scouts

(1025) Engagement, Snake or Eagle Creek, near Bear Paw Mountains, Montana Territory (September 30, 1877)[81]
  — Colonel Nelson A. Miles (5th U.S. Infantry)
    — 2nd U.S. Cavalry Co. F, G and H
    — 7th U.S. Cavalry Co. A, D and K
    — 5th U.S. Infantry Co. B, F, G, I and K, Detachment Co. D
    — Detachment of Indian Scouts
 — 24 KILLED[82]
    — Captain Owen Hale (Co. K 7th U.S. Cavalry)
    — 2nd Lieutenant Jonathan W. Biddle (Co. K 7th U.S. Cavalry)

    — First Sergeant George W. McDermott (Co. A 7th U.S. Cavalry)
    — Sergeant Otto Deshler (Co. A 7th U.S. Cavalry)
    — Private John E. Cleveland (Co. A 7th U.S. Cavalry)

---

[75] Indians. *Annual Report of Secretary of War (1877)*, 557; Chronological List, 65; Heitman (Volume 2), 443; Record of Engagements, 73; Greene, *Nez Perce Summer*, 236-238.
[76] Register of Deaths Regular Army, 1860-1889 (Volume 8).
[77] Greene, *Nez Perce Summer*, 367.
[78] Indians. *Annual Report of Secretary of War (1877)*, 557; Chronological List, 65; Record of Engagements, 73; Greene, *Nez Perce Summer*, 239-240.
[79] Greene, *Nez Perce Summer*, 367.
[80] Indians. Chronological List, 65; Heitman (Volume 2), 443; Record of Engagements, 75; Mulroy, *Freedom on the Border*, 127; Smith, *Old Army in Texas*, 162; Williams, *Texas' Last Frontier*, 214.
[81] Indians. *Annual Report of Secretary of War (1877)*, 634; *Annual Report of Secretary of War (1878)*, 429; Chronological List, 65; Heitman (Volume 2), 443; Record of Engagements, 73-74; Arnold, *Indian Wars of Idaho*, 142-143; Greene, *Nez Perce Summer*, 271-291; Miles, *Personal Recollections*, 267-273; Zimmer, *Frontier Soldier*, 121-123.
[82] Reports of Diseases and Individual Cases, F 480; Register of Deaths Regular Army, 1860-1889 (Volume 8).

— Private Lewis Kelly (Co. A 7th U.S. Cavalry)
— Private Samuel McIntyre (Co. A 7th U.S. Cavalry)

— First Sergeant Michael Martin (Co. D 7th U.S. Cavalry)
— Sergeant James S. Alberts (Co. D 7th U.S. Cavalry)
— Private William R. Randall (Co. D 7th U.S. Cavalry)
— Private David E. Dorsey (Co. D 7th U.S. Cavalry)

— First Sergeant Otto Wilde (Co. K 7th U.S. Cavalry)
— Sergeant Max Mielke (Co. K 7th U.S. Cavalry)
— Sergeant Henry W. Rachael (Co. K 7th U.S. Cavalry)
— Private William Whitlow (Co. K 7th U.S. Cavalry)
— Private Francis Roth (Co. K 7th U.S. Cavalry)
— Private George Hundick (Co. K 7th U.S. Cavalry)
— Private Frank Knaupp (Co. K 7th U.S. Cavalry)

— Corporal John Hadde (Co. B 5th U.S. Infantry)
— Private Thomas Geoghegan (Co. C 5th U.S. Infantry)
— Private Richard M. Pershall (Co. G 5th U.S. Infantry)
— Sergeant Joseph A. Cable (Co. I 5th U.S. Infantry) — d. 10-15-1877
— Private Joseph Kohler (Co. I 5th U.S. Infantry) — d. 10-01-1877

— Private John Irving (Co. G 2nd U.S. Cavalry) — d. 10-01-1877

— 49 WOUNDED[83]
— Captain Myles Moylan (Co. A 7th U.S. Cavalry)
    — *gunshot wound, right thigh, severe wound*
— Captain Edward S. Godfrey (Co. D 7th U.S. Cavalry)
    — *gunshot wound, left lumbar region, slight wound*
— 1st Lieutenant Henry Romeyn (Co. A 5th U.S. Infantry)
    — *gunshot wound, right chest, severe wound*
— 1st Lieutenant George W. Baird (5th U.S. Infantry)
    — *gunshot wound, left arm, fracture, left ear, severe wound*

— Private James Farrell (Co. F 2nd U.S. Cavalry)
    — *gunshot wound, right elbow*
— Private Patrick Martin (Co. F 2nd U.S. Cavalry)

— Sergeant Thomas D. Godman (Co. A 7th U.S. Cavalry)
    — *gunshot wound, left hand and left shoulder, slight wound*
— Trumpeter James E. Christopher (Co. A 7th U.S. Cavalry)
    — *gunshot wound, left knee, severe wound*

[83] Reports of Diseases and Individual Cases, F 480; Greene, *Nez Perce Summer*, 368-371.

— Private Daniel S. Wright (Co. A 7th U.S. Cavalry)
    — *gunshot wound, right thigh, severe wound*
— Private Thomas Denning (Co. A 7th U.S. Cavalry)
    — *gunshot wound, right popliteal region, slight wound*
— Private Charles Miller (Co. A 7th U.S. Cavalry)
    — *gunshot wound, neck and right shoulder, severe wound*
— Private Michael Gilbert (Co. A 7th U.S. Cavalry)
    — *gunshot wound, right shoulder, severe wound*
— Private George W. Savage (Co. A 7th U.S. Cavalry)
    — *gunshot wounds, both thighs, severe wound*
— Private Howard H. Weaver (Co. A 7th U.S. Cavalry)
    — *gunshot wound, right arm, slight wound*

— Sergeant Charles H. Welch (Co. D 7th U.S. Cavalry)
    — *gunshot wound, right thigh and left thigh, severe wound*
— Corporal John Quinn (Co. D 7th U.S. Cavalry)
    — *gunshot wound, left shoulder, severe wound*
— Trumpeter Thomas Herwood (Co. D 7th U.S. Cavalry)
    — *gunshot wound, left side chest, severe wound*
— Private James Clark (Co. D 7th U.S. Cavalry)
    — *gunshot wound, right shoulder, severe wound*
— Private Frederick W. Deetline (Co. D 7th U.S. Cavalry)
    — *gunshot wound, right shoulder and left elbow, severe wound*
— Private John Curran (Co. D 7th U.S. Cavalry)
    — *gunshot wound, left hand, index finger amputated*
— Private Uriah S. Lewis (Co. D 7th U.S. Cavalry)
    — *gunshot wound, right calf, slight wound*
— Private John M. Jones (Co. D 7th U.S. Cavalry)
    — *gunshot wound, left shoulder and left arm, slight wound*
— Private David E. Baker (Co. D 7th U.S. Cavalry)
    — *gunshot wound, right thigh, severe wound*

— Sergeant John Nolan (Co. K 7th U.S. Cavalry)
    — *gunshot wound, left hip*
— Corporal Michael Delany (Co. K 7th U.S. Cavalry)
    — *gunshot wound, right chest, severe wound*
— Saddler John Meyers (Co. K 7th U.S. Cavalry)
    — *gunshot wound, left hand*
— Private Peter Allen (Co. K 7th U.S. Cavalry)
    — *gunshot wound, left arm, fracture, severe wound*
— Private William H. McGee (Co. K 7th U.S. Cavalry)
    — *gunshot wound, right leg*
— Private John Schwerer (Co. K 7th U.S. Cavalry)
    — *gunshot wound, left leg*
— Private George A. Sorrell (Co. K 7th U.S. Cavalry)
    — *gunshot wound, left hand*
— Private John Shawer (Co. K 7th U.S. Cavalry)
    — *gunshot wound, left heel, slight wound*
— Private Emil Taube (Co. K 7th U.S. Cavalry)
    — *gunshot wound, scalp, slight wound*
— Private Michael Murphy (Co. K 7th U.S. Cavalry)
    — *gunshot wound, chest and abdomen, severe wound*
— Private John Foley (Co. K 7th U.S. Cavalry)
— Private Charles Smith (Co. K 7th U.S. Cavalry)
    — *gunshot wound, left thigh, severe wound*

— Private Charles A. Dowell (Co. K 7th U.S. Cavalry)
    — *right wrist and left hand, slight wound*
— Private (Hospital Steward) Jean B.D. Gallenne (Co. M 7th U.S. Cavalry)
    — *gunshot wound, left ankle, fracture, severe wound*

— Private John Ferrons (Co. D 5th U.S. Infantry)
    — *gunshot wound, left leg, slight wound*

— Sergeant George Krager (Co. G 5th U.S. Infantry)
    — *gunshot wound, left side face, right hand, severe wound*
— Musician Jesse O'Neill (Co. G 5th U.S. Infantry)
    — *gunshot wound, left thigh, fracture, severe wound*
— Private Daniel Horgan (Co. G 5th U.S. Infantry)
    — *gunshot wound, right leg, slight wound*
— Private Fleming S. Griffith (Co. G 5th U.S. Infantry)

— Private Lewis Gensler (Co. I 5th U.S. Infantry)
    — *gunshot wound, left forearm, fracture, severe wound*
— Private Patrick McCanna (Co. I 5th U.S. Infantry)
    — *gunshot wound, right hip, slight wound*
— Private John Andrews (Co. I 5th U.S. Infantry)
    — *gunshot wound, left side of face*
— Private Nicholas B. Ward (Co. I 5th U.S. Infantry)
    — *gunshot wound, both thighs, severe wound*

— Hump (Indian Scout)
    — *right shoulder, slight*
— White Wolf (Indian Scout)
    — *fractured skull*

— *1st Lieutenant George W. Baird (5th U.S. Infantry) received MOH: Most distinguished gallantry in action with the Nez Perce Indians (Bear Paw Mountain, Montana, September 30, 1877).*

— *1st Lieutenant Mason Carter (5th U.S. Infantry) brevet promotion to Major for gallant service in action against Indians (Bear Paw Mountains, Montana, September 30, 1877).*

— *1st Lieutenant Mason Carter (5th U.S. Infantry) received MOH: Led a charge under a galling fire, in which he inflicted great loss upon the enemy (Bear Paw Mountain, Montana, September 30, 1877).*

— *Captain Edward S. Godfrey (7th U.S. Cavalry) brevet promotion to Major for gallant service in action against Indians (Bear Paw Mountains, September 30, 1877, where he was wounded).*

— *Captain Edward S. Godfrey (7th U.S. Cavalry) received MOH: Led his command into action when he was severely wounded (Bear Paw Mountain, Montana, September 30, 1877).*

— *2nd Lieutenant Oscar F. Long (5th U.S. Infantry) received MOH: Having been directed to order a troop of cavalry to advance, and finding both its officers killed, he voluntarily assumed command, and under a heavy fire from the Indians advanced the troop to its proper position (Bear Paw Mountain, Montana, September 30, 1877).*

— *First Sergeant Henry Hogan (Co. G 5th U.S. Infantry) received MOH: Carried Lieutenant Romeyn, who was severely wounded, off the field of battle under heavy fire (Bear Paw Mountain, September 30, 1877).*

— *2nd Lieutenant Edward J. McClernand (2nd U.S. Cavalry) received MOH: Gallantly attacked a band of hostiles and conducted the combat with excellent skill and boldness (Bear Paw Mountain, Montana, September 30, 1877).*

— *2ⁿᵈ Lieutenant Edward J. McClernand (2ⁿᵈ U.S. Cavalry) brevet promotion to 1ˢᵗ Lieutenant for gallantry in the pursuit of Indians and in action against them (Bear Paw Mountains, Montana, September 30, 1877).*

— *Captain Myles Moylan (7ᵗʰ U.S. Cavalry) received MOH: Gallantly led his command in action against Nez Perce Indians until he was severely wounded (Bear Paw Mountain, Montana, September 30, 1877).*

— *Captain Myles Moylan (7ᵗʰ U.S. Cavalry) brevet promotion to Major for gallant service in action against Indians (Bear Paw Mountain, Montana, September 30, 1877, where he was severely wounded).*

— *1ˢᵗ Lieutenant Henry Romeyn (5ᵗʰ U.S. Infantry) received MOH: Led his command into close range of the enemy, there maintained his position and vigorously prosecuted the fight until he was severely wounded (Bear Paw Mountain, Montana, September 30, 1877).*

— *1ˢᵗ Lieutenant Henry Romeyn (5ᵗʰ U.S. Infantry) brevet promotion to Major for gallant service in actions against Indians at their village where he was severely wounded (Bear Paw Mountains, Montana, September 30, 1877).*

— *Captain Simon Snyder (5ᵗʰ U.S. Infantry) brevet promotion to Major for gallant service in action against Indians (Bear Paw Mountain, Montana, September 30, 1877).*

— *Major Henry R. Tilton (Surgeon) received MOH: Fearlessly risked his life and displayed great gallantry in rescuing and protecting the wounded men (Bear Paw Mountain, Montana, September 30, 1877).*

— *2ⁿᵈ Lieutenant Thomas M. Woodruff (5ᵗʰ U.S. Infantry) brevet promotion to 1ˢᵗ Lieutenant for gallant service in action against Indians (Bear Paw Mountain, Montana, September 30, 1877).*

(1026) Surrender of Joseph and 418 Indians, Bear Paw Mountains, Montana Territory (October 4 and 5, 1877) [84]

(1027) Citizens, near Flat Rocks, Texas (October 22, 1877) [85]
— (1) Citizen Killed

(1028) Skirmish, Big Bend of Rio Grande, Texas (November 1, 1877) [86]
— 1ˢᵗ Lieutenant John L. Bullis (24ᵗʰ U.S. Infantry)
— Detachment of Indian Scouts

(1029) Citizens, near Indian Creek, Texas (November 16, 1877) [87]
— (1) Citizen Killed

(1030) Citizens, near Sauz Ranch, Texas (November 18, 1877) [88]
— (2) Citizens Killed

[84] Indians. Chronological List, 65; Record of Engagements, 75; Arnold, *Indian Wars of Idaho*, 143-144; Miles, *Personal Recollections*, 275.
[85] Indians. Killed was stagecoach driver John Sanders. *Annual Report of Secretary of War (1878)*, 82; Chronological List, 66; Heitman (Volume 2), 443.
[86] Indians. Chronological List, 66; Record of Engagements, 75; Leckie, *Buffalo Soldiers*, 155; Mulroy, *Freedom on the Border*, 127-128; Smith, *Old Army in Texas*, 162.
[87] Indians. *Annual Report of Secretary of War (1878)*, 82; Chronological List, 66; Record of Engagements, 75.
[88] Indians. Killed were two herders. *Annual Report of Secretary of War (1878)*, 82; Chronological List, 66; Record of Engagements, 75.

(1031) Citizens, near Fort Hall Indian Agency, Idaho Territory (November 23, 1877)[89]
— (1) Citizens Killed

(1032) Action, Sierra del Carmen, Coahuila, Mexico (November 29 and 30, 1877)[90]
— Captain Samuel B.M. Young (8th U.S. Cavalry)
— 8th U.S. Cavalry Co. A and K
— 10th U.S. Cavalry Co. C
— Detachment of Indian Scouts
— **1 WOUNDED**[91]
— First Sergeant Wilson (Co. K 8th U.S. Cavalry)

(1033) Skirmish, Ralston Flat, New Mexico Territory (December 13, 1877)[92]
— 2nd Lieutenant John A. Rucker (6th U.S. Cavalry)
— 6th U.S. Cavalry Detachments Co. C, G, H and L
— Detachment of Indian Scouts

— *Sergeant James Brogan (Co. G 6th U.S. Cavalry) received MOH: Engaged single handed two renegade Indians until his horse was shot under him and then pursued them so long as he was able (Simon Valley, Arizona, December 14, 1877).*

(1034) Skirmish, Las Animas Mountains, Sonora, Mexico (December 18, 1877)[93]
— 2nd Lieutenant John A. Rucker (6th U.S. Cavalry)
— 6th U.S. Cavalry Detachments Co. C, G, H and L
— Detachment of Indian Scouts

(1035) Citizens, Bass Canyon, near Van Horn's Wells, Texas (December 23, 1877)[94]
— (2) Citizens Killed

TOTAL KILLED 1877 — 7/118/2/12 (OFFICERS, ENLISTED MEN, INDIAN SCOUTS, CITIZENS)

[89] Indians. Killed was Alexander Rhodan. *Annual Report of Commissioner of Indian Affairs (1878)*, xiii, 49; Brimlow, *Bannock Indian War*, 62.
[90] Indians. Chronological List, 66; Heitman (Volume 2), 443; Record of Engagements, 75; Leckie, *Buffalo Soldiers*, 155-158; Smith, *Old Army in Texas*, 162; Williams, *Texas' Last Frontier*, 214-215.
[91] 3rd U.S. Cavalry Regimental Return November 1877.
[92] Indians. Chronological List, 66; Heitman (Volume 2), 443; Record of Engagements, 75; Carter, *From Yorktown to Santiago*, 194-195, 278; Sweeney, *Cochise to Geronimo*, 107-108.
[93] Indians. Chronological List, 66; Heitman (Volume 2), 443; Record of Engagements, 75; Carter, *From Yorktown to Santiago*, 195, 278; Rathbun, *New Mexico Frontier Military Place Names*, 6; Sweeney, *Cochise to Geronimo*, 108-110; Thrapp, *Conquest of Apacheria*, 176.
[94] Indians. Killed were Gabriel Valdez and Horan Parsons. *Annual Report of Secretary of War (1878)*, 82; Chronological List, 66; Record of Engagements, 75.

1878

"With the Bannocks and Shoshones our Indian policy has resolved itself into a question of war-path or starvation, and, being merely human, many [Indians] will always chose the former alternative, where death shall at least be glorious."
— George Crook, U.S. Army[1]

---

[1] Official Report of Brigadier General George Crook, 23 September 1878. *Annual Report of Secretary of War (1878)*, 90.

(1036) Citizens, sixty-three miles northwest of Presidio del Norte, Texas (January 5, 1878)[2]
— (6) Citizens Killed

(1037) Skirmish, near Tonto Creek, Arizona Territory (January 7, 1878)[3]
— Captain Charles Porter (8th U.S. Infantry)
— 6th U.S. Cavalry Co. A
— 8th U.S. Infantry Co. B
— Detachment of Indian Scouts

— *Captain Charles Porter (8th U.S. Infantry) brevet promotion to Major for gallant service in actions against Indians (Arizona, August 15, 1876; January 1, 1878 and April 3, 1878).*

(1038) Citizens, Mason County, Texas (January 16, 1878)[4]
— (2) Citizens Killed

(1039) Citizens, Brady City, Texas (January 16, 1878)[5]
— (1) Citizen Killed

(1040) Skirmish, Russell's Ranch, Rio Grande, Texas (January 16, 1878)[6]
— Captain Michael L. Courtney (25th U.S. Infantry)
— 10th U.S. Cavalry Co. H
— 25th U.S. Infantry Co. A and H

(1041) Surrender of 10 Indians, Ross Fork Agency, Idaho Territory (January 16, 1878)[7]

(1042) Skirmish, Headwaters of Sunday Creek, Montana Territory (February 5, 1878)[8]
— UNKNOWN
— Detachment of Indian Scouts

(1043) Action, near Fort Keogh, Montana Territory (February 13, 1878)[9]
— UNKNOWN
— Detachment of Indian Scouts
— **1 KILLED**[10]
— Indian Scout

— **1 WOUNDED**[11]
— Indian Scout

(1044) Citizens, Point of Rocks, Limpia Canyon, Texas (February 16, 1878)[12]
— (2) Citizens Killed

(1045) Citizens, Laredo Road, near Fort Duncan, Texas (February 23, 1878)[13]

[2] Indians. Killed were Librado Galindo, Petro Rentirio, Julian Molino, Martin Lara, Remulo Meontoga, Madaleno Villalobas. *Annual Report of Secretary of War (1878)*, 82; Chronological List, 66; Record of Engagements, 76; Williams, *Texas' Last Frontier*, 220; Wooster, *Frontier Crossroads*, 99.
[3] Indians. Chronological List, 66; Heitman (Volume 2), 444; Carter, *From Yorktown to Santiago*, 278.
[4] Indians. *Annual Report of Secretary of War (1878)*, 82; Chronological List, 66.
[5] Indians. *Annual Report of Secretary of War (1878)*, 82; Chronological List, 66.
[6] Indians. Chronological List, 66; Record of Engagements, 76; Williams, *Texas' Last Frontier*, 222.
[7] Indians. *Annual Report of Commissioner of Indian Affairs (1878)*, xiii-xv, 50; Chronological List, 66; Heitman (Volume 2), 444; Record of Engagements, 76.
[8] Indians. Chronological List, 66; Heitman (Volume 2), 444.
[9] Indians. Chronological List, 66.
[10] Chronological List, 66.
[11] Chronological List, 66.
[12] Indians. Killed were Victorius Rios and Severiano Elivario. *Annual Report of Secretary of War (1878)*, 82; Chronological List, 67; Record of Engagements, 76; Williams, *Texas' Last Frontier*, 222.
[13] Indians. Killed were R.W. Barry and Juan Dias. *Annual Report of Secretary of War (1878)*, 82; Chronological List, 67; Record of Engagements, 76.

— (2) Citizens Killed

(1046) Skirmish, Mogollon Mountains, Arizona Territory (April 5, 1878)[14]
    — Captain Charles Porter (8th U.S. Infantry)
        — 6th U.S. Cavalry Detachment Co. A
        — 8th U.S. Infantry Detachment Co. B
    — Detachment of Indian Scouts

    — *Captain Charles Porter (8th U.S. Infantry) brevet promotion to Major for gallant service in actions against Indians (Arizona, August 15, 1876; January 1, 1878 and April 3, 1878).*

(1047) Citizens, Steele's Ranch, Nueces River, Texas (April 17, 1878)[15]
    — (2) Citizens Killed

(1048) Citizens, near Fort Quitman, Texas (April 17, 1878)[16]
    — (1) Citizen Killed

(1049) Citizens, San Ygnacio, Texas (April 17, 1878)[17]
    — (1) Citizen Killed

(1050) Citizens, near Brown's Ranch, Texas (April 17, 1878)[18]
    — (1) Citizen Killed

(1051) Citizens, Rancho Soledad, Texas (April 18, 1878)[19]
    — (3) Citizens Killed

(1052) Citizens, Charco Escondido, Texas (April 18, 1878)[20]
    — (1) Citizen Killed

(1053) Citizens, Quijotes Gordes, Texas (April 19, 1878)[21]
    — (1) Citizen Killed

(1054) Citizens, near Charco Escondido, Texas (April 19, 1878)[22]
    — (1) Citizen Killed

(1055) Citizens, Point of Rocks, Texas (April 20, 1878)[23]
    — (3) Citizens Killed

(1056) Skirmish, Smith's Mills, near Wickenburg, Arizona Territory (May 20, 1878)[24]
    — 2nd Lieutenant Edward E. Dravo (6th U.S. Cavalry)
        — 6th U.S. Cavalry Detachment Co. I

[14] Indians. Chronological List, 67; Heitman (Volume 2), 444; Carter, *From Yorktown to Santiago*, 196, 278; Thrapp, *Al Sieber*, 201-202.
[15] Indians. Killed were George and Dick Taylor. Annual *Report of Secretary of War (1878)*, 82; Chronological List, 67; Record of Engagements, 76.
[16] Indians. Killed was W. McCall. *Annual Report of Secretary of War (1878)*, 82; Chronological List, 67; Record of Engagements, 76; Williams, *Texas' Last Frontier*, 223.
[17] Indians. Killed was Frederick B. Moore. *Annual Report of Secretary of War (1878)*, 82; Chronological List, 67; Record of Engagements, 76.
[18] Indians. Killed was Vicenti Robledo. *Annual Report of Secretary of War (1878)*, 82; Chronological List, 67; Record of Engagements, 76.
[19] Indians. Killed were shepherd Guadaloupe Basan and his wife. *Annual Report of Secretary of War (1878)*, 82; Chronological List, 67; Record of Engagements, 77.
[20] Indians. Killed was John Jordan. *Annual Report of Secretary of War (1878)*, 82; Chronological List, 67; Record of Engagements, 77.
[21] Indians. Killed was Jose Maria Canales. *Annual Report of Secretary of War (1877)*, 82; Chronological List, 67; Record of Engagements, 77.
[22] Indians. Killed was Margarito Rodriquez. *Annual Report of Secretary of War (1878)*, 82; Chronological List, 67; Record of Engagements, 77.
[23] Indians. Killed in separate attacks were mail carrier Lonjinio Gonzales, a man named Florentino and a third man. *Annual Report of Secretary of War (1878)*, 82; Chronological List, 67; Record of Engagements, 77; Williams, *Texas' Last Frontier*, 223.
[24] Indians. Chronological List, 67; Heitman (Volume 2), 444; Alexander, *Arizona Frontier Military Place Names*, 111; Carter, *From Yorktown to Santiago*, 196, 278.

(1057) Skirmish, Head of White's Gulch, Montana Territory (May 20, 1878)[25]
— Captain Walter Clifford (7th U.S. Infantry)
— 7th U.S. Infantry Detachments Co. D and E

(1058) Citizens, near Camp Wood, Texas (June 1, 1878)[26]
— (2) Citizens Killed

(1059) Citizens, Stein's Mountain, Oregon (June 17, 1878)[27]
— (2) Citizens Killed

(1060) Action, Silver Creek, Oregon (June 23, 1878)[28]
— Captain Reuben F. Bernard (1st U.S. Cavalry)
— 1st U.S. Cavalry Co. A, F, G and L
— Detachment of Volunteers
— **4 KILLED**[29]
— Corporal Peter F. Gruntzinger (Co. A 1st U.S. Cavalry)
— Saddler Joseph Schultz (Co. F 1st U.S. Cavalry)
— Private William M. Marriott (Co. F 1st U.S. Cavalry)

— Scout William Myers (Citizen)

— **2 WOUNDED**[30]
— Private Christian Hanson (Co. G 1st U.S. Cavalry)
— *gunshot wound, shoulder, slight wound*
— Private George Foster (Co. L 1st U.S. Cavalry)
— *gunshot wound, left thigh, slight wound*

— *Captain Reuben F. Bernard (1st U.S. Cavalry) brevet promotion to Brigadier General for gallant service in action against Indians (Chiricahua Mountains, Arizona, October 20, 1869) and in actions against Indians (Silver River, Oregon, June 23, 1878 and Birch Creek, Oregon, July 8, 1878).*

(1061) Citizens, near Fort Simcoe, Washington Territory (July 1878)[31]
— (2) Citizens Killed

(1062) Action, Birch Creek, Oregon (July 8, 1878)[32]
— Brigadier General Oliver O. Howard (Commander Department of Columbia)
— 1st U.S. Cavalry Co. A, E, F, G, H, K and L
— Detachment of Scouts
— **1 KILLED**[33]
— Private Richard Smith (1st U.S. Cavalry)

— **4 WOUNDED**[34]
— Private Joseph S. Howard (Co. E 1st U.S. Cavalry)

[25] Indians. Chronological List, 67; Heitman (Volume 2), 444.
[26] Indians. Killed were two herders. *Annual Report of Secretary of War (1878)*, 82; Chronological List, 67; Record of Engagements, 77.
[27] Indians. Killed were G.C. Smith and his son. *Annual Report of Commissioner of Indian Affairs (1878)*, 120.
[28] Indians. *Annual Report of Secretary of War (1878)*, 159, 429; Chronological List, 67; Heitman (Volume 2), 444; Arnold, *Indian Wars of Idaho*, 193-197; Brimlow, *Bannock Indian War*, 125-127; Russell, *One Hundred and Three Fights*, 124-126. Chronological List lists 28 June 1878. Chronological List lists 1st U.S. Cavalry Co. A, F, G, L.
[29] Reports of Diseases and Individual Cases, F 484; Register of Deaths Regular Army, 1860-1889 (Volume 8).
[30] Reports of Diseases and Individual Cases, F 484.
[31] Indians. Killed were Mr. and Mrs. Perkins. *Annual Report of Commissioner of Indian Affairs (1879)*, 157.
[32] Indians. *Annual Report of Secretary of War (1878)*, 170, 222; *Annual Report of Secretary of War (1879)*, 407-408; Chronological List, 67; Heitman (Volume 2), 444; Arnold, *Indian Wars of Idaho*, 200-202; Brimlow, *Bannock Indian War*, 142-144; Russell, *One Hundred and Three Fights*, 129-130. Chronological List lists 1st U.S. Cavalry Co. A, E, F, G, H, K, L.
[33] Reports of Diseases and Individual Cases, F 485.

— gunshot wound, right thigh, severe wound
— Sergeant William H. Havens (Co. H 1ˢᵗ U.S. Cavalry)
 — gunshot wound, right leg, severe wound
— Private Andrew Turges (Co. H 1ˢᵗ U.S. Cavalry)
 — gunshot wound, left thigh, severe wound
 — Private Clarence Coon (Co. K 1ˢᵗ U.S. Cavalry)
 — gunshot wound, left hand, slight wound

 — Captain Reuben F. Bernard (1ˢᵗ U.S. Cavalry) brevet promotion to Brigadier General for gallant service in action against Indians (Chiricahua Mountains, Arizona, October 20, 1869) and in actions against Indians (Silver River, Oregon, June 28, 1878 and Birch Creek, Oregon, July 8, 1878).

"The advance was made along several approaches in a handsome manner, not a man falling out of ranks. The different sides of the hill were steeper than Missionary Ridge, still the troops, though encountering a severe fire that emptied some saddles and killed many horses, did not waver, but skirmished to the very top."
 — Oliver O. Howard, U.S. Army[35]

(1063) Skirmish, Upper Columbia River, Oregon (July 8, 1878)[36]
 — Captain John A. Kress (Ordinance Department)
  — 21ˢᵗ U.S. Infantry Detachment
  — Ordinance Department Detachment

 — Captain John A. Kress (Ordinance Department) brevet promotion to Lt. Colonel for gallant service in action against Indians (Columbia River, Oregon, July 8, 1878).

 — Captain John A. Kress (Ordnance Department) received Distinguished Service Cross: For distinguished conduct in action. Kress volunteered, though not charged with combat duties, to organize and lead an expedition against bands of hostile Piute-Bannock Indians and to prevent their crossing the Columbia River. Kress seized a river boat and equipped it as a gunboat and by his gallant and fearless leadership in patrolling the Columbia River was successful in five attacks upon the Indians, both on land and from the river; succeeded in capturing and killing their horses, destroyed their boats, arms, ammunition and camp equipage thus frustrating their plan of spreading the war among the Indians to the North (Columbia River, Oregon, July 8, 1878).

(1064) Skirmish, Ladd's Canyon, Oregon (July 12, 1878)[37]
 — Captain John L. Viven (12ᵗʰ U.S. Infantry)
  — 12ᵗʰ U.S. Infantry Co. C

(1065) Action, Umatilla Agency, Oregon (July 13, 1878)[38]
 — Captain Evan Miles (21ˢᵗ U.S. Infantry)
  — 1ˢᵗ U.S. Cavalry Co. K
  — 21ˢᵗ U.S. Infantry Co. B, D, E, G, H, I and K
  — 4ᵗʰ U.S. Artillery Co. D and G

[34] Reports of Diseases and Individual Cases, F 485.
[35] Utley, *Frontier Regulars*, 326-327, 342.
[36] Indians. Webb, *Chronological List of Engagements*, 83.
[37] Indians. Chronological List, 67; Heitman (Volume 2), 444.
[38] Indians. *Annual Report of Secretary of War (1878)*, 174, 178, 224-226; *Annual Report of Secretary of War (1879)*, 408; Chronological List, 67; Heitman (Volume 2), 444; Arnold, *Indian Wars of Idaho*, 204-207; Brimlow, *Bannock Indian War*, 149-151. Chronological List lists 1ˢᵗ U.S. Cavalry Co. K; 21ˢᵗ U.S. Infantry Co. B, D, E, G, H, I, K; 4th U.S. Artillery Co. D, G.

— Detachment of Volunteers
— **2 WOUNDED**[39]
— Corporal Charles Brown (Co. K 1st U.S. Cavalry)
— *gunshot wound, fracture, severe wound*
— Corporal William Roberts (Co. F 21st U.S. infantry)
— *gunshot wound, severe wound*

— *1st Lieutenant Frederick H.E. Ebstein (21st U.S. Infantry) brevet promotion to Captain for gallant service in actions against Indians (Cottonwood Ranch, Idaho, July 4, 1877; Camas Meadows, Idaho, August 20, 1877 and the Umatilla Agency, Oregon, July 13, 1878).*

— *Captain Evan Miles (21st U.S. Infantry) brevet promotion to Major for gallant service in actions against Indians (Clearwater, Idaho, July 11 and 12, 1877 and the Umatilla Agency, Oregon, July 13, 1878).*

— *2nd Lieutenant Robert P.P. Wainwright (1st U.S. Cavalry) brevet promotion to 1st Lieutenant for gallant service in action against Indians (Umatilla Agency, Oregon, July 13, 1878).*

(1066) Action, North Fork of John Day River, Oregon (July 20, 1878)[40]
— Lt. Colonel James W. Forsyth (1st U.S. Cavalry)
— 1st U.S. Cavalry Co. A, E, F, G, H and L
— Detachment of Volunteers
— **1 KILLED**[41]
— Scout A.A. Frohman (Citizen)

— **2 WOUNDED**[42]
— Private William Schaffer (Co. E 1st U.S. Cavalry)
— *gunshot wound, head, slight wound*

— Scout John Campbell (Citizen)
— *severe wound*

(1067) Skirmish, Middle Fork of Clearwater River, Montana Territory (July 21, 1878)[43]
— 1st Lieutenant Thomas S. Wallace (3rd U.S. Infantry)
— 3rd U.S. Infantry Detachments Co. B, H and I

(1068) Skirmish, near Baker City, Idaho Territory (July 26, 1878)[44]
— Captain William F. Drum (2nd U.S. Infantry)
— 2nd U.S. Infantry Co. C, Detachment Co. K

(1069) Skirmish, Sacramento Mountains, Arizona Territory (July 29, 1878)[45]
— 2nd Lieutenant Henry H. Wright (9th U.S. Cavalry)
— Detachment of Indian Scouts

[39] Reports of Diseases and Individual Cases, F 486.
[40] Indians. *Annual Report of Secretary of War (1878)*, 227-228; *Annual Report of Secretary of War (1879)*, 408; Chronological List, 67; Heitman (Volume 2), 444; Brimlow, *Bannock Indian War*, 155-156; Russell, *One Hundred and Three Fights*, 131-132. Chronological List lists 1st U.S. Cavalry Co. A, E, F, G, H, L. Heitman lists 1st U.S. Cavalry Co. A, E, F, G, H.
[41] *Annual Report of Secretary of War (1878)*, 228.
[42] Reports of Diseases and Individual Cases, F 487; *Annual Report of Secretary of War (1878)*, 228.
[43] Indians. Chronological List, 67; Heitman (Volume 2), 444; Record of Engagements, 78; Arnold, *Indian Wars of Idaho*, 215.
[44] Indians. Chronological List, 67; Heitman (Volume 2), 444.

— 2ⁿᵈ Lieutenant Henry H. Wright (9ᵗʰ U.S. Cavalry) brevet promotion to 1ˢᵗ Lieutenant for gallant service in actions against Indians (Florida Mountains, New Mexico, January 24, 1877; Sacramento Mountains, New Mexico, July 29, 1878 and Miembres Mountains, New Mexico, May 29, 1879).

(1070) Skirmish, Dog Canyon, New Mexico Territory (August 5, 1878)[46]
— Captain Henry Carroll (9ᵗʰ U.S. Cavalry)
    — 9ᵗʰ U.S. Cavalry Co. F and H
    — Detachment of Indian Scouts

(1071) Action, Bennett Creek, Idaho Territory (August 9, 1878)[47]
— Captain William E. Dove (12ᵗʰ U.S. Infantry)
    — 12ᵗʰ U.S. Infantry Detachment Co. K
— **1 WOUNDED**[48]
    — Enlisted Man (12ᵗʰ U.S. Infantry)

(1072) Action, Big Creek, Idaho Territory (August 20, 1878)[49]
— 1ˢᵗ Lieutenant Henry Catley (2ⁿᵈ U.S. Infantry)
    — 2ⁿᵈ U.S. Infantry Co. C, Detachment Co. K
— **1 KILLED**[50]
    — Enlisted Man (2ⁿᵈ U.S. Infantry)

(1073) Skirmish, Henry's Lake, Idaho Territory (August 27, 1878)[51]
— Captain James Egan (2ⁿᵈ U.S. Cavalry)
    — 2ⁿᵈ U.S. Cavalry Co. K

(1074) Skirmish, Index Peak, Wyoming Territory (August 29 and 30, 1878)[52]
— 1ˢᵗ Lieutenant William P. Clark (2ⁿᵈ U.S. Cavalry)
    — 5ᵗʰ U.S. Infantry Detachment
    — Detachment of Indian Scouts

(1075) Action, Clark's Fork, Montana Territory (September 4, 1878)[53]
— Colonel Nelson A. Miles (5ᵗʰ U.S. Infantry)
    — 5ᵗʰ U.S. Infantry Detachments Co. A, C, F, G, I and K
    — Detachment of Indian Scouts
— **2 KILLED**[54]
    — Captain Andrew S. Bennett (5ᵗʰ U.S. Infantry)

    — Rock (Indian Scout)

— **1 WOUNDED**[55]
    — Private William McAtee (Co. G 5ᵗʰ U.S. Infantry)
      — gunshot wound, right arm, slight wound

[45] Indians. Chronological List, 68; Heitman (Volume 2), 444.
[46] Indians. Chronological List, 68; Heitman (Volume 2), 444; Billington, *New Mexico's Buffalo Soldiers*, 56-57; Leckie, *Buffalo Soldiers*, 194; Rathbun, *New Mexico Frontier Military Place Names*, 58-59.
[47] Indians. Chronological List, 68; Heitman (Volume 2), 444; Brimlow, *Bannock Indian War*, 159-160.
[48] Chronological List, 68.
[49] Indians. Chronological List, 68.
[50] Chronological List, 68.
[51] Indians. Chronological List, 68; Heitman (Volume 2), 444; Record of Engagements, 78.
[52] Indians. Chronological List, 68; Heitman (Volume 2), 444; Record of Engagements, 78.
[53] Indians. *Annual Report of Secretary of War (1879)*, 408; Chronological List, 68; Heitman (Volume 2), 444; Record of Engagements, 78; Brimlow, *Bannock Indian War*, 183-184; Miles, *Personal Recollections*, 297-300. Chronological List lists 5ᵗʰ U.S. Infantry Detachments; Detachment of Indian Scouts.
[54] Reports of Diseases and Individual Cases, F 488; Register of Deaths Regular Army, 1860-1889 (Volume 9).
[55] Reports of Diseases and Individual Cases, F 488.

(1076) Skirmish, near Big Wind or Snake River, Wyoming Territory (September 12, 1878)[56]
— 2nd Lieutenant Hoel S. Bishop (5th U.S. Cavalry)
— 5th U.S. Cavalry Detachment Co. G
— Detachment of Indian Scouts

(1077) Action, near Turkey Springs, Indian Territory (September 13, 1878)[57]
— Captain Joseph Rendlebrock (4th U.S. Cavalry)
— 4th U.S. Cavalry Co. G and H
— Detachment of Indian Scouts
— **2 KILLED**[58]
— Corporal Patrick Lynch (Co. G 4th U.S. Cavalry)
— Private Frank Struad (Co. G 4th U.S. Cavalry)

—**2 WOUNDED**[59]
— Blacksmith George Burrows (Co. G 4th U.S. Cavalry)
— *gunshot wound, leg, slight wound*
— Private George Leonard (Co. G 4th U.S. Cavalry)
— *gunshot wound, thorax, severe wound*

(1078) Action, Red Hill, Indian Territory (September 14, 1878)[60]
— Captain Joseph Rendlebrock (4th U.S. Cavalry)
— 4th U.S. Cavalry Co. G and H
— Detachment of Indian Scouts
— **1 KILLED**[61]
— Blacksmith Francis Burton (Co. H 4th U.S. Cavalry)

(1079) Action, Bear Creek, New Mexico Territory (September 17, 1878)[62]
— 1st Lieutenant Henry P. Perrine (6th U.S. Cavalry)
— 6th U.S. Cavalry Detachment
— Detachment of Indian Scouts
— **1 KILLED**[63]
— Indian Scout

(1080) Action, Bear Creek or Bluff Creek, Kansas (September 18, 1878)[64]
— Captain William C. Hemphill (4th U.S. Cavalry)
— 4th U.S. Cavalry Co. I
— Detachment of Volunteers
— **1 WOUNDED**[65]
— Private Adolph Esslinger (Co. I 4th U.S. Cavalry)
— *gunshot wound, left hip, severe wound*

---

[56] Indians. Chronological List, 68; Heitman (Volume 2), 444; Record of Engagements, 78; Brimlow, *Bannock Indian War*, 186-187.
[57] Indians. *Annual Report of Secretary of War (1879)*, 408; Chronological List, 68; Heitman (Volume 2), 444; Buecker, *Fort Robinson*, 128; Hoig, *Perilous Pursuit*, 67-72; Maddux, *In Dull Knife's Wake*, 34-42; Monnett, *Tell Them We Are Going Home*, 53-54. Chronological List lists 4th U.S. Cavalry Co. G, H.
[58] Reports of Diseases and Individual Cases, F 489; Register of Deaths Regular Army, 1860-1889 (Volume 9).
[59] Reports of Diseases and Individual Cases, F 489.
[60] Indians. *Annual Report of Secretary of War (1879)*, 408; Chronological List, 68; Heitman (Volume 2), 444; Buecker, *Fort Robinson*, 128; Hoig, *Perilous Pursuit*, 73-80; Maddux, *In Dull Knife's Wake*, 34-42; Monnett, *Tell Them We Are Going Home*, 55. Chronological List lists 4th U.S. Cavalry Co. G, H.
[61] Reports of Diseases and Individual Cases, F 489; Register of Deaths Regular Army, 1860-1889 (Volume 9).
[62] Indians. *Annual Report of Secretary of War (1879)*, 169; Chronological List, 68; Heitman (Volume 2), 444; Carter, *From Yorktown to Santiago*, 199. Chronological List and Heitman both list Detachment of Indian Scouts.
[63] Chronological List, 68.
[64] Indians. *Annual Report of Secretary of War (1879)*, 408; Chronological List, 68; Heitman (Volume 2), 444; Buecker, *Fort Robinson*, 128; Hoig, *Perilous Pursuit*, 97; Maddux, *In Dull Knife's Wake*, 64-66; Monnett, *Tell Them We Are Going Home*, 62. Chronological List lists 4th U.S. Cavalry Co. I.

(1081) Skirmish, Sand Creek, Kansas (September 21 and 22, 1878)[66]
    — Captain Joseph Rendlebrock (4th U.S. Cavalry)
        — 4th U.S. Cavalry Co. F, G, H and I
        — 16th U.S. Infantry Co. A
        — 19th U.S. Infantry Detachment Co. F
        — Detachment of Indian Scouts
        — Detachment of Volunteers

    — *1st Lieutenant Abram E. Wood (4th U.S. Cavalry) brevet promotion to Captain for gallant service in actions against Indians (Sand Creek, Kansas, September 21, 1878 and Punished Woman's Fork, September 27, 1878).*

(1082) Action, Famished Woman's Fork, Kansas (September 27, 1878)[67]
    — Lt. Colonel William H. Lewis (19th U.S. Infantry)
    — Captain Clarence Mauck (4th U.S. Cavalry)
        — 4th U.S. Cavalry Detachments Co. B, F, G, H and I
        — 19th U.S. Infantry Detachments Co. D, F and G
    — **1 KILLED**[68]
        — Lt. Colonel William H. Lewis (19th U.S. Infantry) — d. 09-28-1878

    — **2 WOUNDED**[69]
        — Private Jack Loan (Co. F 4th U.S. Cavalry)
            — *gunshot wound, left shoulder, slight wound*
        — Private John R. Danneker (Co. G 4th U.S. Cavalry)
            — *gunshot wound, shoulder, slight wound*

    — *Private Joseph Sudsburger (Co. B 4th U.S. Cavalry) received Certificate of Merit: For bravery in action with hostile Indians (Punished Woman's Fork, Kansas, September 27, 1878).*

    — *1st Lieutenant Abram E. Wood (4th U.S. Cavalry) brevet promotion to Captain for gallant service in actions against Indians (Sand Creek, Kansas, September 21, 1878 and Punished Woman's Fork, September 27, 1878).*

> **"[Lt. Colonel William H. Lewis] was a man very much beloved by his fellow officers and by the men under his command. He was a man of sterling integrity and correct habits. Twenty-nine years of continuous service on the frontier gave him an experience which with his great personal bravery and good judgment, makes his loss at his juncture a peculiarly great one."**
> — Editor, *Ford County Globe*, Citizen[70]

(1083) Citizens, Johnson's Fork, Guadalupe River, Texas (October 5, 1878)[71]
    — (4) Citizens Killed

TOTAL KILLED 1878 — 2/9/3/2 (Officers, Enlisted Men, Indian Scouts, Citizens)

---

[65] Reports of Diseases and Individual Cases, F 490.
[66] Indians. Chronological List, 68; Heitman (Volume 2), 444; Record of Engagements, 80; Buecker, *Fort Robinson*, 128; Hoig, *Perilous Pursuit*, 100-106; Maddux, *In Dull Knife's Wake*, 69-75; Monnett, *Tell Them We Are Going Home*, 63-66. Chronological List lists 4th U.S. Cavalry Co. F, G, H, I; 16th U.S. Infantry Co. A; 19th U.S. Infantry Detachments; Detachment of Indian Scouts.
[67] Indians. *Annual Report of Secretary of War (1879)*, 408; Chronological List, 68; Heitman (Volume 2), 444; Record of Engagements, 80; Buecker, *Fort Robinson*, 128-129; Hoig, *Perilous Pursuit*, 113-123; Maddux, *In Dull Knife's Wake*, 84-94; Monnett, *Tell Them We Are Going Home*, 67-73.
[68] Reports of Diseases and Individual Cases, F 491; Register of Deaths Regular Army, 1860-1889 (Volume 9).
[69] Reports of Diseases and Individual Cases, F 491.
[70] *Ford County Globe*, 1 October 1878.
[71] Indians. Killed were four children of the Dowdy family, one boy and three girls. *Annual Report of Secretary of War (1879)*, 114; Chronological List, 68; Record of Engagements, 82.

1879

"There is no doubt that these Indians were starving and dying of fever and were justified in leaving their reservations peaceably... Our sympathies were therefore with them at first, but when we reached their trail of murder, rapine and desolation our blood rose against them and there was not a man who would not gladly have risked his life to avenge the defenseless men, woman end children who had been barbarously murdered and outraged."

— Calvin D. Cowles, U.S. Army[1]

---

[1] 2nd Lieutenant Calvin D. Cowles (23rd U.S. Infantry) shared his sentiments with his father in a letter written home. Monnett, *Tell Them We are Going Home*.

(1084) Citizens, near Porcupine Bottoms, Montana Territory (January 1879)[2]
— (1) Citizen Killed

(1085) Action, Fort Robinson, Nebraska (January 9 and 10, 1879)[3]
— Captain Henry W. Wessels, Jr. (3rd U.S. Cavalry)
     — 3rd U.S. Cavalry Co. A, C, E, F, H and L
— **5 KILLED**[4]
     — Private Frank Amish (Co. A 3rd U.S. Cavalry)
     — Private Peter Hulse (Co. A 3rd U.S. Cavalry)
     — Private Frank Schmidt (Co. A 3rd U.S. Cavalry)
     — Private William W. Everett (Co. H 3rd U.S. Cavalry) — d. 01-11-1879
     — Private William H. Good (Co. L 3rd U.S. Cavalry) — d. 01-10-1879

— **6 WOUNDED**[5]
     — Private James Emory (Co. C 3rd U.S. Cavalry)
         — *gunshot wound, right thigh, severe wound*
     — Private Thomas Ferguson (Co. E 3rd U.S. Cavalry)
         — *knife wound, chest, slight wound*
     — Private Edward Glavin (Co. E 3rd U.S. Cavalry)
         — *gunshot wound, right hand*
     — Private Daniel Trimany (Co. E 3rd U.S. Cavalry)
         — *gunshot wound, right arm, severe wound*
     — Private James McHale (Co. F 3rd U.S. Cavalry)
         — *gunshot wound, right thigh, slight wound*
     — Corporal Edward Pulver (Co. L 3rd U.S. Cavalry)
         — *gunshot wound, right arm, slight wound*

(1086) Action, twenty miles from Fort Robinson, Nebraska (January 11, 1879)[6]
— Captain Henry W. Wessels, Jr. (3rd U.S. Cavalry)
     — 3rd U.S. Cavalry Co. A, C, E, F, H and L
— **2 KILLED**[7]
     — Corporal Henry P. Orr (Co. A 3rd U.S. Cavalry) — d. 01-12-1879
     — Private Bernard Kelley (Co. E 3rd U.S. Cavalry) — d. 01-12-1879

— **1 WOUNDED**[8]
     — Farrier Peter N. Painter (Co. C 3rd U.S. Cavalry)
         — *gunshot wound, shoulder, slight wound*

(1087) Skirmish, Cormedos Mountains, New Mexico Territory (January 15, 1879)[9]
— 2nd Lieutenant Mathias W. Day (9th U.S. Cavalry)
     — 9th U.S. Cavalry Co. A

[2] Indians. Killed was Phillip Lynch. *Annual Report of Secretary of War (1879)*, 69.
[3] Indians. *Annual Report of Secretary of War (1879)*, 78-79, 408; Chronological List, 69; Heitman (Volume 2), 444; Record of Engagements, 83; Hoig, *Perilous Pursuit*, 170-180; Monnett, *Tell Them We Are Going Home*, 124-137. Chronological List and Heitman both list a single entry 9 to 22 January 1879.
[4] Reports of Diseases and Individual Cases, F 492; Register of Deaths Regular Army, 1860-1889 (Volume 9); 3rd U.S. Cavalry Regimental Return January 1877.
[5] Reports of Diseases and Individual Cases, F 492.
[6] Indians. Annual Report of Secretary of War (1879), 408; Chronological List, 69; Heitman (Volume 2), 444; Record of Engagements, 83; Hoig, *Perilous Pursuit*, 181-184; Monnett, *Tell Them We Are Going Home*, 142-159. Chronological List and Heitman both list a single entry 9 to 22 January 1879.
[7] Reports of Diseases and Individual Cases, F 492; Register of Deaths Regular Army, 1860-1889 (Volume 9).
[8] Reports of Diseases and Individual Cases, F 492.
[9] Indians. Chronological List, 69; Heitman (Volume 2), 444.

(1088) Action, thirty miles from Fort Robinson, Nebraska (January 17, 1879)[10]
    — Captain Henry W. Wessels, Jr. (3rd U.S. Cavalry)
        — 3rd U.S. Cavalry Co. A, C, E, F, H and L
    — **1 KILLED**[11]
        — Private Amos J. Barber (Co. H 3rd U.S. Cavalry)

(1089) Skirmish, near Bluff Station, Wyoming Territory (January 20, 1879)[12]
    — Major Andrew W. Evans (3rd U.S. Cavalry)
        — 3rd U.S. Cavalry Co. B and D

(1090) Action, forty miles from Fort Robinson, Nebraska (January 22, 1879)[13]
    — Captain Henry W. Wessels, Jr. (3rd U.S. Cavalry)
        — 3rd U.S. Cavalry Co. A, E, F and H
        — Detachment of Indian Scouts
    — **4 KILLED**[14]
        — Sergeant James Taggert (Co. A 3rd U.S. Cavalry)
        — Farrier George Brown (Co. A 3rd U.S. Cavalry)
        — Private George Nelson (Co. A 3rd U.S. Cavalry)
        — Private Henry A. Deblois (Co. H 3rd U.S. Cavalry) — d. 01-24-1879

    — **4 WOUNDED**[15]
        — Captain Henry W. Wessels, Jr. (3rd U.S. Cavalry)
            — *gunshot wound, head, severe wound*

        — First Sergeant Edward Ambrose (Co. E 3rd U.S. Cavalry)
            — *gunshot wound, arm, severe wound*
        — Sergeant William D. Reed (Co. H 3rd U.S. Cavalry)
            — *gunshot wound, thigh, severe wound*

        — Woman's Dress (Indian Scout)
            — *gunshot wound, arm, severe wound*

    — *Private Marcus Magerlein (Co. E 3rd U.S. Cavalry) received Certificate of Merit: For bravery in action against hostile Cheyenne Indians, dashing ahead of the troops under severe fire and being the first to gain a position on the edge of the Indian stronghold, whence he kept up a steady effective fire, being himself exposed to two fires; also great presence of mind saving the life of Corporal Krause (Co. A 5th U.S. Cavalry) in the same action (Bluff Station, Wyoming, January 22, 1879).*

[10] Indians. *Annual Report of Secretary of War (1879)*, 408-409; Chronological List, 69; Heitman (Volume 2), 444; Hoig, *Perilous Pursuit*, 185-186; Monnett, *Tell Them We Are Going Home*, 142-159.
[11] Reports of Diseases and Individual Cases, F 492; Register of Deaths Regular Army, 1860-1889 (Volume 9).
[12] Indians. Chronological List, 69; Heitman (Volume 2), 444; Record of Engagements, 84; Hoig, *Perilous Pursuit*, 187-188; Monnett, *Tell Them We Are Going Home*, 149.
[13] Indians. *Annual Report of Secretary of War (1879)*, 409; Chronological List, 69; Heitman (Volume 2), 444; Record of Engagements, 84; Hoig, *Perilous Pursuit*, 181-194; Monnett, *Tell Them We Are Going Home*, 142-159. Chronological List and Heitman both list a single entry January 9 to 22, 1879. Chronological List lists 3rd U.S. Cavalry Co. A, C, E, F, H, L. Record of Engagements lists 3rd U.S. Cavalry Co. A, E, F, I.
[14] Reports of Diseases and Individual Cases, F 492; Register of Deaths Regular Army, 1860-1889 (Volume 9).
[15] Reports of Diseases and Individual Cases, F 492.
[16] Indians. Chronological List, 69; Heitman (Volume 2), 444; Record of Engagements, 84.
[17] Indians. Killed was a herder. *Annual Report of Secretary of War (1879)*, 114; Chronological List, 69; Record of Engagements, 84.

(1091) Surrender of Victoria and 22 Indians, Ojo Caliente, New Mexico Territory (March 8, 1879)[16]

(1092) Citizens, fifty miles from Fort Ewell, Texas (March 15, 1879)[17]
— (1) Citizen Killed

(1093) Surrender of Little Wolf and 114 Indians, Box Elder Creek, Montana Territory (March 25, 1879)[18]

(1094) Citizens, Buffalo Station, Yellowstone River, Montana Territory (March 28, 1879)[19]
— (1) Citizen Killed

(1095) Citizens, near Mouth of Big Horn River, Montana Territory (March 28, 1879)[20]
— (1) Citizen Killed

(1096) Action, Mizpah Creek, Montana Territory (April 5, 1879)[21]
— Sergeant Dennis Kennedy (Signal Corps)
— 2nd U.S. Cavalry Detachment Co. E
— Signal Corps Detachment
— **1 KILLED**[22]
— Private Leo Baader (Co. E 2nd U.S. Cavalry)

— **1 WOUNDED**[23]
— Sergeant Dennis Kennedy (Signal Corps)
— *gunshot wound, right thigh, slight wound*

(1097) Citizens, near Powder River, Montana Territory (April 6, 1879)[24]
— (1) Citizen Killed

(1098) Skirmish, near Fort Keogh, Montana Territory (April 10, 1879)[25]
— Sergeant Thomas B. Glover (2nd U.S. Cavalry)
— 2nd U.S. Cavalry Detachments Co. B and I
— Detachment of Indian Scouts

— *Sergeant Thomas B. Glover (Co. B 2nd U.S. Cavalry) received MOH: While in charge of small scouting parties, fought, charged, surrounded, and captured war parties of Sioux Indians (Mizpah Creek, Montana, April 10, 1879; Pumpkin Creek, Montana, February 10. 1880).*

(1099) Action, near Careless Creek, Musselshell River, Montana Territory (April 17, 1879)[26]
— 2nd Lieutenant Samuel H. Loder (7th U.S. Infantry)
— 3rd U.S. Infantry Detachment Co. K
— 7th U.S. Infantry Detachment Co. D
— Detachment of Indian Scouts
— **2 KILLED**[27]

[18] Indians. *Annual Report of Secretary of War (1879)*, 57-58; Chronological List, 69; Heitman (Volume 2), 444; Record of Engagements, 84; Monnett, *Tell Them We Are Going Home*, 165-169.
[19] Indians. Killed was David Henderson. Chronological List, 69; Record of Engagements, 85.
[20] Indians. Killed was H.D. Johnson. Chronological List, 69; Record of Engagements, 85.
[21] Indians. *Annual Report of Secretary of War (1879)*, 52-53, 409; Chronological List, 69; Heitman (Volume 2), 444; Record of Engagements, 85; Brown, *Plainsmen of the Yellowstone*, 321; Hoig, *Perilous Pursuit*, 202; Monnett, *Tell Them We Are Going Home*, 170. Chronological List lists 2nd U.S. Cavalry Detachment.
[22] Reports of Diseases and Individual Cases, F 493; Register of Deaths Regular Army, 1860-1889 (Volume 9).
[23] Reports of Diseases and Individual Cases, F 493.
[24] Indians. Killed was rancher named Sebbesze. *Annual Report of Secretary of War (1879)*, 69; Chronological List, 69; Record of Engagements, 85.
[25] Indians. *Annual Report of Secretary of War (1879)*, 53; Chronological List, 69; Heitman (Volume 2), 444; Record of Engagements, 85; Brown, *Plainsmen of the Yellowstone*, 321-322; Hoig, *Perilous Pursuit*, 202; Monnett, *Tell Them We Are Going Home*, 170. Chronological List lists 2nd U.S. Cavalry Detachment Co. B.
[26] Indians. *Annual Report of Secretary of War (1879)*, 53; Chronological List, 69; Heitman (Volume 2), 444; Record of Engagements, 85. Chronological List lists 3rd U.S. Infantry Detachment Co. K; 7th U.S. Infantry Detachments Co. D, E; Detachment of Indian Scouts.
[27] Chronological List, 69.

— Indian Scout
— Indian Scout

— 1 WOUNDED[28]
— Indian Scout

(1100) Skirmish, Countryman's Ranch, Montana Territory (April 22, 1879)[29]
— UNKNOWN
— Detachment of Indian Scouts

(1101) Citizens, between Fort Ewell and Corpus Christi, Texas (May 1, 1879)[30]
— (1) Citizen Killed

(1102) Citizens, near Fort McIntosh, Texas (May 1, 1879)[31]
— (1) Citizen Killed

(1103) Action, Miembres Mountains, New Mexico Territory (May 2, 1879)[32]
— UNKNOWN
— Detachment of Indian Scouts
— 1 KILLED[33]
— Lewis Wellington (Indian Scout)

(1104) Citizen, near Van Horn's Wells, Texas (May 18, 1879)[34]
— (1) Citizen Killed

(1105) Action, Black Range, Miembres Mountains, New Mexico Territory (May 29, 1879)[35]
— Captain Charles D. Beyer (9th U.S. Cavalry)
— 9th U.S. Cavalry Detachments Co. C and I
— Detachment of Indian Scouts
— 1 KILLED[36]
— Private Frank Dorsey (Co. C 9th Cavalry)

— 2 WOUNDED[37]
— Private George H. Moore (Co. C 9th U.S. Cavalry)
— *gunshot wound, right hip, severe wound*
— Private John Scott (Co. I 9th U.S. cavalry)
— *gunshot wound, abdomen, slight wound*

— *Sergeant Thomas Boyne (Co. C 9th U.S. Cavalry) received MOH: Bravery in action (Miembres Mountains, New Mexico, May 29, 1879; Cuchillo Negro River near Ojo Caliente, New Mexico, September 29, 1879).*

---

[28] Chronological List, 69.
[29] Indians. Chronological List, 69; Heitman (Volume 2), 444; Record of Engagements, 85.
[30] Indians. Killed was a teamster. *Annual Report of Secretary of War (1879)*, 114; Chronological List, 69; Record of Engagements, 86.
[31] Indians. Killed was a teamster. Chronological List, 69.
[32] Indians. *Annual Report of Secretary of War (1879)*, 409; Chronological List, 69; Heitman (Volume 2), 444. Chronological List and Heitman both lists 30 April 1879.
[33] Killed was Lewis Wellington "a negro enlisted in the Navajo Scouts." Reports of Diseases and Individual Cases, F 495; Register of Deaths Regular Army, 1860-1889 (Volume 9).
[34] Indians. Killed was John Clarkson. *Annual Report of Secretary of War (1879)*, 114; Record of Engagements, 86.
[35] Indians. *Annual Report of Secretary of War (1879)*, 409; Chronological List, 69; Heitman (Volume 2), 444; Record of Engagements, 86; Billington, *New Mexico's Buffalo Soldiers*, 88-89; Burton, *Black, Buckskin and Blue*, 157-158; Stout, *Apache Lightning*, 88; Thrapp, *Victorio*, 216. Chronological List lists 9th U.S. Cavalry Detachments Co. C, I.
[36] Reports of Diseases and Individual Cases, F 494; Register of Deaths Regular Army, 1860-1889 (Volume 9).
[37] Reports of Diseases and Individual Cases, F 494.

— *2nd Lieutenant Henry H. Wright (9th U.S. Cavalry) brevet promotion to 1st Lieutenant for gallant service in actions against Indians (Florida Mountains, New Mexico, January 24, 1877; Sacramento Mountains, New Mexico, July 29, 1878 and Miembres Mountains, New Mexico, May 29, 1879).*

(1106) Citizens, Colson's Ranch, near Camp Wood, Texas (June 1, 1879)[38]
— (3) Citizens Killed

(1107) Skirmish, Tonto Basin, Arizona Territory (June 25, 1879)[39]
— 1st Lieutenant Frederick Von Schrader (12th U.S. Infantry)
— Detachment of Indian Scouts

(1108) Action, Alkali Creek, Montana Territory (June 29, 1879)[40]
— UNKNOWN
— Detachment of Indian Scouts
— **1 KILLED**[41]
— Indian Scout

— **4 WOUNDED**[42]
— Indian Scout
— Indian Scout
— Indian Scout
— Indian Scout

(1109) Citizens, Headwaters of North Concho River, Texas (June 30, 1879)[43]
— (1) Citizen Killed

(1110) Citizen, Deutscheurer Ranch, northwest of Fort Davis, Texas (July 14, 1879)[44]
— (1) Citizen Killed

(1111) Action, Milk River, Montana Territory (July 17, 1879)[45]
— Colonel Nelson A. Miles (5th U.S. Infantry)
— 2nd U.S. Cavalry Co. A, B, C, E, G, I and M
— 5th U.S. Infantry Co. A, B, C, G, H, I and K
— 6th U.S. Infantry Co. C and K
— Detachment of Indian Scouts
— **3 KILLED**[46]
— Magpie (Indian Scout)
— Medicine Stand (Indian Scout)
— Shadow Comes Out (Indian Scout) — d. 07-18-1879

---

[38] Indians. Killed were the wife and two daughters of Nick Colson. *Annual Report of Secretary of War (1879)*, 114; Chronological List, 69; Record of Engagements, 86.

[39] Indians. Chronological List, 69; Heitman (Volume 2), 444.

[40] Indians. Chronological List, 69; Heitman (Volume 2), 445; Record of Engagements, 86.

[41] Chronological List, 69.

[42] Chronological List, 69.

[43] Indians. Killed was a Texas Ranger named W.B. Anglin. *Annual Report of Secretary of War (1879)*, 114; Chronological List, 69; Record of Engagements, 86; Nye, *Carbine and Lance*, 237-239

[44] Indians. Killed was Juan Jose. *Annual Report of Secretary of War (1879)*, 114; Record of Engagements, 86.

[45] Indians. *Annual Report of Secretary of War (1879)*, 62, 71-72; *Annual Report of Secretary of War (1880)*, 519; Chronological List, 69; Heitman (Volume 2), 445; Record of Engagements, 87; Hoig, *Perilous Pursuit*, 231; Miles, *Personal Recollections*, 306-309.

[46] Reports of Diseases and Individual Cases, F 496; Register of Deaths Regular Army, 1860-1889 (Volume 11).

— **3 WOUNDED**[47]
— Private Gene Etienne (Co. C 2nd U.S. Cavalry)
— *gunshot wound, shoulder, slight wound*
— Private P.M. Hardimann (Co. C 2nd U.S. Cavalry)
— *gunshot wound, shoulder, slight wound*

— Blue Cloud (Indian Scout)
— *gunshot wound, thigh, severe wound*

(1112) Skirmish, near Camp Loder, Montana Territory (July 19, 1879)[48]
— 1st Lieutenant John T. Van Orsdale (7th U.S. Infantry)
— 7th U.S. Infantry Detachment Co. I

(1113) Action, near Salt Lake or Sulphur Springs, Texas (July 25, 1879)[49]
— Captain Michael L. Courtney (25th U.S. Infantry)
— 10th U.S. Cavalry Detachment Co. H
— 25th U.S. Infantry Detachment Co. H
— **2 WOUNDED**[50]
— Corporal J.W. Webb (Co. F 10th U.S. Cavalry)
— *gunshot wound, right thigh, slight wound*
— Private G.W. Foster (Co. F 10th U.S. Cavalry)
— *gunshot wound, thorax, slight wound*

(1114) Action, Big Creek, Idaho Territory (July 29, 1879)[51]
— 1st Lieutenant Henry Catley (2nd U.S. Infantry)
— 2nd U.S. Infantry Co. C, Detachment Co. K
— **2 WOUNDED**[52]
— Private James Doyes (2nd U.S. Infantry)
— *gunshot wound, left thigh, slight wound*
— Private William A.R. Hollis (2nd U.S. Infantry)
— *gunshot wound, left ankle, fracture, severe wound*

— *Private John Benson (Co. K 2nd U.S. Infantry) received Certificate of Merit: For bravery in action against hostile Sheepeater Indians, in voluntarily remaining with the wounded when the command had retreated until a detail had been sent to their relief and for bravery in campaign (Big Creek, Idaho, July 29, 1879 and August 20, 1879).*

(1115) Surrender of Fast Bull and 57 Indians, Missouri River near Poplar Creek, Montana Territory (August 10, 1879)[53]

(1116) Citizens, Raines Ranch, Idaho Territory (August 15, 1879)[54]
— (3) Citizens Killed

[47] Reports of Diseases and Individual Cases, F 496.
[48] Indians. *Annual Report of Secretary of War (1879)*, 54; Chronological List, 70; Heitman (Volume 2), 445. Chronological List lists 7th U.S. Infantry Detachment.
[49] Indians. *Annual Report of Secretary of War (1880)*, 519; Chronological List, 70; Heitman (Volume 2), 445; Record of Engagements, 86; Nankivell, *Buffalo Soldier Regiment*, 30; Smith; *Old Army in Texas*, 162; Wooster, *Frontier Crossroads*, 100.
[50] Reports of Diseases and Individual Cases, F 497.
[51] Indians. *Annual Report of Secretary of War (1879)*, 158; *Annual Report of Secretary of War (1880)*, 519; Chronological List, 70; Heitman (Volume 2), 445; Arnold, *Indian Wars of Idaho*, 229-231; Russell, *One Hundred and Three Fights*, 149-150.
[52] Reports of Diseases and Individual Cases, F 498.
[53] Indians. *Annual Report of Secretary of War (1879)*, 63, 73; Chronological List, 70; Record of Engagements, 87-88.
[54] Indians. Killed were James Edwards, James F. Rains and Albert Webber. *Annual Report of Secretary of War (1879)*, 159; Arnold, *Indian Wars of Idaho*, 238-239; Glassley, *Indian Wars of the Pacific Northwest*, 245-246.

(1117) Skirmish, Big Creek, Idaho Territory (August 19, 1879)[55]
— 2nd Lieutenant William C. Brown (1st U.S. Cavalry)
— 2nd Lieutenant Edmund S. Farrow (21st U.S. Infantry)
— Detachment of Indian Scouts

— 2nd Lieutenant William C. Brown (1st U.S. Cavalry) brevet promotion to 1st Lieutenant for gallant service in action against Indians (Big Creek, Idaho, August 19, 1879) and in reconnaissance (August 17, 1879 and September 25, 1879).

— 2nd Lieutenant Edmund S. Farrow (21st U.S. Infantry) brevet promotion to 1st Lieutenant for gallant service in actions against Indians (Big Creek, Idaho, August 19, 1879 and Big Meadows, Idaho, October 8, 1879).

(1118) Action, Soldier Bar or Big Creek, Idaho Territory (August 20, 1879)[56]
— Corporal Charles B. Hardin (1st U.S. Cavalry)
— Sergeant (2nd U.S. Infantry)
— 1st U.S. Cavalry Detachments Co. D and G
— 2nd U.S. Infantry Detachments Co. C and K
— 1 KILLED[57]
— Private Harry Eagan (Co. C 2nd U.S. Infantry)

— Private John Benson (Co. K 2nd U.S. Infantry) received Certificate of Merit: For bravery in action against hostile Sheepeater Indians, in voluntarily remaining with the wounded when the command had retreated until a detail had been sent to their relief and for bravery in campaign (Big Creek, Idaho, July 29, 1879 and August 20, 1879).

(1119) Skirmish, Salmon River, Idaho Territory (August 20, 1879)[58]
— Captain Reuben F. Bernard (1st U.S. Cavalry)
— 1st U.S. Cavalry Co. D and G

(1120) Engagement, Ojo Caliente, New Mexico Territory (September 4, 1879)[59]
— Sergeant Silas S. Chapman (9th U.S. Cavalry)
— 9th U.S. Cavalry Detachment Co. E
— 8 KILLED[60]
— Sergeant Silas S. Chapman (Co. E 9th Cavalry)
— Private Silas Graddon (Co. E 9th Cavalry)
— Private Lafayette Hoke (Co. E 9th Cavalry)
— Private William Murphy (Co. E 9th Cavalry)
— Private Abram Percival (Co. E 9th Cavalry)

— (3) Citizens

[55] Indians. Heitman (Volume 2), 445; Arnold, *Indian Wars of Idaho*, 239-240; Russell, *One Hundred and Three Fights*, 149-150.
[56] Indians. *Annual Report of Secretary of War (1879)*, 161; *Annual Report of Secretary of War (1880)*, 519; Chronological List, 70; Heitman (Volume 2), 445; Nelson, *Fighting for Paradise*, 236; Russell, *One Hundred and Three Fights*, 151-152. Heitman lists 2nd U.S. Infantry Co. C, Detachment Co. K.
[57] Reports of Diseases and Individual Cases, F 499; Register of Deaths Regular Army, 1860-1889 (Volume 10).
[58] Indians. Chronological List, 70; Heitman (Volume 2), 445; Arnold, *Indian Wars of Idaho*, 240; Russell, *One Hundred and Three Fights*, 151-152.
[59] Indians. *Annual Report of Secretary of War (1880)*, 86; Chronological List, 70; Heitman (Volume 2), 445; Record of Engagements, 92; Billington, *New Mexico's Buffalo Soldiers*, 89; Lockwood, *Apache Indians*, 230; Rathbun, *New Mexico Frontier Military Place Names*, 132-133; Stout, *Apache Lightning*, 93-94; Thrapp, *Victorio*, 220-237.
[60] Register of Deaths Regular Army, 1860-1889 (Volume 12); Chronological List, 70.

(1121) Citizens, McEver's Ranch, New Mexico Territory (September 10, 1879)[61]
— (7) Citizens Killed

(1122) Citizens, Arroyo Seco, New Mexico Territory (September 10, 1879)[62]
— (2) Citizens Killed

(1123) Skirmish, Van Horn Mountains, Texas (September 16, 1879)[63]
— Captain Michael L. Courtney (25th U.S. Infantry)
— 10th U.S. Cavalry Detachment Co. H
— 25th U.S. Infantry Co. H

(1124) Citizens, Black Range, New Mexico Territory (September 17, 1879)[64]
— (2) Citizens Killed

(1125) Action, Las Animas River, New Mexico Territory (September 18, 1879)[65]
— Captain Charles D. Beyer (9th U.S. Cavalry)
— 9th U.S. Cavalry Co. A, B, C and G
— Detachment of Indian Scouts
— **5 KILLED**[66]
— Private Jeremiah Crump (Co. B 9th U.S. Cavalry)
— Private Deter Haines (Co. G 9th U.S. Cavalry)

— Barrajo (Indian Scout)
— Sam (Indian Scout)

— Jack Hagan (Citizen)

— **1 WOUNDED**[67]
— Private Alfred Freeland (Co. B 9th U.S. Cavalry)
— *gunshot wound, right thigh, severe wound*

— *2nd Lieutenant Matthias W. Day (9th U.S. Cavalry) received MOH: Advanced alone into the enemy's lines and carried a wounded soldier of his command under a hot fire after he had been ordered to retreat (Las Animas Canyon, New Mexico, September 18, 1879).*

— *Sergeant John Denny (Co. C 9th U.S. Cavalry) received MOH: Removed a wounded comrade, under a heavy fire, to a place of safety (Las Animas Canyon, New Mexico, September 18, 1879).*

— *2nd Lieutenant Robert Temple Emmet (9th U.S. Cavalry) received MOH: Lt. Emmet was in G Troop which was sent to relieve a detachment of soldiers under attack by hostile Apaches. During a flank attack on the Indian camp, made to divert the hostiles, Lt. Emmet and five of his men became surrounded when the Indians returned to defend their camp. Finding that the Indians were making for a position from which they could direct*

---

[61] Indians. Killed were Steve Hanlon, Thomas Huges, Dr. Williams, I. Chavez, a man named Thornton, a man named Pressier, and a man named Green. *Annual Report of Secretary of War (1880)*, 106; Chronological List, 70; Record of Engagements, 92; Leckie, *Buffalo Soldiers*, 212; Rathbun, *New Mexico Frontier Military Place Names*, 115-116; Stout, *Apache Lightning*, 92; Sweeney, *Cochise to Geronimo*, 140; Thrapp, *Victorio*, 237.
[62] Indians. Killed were Refugia Arvies and Jose Morena. *Annual Report of Secretary of War (1880)*, 106; Chronological List, 70; Rathbun, *New Mexico Frontier Military Place Names*, 115; Leckie, *Buffalo Soldiers*, 212.
[63] Indians. Chronological List, 70; Heitman (Volume 2), 445; Smith, *Old Army in Texas*, 162; Wooster, *Frontier Crossroads*, 100. Heitman lists 10th U.S. Cavalry Detachment Co. H.
[64] Indians. *Annual Report of Secretary of War (1880)*, 106; Chronological List, 70.
[65] Indians. *Annual Report of Secretary of War (1880)*, 519; Chronological List, 70; Heitman (Volume 2), 445; Record of Engagements, 92; Billington, *New Mexico's Buffalo Soldiers*, 90-91; Burton, *Black, Buckskin and Blue*, 159-160; Rathbun, *New Mexico Frontier Military Place Names*, 102-104; Thrapp, *Victorio*, 239-241. Chronological List lists 9th U.S. Cavalry Co. A, B, C, G.
[66] Reports of Diseases and Individual Cases, F 500; Register of Deaths Regular Army, 1860-1889 (Volume 12).
[67] Reports of Diseases and Individual Cases, F 500.

their fire on the retreating troop, the Lieutenant held his point with his party until the soldiers reached the safety of a canyon. Lt. Emmet then continued to hold his position while his party recovered their horses. The enemy force consisted of approximately 200 (Las Animas Canyon, New Mexico, September 18, 1879).

(1126) Action, Miembres Mountains, New Mexico Territory (September 19, 1879)[68]
— 2nd Lieutenant Robert T. Emmett (9th U.S. Cavalry)
— Detachment of Indian Scouts
— **2 KILLED**[69]
— Indian Scout
— Indian Scout

(1127) Skirmish, Middle Fork of Salmon River, Idaho Territory (September 21 and 22, 1879)[70]
— 2nd Lieutenant William C. Brown (1st U.S. Cavalry)
— 2nd Lieutenant Edward S. Farrow (21st U.S. Infantry)
— Detachment of Indian Scouts

— *2nd Lieutenant William C. Brown (1st U.S. Cavalry) brevet promotion to 1st Lieutenant for gallant service in action against Indians (Big Creek, Idaho, August 19, 1879) and in reconnaissance (Idaho, August 17, 1879 and September 25, 1879).*

(1128) Skirmish, Black Range Mountains, New Mexico Territory (September 23, 1879)[71]
— 2nd Lieutenant Eugene D. Dimmick (9th U.S. Cavalry)
— Detachment of Indian Scouts

— *2nd Lieutenant Eugene D. Dimmick (9th U.S. Cavalry) brevet promotion to Captain for gallant service in action against Indians (Black Range Mountains, New Mexico, September 23, 1879).*

(1129) Citizens, White River Agency, Colorado (September 29, 1879)[72]
— (11) Citizens Killed

(1130) Engagement, Milk River, Colorado (September 29 to October 1, 1879)[73]
— Major Thomas T. Thornburgh (4th U.S. Infantry)
— Captain John S. Payne (5th U.S. Cavalry)
— 3rd U.S. Cavalry Co. E
— 5th U.S. Cavalry Co. D and F
— **13 KILLED**[74]
— Major Thomas T. Thornburgh (4th U.S. Infantry)

— Private Dominick Cuff (Co. E 3rd U.S. Cavalry)
— Private Michael Lynch (Co. D 5th U.S. Cavalry)
— Private Thomas Mooney (Co. D 5th U.S. Cavalry)
— Private Charles Wright (Co. D 5th U.S. Cavalry)

[68] Indians. Chronological List, 70; Heitman (Volume 2), 445.
[69] Chronological List, 70.
[70] Indians. Heitman (Volume 2), 445; Arnold, *Indian Wars of Idaho*, 242-247; Nelson, *Fighting for Paradise*, 236.
[71] Indians. Webb, *Chronological List of Engagements*, 87.
[72] Indians. Killed were agent Nathan C. Meeker, Frank Dresser, Harry Dresser, Carl Goldstein, Julius Moore, Wilmer Eskridge, Arthur Thompson, Shadrach Price, William Post, Fred Shepard and George Eaton. Arvilla Meeker, Josie Meeker, Flora Price, Johnnie Price and May Price were all kidnapped and eventually recovered. *Annual Report of Secretary of War (1880)*, 82-83; Michno, *Fate Worse Than Death*, 442-449; Miller, *Hollow Victory*, 143; Sprague, *Massacre*, 226-238.
[73] Indians. *Annual Report of Secretary of War (1880)*, 79-83; 519-520; Chronological List, 70; Heitman (Volume 2), 445; Record of Engagements, 88-90; Miller, *Hollow Victory*, 53-93; Sprague, *Massacre*, 209-217. Heitman lists 29 September to 5 October 1879.
[74] Reports of Diseases and Individual Cases, F 501; Register of Deaths Regular Army, 1860-1889 (Volume 10); Miller, *Hollow Victory*, 178.

— First Sergeant John Dolan (Co. F 5th U.S. Cavalry)
— Private John Burns (Co. F 5th U.S. Cavalry)
— Private Michael Firestone (Co. F 5th U.S. Cavalry)
— Private Samuel McKee (Co. F 5th U.S. Cavalry)
— Wagoner Amos D. Miller (Co. F 5th U.S. Cavalry)

— Guide Charlie G. Lowry (Citizen)
— Wagon Master William McKinstry (Citizen)
— Teamster Thomas McGuire (Citizen)

— 44 WOUNDED[75]

— Captain John S. Payne (Co. F 5th U.S. Cavalry)
   — *gunshot wound, left shoulder, arm, abrasion to abdomen*
— 2nd Lieutenant James V.S. Paddock (Co. D 5th U.S. Cavalry)
   — *gunshot wounds, right thigh, slight wounds*

— Sergeant Allen Lupton (Co. E 3rd U.S. Cavalry)
   — *gunshot wound, right thigh, slight wound*
— Sergeant James Montgomery (Co. E 3rd U.S. Cavalry)
   — *gunshot wound, left ankle, fracture, severe wound*
— Corporal Charles Eichwurgel (Co. E 3rd U.S. Cavalry)
   — *gunshot wound, right, left arms, slight wounds*
— Corporal Frank Hunter (Co. E 3rd U.S. Cavalry)
   — *gunshot wound, right foot, slight wound*
— Farrier William M. Schubert (Co. E 3rd U.S. Cavalry)
   — *gunshot wound, left thigh, arm, slight wounds*
— Private Joseph Budka (Co. E 3rd U.S. Cavalry)
   — *gunshot wound, neck, slight wound*
— Private William H. Clark (Co. E 3rd U.S. Cavalry)
   — *gunshot wound, left side*
— Private James Conway (Co. E 3rd U.S. Cavalry)
   — *gunshot wound, left temple, slight wound*
— Private John Crowley (Co. E 3rd U.S. Cavalry)
   — *gunshot wound, left ear, slight wound*
— Private John Donovan (Co. E 3rd U.S. Cavalry)
   — *gunshot wound, left foot, slight wound*
— Private Orlando H. Duren (Co. E 3rd U.S. Cavalry)
   — *gunshot wound, right arm, slight wound*
— Private Thomas Furgeson (Co. E 3rd U.S. Cavalry)
   — *gunshot wounds, left side, left hand, slight wounds*
— Private Marcus Hansen (Co. E 3rd U.S. Cavalry)
   — *gunshot wound, back, slight wound*

---

[75] Reports of Diseases and Individual Cases, F 501; Miller, *Hollow Victory*, 178-180.

— Private Edward Lavalle (Co. E 3rd U.S. Cavalry)
    — *gunshot wound, right ankle, slight wound*
— Private Thomas Lewis (Co. E 3rd U.S. Cavalry)
    — *gunshot wound, right ankle, slight wound*
— Private John Mahoney (Co. E 3rd U.S. Cavalry)
    — *gunshot wound, right leg, fracture, severe wound*
— Private Willard W. Mitchell (Co. E 3rd U.S. Cavalry)
    — *gunshot wound, left leg, slight wound*
— Private Thomas McNamara (Co. E 3rd U.S. Cavalry)
    — *gunshot wound, right thigh, slight wound*
— Private Joseph Patterson (Co. E 3rd U.S. Cavalry)
    — *gunshot wound, left leg, slight wound*

— Sergeant John S. Lawton (Co. D 5th U.S. Cavalry)
    — *crushed right foot*
— Private Frederick Bernhardt (Co. D 5th U.S. Cavalry)
    — *gunshot wound, left hand, fracture, severe wound*
— Private N. H. Heeney (Co. D 5th U.S. Cavalry)
    — *gunshot wound, right leg, slight wound*
— Private Richard Lynch (Co. D 5th U.S. Cavalry)
    — *gunshot wound, face, slight wound*
— Private Ernest Muller (Co. D 5th U.S. Cavalry)
    — *gunshot wound, scalp wound, slight wound*

— Sergeant John Merrill (Co. F 5th U.S. Cavalry)
    — *gunshot wound, left shoulder, slight wound*
— Trumpeter John McDonald (Co. F 5th U.S. Cavalry)
    — *gunshot wound, left thigh, slight wound*
— Trumpeter Frederick Sutcliffe (Co. F 5th U.S. Cavalry)
    — *gunshot wound, left leg, slight wound*
— Private William Esser (Co. F 5th U.S. Cavalry)
    — *gunshot wounds, face, back of neck, mouth, cheek, slight wounds*
— Private James F. Gibbs (Co. F 5th U.S. Cavalry)
    — *gunshot wound, left foot, fracture, severe wound*
— Private John Hoaxey (Co. F 5th U.S. Cavalry)
    — *gunshot wound, left leg, slight wound*
— Private Emil Kussman (Co. F 5th U.S. Cavalry)
    — *gunshot wound, left arm, fracture, severe wound*
— Private Eugene Patterson (Co. F 5th U.S. Cavalry)
    — *gunshot wound, right ankle, slight wound*
— Private Walter Peterson (Co. F 5th U.S. Cavalry)
— Private Eugene Schickedonz (Co. F 5th U.S. Cavalry)
    — *gunshot wound, right forearm, slight wound*
— Private Frank E. Simmons (Co. F 5th U.S. Cavalry)
    — *gunshot wound, chest, slight wound*
— Private Gottleib Steiger (Co. F 5th U.S. Cavalry)
    — *gunshot wound, right leg, slight wound*

— Acting Assistant Surgeon Robert Grimes (Citizen)
    — *gunshot wound, left shoulder, slight wound*
— Sutler John C. Davis (Citizen)
    — *gunshot wound, left foot, slight wound*
— Teamster Thomas Kane (Citizen)
    — *gunshot wound, left breast, slight wound*

— Teamster Frederick Nelson (Citizen)
    — *gunshot wounds, left shoulder, leg, slight wounds*
— Blacksmith Rodney (Citizen)
— Blacksmith Robin Saunder (Citizen)
    — *right leg*

— *Private John Brennan (Co. E 3rd U.S. Cavalry) received Certificate of Merit: For great gallantry in action against hostile Ute Indians, being everywhere in the thickest of the fight and by his coolness saving the lives of the helpless wounded (Milk River, Colorado, September 29, 1879).*

— *Private Clarence E. Carpenter (Co. F 5th U.S. Cavalry) received Certificate of Merit: For conspicuous gallantry in action against hostile Ute Indians. He went to the relief of his captain who was dismounted while leading a charge, and under a severe fire from the enemy held the horse until the captain was able to mount, thus doubtless saving his life (Milk River, Colorado, September 29, 1879).*

— *Private Charles Clark (Co. F 5th U.S. Cavalry) received Certificate of Merit: For conspicuous gallantry displayed during an engagement with hostile Ute Indians, he voluntarily went to the rescue of a wounded comrade who had fallen near the enemy's lines and assisted in carrying hum until life was extinct, although exposed to a severe crossfire from the Indians, without shelter or protection of any kind (Milk River, Colorado, September 29, 1879).*

— *Private Kenrick B. Combs (Co. F 5th U.S. Cavalry) received Certificate of Merit: For conspicuous gallantry in action against hostile Ute Indians, he voluntarily went to the rescue of a wounded comrade fallen near the enemy's lines and assisted in carrying him through a heavy crossfire of the enemy (Milk River, Colorado, September 29, 1879).*

— *Private Henry B. Combs (Co. F 5th U.S. Cavalry) received Distinguished Service Medal: For gallantry in action (Milk River, Colorado, September 29, 1879).*[76]

— *Private John Crowley (Co. E 3rd U.S. Cavalry) received Certificate of Merit: For great gallantry in action against hostile Ute Indians, being wounded, saving the lives of many men by determinedly resisting the enemy (Milk River, Colorado, September 29, 1879).*

— *Captain Francis S. Dodge (9th U.S. Cavalry) brevet promotion to Major for gallant service in action against Indians (Milk River, Colorado, September 29 to October 1, 1879).*

— *Private Samuel P. Eakle (Co. F 5th U.S. Cavalry) received Certificate of Merit: For conspicuous gallantry in action against hostile Ute Indians, when left alone in an exposed position, surrounded by Indians he resisted their attack and on foot fought his way to the command more than a mile distant (Milk Creek, Colorado, September 29, 1879).*

[76] The medal was received in lieu of the Certificate of Merit under the provisions of the act of Congress, approved 9 July 1918. *American Decorations (1862-1926).*

— *Sergeant Edward P. Grimes (Co. F 5th U.S. Cavalry) received MOH: The command being almost out of ammunition and surrounded on three sides by the enemy, he voluntarily brought up a supply under heavy fire at almost point blank range (Milk River, Colorado, September 29, to October 5, 1879).*

— *Private Samuel W. Hagerman (Co. H 4th U.S. Infantry) received Certificate of Merit: For special bravery and good conduct, in action against hostile Ute Indians, while driving an ambulance containing two sick soldiers and cut off by the train by ten or twelve Indians, he fought his way through, delivering the sick at the train, then volunteered to charge the bluffs with the men of troop D, 5th Cavalry, doing good fighting, and exhibiting conspicuous coolness in building breastworks and fighting off the fire which started to burn out the troops (Milk Creek, Colorado, September 29, 1879).*

— *Private Thomas Hogan (Co. E 3rd U.S. Cavalry) received Certificate of Merit: For bravery in action against hostile Ute Indians (Milk River, Colorado, September 29, 1879).*

— *Private Samuel Klingensmith(Co. F 5th U.S. Cavalry) received Certificate of Merit: For gallantry in action with Indians, in voluntarily carrying a wounded comrade from near the enemy's lines, through a severe crossfire (Milk River, Colorado, September 29, 1879).*

— *Sergeant John S. Lawton (Co. D 5th U.S. Cavalry) received MOH: Coolness and steadiness under fire, volunteered to accompany a small detachment on a very dangerous mission (Milk River, Colorado, September 29, 1879).*

— *Private Thomas Lewis (Co. E 3rd U.S. Cavalry) received Certificate of Merit: For conspicuous bravery before hostile Ute Indians (Milk River, Colorado, September 29, 1879).*

— *Private Thomas Lewis (Co. E 3rd U.S. Cavalry) received Distinguished Service Medal: For conspicuous bravery before hostile Ute Indians (Milk River, Colorado, September 29, 1879).*[77]

— *Private John Mahoney (Co. E 3rd U.S. Cavalry) received Certificate of Merit: For conspicuous gallantry in action against hostile Ute Indians, in fighting alone and unaided, for ¾ of an hour and over every inch of the ground for nearly a mile, a force ten times their own number (Milk River, Colorado, September 29, 1879).*

— *Private John Maloney (Co. E 3rd U.S. Cavalry) received Certificate of Merit: For great gallantry in action against hostile Ute Indians, being wounded, saving the lives of many men by determinedly resisting the enemy (Milk River, Colorado, September 29, 1879).*

— *Private John McDonald (Co. F 5th U.S. Cavalry) received Certificate of Merit: For gallantry and great coolness in action against Ute Indians, going alone and unaided to the assistance of a wounded comrade, giving him his horse and fighting his way to the wagons on foot, though wounded in the hip (Milk Creek, Colorado, September 29, 1879).*

---

[77] The medal was received in lieu of the Certificate of Merit under the provisions of the act of Congress, approved 9 July 1918. *American Decorations (1862-1926).*

— Private Thomas McNamara (Co. E 3rd U.S. Cavalry) received Certificate of Merit: For gallantry in action with Indians, though wounded in the right thigh, and having had his horse shot under him, and having been ordered to the rear, he remained in the fight, and, under heavy fire, he risked his own life to aid a severely wounded comrade (Milk River, September 29, 1879).

— Sergeant John Merrill (Co. F 5th U.S. Cavalry) received MOH: Though painfully wounded, he remained on duty and rendered gallant and valuable service (Milk River, Colorado, September 29, 1879).

— Corporal George Moquin (Co. F 5th U.S. Cavalry) received MOH: Gallantry in action (Milk River, Colorado, September 29, 1879 to October 5, 1879).

— Corporal Edward F. Murphy (Co. D 5th U.S. Cavalry) received MOH: Gallantry in action (Milk River, Colorado, September 29, 1879).

— Private Eugene Patterson (Co. F 5th U.S. Cavalry) received Certificate of Merit: For conspicuous gallantry in action against hostile Ute Indians, although dismounted and wounded, he fought his way alone to the wagons, over a mile distant, and hemmed in by the enemy, broke up the arms abandoned by the wounded to keep them from falling into the hands of the Indians in a serviceable condition; also rendering valuable service in subsequent siege, though severely suffering from his wounds (Milk Creek, Colorado, September 29, 1879).

— Private Joseph Patterson (Co. E 3rd U.S. Cavalry) received Certificate of Merit: For gallantry in action with Indians, in covering the retreat of the wounded and holding a much superior force of the enemy in check until severely wounded in the left leg (Milk River, Colorado, September 29, 1879).

— Captain John S. Payne (5th U.S. Cavalry) brevet promotion to Major for gallant service in action against Indians (Milk River, Colorado, September 29 to October 1, 1879).

— Blacksmith Wilhelm O. Philipsen (Co. D 5th U.S. Cavalry) received MOH: With nine others voluntarily attacked and captures a strong position held by Indians (Milk River, Colorado, September 29, 1879).

— Sergeant John A. Poppe (Co. F 5th U.S. Cavalry) received MOH: Gallantry in action (Milk River, Colorado, September 29 to October 1, 1879).

— Corporal Hampton M. Roach (Co. F 5th U.S. Cavalry) received MOH: Erected breastworks under fire, also kept the command supplied with water three consecutive nights while exposed to fire from ambushed Indians at close range (Milk River, Colorado, September 29 to October 5, 1879).

— First Sergeant Jacob Widmer (Co. D 5th U.S. Cavalry) received MOH: Volunteered to accompany a small detachment on a very dangerous mission (Milk River, Colorado, September 29, 1879).

"This command, composed of three companies of cavalry, was met a mile south of Milk River by several hundred Ute Indians who attacked and drove us to the wagon train with great loss. It becomes my painful duty to announce the death of [Major Thomas T. Thornburgh], who fell in harness; the painful but not serious wounding of [2nd Lieutenant James V.S. Paddock] and [Acting Assistant Surgeon Robert Grimes], and the killing of ten enlisted men and wagon master, with the wounding of about twenty men and teamsters… Officers and men behaved with greatest gallantry."
— John S. Payne, U.S. Army[78]

(1131) Action, Cuchillo Negro River, Miembres Mountains, New Mexico Territory (September 29 and 30, 1879)[79]

— Major Albert P. Morrow (9th U.S. Cavalry)
    — 6th U.S. Cavalry Detachment Co. A
    — 9th U.S. Cavalry Detachments Co. B, C, E and L
    — Detachment of Indian Scouts
— **2 KILLED**[80]
    — Private John Johnson (Co. L 9th U.S. Cavalry) — d. 9-30-1879
    — Private Major Woodard (Co. L 9th U.S. Cavalry) — d. 9-30-1879

— Sergeant Thomas Boyne (Co. C 9th U.S. Cavalry) received MOH: Bravery in action (Miembres Mountains, New Mexico, May 29, 1879; Cuchillo Negro River near Ojo Caliente, New Mexico, September 29, 1879).

(1132) Operations, Chamberlain Basin, Idaho Territory (October 1 to 6, 1879)[81]
    — 2nd Lieutenant Edmund S. Farrow (21st U.S. Infantry)
        — Detachment of Indian Scouts

— 2nd Lieutenant Edmund S. Farrow (21st U.S. Infantry) brevet promotion to 1st Lieutenant for gallant service in actions against Indians (Big Creek, Idaho, August 19, 1879 and Big Meadows, Idaho, October 8, 1879).

(1133) Operations, Milk Creek, Colorado (October 2 to 4, 1879)[82]
    — Captain Francis S. Dodge (9th U.S. Cavalry)
        — 3rd U.S. Cavalry Co. E
        — 5th U.S. Cavalry Co. D and F
        — 9th U.S. Cavalry Co. D

— Captain Francis S. Dodge (9th U.S. Cavalry) brevet promotion to Major for gallant service in action against Indians (Milk River, Colorado, September 29 to October 1, 1879).

— Captain Frances S. Dodge (9th U.S. Cavalry) received MOH: With a force of forty men road all night to the relief of a command that had been defeated and besieged by an overwhelming force of Indians, reached the field at daylight, joined in the action and fought for three days (White River Agency, Colorado, September 29, 1879).

— Sergeant Henry Johnson (Co. D 9th U.S. Cavalry) received MOH: Voluntarily left fortified shelter and under heavy fire at close range made the rounds of the pits to instruct the guards, fought his way to the creek and back to bring water to the wounded (Milk River, Colorado, October 2 to 5, 1879).

"I wish to say a word in favor of the enlisted men of my command whose conduct throughout was exemplary. They endured a forced march of seventy miles, loss of sleep, lack of food, and the dispositions attendant on their situation without a murmur and have proven themselves good soldiers and reliable men."
        — Francis S. Dodge, U.S. Army [83]

---

[78] Captain John S. Payne's message to Brigadier General George Crook, 29 September 1879. Sprague, *Massacre*, 214-215.

[79] Indians. *Annual Report of Secretary of War (1880)*, 520; Chronological List, 70; Heitman (Volume 2), 445; Record of Engagements, 92; Billington, *New Mexico's Buffalo Soldiers*, 91; Carter, *From Yorktown to Santiago*, 278; Leckie, *Buffalo Soldiers*, 212-213; Thrapp, *Victorio*, 242-244. Chronological List lists 26 to 30 September 1879. Heitman lists 29 September to 1 October 1879. Chronological List lists 6th U.S. Cavalry Detachments; 9th U.S. Cavalry Detachments; Detachment of Indian Scouts. Heitman lists 9th U.S. Cavalry Detachments Co. B, C, G, L.

[80] Reports of Diseases and Individual Cases, F 502; Register of Deaths Regular Army, 1860-1889 (Volume 11).

[81] Indians. Heitman (Volume 2), 445; Arnold, *Indian Wars of Idaho*, 242-247.

[82] Indians. *Annual Report of Commissioner of Indian Affairs (1879)*, xxxiii; Chronological List, 71; Heitman (Volume 2), 445; Record of Engagements, 90-91; Burton, *Black, Buckskin and Blue*, 217-220; Leckie, *Buffalo Soldiers*, 209-210; Miller, *Hollow Victory*, 95-103; Sprague, *Massacre*, 218-222.

[83] Official Report of Captain Francis S. Dodge, In the Field, Rawlins Springs, Wyoming Territory, 19 October 1879. Miller, *Hollow Victory*, 207.

(1134) Skirmish, Milk Creek, Colorado (October 5, 1879)[84]
— Colonel Wesley Merritt (5th U.S. Cavalry)
— 3rd U.S. Cavalry Co. E
— 5th U.S. Cavalry Co. A, B, D, F, I and M
— 9th U.S. Cavalry Co. D
— 4th U.S. Infantry Co. B, C, E, F and I

(1135) Skirmish, White River, Colorado (October 10, 1879)[85]
— Colonel Wesley Merritt (5th U.S. Cavalry)
— 3rd U.S. Cavalry Co. E
— 5th U.S. Cavalry Co. A, B, D, F, H, I and M
— 9th U.S. Cavalry Co. D
— 4th U.S. Infantry Co. B, C, E, F and I

(1136) Citizens, Slocum's Ranch, New Mexico Territory (October 13, 1879)[86]
— (11) Citizens Killed

(1137) Citizens, Lloyd's Ranch, New Mexico Territory (October 13, 1879)[87]
— (6) Citizens Killed

(1138) Action, Rifle Creek, near White River Agency, Colorado (October 20, 1879)[88]
— 1st Lieutenant William P. Hall (5th U.S. Cavalry)
— Detachment of Indian Scouts
— **2 KILLED**[89]
— 1st Lieutenant William B. Weir (Ordnance Department)

— Humme (Indian Scout)

— *1st Lieutenant William P. Hall (5th U.S. Cavalry) received MOH: With a reconnoitering party of three men, was attacked by thirty-five Indians and several times exposed himself to draw fire of the enemy, giving his small party opportunity to reply with much effect (Near camp on White River, Colorado, October 20, 1879).*

(1139) Action, Guzman Mountains, near Corralitos River, Mexico (October 27, 1879)[90]
— Major Albert P. Morrow (9th U.S. Cavalry)
— 6th U.S. Cavalry Detachment Co. A
— 9th U.S. Cavalry Detachments Co. B, C, G and H
— Detachment of Indian Scouts

[84] Indians. *Annual Report of Secretary of War (1880)*, 83; Heitman (Volume 2), 445; Record of Engagements, 91; Leckie, *Buffalo Soldiers*, 210; Miller, *Hollow Victory*, 125-143; Sprague, *Massacre*, 222-226.
[85] Indians. Chronological list, 71; Heitman (Volume 2), 445; Record of Engagements, 91; Miller, *Hollow Victory*, 143; Sprague, *Massacre*, 223-225.
[86] Indians. *Annual Report of Secretary of War (1880)*, 106; Chronological list, 71; Thrapp, *Victorio*, 246.
[87] Indians. Killed were David Chandler, Will Jones, A. Sanchoz, N. Baragan, F. Beltran and a sixth man. *Annual Report of Secretary of War (1880)*, 105-106; Chronological list, 71; Rathbun, *New Mexico Frontier Military Place Names*, 113; Thrapp, *Conquest of Apacheria*, 186.
[88] Indians. Chronological list, 71; Heitman (Volume 2), 445; Record of Engagements, 91.
[89] Register of Deaths Regular Army, 1860-1889 (Volume 11).
[90] Indians. *Annual Report of Secretary of War (1880)*, 221, 520; Chronological list, 71; Heitman (Volume 2), 445; Record of Engagements, 92; Carter, *From Yorktown to Santiago*, 278; Leckie, *Buffalo Soldiers*, 213-214; Stout, *Apache Lightning*, 107-108; Sweeney, *Cochise to Geronimo*, 141-142; Thrapp, *Conquest of Apacheria*, 186-189. Chronological List lists 6th U.S. Cavalry Detachments; 9th U.S. Cavalry Detachments; Detachment of Indian Scouts.

— 2 KILLED[91]
   — Private Reinhold W. Cochlovius (Co. A 6th U.S. Cavalry)

   — Skilly (Indian Scout)

— 1 WOUNDED[92]
   — Jack (Indian Scout)
      — *gunshot wound, right arm, slight wound*

(1140) Citizens, thirty miles south of Fort Cummings, New Mexico Territory (December 1879)[93]
   — (1) Citizen Killed

TOTAL KILLED 1879 — 2/34/13/7 (Officers, Enlisted Men, Indian Scouts, Citizens)

[91] Reports of Diseases and Individual Cases, F 504; Register of Deaths Regular Army, 1860-1889 (Volume 10).
[92] Reports of Diseases and Individual Cases, F 504.
[93] Indians. *Annual Report of Secretary of War (1880)*, 106.

1880

"I am heartily sick of this business and am convinced that the most expeditious and least expensive way to settle the [Apache] troubles in this section is to employ about one hundred and fifty Apache Indian Scouts and turn them loose on Victorio without interference from troops... I have had eight engagements with the Victorio Indians in the Mountains since their return from Mexico and in each have driven and beaten them but there is no appreciable advantage gained. They run but make another stand on another point where possibly ten men can stand off a hundred, kill a number and lose none."

— Albert P. Morrow, U.S. Army[1]

---

[1] Major Albert Morrow (9th U.S. Cavalry) shared his sentiments to a friend, Captain Charles Steelhammer (15th U.S. Infantry), in a letter dated 8 February 1880. Thrapp, *Victorio*, 368.

(1141) Citizens, near La-Ma-Parsa, New Mexico Territory (January 1880)[2]
— (1) Citizens Killed

(1142) Action, Rio Puerco, New Mexico Territory (January 12, 1880)[3]
— Major Albert P. Morrow (9th U.S. Cavalry)
— 9th U.S. Cavalry Co. B, C, F, G, H and M
— Detachment of Indian Scouts
— **1 KILLED**[4]
— Sergeant Daniel J. Gross (Co. F 9th U.S. Cavalry)

— **1 WOUNDED**[5]
— Frank (Indian Scout)
— *gunshot wound, left thigh, slight wound*

(1143) Action, San Mateo Mountains, New Mexico Territory (January 17, 1880)[6]
— Major Albert P. Morrow (9th U.S. Cavalry)
— 9th U.S. Cavalry Co. B, C, F, H and M
— Detachment of Indian Scouts
— **1 KILLED**[7]
— 2nd Lieutenant James H. French (9th U.S. Cavalry)

— **2 WOUNDED**[8]
— Jim (Indian Scout)
— *gunshot wound, left foot, fracture, severe wound*
— Nobildetinda (Indian Scout)
— *gunshot wound, right leg, slight wound*

(1144) Action, Cabello Mountains, New Mexico Territory (January 30, 1880)[9]
— Captain Louis H. Rucker (9th U.S. Cavalry)
— 9th U.S. Cavalry Detachments Co. B and M
— **1 WOUNDED**[10]
— Sergeant Albert Shout (Co. M 9th U.S. Cavalry)
— *gunshot wound, left shoulder, slight wound*

(1145) Action, San Andreas Mountains, New Mexico Territory (February 3, 1880)[11]
— Major Albert P. Morrow (9th U.S. Cavalry)
— 9th U.S. Cavalry Co. B, C, F, H and M
— Detachment of Indian Scouts

[2] Indians. Killed was Green Woetley. *Annual Report of Secretary of War (1880)*, 105.
[3] Indians. *Annual Report of Secretary of War (1880)*, 520; Chronological list, 71; Heitman (Volume 2), 445; Record of Engagements, 93; Leckie, *Buffalo Soldiers*, 215-216; Rathbun, *New Mexico Frontier Military Place Names*, 138; Stout, *Apache Lightning*, 121; Sweeney, *Cochise to Geronimo*, 149; Thrapp, *Conquest of Apacheria*, 191-192. Chronological List lists 9th U.S. Cavalry Co. B, C, F, G, H, M. Heitman lists 9th U.S. Cavalry Co. B, C, F, H, M; Detachment of Indian Scouts.
[4] Report of Diseases and Individual Cases, F507; Register of Deaths Regular Army, 1860-1889 (Volume 10).
[5] Reports of Diseases and Individual Cases, F507.
[6] Indians. *Annual Report of Secretary of War (1880)*, 520; Chronological list, 71; Heitman (Volume 2), 445; Record of Engagements, 93; Leckie, *Buffalo Soldiers*, 215-216; Stout, *Apache Lightning*, 121-122; Sweeney, *Cochise to Geronimo*, 150; Thrapp, *Conquest of Apacheria*, 192. Chronological List lists 9th U.S. Cavalry Co. B, C, F, H, M.
[7] Reports of Diseases and Individual Cases, F508; Register of Deaths Regular Army, 1860-1889 (Volume 10).
[8] Reports of Diseases and Individual Cases, F508.
[9] Indians. *Annual Report of Secretary of War (1880)*, 520; Chronological list, 71; Heitman (Volume 2), 445; Leckie, *Buffalo Soldiers*, 215-216; Rathbun, *New Mexico Frontier Military Place Names*, 27; Stout, *Apache Lightning*, 122-123; Thrapp, *Victorio*, 262.
[10] Reports of Diseases and Individual Cases, F509.
[11] Indians. *Annual Report of Secretary of War (1880)*, 520; Chronological list, 71; Heitman (Volume 2), 445; Leckie, *Buffalo Soldiers*, 215-216; Stout, *Apache Lightening*, 124-125; Sweeney, *Cochise to Geronimo*, 150; Thrapp, *Conquest of Apacheria*, 192.

— **1 KILLED**[12]
— Chilchuene (Indian Scout)

— **4 WOUNDED**[13]
— Private Stephen H. Garnet (Co. B 9th U.S. Cavalry)
— *gunshot wound, left arm, severe wound*
— Private Brent Woods (Co. B 9th U.S. Cavalry)
— *gunshot wound, left thigh, severe wound*
— Private James Johnson (Co. F 9th U.S. Cavalry)
— *gunshot wound, right hand, slight wound*
— Private Stanley Osborne (Co. F 9th U.S. Cavalry)
— *gunshot wound, left thigh, severe wound*

(1146) Action, near Pumpkin Creek, Montana Territory (February 7, 1880)[14]
— Sergeant Thomas B. Glover (2nd U.S. Cavalry)
— 2nd U.S. Cavalry Detachment Co. B
— Detachment of Indian Scouts
— **1 KILLED**[15]
— Private George E. Douglas (Co. E 2nd U.S. Cavalry)

— **1 WOUNDED**[16]
— Private Charles W. Gurnsey (Co. B 2nd U.S. Cavalry)
— *gunshot wound, thorax and left wrist, severe wound*

— *Sergeant Thomas B. Glover (Co. B 2nd U.S. Cavalry) received MOH: While in charge of small scouting parties, fought, charged, surrounded, and captured war parties of Sioux Indians (Mizpah Creek, Montana, April 10, 1879; Pumpkin Creek, Montana, February 10. 1880)*

(1147) Skirmish, Sacramento Mountains, New Mexico Territory (February 28, 1880)[17]
— 1st Lieutenant John Conline (9th U.S. Cavalry)
— 9th U.S. Cavalry Co. A

(1148) Citizens, near La Luz, New Mexico Territory (March 1880)[18]
— (3) Citizens Killed

(1149) Action, Rosebud Creek, Montana Territory (March 9, 1880)[19]
— 2nd Lieutenant Samuel W. Miller (5th U.S. Infantry)
— 5th U.S. Infantry Detachment Co. E
— Detachment of Indian Scouts

[12] Reports of Diseases and Individual Cases, F510; Register of Deaths Regular Army, 1860-1889 (Volume 10).
[13] Reports of Diseases and Individual Cases, F510.
[14] Indians. *Annual Report of Secretary of War (1880)*, 62, 74-75, 520; Chronological list, 71; Heitman (Volume 2), 445; Record of Engagements, 93; Brown, *Plainsmen of the Yellowstone*, 324; Miles, *Personal Recollections*, 316. Chronological List lists New Mexico Territory. Chronological List lists 12 February 1880.
[15] Reports of Diseases and Individual Cases, F506; Register of Deaths Regular Army, 1860-1889 (Volume 10).
[16] Reports of Diseases and Individual Cases, F506.
[17] Indians. Chronological List, 71; Heitman (Volume 2), 445.
[18] Indians. Killed were Vincento Luna, M. Sanchez and an unknown. *Annual Report of Secretary of War (1880)*, 106; Chronological List, 71.
[19] Indians. *Annual Report of Secretary of War (1880)*, 63, 75, 520; Chronological List, 71; Heitman (Volume 2), 445; Record of Engagements, 93; Brown, *Plainsmen of the Yellowstone*, 325. Chronological List lists 8 March 1880.

— **2 KILLED**[20]
    — Black Eagle (Indian Scout)
    — Little Horse (Indian Scout)

(1150) Skirmish, Porcupine Creek, Montana Territory (March 10, 1880)[21]
    — Captain Frank D. Baldwin (5th U.S. Infantry)
        — 5th U.S. Infantry Co. I and K

(1151) Citizens, Russell's Ranch, Texas (March 13, 1880)[22]
    — (1) Citizen Killed

(1152) Citizens, Blazer's Mill, New Mexico Territory (March 15, 1880)[23]
    — (1) Citizen Killed

(1153) Action, O'Fallon's Creek, Montana Territory (April 1, 1880)[24]
    — Captain Eli L. Huggins (2nd U.S. Cavalry)
        — 2nd U.S. Cavalry Detachments Co. C and E
— **1 KILLED**[25]
    — Sergeant Joseph Johnson (Co. C 2nd U.S. Cavalry)

    — *2nd Lieutenant Lloyd M. Brett (2nd U.S. Cavalry) received MOH: Fearless exposure and dashing bravery in cutting off the Indian's pony herd, thereby greatly crippling the hostiles (O'Fallon's Creek, Montana, April 1, 1880).*

    — *Captain Eli L. Huggins (2nd U.S. Cavalry) received MOH: Surprised the Indians in their strong position and fought them until dark with great boldness (O'Fallon's Creek, Montana, April 1, 1880).*

(1154) Skirmish, near Pecos Falls, Texas (April 3, 1880)[26]
    — 2nd Lieutenant Calvin Esterly (10th U.S. Cavalry)
        — 10th U.S. Cavalry Co. F and L

(1155) Action, Miembrillo Canyon, San Andreas Mountains, New Mexico Territory (April 5, 1880)[27]
    — 1st Lieutenant John Conline (9th U.S. Cavalry)
        — 9th U.S. Cavalry Co. A
— **2 WOUNDED**[28]
    — Corporal D. Hawkins (Co. A 9th U.S. Cavalry)
        — *gunshot wound, buttocks, severe wound*

    — (1) Citizen

[20] Reports of Diseases and Individual Cases, F511; Register of Deaths Regular Army, 1860-1889 (Volume 10).
[21] Indians. *Annual Report of Secretary of War (1880)*, 63, 75; Chronological List, 71; Heitman (Volume 2), 445; Record of Engagements, 93. Chronological List lists 8 March 1880.
[22] Indians. Killed was a sheep-herder. *Annual Report of Secretary of War (1880)*, 149; Chronological List, 71; Record of Engagements, 94.
[23] Indians. Killed was William Smith. *Annual Report of Secretary of War (1880)*, 106; Chronological List, 72.
[24] Indians. *Annual Report of Secretary of War (1880)*, 63, 75, 520; Chronological List, 72; Heitman (Volume 2), 445; Record of Engagements, 94; Brown, *Plainsmen of the Yellowstone*, 325; Miles, *Personal Recollections*, 311.
[25] Reports of Diseases and Individual Cases, F519; Register of Deaths Regular Army, 1860-1889 (Volume 10).
[26] Indians. Chronological List, 72; Heitman (Volume 2), 445; Record of Engagements, 94; Leckie, *Buffalo Soldiers*, 222; Williams, *Texas' Last Frontier*, 235.
[27] Indians. Chronological List, 72; Heitman (Volume 2), 445; Rathbun, *New Mexico Frontier Military Place Names*, 85-86; Stout, *Apache Lightning*, 129-130.
[28] Reports of Diseases and Individual Cases, F513; 9th U.S. Cavalry Regimental Return April 1880; Chronological List, 72.

(1156) Action, Miembrillo Canyon, San Andreas Mountains, New Mexico Territory (April 6 and 7, 1880)[29]
— Captain Henry Carroll (9th U.S. Cavalry)
— 1st Lieutenant Patrick Cusack (9th U.S. Cavalry)
— 9th U.S. Cavalry Co. A, D, F and G
— **2 KILLED**[30]
— Farrier Isaac James (Co. F 9th U.S. Cavalry)
— Private William Saunders (Co. F 9th U.S. Cavalry)

— **6 WOUNDED**[31]
— Captain Henry Carroll (9th U.S. Cavalry)
— *gunshot wounds, shoulder and knee, severe wounds*

— Private Zeik Guddy (Co. D 9th U.S. Cavalry)
— *gunshot wound, thigh, severe wound*
— Private Jenny E. Morgan (Co. D 9th U.S. Cavalry)
— *gunshot wound, leg, severe wound*
— Private James H. Johnson (Co. F 9th U.S. Cavalry)
— *gunshot wound, thigh, severe wound*
— Private Benjamin Robinson (Co. F 9th U.S. Cavalry)
— *contusion, back, severe wound*
— Private George Syles (Co. F 9th U.S. Cavalry)
— *gunshot wound, leg, severe wound*

— *Captain Henry Carroll (9th U.S. Cavalry) brevet promotion to Major for gallant service in action against Indians (Main Fork of Brazos River, Texas, September 16, 1869) and against Indians (San Andreas Mountains, New Mexico, April 7, 1880, where he was severely wounded).*

— *1st Lieutenant John Conline (9th U.S. Cavalry) brevet promotion to Captain for gallant service in action against Indians (San Andreas Mountains, New Mexico, April 7, 1880).*

— *1st Lieutenant Patrick Cusack (9th U.S. Cavalry) brevet promotion to Major for gallant service in action against Indians (San Andreas Mountains, New Mexico, April 7, 1880).*

— *1st Lieutenant Martin B. Hughes (9th U.S. Cavalry) brevet promotion to Captain for gallant service in action against Indians (San Andreas Mountains, New Mexico, April 7, 1880).*

— *2nd Lieutenant Stephen C. Mills (12th U.S. Infantry) brevet promotion to 1st Lieutenant for gallant service in actions against Indians (San Andreas Mountains, New Mexico, April 7, 1880 and Las Animas Mountains, April 28, 1882).*

[29] Indians. *Annual Report of Secretary of War (1880)*, 95, 217, 520; Chronological List, 72; Heitman (Volume 2), 445; Record of Engagements, 94; Cruse, *Apache Days*, 72-75; King, *War Eagle*, 191; Leckie, *Buffalo Soldiers*, 216-221; Rathbun, *New Mexico Frontier Military Place Names*, 85-86; Stout, *Apache Lightning*, 130-131; Sweeney, *Cochise to Geronimo*, 151-152; Thrapp, *Victorio*, 268-270. Chronological List lists 6 to 9 April 1880.
[30] Reports of Diseases and Individual Cases, F513; Register of Deaths Regular Army, 1860-1889 (Volume 10).
[31] Reports of Diseases and Individual Cases, F513.
[32] Indians. *Annual Report of Secretary of War (1880)*, 35, 221; Chronological List, 72; Heitman (Volume 2), 446; Carter, *From Yorktown to Santiago*, 278; King, *War Eagle*, 191; Leckie, *Buffalo Soldiers*, 221; Rathbun, *New Mexico Frontier Military Place Names*, 85-86; Stout, *Apache Lightning*, 130-131; Sweeney, *Cochise to Geronimo*, 152; Williams, *Texas' Last Frontier*, 235. Chronological List lists 9 April 1880. Chronological List lists 6th U.S. Cavalry Co. L; Detachment of Indian Scouts.

— *2nd Lieutenant Charles W. Taylor (9th U.S. Cavalry) brevet promotion to 1st Lieutenant for gallant service in actions against Indians (San Andreas Mountains, New Mexico, April 7, 1880).*

(1157) Skirmish, San Andreas Mountains, New Mexico Territory (April 7 and 8, 1880)[32]
    — Captain Curwen B. McClellan (6th U.S. Cavalry)
        — 6th U.S. Cavalry Detachments Co. D and E
        — 9th U.S. Cavalry Detachment
        — Detachment of Indian Scouts

    — *Captain Curwen B. McClellan (6th U.S. Cavalry) brevet promotion to Lt. Colonel for gallant service in actions against Indians (Red River, Indian Territory, August 30, 1874 and San Andreas Mountains, New Mexico, April 8, 1880).*

(1158) Skirmish, Shakehand Springs, New Mexico Territory (April 9, 1880)[33]
    — Captain Thomas C. Lebo (10th U.S. Cavalry)
        — 10th U.S. Cavalry Co. K

(1159) Citizens, Pato Spring, New Mexico Territory (April 15, 1880)[34]
    — (1) Citizen Killed

(1160) Skirmish, near South Fork, New Mexico Territory (April 16, 1880)[35]
    — Captain Charles Steelhammer (15th U.S. Infantry)
        — 9th U.S. Cavalry Detachment Co. G
        — 15th U.S. Infantry Co. G

(1161) Skirmish, Mescalero Agency, New Mexico Territory (April 16, 1880)[36]
    — Colonel Edward Hatch (9th U.S. Cavalry)
        — 9th U.S. Cavalry Detachments Co. H and L
        — 10th U.S. Cavalry Co. D, E, F, K and L
        — 25th U.S. Infantry Detachments

(1162) Skirmish, near Dog Canyon, New Mexico Territory (April 17, 1880)[37]
    — Major Albert P. Morrow (9th U.S. Cavalry)
        — 6th U.S. Cavalry Co. L
        — 9th U.S. Cavalry Co. L
        — Detachment of Indian Scouts

(1163) Skirmish, Sacramento Mountains, New Mexico Territory (April 20, 1880)[38]
    — 1st Lieutenant Mason M. Maxon (10th U.S. Cavalry)
        — 10th U.S. Cavalry Detachment Co. L

[33] Indians. *Annual Report of Secretary of War (1880)*, 155; Chronological List, 72; Heitman (Volume 2), 446; Record of Engagements, 94; Cruse, *Apache Days*, 78; Leckie, *Buffalo Soldiers*, 222; Rathbun, *New Mexico Frontier Military Place Names*, 65; Smith, *Old Army in Texas*, 162; Williams, *Texas' Last Frontier*, 235-236.

[34] Indians. Killed was Samuel Smith. *Annual Report of Secretary of War (1880)*, 106; Chronological List, 72.

[35] Indians. *Annual Report of Secretary of War (1880)*, 95-96, 156; Chronological List, 72; Heitman (Volume 2), 446; Thrapp, *Victorio*, 272. Chronological List lists 9th U.S. Cavalry Detachments; 15th U.S. Infantry Co. G.

[36] Indians. *Annual Report of Secretary of War (1880)*, 95-96, 156; Chronological List, 72; Heitman (Volume 2), 446; Record of Engagements, 95; Leckie, *Buffalo Soldiers*, 223-224; Stout, *Apache Lightning*, 135. Chronological List lists 9th U.S. Cavalry Detachments; 10th U.S. Cavalry Co. D, E, F, K, L; 25th U.S. Infantry Detachment. Heitman lists 9th U.S. Cavalry Co. H, L; 10th U.S. Cavalry Co. D, E, F, K, L.

[37] Indians. *Annual Report of Secretary of War (1880)*, 96, 100; Chronological List, 72; Heitman (Volume 2), 446; Record of Engagements, 95; Cruse, *Apache Days*, 79; Leckie, *Buffalo Soldiers*, 224; Rathbun, *New Mexico Frontier Military Place Names*, 59; Stout, *Apache Lightning*, 136. Heitman lists 9th U.S. Cavalry Co. H, L; Detachment of Indian Scouts.

[38] Indians. Chronological List, 72; Heitman (Volume 2), 446; Record of Engagements, 95.

(1164) Citizens, near Ojo Caliente, New Mexico Territory (April 27, 1880)[39]
— (3) Citizens Killed

(1165) Citizens, near Headwaters of Rio Gilitfe, New Mexico Territory (April 28, 1880)[40]
— (6) Citizens Killed

(1166) Citizens, Mogollon Mountains, New Mexico Territory (April 29, 1880)[41]
— (3) Citizens Killed

(1167) Citizens, James Kelher's House, New Mexico Territory (April 29, 1880)[42]
— (1) Citizen Killed

(1168) Citizens, Bacon Ranch, New Mexico Territory (May 2, 1880)[43]
— (2) Citizens Killed

(1169) Citizens, San Francisco River, New Mexico Territory (May 2, 1880)[44]
— (2) Citizens Killed

(1170) Citizens, San Francisco River, New Mexico Territory (May 2, 1880)[45]
— (5) Citizens Killed

(1171) Citizens, Las Lentes, New Mexico Territory (May 4, 1880)[46]
— (6) Citizens Killed

(1172) Citizens, Ash Creek, Arizona Territory (May 7, 1880)[47]
— (2) Citizens Killed

(1173) Action, Ash Creek Valley, Arizona Territory (May 7, 1880)[48]
— Captain Adam Kramer (6th U.S. Cavalry)
— 6th U.S. Cavalry Detachments Co. D and E
— Detachment of Indian Scouts
— **1 KILLED**[49]
— Sergeant Daniel Griffin (Co. E 6th U.S. Cavalry) – d. 5-08-1880

— *2nd Lieutenant Augustus P. Blocksom (6th U.S. Cavalry) brevet promotion to 1st Lieutenant for gallant service in action against hostile Indians (Ash Creek, Arizona, May 7, 1880).*

[39] Indians. Killed were three herders of Manuel Vigilo. *Annual Report of Secretary of War (1880)*, 105; Chronological List, 72.
[40] Indians. Killed was Mal Charez, Jose and four herders. *Annual Report of Secretary of War (1880)*, 105; Chronological List, 72.
[41] Indians. Killed were three miners, Jim Cooney and men named Chick and Wilcox. *Annual Report of Secretary of War (1880)*, 105; Chronological List, 72; Rathbun, *New Mexico Frontier Military Place Names*, 47; Stout, *Apache Lightning*, 137; Sweeney, *Cochise to Geronimo*, 153; Thrapp, *Victorio*, 275.
[42] Indians. *Annual Report of Secretary of War (1880)*, 105; Sweeney, *Cochise to Geronimo*, 153.
[43] Indians. Killed were two herders. *Annual Report of Secretary of War (1880)*, 105.
[44] Indians. Killed was Miguel Pacheco and his family. *Annual Report of Secretary of War (1880)*, 105; Chronological List, 72. Chronological List combines the two 2 May 1880 events on the San Francisco River.
[45] Indians. Killed was G. Matta and his family. *Annual Report of Secretary of War (1880)*, 105; Chronological List, 72. Chronological List combines the two 2 May 1880 events on the San Francisco River.
[46] Indians. Killed were two women and four children. *Annual Report of Secretary of War (1880)*, 105; Chronological List, 72.
[47] Indians. *Annual Report of Commissioner of Indian Affairs (1880)*, 7.
[48] Indians. *Annual Report of Secretary of War (1880)*, 217, 520; Chronological List, 73; Heitman (Volume 2), 446; Alexander, *Arizona Military Place Names*, 8; Carter, *From Yorktown to Santiago*, 203, 278; Thrapp, *Victorio*, 275-276. Heitman lists 6th U.S. Cavalry Detachment Co. D; Detachment of Indian Scouts.
[49] Reports of Diseases and Individual Cases, F 518; Register of Deaths Regular Army, 1860-1889 (Volume 10).

— *Captain Adam Kramer (6ᵗʰ U.S. Cavalry) brevet promotion to Major for gallant service in actions against Indians (Ash Creek, Arizona, May 7, 1880 and Big Dry Wash, Arizona, July 17, 1882).*

(1174) Citizens, Bass Canyon, Texas (May 13, 1880)[50]
— (2) Citizens Killed

(1175) Skirmish, Old Fort Tularosa, New Mexico Territory (May 14, 1880)[51]
— Sergeant George Jordan (9ᵗʰ U.S. Cavalry)
— 9ᵗʰ U.S. Cavalry Detachments Co. E, I and K

— *Sergeant George Jordan (Co. K 9ᵗʰ U.S. Cavalry) received MOH: While commanding a detachment of twenty-five men at Fort Tularosa, New Mexico, repulsed a force of more the one hundred Indians (May 14, 1880). At Carrizo Canyon, New Mexico while commanding the right of a detachment of nineteen men, he stubbornly held his ground in an extremely exposed position and gallantry forced back a much superior number of the enemy, preventing them from surrounding the command (August 12, 1881).*

(1176) Citizens, near Gila, New Mexico Territory (May 15, 1880)[52]
— (2) Citizens Killed

(1177) Citizens, Kelly's Ranch, New Mexico Territory (May 15, 1880)[53]
— (3) Citizens Killed

(1178) Skirmish, Headwaters of Polomas River, New Mexico Territory (May 24, 1880)[54]
— Chief Scout Henry K. Parker (Citizen)
— Detachment of Indian Scouts

(1179) Citizens, Beaver Station, near Little Missouri River, Montana Territory (May 27, 1880)[55]
— (2) Citizens Killed

(1180) Citizens, Cooke's Canyon, New Mexico Territory (May 29, 1880)[56]
— (2) Citizens Killed

(1181) Citizens, Cooke's Canyon, New Mexico Territory (May 29, 1880)[57]
— (3) Citizens Killed

(1182) Action, Ojo Viejo, Texas (June 11 and 12, 1880)[58]
— 1ˢᵗ Lieutenant Frank H. Mills (24ᵗʰ U.S. Infantry)
— Detachment of Indian Scouts

[50] Indians. Killed were James Grant and Margaret Graham. *Annual Report of Secretary of War (1880)*, 138-139, 149; Record of Engagements, 95; Leckie, *Buffalo Soldiers*, 227; Williams, *Texas' Last Frontier*, 239-240.

[51] Indians. Chronological List, 73; Heitman (Volume 2), 446; Billington, *New Mexico's Buffalo Soldiers*, 95-96; Burton, *Black, Buckskin and Blue*, 160; Leckie, *Buffalo Soldiers*, 225; Rathbun, *New Mexico Frontier Military Place Names*, 180.

[52] Indians. Killed were Perfeto Martinez and another man. *Annual Report of Secretary of War (1880)*, 105.

[53] Indians. Killed were Fras Pacheco, Louis Silva and "a boy". *Annual Report of Secretary of War (1880)*, 106; Chronological List, 73.

[54] Indians. *Annual Report of Secretary of War (1880)*, 99-100; Chronological List, 73; Heitman (Volume 2), 446; Record of Engagements, 95; Billington, *New Mexico's Buffalo Soldiers*, 96; Leckie, *Buffalo Soldiers*, 226; Rathbun, *New Mexico Frontier Military Place Names*, 135; Stout, *Apache Lightning*, 139-140; Sweeney, *Cochise to Geronimo*, 164; Thrapp, *Victorio*, 277-281.

[55] Indians. *Annual Report of Secretary of War (1880)*, 75.

[56] Indians. Killed were S.I. Lyons and Sam Chambers. *Annual Report of Secretary of War (1880)*, 106; Chronological List, 73; Stout, *Apache Lightning*, 144; Thrapp, *Victorio*, 282. Chronological List combines the two 29 May 1880 events in Cooke's Canyon.

[57] Indians. Killed were a man named Vigil and two others. *Annual Report of Secretary of War (1880)*, 106; Chronological List, 73; Stout, *Apache Lightning*, 144; Thrapp, *Victorio*, 282. Chronological List combines the two 29 May 1880 events in Cooke's Canyon.

[58] Indians. *Annual Report of Secretary of War (1880)*, 149; Chronological List, 73; Heitman (Volume 2), 446; Record of Engagements, 95; Leckie, *Buffalo Soldiers*, 227; Smith, *Old Army in Texas*, 163; Williams, *Texas' Last Frontier*, 241; Wooster, *Frontier Crossroads*, 102.

— **1 KILLED**[59]
  — Simon Olgin (Indian Scout)

— **2 WOUNDED**[60]
  — Indian Scout
  — Indian Scout

(1183) Citizens, between Pennel and O'Fallon Stations, Montana Territory (July 11, 1880)[61]
  — (1) Citizen Killed

(1184) Action, Rocky Ridge or Eagle Pass, Texas (July 30, 1880)[62]
  — Colonel Benjamin H. Grierson (10th U.S. Cavalry)
    — 10th U.S. Cavalry Detachments Co. C and G
    — Detachment of Indian Scouts
— **1 KILLED**[63]
  — Private Martin Davis (Co. C 10th U.S. Cavalry)

— **2 WOUNDED**[64]
  — 1st Lieutenant Samuel R. Collady (10th U.S. Cavalry)
    — *gunshot wound, thigh, severe wound*

  — Private Samuel Prescott (Co. G 10th U.S. Cavalry)
    — *gunshot wound, hand, slight wound*

(1185) Citizens, near Eagle Springs, Texas (July 31, 1880)[65]
  — (2) Citizens Killed

(1186) Skirmish, Sierra Diablo, Texas (August 3, 1880)[66]
  — Captain Thomas C. Lebo (10th U.S. Cavalry)
    — 10th U.S. Cavalry Co. K

(1187) Action, Alamo Springs, Texas (August 3, 1880)[67]
  — Corporal Asa Weaver (10th U.S. Cavalry)
    — 10th U.S. Cavalry Detachments Co. B, C, G and H
    — Detachment of Indian Scouts
— **1 KILLED**[68]
  — Private George Tockes (Co. C 10th U.S. Cavalry)

[59] *Annual Report of Secretary of War (1880)*, 149.
[60] Chronological List, 73.
[61] Indians. *Annual Report of Secretary of War (1880)*, 75.
[62] Indians. *Annual Report of Secretary of War (1880)*, 149, 159-160; *Annual Report of Secretary of War (1881)*, 527-528; Chronological List, 73; Heitman (Volume 2), 446; Record of Engagements, 95; Burton, *Black, Buckskin and Blue*, 189; Leckie, *Buffalo Soldiers*, 227-229; Stout, *Apache Lightning*, 154-155; Thrapp, *Victorio*, 286-287; Wooster, *Frontier Crossroads*, 102-103. Chronological List lists 10th U.S. Cavalry Co. A, C, D, G; Detachment of Indian Scouts.
[63] Reports of Diseases and Individual Cases, F 514; Register of Deaths Regular Army, 1860-1889 (Volume 11).
[64] Reports of Diseases and Individual Cases, F 514.
[65] Indians. Killed were stagecoach driver E.C. Baker and passenger Frank Wyant. *Annual Report of Secretary of War (1880)*, 149; Chronological List, 73; Record of Engagements, 95.
[66] Indians. *Annual Report of Secretary of War (1880)*, 161; Chronological List, 73; Record of Engagements, 96; Leckie, *Buffalo Soldiers*, 230; Wooster, *Frontier Crossroads*, 104.
[67] Indians. *Annual Report of Secretary of War (1880)*, 160; *Annual Report of Secretary of War (1881)*, 528; Chronological List, 73; Heitman (Volume 2), 446; Record of Engagements, 95-96; Leckie, *Buffalo Soldiers*, 229; Smith, *Old Army in Texas*, 163; Wooster, *Frontier Crossroads*, 103-104. Chronological List lists 10th U.S. Cavalry Detachments; Detachment of Scouts.
[68] Reports of Diseases and Individual Cases, F 517; Register of Deaths Regular Army, 1860-1889 (Volume 11).

— **1 WOUNDED**[69]
　　　— Private Julius Lundun (Co. G 10th U.S. Cavalry)
　　　　— *gunshot wound, right heel, slight wound*

(1188) Action, Camp Safford, Guadalupe Mountains, Texas (August 4, 1880)[70]
　　　— Sergeant William Richardson (10th U.S. Cavalry)
　　　　— 10th U.S. Cavalry Detachment Co. F
— **1 KILLED**[71]
　　　— Private William Taylor (Co. F 10th U.S. Cavalry)

— **1 WOUNDED**[72]
　　　— Private Havermond Dickerson (Co. F 10th U.S. Cavalry)
　　　　— *sprain, right knee, slight wound*

(1189) Skirmish, Guadalupe Mountains, Texas (August 6, 1880)[73]
　　　— Captain William B. Kennedy (10th U.S. Cavalry)
　　　　— 10th U.S. Cavalry Co. F

(1190) Skirmish, Rattlesnake Canyon, Texas (August 6, 1880)[74]
　　　— Captain Louis H. Carpenter (10th U.S. Cavalry)
　　　　— 10th U.S. Cavalry Co. B, C, G and H

(1191) Action, near Rattlesnake Spring, Texas (August 6, 1880)[75]
　　　— Captain John C. Gilmore (24th U.S. Infantry)
　　　　— 10th U.S. Cavalry Detachment Co. H
　　　　— 24th U.S. Infantry Detachment Co. H
— **1 KILLED**[76]
　　　— Private Wesley Hardy (Co. H 10th U.S. Cavalry)

(1192) Citizens, near old Fort Quitman, Texas (August 9, 1880)[77]
　　　— (1) Citizen Killed

(1193) Skirmish, Little Missouri River, Montana Territory (August 17, 1880)[78]
　　　— Sergeant E. Davern (7th U.S. Cavalry)
　　　　— 7th U.S. Cavalry Detachment Co. F

---

[69] Reports of Diseases and Individual Cases , F 517.
[70] Indians. *Annual Report of Secretary of War (1881)*, 528; Chronological List, 73; Heitman (Volume 2), 446; Smith, *Old Army in Texas*, 163.
[71] Reports of Diseases and Individual Cases, F 522; Register of Deaths Regular Army, 1860-1889 (Volume 11).
[72] Reports of Diseases and Individual Cases, F 522.
[73] Indians. *Annual Report of Secretary of War (1880)*, 161; Chronological List, 73; Heitman (Volume 2), 446; Record of Engagements, 96; Leckie, *Buffalo Soldiers*, 230; Smith, *Old Army in Texas*, 163-164; Wooster, *Frontier Crossroads*, 104.
[74] Indians. *Annual Report of Secretary of War (1880)*, 161; Chronological List, 73; Heitman (Volume 2), 446; Record of Engagements, 96; Burton, *Black, Buckskin and Blue*, 190; Leckie, *Buffalo Soldiers*, 230; Stout, *Apache Lightning*, 155-156; Thrapp, *Conquest of Apacheria*, 205.
[75] Indians. *Annual Report of Secretary of War (1880)*, 161; Chronological List, 73; Heitman (Volume 2), 446; Record of Engagements, 96; Burton, *Black, Buckskin and Blue*, 190; Leckie, *Buffalo Soldiers*, 230; Stout, *Apache Lightning*, 156-157; Thrapp, *Conquest of Apacheria*, 205-206; Wooster, *Frontier Crossroads*, 104-105. Chronological List lists 10th U.S. Cavalry Detachments; 24th U.S. Infantry Co. H.
[76] 10th U.S. Cavalry Regimental Return August 1880.
[77] Indians. Killed was James J. Byrne, Brevet Brigadier General Volunteers, American Civil War. *Annual Report of Secretary of War (1880)*, 161; Chronological List, 73; Record of Engagements, 96; Leckie, *Unlikely Warriors*, 268; Fowler, *Black Infantry*, 37-38; Stout, *Apache Lightning*, 158-159; Thrapp, *Victorio*, 290; Williams, *Texas' Last Frontier*, 243-245; Wooster, *Frontier Crossroads*,105.
[78] Indians. Chronological List, 73; Heitman (Volume 2), 446; Record of Engagements, 96. Chronological List lists 7th U.S. Cavalry Co. F.

(1194) Action, Agua Chiquita Canyon, Sacramento Mountains, New Mexico Territory (September 1, 1880)[79]

— Sergeant James Robinson (9th U.S. Cavalry)
— 9th U.S. Cavalry Detachment Co. G
— 15th U.S. Infantry Detachment Co. C
— **2 KILLED**[80]
— Private Robert A. Smith (Co. G 9th U.S. Cavalry)
— Private Daniel Stanton (Co. G 9th U.S. Cavalry)

(1195) Action, near Fort Cummings, New Mexico Territory (September 7, 1880)[81]

— Captain Leopold O. Parker (4th U.S. Cavalry)
— 4th U.S. Cavalry Co. A
— Detachment of Indian Scouts
— **3 KILLED**[82]
— Private William F. McFee (Co. A 4th U.S. Cavalry)

— Dick (Indian Scout)
— Monte Jack (Indian Scout)

—**2 WOUNDED**[83]
— Private William A. Aker (Co. A 4th U.S. Cavalry)
— *gunshot wound, right thigh and scrotum, severe wound*
— Private Joseph Peacock (Co. A 4th U.S. Cavalry)
— *gunshot wound, left arm, slight wound*

(1196) Action, Ojo Caliente, Texas (October 28, 1880)[84]

— Sergeant Charles Perry (10th U.S. Cavalry)
— 10th U.S. Cavalry Detachments Co. B, I and K
— **5 KILLED**[85]
— Private Carter Burns (Co. B 10th U.S. Cavalry)
— Private George Mills (Co. B 10th U.S. Cavalry)

— Corporal William Backus (Co. K 10th U.S. Cavalry)
— Private Jeremiah K. Griffin (Co. K 10th U.S. Cavalry)
— Private James Stanley (Co. K 10th U.S. Cavalry)

(1197) Skirmish, Mouth of Musselshell River, Montana Territory (November 7, 1880)[86]

— 2nd Lieutenant Frederick F. Kislingbury (11th U.S. Infantry)
— 2nd U.S. Cavalry Detachment Co. M
— Detachment of Indian Scouts

[79] Indians. *Annual Report of Secretary of War (1881)*, 528; Chronological List, 73; Heitman (Volume 2), 446; Billington, *New Mexico's Buffalo Soldiers*, 97-98.
[80] Reports of Diseases and Individual Cases , F 516; Register of Deaths Regular Army, 1860-1889 (Volume 11).
[81] Indians. *Annual Report of Secretary of War (1881)*, 528; Chronological List, 73; Heitman (Volume 2), 446; Stout, *Apache Lightning*, 162; Thrapp, *Conquest of Apacheria*, 207.
[82] Reports of Diseases and Individual Cases, F 515; Register of Deaths Regular Army, 1860-1889 (Volume 11).
[83] Reports of Diseases and Individual Cases, F 515.
[84] Indians. *Annual Report of Secretary of War (1881)*, 528; Chronological List, 73; Heitman (Volume 2), 446; Leckie, *Buffalo Soldiers*, 234; Smith, *Old Army in Texas*, 164; Sweeney, *Cochise to Geronimo*, 168; Wooster, *Frontier Crossroads*, 106. Heitman lists 10th U.S. Cavalry Detachments Co. B, K.
[85] Reports of Diseases and Individual Cases, F 520; Register of Deaths Regular Army, 1860-1889 (Volume 11).
[86] Indians. *Annual Report of Secretary of War (1881)*, 89-90; Chronological List, 73; Heitman (Volume 2), 446. Chronological List lists 11 November 1880.

(1198) Action, South Fork in White Mountains, New Mexico Territory (December 2, 1880)[87]
    — Captain Casper H. Conrad (15th U.S. Infantry)
        — 15th U.S. Infantry Co. C
  — **3 WOUNDED**[88]
        — Private Robert Nelson (Co. A 9th U.S. Cavalry)
            — *gunshot wound, chest, severe wound*
        — Private William Fett (Co. C 15th U.S. Infantry)
            — *gunshot wound, thigh, slight wound*
        — Private Lewis Monroe (Co. C 15th U.S. Infantry)
            — *gunshot wound, shoulder, slight wound*

TOTAL KILLED 1880 — 1/18/6/0

---

[87] Indians. *Annual Report of Secretary of War (1881)*, 528; Chronological List, 73; Heitman (Volume 2), 446.
[88] Reports of Diseases and Individual Cases, F 521.

1881

"I beg to assure you that the enlisted man and officers of the present Army of the United States, in physique, in intelligence, in patriotic devotion to the honor and flag of the country, will compare favorably with any similar establishment on earth, and with our own Army at any previous period of our history."

— William T. Sherman, U.S. Army[1]

---

[1] Official Report of General of the Army William T. Sherman, 3 November 1881. *Annual Report of Secretary of War (1881)*, 39.

(1199) Skirmish, Poplar River, Montana Territory (January 2, 1881)[2]
— Major Guido Ilges (5th U.S. Infantry)
— 7th U.S. Cavalry Co. F
— 5th U.S. Infantry Co. A, B, C, F and G
— 7th U.S. Infantry Detachments Co. A, B and E
— 11th U.S. Infantry Detachment Co. F
— Detachment of Indian Scouts
— Detachment of Volunteers

"I cannot speak too highly of the coolness and gallantry with which the officers and enlisted men of my command went to the scene of action and proceeded to their duties in the expectation of a severe encounter with these savage people, who were supposed to defend their stronghold to the last. Where all did so well I cannot discriminate in favor of one, but recommend them all to the favorable consideration of the authorities. They are good soldiers and I congratulate myself to have been their commanding officer..."
— Guido Ilges, U.S. Army[3]

(1200) Skirmish, near Canada Alamosa, New Mexico Territory (January 23, 1881)[4]
— Sergeant Madison Ingorman (9th U.S. Cavalry)
— 9th U.S. Cavalry Detachment Co. D

— *Sergeant Madison Ingorman (Co. D 9th U.S. Cavalry) awarded Certificate of Merit: For gallantry in two actions against hostile [Apache] Indians; while in command of a detachment of six men of his troop, escorting a wagon train, was attacked by twenty-five Indians, January 23, 1881, while en route to Ojo Caliente, and again by fifteen Indians, January 25, 1881, in the canyon of Canada Alamosa, in both instances promptly charging and routing the enemy and saving his train (New Mexico, January 23 and 25, 1881).*

(1201) Action, near Canada Alamosa, New Mexico Territory (January 25, 1881)[5]
— Sergeant Madison Ingorman (9th U.S. Cavalry)
— 9th U.S. Cavalry Detachment Co. D
— **1 KILLED**[6]
— Private William Jones (Co. D 9th U.S. Cavalry)

— *Sergeant Madison Ingorman (Co. D 9th U.S. Cavalry) awarded Certificate of Merit: For gallantry in two actions against hostile [Apache] Indians; while in command of a detachment of six men of his troop, escorting a wagon train, was attacked by twenty-five Indians, January 23, 1881, while en route to Ojo Caliente, and again by fifteen Indians, January 25, 1881, in the canyon of Canada Alamosa, in both instances promptly charging and routing the enemy and saving his train (New Mexico, January 23 and 25, 1881).*

(1202) Surrender of Iron Dog and 64 Indians, Camp Poplar River, Montana Territory (January 29, 1881)[7]

[2] Indians. *Annual Report of Secretary of War (1881)*, 92, 102-104; Chronological List, 74; Heitman (Volume 2), 446; Record of Engagements, 98; Utley, *Lance and Shield*, 219-220. Chronological List lists 7th U.S. Cavalry Co. F; 5th U.S. Infantry Co. A, B, C, F, G; 7th U.S. Infantry Detachments; 11th U.S. Infantry Co. F. Heitman lists 7th U.S. Cavalry Co. F; 5th U.S. Infantry Co. A, B, C, F, G; 7th U.S. Infantry Detachment Co. A; 11th U.S. Infantry Detachment Co. F.
[3] Official Report of Major Guido Ilges (5th U.S. Infantry), 31 January 1881. *Annual Report of Secretary of War (1881)*, 103-104.
[4] Indians. *Annual Report of Secretary of War (1881)*, 528; Chronological List, 74; Heitman (Volume 2), 446; Billington, *New Mexico's Buffalo Soldiers*, 101. Chronological List and Heitman both list a single entry near Canada Alamosa, New Mexico Territory on 24 January 1881.
[5] Indians. *Annual Report of Secretary of War (1881)*, 528; Chronological List, 74; Heitman (Volume 2), 446; Billington, *New Mexico's Buffalo Soldiers*, 101. Chronological List and Heitman both list a single entry near Canada Alamosa, New Mexico Territory on 24 January 1881.
[6] Reports of Diseases and Individual Cases, F 523; Register of Deaths Regular Army, 1860-1889 (Volume 11).
[7] Indians. *Annual Report of Secretary of War (1881)*, 105; Chronological List, 74; Record of Engagements, 98.

(1203) Skirmish, Candelaria Mountains, Sonora, Mexico (February 5, 1881)[8]
     — 2nd Lieutenant James A. Maney (15th U.S. Infantry)
         — 9th U.S. Cavalry Detachment Co. K
         — Detachment of Indian Scouts

(1204) Surrender of 325 Indians, Fort Buford, Dakota Territory (February 6, 1881)[9]

(1205) Surrender of 185 Indians, Yanktonnais Camp, Montana Territory (February 12, 1881)[10]

(1206) Surrender of Low Dog and 135 Indians, Fort Buford, Dakota Territory (March 11, 1881)[11]

    (1207) Citizens, near Terry Point, Dakota Territory (April 1881)[12]
     — (2) Citizens Killed

(1208) Surrender of 156 Indians, Fort Keogh, Montana Territory (April 18, 1881)[13]

    (1209) Citizens, McLauren Ranch, Headwaters of Rio Frio, Texas (April 24, 1881)[14]
     — (2) Citizens Killed

(1210) Action, near Mexican Line, New Mexico Territory (April 30, 1881)[15]
     — 2nd Lieutenant James A. Maney (15th U.S. Infantry)
         — 9th U.S. Cavalry Detachment Co. K
         — Detachment of Indian Scouts
     — **1 KILLED**[16]
         — Private Thomas Duke (Co. B 9th U.S. Cavalry)

(1211) Skirmish, Sierra del Burro Mountains, Coahuila, Mexico (May 3, 1881)[17]
     — 1st Lieutenant John L. Bullis (24th U.S. Infantry)
         — Detachment of Indian Scouts

     — *1st Lieutenant John L. Bullis (24th U.S. Infantry) brevet promotion to Major for gallant service in actions against Indians (Saragossa, Mexico, July 30, 1876 and Sierra del Burro Mountains, Coahuila, Mexico, May 3, 1881).*

    (1212) Citizens, near Fort Niobrara, Nebraska (May 9, 1881)[18]
     — (1) Citizen Killed

[8] Indians. Chronological List, 74; Heitman (Volume 2), 446; Billington, *New Mexico's Buffalo Soldiers*, 103; Sweeney, *Cochise to Geronimo*, 169-170. Chronological List lists 9th U.S. Cavalry Detachments; Detachment of Indian Scouts.
[9] Indians. *Annual Report of Secretary of War (1881)*, 93, 105; Chronological List, 74; Record of Engagements, 98-99; Utley, *Lance and Shield*, 220. Chronological List lists 26 February 1881.
[10] Indians. *Annual Report of Secretary of War (1881)*, 93, 105; Chronological List, 74; Record of Engagements, 99.
[11] Indians. *Annual Report of Secretary of War (1881)*, 94; Chronological List, 74; Record of Engagements, 99; Utley, *Lance and Shield*, 222. Chronological List lists 11 April 1881.
[12] Indians. Killed were two hunters. *Annual Report of Secretary of War (1881)*, 94.
[13] Indians. *Annual Report of Secretary of War (1881)*, 94; Chronological List, 74; Record of Engagements, 99.
[14] Indians. Killed were Mrs. McLauren and Allen Reiss. *Annual Report of Secretary of War (1881)*, 128; Record of Engagements, 100; Mulroy, *Freedom on the Border*, 130.
[15] Indians. *Annual Report of Secretary of War (1881)*, 528; Chronological List, 74; Heitman (Volume 2), 446. Chronological List and Heitman both list 29 April 1881. Chronological List lists 9th U.S. Cavalry Detachments; Detachment of Indian Scouts.
[16] Reports of Diseases and Individual Cases, F 528; Register of Deaths Regular Army, 1860-1889 (Volume 11).
[17] Indians. *Annual Report of Secretary of War (1881)*, 128; Chronological List, 74; Heitman (Volume 2), 446; Burton, *Black, Buckskin and Blue*, 100-101; Mulroy, *Freedom on the Border*, 130; Smith, *Old Army in Texas*, 164.
[18] Bandits. Killed was Chief Herder John Bordeau. *Annual Report of Commissioner of Indian Affairs (1881)*, 54.

(1213) Action, near White Lake, Dakota Territory (May 11, 1881)[19]
— 2nd Lieutenant Samuel A. Cherry (5th U.S. Cavalry)
— 5th U.S. Cavalry Detachment
— **1 KILLED**[20]
— 2nd Lieutenant Samuel A. Cherry (5th U.S. Cavalry)

— **1 WOUNDED**[21]
— Private James Conroy (5th U.S. Cavalry)
— *gunshot wound, thigh*

"The career of [2nd Lieutenant Samuel A. Cherry], though brief, has been most honorable, and marked by a cheerful, vigorous and soldiery discharge of duty. His character was most free from defects. He made friends of all who knew him well, and it is certain he never gave cause for the enmity of anyone. He was positive, though happy in disposition as a man, loyal and devoted as a friend, brave, capable and chivalrous as an officer — one in short whose sad death will long be felt in the regiment as an irreparable loss in every way."
— Wesley Merritt, U.S. Army[22]

(1214) Surrender of 50 Indians, Camp Poplar River, Montana Territory (May 24, 1881)[23]

(1215) Surrender of 32 Indians, Fort Buford, Dakota Territory (May 26, 1881)[24]

(1216) Action, Alamo Canyon, New Mexico Territory (July 17, 1881)[25]
— 2nd Lieutenant John F. Guilfoyle (9th U.S. Cavalry)
— 9th U.S. Cavalry Detachment Co. L
— Detachment of Indian Scouts
— **1 WOUNDED**[26]
— Chief Packer Burgess (Citizen)
— *gunshot wound, hip*

(1217) Citizens, Arena Blanca, New Mexico Territory (July 19, 1881)[27]
— (3) Citizens Killed

(1218) Skirmish, Arena Blanca, New Mexico Territory (July 19, 1881)[28]
— 2nd Lieutenant John F. Guilfoyle (9th U.S. Cavalry)
— 9th U.S. Cavalry Detachment Co. L
— Detachment of Indian Scouts

— *2nd Lieutenant John F. Guilfoyle (9th U.S. Cavalry) brevet promotion to 1st Lieutenant for gallant service in actions against Indians (White Sands, New Mexico, July 19, 1881, San Andreas Mountains, New Mexico, July 25, 1881 and Monica Springs, New Mexico, August 3, 1881).*

[19] Bandits. *Annual Report of Commissioner of Indian Affairs (1881)*, 54; *LaGrange (Indiana) Standard*, 19 May 1881.
[20] Register of Deaths Regular Army, 1860-1889 (Volume 11); *LaGrange (Indiana) Standard*, 19 May 1881.
[21] *LaGrange (Indiana) Standard*, 19 May 1881.
[22] Battey, *Counties of LaGrange and Noble, Indiana*, 100-101.
[23] Indians. Chronological List, 74; Record of Engagements, 99.
[24] Indians. Chronological List, 74; Record of Engagements, 99.
[25] Indians. *Annual Report of Secretary of War (1881)*, 117, 126; Chronological List, 74; Heitman (Volume 2), 446; Record of Engagements, 99; Billington, *New Mexico's Buffalo Soldiers*, 103; Lekson, *Nana's Raid*, 13; Rathbun, *New Mexico Frontier Military Place Names*, 3; Sweeney, *Cochise to Geronimo*, 173; Thrapp, *Conquest of Apacheria*, 212-213. Chronological List lists 9th U.S. Cavalry Detachments.
[26] Lekson, *Nana's Raid*, 13.
[27] Indians. Killed were two men, Jose Provencio and Victoiano Albillar, and an unnamed woman. *Annual Report of Secretary of War (1881)*, 117, 126; Chronological List, 74; Record of Engagements, 99; Billington, *New Mexico's Buffalo Soldiers*, 105; Lekson, *Nana's Raid*, 15; Rathbun, *New Mexico Frontier Military Place Names*, 101; Thrapp, *Conquest of Apacheria*, 213. Chronological List combines the events at Arena Blanca, New Mexico Territory on 19 July 1881.
[28] Indians. *Annual Report of Secretary of War (1881)*, 117, 126; Chronological List, 74; Heitman (Volume 2), 446; Record of Engagements, 99; Rathbun, *New Mexico Frontier Military Place Names*, 101; Thrapp, *Conquest of Apacheria*, 213. Chronological List combines the events at Arena Blanca, New Mexico Territory on 19 July 1881. Chronological List lists 9th U.S. Cavalry Detachments; Detachment of Indian Scouts.

(1219) Surrender of Sitting Bull and 185 Indians, Fort Buford, Dakota Territory (July 20, 1881)[29]

(1220) Action, San Andreas Mountains, New Mexico Territory (July 25, 1881)[30]
— 2nd Lieutenant John F. Guilfoyle (9th U.S. Cavalry)
— 9th U.S. Cavalry Detachment Co. L
— Detachment of Indian Scouts
— **3 WOUNDED**[31]
— (3) Citizens

— 2nd Lieutenant John F. Guilfoyle (9th U.S. Cavalry) brevet promotion to 1st Lieutenant for gallant service in actions against Indians (White Sands, New Mexico, July 19, 1881, San Andreas Mountains, New Mexico, July 25, 1881 and Monica Springs, New Mexico, August 3, 1881).

(1221) Skirmish, White Sands, New Mexico Territory (July 25, 1881)[32]
— 2nd Lieutenant John F. Guilfoyle (9th U.S. Cavalry)
— 9th U.S. Cavalry Detachment Co. L
— Detachment of Indian Scouts

(1222) Skirmish, San Andreas Mountains, New Mexico Territory (July 26, 1881)[33]
— 2nd Lieutenant John F. Guilfoyle (9th U.S. Cavalry)
— 9th U.S. Cavalry Detachment Co. L
— Detachment of Indian Scouts

(1223) Citizens, San Mateo Mountains, New Mexico Territory (July 30, 1881)[34]
— (4) Citizens Killed

(1224) Citizens, Red Canyon, San Mateo Mountains, New Mexico Territory (August 1, 1881)[35]
— (1) Citizen Killed

(1225) Skirmish, Monica Springs, New Mexico Territory (August 3, 1881)[36]
— 2nd Lieutenant John F. Guilfoyle (9th U.S. Cavalry)
— 9th U.S. Cavalry Detachment Co. L
— Detachment of Indian Scouts

— 2nd Lieutenant John F. Guilfoyle (9th U.S. Cavalry) brevet promotion to 1st Lieutenant for gallant service in actions against Indians (White Sands, New Mexico, July 19, 1881, San Andreas Mountains, New Mexico, July 25, 1881 and Monica Springs, New Mexico, August 3, 1881).

[29] Indians. *Annual Report of Secretary of War (1881)*, 98, 107-108; Chronological List, 74; Record of Engagements, 99; Brown, *Plainsmen of the Yellowstone*, 330-331; Rockwell, *U.S. Army in Frontier Montana*, 483; Utley, *Lance and the Shield*, 231-233.
[30] Indians. *Annual Report of Secretary of War (1881)*, 117, 126; Chronological List, 75; Record of Engagements, 99; Leckie, *Buffalo Soldiers*, 235; Lekson, *Nana's Raid*, 16; Rathbun, *New Mexico Frontier Military Place Names*, 128-129; Sweeney, *Cochise to Geronimo*, 173-174; Thrapp, *Conquest of Apacheria*, 212-214. Chronological List lists 9th U.S. Cavalry Detachments; Detachment of Indian Scouts.
[31] Chronological List, 75.
[32] Indians. *Annual Report of Secretary of War (1881)*, 117, 126; Chronological List, 75; Heitman (Volume 2), 446; Record of Engagements, 99; Leckie, *Buffalo Soldiers*, 235; Lekson, *Nana's Raid*, 16; Rathbun, *New Mexico Frontier Military Place Names*, 128-129; Thrapp, *Conquest of Apacheria*, 212-214. Chronological List lists 9th U.S. Cavalry Detachment Co. L.
[33] Indians. *Annual Report of Secretary of War (1881)*, 117, 126; Chronological List, 75; Heitman (Volume 2), 446; Thrapp, *Conquest of Apacheria*, 212-214. Chronological List lists 9th U.S. Cavalry Detachment Co. L.
[34] Indians. Chronological List, 75; Record of Engagements, 99; Thrapp, *Conquest of Apacheria*, 213.
[35] Indians. Chronological List, 75; Record of Engagements, 100; Leckie, *Buffalo Soldiers*, 235; Sweeney, *Cochise to Geronimo*, 174; Thrapp, *Conquest of Apacheria*, 213-214.
[36] Indians. *Annual Report of Secretary of War (1881)*, 117, 126; Chronological List, 75; Heitman (Volume 2), 446; Record of Engagements, 100; Billington, *New Mexico's Buffalo Soldiers*, 105; Lekson, *Nana's Raid*, 19-20; Rathbun, *New Mexico Frontier Military Place Names*, 127-128; Sweeney, *Cochise to Geronimo*, 176; Thrapp, *Conquest of Apacheria*, 214.

(1226) Action, Carrizo Canyon, New Mexico Territory (August 12, 1881)[37]
    — Captain Charles Parker (9th U.S. Cavalry)
        — 9th U.S. Cavalry Detachment Co. K
    — **2 KILLED**[38]
        — Private Charles Perry (Co. K 9th U.S. Cavalry)
        — Private Guy Temple (Co. K 9th U.S. Cavalry)

    — **3 WOUNDED**[39]
        — Private Washington Pennington (Co. K 9th U.S. Cavalry)
            — *gunshot wound, abdomen, severe wound*
        — Private John Slydell (Co. K 9th U.S. Cavalry)
            — *gunshot wound, abdomen, severe wound*
        — Private Berry Smith (Co. K 9th U.S. Cavalry)
            — *gunshot wound, back, slight wound*

    — *Sergeant George Jordan (Co. K 9th U.S. Cavalry) received MOH: While commanding a detachment of twenty-five men at Fort Tularosa, New Mexico, repulsed a force of more the one hundred Indians (May 14, 1880). At Carrizo Canyon, New Mexico while commanding the right of a detachment of nineteen men, he stubbornly held his ground in an extremely exposed position and gallantry forced back a much superior number of the enemy, preventing them from surrounding the command (August 12, 1881).*

    — *Sergeant George Jordan (Co. K 9th U.S. Cavalry) awarded Certificate of Merit: For gallantry in action against hostile Apache Indian, while commanding the right of a detachment of nineteen men, stubbornly holding his ground in an extremely exposed position and gallantly forcing back a much superior number of the enemy and preventing them from surrounding the command (Carrizo Canyon, New Mexico, August 12, 1881).*

    — *Sergeant Thomas Shaw (Co. K 9th U.S. Cavalry) received MOH: Forced the enemy back after stubbornly holding his ground in an extremely exposed position and prevented the enemy's superior numbers from surrounding his command (Carrizo Canyon, New Mexico, August 12, 1881).*

(1227) Action, Rio Cuchillo Negro, New Mexico Territory (August 15, 1881)[40]
    — 1st Lieutenant Gustavus Valois (9th U.S. Cavalry)
        — 9th U.S. Cavalry Co. I
        — Detachment of Volunteers
    — **2 WOUNDED**[41]
  — Corporal Monroe Johnson (Co. I 9th U.S. Cavalry)
            — *gunshot wound, right leg, slight wound*
        — Private Norman Gaines (Co. I 9th U.S. Cavalry)
            — *gunshot wound, chest, severe wound*

[37] Indians. *Annual Report of Secretary of War (1881)*, 126; *Annual Report of Secretary of War (1882)*, 476; Chronological List, 75; Heitman (Volume 2), 446; Record of Engagements, 100; Billington, *New Mexico's Buffalo Soldiers*, 105; Burton, *Black, Buckskin and Blue*, 160-161; Lekson, *Nana's Raid*, 22-23; Rathbun, *New Mexico Frontier Military Place Names*, 33; Thrapp, *Conquest of Apacheria*, 214.
[38] Reports of Diseases and Individual Cases, F 524; Register of Deaths Regular Army, 1860-1889 (Volume 12).
[39] Reports of Diseases and Individual Cases, F 524.
[40] Indians. *Annual Report of Secretary of War (1881)*, 127; *Annual Report of Secretary of War (1882)*, 476; Chronological List, 75; Heitman (Volume 2), 446; Record of Engagements, 100; Billington, *New Mexico's Buffalo Soldiers*, 106; Burton, *Black, Buckskin and Blue*, 161-164; Lekson, *Nana's Raid*, 23-24; Rathbun, *New Mexico Frontier Military Place Names*, 53-55; Thrapp, *Conquest of Apacheria*, 214. Heitman lists 16 August 1881. Chronological List lists 9th U.S. Cavalry Co. I.
[41] Reports of Diseases and Individual Cases, F 525. Chronological List lists 2nd Lieutenant George R. Burnett (9th U.S. Cavalry) as WIA. His name does not appear on Reports of Diseases and Individual Cases, F 525.

— 2nd Lieutenant George R. Burnett (9th U.S. Cavalry) received MOH: Saved the life of a dismounted soldier, who was in imminent danger of being cut off, by alone galloping quickly to his assistance under heavy fire and escorting him to a place of safety, his horse being twice shot in this action (Cuchillo Negro Mountains, New Mexico, August 15, 1881).

— Trumpeter John Rogers (Co. I 9th U.S. Cavalry) awarded Certificate of Merit: For distinguished gallantry in action against hostile Apache Indians, voluntarily carrying a dispatch for succor, under a severe fire, through the lines of the hostile Indians encircling the command (Cuchillo Negro Mountains, New Mexico, August 15, 1881).

— Private Augustus Walley (Co. I 9th U.S. Cavalry) received MOH: Bravery in action with hostile Apaches (Cuchillo Negro Mountains, New Mexico, August 15, 1881).

— First Sergeant Moses Williams (Co. I 9th U.S. Cavalry) received MOH: Rallied a detachment, skillfully conducted a running fight of three or four hours, and by his coolness, bravery, and unflinching devotion to duty in standing by his commanding officer in an exposed position under a heavy fire from a large party of Indians saved the lives of at least three of his comrades (Cuchillo Negro Mountains, New Mexico, August 15, 1881).

(1228) Skirmish, San Mateo Mountains, near Black Range, New Mexico Territory (August 16, 1881)[42]
— 2nd Lieutenant Charles W. Taylor (9th U.S. Cavalry)
— 9th U.S. Cavalry Detachments Co. B and H
— Detachment of Indian Scouts

(1229) Action, McEver's Ranch, Guerillo Canyon, New Mexico Territory (August 19, 1881)[43]
— 2nd Lieutenant George W. Smith (9th U.S. Cavalry)
— Sergeant Brent Woods (9th U.S. Cavalry)
— 9th U.S. Cavalry Detachments Co. B and H
— Detachment of Volunteers
— **5 KILLED**[44]
— 2nd Lieutenant George W. Smith (9th U.S. Cavalry)

— Saddler Thomas Golding (Co. B 9th U.S. Cavalry)
— Private James Brown (Co. B 9th U.S. Cavalry)
— Private Monroe Overstreet (Co. B 9th U.S. Cavalry)

— George Daly (Citizen)

— **3 WOUNDED**[45]
— Private Wesley Harris (Co. H 9th U.S. Cavalry)
— gunshot wound, ride side, slight wound
— Private William A. Hollins (Co. H 9th U.S. Cavalry)
— gunshot wound, chest, severe wound
— Private John Williams (Co. H 9th U.S. Cavalry)

[42] Indians. *Annual Report of Secretary of War (1881)*, 127; Chronological List, 75; Heitman (Volume 2), 446; Record of Engagements, 100; Billington, *New Mexico's Buffalo Soldiers*, 105; Lekson, *Nana's Raid*, 27; Thrapp, *Conquest of Apacheria*, 215.
[43] Indians. *Annual Report of Secretary of War (1881)*, 83, 117, 127; *Annual Report of Secretary of War (1882)*, 476; Chronological List, 75; Heitman (Volume 2), 446; Record of Engagements, 100; Billington, New *Mexico's Buffalo Soldiers*, 106-107; Burton, *Black, Buckskin and Blue*, 164-165; Lekson, *Nana's Raid*, 30-31; Rathbun, *New Mexico Frontier Military Place Names*, 73-75; Thrapp, *Conquest of Apacheria*, 215. Chronological List lists 2nd Lieutenant George W. Smith (9th U.S. Cavalry) C/O. Chronological List lists 9th U.S. Cavalry Detachments Co. B, F; Detachment of Volunteers. Heitman lists 9th U.S. Cavalry Co. B, H.
[44] Reports of Diseases and Individual Cases, F 526; Register of Deaths Regular Army, 1860-1889 (Volume 12).
[45] Reports of Diseases and Individual Cases, F 526.

— gunshot wound, right leg, fracture, severe wound

— Sergeant Brent Woods (Co. B 9ᵗʰ U.S. Cavalry) received MOH: Saved the lives of his comrades and citizens of the detachment (New Mexico Territory, August 19, 1881).

"The party were under fire from ten in the morning until half past two in the afternoon. His command continued to fight, and by their bravery without a commander (God bless them) saved the body of their heroic commander. They were colored troops, soldiers of the 9ᵗʰ U.S. Cavalry, and a braver set of men never lived."
— Jennie T. (Ridgeway) Smith, Citizen[46]

(1230) Action, Cibicu Creek, Arizona Territory (August 30, 1881)[47]
— Colonel Eugene A. Carr (6ᵗʰ U.S. Cavalry)
— 6ᵗʰ U.S. Cavalry Co. D and E
— Detachment of Indian Scouts
— 7 KILLED[48]
— Captain Edmund C. Hentig (Co. D 6ᵗʰ U.S. Cavalry)

— Private Henry C. Bird (Co. D 6ᵗʰ U.S. Cavalry)
— Private Thomas J.F. Foran (Co. D 6ᵗʰ U.S. Cavalry)
— Private Edward D. Livingston (Co. D 6ᵗʰ U.S. Cavalry)
— Private William Miller (Co. D 6ᵗʰ U.S. Cavalry)
— Private John Sanderegger (Co. D 6ᵗʰ U.S. Cavalry)
— Private John Sullivan (Co. D 6ᵗʰ U.S. Cavalry)

— 2 WOUNDED[49]
— Sergeant John McDonald (Co. E 6ᵗʰ U.S. Cavalry)
— gunshot wound, leg, slight wound
— Private Ludwig Baege (Co. D 6ᵗʰ U.S. Cavalry)
— gunshot wound, shoulder, slight wound

— Sergeant Alonzo Bowman (Co. D 6ᵗʰ U.S. Cavalry) received MOH: Conspicuous and extraordinary bravery in attacking mutinous scouts (Cibicu Creek, Arizona, August 30, 1881).

— 1ˢᵗ Lieutenant William H. Carter (6ᵗʰ U.S. Cavalry) received MOH: Rescued, with the voluntary assistance of two soldiers, the wounded from under a heavy fire (Cibicu Creek, Arizona, August 30, 1881).

— Private Richard Heartery (Co. D 6ᵗʰ U.S. Cavalry) received MOH: Bravery in action (Cibicu Creek, Arizona, August 30, 1881).

— Blacksmith John Martin (Co. E 6ᵗʰ U.S. Cavalry) received Certificate of Merit: For gallantry in action against hostile Apache Indians (Cibicu Creek, Arizona, August 30, 1881).

---

[46] Jennie T. (Ridgeway) Smith's words were written in the late 1890's as part of a short biographical sketch of her husband published by his American Civil War unit for reunions. *Proceedings of Reunions Held*, 124-125.
[47] Indians. *Annual Report of Secretary of War (1881)*, 120-121, 139-146, 153-155; *Annual Report of Secretary of War (1882)*, 146, 476; Chronological List, 75; Heitman (Volume 2), 446; Alexander, *Arizona Frontier Military Place Names*, 35-36; Carter, *From Yorktown to Santiago*, 278; Collins, *Apache Nightmare*, 45-69; Cruse, *Apache Days*, 111-117; King, *War Eagle*, 209-212; Lockwood, *Apache Indians*, 236-240; Sweeney, *Cochise to Geronimo*, 178; Thrapp, *Conquest of Apacheria*, 222-225.
[48] Reports of Diseases and Individual Cases, F 529; Register of Deaths Regular Army, 1860-1889 (Volume 12).
[49] Reports of Diseases and Individual Cases, F 529.

"The command behaved with the utmost coolness and gallantry, and encountered danger, hardship, and fatigue with the greatest cheerfulness. In spite of the sudden and most traitorous nature of the attack in the midst of the camp, officers and soldiers sprang to their arms and defeated their plan...."
— Eugene A. Carr, U.S. Army[50]

(1231) Citizens, near Fort Apache, Arizona Territory (August 31, 1881)[51]
— (7) Citizens Killed

(1232) Action, Black River Ferry, near Fort Apache, Arizona Territory (August 31, 1881)[52]
— UNKNOWN
— 6th U.S. Cavalry Detachment Co. D
— 12th U.S. Infantry Detachment Co. D
— **3 KILLED[53]**
— Private John Dorman (Co. D 6th U.S. Cavalry)
— Private Paul Winkler (Co. D 12th U.S. Infantry)
— Private Peter J. Bladt (Co. D 12th U.S. Infantry)

(1233) Action, Fort Apache, Arizona Territory (September 1, 1881)[54]
— Colonel Eugene A. Carr (6th U.S. Cavalry)
— 6th U.S. Cavalry Co. D and E
— 12th U.S. Infantry Co. D
— Detachment of Indian Scouts
— **1 WOUNDED[55]**
— 1st Lieutenant Charles G. Gordon (6th U.S. Cavalry)
— *gunshot wound, leg, slight wound*

— *Private Will C. Barnes (U.S. Army Signal Corps) received MOH: Bravery in action (Fort Apache, Arizona, September 1, 1881).*

— *Captain Alexander B. MacGowan (12th U.S. Infantry) brevet promotion to Major for gallant service in action against Indians (Fort Apache, Arizona, September 1, 1881).*

(1234) Surrender of 47 Indians, near San Carlos, Arizona Territory (September 30, 1881)[56]

(1235) Action, near Cedar Springs, Arizona Territory (October 2, 1881)[57]
— UNKNOWN
— 6th U.S. Cavalry Detachment
— 8th U.S. Infantry Detachment
— **4 KILLED[58]**
— Private Anton F. Linderkrantz (Co. A 6th U.S. Cavalry)
— Private Thomas Welsh (6th U.S. Cavalry)

[50] Official Report of Colonel Eugene A. Carr (6th U.S. Cavalry), Fort Apache, Arizona Territory 2 September 1881. *Annual Report of Secretary of War (1881)*, 143.
[51] Indians. Killed in separate engagements were mail carrier Thomas Owens, three Mormon freighters named Henderson, Chelsey and Daniels; Johnny Cowden, an employee of the Phipps's ranch, George Turner and Henry Moody. Chronological List, 75; Collins, *Apache Nightmare*, 70-81; King, *War Eagle*, 213; Lockwood, *Apache Indians*, 241-242; Sweeney, *Cochise to Geronimo*, 178. Chronological List combines the events near Fort Apache, Arizona Territory on 31 August 1881.
[52] Indians. *Annual Report of Secretary of War (1882)*, 476; Chronological List, 75; Heitman (Volume 2), 446; Alexander, *Arizona Frontier Military Place Names*, 16; Carter, *From Yorktown to Santiago*, 278; King, *War Eagle*, 213; Sweeney, *Cochise to Geronimo*, 178; Thrapp, *Conquest of Apacheria*, 226. Chronological List combines the events near Fort Apache, Arizona Territory on 31 August 1881.
[53] Reports of Diseases and Individual Cases, F 531; Register of Deaths Regular Army, 1860-1886 (Volume 12).
[54] Indians. Annual Report of Secretary of War (1882), 476; Chronological List, 75; Heitman (Volume 2), 446; Carter, *From Yorktown to Santiago*, 278; Cruse, *Apache Days*, 130-133; King, *War Eagle*, 213-214; Sweeney, *Cochise to Geronimo*, 178; Thrapp, *Conquest of Apacheria*, 226-227.
[55] Reports of Diseases and Individual Cases, F 531.
[56] Indians. Chronological List, 75; Heitman (Volume 2), 446.
[57] Indians. *Annual Report of Secretary of War (1882)*, 476-477; Lockwood, *Apache Indians*, 241-242; Ludwig, *Battle of K-H Butte*, 8; Sweeney, *Cochise to Geronimo*, 187.
[58] Reports of Diseases and Individual Cases, F 532; Register of Deaths Regular Army, 1860-1886 (Volume 12).

— Recruit August Ensner (6th U.S. Cavalry)
— Private John M. Yandell (Co. B 8th U.S. Infantry)

(1236) Action, Cedar Springs, Arizona Territory (October 2, 1881)[59]
— Colonel Orlando B. Willcox (12th U.S. Infantry)
— 1st U.S. Cavalry Co. G
— 6th U.S. Cavalry Co. A and F
— Detachment of Indian Scouts
— **1 KILLED**[60]
— Sergeant Albert Buford (Co. F 6th U.S. Cavalry)

— **3 WOUNDED**[61]
— Private William H. Humphreys (Co. G 1st U.S. Cavalry)
— *gunshot wound, thigh, slight wound*
— Private James C. Rencard (Co. G 1st U.S. Cavalry)
— *gunshot wound, eye, severe wound*
— Private John Hunt (Co. F 6th U.S. Cavalry)
— *gunshot wound, metalascus, severe wound*

(1237) Action, South Pass of Dragoon Mountains, Arizona Territory (October 4, 1881)[62]
— Colonel Orlando B. Willcox (12th U.S. Infantry)
— 1st U.S. Cavalry Co. G and I
— 9th U.S. Cavalry Co. F and H
— Detachment of Indian Scouts
— **4 WOUNDED**[63]
— Private William Carroll (9th U.S. Cavalry)
— *gunshot wound, thumb, slight wound*
— Private James Goodlow (9th U.S. Cavalry)
— *gunshot wound, wrist, hand, severe wound*
— Private Henry Harrison (9th U.S. Cavalry)
— *gunshot wound, leg, severe wound*

— Conzozzee (Indian Scout)
— *gunshot wound, left arm, slight wound*

(1238) Operations, near Milk River, Montana Territory (October 8 to 26, 1881)[64]
— Captain Jacob Kline (18th U.S. Infantry)
— 2nd U.S. Cavalry Co. H and L
— 18th U.S. Infantry Co. A, D, E and H

TOTAL KILLED 1881 — 3/21/0/1 (Officers, Enlisted Men, Indian Scouts, Citizens)

[59] Indians. *Annual Report of Secretary of War (1881)*, 146-147; *Annual Report of Secretary of War (1882)*, 476-477; Chronological List, 75; Heitman (Volume 2), 447; Carter, *From Yorktown to Santiago*, 278; Lockwood, *Apache Indians*, 246; Russell, *One Hundred and Three Fights*, 161-162; Sweeney, *Cochise to Geronimo*, 187-188; Thrapp, *Conquest of Apacheria*, 233-234. Chronological List and Heitman both list 1st U.S. Cavalry Co. G; 6th U.S. Cavalry Co. A, F; 8th U.S. Infantry Detachment; Detachment of Indian Scouts.
[60] Reports of Diseases and Individual Cases, F 532; Register of Deaths Regular Army, 1860-1886 (Volume 12).
[61] Reports of Diseases and Individual Cases, F 532.
[62] Indians. *Annual Report of Secretary of War (1882)*, 477; Chronological List, 75; Heitman (Volume 2), 447; Leckie, *Buffalo Soldiers*, 237-238; Russell, *One Hundred and Three Fights*, 163-164; Sweeney, *Cochise to Geronimo*, 189. Heitman lists 1st U.S. Cavalry Co. G, I; 6th U.S. Cavalry Co. A, F; 9th U.S. Cavalry Co. F, H; Detachment of Indian Scouts.
[63] Reports of Diseases and Individual Cases, F 530.
[64] Indians. *Annual Report of Secretary of War (1882)*, 84, 94; Chronological List, 75; Heitman (Volume 2), 447. Chronological List and Heitman both list 8 October 1881. Chronological List lists Captain Randolph Norwood (2nd U.S. Cavalry) C/O. Chronological List and Heitman both list 2nd U.S. Cavalry Co. H, L.

1882

"To show how inadequate our numbers were to effectually guard at once the San Carlos Reservation, embracing 4,550 square miles, the settlements and the Mexican border... to watch, pursue, head off and destroy the Apaches, on all sides, celebrated for their fleetness over such an immense range of rough country as Arizona... there were for duty at their post 487 [enlisted men and scouts], on extra or daily duty 318, and in the field or otherwise on detached service 379 — all told 1,184 in the whole department."

— Orlando B. Willcox, U.S. Army[1]

---

[1] Official Report of Colonel Orlando B. Wilcox, Department of Arizona, 31 August 1882. *Annual Report of Secretary of War (1882)*, 147.

(1239) Action, near San Carlos Agency, New Mexico Territory (April 19, 1882)[2]
    — Albert Sterling (Chief of Indian Police)
        — Detachment of Indian Police
  — **2 KILLED**[3]
        — Albert Sterling (Indian Police)
        — Sagotal (Indian Police)

(1240) Skirmish, near Fort Thomas, Arizona Territory (April 20, 1882)[4]
    — 2nd Lieutenant George H. Sands (6th U.S. Cavalry)
        — 6th U.S. Cavalry Co. B

(1241) Action, near Stein's Pass, Arizona Territory (April 23, 1882)[5]
    — 1st Lieutenant Donald N. McDonald (4th U.S. Cavalry)
        — 4th U.S. Cavalry Detachment
        — Detachment of Indian Scouts
  — **4 KILLED**[6]
        — Ceguania (Indian Scout)
        — Kaloh Vichajo (Indian Scout)
        — Panocha (Indian Scout)
        — Yuma Bill (Indian Scout)

  — **2 WOUNDED**[7]
        — Private William F. Downing (Co. H 4th U.S. Cavalry)
          — *gunshot wound, right thigh, slight wound*
        — Private John Sullivan (Co. H 4th U.S. Cavalry)
          — *gunshot wound, right thigh, severe wound*

(1242) Action, Horseshoe Canyon, New Mexico Territory (April 23, 1882)[8]
    — Lt. Colonel George A. Forsyth (4th U.S. Cavalry)
        — 4th U.S. Cavalry Co. C and G
        — Detachment of Indian Scouts
  — **2 KILLED**[9]
        — Sergeant Harry Morby (Co. C 4th U.S. Cavalry)
        — Private William Kurtz (Co. C 4th U.S. Cavalry) — d. 4-25-1882

  — **1 WOUNDED**[10]
        — Private Edward Leonard (Co. G 4th U.S. Cavalry)
          — *gunshot wound, right leg, severe wound*

  — *Wagoner John Schnitzer (Co. G 4th U.S. Cavalry) received MOH: Assisted, under a heavy fire, to rescue a wounded comrade (Horseshoe Canyon, New Mexico, April 23, 1882).*

---

[2] Indians. *Annual Report of Secretary of War (1882)*, 147; Alexander, *Arizona Frontier Military Place Names*, 70; Sweeney, *Cochise to Geronimo*, 211-213; Thrapp, *Conquest of Apacheria*, 236.
[3] Thrapp, *Conquest of Apacheria*, 236.
[4] Indians. *Annual Report of Secretary of War (1882)*, 147-148; Chronological List, 76; Heitman (Volume 2), 447; Carter, *From Yorktown to Santiago*, 278; Sweeney, *Cochise to Geronimo*, 214.
[5] Indians. *Annual Report of Secretary of War (1882)*, 477; Chronological List, 76; Heitman (Volume 2), 447; Record of Engagements, 101; Rathbun, *New Mexico Frontier Military Place Names*, 87-88; Sweeney, *Cochise to Geronimo*, 215-216; Thrapp, *Conquest of Apacheria*, 240-244. Chronological List and Heitman both list 4th U.S. Cavalry Detachment Co. M; Detachment of Indian Scouts.
[6] Reports of Diseases and Individual Cases, F 534; Register of Deaths Regular Army, 1860-1886 (Volume 12).
[7] Reports of Diseases and Individual Cases, F 534.
[8] Indians. *Annual Report of Secretary of War (1882)*, 148, 477; Chronological List, 76; Heitman (Volume 2), 447; Record of Engagements, 101; Alexander, *Arizona Frontier Military Place Names*, 70; Dixon, *Hero of Beecher Island*, 150-155; Lockwood, *Apache Indians*, 247-248; Rathbun, *New Mexico Frontier Military Place Names*, 88; Sweeney, *Cochise to Geronimo*, 216-217; Thrapp, *Conquest of Apacheria*, 244-245. Chronological List and Heitman both list 4th U.S. Cavalry Co. C, F, G, H, M; Detachment of Indian Scouts.
[9] Reports of Diseases and Individual Cases, F 533.
[10] Reports of Diseases and Individual Cases, F 533. Chronological List lists 1st Lieutenant John W. Martin (4th U.S. Cavalry) WIA. His name does not appear on F 533.

— *1ˢᵗ Lieutenant Wilber E. Wilder (4ᵗʰ U.S. Cavalry) brevet promotion to Captain for gallant service in action against Indians, inclusive of the rescue, while under heavy fire, of an enlisted man who was severely wounded (Horseshoe Canyon, New Mexico, April 23, 1882).*

— *1ˢᵗ Lieutenant Wilber E. Wilder (4ᵗʰ U.S. Cavalry) received MOH: Assisted, under heavy fire, to rescue a wounded comrade (Horseshow Canyon, New Mexico, April 23, 1882).*

(1243) Action, Hatchett Mountains, near Mexican Line, New Mexico Territory (April 28, 1882)[11]
    — Captain Tullius C. Tupper (6ᵗʰ U.S. Cavalry)
        — 6ᵗʰ U.S. Cavalry Detachments Co. G and M
        — Detachment of Indian Scouts
— **1 KILLED**[12]
    — Private William W. Goldrick (Co. M 6ᵗʰ U.S. Cavalry)

— **1 WOUNDED**[13]
    — Private Sandora Miller (Co. M 6ᵗʰ U.S. Cavalry)
        — *gunshot wound, left leg, fracture, severe wound*

— *Private Jeremiah H. Angel (Co. G 6ᵗʰ U.S. Cavalry) awarded Certificate of Merit: For gallantry in action with Indians, in distributing ammunition along the line of skirmishers under a severe fire of the enemy (Hatchet Mountains, New Mexico, April 28, 1882).*

— *Private John C. Hubbard (Co. G 6ᵗʰ U.S. Cavalry) awarded Certificate of Merit: For gallantry in action with Indians, in distributing ammunition along the line of skirmishers under a severe fire of the enemy (Hatchet Mountains, New Mexico, April 28, 1882).*

— *Private John C. Hubbard (Co. G 6ᵗʰ U.S. Cavalry) awarded Distinguished Service Cross: For bravery in action with Indians (Huachuca Mountains, Arizona Territory, April 28, 1882).*

— *Private Samuel D. Lawrence (Co. M 6ᵗʰ U.S. Cavalry) awarded Certificate of Merit: Rescuing his comrades under a heavy fire (Hatchet Mountains, New Mexico, April 28, 1882).*

— *Private Edward T. Lynch (Co. M 6ᵗʰ U.S. Cavalry) awarded Certificate of Merit: For rescuing under a heavy fire two of his comrades (Hatchet Mountains, New Mexico, April 28, 1882).*

— *2ⁿᵈ Lieutenant Stephen C. Mills (12ᵗʰ U.S. Infantry) brevet promotion to 1ˢᵗ Lieutenant for gallant service in actions against Indians (San Andreas Mountains, New Mexico, April 7, 1880 and Las Animas Mountains, April 28, 1882).*

— *Captain William A. Rafferty (6ᵗʰ U.S. Cavalry) brevet promotion to Major for gallant service in actions against Indians (Little Wichita River, Texas, October 5, 1870 and Hatchet Mountain, New Mexico, April 28, 1882).*

[11] Indians. *Annual Report of Secretary of War (1882)*, 72, 148-149, 477; Chronological List, 76; Heitman (Volume 2), 447; Record of Engagements, 101; Carter, *From Yorktown to Santiago*, 278; Sweeney, *Cochise to Geronimo*, 218-222; Thrapp, *Conquest of Apacheria*, 245-247.
[12] Reports of Diseases and Individual Cases, F 535; Register of Deaths Regular Army, 1860-1886 (Volume 12).
[13] Reports of Diseases and Individual Cases, F 535.

— *Captain Tullius C. Tupper (6th U.S. Cavalry) brevet promotion to Lt. Colonel for gallant service in successfully leading a cavalry charge against Indians (Red River, Texas, August 30, 1874) and for gallant service in action against Indians (Las Animas Mountain, New Mexico, April 28, 1882).*

(1244) Action, Shoshone Agency, near Fort Washakie, Wyoming Territory (April 29, 1882)[14]
— 2nd Lieutenant George H. Morgan (3rd U.S. Cavalry)
    — 3rd U.S. Cavalry Detachments Co. H and K
    — Detachment of Indian Scouts
— **1 KILLED**[15]
    — Sergeant Richard J. Casey (Co. K 3rd U.S. Cavalry)

(1245) Skirmish, near Cloverdale, New Mexico Territory (June 1, 1882)[16]
— 1st Lieutenant William Stanton (6th U.S. Cavalry)
    — 6th U.S. Cavalry Co. A
    — Detachment of Indian Scouts

(1246) Action, Mescalero Agency, Fort Stanton, New Mexico Territory (June 22, 1882)[17]
— Indian Agent William H.H. Llewellyn (Citizen)
    — Detachment of Indian Police
— **1 WOUNDED**[18]
    — Indian Agent William H.H. Llewellyn (Citizen)
      — *gunshot wounds, left arm*

(1247) Operations, Big Bend of Milk River, Montana Territory (July 1 to August 14, 1882)[19]
— Captain Edgar R. Kellogg (18th U.S. Infantry)
    — 2nd U.S. Cavalry Co. H and L
    — 18th U.S. Infantry Co A, F, H and K

(1248) Action, near San Carlos Agency, New Mexico Territory (July 6, 1882)[20]
— Chief of Scouts John L. Colvig (aka Cibicu Charley, Chief of Indian Police)
    — Detachment of Indian Police
— **4 KILLED**[21]
    — Chief of Scouts John L. "Cibicu Charlie" Colvig (Indian Police)

    — Indian Police
    — Indian Police
    — Indian Police

(1249) Action, Big Dry Wash or Chevelon's Fork, Arizona Territory (July 17, 1882)[22]
— Major Andrew W. Evans (3rd U.S. Cavalry)
    — 3rd U.S. Cavalry Co. D, E and I
    — 6th U.S. Cavalry Co. E, I and K

[14] Indians. *Annual Report of Secretary of War (1882)*, 96; Chronological List, 76; Heitman (Volume 2), 447; Record of Engagements, 101-102.
[15] Register of Deaths Regular Army, 1860-1889 (Volume 12).
[16] Indians. Chronological List, 76; Heitman (Volume 2), 447; Carter, *From Yorktown to Santiago*, 278.
[17] Indians. *Annual Report of Commissioner of Indian Affairs (1882)*, 123, 125-126; Chronological List, 76; Heitman (Volume 2), 447; Record of Engagements, 102. Chronological List and Heitman both list 23 July 1882.
[18] *Annual Report of Commissioner of Indian Affairs (1882)*, 123.
[19] Indians. *Annual Report of Secretary of War (1882)*, 90, 95; Chronological List, 76; Heitman (Volume 2), 447. Chronological List and Heitman both list 9 July 1882. Chronological List lists Captain Randolph Norwood (2nd U.S. Cavalry) C/O. Chronological List and Heitman both list 2nd U.S. Cavalry Co. L.
[20] Indians. *Annual Report of Secretary of War (1882)*, 72, 150; Cruse, *Apache Days*, 158; King, *War Eagle*, 227; Thrapp, *Conquest of Apacheria*, 254; Wellman, *Death in the Desert*, 222-223.
[21] *Annual Report of Secretary of War (1882)*, 72, 150; Collins, *Apache Nightmare*, 207.
[22] Indians. *Annual Report of Secretary of War (1882)*, 72, 150; *Annual Report of Secretary of War (1883)*, 614; Chronological List, 76; Heitman (Volume 2), 447; Alexander, *Arizona Military Place Names*, 14; Carter, *From Yorktown to Santiago*, 278; Cruse, *Apache Days*, 162-169; Davis, *Truth About Geronimo*, 16-24; Lockwood, *Apache Indians*, 249-255; Thrapp, *Al Sieber*, 244-257; Wellman, *Death in the Desert*, 225.

— Detachment of Indian Scouts
— **2 KILLED**[23]
— Private Joseph McLernon (Co. E 6th U.S. Cavalry)

— Pete (Indian Scout)

— **8 WOUNDED**[24]
— 2nd Lieutenant George Converse (Co. I 3rd U.S. Cavalry)
— *gunshot wound, head, slight wound*
— 2nd Lieutenant George Morgan (Co. K 3rd U.S. Cavalry)
— *gunshot wound arm, fracture, severe wound*

— First Sergeant Charles Taylor (Co. D 3rd U.S. Cavalry)
— *gunshot wound, arm, slight wound*
— Sergeant Daniel Conn (Co. E 6th U.S. Cavalry)
— *gunshot wound, neck, severe wound*

— Private Timothy Foley (Co. K 6th U.S. Cavalry)
— *gunshot wound, neck, slight wound*
— Private James Mullica (Co. K 6th U.S. Cavalry)
— *gunshot wound, chest, severe wound*
— Private John Witt (Co. K 6th U.S. Cavalry)
— *gunshot wound, chest, severe wound*

— Toggey (Indian Scout)
— *gunshot wound, leg, slight wound*

— *Captain Lemuel A. Abbot (6th U.S. Cavalry) brevet promotion to Major for gallant service in action against Indians (Big Dry Wash, Arizona, July 17, 1882).*

— *Captain Adna R. Chaffee (6th U.S. Cavalry) brevet promotion to Lt. Colonel for gallant service in leading a cavalry charge over rough and precipitous bluffs held by Indians (Red River, Texas, August 30, 1874) and gallant service in action against Indians (Big Dry Wash, Arizona, July 17, 1882).*

— *2nd Lieutenant George L. Converse Jr. (3rd U.S. Cavalry) brevet promotion to 1st Lieutenant for gallant service in action against Indians (Big Dry Wash, Arizona, July 17, 1882).*

— *2nd Lieutenant Thomas Cruse (6th U.S. Cavalry) brevet promotion to 1st Lieutenant for gallant service in action against Indians (Big Dry Wash, Arizona, July 17, 1882).*

[23] Reports of Diseases and Individual Cases, F 536; Register of Deaths Regular Army, 1860-1886 (Volume 13).
[24] Reports of Diseases and Individual Cases, F 536.

— *2ⁿᵈ Lieutenant Thomas Cruse (6ᵗʰ U.S. Cavalry) received MOH: Gallantly charged hostile Indians, and with his carbine compelled a party of them to keep under cover of their breastworks, thus being enabled to recover a severely wounded soldier (Big Dry Wash, Arizona, July 17, 1882).*

— *Major Andrew W. Evans (3ʳᵈ U.S. Cavalry) brevet promotion to Brigadier General for gallant service in action against Indians (Big Dry Wash, Arizona, July 17, 1782).*

— *Private Timothy Foley (Co. K 6ᵗʰ U.S. Cavalry) awarded Certificate of Merit: For gallant and distinguished conduct in action against hostile Apache Indians, where he was wounded through the neck during the second charge of his troop (Big Dry Wash, Arizona, July 17, 1885).*

— *Captain Adam Kramer (6ᵗʰ U.S. Cavalry) brevet promotion to Major for gallant service in actions against Indians (Ash Creek, Arizona, May 7, 1880 and Big Dry Wash, Arizona, July 17, 1882).*

— *2ⁿᵈ Lieutenant George H. Morgan (3ʳᵈ U.S. Cavalry) brevet promotion to 1ˢᵗ Lieutenant for gallant service in action against Indians (Big Dry Wash, Arizona, July 17, 1882, where he was severely wounded).*

— *2ⁿᵈ Lieutenant George H. Morgan (3ʳᵈ U.S. Cavalry) received MOH: Gallantly held his ground at a critical moment and fired upon the advancing enemy (hostile Indians) until he was disabled by a shot (Big Dry Fork, Arizona, July 17, 1882).*

— *Private James Mullica (Co. K 6ᵗʰ U.S. Cavalry) awarded Certificate of Merit: For gallant and distinguished conduct in action against hostile Apache Indians. Was dangerously wounded through the lungs in the first charge, and fallen to the ground on the enemy's skirmish line, with great coolness encouraged the men under fire (Big Dry Wash, Arizona, July 17, 1882).*

— *First Sergeant Charles Taylor (Co. D 3ʳᵈ U.S. Cavalry) received MOH: Gallantry in action (Big Dry Wash, Arizona, July 17, 1882).*

— *1ˢᵗ Lieutenant Frank West (6ᵗʰ U.S. Cavalry) received MOH: Rallied his command and led it in advance against the enemies fortified position (Big Dry Wash, Arizona, July 17, 1882).*

— *Private John Witt (Co. K 6ᵗʰ U.S. Cavalry) awarded Certificate of Merit: For gallant and distinguished conduct in action against hostile Apache Indians. He was dangerously wounded through the body during the first charge and with great coolness and self- possession kept his place in line (Big Dry Wash, Arizona, July 17, 1882).*

(1250) Citizens, near San Carlos Agency, New Mexico Territory (July 20, 1882)[25]
— (1) Citizen Killed

---

[25] Indians. Killed was teamster Jacob Finner. *Annual Report of Secretary of War (1882)*, 151.

(1251) Action, near Tullock's Fork, Montana Territory (November 8, 1882)[26]
    — UNKNOWN
        — Detachment of Indian Scouts
    — **1 WOUNDED**[27]
        — Crooked Face (Indian Scout)
            — *gunshot wound, left thigh, severe wound*

TOTAL KILLED 1882 — 0/7/11/0 (Officers, Enlisted Men, Indian Scouts, Citizens)

[26] Indians. *Annual Report of Secretary of War (1883)*, 109, 614; Chronological List, 76; Heitman (Volume 2), 447.
[27] Reports of Diseases and Individual Cases, F 537.

1883

"From my experience of late years, I can state unhesitatingly that... in almost every Indian War which I have known anything about, the prime cause therefore has been either the failure of the Government to make good it pledges, or the wrongs perpetuated upon [Indians] by unscrupulous whites. This condition of affairs can no longer continue."

— George Crook, U.S. Army[1]

---

[1] Official Report of Brigadier General George Crook, Whipple Barracks, Arizona Territory, 27 September 1883. *Annual Report of Secretary of War (1883)*, 165.

(1252) Citizens, Canelo Hills, near Fort Huachuca, Arizona Territory (March 21, 1883)[2]
— (4) Citizens Killed

(1253) Citizens, Total Wreck Mine, West Side of Whetstone Mountains, Arizona Territory (March 22, 1883)[3]
— (6) Citizens Killed

(1254) Citizens, Point of Mountain, South End of Galiuro Range, Arizona Territory (March 23, 1883)[4]
— (2) Citizens Killed

(1255) Citizens, near Gila River, Arizona Territory (March 26, 1883)[5]
— (3) Citizens Killed

(1256) Citizens, near Gila River, Arizona Territory (March 27, 1883)[6]
— (5) Citizens Killed

(1257) Citizens, Thompson Canyon, between Silver City and Lordsburg, New Mexico Territory (March 28, 1883)[7]
— (2) Citizens Killed

(1258) Surrender of 69 Indians, Beaver Creek or Sweetgrass Hills, Montana Territory (April 14, 1883)[8]

(1259) Skirmish, Wild Horse Lake, near Canadian Line, Montana Territory (April 19, 1883)[9]
— Captain Randolph Norwood (2nd U.S. Cavalry)
— 2nd U.S. Cavalry Detachment Co. L
— Detachment of Indian Scouts

(1260) Skirmish, Babispe River, Sierra Madre Mountains, Sonora, Mexico (May 15, 1883)[10]
— Captain Emmet Crawford (3rd U.S. Cavalry)
— Detachment of Indian Scouts

TOTAL KILLED 1883 — 0/0/0/22 (Officers, Enlisted Men, Indian Scouts, Citizens)

---

[2] Indians. Killed were William Murray, Ged Owens, Joseph Woelfolk, and a man named Armstrong. *Annual Report of Secretary of War (1883)*, 161; Chronological List, 76; Alexander, *Arizona Frontier Military Place Names*, 24-26; Lockwood, *Apache Indians*, 264; Simmons, *Massacre on the Lordsburg Road*, 90-91; Sweeney, *Cochise to Geronimo*, 291.

[3] Indians. Killed in two separate attacks were pack master Stephen Barthand and three drovers, as well as S.E. James and C.M. Thorndykeson. *Annual Report of Secretary of War (1883)*, 162; Chronological List, 77; Lockwood, *Apache Indians*, 264; Simmons, *Massacre on the Lordsburg Road*, 91-92; Sweeney, *Cochise to Geronimo*, 291.

[4] Indians. Killed were two men named Dibble and Bateman. *Annual Report of Secretary of War (1883)*, 162; Chronological List, 77; Lockwood, *Apache Indians*, 264; Simmons, *Massacre on the Lordsburg Road*, 92-93; Sweeney, *Cochise to Geronimo*, 291-292.

[5] Indians. Killed were miners John Emerick, Walter Jones and Harlan Haynes. *Annual Report of Secretary of War (1883)*, 141; Simmons, *Massacre on the Lordsburg Road*, 98; Sweeney, *Cochise to Geronimo*, 294.

[6] Indians. *Annual Report of Secretary of War (1883)*, 141; Simmons, *Massacre on the Lordsburg Road*, 99; Sweeney, *Cochise to Geronimo*, 294.

[7] Indians. Killed were Judge Hamilton McComas and wife Juniata. Their son Charley was kidnapped and never recovered. *Annual Report of Secretary of War (1883)*, 141-142, 162; Chronological List, 77; Cruse, *Apache Days*, 184; Davis, *Truth About Geronimo*, 56-57, 68; Michno, *Fate Worse Than Death*, 450-453; Rathbun, *New Mexico Frontier Military Place Names*, 175-176; Simmons, *Massacre on the Lordsburg Road* , 109-117; Sweeney, *Cochise to Geronimo*, 294-295; Thrapp, *Conquest of Apacheria*, 270.

[8] Indians. *Annual Report of Secretary of War (1883)*, 112, 120; Chronological List, 77; Heitman (Volume 2), 447.

[9] Indians. *Annual Report of Secretary of War (1883)*, 112, 120-121; Chronological List, 77; Heitman (Volume 2), 447. Chronological List and Heitman both list 2nd U.S. Cavalry Detachment Co. L.

[10] Indians. *Annual Report of Secretary of War (1883)*, 175-176; Chronological List, 77; Heitman (Volume 2), 447; Bourke, *Apache Campaign*, 75-79; Cruse, *Apache Days*, 189-190; Davis, *Truth About Geronimo*, 67-69; Lockwood, *Apache Indians*, 268; Simmons, *Massacre on the Lordsburg Road* , 162; Sweeney, *Cochise to Geronimo*, 306; Thrapp, *Conquest of Apacheria*, 286-287.

1884

"Justice and humanity toward the Indians are the surest and least expensive means of preventing any further trouble. Starvation must necessarily drive the Indians to commit depredations upon the settlements in their vicinity. Retribution followed by war and ending in the destruction of the white settlements must be the result of any illiberal policy toward these natives of the plains. They have been deprived of their primitive means of support to make room for vast herds of cattle...."

— John M. Schofield, U.S. Army[1]

---

[1] Official Report of Major General John M. Schofield, Division of Missouri, 14 October 1884. *Annual Report of Secretary of War (1884)*, 104.

(1261) Action, near Fort Buford, Dakota Territory (May 14, 1884)[2]
    — Major Charles H. Whipple (Paymaster)
        — 7th U.S. Cavalry Detachment
    — 1 KILLED[3]
        — Sergeant Aquilla Coonrod (Co. F 7th U.S. Cavalry)

    — 1 WOUNDED[4]
        — Private James Birch (Co. L 7th U.S. Cavalry)
            — *gunshot wound, right forearm*

(1262) Action, Wormington Canyon, Colorado (July 15, 1884)[5]
    — 1st Lieutenant Henry P. Perrine (6th U.S. Cavalry)
        — 6th U.S. Cavalry Co. F, Detachment Co. B
        — Detachment of Volunteers
    — 2 KILLED[6]
        — James Rowdy Higgins (Citizen)
        — Joe Wormington (Citizen)

TOTAL KILLED 1884 — 0/1/0/2 (Officers, Enlisted Men, Indian Scouts, Citizens)

---

[2] Bandits. *Annual Report of Secretary of War (1884)*, 111-112.
[3] Register of Deaths Regular Army, 1860-1886 (Volume 16); 7th U.S. Cavalry Regimental Return May 1884; Fort Buford Post Return May 1884.
[4] Fort Buford Post Return May 1884.
[5] Indians. *Annual Report of Secretary of War (1884)*, 121-122; Chronological List, 77; Heitman (Volume 2), 447; Carter, *From Yorktown to Santiago*, 278. Chronological List and Heitman both list 6th U.S. Cavalry Co. B, F.
[6] "In the skirmish at this point, one packer and one cowboy were killed trying to crawl upon the Indians without orders." *Annual Report of Secretary of War (1884)*, 121; Michno, *Forgotten Fights*, 317

1885

"I wish to say a word to stem the torrent of invective and abuse which has almost universally been indulged in against the whole Apache race. This is not strange on the frontier from a certain class of vampires who prey on the misfortunes of their fellow man and who live best and easiest in time of Indian troubles. With them peace kills the goose that lays the golden egg. Greed and avarice on the part of whites - in other words the almighty dollar - is at the bottom of nine-tenths of all our Indian troubles."

— George Crook, U.S. Army[1]

---

[1] *Annual Report of Secretary of War (1885)*, 178.

(1263) Action, Devil's Creek, Mogollon Mountains, New Mexico Territory (May 22, 1885)[2]
— Captain Allen Smith (4th U.S. Cavalry)
— 4th U.S. Cavalry Co. A and K
— Detachment of Indian Scouts
— **2 WOUNDED**[3]
— Private Herman Haag (Co. A 4th U.S. Cavalry)
— *gunshot wound, right hand, slight wound*

— Yah-To-Et (Indian Scout)
— *gunshot wound, left arm, severe wound*

(1264) Action, Guadalupe Canyon, Sonora, Mexico (June 8, 1885)[4]
— Sergeant Peter Munich (4th U.S. Cavalry)
— 4th U.S. Cavalry Detachments Co. C, D and G
— **3 KILLED**[5]
— Sergeant Peter Munich (Co. G 4th U.S. Cavalry)
— Saddler Henry Niehouse (Co. D 4th U.S. Cavalry)
— Private D. Vislaoki (Co. C 4th U.S. Cavalry)

— *Private John Schnitzer (Co. G 4th U.S. Cavalry) awarded Certificate of Merit: For gallant conduct in action against hostile Chiricahua Indians in carrying the sergeant commanding the party, who had been three times wounded, from the bottom to the top of the canyon, where the sergeant received a fatal wound; this within a short distance of the hostile Indians concealed in the rocks (Guadalupe Canyon, Sonora, Mexico, June 8, 1885).*

(1265) Action, Oputo, Sonora, Mexico (June 21, 1885)[6]
— 2nd Lieutenant Britton Davis (3rd U.S. Cavalry)
— Detachment of Indian Scouts
— **1 KILLED**[7]
— Indian Scout

(1266) Action, Babispe Mountains, Sonora, Mexico (June 23, 1885)[8]
— Captain Emmet Crawford (3rd U.S. Cavalry)
— Detachment of Indian Scouts
— **1 WOUNDED**[9]
— Big Dave (Indian Scout)
— *gunshot wound, arm, fracture, severe wound*

(1267) Skirmish, Sierra Madre, Sonora, Mexico (July 28, 1885)[10]
— Captain Wirt Davis (4th U.S. Cavalry)
— Detachment of Indian Scouts

[2] Indians. *Annual Report of Secretary of War (1885)*, 161; *Annual Report of Secretary of War (1886)*, 148, 603; Chronological List, 77; Heitman (Volume 2), 447; Gatewood, *Lt. Charles Gatewood*, 64-65; Rathbun, *New Mexico Frontier Military Place Names*, 127; Sweeney, *Cochise to Geronimo*, 416-418; Thrapp, *Conquest of Apacheria*, 318-319.
[3] Reports of Diseases and Individual Cases, F 538.
[4] Indians. *Annual Report of Secretary of War (1886)*, 149; Chronological List, 77; Heitman (Volume 2), 447; Cruse, *Apache Days*, 210-211; Faulk, *Geronimo Campaign*, 64-65; Rathbun, *New Mexico Frontier Military Place Names*, 80-81; Sweeney, *Cochise to Geronimo*, 425-427; Thrapp, *Conquest of Apacheria*, 324-325. Chronological List lists 4th U.S. Cavalry Detachments.
[5] 4th U.S. Cavalry Regimental Return June 1885.
[6] Indians. Chronological List, 77; Heitman (Volume 2), 447; Sweeney, *Cochise to Geronimo*, 433-434; Thrapp, *Conquest of Apacheria*, 328.
[7] Chronological List, 77.
[8] Indians. *Annual Report of Secretary of War (1886)*, 149-150, 603; Chronological List, 77; Heitman (Volume 2), 447; Carter, *From Yorktown to Santiago*, 244-245; Cruse, *Apache Days*, 219; Davis, *Truth About Geronimo*, 166-169; Faulk, *Geronimo Campaign*, 65; Lockwood, *Apache Indians*, 282; Sweeney, *Cochise to Geronimo*, 434-435; Thrapp, *Conquest of Apacheria*, 328-329. Chronological List lists 3rd U.S. Cavalry Detachment; 6th U.S. Cavalry Detachment; Detachment of Indian Scouts.
[9] Reports of Diseases and Individual Cases, F 540.
[10] Indians. *Annual Report of Secretary of War (1886)*, 150; Chronological List, 77; Heitman (Volume 2), 447; Faulk, *Geronimo Campaign*, 67; Sweeney, *Cochise to Geronimo*, 443; Thrapp, *Conquest of Apacheria*, 330-331.

(1268) Skirmish, Sierra Madre, Sonora, Mexico (August 7, 1885)[11]
— 1st Lieutenant Matthias W. Day (9th U.S. Cavalry)
— Detachment of Indian Scouts

— *1st Lieutenant Matthias W. Day (9th U.S. Cavalry) brevet promotion to Captain for gallant service in actions against Indians during the attacks on Geronimo's stronghold (Sierra Madre, Mexico, August 7, 1885 and Terres Mountains, Mexico, September 22, 1885).*

(1269) Citizens, near Lake Valley, New Mexico Territory (September 11, 1885)[12]
— (1) Citizen Killed

(1270) Action, Terres Mountains, Sonora, Mexico (September 22, 1885)[13]
— 1st Lieutenant Matthias W. Day (9th U.S. Cavalry)
— Detachment of Indian Scouts
— **1 KILLED**[14]
— Skon-ab-toza (Indian Scout)

— **1 WOUNDED**[15]
— Spetcle (Indian Scout)
— *gunshot wound, thigh, slight wound*

— *1st Lieutenant Matthias W. Day (9th U.S. Cavalry) brevet promotion to Captain for gallant service in actions against Indians during the attacks on Geronimo's stronghold (Sierra Madre, Mexico, August 7, 1885 and Terres Mountains, Mexico, September 22, 1885).*

(1271) Action, near Lang's Ranch, New Mexico Territory (October 10, 1885)[16]
— UNKNOWN
— 4th U.S. Cavalry Detachment Co. F
— **1 KILLED**[17]
— Private Samuel Hickman (Co. F 4th U.S. Cavalry)

— **1 WOUNDED**[18]
— Private Sylvester Grover (Co. F 4th U.S. Cavalry)

— *Private Sylvester Grover (Co. F 4th U.S. Cavalry) awarded Certificate of Merit: For coolness and bravery in defending himself and the dispatches he was carrying, when ambushed by approximately fourteen hostile Chiricahua Indians, he being wounded and a second dispatch rider killed in the engagement (Cow Boy Pass, New Mexico, October 10, 1885).*

[11] Indians. *Annual Report of Secretary of War (1886)*, 603; Chronological List, 77; Heitman (Volume 2), 447; Faulk, *Geronimo Campaign*, 67; Sweeney, *Cochise to Geronimo*, 444-445; Thrapp, *Conquest of Apacheria*, 330-331. Chronological List lists Captain Wirt Davis (4th U.S. Cavalry) C/O.
[12] Indians. *Annual Report of Secretary of War (1886)*, 182.
[13] Indians. *Annual Report of Secretary of War (1886)*, 150, 603; Chronological List, 77; Heitman (Volume 2), 447; Sweeney, *Cochise to Geronimo*, 450-453; Thrapp, *Conquest of Apacheria*, 332. Chronological List lists 27 September 1885. Chronological List lists Captain Wirt Davis (4th U.S. Cavalry) C/O.
[14] Reports of Diseases and Individual Cases, F 539.
[15] Reports of Diseases and Individual Cases, F 539; Register of Deaths Regular Army, 1860-1886 (Volume 16).
[16] Indians. Chronological List, 77; Heitman (Volume 2), 447; Sweeney, *Cochise to Geronimo*, 478.
[17] Register of Deaths Regular Army, 1860-1886 (Volume 16); 4th U.S. Cavalry Regimental Return October 1885.
[18] Private Sylvester Grover (4th U.S. Cavalry) Certificate of Merit Citation.

(1272) Action, Florida Mountains, New Mexico Territory (November 7, 1885)[19]
     — Captain Henry M. Kendall (6th U.S. Cavalry)
         — 6th U.S. Cavalry Detachment Co. A
         — Detachment of Indian Scouts
     — **1 KILLED**[20]
         — Antonio (Indian Scout)

     — **1 WOUNDED**[21]
         — Private John Abbott (Co. A 6th U.S. Cavalry)
            — *gunshot wound, chest*

(1273) Skirmish, Lillie's Ranch, Clear Creek, New Mexico Territory (December 9, 1885)[22]
     — 1st Lieutenant Samuel W. Fountain (8th U.S. Cavalry)
         — 8th U.S. Cavalry Detachment Co. C
         — Detachment of Indian Scouts

(1274) Action, Little Dry Creek or White House, New Mexico Territory (December 19, 1885)[23]
     — 1st Lieutenant Samuel W. Fountain (8th U.S. Cavalry)
         — 8th U.S. Cavalry Detachment Co. C
         — Detachment of Indian Scouts
     — **5 KILLED**[24]
         — 1st Lieutenant Thomas J.C. Maddox (Assistant Surgeon)

         — Blacksmith Daniel Collins (Co. C 8th U.S. Cavalry)
         — Wagoner Frank E. Hutton (Co. C 8th U.S. Cavalry)
         — Private George Gibson (Co. C 8th U.S. Cavalry)
         — Private Harry E. McMillan (Co. C 8th U.S. Cavalry)

     — **3 WOUNDED**[25]
         — 2nd Lieutenant DeRosey C. Cabell (Co. C 8th U.S. Cavalry)
            — *gunshot wound, right hand, slight wound*

         — Corporal Wallace McFarland (Co. C 8th U.S. Cavalry)
            — *gunshot wound, right leg, slight wound*
         — Trumpeter Julius Hirschfield (Co. C 8th U.S. Cavalry)
            — *gunshot wound, right ankle, slight wound*

[19] Indians. *Annual Report of Secretary of War (1886)*, 604; Chronological List, 77; Heitman (Volume 2), 447; Carter, *From Yorktown to Santiago*, 278; Sweeney, *Cochise to Geronimo*, 481. Heitman lists 8 November 1885. Chronological List does not list C/O. Chronological List lists 6th U.S. Cavalry Co. A; Detachment of Indian Scouts.
[20] Register of Deaths Regular Army, 1860-1886 (Volume 16); 6th U.S. Cavalry Regimental Return November 1885.
[21] 6th U.S. Cavalry Regimental Return November 1885; Sweeney, *Cochise to Geronimo*, 481.
[22] Indians. *Annual Report of Secretary of War (1886)*, 183, 604; Chronological List, 77; Heitman (Volume 2), 447; Faulk, *Geronimo Campaign*, 73; Sweeney, *Cochise to Geronimo*, 507-508; Thrapp, *Conquest of Apacheria*, 336-337. Chronological List and Heitman both list 8th U.S. Cavalry Co. C.
[23] Indians. *Annual Report of Secretary of War (1886)*, 183, 604, 615; Chronological List, 77; Heitman (Volume 2), 447; Carter, *From Yorktown to Santiago*, 246; Cruse, *Apache Days*, 220; Davis, *Truth About Geronimo*, 196; Rathbun, *New Mexico Frontier Military Place Names*, 17; Sweeney, *Cochise to Geronimo*, 508-509; Thrapp, *Conquest of Apacheria*, 337. Chronological List and Heitman both list 8th U.S. Cavalry Co. C.
[24] Reports of Diseases and Individual Cases, F 542; Register of Deaths Regular Army, 1860-1886 (Volume 16).
[25] Reports of Diseases and Individual Cases, F 542.

"[1ˢᵗ Lieutenant Thomas J.C. Maddox] is the only commissioned officer killed in New Mexico during the Apache raids. By his death the service lost an officer of great promise and usefulness and one who was universally esteemed among his brother officers."

— Luther P. Bradley, U.S. Army[26]

(1275) Citizens, near Carlisle, New Mexico Territory (December 25, 1885)[27]
— (2) Citizens Killed

TOTAL KILLED 1885 — 1/8/3/0 (Officers, Enlisted Men, Indian Scouts, Citizens)

[26] *Annual Report of Secretary of War (1886)*, 183.
[27] Indians. *Annual Report of Secretary of War (1886)*, 183.

1886

*"The Southern Utes, living in Southwestern Colorado, number about one thousand ,
and they are entirely dependent on the Government. They have been neglected in past
years and have come near breaking out several times through starvation. At the beginning
of the last fiscal year the Utes received less than half-rations... This tribe should be
furnished full rations, and nothing but ample food will keep them on their reservation.
They are a spirited and warlike people, and they will not submit to starvation."*

— Luther P. Bradley, U.S. Army[1]

---

[1] Official Report of Colonel Luther P. Bradley, Headquarters Department
of New Mexico, 13 September 1886. *Annual Report of Secretary of War
(1886)*, 184.

(1276) Skirmish, near Aros River, Sonora, Mexico (January 10, 1886)[2]
    — Captain Emmet Crawford (3rd U.S. Cavalry)
        — Detachment of Indian Scouts

(1277) Action, near Aros River, Sonora, Mexico (January 11, 1886)[3]
    — Captain Emmet Crawford (3rd U.S. Cavalry)
    — 1st Lieutenant Marion P. Maus (1st U.S. Infantry)
        — Detachment of Indian Scouts
    — **1 KILLED**[4]
        — Captain Emmet Crawford (3rd U.S. Cavalry) — d. 1-18-1886

    — **4 WOUNDED**[5]
        — Chief of Scouts Thomas Horn (Citizen)
           — *gunshot wound, left arm, severe wound*

        — Brn-Ayal-Thay (Indian Scout)
           — *gunshot wound, left thigh, severe wound*
        — Kay-Was-Laze (Indian Scout)
           — *gunshot wound, left leg, severe wound*
        — No-Fan (Indian Scout)
           — *gunshot wound, left wrist, slight wound*

    — *1st Lieutenant Marion P. Maus (1st U.S. Infantry) received MOH: Most distinguished gallantry in action with hostile Apaches led by Geronimo and Natchez (Sierra Madre Mountains, Mexico, January 11, 1886).*

"With feelings of the deepest sorrow, the Brigadier General Commanding announces the death of Captain Emmet Crawford (3rd U.S. Cavalry)… His loss is irrepressing… Brave as a lion, tender and gentle as a woman, always averse to alluding to his own achievements, temperate, noble, and wise, who was during his life, an honor to his profession and in death is an example to his comrades."
           — George Crook, U.S. Army[6]

(1278) Citizens, Peck Ranch, Santa Cruz Valley, New Mexico Territory (April 27, 1886)[7]
    — (2) Citizens Killed

[2] Indians. *Annual Report of Secretary of War (1886)*, 72, 152, 155; Chronological List, 78; Heitman (Volume 2), 447; Alexander, *Arizona Frontier Military Place Names*, 43-44; Carter, *From Yorktown to Santiago*, 247; Cruse, *Apache Days*, 221-222; Davis, *Truth About Geronimo*, 197-198; Faulk, *Geronimo Campaign*, 78-79; Lockwood, *Apache Indians*, 283-285; Sweeney, *Cochise to Geronimo*, 497-499; Thrapp, *Conquest of Apacheria*, 341-342. Chronological List and Heitman both combine the events near Aros River, Sonora, Mexico on 10 and 11 January 1886.
[3] Mexican Irregulars. *Annual Report of Secretary of War (1886)*, 9-10, 72-73, 152-153, 156-157, 160-164; Chronological List, 78; Heitman (Volume 2), 447; Alexander, *Arizona Frontier Military Place Names*, 43-44; Carter, *From Yorktown to Santiago*, 247-248; Cruse, *Apache Days*, 221-222; Davis, *Truth About Geronimo*, 197-198; Faulk, *Geronimo Campaign*, 79-82; Lockwood, *Apache Indians*, 283-285; Sweeney, *Cochise to Geronimo*, 500-504; Thrapp, *Conquest of Apacheria*, 341-342. Chronological List and Heitman both combine the events near Aros River, Sonora, Mexico on 10 and 11 January 1886. Chronological List lists Captain Emmet Crawford (3rd U.S. Cavalry) C/O.
[4] Reports of Diseases and Individual Cases, F 543; Register of Deaths Regular Army, 1860-1886 (Volume 16).
[5] Reports of Diseases and Individual Cases, F 543.
[6] Brigadier General George Crook, General Field Orders No. 2, Fort Bowie, Arizona Territory, 30 January 1886. Sweeney, *Cochise to Geronimo*, 507.
[7] Indians. Killed were the wife and child of Arthur L. Peck. Peck and his daughter were kidnapped. *Annual Report of Secretary of War (1886)*, 167; Alexander, *Arizona Frontier Military Place Names*, 94; Burton, *Black, Buckskin and Blue*, 194; Faulk, *Geronimo Campaign*, 103-104; Leckie, *Buffalo Soldiers*, 249; Miles, *Personal Recollections*, 506-507; Sweeney, *Cochise to Geronimo*, 537-538; Wellman, *Death in the Desert*, 260.

(1279) Action, near Pinto Mountains, Sonora, Mexico (May 3, 1886)[8]
— Captain Thomas C. Lebo (10th U.S. Cavalry)
— 10th U.S. Cavalry Co. K
— 1 KILLED[9]
— Private Joseph Hollis (Co. K 10th U.S. Cavalry)

— 1 WOUNDED[10]
— Corporal Edward Scott (Co. K 10th U.S. Cavalry)
— *gunshot wounds, left foot, right knee, fracture, severe wounds*

— *2nd Lieutenant Powhatan H. Clarke (10th U.S. Cavalry) received MOH: Rushed forward to the rescue of a soldier who was severely wounded and lay, disabled, exposed to the enemy's fire, and carried him to a place of safety (Penito Mountains, Sonora, Mexico, May 3, 1886).*

— *2nd Lieutenant Powhatan H. Clarke (10th U.S. Cavalry) brevet promotion to 1st Lieutenant for gallant service in actions against Indians (Penito Mountains, Sonora, Mexico, May 3, 1886).*

(1280) Action, Pinto Mountains or Santa Cruz Mountains, Sonora, Mexico (May 15, 1886)[11]
— Captain Charles A. P. Hatfield (4th U.S. Cavalry)
— 4th U.S. Cavalry Co. D
— 2 KILLED[12]
— Blacksmith John H. Conradi (Co. D 4th U.S. Cavalry)
— Private Gustav A.F. Liebenaw (Co. D 4th U.S. Cavalry)

— 2 WOUNDED[13]
— First Sergeant Samuel Adams (Co. D 4th U.S. Cavalry)
— *gunshot wound, right thigh, slight wound*
— Sergeant Samuel H. Craig (Co. D 4th U.S. Cavalry)
— *gunshot wound, right arm, fracture, severe wound*

— *Private John Coghlan (Co. D 4th U.S. Cavalry) awarded Certificate of Merit: For gallant and meritorious conduct at the fight at Santa Cruz Mountains, he together with citizen packer Bowman attempted to rescue Blacksmith Conradi under fire (Santa Cruz Mountains, Mexico, May 15, 1886).*

— *Sergeant Samuel H. Craig (Co. D 4th U.S. Cavalry) received MOH: Conspicuous gallantry during an attack on a hostile Apache Indian camp, seriously wounded (Santa Cruz Mountains, Mexico, May 15, 1886).*

— *Captain Charles A.P. Hatfield (4th U.S. Cavalry) brevet promotion to Major for gallant service in action against Indians in the attack on Geronimo's camp (Santa Cruz Mountains, Mexico, May 15, 1886).*

---

[8] Indians. *Annual Report of Secretary of Wars (1886)*, 143, 167, 177; Chronological List, 78; Heitman (Volume 2), 447; Burton, *Black, Buckskin and Blue*, 194; Cruse, *Apache Days*, 225; Davis, *Truth About Geronimo*, 219; Faulk, *Geronimo Campaign*, 104-105; Gale, "Lebo in Pursuit," *Journal of Arizona History* 21 (Spring 1980): 19-21; Leckie, *Buffalo Soldiers*, 249; Miles, *Personal Recollections*, 489-490; Sweeney, *Cochise to Geronimo*, 538-539.
[9] 10th U.S. Cavalry Regimental Return May 1886.
[10] Gale, "Lebo in Pursuit," *Journal of Arizona History* 21 (Spring 1980): 19-21; Leckie, *Buffalo Soldiers*, 250.
[11] Indians. *Annual Report of Secretary of War (1886)*, 143, 167-168; Chronological List, 78; Heitman (Volume 2), 448; Cruse, *Apache Days*, 225; Davis, *Truth About Geronimo*, 219-220; Faulk, *Geronimo Campaign*, 107-108; Gale, "Hatfield Under Fire," *Journal of Arizona History* 17 (Winter 1977): 447-468; Leckie, *Buffalo Soldiers*, 250; Miles, *Personal Recollections*, 490; Sweeney, *Cochise to Geronimo*, 540-541; Thrapp, *Conquest of Apacheria*, 351.
[12] Reports of Diseases and Individual Cases, F 544; Register of Deaths Regular Army, 1860-1886 (Volume 16).
[13] Reports of Diseases and Individual Cases, F 544.

(1281) Skirmish, Patagonia Mountains, Arizona Territory (June 6, 1886)[14]
　　— 2nd Lieutenant Robert D. Walsh (4th U.S. Cavalry)
　　　　— 4th U.S. Cavalry Co. B

　　— *2nd Lieutenant Robert D. Walsh (4th U.S. Cavalry) brevet promotion to 1st Lieutenant for gallant service in action against Indians (Patagonia Mountains, Arizona, June 6, 1886).*

"I desire to particularly invite the attention of the Department Commander to... [2nd Lieutenant Robert D. Walsh], for successfully intercepting a party of hostiles and capturing their animals and equipage, and for continued faithful service when his physical condition was such as would have justified him in asking relief on account of sickness. Lieutenant Walsh has been in the field against these hostile Indians since the outbreak, May 17, 1885, longer than any other officer in the department."
　　　　　　　　　　　　　　　　　　　— Henry W. Lawton, U.S. Army[15]

(1282) Skirmish, Yakin River, Sonora, Mexico (July 13, 1886)[16]
　　— 2nd Lieutenant Robert A. Brown (4th U.S. Cavalry)
　　　　— Detachment of Indian Scouts

(1283) Surrender of Geronimo and 38 Indians, Skeleton Canyon, Arizona Territory (September 4, 1886)[17]

　　　— *1st Lieutenant Abiel L. Smith (4th U.S. Cavalry) brevet promotion to Captain for gallant service in the campaign against Geronimo's band of Indians (Sonora, Mexico, July, 1886 to September, 1886).*

　　　— *Assistant Surgeon Leonard Wood (U.S. Army) received MOH: Voluntarily carried dispatches through a region infested with hostile Indians, making a journey of seventy miles one night and walking thirty miles the next day. Also, for several weeks, while in close pursuit of Geronimo's band and constantly expecting an encounter, commanded a detachment of infantry, which was then without an officer, and to the command of which he was assigned upon his request (Apache Campaign, Summer of 1886).*

(1284) Surrender of Mangus and 12 Indians, Black River Mountains, Arizona Territory (October 19, 1886)[18]

TOTAL KILLED 1886 — 1/3/0/0 (Officers, Enlisted Men, Indian Scouts, Citizens)

[14] Indians. *Annual Report of Secretary of War (1886)*, 169, 177; Chronological List, 78; Heitman (Volume 2), 448; Miles, *Personal Recollections*, 491; Thrapp, *Conquest of Apacheria*, 352.
[15] *Annual Report of Secretary of War (1886)*, 180.
[16] Indians. *Annual Report of Secretary of War (1886)*, 144, 170, 179; Chronological List, 78; Heitman (Volume 2), 448; Davis, *Truth About Geronimo*, 220-221; Miles, *Personal Recollections*, 493, 510; Sweeney, *Cochise to Geronimo*, 554; Thrapp, *Conquest of Apacheria*, 352. Chronological List lists Captain Henry W. Lawton (4th U.S. Cavalry) C/O. Chronological List and Heitman both list 8th U.S. Infantry Detachments Co. D, K; Detachment of Indian Scouts.
[17] Indians. *Annual Report of Secretary of War (1886)*, 12, 73, 144, 172-173, 179-180; *Annual Report of Secretary of War (1888)*, 7; Chronological List, 78; Alexander, *Arizona Frontier Military Place Names*, 109; Carter, *From Yorktown to Santiago*, 250; Cruse, *Apache Days*, 228-233; Faulk, *Geronimo Campaign*, 132-151; Gatewood, *Lt. Charles Gatewood*, 143-157; Sweeney, *Cochise to Geronimo*, 572-573; Thrapp, *Conquest of Apacheria*, 360-364.
[18] Indians. *Annual Report of Secretary of War (1887)*, 14, 156-158; Chronological List, 78; Heitman (Volume 2), 448; Alexander, *Arizona Frontier Military Place Names*, 16-17; Burton, *Black, Buckskin and Blue*, 195; Miles, *Personal Recollections*, 530; Thrapp, *Conquest of Apacheria*, 366. Chronological List and Heitman both list 18 October 1886.

1887

"I believe that three battalions of four companies each is the best organization for infantry troops that has yet been devised. It is more than any other suited to the peculiar needs of our country and is the one most capable of expansion in case of emergencies. But with our present force, and present organization, no degree of expansion would suffice to put our Army on an effective war footing. An increase in enlisted strength is, in my opinion, not nearly a desideratum but a necessity."

— George Crook, U.S. Army[1]

---

[1] Official Report of Brigadier General George Crook, Department of the Platte, Omaha, Nebraska, 27 August 1887. *Annual Report of Secretary of War (1887)*, 134.

(1285) Action, San Carlos Agency, Arizona Territory (March 10, 1887)[2]
— 1 KILLED[3]
— 2nd Lieutenant Seward Mott (10th U.S. Cavalry) — d. 3-11-1887

"2nd Lieutenant Seward Mott (10th U.S. Cavalry)... in charge of Indians farming on the Upper Gila River, was shot by a young Indian named Nah-diz-az, receiving wounds from which he died the following day at the agency; and thus an intelligent young officer gave up his life while in the performance of duty, endeavoring to benefit and guide wild Indians in peaceful pursuits."
— Nelson A. Miles, U.S. Army[4]

(1286) Citizens, near Mammoth Mines, Arizona Territory (June 3, 1887)[5]
— (1) Citizen Killed

(1287) Citizens, near Fort Huachuca, Arizona Territory (June 8, 1887)[6]
— (1) Citizen Killed

(1288) Skirmish, Rincon Mountains, Arizona Territory (June 11, 1887)[7]
— 2nd Lieutenant Carter P. Johnson (10th U.S. Cavalry)
— 10th U.S. Cavalry Detachments Co. E and L

(1289) Citizens, near Mouth of Jocko River, Montana Territory (July 1887)[8]
— (2) Citizens Killed

— Private Timothy Sullivan (Co. L 7th U.S. Cavalry) awarded Certificate of Merit: For distinguished service in carrying dispatches through an almost unknown country infested with hostile Indians (Montana, September 17, 1887).

(1290) Action, Crow Agency, Montana Territory (November 5, 1887)[9]
— Brigadier General Thomas H. Ruger
— 1st U.S. Cavalry Co. A, B, D, E, G and K
— 7th U.S. Cavalry Co. A
— 9th U.S. Cavalry Co. H
— 3rd U.S. Infantry Co. B and E
— 5th U.S. Infantry Co. D, G and I
— 7th U.S. Infantry Co. C

---

[2] Indians. *Annual Report of Secretary of War (1887)*, 159; Chronological List, 78.
[3] Register of Deaths Regular Army, 1860-1886 (Volume 16)
[4] Brigadier General Nelson A. Miles, Department of Arizona, Los Angeles, California, September 3, 1887. *Annual Report of Secretary of War (1887)*, 159
[5] Indians. Killed was William Diehl. *Annual Report of Secretary of War (1887)*, 156, 160.
[6] Indians. Killed was Mike Grace. *Annual Report of Secretary of War (1887)*, 156, 160.
[7] Indians. *Annual Report of Secretary of War (1887)*, 156, 160; Chronological List, 78; Heitman (Volume 2), 448. Chronological List lists 10th U.S. Cavalry Detachments.
[8] Indians. *Annual Report of Secretary of War (1889)*, 162.
[9] Indians. *Annual Report of Secretary of War (1888)*, 148-150, 152-153; Chronological List, 78; Heitman (Volume 2), 448; Brown, *Plainsmen of the Yellowstone*, 441-442, Calloway, "Sword Bearer," *Montana, the Magazine of Western History* 36 (Autumn 1986): 46-47.

— **1 KILLED**[10]
    — Corporal Charles Sampson (Co. K 1st U.S. Cavalry)

— **1 WOUNDED**[11]
    — Private Eugene Malloy (Co. K 1st U.S. Cavalry)
        — *gunshot wounds, right ear, back, right arm, slight wounds*

"The result of the fight, including the killing of the [Sword Bearer], was most fortunate; the Indians inclined to hostility were completely subdued and the authority of those well disposed was restored... It would do but partial justice to all concerned to commend only those actually engaged and for the deeds done; what was forborne by others as well, from humane motives under circumstances of provocation, is as praiseworthy as what was actually done against these Crow Indians. The forbearance shown impressed the Indians, who said they would ever "be friends of the soldiers who spared them when they might have killed them all."
                                                    — Thomas H. Ruger, U.S. Army[12]

TOTAL KILLED 1887 — 1/1/0/0 (OFFICERS, ENLISTED MEN, INDIAN SCOUTS, CITIZENS)

---

[10] Reports of Diseases and Individual Cases, F 547; Register of Deaths Regular Army, 1860-1886 (Volume 16).
[11] Reports of Diseases and Individual Cases, F 547.
[12] Official Report of Brigadier General Thomas H. Ruger, Department of Dakota, Saint Paul, Minnesota, 15 September 1888. *Annual Report of Secretary of War (1888)*, 150.

1888

"Substantial progress is being made toward a solution of the great Indian problem. Danger of [Indian] warfare is continually diminishing and the time is not very distant when, it may be hoped, that danger may disappear. But for the present and near future increased vigilance, caution and preparation are and will be necessary, for the reason that the rich settlements now surrounding the Indian reservations render possible greater destruction of life and property in a few days than was formerly possible during a long period of hostilities."

— John M. Schofield, U.S. Army[1]

---

[1] Official Report of Major General John M. Schofield, Headquarters of the Army, Washington D.C., 25 October 1888. *Annual Report of Secretary of War (1888)*, 69.

(1291) Skirmish, Pompey's Pillar, Yellowstone River, Montana Territory (June 15, 1888)[2]
    — Interpreter Charles Cacely (Citizen)
        — Detachment of Indian Scouts

(1292) Skirmish, near San Carlos Agency, Arizona Territory (July 28, 1888)[3]
    — UNKNOWN
        — Detachment of Indian Scouts
    — 2 WOUNDED[4]
        — Rowdy (Indian Scout)
            — gunshot wound, left arm, slight wound
        — Nai-Tah (Indian Scout)
            — gunshot wounds, chest, severe wound, side, slight wound

TOTAL KILLED 1888 — 0/0/0/0 (OFFICERS, ENLISTED MEN, INDIAN SCOUTS, CITIZENS)

[2] Indians. *Annual Report of Secretary of War (1888)*, 156; Chronological List, 78; Heitman (Volume 2), 448. Chronological List and Heitman both list June 16, 1888.
[3] Indians. Chronological List, 78; Heitman (Volume 2), 448.
[4] Reports of Diseases and Individual Cases, F 548.

1889

"The Army is now in a transitory state. During the past twenty-three years... it has been largely occupied in what has been known as "the battle of civilization." It has been pushed forward in advance of the building of the transcontinental railways, occupying every dangerous mountain pass, guarding every surveying expedition, working party, and settlement that has been established westward from the Missouri River to the Pacific. Wherever danger threatened, whether a miner's camp, a settler's ranch or home, or where a detachment of railroad men were located, the Army has been hurried from point to point to defend them from [Indians] until the entire wilderness has been traversed, overrun, and occupied by civilized communities."

— Nelson A. Miles, U.S. Army[1]

---

[1] Official Report of Brigadier General Nelson A. Miles, Headquarters Division of the Pacific, San Francisco, California, 16 September 1889. *Annual Report of Secretary of War (1889)*, 171.

(1293) Citizens, near Globe, Arizona Territory (February 1889)[2]
— (1) Citizen Killed

(1294) Action, Cedar Springs, Arizona Territory (May 11, 1889)[3]
— Sergeant Benjamin Brown (24th U.S. Infantry)
— 10th U.S. Cavalry Detachments Co. C and G
— 24th U.S. Infantry Detachments Co. B, C, E and K
— **7 WOUNDED**[4]
— Private Thornton Hams (Co. C 10th U.S. Cavalry)
— *gunshot wound, right arm, slight wound*
— Private James Wheeler (Co. G 10th U.S. Cavalry)
— *gunshot wound, left arm, severe wound*

— Private Hamilton Lewis (Co. B 24th U.S. Infantry)
— *gunshot wound, side*
— Sergeant Benjamin Brown (Co. C 24th U.S. Infantry)
— *gunshot wounds, side, severe wound, arm, slight wound*
— Private George Arrington (Co. C 24th U.S. Infantry)
— *gunshot wound, right shoulder, severe wound*
— Private Benjamin Burge (Co. E 24th U.S. Infantry)
— *gunshot wounds, leg, arm*
— Private Squire Williams (Co. K 24th U.S. Infantry)
— *gunshot wound, left leg, severe wound*

— *Private George Arrington (Co. C 24th U.S. Infantry) awarded Distinguished Service Cross: For gallant and meritorious conduct while serving with a detachment escorting Major Joseph W. Wham, paymaster, U.S. Army, in an encounter with a band of robbers (Between Fort Grant and Fort Thomas, Arizona, May 11, 1889).*

— *Private George Arrington (Co. C 24th U.S. Infantry) awarded Certificate of Merit: For gallant and meritorious conduct while serving with a detachment escorting Major Joseph W. Wham, paymaster, U.S. Army, in an encounter with a band of robbers, by whom the party was attacked.(Between Fort Grant and Fort Thomas, Arizona, May 11, 1889).*

— *Sergeant Benjamin Brown (Co. C 24th U.S. Infantry) received MOH: Although shot in the abdomen, in a fight between a paymaster's escort and robbers, did not leave the field until again wounded through both arms (Arizona, May 11, 1889).*

— *Private Benjamin Burge (Co. E 24th U.S. Infantry) awarded Certificate of Merit: For gallant and meritorious conduct while serving with a detachment escorting Major Joseph W. Wham, paymaster, U.S. Army,*

[2] Indians. Killed was teamster Gasper T. Freeman. *Annual Report of Secretary of War (1889)*, 178-179.
[3] Bandits. *Annual Report of Secretary of War (1889)*, 185-186; Chronological List, 79; Heitman (Volume 2), 448; Alexander, *Arizona Frontier Military Place Names*, 31; Ball, *Ambush at Bloody Run*, 1-18; Burton, *Black, Buckskin and Blue*, 143-146; Fowler, *Black Infantry*, 85-86. Chronological List lists 10th U.S. Cavalry Detachments Co. C, G; 24th U.S. Infantry Detachments.
[4] Reports of Diseases and Individual Cases, F 549.

in an encounter with a band of robbers, by whom the party was attacked.(Between Fort Grant and Fort Thomas, Arizona, May 11, 1889).

— Private Thornton Hams (Co. C 10th U.S. Cavalry) awarded Certificate of Merit: For gallant and meritorious conduct while serving with a detachment escorting Major Joseph W. Wham, paymaster, U.S. Army, in an encounter with a band of robbers, by whom the party was attacked.(Between Fort Grant and Fort Thomas, Arizona, May 11, 1889).

— Private Julius Harrison (Co. B 24th U.S. Infantry) awarded Certificate of Merit: For gallant and meritorious conduct while serving with a detachment escorting Major Joseph W. Wham, paymaster, U.S. Army, in an encounter with a band of robbers, by whom the party was attacked.(Between Fort Grant and Fort Thomas, Arizona, May 11, 1889).

— Private Hamilton Lewis (Co. B 24th U.S. Infantry) awarded Certificate of Merit: For gallant and meritorious conduct while serving with a detachment escorting Major Joseph W. Wham, paymaster, U.S. Army, in an encounter with a band of robbers, by whom the party was attacked.(Between Fort Grant and Fort Thomas, Arizona, May 11, 1889).

— Corporal Isaiah Mays (Co. B 24th U.S. Infantry) received MOH: Gallantry in the fight between paymaster Wham's escort and robbers. Mays walked and crawled two miles to a Ranch for help (Arizona, May 11, 1889).

— Private James Wheeler (Co. G 10th U.S. Cavalry) awarded Certificate of Merit: For gallant and meritorious conduct while serving with a detachment escorting Major Joseph W. Wham, paymaster, U.S. Army, in an encounter with a band of robbers, by whom the party was attacked.(Between Fort Grant and Fort Thomas, Arizona, May 11, 1889).

— Private Squire Williams (Co. K 24th U.S. Infantry) awarded Certificate of Merit: For gallant and meritorious conduct while serving with a detachment escorting Major Joseph W. Wham, paymaster, U.S. Army, in an encounter with a band of robbers, by whom the party was attacked.(Between Fort Grant and Fort Thomas, Arizona, May 11, 1889).

— Private James Young (Co. K 24th U.S. Infantry) awarded Certificate of Merit: For gallant and meritorious conduct while serving with a detachment escorting Major Joseph W. Wham, paymaster, U.S. Army, in an encounter with a band of robbers, by whom the party was attacked.(Between Fort Grant and Fort Thomas, Arizona, May 11, 1889).

(1295) Surrender of Black Moon and 34 Indians, North Bank of Missouri River, North Dakota (June 2, 1889) [5]

---

[5] Indians. *Annual Report of Secretary of War (1889)*, 161; Chronological List, 79; Heitman (Volume 2), 448.

— Private James Settlers (Co. E 9ᵗʰ U.S. Cavalry) awarded Certificate of Merit: For saving the life of his commanding officer from drowning (Wind River, Wyoming, July 19, 1889).

(1296) Action, Mescal Springs, Arizona Territory (October 8, 1889)[6]
    — UNKNOWN
        — 4ᵗʰ U.S. Cavalry Detachment Co. I
    — 1 KILLED[7]
        — Private A.J. Ponca (Co. I 4ᵗʰ U.S. Cavalry)

    — 1 WOUNDED[8]
        — Enlisted Man (4ᵗʰ U.S. Cavalry)

(1297) Citizens, Gila River, near Riverside, Arizona Territory (November 2, 1889)[9]
    — (2) Citizens Killed

TOTAL KILLED 1889 — 0/1/0/0 (Officers, Enlisted Men, Indian Scouts, Citizens)

---

[6] Bandits. *Annual Report of Secretary of War (1890)*, 164.
[7] 4ᵗʰ U.S. Cavalry Regimental Return October 1889.
[8] *Annual Report of Secretary of War (1890)*, 164.
[9] Bandits. Killed while transferring nine prisoners to Yuma penitentiary were Sheriff Glenn Reynolds and deputy W.A. (Hunkydory) Holmes. *Annual Report of Secretary of War (1890)*, 165, 176; Griffith, *Mickey Free*, 173-174; Hayes, *Apache Vengeance*, 92-102.

1890

"From the close of the great civil war in 1865 until near the present time the Army was very actively employed in subduing the warlike tribes of Indians which roamed over a great part of the vast territory between the Mississippi River and the Pacific Ocean, in giving necessary protection to the numerous railroads in process of construction across that territory and to tide the emigration constantly spreading over it. That work appears now to have been nearly accomplished, and it remains only to adequately guard the adjacent settlements from possible injury by the Indian tribes, heretofore hostile and now but partially civilized, assembled upon comparatively small reservations."

— John M. Schofield, U.S. Army[1]

[1] Official Report of Major General John M. Schofield, Headquarters of the Army, Washington, D.C., 23 October 1890. *Annual Report of Secretary of War (1890)*, 43-44.

(1298) Citizens, near Fort Thomas, Arizona Territory (March 2, 1890)[2]
— (1) Citizen Killed

(1299) Skirmish, Salt River, near Mouth of Cherry Creek, Arizona Territory (March 7, 1890)[3]
— 1st Lieutenant James W. Watson (10th U.S. Cavalry)
    — 4th U.S. Cavalry Detachment Co. L
    — 10th U.S. Cavalry Detachment Co. K
    — Detachment of Indian Scouts

— *Sergeant James T. Daniels (Co. L 4th U.S. Cavalry) received MOH: Untiring energy and cool gallantry under fire in an engagement with Apache Indians (Arizona, March 7, 1890).*

— *Sergeant William McBryar (Co. K 10th U.S. Cavalry) received MOH: Distinguished himself for coolness, bravery and marksmanship while his troop was in pursuit of hostile Apache Indians (Arizona, March 7, 1890).*

— *Sergeant Rowdy (Indian Scout) received MOH: Bravery in action with Apache Indians (Arizona, March 7, 1890).*

— *1st Lieutenant James W. Watson (10th U.S. Cavalry) brevet promotion to Captain for gallant service in action against Indians (Salt River, Arizona, March 7, 1890).*

(1300) Citizens, near Tongue River Agency, Montana (September 1890)[4]
— (1) Citizen Killed

(1301) Skirmish, Tongue River Agency, Montana (September 13, 1890)[5]
— 1st Lieutenant John Pitcher (1st U.S. Cavalry)
    — 1st U.S. Cavalry Co. E and G

(1302) Action, Grand River, near Standing Rock, North Dakota (December 15, 1890)[6]
— Captain Edmond G. Fechet (8th U.S. Cavalry)
    — 8th U.S. Cavalry Co. F and G
    — Detachment of Indian Police
— **6 KILLED**[7]
    — 1st Lieutenant Bull Head or Henry Tatankapah (Indian Police)

    — First Sergeant Shave Head or Charles Kashlah (Indian Police) — d. 12-17-1890
    — Forth Sergeant Little Eagle or James Wambdichigalah (Indian Police)
    — Private Afraid-of-Soldier or Paul Akichitah (Indian Police)
    — Private Hawk Man No. 2 (Indian Police)
    — Private John Armstrong (Indian Police)

[2] Indians. Killed was a freighter named Herbert. *Annual Report of Secretary of War (1890)*, 167, 176; Hayes, *Apache Vengeance*, 133.
[3] Indians. *Annual Report of Secretary of War (1890)*, 167; Chronological List, 79; Heitman (Volume 2), 448; Alexander, *Arizona Frontier Military Place Names*, 32; Burton, *Black, Buckskin and Blue*, 197; Hayes, *Apache Vengeance*, 134-140; Leckie, *Buffalo Soldiers*, 252. Chronological List lists 11 March 1890.
[4] Indians. Killed was Hugh Boyle. *Annual Report of Secretary of War (1891)*, 163.
[5] Indians. *Annual Report of Secretary of War (1891)*, 163; Chronological List, 79; Heitman (Volume 2), 448.
[6] Indians. *Annual Report of Secretary of War (1891)*, 146-147, 167-168, 182-183, 194-199; Chronological List, 79; Heitman (Volume 2), 448; Utley, *Last Days of the Sioux Nation*, 146-166. Chronological List lists Standing Rock, Montana. Heitman lists 8th U.S. Cavalry Co. E, G; Detachment of Indian Scouts.
[7] *Annual Report of Secretary of War (1891)*, 199.
[8] *Annual Report of Secretary of War (1891)*, 199.

— 1 WOUNDED[8]
    — Private Middle or Alexander Hochokah (Indian Police)

"I cannot too strongly commend the splendid courage and ability which characterized the conduct of the Indian police commanded by Bull Head and Shave Head throughout the encounter. The attempt to arrest Sitting Bull was so managed as to place the responsibility for the fight that ensued upon Sitting Bull's band, which began the firing... After the fight, no demoralization seemed to exist among them, and they were ready and willing to cooperate with the troops to any extent desired."
    — Edmond G. Fechet, U.S. Army[9]

(1303) Surrender of 294 Indians, Cherry Creek, South Dakota (December 22, 1890)[10]

(1304) Surrender of Big Foot and 106 Indians, Porcupine Creek, South Dakota (December 28, 1890)[11]

(1305) Engagement, Wounded Knee Creek, South Dakota (December 29, 1890)[12]
    — Colonel James W. Forsyth (7th U.S. Cavalry)
        — 7th U.S. Cavalry Co. A, B, C, D, E, G, I and K
        — 1st U.S. Artillery Co. E
    — 33 KILLED[13]
        — Captain George D. Wallace (7th U.S. Cavalry)

        — Sergeant Major Richard W. Corwine (F&S)
        — Hospital Steward Oscar Pollock (F&S)

        — Sergeant Arthur C. Dyer (Co. A 7th U.S. Cavalry)
        — Private Henry Frey (Co. A 7th U.S. Cavalry)
        — Private Herman Granberg (Co. A 7th U.S. Cavalry)
        — Private George P. Johnson (Co. A 7th U.S. Cavalry)
        — Private James Logan (Co. A 7th U.S. Cavalry)
        — Private Michael Regan (Co. A 7th U.S. Cavalry)

        — First Sergeant Dora S. Coffey (Co. B 7th U.S. Cavalry)
        — Corporal Harry R. Forrest (Co. B 7th U.S. Cavalry)
        — Corporal Charles H. Newell (Co. B 7th U.S. Cavalry)
        — Private Ralph L. Cook (Co. B 7th U.S. Cavalry)
        — Private John Costello (Co. B 7th U.S. Cavalry)
        — Private William S. Mezo (Co. B 7th U.S. Cavalry)
        — Private Harry B. Stone (Co. B 7th U.S. Cavalry)[14] — d. 1-13-1891

        — Private James DeVreede (Co. C 7th U.S. Cavalry)

[9] Official Report of Captain Edmond G. Fechet (8th U.S. Cavalry).
[10] Indians. *Annual Report of Secretary of War (1891)*, 147, 168-169, 184; 200-209, 223-228, 233-238; Chronological List, 79; Utley, *Last Days of the Sioux Nation*, 179-186.
[11] Indians. *Annual Report of Secretary of War (1891)*, 150, 170, 210-216; Chronological List, 79; Heitman (Volume 2), 448; Utley, *Last Days of the Sioux Nation*, 187-199.
[12] Indians. *Annual Report of Secretary of War (1891)*, 150, 170, 216-219, 600; Chronological List, 79; Heitman (Volume 2), 448; Utley, *Last Days of the Sioux Nation*, 200-230.
[13] Telegraph, General Nelson A. Miles to Adjutant General's Office, Washington, D.C., 3 January 1891. Reports and Correspondence Relating to the Army Investigations of the Battle of Wounded Knee and the Sioux Campaign, 1890-1891; *Annual Report of Secretary of War (1891)*, 56, 154.
[14] *Army and Navy Journal*, 17 January 1891.

— Private Frank T. Reinecky (Co. D 7th U.S. Cavalry)
— Sergeant Robert H. Nettles (Co. E 7th U.S. Cavalry)
— Private August Kellner (Co. E 7th U.S. Cavalry)

— Sergeant Henry Howard (Co. I 7th U.S. Cavalry)[15] — d. 1-30-1891
— Corporal Albert S. Bone (Co. I 7th U.S. Cavalry)
— Blacksmith Gustav Korn (Co. I 7th U.S. Cavalry)
— Private Pierce Cummings (Co. I 7th U.S. Cavalry)
— Private James E. Kelley (Co. I 7th U.S. Cavalry)
— Private Daniel Twohig (Co. I 7th U.S. Cavalry)
— Private Bernhard Zolinder (Co. I 7th U.S. Cavalry)

— Sergeant William T. Hodges (Co. K 7th U.S. Cavalry)
— Private William F. McClintock (Co. K 7th U.S. Cavalry)
— Private John M. McCue (Co. K 7th U.S. Cavalry)
— Private Joseph Murphy (Co. K 7th U.S. Cavalry)
— Private Philip Schwenkey (Co. K 7th U.S. Cavalry)

— High Backbone (Indian Scout)

— **29 WOUNDED**[16]
— 1st Lieutenant Ernest A. Garlington (7th U.S. Cavalry)
— 1st Lieutenant John C. Gresham (7th U.S. Cavalry)
— 1st Lieutenant John C. Kinzie (2nd U.S. Infantry)
— 2nd Lieutenant Harry L. Hawthorne (2nd U.S. Artillery)[17]

— Sergeant A.H. Hazlewood (Co. A 7th U.S. Cavalry)
— Private Harry L. Duncan (Co. A 7th U.S. Cavalry)
— Private Daniel McMahon (Co. A 7th U.S. Cavalry)
— Private Adam Neder (Co. A 7th U.S. Cavalry)

— Sergeant William H. Toohey (Co. B 7th U.S. Cavalry)
— Sergeant James Ward (Co. B 7th U.S. Cavalry)
— Private Frank Lewis (Co. B 7th U.S. Cavalry)
— Private John McKenzie (Co. B 7th U.S. Cavalry)

— Private William H. Green (Co. C 7th U.S. Cavalry)
— Private Ervin Schriver (Co. C 7th U.S. Cavalry)
— Wagoner George York (Co. D 7th U.S. Cavalry)
— Sergeant John F. Tritle (Co. E 7th U.S. Cavalry)

[15] *Army and Navy Journal*, 7 February 1891.
[16] Telegraph, General Nelson A. Miles to Adjutant General's Office, Washington, D.C., January 3, 1891. M983 Reports and Correspondence Relating to the Army Investigations of the Battle of Wounded Knee and the Sioux Campaign, 1890-1891; *Annual Report of Secretary of War (1891)*, 56, 154.
[17] Attached to 1st U.S. Artillery Co. E. *Army and Navy Journal*, 1 January 1891.

— Sergeant George Lloyd (Co. I 7ᵗʰ U.S. Cavalry)
— Private Gottlieb Hipp (Co. I 7ᵗʰ U.S. Cavalry)
— Private Harvey H. Thomas (Co. I 7ᵗʰ U.S. Cavalry)

— Corporal Harold L. Clifton (Co. K 7ᵗʰ U.S. Cavalry)
— Trumpeter James Christianson (Co. K 7ᵗʰ U.S. Cavalry)
— Private William Adams (Co. K 7ᵗʰ U.S. Cavalry)
— Private William J. Davis (Co. K 7ᵗʰ U.S. Cavalry)
— Private George Elliott (Co. K 7ᵗʰ U.S. Cavalry)
— Private C.P. Martin (Co. K 7ᵗʰ U.S. Cavalry)
— Private Samuel F. Smith (Co. K 7ᵗʰ U.S. Cavalry)
— Private Edward A. Sullivan (Co. K 7ᵗʰ U.S. Cavalry)
— Private Frederick F. Yoder (Co. K 7ᵗʰ U.S. Cavalry)

— Father Francis M.J. Craft (Citizen)
— *knife wound*

— *Sergeant William G. Austin (Co. E 7ᵗʰ U.S. Cavalry) received MOH: While the Indians were concealed in a ravine, assisted men on the skirmish line, directing their fire, etc., and using every effort to dislodge the infantry (Wounded Knee Creek, South Dakota, December 29, 1890).*

— *Corporal Harry W. Capron (Co. B 7ᵗʰ U.S. Cavalry) awarded Certificate of Merit: For gallantry in action against hostile Sioux Indians, rushing forward and saving the life of a wounded sergeant of his troop by disabling his assailant (Wounded Knee Creek, South Dakota, December 29, 1890).*

— *Corporal Harry W. Capron (Co. B 7ᵗʰ U.S. Cavalry) awarded Distinguished Service Cross: For extraordinary gallantry in action (Wounded Knee Creek, South Dakota, December 29, 1890).*

— *Musician John E. Clancy (Co. E 1ˢᵗ U.S. Artillery) received MOH: Twice voluntarily rescued wounded comrades under fire of the enemy (Wounded Knee Creek, South Dakota, December 29, 1890).*

— *Private Mosheim Feaster (Co. E 7ᵗʰ U.S. Cavalry) received MOH: Extraordinary gallantry (Wounded Knee Creek, South Dakota, December 29, 1890).*

— *Private Nathan Fellman (Co. K 7ᵗʰ U.S. Cavalry) awarded Certificate of Merit: For special bravery after the action against hostile Sioux Indians, in voluntarily accompanying an officer carrying dispatches on a most dangerous and difficult trip (Wounded Knee Creek, South Dakota, December 29, 1890).*

— *1ˢᵗ Lieutenant Ernest A. Garlington (7ᵗʰ U.S. Cavalry) received MOH: Distinguished gallantry (Wounded Knee Creek, South Dakota, December 29, 1890).*

— *1ˢᵗ Lieutenant John C. Gresham (7ᵗʰ U.S. Cavalry) received MOH: Voluntarily led a party into a ravine to dislodge Sioux Indians concealed therein. He was wounded during this action (Wounded Knee Creek, South Dakota, December 29, 1890).*

— *Private Matthew H. Hamilton (Co. G 7ᵗʰ U.S. Cavalry) received MOH: Bravery in action (Wounded Knee Creek, South Dakota, December 29, 1890).*

— *Private Joshua B. Hartzog (Co. E 1ˢᵗ U.S. Artillery) received MOH: Went to the rescue of the commanding officer who had fallen severely wounded, picked him up, and carried him out of range of the hostile guns (Wounded Knee Creek, South Dakota, December 29, 1890).*

— *2ⁿᵈ Lieutenant Harry L. Hawthorne (2ⁿᵈ U.S. Artillery) received MOH: Distinguished conduct in battle with hostile Indians (Wounded Knee Creek, South Dakota, December 29, 1890).*

— *Private Marvin C. Hillock (Co. B 7ᵗʰ U.S. Cavalry) received MOH: Distinguished bravery (Wounded Knee Creek, South Dakota, December 29, 1890).*

— *Private George Hobday (Co. A 7ᵗʰ U.S. Cavalry) received MOH: Conspicuous and gallant conduct in battle (Wounded Knee Creek, South Dakota, December 29, 1890).*

— *Captain John V.R. Hoff (Medical Corps) awarded Distinguished Service Cross: For ext6raordunary heroism while serving as Assistant Surgeon, Medical Corps. When the Indians made a sudden treacherous attack upon the troops, Captain Hoff, with utter disregard for his personal safety, attended to the dressing of the wounds of fallen soldiers (Wounded Knee Creek, South Dakota, December 29, 1890).*

— *Sergeant George Loyd (Co. I 7ᵗʰ U.S. Cavalry) received MOH: Bravery, especially after having been severely wounded through the lung (Wounded Knee Creek, South Dakota, December 29, 1890).*

— *Sergeant Albert W. McMillan (Co. E 7ᵗʰ U.S. Cavalry) received MOH: While engaged with Indians concealed in a ravine, he assisted the men on the skirmish line, directed their fire, encouraged them by example, and used every effort to dislodge the enemy (Wounded Knee Creek, South Dakota, December 29, 1890).*

— *Private Thomas Sullivan (Co. E 7ᵗʰ U.S. Cavalry) received MOH: Conspicuous bravery in action concealed in a ravine (Wounded Knee Creek, South Dakota, December 29, 1890).*

— *First Sergeant Frederick E. Toy (Co. C 7ᵗʰ U.S. Cavalry) received MOH: Bravery (Wounded Knee Creek, South Dakota, December 29, 1890).*

— *Sergeant John F. Trittle (Co. E 7ᵗʰ U.S. Cavalry) awarded Certificate of Merit: For conspicuously gallant and meritorious conduct in action against hostile Sioux Indians, though slightly wounded in the right hand, he continued his efforts until disabled by a severe wound in the right shoulder (Wounded Knee Creek, South Dakota, December 29, 1890).*

— *First Sergeant Jacob Trautman (Co. I 7ᵗʰ U.S. Cavalry) received MOH: Killed a hostile Indian lose quarters, and, although entitled to retirement from service, remained to the close of the campaign (Wounded Knee Creek, South Dakota, December 29, 1890).*

— *Sergeant James Ward (Co. B 7ᵗʰ U.S. Cavalry) received MOH: Continued to fight after being severely wounded (Wounded Knee Creek, South Dakota, December 29, 1890).*

— *Corporal Paul H. Weinert (Co. E 1ˢᵗ U.S. Artillery) received MOH: Taking the place of his commanding officer, who had fallen severely wounded, he gallantry served his piece, after each fire advancing it to a better position (Wounded Knee Creek, South Dakota, December 29, 1890).*

— *Private Hermann Zeigner (Co. E 7ᵗʰ U.S. Cavalry) received MOH: Conspicuous bravery (Wounded Knee Creek and White Clay Creek, South Dakota, December 29 and 30, 1890).*

(1306) Action, near Pine Ridge Agency, South Dakota (December 29, 1890)[18]
    — Colonel Frank Wheaton (2ⁿᵈ U.S. Infantry)
        — 2ⁿᵈ U.S. Infantry
    — **5 WOUNDED**[19]
        — Private Hahn (Co. B 2ⁿᵈ U.S. Infantry)
        — Private Haran (Co. B 2ⁿᵈ U.S. Infantry)
        — Private Gruner (Co. B 2ⁿᵈ U.S. Infantry)

        — Corporal Boyle (Co. G 2ⁿᵈ U.S. Infantry)
        — Corporal Cowley (Co. G 2ⁿᵈ U.S. Infantry)

(1307) Action, near Pine Ridge Agency, South Dakota (December 30, 1890)[20]
    — Captain John S. Loud (9th U.S. Cavalry)
        — 9th U.S. Cavalry Co. D
— 1 KILLED[21]
        — Private Charles Haywood (Co. D 9th U.S. Cavalry)

(1308) Action, White Clay Creek or Old Catholic Mission, South Dakota (December 30, 1890)[22]
    — Colonel James W. Forsyth (7th U.S. Cavalry)
        — 7th U.S. Cavalry Co. A, B, C, D, E, G, I and K
        — 9th U.S. Cavalry Co. D, F, I and K
        — 1st U.S. Artillery Co. E
— 2 KILLED[23]
        — 1st Lieutenant James D. Mann (7th U.S. Cavalry) — d. 01-15-1891

        — Private Dominick Franceshetti (Co. G 7th U.S. Cavalry)

— 6 WOUNDED[24]
        — Private Marvin C. Hillock (Co. B 7th U.S. Cavalry)
        — Private William S. Kirkpatrick (Co. B 7th U.S. Cavalry)
        — Private Peter Clausen (Co. C 7th U.S. Cavalry)
        — Private Richard Kern (Co. D 7th U.S. Cavalry)
        — Farrier Richard J. Nolan (Co. I 7th U.S. Cavalry)

        — First Sergeant Theodore Ragnar (Co. K 7th U.S. Cavalry)

    — Private Richard Costner (Hospital Corps) awarded Certificate of Merit: For gallantry in action against hostile Sioux Indians, in taking the ambulance, abandoned by its civilian teamster, and rescuing a wounded officer under fire, on the battlefield (White Clay Creek, South Dakota, December 30, 1890).

    — Private William Girdwood (Hospital Corps) awarded Certificate of Merit: For gallantry in action against hostile Sioux Indians, in taking the ambulance, abandoned by its civilian teamster, and rescuing a wounded officer under fire, on the battlefield (White Clay Creek, South Dakota, December 30, 1890).

    — Farrier Richard J. Nolan (Co. I 7th U.S. Cavalry) received MOH: Bravery (White Clay Creek, South Dakota, December 30, 1890).

    — First Sergeant Theodore Ragnar (Co. K 7th U.S. Cavalry) received MOH: Bravery (White Clay Creek, South Dakota, December 30, 1890).

    — Captain Charles A. Varnum (Co. B 7th U.S. Cavalry) received MOH: While executing an order to withdraw, seeing that a continuance of the movement would expose another troop of his regiment to being cut off and surrounded, he disregarded orders to retire, placed himself in front of his men, led a charge upon

[18] Indians. Chronological List, 79; Heitman (Volume 2), 448; Utley, *Last Days of the Sioux Nation*, 232.
[19] *Army and Navy Journal*, 17 January 1891.
[20] Indians. *Annual Report of Secretary of War (1891)*, 151; Chronological List, 79; Heitman (Volume 2), 448; Leckie, *Buffalo Soldiers*, 275; Utley, *Last Days of the Sioux Nation*, 235-236.
[21] 9th U.S. Cavalry Regimental Return December 1890.
[22] Indians. *Annual Report of Secretary of War (1891)*, 151, 170; Chronological List, 79; Heitman (Volume 2), 448; Leckie, *Buffalo Soldiers*, 275-276; Utley, *Last Days of the Sioux Nation*, 231-241. Heitman lists 7th U.S. Cavalry Co. A, B, C, D, E, G, I, K; 9th U.S. Cavalry Co. D, E, I, K; 1st U.S. Artillery Co. E; Detachment of Indian Scouts.
[23] Telegraph, General Nelson A. Miles to Adjutant General's Office, Washington, D.C., 3 January 1891. Reports and Correspondence Relating to the Army Investigations of the Battle of Wounded Knee and the Sioux Campaign, 1890-1891.
[24] Telegraph, General Nelson A. Miles to Adjutant General's Office, Washington, D.C., 3 January 1891. Reports and Correspondence Relating to the Army Investigations of the Battle of Wounded Knee and the Sioux Campaign, 1890-1891.

the advancing Indians, regained a commanding position that had just been vacated, and thus insured a safe withdrawal of both detachments without further loss (White Clay Creek, South Dakota, December 30, 1890).

— Sergeant Bernard Jetter (Co. K 7ᵗʰ U.S. Cavalry) received MOH: Distinguished bravery (Sioux Campaign, December 1890).

— Private Adam Neder (Co. A 7ᵗʰ U.S. Cavalry) received MOH: Distinguished bravery (Sioux Campaign, December 1890).

— Corporal William O. Wilson (Co. I 9ᵗʰ U.S. Cavalry) received MOH: Bravery (Sioux Campaign, December 1890).

TOTAL KILLED 1890 — 2/33/7/1 (OFFICERS, ENLISTED MEN, INDIAN SCOUTS, CITIZENS)

1891-1898

"There is... a well-grounded belief that, by the constant exercise of discretion in the management of the Indians, coupled with justice in all dealings of the Government with them, and the presence of a sufficient military force to overawe the turbulent minority among them, there need be no serious apprehension of an extended uprising of the Sioux, and, probably, not of any other Indian tribe."

— John M. Schofield, U.S. Army[1]

---

[1] Official Report of Major General Commanding the Army, Major General John M. Schofield, Headquarters of the Army, Washington, D.C., September 24, 1891. *Annual Report of Secretary of War (1891)*, 56. 231

(1309) Skirmish, White River, near Wounded Knee Creek, South Dakota (January 1, 1891)[2]
     — Captain John B. Kerr (6th U.S. Cavalry)
         — 6th U.S. Cavalry Co. K

     — *2nd Lieutenant Robert L. Howze (Co. K 6th U.S. Cavalry) received MOH: Bravery in action (White River, South Dakota, January 1, 1891).*

     — *Captain John B. Kerr (6th U.S. Cavalry) received MOH: For distinguished bravery while in command of his troop in action against hostile Sioux Indians on the north bank of the White River, near the mouth of Little Grass Creek, South Dakota, where he defeated a force of three hundred Brule Sioux warriors, and turned the Sioux tribe, which was endeavoring to enter the Bad Lands, back into the Pine Ridge Agency (White River, South Dakota, January 1, 1891).*

     — *Sergeant Fred Myers (Co. K 6th U.S. Cavalry) received MOH: With five mean repelled a superior force of the enemy and held his position against their repeated efforts to recapture it (White River, South Dakota, January 1, 1891).*

     — *Corporal Cornelius C. Smith (Co. K 6th U.S. Cavalry) received MOH: With four men of his troop drove off a superior force of the enemy and held his position against their repeated efforts to recapture it, and subsequently pursued them a great distance (White River, South Dakota, January 1, 1891).*

(1310) Skirmish, near Mouth of Little Grass Creek, South Dakota (January 1, 1891)[3]
     — Major Tullius C. Tupper (6th U.S. Cavalry)
         — 6th U.S. Cavalry Co. A, F, H, I and K

     — *1st Lieutenant Benjamin H. Cheever Jr. (6th U.S. Cavalry) received MOH: Headed the advance across White River partly frozen, in a spirited movement to the effective assistance of Troop K, 6th U.S. Cavalry (White River, South Dakota, January 1, 1891).*

     — *Sergeant Jospeh Knight (Co. F 6th U.S. Cavalry) received MOH: Led the advance in a spirited movement to the assistance of Troop K, 6th U.S. Cavalry (White River, South Dakota, January 1, 1891).*

(1311) Action, near Pine Ridge Agency, South Dakota (January 7, 1891)[4]
     — 1st Lieutenant Edward W. Casey (22nd U.S. Infantry)
         — Detachment of Indian Scouts
     — **1 KILLED**[5]
         — 1st Lieutenant Edward W. Casey (22nd U.S. Infantry)

(1312) Skirmish, near Fort Buford, South Dakota (January 9, 1891)[6]
     — 1st Lieutenant Henry F. Kendall (8th U.S. Cavalry)
         — 8th U.S. Cavalry Detachment Co. E

[2] Indians. *Annual Report of Secretary of War (1891)*, 151; Chronological List, 79; Carter, *From Yorktown to Santiago*, 278; Utley, *Last Days of the Sioux Nation*, 253. Chronological List combines the events of 1 January 1891.
[3] Indians. *Annual Report of Secretary of War (1891)*, 151; Heitman (Volume 2), 448; Carter, *From Yorktown to Santiago*, 278; Utley, *Last Days of the Sioux Nation*, 253. Chronological List combines the events of 1 January 1891.
[4] Indians. *Annual Report of Secretary of War (1891)*, 171, 250-251; Chronological List, 79; Heitman (Volume 2), 448; Di Silvestro, *In the Shadow of Wounded Knee*, 97-101; Utley, *Last Days of the Sioux Nation*, 256-258.
[5] *Annual Report of Secretary of War (1891)*, 56.
[6] Indians. *Annual Report of Secretary of War (1891)*, 171; Heitman (Volume 2), 448.

(1313) Action, Retamal, Texas (December 21 and 22, 1891)[7]
— Captain John G. Bourke (3rd U.S. Cavalry)
— 3rd U.S. Cavalry Detachment Co. C
— 18th U.S. Infantry Detachment Co. E
— 1 KILLED[8]
— Corporal Charles H. Edstrome (Co. C 3rd U.S. Cavalry)

— 2 WOUNDED[9]
— 2nd Lieutenant Charles E. Hays (18th U.S. Infantry)
— *gunshot wound, right side, slight wound*

— Private David Lloyd (Co. C 3rd U.S. Cavalry)
— *gunshot wound, right knee, slight wound*

(1314) Skirmish, Charco Renondo, Texas (December 29, 1891)[10]
— UNKNOWN
— 3rd U.S. Cavalry Detachment Co. C

— *Private Allen Walker (Co. C 3rd U.S. Cavalry) received MOH: While carrying dispatches, he attacked a party of three armed men and secured papers valuable to the United States (Texas, December 30, 1891).*

(1315) Skirmish, Rancho Rendado Zapata, Texas (December 30, 1891)[11]
— Captain Francis Hardie (3rd U.S. Cavalry)
— 3rd U.S. Cavalry Detachments Co. A and G
— Detachment of Volunteers

TOTAL KILLED 1891 — 1/1/0/0 (Officers, Enlisted Men, Indian Scouts, Citizens)

"The Army, under favorable conditions, should be one of the most desirable trades of youth; and there can scarcely be a doubt that bright and adventurous young men would seek our colors in considerable numbers if it were generally understood that courage and merit would be suitably rewarded. Under present conditions there is scarcely any pecuniary benefit to attract a man to the ranks."
— Stephen B. Elkins, Citizen[12]

(1316) Skirmish, Rancho Grominito, Texas (January 24, 1892)[13]
— UNKNOWN
— 3rd U.S. Cavalry Detachment Co. C

[7] Bandits. *Annual Report of Secretary of War (1892)*, 133-134; Heitman (Volume 2), 448; Neal, *Valor Across the Lone Star*, 241-245; Porter, *Paper Medicine Man*, 286-287.
[8] *Annual Report of Secretary of War (1892)*, 134.
[9] *Annual Report of Secretary of War (1892)*, 134.
[10] Bandits. *Annual Report of Secretary of War (1892)*, 134-135; Heitman (Volume 2), 448.
[11] Bandits. *Annual Report of Secretary of War (1892)*, 134-135; Heitman (Volume 2), 448; Neal, *Valor Across the Lone Star*, 241-245. Heitman lists 3rd U.S. Cavalry Co. A, G.
[12] Official Report of the Secretary of War Stephen Elkins. *Annual Report of Secretary of War (1892)*, 5.
[13] Bandits. Heitman (Volume 2), 448.

(1317) Operations, near Grande, Texas (February 6 to 15, 1892)[14]
— UNKNOWN
— 3rd U.S. Cavalry Detachment Co. C

(1318) Skirmish, northeast of Palito Blanco, Texas (February 18, 1892)[15]
— UNKNOWN
— 3rd U.S. Cavalry Co. D

— Private James Donnelly (Co. G 18th U.S. Infantry) awarded Certificate of Merit: For zeal, energy, and devotion in duty in saving, at great personal risk, the public buildings at Fort Clark for destruction by fire (Fort Clark, Texas, March 31, 1892).

(1319) Citizens, Davenport Ranch, near Deming, New Mexico (August 8, 1892)[16]
— (2) Citizens Killed

— Corporal Andrew J. Bannon (Co. F 3rd U.S. Artillery) received Certificate of Merit: For hazardous service preformed by him during the progress of the fire at Fort Sam Houston on the night of August 12, 1892, in remaining in imminent danger of being enveloped in flame, and with wet blankets protecting the end of the battery stable from fire (Fort Same Houston, Texas, August 12, 1892).

— Private Henry N. Clarke (Co. D 3rd U.S. Cavalry) awarded Certificate of Merit: For courage, endurance, and determination in saving, at the risk of their lives, the stables at Fort Sam Houston from destruction by fire (Fort Sam Houston, Texas, August 12, 1892).

— Blacksmith Elwood Donley (Co. D 3rd U.S. Cavalry) awarded Certificate of Merit: For courage, endurance, and determination in saving, at the risk of their lives, the stables at Fort Sam Houston from destruction by fire (Fort Sam Houston, Texas, August 12, 1892).

— Sergeant Michael Gannon (Co. F 3rd U.S. Artillery) awarded Certificate of Merit: For hazardous service preformed by him during the progress of the fire at Fort Sam Houston on the night of August 12, 1892, in remaining in imminent danger of being enveloped in flame, and with wet blankets protecting the end of the battery stable from fire (Fort Same Houston, Texas, August 12, 1892).

— Musician Oskar Hoffman (23rd U.S. Infantry) awarded Certificate of Merit: For distinguished service at a fire at Fort Sam Houston, making every possible exertion at the risk of his life in the hottest place on the roof of the burning troop stables for more than an hour, and thus greatly assisting in saving the building from destruction (Fort Sam Houston, Texas, August 12, 1892).

— Artificer John Long (Co. F 3rd U.S. Artillery) awarded Certificate of Merit: For services received during the fire at Fort Sam Houston (Fort Sam Houston, Texas, August 12, 1892).

---

[14] Bandits. Heitman (Volume 2), 448.
[15] Bandits. Heitman (Volume 2), 448.
[16] Indians. Killed were two cowboys. *Annual Report of Secretary of War (1892)*, 130; Simmons, *Massacre on the Lordsburg Road*, 183.

— *Corporal William Murray (Co. F 3rd U.S. Artillery) awarded Certificate of Merit: For distinguished service at a fire, in assisting, at the risk of his life, to remove from a burning building two barrels of gunpowder (Fort Sam Houston, Texas, August 12, 1892).*

— *Private Newcomb R. Nowlin (Co. H 23rd U.S. Infantry) awarded Certificate of Merit: For distinguished service at a fire which occurred at the Quartermaster's Dept, by service conspicuous for skill, courage and fortitude, being the hose man of his company he led an almost forlorn hope in an effort to save the main storehouse on the East side, remaining at his post and doing fierce battle with the flames at the sacrifice of his personal safety and comfort, and his clothing (Fort Sam Houston, Texas, August 12, 1892).*

(1320) Citizens, near Moore's Ranch, south of Fort Bowie, Arizona Territory (October 9, 1892)[17]
— (1) Citizen Killed

(1321) Citizens, Animas Mountains, Arizona Territory (December 8, 1892)[18]
— (1) Citizen Killed

(1322) Skirmish, El Alazan, near Roma, Texas (December 24, 1892)[19]
— 1st Lieutenant Parker W. West (3rd U.S. Cavalry)
— 3rd U.S. Cavalry Co. I
— Detachment of Indian Scouts

TOTAL KILLED 1892 — 0/0/0/0 (OFFICERS, ENLISTED MEN, INDIAN SCOUTS, CITIZENS)

"The most arduous service which has been rendered by troops during the past year… has been that required to suppress and punish violations of the neutrality laws between [the United States] and Mexico…." — John M. Schofield, U.S. Army[20]

(1323) Skirmish, near Baluarte Ranch, Texas (January 21, 1893)[21]
— 1st Lieutenant Joseph T. Dickman (3rd U.S. Cavalry)
— 3rd U.S. Cavalry Detachments Co. D and K

(1324) Skirmish, Las Tajitos Ranch, near Brownville, Texas (January 22, 1893)[22]
— 1st Lieutenant Joseph T. Dickman (3rd U.S. Cavalry)
— 3rd U.S. Cavalry Detachments Co. D and K

(1325) Skirmish, Las Mulas Ranch, Starr County, Texas (February 23, 1893)[23]
— 2nd Lieutenant Percival G. Lowe (18th U.S. Infantry)
— Detachment of Indian Scouts

[17] Indians. Killed was teamster Florentio Mongarro. *Annual Report of Secretary of War (1893)*, 139.
[18] Indians. Killed was Bud Taylor. *Annual Report of Secretary of War (1893)*, 139.
[19] Bandits. *Annual Report of Secretary of War (1893)*, 142; Heitman (Volume 2), 448.
[20] Official Report of the Major General John M. Schofield, Headquarters of the Army, Washington, D.C., 4 October 1893. *Annual Report of Secretary of War (1893)*, 61.
[21] Bandits. *Annual Report of Secretary of War (1893)*, 142-143; Heitman (Volume 2), 448.
[22] Bandits. *Annual Report of Secretary of War (1893)*, 142-143; Heitman (Volume 2), 448.
[23] Bandits. *Annual Report of Secretary of War (1893)*, 142-143; Heitman (Volume 2), 449.

— *First Sergeant Patrick Kaine (Co. D 3rd U.S. Infantry) awarded Certificate of Merit: For saving the life of a comrade from drowning, at the risk of his own life (Leech Lake, Minnesota, June 16, 1893).*

— *Private Frank Bell (Co. A 7th U.S. Cavalry) awarded Certificate of Merit: For courage and determination in saving, at the risk of his life, the Post Exchange building from destruction (Fort Riley, Kansas, November 3, 1893).*

TOTAL KILLED 1893 — 0/0/0/0 (OFFICERS, ENLISTED MEN, INDIAN SCOUTS, CITIZENS)

"It is certainly manifest that the present condition of the country, with a population of nearly seventy millions, under the danger of disorder now known to exist, cannot be met by the same force that was deemed adequate twenty-five years ago… one man to fourteen square miles of territory, or one man to twenty eight hundred of population, is surely a very small guard to protect property and prevent violation of law…."

— John M. Schofield, U.S. Army[24]

(1326) Citizens, near Defiance Station, Atlantic and Pacific Railroad, New Mexico Territory (March 17, 1894)[25]

— (1) Citizens Killed

(1327) Action, near Sacramento, California (July 11, 1894)[26]

— 2nd Lieutenant Delamere Skerrett (5th U.S. Artillery)

— 5th U.S. Artillery Detachment Co. L

— 5 KILLED[27]

— Private James Byrne (Co. L 5th U.S. Artillery)
— Private Peter Clark (Co. L 5th U.S. Artillery)
— Private Wesley C. Dougan (Co. L 5th U.S. Artillery)
— Private George W. Lubberden (Co. L 5th U.S. Artillery)

— Engineer Sam B. Clark (Citizen)

— 3 WOUNDED[28]

— Private Daumier (Co. L 5th U.S. Artillery)
— Private Ellis (Co. L 5th U.S. Artillery)
— Private Wilson (Co. L 5th U.S. Artillery)

TOTAL KILLED 1894 — 0/4/0/1

---

[24] Official Report of Major General John M. Schofield, Headquarters of the Army, Washington, D.C., 1 October 1894. *Annual Report of Secretary of War (1894)*, 59.
[25] Indians. Killed was storekeeper William Smith. *Annual Report of Secretary of War (1894)*, 140.
[26] Bandits. *Annual Report of Secretary of War (1894)*, 113-114.
[27] *Annual Report of Secretary of War (1894)*, 114; *Sacramento Union*, 11 July 1894; *Sacramento Bee*, 12 July 1894.
[28] *Sacramento Union*, 11 July 1894; *Sacramento Bee*, 12 July 1894.

"The Army has been kept at [25,000 men] for twenty-one years, and is the same today as when we had thirty million less population than we have now, with all our increasing wealth during that time... The Army should grow as the nation grows. There is no reason why it should become crystallized. It is one of the pillars of the nation. It is the main dependence of the civil government, that guarantees protection to life and property, and is the main reliance of the nation in case of war with any foreign Power." —
Nelson A. Miles, U.S. Army[29]

(1328) Citizens, near Duncan, Arizona Territory (December 3, 1895)[30]
— (2) Citizens Killed

TOTAL KILLED 1895 — 0/0/0/0 (OFFICERS, ENLISTED MEN, INDIAN SCOUTS, CITIZENS)

"During the past year the country has fortunately been free from any serious outbreak of Indians... I attribute this to three causes. The first, the presence of and knowledge on the part of the Indians of the strength and efficiency of, the military forces that are within reach of all the tribes... The second is the fact that the Indians are receiving more benefits from the General Government and a just, intelligent, and judicious administration of their affairs. The third is that many of the most turbulent and heretofore hostile Indian tribes have been under the care and control of experienced, judicious, and conscientious officers of the Army, who have had years of experience with these people, have administered their affairs with intelligence and fidelity, and command the respect and confidence of the Indians."
— Nelson A. Miles, U.S. Army[31]

(1329) Citizens, Chiricahua Mountains, Arizona Territory (March 28, 1896)[32]
— (1) Citizen Killed

— Private Adolphus A. Schwarz (Co. K 3rd U.S. Cavalry) awarded Certificate of Merit: For distinguished service at a fire at Jefferson Barracks, where in his efforts to save the burning buildings from destruction, he stood his ground until entirely overcome by the smoke and heat (Jefferson Barracks, Missouri, April 22, 1896).

(1330) Skirmish, near Lang's Ranch, Arizona Territory (May 8, 1896)[33]
— 2nd Lieutenant Nathan K. Averill (7th U.S. Cavalry)
— 7th U.S. Cavalry Detachment Co. E
— Detachment of Indian Scouts

[29] Official Report of Major General Nelson A. Miles, Headquarters of the Army, Washington, D.C., 5 November 1895. *Annual Report of Secretary of War (1895)*, 69.
[30] Indians. Killed were sheep herder Horatio H. Merrill and his daughter Elizabeth. *Annual Report of Secretary of War (1896)*, 4, 142; Alexander, *Arizona Military Place Names*, 8; Wilson, "Soldiers vs. Apaches One Last Time," *Wild West Magazine* (October 2001): 25-30.
[31] Official Report of Major General Nelson A. Miles, Headquarters of the Army, Washington, D.C., 10 November 1896. *Annual Report of Secretary of War (1896)*, 75.
[32] Indians. Killed was sheep herder Alfred Hands. *Annual Report of Secretary of War (1896)*, 4, 142; Wilson, "Soldiers vs. Apaches One Last Time," *Wild West Magazine* (October 2001): 25-30.
[33] Indians. *Annual Report of Secretary of War (1896)*, 143; Heitman (Volume 2), 449; Chandler, *Of Garryowen in Glory*, 97-98.

(1331) Skirmish, Guadalupe Canyon, Peloncillo Mountains, Arizona Territory (May 17, 1896)[34]
— 1st Lieutenant Sedgwick Rice (7th U.S. Cavalry)
— 7th U.S. Cavalry Detachments Co. C, E and I
— Detachment of Indian Scouts
— Detachment of Volunteers

— *Sergeant Major John C. Young (3rd U.S. Infantry) awarded Certificate of Merit: For distinguished service in saving the life of a comrade who was drowning (Minnesota River, Minnesota, November 19, 1896).*

TOTAL KILLED 1896 — 0/0/0/0 (OFFICERS, ENLISTED MEN, INDIAN SCOUTS, CITIZENS)

— *Sergeant Walter S. Volkmar (Signal Corps) awarded Certificate of Merit: For bravery at the fire at Fort Sam Houston (Fort Sam Houston, Texas, March 15, 1898).*

(1332) Engagement, Sugar Point, Leech Lake, Minnesota (October 5 and 6, 1898)[35]
— Brigadier General of Volunteers John M. Bacon
— 3rd U.S. Infantry Detachments Co. A, B, C, D, E, F, G and H
— Detachment of Indian Police
— 7 KILLED[36]
— Captain Melville C. Wilkinson (3rd U.S. Infantry)

— Private John Schwallenstocker (Co. C 3rd U.S. Infantry)
— Private Edward Lowe (Co. D 3rd U.S. Infantry)
— Sergeant William S. Butler (Co. E 3rd U.S. Infantry)
— Private John Olmstead (Co. E 3rd U.S. Infantry)
— Private Albert Zehell (Co. E 3rd U.S. Infantry)

— Gway-Bah-Be-Pung or William Russell (Indian Police)

— 10 WOUNDED[37]
— Sergeant Leroy Ayres (Co. E 3rd U.S. Infantry)
— *gunshot wound, neck*
— Private E.G Antonello (Co. E 3rd U.S. Infantry)
— *gunshot wound, left leg*
— Private John Daily (Co. E 3rd U.S. Infantry)
— *gunshot wound, right thigh*
— Private Charles Francis (Co. E 3rd U.S. Infantry)

---

[34] Indians. *Annual Report of Secretary of War (1896)*, 144; Heitman (Volume 2), 449; Chandler, *Of Garryowen in Glory*, 98. Heitman lists 7th U.S. Cavalry Detachments Co. C, E, I; Detachment of Indian Scouts.
[35] Indians. *Annual Report of Secretary of War (1899)*, 23-25; Heitman (Volume 2), 449; McKeig, *Battle of Sugar Point*, 20-42; Roddis, "Last Indian Uprising," *Minnesota History Bulletin* 3 (February 1920): 275-290. Heitman lists 4 to 7 October 1898. Heitman lists 3rd U.S. Infantry Co. A, B, C, D, E, F, G, H.
[36] *Army and Navy Journal* (Volume 36), 130; McKeig, *Battle of Sugar Point*, 59.
[37] *Army and Navy Journal* (Volume 36), 130; McKeig, *Battle of Sugar Point*, 59.

— Private Jesse Jelsen (Co. E 3rd U.S. Infantry)
— *gunshot wound, left shoulder*
— Private John Truner (Co. E 3rd U.S. Infantry)
— *gunshot wound, right shoulder*
— Private George Wicker (Co. E 3rd U.S. Infantry)
— *gunshot wound, left leg, slight wound*

— Private Richard Boucher (Co. G 3rd U.S. Infantry)
— *gunshot wound, shoulder*
— Private Edward Brown (3rd U.S. Infantry)
— *gunshot wound, face*

— Albert Schuyler (Citizen)

— *Private Oscar Burkard (Hospital Corps, U.S. Army) received MOH: For distinguished bravery in action against hostile Indians (Hay Creek, Minnesota, October 5, 1898).*

— *First Sergeant Thomas Kelly (Co. E 3rd U.S. Infantry) awarded Distinguished Service Cross: Sergeant Kelly displayed extraordinary heroism in assuming, upon the death of his commanding officer, the command of the skirmishers on the right side of the line. With utter disregard for his own personal safety he so gallantly led and directed his men. This action had much to do with the subsequent victorious result of the engagement (Leech Lake, Minnesota, October 5 and 6, 1898).*

TOTAL KILLED 1898 — 1/5/1/0 (OFFICERS, ENLISTED MEN, INDIAN SCOUTS, CITIZENS)

— CONCLUSION —

And they who for their country die shall fill an honored grave,
for glory lights the soldier's tomb, and beauty weeps the brave.

— Joseph Drake, Citizen

Between the end of the American Civil War in 1865 and the turn of the century, first state volunteers and then soldiers of the United States Army fought over 1400 battles in the West, mostly with Indians, but also with bandits and men of "bad character". Only a few of these battles are remembered, most having resulted in neither grand victories nor epic defeats; instead, the results of most are forgotten, being of little consequence, with few casualties taken or caused and no grand objectives won. But taken together, the service and sacrifice of the frontier soldier and the battles he fought had a long lasting and undeniable effect upon the history of the United States, for with the soldier came civilization and all that followed to the West. With battle came order. Of these once lawless lands, twelve states would be admitted to the Union, and millions, pushed ever westward, would find a new life and new opportunity.

At the end of the Civil War, much of the vast West remained untamed and unexplored. The Western plains were a largely impenetrable barrier, as were the rugged mountains of the Pacific Northwest and desolate desert Southwest. Into this wilderness went the Army, building posts and forts, around which would one day grow towns and cities. The soldier escorted the wagon trains and stagecoaches, further speeding the arrival of civilization. Following the soldiers, the posts, and the forts were the surveyors and the track layers. Soon the nation would be crossed by rail, connected from sea to sea. Too followed the hunter and the buffalo, so vital to the Indian way of life, the herds of which once covered the open plains; they were hunted to near extinction, the hides shipped East. The once open plains were fenced by barbed wire, the endless buffalo herds replaced by herds of cattle and farms.

By the end of the American Civil War the once free-roaming Indians had been pushed ever westward, but by 1865 the Indian could be pushed no further. Settler and Indian more and more came into contact and conflict, with tragic results for both. Innocents died. The Army was tasked with forcing the Indian on to reservation, where the Indian might be protected from all that came with civilization, and civilization might be protected from the Indian. For civilization had forever changed the Indian, both for good and bad, and it would continue to do so. The horse forever changed Indian society, as did the firearm. Alcohol and disease had and would continue to do so. The Army was able to shelter and even protect the Indian from some of the more extreme influences of civilization, for there were those that believed the Indian stood in the way of civilization and needed to be eliminated.

In carrying out their mission, in bringing civilization to the West, approximately 1,200 soldiers paid the ultimate price, killed in action with Indians or bandits. Countless more would forever bear the scars, both physical and emotional, of their service. It can truly be said that these men answered their nation's greatest calling. But for all of their service, for all of their sacrifice, they received no parade, no thanks of a grateful nation, no monuments on town squares. To both those of their own generation and the generations that followed they were alternately celebrated as heroes and reviled as villains. The truth is they were neither. They were soldiers. Those who fell often were laid to rest in graves unmarked and unattended, forgotten. Those fortunate ones received a pension: twenty dollars a month and twelve dollars for widows. These men, immigrants and sons of immigrants, freemen and freed slaves, white, black, and Indian, these soldiers who did all that their nation asked of them, deserved more. They deserved and continue to deserve that a nation remember them, that a nation remember the sacrifice they made and the heroism they exhibited. For men so key in shaping a nation, there can be no less.

APPENDIX A: WESTERN INDIAN WAR CASUALTY ROSTER (1865-1898)

— OFFICERS —

(0001) Adair, Lewis D. Born April 11 1835 in Ohio. Ohio. 1st Lieutenant 26th Ohio Infantry 24 July 1861; Captain 1 December 1861; honorably mustered out 25 July 1864; 1st Lieutenant 22nd U.S. Infantry 28 July 1866; died 5 October 1872 of wounds received 4 October 1872 in action with Sioux Indians near Heart River Crossing Dakota Territory.[1]

— Buried: Grandview Cemetery, Chillicothe, Ohio

(0002) Almy, Jacob. Born 20 November 1842 in New Bedford Massachusetts. Corporal Co. I 33rd Massachusetts Infantry 4 August 1862 to 5 February 1863; Cadet U.S. Military Academy 1 July 1863 (41/63); 2nd Lieutenant 5th U.S. Cavalry 17 June 1867; 1st Lieutenant 15 April 1869; Regimental Commissary of Subsistence 22 November 1869 to 15 July 1870; murdered by an Indian 27 May 1873 at San Carlos Agency Arizona Territory.[2]

— Buried: Rural Cemetery, New Bedford, Massachusetts

(0003) Beecher, Frederick Henry. Born 22 June 1841 in New Orleans Louisiana. Massachusetts. Sergeant Co. B 16 Maine Infantry 14 August 1862; 2nd Lieutenant 1 February 1863; 1st Lieutenant 11 April 1863; resigned 20 September 1864; 2nd Lieutenant Veteran Reserve Corps 22 August 1864; brevet 1st Lieutenant and Captain Volunteers 5 December 1865 for gallant and meritorious service; honorably mustered out 3 March 1866; 2nd Lieutenant 3rd U.S. Infantry 29 November 1865; 1st Lieutenant 28 July 1866; killed 17 September 1868 in action with Indians at Delaware Creek Kansas.[3]

— Buried: Harmony Cemetery, Georgetown, Massachusetts

(0004) Bennett, Andrew S. New York. Wisconsin. 2nd Lieutenant 5th Wisconsin Infantry 12 July 1861; 1st Lieutenant 25 December 1862; honorably mustered out 2 Aug 1864; 1st Lieutenant 15th U.S. Infantry 7 March 1867; Captain 28 February 1869; unassigned 12 August 1869; assigned to 5th U.S. Infantry 1 January 1871; killed 4 September 1878 in action with Bannock Indians at Clark's Fork Montana Territory.[4]

— Buried: Prairie Home Cemetery, Waukesha, Wisconsin

(0005) Biddle, Jonathan Williams. Born in Philadelphia Pennsylvania. Pennsylvania. 2nd Lieutenant 7th U.S. Cavalry 31 August 1876; killed 30 September 1877 in action with Nez Perce Indians at Snake River Montana Territory.[5]

— Buried: Laurel Hill Cemetery, Philadelphia, Pennsylvania

(0006) Bingham, Horatio S. Canada. Minnesota. 2nd Lieutenant 2nd Minnesota Cavalry 23 December 1863; Captain 4 January 1864; honorably mustered out 19 April 1866; 2nd Lieutenant 2nd U.S. Cavalry 23 February 1866; killed 6 December 1866 in action with Sioux Indians near Ft Phil Kearny Dakota Territory.[6]

— Buried: Custer National Cemetery, Crow Agency, Montana

(0007) Bradley, James Howard. Born 25 May 1844 in Sandusky Ohio. Ohio. Private 14th Ohio Infantry 23 April 1861; honorably mustered out 13 August 1861; Private, Corporal and Sergeant Co. F 45th Ohio Infantry 19 August 1862; honorably mustered out 5 July 1865; 2nd Lieutenant 18th U.S. Infantry 23 February 1866; 1st Lieutenant 29 July 1866; transferred to 7th

U.S. Infantry 28 November 1871; killed 9 August 1877 in action with Nez Perce Indians at Big Hole Pass Montana Territory.[7]

— Buried: Oakwood Cemetery, Stryker, Ohio

(0008) Brown, Frederick Hallam. New York. Army. Private and Quartermaster Sergeant 18th U.S. Infantry 18 July 1861; 2nd Lieutenant 18th U.S. Infantry 30 October 1861; 1st Lieutenant 24 March 1862; Regimental Quartermaster 4 November 1861 to 15 May 1866; Captain 15 May 1866; brevet Captain 1 September 1864 for gallant and meritorious service during the Atlanta campaign; killed 21 December 1866 in action with Indians near Ft Phil Kearny Dakota Territory.[8]

— Buried: Custer National Cemetery, Crow Agency, Montana

(0009) Buel, David Hillhouse. Michigan. New York. Cadet U.S. Military Academy 1 September 1857 (10/xy); brevet 2nd Lieutenant and 2nd Lieutenant 1st U.S. Dragoons 24 June 1861; 1st U.S. Cavalry 3 August 1861; transferred to 3rd U.S. Artillery 23 October 1861; transferred to Ordnance Department 24 October 1861; 1st Lieutenant 3 March 1863; Captain 30 July 1863; brevet Major 22 July 1864 for gallant and meritorious service in action in front of Atlanta Georgia and Lieutenant Colonel 13 March 1865 for meritorious and distinguished service in the campaign from Atlanta Georgia to Goldsboro North Carolina; assassinated 22 July 1870.[9]

— Buried: Fort Leavenworth National Cemetery, Fort Leavenworth, Kansas

(0010) Calhoun, James. Born 24 August, 1845 in Cincinnati, Ohio. Ohio. Private Co. D 23rd U.S. Infantry 14 January, 1864; appointed First Sergeant 1 February, 1865 to 24 October 1867; 2nd Lieutenant 32nd U.S. Infantry 31 July 1867; transferred to 21st U.S. Infantry 19 April 1869; unassigned 29 October 1870; assigned to 7th U.S. Cavalry 1 January 1871; 1st Lieutenant 9 January 1871; killed 25 June 1876 in action with Sioux Indians on Little Big Horn River Montana Territory.[10]

— Buried: Fort Leavenworth National Cemetery, Fort Leavenworth, Kansas

(0011) Canby, Edward Richard Sprigg. Born 9 November 1817 in Piatt's Landing Kentucky. Indiana. Cadet U.S. Military Academy 1 July 1835 (30/31); 2nd Lieutenant 2nd U.S. Infantry 1 July 1839; 1st Lieutenant 18 June 1846; Regimental Adjutant 24 Mar 1846 to 3 Mar 1847; brevet Captain Assistant Adjutant General 3 March 1847; Major 10th U.S. Infantry 3 March 1855; Colonel 19th U.S. Infantry 14 May 1861; Brigadier General Volunteers 31 March 1862; Major General Volunteers 7 May 1864; honorably mustered out of volunteer service 1 September 1866; Brigadier General USA 28 July 1866; brevet Major 20 August 1847 for gallant and meritorious conduct at the battles of Contreras and Churubusco; Lieutenant Colonel 13 September 1847 for gallant conduct at Belen Gate of City of Mexico; Brigadier General 13 March 1865 for gallant and meritorious service at the battle of Valverde New Mexico and Major General 13 Mar 1865 for gallant and meritorious service in the capture of Ft Blakely and Mobile Alabama; murdered 11 April 1873 by Modoc Indians near Van Bremmer's Ranch California while engaged in a peace conference.[11]

— Buried: Crown Hill Cemetery, Indianapolis, Indiana

[1] Heitman (Volume 1), 151; Grandview Cemetery Records.
[2] Heitman (Volume 1), 161; Altshuler, *Cavalry Yellow*, 7-8; Cullum, *Biographical Register (Volume 2)*, 641; Price, *Across the Continent*, 519-523; Thrapp, *Encyclopedia of Frontier Biography (Volume 1)*, 18.
[3] Heitman (Volume 1), 206; Thrapp, *Encyclopedia of Frontier Biography (Volume 1)*, 87.
[4] Heitman (Volume 1), 211; Thrapp, *Encyclopedia of Frontier Biography (Volume 4)*, 41.
[5] Heitman (Volume 1), 217; Thrapp, *Encyclopedia of Frontier Biography (Volume 1)*, 106.
[6] Heitman (Volume 1), 218; McDermott, *Red Clouds War (Volume 1)*, 167; Thrapp, *Encyclopedia of Frontier Biography (Volume 1)*, 114.
[7] Heitman (Volume 1), 238; Bradley, *March of the Montana Column*, 3-6; Thrapp, *Encyclopedia of Frontier Biography (Volume 1)*, 156-157.
[8] Heitman (Volume 1), 251; McDermott, *Red Clouds War (Volume 1)*, 24; Thrapp, *Encyclopedia of Frontier Biography (Volume 1)*, 175.
[9] Heitman (Volume 1), 259; Kirshner, *Class of 1862*, 163.
[10] Heitman (Volume 1), 274; Altshuler, *Cavalry Yellow*, 52-53; Nichols, *Men with Custer*, 47; Thrapp, *Encyclopedia of Frontier Biography (Volume 1)*, 211.
[11] Heitman (Volume 1), 279; Cullum, *Biographical Register (Volume 1)*, 590-591; Heyman, *Prudent Soldier*; Thrapp, *Encyclopedia of Frontier Biography (Volume 1)*, 218-219.

(0012) Carroll, John Cuthbert. Born in Kentucky. First Sergeant 15th Kentucky Infantry 14 December 1861; 2nd Lieutenant 25 April 1862; 1st Lieutenant 11 December 1862; Captain 17 March 1863; honorably mustered out 14 January 1865; 2nd Lieutenant and 1st Lieutenant 14th U.S. Infantry 23 February 1866; transferred to 32nd U.S. Infantry 21 September 1866; killed 5 November 1867 in action with Apache Indians near Ft Bowie Arizona Territory.[12]

— Buried: San Francisco National Cemetery, San Francisco, California

(0013) Casey, Edward Wanton. Born 1 December 1850 in Benicia California. Louisiana. Cadet U.S. Military Academy 1 July 1869 (34/41); 2nd Lieutenant 22nd U.S. Infantry 13 June 1873; 1st Lieutenant 11 January 1880; regimental adjutant 1 September 1884 to 31 January 1887; brevet 1st Lieutenant 27 February 1890 for gallant service in action against Indians at Muddy Creek Montana Territory 7 May 1877; murdered by Brule Indians 7 January 1891 near Pine Ridge Agency South Dakota.[13]

— Buried: Casey Family Farm, Warwick, Rhode Island

(0014) Cherry, Samuel Austin. Born in Indiana. Indiana. Cadet U.S. Military Academy July1870 (35); 2nd Lieutenant 23rd U.S. Infantry 16 June 1875; transferred to 5th U.S. Cavalry 28 July 1876; murdered by a soldier 11 May 1881.[14]

— Buried: Greenwood Cemetery, Lagrange, Indiana

(0015) Cole, Osmer F. Killed 31 August 1865 on Tongue River Dakota Territory.[15]

— Buried: Near Tongue River, Montana[16]

(0016) Collins, Caspar Wever. Born 30 September 1844 in Hillsboro Ohio. Ohio. Killed 26 July 1865 in action with Cheyenne Indians at Platte River Bridge Dakota Territory.[17]

— Buried: Hillsboro Cemetery, Hillsboro, Ohio

(0017) Cooke, William Winer. Born 29 May 1846 in Mount Pleasant Ontario Canada. New York. 24th New York Volunteer Cavalry 1863; 2nd Lieutenant 24th New York Cavalry 26 January 1864; 1st Lieutenant 14 December 1864; wounded at Battle of Petersburg, honorably mustered out 24 June 1865; 2nd Lieutenant 7th U.S. Cavalry 28 July 1866; 1st Lieutenant 31 July 1867; Regimental Adjutant 8 December 1866 to 21 February 1867 and 1 January 1871 to 25 June 1876; brevet Captain 2 March 1867 for gallant and meritorious service in the battle of Petersburg Virginia 17 June 1864; Major 2 March 1867 for gallant and meritorious service in the battle of Dinwiddie Court House Virginia 29 March 1865 and Lieutenant Colonel 2 March 1867 for gallant and meritorious service in the battle of Sailors Creek Virginia 6 April 1865; killed 25 June 1876 in action with Sioux Indians on Little Big Horn River Montana Territory.[18]

— Buried: Hamilton Cemetery, Hamilton, Ontario, Canada

(0018) Cranston, Arthur. Born 1843 in Massachusetts. Ohio. Private Co. E 7th Ohio Infantry 25 April 1861 to 22 August 1861; 2nd Lieutenant 55th Ohio Infantry 16 October 1861; resigned 15 March 1862; Cadet U.S. Military Academy 1 July 1862 (35/63) ; 2nd Lieutenant 4th U.S. Artillery 17 June 1867; 1st Lieutenant 30 November 1871; killed 26 April 1873 in action with Modoc Indians at Lava Beds California.[19]

— Buried: San Francisco National Cemetery, San Francisco, California

(0019) Crawford, Emmett. Born 6 September, 1844, Philadelphia, Pennsylvania. Pennsylvania. Private Co. F 71st Pennsylvania Infantry 28 May 1861 to 2 July 1864; First Sergeant Co. K 197th Pennsylvania Infantry 11 July to 11 November 1864; 1st Lieutenant 13th U.S. Colored Infantry 23 November 1864; honorably mustered out 18 November 1865; 2nd Lieutenant 37th U.S. Colored Infantry 16 February 1866; brevet Captain and Major Volunteers

13 March 1865 for meritorious service during the war; honorably mustered out 19 May 1867; 2nd Lieutenant 39th U.S. Infantry 22 January 1867; 1st Lieutenant 5 June 1868; transferred to 25th U.S. Infantry 20 April 1869; unassigned June 1869; assigned to 3rd U.S. Cavalry 31 December 1870; Captain 20 March 1879; died 18 January 1886 of wounds received from Mexican troops 11 January 1886 near Nacori Mexico while in pursuit of Indians.[20]

— Buried: Arlington National Cemetery, Washington, D.C.

(0020) Crittenden, John Jordan. Born 7 June 1854 in Frankfort, Kentucky. Kentucky. Cadet U.S. Military Academy 1 July 1871; Discharged 26 June 1874; 2nd Lieutenant 20th U.S. Infantry 15 October, 1875; killed 25 June 1876 in action with Sioux Indians at the Little Big Horn River, Montana.[21]

— Buried: Custer National Cemetery, Crow Agency, Montana

(0021) Crosby, Eben. Maine. Maine. Private Sergeant and First Sergeant Co. I 6th Maine Infantry 15 July 1861 to 17 January 1864; 2nd Lieutenant Veteran Reserve Corps 30 March 1864; honorably mustered out 30 June 1866; 2nd Lieutenant 44th U.S. Infantry 28 July 1866; transferred to 17th U.S. Infantry 27 May 1869; 1st Lieutenant 30 June 1872; killed 3 October 1872 while on railroad survey Dakota Territory.[22]

— Buried: Custer National Cemetery, Crow Agency, Montana

(0022) Cushing, Howard Bass. Born 22 August 1838 in Milwaukee, Wisconsin. Army. Private Co. B 1st Illinois Artillery 24 March 1862 to 30 November 1863; Private Co. B 4th U.S. Artillery 30 November 1863; 2nd Lieutenant 4th U.S. Artillery 30 November 1863; transferred to 3rd U.S. Cavalry 7 Sept 1867; 1st Lieutenant 16 December 1867; killed 5 May 1871 in action with Apache Indians in Whetstone Mountains Arizona Territory.[23]

— Buried: San Francisco National Cemetery, San Francisco, California

(0023) Custer, George Armstrong. Born 5 December 1839 in New Rumley, Ohio. Ohio. Cadet U.S. Military Academy 1 July 1857 (34/34); 2nd Lieutenant 2nd U.S. Cavalry 24 June 1861; 5th U.S. Cavalry 3 Aug 1861; 1st Lieutenant 17 July 1862; Captain Additional Aide-de-Camp 5 June 1862; honorably discharged as Additional Aide-de-Camp 31 Mar 1863; Brigadier General Volunteers 29 June 1863; Major General Volunteers 15 April 1865; honorably mustered out of Volunteer service 1 February 1866; Captain 5th U.S. Cavalry 8 May 1864; Lieutenant Colonel 7th U.S. Cavalry 28 July 1866; brevet Major 3 July 1863 for gallant and meritorious service in the battle of Gettysburg Pennsylvania; Lieutenant Colonel 11 May 1864 for gallant and meritorious ser in the battle of Yellow Tavern Virginia; Colonel 19 September 1864 for gallant and meritorious service in the battle of Winchester Virginia; Brigadier General 13 March 1865 for gallant and meritorious service in the battle of Five Forks Virginia; Major General 13 Mar 1865 for gallant and meritorious service during the campaign ending in the surrender of the insurgent Army of Northern Virginia and Major General Volunteers 19 October 1864 for gallant and meritorious service at the battles of Winchester and Fishers Hill Virginia; killed 25 June 1876 and his whole command massacred in action with Sioux Indians at Little Big Horn River Montana Territory.[24]

— Buried: U.S. Military Academy Post Cemetery, West Point, New York

(0024) Custer, Thomas Ward. Born 15 March 1845 in New Rumley, Ohio. Michigan. Private Co. H 21st Ohio Infantry 2 September 1861 to 10 October 1864; 2nd Lieutenant 6th Michigan Cavalry 8 November 1864; brevet 1st Lieutenant Captain and Major Volunteers 13 Mar 1865 for distinguished and gallant conduct; honorably mustered out 24 Nov 1865; 2nd Lieutenant 1st U.S. Infantry 23 Feb 1866; 1st Lieutenant 7th U.S. Cavalry 28 July 1866; Regimental Quartermaster 3 December 1866 to 10 March 1867; Captain 2 December 1875; brevet Captain 2 March 1867 for gallant and distinguished conduct in the engagement with the enemy at Waynesboro Virginia 2 March 1865; Major 2 March 1867 for distinguished conduct in the engagement with the enemy at Namozine Church Virginia 3 April 1865 and Lieutenant Colonel 2 March 1867 for distinguished courage and service at the battle of Sailors Creek Virginia; received Medal of Honor 24 Apr 1865 for the capture of a flag at Namozine

[12] Heitman (Volume 1), 286; Altshuler, *Cavalry Yellow*, 62; Thrapp, *Encyclopedia of Frontier Biography (Volume 1)*, 232.
[13] Heitman (Volume 1), 289; Cullum, *Biographical Register (Volume 3)*, 461; Silvestro, *In the Shadow of Wounded Knee*, 7-20; Thrapp, *Encyclopedia of Frontier Biography (Volume 1)*, 239.
[14] Heitman (Volume 1), 298.
[15] *Official Records, Series I, Volume 48, Part I*, 329-389.
[16] " On [3 September 1865] we buried Captain Cole on the north side of the corral, in a rifle pit…" Sawyer's Official Report September 6, 1865. Hafen and Hafen, *Powder River Campaigns*, 263.
[17] Spring, *Caspar Collins*.
[18] Heitman (Volume 1), 324; Nichols, *Men with Custer*, 62; Thrapp, *Encyclopedia of Frontier Biography (Volume 1)*, 314-315.
[19] Heitman (Volume 1), 336; Cullum, *Biographical Register (Volume 2)*, 640; Thrapp, *Encyclopedia of Frontier Biography*, 337.
[20] Heitman (Volume 1), 336; Altshuler, *Cavalry Yellow*, 84-85; Thrapp, *Encyclopedia of Frontier Biography (Volume 1)*, 338.
[21] Heitman (Volume 1), 338; Nichols, *Men with Custer*, 69; Thrapp, *Encyclopedia of Frontier Biography (Volume 1)*, 346.
[22] Heitman (Volume 1), 340.
[23] Heitman (Volume 1), 347; Altshuler, *Cavalry Yellow*, 91; Randall, *Only the Echoes*; Thrapp, *Encyclopedia of Frontier Biography (Volume 1)*, 361.
[24] Heitman (Volume 1), 348; Cullum, *Biographical Register (Volume 2)*, 568-569; Kirshner, *Class of 1861*, 66-86, 111-119; Nichols, *Men with Custer*, 74-75; Thrapp, *Encyclopedia of Frontier Biography (Volume 1)*, 363-364; Utley, *Cavalier in Buckskin*; Wert, *Custer*.

Church Virginia 2 Apr 1865 and another Medal of Honor 22 May 1865 for the capture of a flag at Sailors Creek Virginia 6 April 1865; killed 25 June 1876 in action with Sioux Indians at Little Big Horn River Montana Territory.[25]

— Buried: Fort Leavenworth National Cemetery,
Fort Leavenworth, Kansas

(0025) **Daniels, Napoleon H**. Louisiana. Indiana. Sergeant Co. B 18th Indiana Infantry 16 August 1861; 1st Lieutenant 12 February1863; honorably mustered out 28 August 1865; 2nd Lieutenant and 1st Lieutenant 18th U.S. Infantry 23 February 1866; killed 21 July 1866 by Indians on Powder River Dakota Territory.[26]

(0026) **Elliott, Joel H**. Born 27 October 1858 in Centerville Indiana. Indiana. Private Co. C 2nd Indiana Cavalry 13 September 1861 to 25 June 1863; 2nd Lieutenant 7th Indiana Cavalry 25 June 1863; Captain 23 October 1863; honorably mustered out 18 February 1866; Major 7th U.S. Cavalry 7 March 1867; killed 27 November 1868 in action with Indians on the Washita River Indian Territory.[27]

— Buried: Fort Gibson National Cemetery, Fort Gibson, Oklahoma

(0027) **English, William Lewis**. Born 1841 in Illinois. Illinois. First Sergeant Co. E 101st Illinois Infantry 2 Sept 1862; 2nd Lieutenant 1 May 1863; 1st Lieutenant 5 March 1864; honorably mustered out 7 June 1865; 2nd Lieutenant 7th U.S. Infantry 18 June 1867; 1st Lieutenant 24 October 1874; died 20 August 1877 of wounds received 9 August 1877 in action with Nez Perce Indians at Big Hole Pass Montana Territory.[28]

— Buried: Diamond Grove Cemetery, Jacksonville, Illinois

(0028) **Fetterman, William Judd**. Born 1833 in Connecticut. Delaware. 1st Lieutenant 18th U.S. Infantry 14 May 1861; Captain 25 October 1861; transferred to 27th U.S. Infantry 21 September 1866; brevet Major 31 December 1862 for gallant and meritorious conduct at the battle of Murfreesboro Tennessee and Lieutenant Colonel 1 September 1864 for gallant and meritorious service during the Atlanta campaign and at the battle of Jonesboro Georgia; killed 21 December 1866 in action with Sioux Indians near Ft Phil Kearny Dakota Territory.[29]

— Buried: Custer National Cemetery, Crow Agency, Montana Territory

(0029) **Fouts, William D**. Killed 14 June 1865 by Indians on Horse Creek Dakota Territory.[30]

— Buried: Fort McPherson National Cemetery, Maxwell, Nebraska

(0030) **French, James Hansell**. Born 14 March 1851 in Philadelphia Pennsylvania. Louisiana. Cadet U.S. Military Academy 1 July 1869 (41/41); 2nd Lieutenant 9th U.S. Cavalry 17 June 1874; resigned 31 August 1876; 2nd Lieutenant 9th U.S. Cavalry 10 August 1878; killed 17 January 1880 in action with Apache Indians in the San Mateo Mountains New Mexico Territory.[31]

— Buried: Laurel Hill Cemetery, Philadelphia, Pennsylvania

(0031) **Grummond, George Washington**. Michigan. Michigan. First Sergeant Co. A 1st Michigan Infantry 1 May to 7 August 1861; Captain 1st Michigan Infantry 12 September 1861; resigned 14 July 1862; Major 14th Michigan Infantry 9 March 1863; Lieutenant Colonel 20 April 1863; honorably mustered out 18 July 1865; 2nd Lieutenant 18th U.S. Infantry 7 May 1866; killed 21 December 1866 in action with Indians near Ft Phil Kearny Dakota Territory.[32]

— Buried: Rest Haven Cemetery, Franklin, Tennessee

(0032) **Hale, Owen**. Born 23 July 1843 in New York. New York. Sergeant Major 7th New York Cavalry 23 October 1861 to 31 March 1862; Private Co. B and Sergeant Major 7th New York Cavalry 14 August 1862 to 9 May 1863; 2nd Lieutenant 7th New York Cavalry 9 May 1863; 1st Lieutenant 19 October 1864; brevet Captain Volunteers 13 March 1865 for gallant and meritorious service during the war; honorably mustered out 29 November 1865; 1st Lieutenant 7th U.S. Cavalry 28 July 1866; Captain 1 March 1869; killed 30 September 1877 in action with Nez Perce Indians at Snake River Montana Territory.[33]

— Buried: Oakwood Cemetery, Troy, New York

(0033) **Hamilton, Louis McLane**. Born 21 July 1844 in New York, New York. Army. Private Co. G 22nd New York State Militia 21 July to 5 September 1862; Private 14th U.S. Infantry 23 September 1862; 2nd Lieutenant 3rd U.S. Infantry 27 September 1862; 1st Lieutenant 6 May 1864; Regimental Quartermaster 8 June 1865 to 21 May 1866; Captain 7th U.S. Cavalry 28 July 1866; brevet 1st Lieutenant 3 May 1863 for gallant and meritorious ser at the battle of Chancellorsville Virginia; Captain 2 July 1863 for gallant and meritorious service at the battle of Gettysburg Pennsylvania and Major 27 November 1868 for gallant and meritorious service in engagement with Indians particularly in the battle with the Cheyenne on the Washita River Indian Territory 27 Nov 1868 where he was killed while gallantly leading his command.[34]

— Buried: Poughkeepsie Rural Cemetery, Poughkeepsie, New York

(0034) **Harris, George Montgomery**. Born 1846 in Pennsylvania. Georgia. Cadet U.S. Military Academy 9 Sept 1863 (45/54); 2nd Lieutenant 10th U.S. Infantry 15 June 1868; unassigned 19 May 1869; assigned to 4th U.S. Artillery 14 July 1869; 1st Lieutenant 1 May 1873; died 12 May 1873 of wounds received 26 April 1873 in action with Modoc Indians at the Lava Beds California.[35]

— Buried: Laurel Hill Cemetery, Philadelphia, Pennsylvania

(0035) **Harrington, Henry Moore**. Born 30 April 1849 in Albion, New York. Michigan. Cadet U.S. Military Academy 1 July 1868 (19/57); 2nd Lieutenant 7th U.S. Cavalry 14 June 1872; killed 25 June 1876 in action with Sioux Indians at Little Big Horn River Montana Territory.[36]

— Buried: Coldwater Cemetery, Coldwater, Michigan

(0036) **Hentig, Edmund Clarence**. Born 24 August 1842 in Marshall, Michigan. Michigan. 2nd Lieutenant 6th U.S. Cavalry 12 June 1867; 1st Lieutenant 23 December 1868; Captain 15 November 1876; killed 30 August 1881 in action with Apache Indians at Cibicu Creek Arizona Territory.[37]

— Buried: Santa Fe National Cemetery, Santa Fe, New Mexico

(0037) **Herkness, Bernard H**. Pennsylvania. Pennsylvania. Private Co. A 20th Pennsylvania Infantry 30 April to 6 August 1861; Sergeant Co. C 6th Pennsylvania Cavalry 10 September 1861; 2nd Lieutenant 1 April 1863; 1st Lieutenant 20 February 1864; Captain 24 December 1864; Major 22 March 1865; honorably mustered out 7 August 1865; 2nd Lieutenant 17th U.S. Infantry 11 May 1866; transferred to 35th U.S. Infantry 21 September 1866; killed 23 April 1869 by deserters.[38]

(0038) **Hodgson, Benjamin Hubert**. Born 30 June 1848 in Philadelphia, Pennsylvania. Pennsylvania. Cadet U.S. Military Academy 1 July 1865 (45/58); 2nd Lieutenant 7th U.S. Cavalry 15 June 1870; killed 25 June 1876 in action with Sioux Indians at Little Big Horn River Montana Territory.[39]

— Buried: Laurel Hill Cemetery, Philadelphia, Pennsylvania

[25] Heitman (Volume 1), 348; Day, *Tom Custer*; Nichols, *Men with Custer*, 76; Thrapp, *Encyclopedia of Frontier Biography (Volume 1)*, 364-365.
[26] Heitman (Volume 1),353.
[27] Heitman (Volume 1), 402; Thrapp, *Encyclopedia of Frontier Biography (Volume 1)*, 460.
[28] Heitman (Volume 1), 406; Thrapp, *Encyclopedia of Frontier Biography (Volume 1)*, 464.
[29] Heitman (Volume 1), 418; McDermott, *Red Clouds War (Volume 1)*, 169-170; Thrapp, *Encyclopedia of Frontier Biography (Volume 1)*, 489.
[30] *Official Records, Series I, Volume 48, Part I*, 324
[31] Heitman (Volume 1), 437; Cullum, *Biographical Register (Volume 3)*, 474; Thrapp, *Encyclopedia of Frontier Biography (Volume 1)*, 520.
[32] Heitman (Volume 1), 482; McDermott, *Red Clouds War (Volume 1)*, 139-140; Thrapp, *Encyclopedia of Frontier Biography (Volume 2)*, 594-595.
[33] Heitman (Volume 1), 487; Thrapp, *Encyclopedia of Frontier Biography (Volume 2)*, 605-606.
[34] Heitman (Volume 1), 494; Thrapp, *Encyclopedia of Frontier Biography (Volume 2)*, 610.
[35] Heitman (Volume 1), 503; Cullum, *Biographical Register (Volume 3)*, 389; Thrapp, *Encyclopedia of Frontier Biography*, 620.
[36] Heitman (Volume 1), 502; Cullum, *Biographical Register (Volume 3)*, 441-442; Nichols, *Men with Custer*, 140; Thrapp, *Encyclopedia of Frontier Biography (Volume 2)*, 618.
[37] Heitman (Volume 1), 524; Altshuler, *Cavalry Yellow*, 166-167; Thrapp, *Encyclopedia of Frontier Biography (Volume 2)*, 649-650.
[38] Heitman (Volume 1), 525.
[39] Heitman (Volume 1), 534; Cullum, *Biographical Register (Volume 3)*, 418; Nichols, *Men with Custer*, 149-150; Thrapp, *Encyclopedia of Frontier Biography (Volume 2)*, 667-668.

(0039) Howe, Albion. Born May 11, 1841 in St. Augustine, Florida. New York. 2nd Lieutenant 14th New York Artillery 16 December 1863; 1st Lieutenant 3 May 1865; Major 26 July 1865; honorably mustered out 26 August 1865; 2nd Lieutenant 4th U.S. Artillery 1 December 1866; 1st Lieutenant 18 November 1869; brevet 1st Lieutenant 2 Mar 1867 for gallant and distinguished service in the battle of Cold Harbor Virginia and Captain 2 March 1867 for gallant and distinguished service in the battle of Petersburg Virginia; killed 26 April 1873 in action with Modoc Indians at the Lava Beds California.[40]

— Buried: Forest Lawn Cemetery, Buffalo, New York

(0040) Jenness, John C. Vermont. New Hampshire. Private and Sergeant Co. A and Quartermaster Sergeant 17th New Hampshire Infantry 25 November 1862 to 16 April 1863; 1st Lieutenant 1st New Hampshire Artillery 19 September 1864; honorably mustered out 15 June 1865; 2nd Lieutenant 27th U.S. Infantry 28 July 1866; 1st Lieutenant 5 March 1867; killed 2 August 1867 in action with Indians near Ft Phil Kearny Dakota Territory.[41]

— Buried: Custer National Cemetery, Crow Agency, Montana

(0041) Keogh, Myles Walter. Born 25 March 1840 in Orchard House, County Carlow, Ireland. District of Columbia. 2nd Lieutenant Forth Company St. Papal Guard 7 August 1860; Captain Additional Aide-de-Camp 9 April 1862; Major Aide-de-Camp Volunteers 7 April 1864; brevet Lieutenant Colonel Volunteers 13 March 1865 for uniform gallantry and good conduct during the war; honorably mustered out 1 September 1866; 2nd Lieutenant 4th U.S. Cavalry 4 May 1866: Captain 7th U.S. Cavalry 28 July 1866; brevet Major 2 March 1867 for gallant and meritorious service in the battle of Gettysburg Pennsylvania and Lieutenant Colonel 2 March 1867 for gallant and meritorious service in the battle of Dallas Georgia; killed 25 June 1876 in action with Sioux Indians at Little Big Horn River Montana Territory.[42]

— Buried: Fort Hill Auburn Cemetery, Auburn, New York

(0042) Kidder, Lyman Stockwell. Born 31 August 1842 in Braintree Vermont. Dakota Territory. Corporal Co. K 5th Iowa Cavalry 1 November 1861; 1st Lieutenant 1st Minnesota Cavalry 6 June 1863; honorably mustered out 28 November 1863; Private Sergeant and First Sergeant Co. E Hatch's Battalion Minnesota Cavalry 20 August 1864; honorably mustered out 1 May 1866; 2nd Lieutenant 2nd U.S. Cavalry 22 January 1867; killed about 21 July 1867 in action with Indians near Beaver Creek Kansas.[43]

— Buried: Oakland Cemetery, St. Paul, Minnesota

(0043) Lewis, William Henry. Born 25 December 1829 in Mobile Alabama. New York. Cadet U.S. Military Academy 1 July 1845 (15/43); brevet 2nd Lieutenant 4th U.S. Infantry 1 July 1849; 2nd Lieutenant 1st U.S. Infantry 31 August 1849; transferred to 5th U.S. Infantry 7 August 1850; 1st Lieutenant 3 March 1855; Regimental Adjutant 1 November 1856 to 6 June 1857; Captain 7 May 1861; Major 18th U.S. Infantry 14 July 1864; transferred to 36th U.S. Infantry 21 September 1866; transferred to 7th U.S. Infantry 15 March 1869; Lieutenant Colonel 19th U.S. Infantry 10 December 1873; brevet Major 28 March 1862 for gallant and meritorious service in the battle of Apache Canyon New Mexico Territory and Lieutenant Colonel 15 April 1862 for gallant and meritorious service at the battle of Peralta New Mexico Territory; died 28 September 1878 of wounds received 27 September 1878 in action with Cheyenne Indians at Punished Woman's Fork Kansas.[44]

— Buried: Union Cemetery, Hudson Falls, New York

(0044) Logan, William. Born 9 December 1832 in Ireland. Army. Private Corporal and Sergeant Co. I 7th U.S. Infantry 27 December 1850 to 12 January 1863 and Hospital Steward to 4 June 1864; 2nd Lieutenant and 1st Lieutenant 7th U.S. Infantry 18 May 1864; Regimental Quartermaster 23 September 1864 to 19 May 1869; Captain 24 October 1874; killed 9 August 1877 in action with Nez Perce Indians at Big Hole Pass Montana Territory.[45]

— Buried: Custer National Cemetery, Crow Agency, Montana

(0045) Lord, George Edwin. Born 17 February 1846 in Boston Massachusetts. Massachusetts. Acting Assistant Surgeon 27 April, 1871; Assistant Surgeon 26 June 1875; killed 25 June 1876 in action with Sioux Indians on Little Big Horn River Montana Territory.[46]

— Buried: Custer National Cemetery, Crow Agency, Montana

(0046) Maddox, Thomas John Claggett. Born 12 December 1852 in Maryland. Maryland. Assistant Surgeon 22 October 1881; killed 19 December 1885 in action with Apache Indians near White House New Mexico Territory.[47]

— Buried: Episcopal Church Graveyard, Lappan's Crossroads, Maryland

(0047) Madigan, John. Born 1840 in Ireland. New Jersey. Private Co. G 88th New York Infantry 12 October 1861; Commissary Sergeant 20 February 1862; 2nd Lieutenant 13 December 1862; honorably mustered out 12 June 1863; 1st Lieutenant 2nd New Jersey Cavalry 12 August 1863; honorably mustered out 1 November 1865; 2nd Lieutenant 1st U.S. Cavalry 23 February 1866; 1st Lieutenant 25 April 1867; brevet Captain 27 September 1867 for conspicuous gallantry in charging a large band of Indians strongly fortified in the Infernal Caverns Pitt River California where he was killed 27 September 1867.[48]

— Buried: Modoc County, California[49]

(0048) Mann, James Defrees. Born 15 May 1854 in Indiana. Indiana. Cadet U.S. Military Academy 1 July 1873 (36/76); 2nd Lieutenant 7th U.S. Cavalry 15 June 1877; 1st Lieutenant 22 July 1890; died 15 January 1891 of wounds received in action with Sioux Indians at White Clay Creek South Dakota 30 December 1890.[50]

— Buried: Arlington National Cemetery, Washington, D.C.

(0049) McDermit, Charles. Born 7 May 1820 in Cambria Country Pennsylvania. Killed 7 August 1865 at Queens River Nevada.[51]

— Buried: Lone Mountain Cemetery, Carson City, Nevada

(0050) McIntosh, Donald. Born 4 September 1838 in Jasper House near Montreal Canada. Washington D.C. 2nd Lieutenant 7th U.S. Cavalry 17 August 1867; 1st Lieutenant 22 March 1870; killed 25 June 1876 in action with Sioux Indians at Little Big Horn River Montana Territory.[52]

— Buried: Arlington National Cemetery, Washington, D.C.

(0051) McKinney, John Augustine. Born 1846 in Memphis, Tennessee. Tennessee. Cadet U.S. Military Academy 1 July 1867 (21/41); 2nd Lieutenant 4th U.S. Cavalry 12 June 1871; 1st Lieutenant 17 May 1876; killed 25 November 1876 in action with Indians on North Fork of Powder River Wyoming Territory.[53]

— Buried: Elmwood Cemetery, Memphis, Tennessee

(0052) Millar, James Franklin. New York. Oregon. Private Co. A 2nd Ohio Infantry 17 April to 20 June 1861; 1st Lieutenant 14th U.S. Infantry 14 May 1861; Captain 17 September 1862; brevet Major 1 August 1864 for gallant and meritorious service at the battle of the Wilderness Virginia; killed 22 March 1866 by Apache Indian while en route from Ft Yuma to Ft Grand Arizona Territory.[54]

— Buried: Riverside Cemetery, Albany, Oregon

(0053) Mott, Seward. Born 21 August 1862 in Mechanicville New York. New York. Cadet U.S. Military Academy 1 July 1881 (73/77); additional 2nd Lieutenant 6th U.S. Cavalry 1 July 1886; 2nd Lieutenant 10th U.S. Cavalry 6 July 1886; died 11 March 1887 from injuries received 10 March 1887 in an assault by an Indian at San Carlos Agency Arizona Territory.[55]

— Buried: Woodlawn Cemetery, Hamilton, New York

[40] Heitman (Volume 1), 547; Howe, *Frontiersman*, 34-36.
[41] Heitman (Volume 1), 572; Thrapp, *Encyclopedia of Frontier Biography (Volume 2)*, 725.
[42] Heitman (Volume 1), 593; Nichols, *Men with Custer*, 177-178; Thrapp, *Encyclopedia of Frontier Biography (Volume 2)*, 772-773.
[43] Heitman (Volume 1), 596; Johnson, *Dispatch to Custer*, 7-26; Thrapp, *Encyclopedia of Frontier Biography (Volume 2)*, 778-779.
[44] Heitman (Volume 1), 612; William Henry Lewis grave marker; Cullum, *Biographical Register (Volume 2)*, xyz; Thrapp, *Encyclopedia of Frontier Biography (Volume 2)*, 853-854.
[45] Heitman (Volume 1), 639; Thrapp, *Encyclopedia of Frontier Biography (Volume 2)*, 868.
[45] Heitman (Volume 1), 641; Nichols, *Men with Custer*, 197-198; Thrapp, *Encyclopedia of Frontier Biography (Volume 2)*, 877.
[47] Heitman (Volume 1), 683; Thomas John Claggett Maddox grave marker; Thrapp, *Encyclopedia of Frontier Biography (Volume 2)*, 928.
[48] Heitman (Volume 1), 683; Thrapp, *Encyclopedia of Frontier Biography (Volume 2)*, 928-929.
[49] *Owyhee Avalanche*, 2 November 1867 in Cozzens, *Eyewitnesses to the Indian Wars (Volume 2)*, 76.
[50] Heitman (Volume 1), 687; Cullum, *Biographical Register (Volume 3)*, 502; Thrapp, *Encyclopedia of Frontier Biography (Volume 2)*, 937.
[51] Rathbun, *Nevada Military Place Names*, 115-117.
[52] Heitman (Volume 1), 669; Nichols, *Men with Custer*, 220; Thrapp, *Encyclopedia of Frontier Biography (Volume 2)*, 909-910.
[53] Heitman (Volume 1), 673; Cullum, *Biographical Register (Volume 3)*, 429; Thrapp, *Encyclopedia of Frontier Biography (Volume 2)*, 915.
[54] Heitman (Volume 1), 709; Thrapp, *Encyclopedia of Frontier Biography (Volume 2)*, 986.
[55] Heitman (Volume 1), 732; Cullum, *Biographical Register (Volume 4)*, 438; Altshuler, *Cavalry Yellow*, 240-241; Thrapp, *Encyclopedia of Frontier Biography (Volume 2)*, 1027.

(0054) **Pike. James.** Ohio. Ohio. Corporal Co. A 4th Ohio Cavalry 20 November 1861 to 1 April 1865; 2nd Lieutenant 1st U.S. Cavalry 31 March 1866; 1st Lieutenant 27 September 1867; died 14 October 1867.[56]

— Buried: Fort Walla Walla Military Cemetery, College Place, Washington

(0055) **Porter, James Ezekiel.** Born 2 February 1847 in Strong Maine. Maine. Cadet U.S. Military Academy 1 September 1864 (16/39); 2nd Lieutenant 7th U.S. Cavalry 15 June 1869; 1st Lieutenant 1 March 1872; killed 25 June 1876 in action with Sioux Indians at Little Big Horn River Montana Territory.[57]

— Buried: Village Cemetery, Strong, Maine

(0056) **Rains, Sevier McClellan.** Born 1851 in Michigan. Georgia. Cadet U.S. Military Academy 1 July 1872 (18/48); 2nd Lieutenant 1st U.S. Cavalry 15 June 1876; killed 3 July 1877 in action with Nez Perce Indians at Craig's Mountain Idaho Territory.[58]

— Buried: Fort Walla Walla Military Cemetery, College Place, Washington

(0057) **Reily, William Van Wyck.** Born 12 December 1853 in Washington D.C. Washington, D.C. Cadet U.S. Naval Academy 22 September, 1868; discharged 17 October, 1872; 2nd Lieutenant 10th U.S. Cavalry 15 October 1875; transferred to 7th U.S. Cavalry 26 January 1876; killed 25 June 1876 in action with Sioux Indians at Little Big Horn River Montana Territory.[59]

— Buried: Mt. Olivet Cemetery, Washington, D.C.

(0058) **Roberts, George.** 1st Lieutenant Fairchild's Detachment California Volunteers; died 9 February 1873 of wounds received 17 January 1873 in action with Modoc Indians at Lava Beds California.[60]

— Buried: San Francisco National Cemetery, San Francisco, California

(0059) **Robinson, Levi H.** Born 2 October 1840 in Swanton Vermont. Sergeant Co. F 10th Vermont Infantry 16 July 1862 to 17 February 1865; 2 lt 119th U.S. Colored Infantry 8 February 1865; honorably mustered out 27 Apr 1866; 2nd Lieutenant 14th U.S. Infantry 19 April 1866; 1st Lieutenant 11 August 1866; killed 9 February 1874 by Indians near Laramie Peak Wyoming Territory.[61]

— Buried: Fairview Cemetery, New Britain, Connecticut

(0060) **Russell, William, Jr.** Born 22 November 1838 in Albany New York. New York. 1st Lieutenant Regimental Quartermaster 18th New York Infantry 21 September 1861 to 22 April 1863; Major Acting Adjutant General Volunteers 15 April 1863; brevet Lieutenant Colonel Volunteers 13 March 1865 for meritorious service during the war; honorably mustered out 10 February 1866; 2nd Lieutenant 4th U.S. Cavalry 25 October 1867; brevet 1st Lieutenant 25 October 1867 for gallant and meritorious service in the battle of Antietam Maryland; Captain 25 October 1867 for gallant and meritorious service at the battle of Gettysburg Pennsylvania and Major 25 October 1867 for gallant and meritorious service in the battle of Petersburg Virginia; died 15 May 1870 of wounds received 14 May 1870 in action with Indians at Mount Adam Texas.[62]

— Buried: Albany Rural Cemetery, Albany, New York

(0061) **Sherwood, William Lord.** Born 3 November 1847 in Buffalo New York. 2nd Lieutenant 21st U.S. Infantry 3 September 1867; 1st Lieutenant 22 July 1872; died 14 April 1873 of wounds received 11 April 1873 from Modoc Indians while receiving a flag of truce at the Lava Beds California.[63]

— Buried: Forest Lawn Cemetery, Buffalo, New York

(0062) **Smith, Algernon Emory.** Born 17 September 1842 in Newport New York. New York. 2nd Lieutenant 117th New York Infantry 20 August 1862; 1st Lieutenant 20 September 1862; Captain 12 October 1864; brevet Major Volunteers 13 March 1865 for gallant and meritorious service at the storming of Ft Fisher North Carolina; honorably mustered out 15 May 1865; 2nd Lieutenant 7th U.S. Cavalry 9 August 1867; 1st Lieutenant 5 December 1868; Regimental Quartermaster 31 March to 7 July 1869; brevet 1st Lieutenant 9 August 1867 for gallant and meritorious service at the battle of Drury's Farm Virginia and Captain 9 August 1867 for gallant and meritorious service in the capture of Ft Fisher North Carolina; killed 25 June 1876 in action with Sioux Indians on Little Big Horn River Montana Territory.[64]

— Buried: Fort Leavenworth National Cemetery, Fort Leavenworth, Kansas

(0063) **Smith, George Washington.** Born 16 October 1836 in Butler Pennsylvania. Kansas. Captain 18th U.S. Infantry 5 August 1861; brevet Major 20 September 1863 for gallant and meritorious service in the battle of Chickamauga Georgia and Lieutenant Colonel 1September 1864 for gallant and meritorious service during the Atlanta campaign and in the battle of Jonesboro Georgia; resigned 15 May 1866; 2nd Lieutenant 9th U.S. Cavalry 6 August 1873; killed 19 August 1881 in action with Apache Indians near McEver's Ranch New Mexico Territory.[65]

— Buried: Oak Hill Cemetery, Lawrence, Kansas

(0064) **Stambaugh, Charles B.** Ohio. Ohio. Private Co. H 11th Ohio Cavalry 8 March 1864 to 2 May 1866; 2nd Lieutenant 2nd U.S. Cavalry 7 March 1867; 1st Lieutenant 5 July1868; killed 4 May 1870 in action with Indians near Miners Delight Wyoming Territory.[66]

(0065) **Sternberg, Sigismund.** Prussia. District of Columbia. 1st Lieutenant 175th New York Infantry 26 September 1862; resigned 13 February 1864; Captain 7th New York Infantry 22 October 1864; honorably mustered out 4 August 1865; 1st Lieutenant 82nd U.S. Colored Infantry 10 September 1865; Captain 30 June 1866; honorably mustered out 10 September 1866: 2nd Lieutenant 27th U.S. Infantry 7 March 1867; killed 1 August 1867 in action with Sioux Indians near Ft CF Smith Montana Territory.[67]

— Buried: Custer National Cemetery, Crow Agency, Montana

(0066) **Stewart, Reid T.** Born 1850 in Pennsylvania. Pennsylvania. Cadet U.S. Military Academy 1 September 1867 (8/41); 2nd Lieutenant 5th U.S. Cavalry 12 June 1871; killed 27 August 1872 in action with Apache Indians at Davidson's Canyon Arizona Territory.[68]

— Buried: Erie Cemetery, Erie, Pennsylvania

(0067) **Sturgis, James Garland.** Born 24 January 1850 in Albuquerque New Mexico. At Large. Cadet U.S. Military Academy 1 July 1871 (29/43); 2nd Lieutenant 7th U.S. Cavalry 16 June 1875; killed 25 June 1876 in action with Sioux Indians at Little Big Horn River Montana Territory.[69]

— Buried: Little Big Horn Battlefield, Hardin, Montana[70]

(0068) **Tappan, Benjamin.** Ohio. California. Surgeon 8th Ohio Infantry 2 May 1861; honorably discharged 24 March 1862; Assistant Surgeon Volunteers 3 December 1864; killed 22 March 1866 in action with Apache Indians near Cottonwood Springs Arizona Territory.[71]

(0069) **Theller, Edward Russell.** Born 1831 in Vermont. California. Capt 2nd California Infantry 25 October 1861; brevet Major Volunteers 13 March 1865 for faithful and meritorious service; honorably mustered out 10 May 1866; 2nd Lieutenant 9th U.S. Infantry 7 March 1867; transferred to 21st U.S. Infantry 30 August 1869; 1st Lieutenant 31 August 1871; killed 17 June 1877 in action with Nez Perce Indians near the Mouth of White Bird Creek Idaho Territory.[72]

[56] Heitman (Volume 1), 792.
[57] Heitman (Volume 1), 799; Cullum, *Biographical Register (Volume 3)*, 397; Nichols, *Men with Custer*, 264-265; Thrapp, *Encyclopedia of Frontier Biography (Volume 3)*, 1163-1164.
[58] Heitman (Volume 1), 813; Cullum, *Biographical Register (Volume 3)*, 488; Thrapp, *Encyclopedia of Frontier Biography (Volume 3)*, 1189.
[59] Heitman (Volume 1), 823; Nichols, *Men with Custer*, 275-276; Thrapp, *Encyclopedia of Frontier Biography (Volume 3)*, 1204-1205.
[60] Reports of Diseases and Individual Cases, F 432.
[61] Heitman (Volume 1), 839; Altshuler, *Cavalry Yellow*, 284-285; Thrapp, *Encyclopedia of Frontier Biography (Volume 4)*, 404.
[62] Heitman (Volume 1), 854.
[63] Heitman (Volume 1), 882; Altshuler, *Cavalry Yellow*, 301.
[64] Heitman (Volume 1), 893; Nichols, *Men with Custer*, 307-308; Thrapp, *Encyclopedia of Frontier Biography (Volume 3)*, 1323.
[65] Heitman (Volume 1), 898; Thrapp, *Encyclopedia of Frontier Biography (Volume 3)*, 1326-1327.
[66] Heitman (Volume 1), 914.
[67] Heitman (Volume 1), 921; Thrapp, *Encyclopedia of Frontier Biography (Volume 3)*, 1366.
[68] Heitman (Volume 1), 925; Cullum, *Biographical Register (Volume 3)*, 425; Altshuler, *Cavalry Yellow*, 319; Thrapp, *Encyclopedia of Frontier Biography (Volume 3)*, 1368-1369.
[69] Heitman (Volume 1), 934; Cullum, *Biographical Register (Volume 3)*, 481; Nichols, *Men with Custer*, 321; Thrapp, *Encyclopedia of Frontier Biography (Volume 3)*, 1384.
[70] "Lt. James G. Sturgis, it may be remembered, fell in Custer's fatal battle, and, at his father's request, was buried on the field of valor where he fell." *Army and Navy Journal (Volume 15)*, 20.
[71] Heitman (Volume 1), 944; Thrapp, *Encyclopedia of Frontier Biography (Volume 3)*, 1401.
[72] Heitman (Volume 1), 952; Altshuler, *Cavalry Yellow*, 329-330; Thrapp, *Encyclopedia of Frontier Biography (Volume 3)*, 1415.

(0070) Thomas, Evan. Born December 1843 in District of Columbia. District of Columbia. 2nd Lieutenant 4th U.S. Artillery 9 April 1861; 1st Lieutenant 14 May 1861; Captain 31 August 1864; brevet Captain 13 December 1862 for gallant and meritorious service at the battle of Fredericksburg Virginia and Major 3 July 1863 for gallant and meritorious service in the battle of Gettysburg Pennsylvania; killed 26 April 1873 in action with Modoc Indians at Lava Beds California.[73]

— Buried: Arlington National Cemetery, Washington, D.C.

(0071) Thompson, John A. Ohio. Virginia. 2nd Lieutenant 1st U.S. Dragoons 25 June 1855; transferred to 1st U.S. Cavalry 29 August 1855; 1st Lieutenant 31 January 1861; Captain 14 May 1861; 4th U.S. Cavalry 3 August 1861; Major 7th U.S. Cavalry 25 August 1867; brevet Major 26 June 1863 for gallant and meritorious service in the battle of Hoover's Gap Tennessee; murdered 14 Nov 1867 by desperadoes near Ft Mason Texas.[74]

— Buried: Thompson Cemetery, Mead Township,
Belmont County, Ohio

(0072) Thornburgh, Thomas Tipton. Born 26 December 1843 in New Market Tennessee. Tennessee. Private Co. A and Sergeant Major 6 Tennessee Infantry 20 April 1862 to 1 September 1863; Cadet U.S. Military Academy 1 September 1863 (26/63); 2nd Lieutenant 2nd U.S. Artillery 17 June l867; 1st Lieutenant 21 April 1870; Major Paymaster 26 April 1875; transferred as Major to 4th U.S. Infantry 23 May 1878; killed 29 September 1879 in action with Ute Indians at Milk River Colorado.[75]

— Buried: Arlington National Cemetery, Washington, D.C.

(0073) Vincent, Frederick R. Prince Edward Island. Missouri. Private and Sergeant Co. F 11th and 2nd Missouri State Militia Cavalry 24 March 1862 to 6 September 1863; 1st Lieutenant 2nd Missouri State Militia Cavalry 6 September 1863; Captain 11 December 1863; honorably mustered out 29 March 1865; 2nd Lieutenant 9th U.S. Cavalry 18 June 1867; 1st Lieutenant 16 July 1869; died 20 April 1872 of wounds received that date in action with Indians near Howards Well Texas.[76]

— Buried: San Antonio National Cemetery, San Antonio, Texas

(0074) Wallace, George Daniel. Born 24 June, 1849 in York County, South Carolina. South Carolina. Cadet U.S. Military Academy 1 September 1868 (9/57); 2nd Lieutenant 7th U.S. Cavalry 14 June 1872; 1st Lieutenant 25 June 25 1876; Regimental Adjutant 25 June 1876 to 6 June 1877; Captain 23 September 1885; killed 29 December 1890 in action with Sioux Indians at Wounded Knee South Dakota.[77]

— Buried: Rose Hill Cemetery, York, South Carolina

(0075) Weir, William Bayard. New York. At Large. Cadet U.S. Military Academy 1 July 1866 (7/58); 2nd Lieutenant 5th U.S. Artillery 15 June 1870; 1st Lieutenant Ordnance Department 1 November 1874; killed 20 October 1879 by Ute Indian near White River Agency Colorado.[78]

— Buried: U.S. Military Academy Post Cemetery, West Point, New York

(0076) Wilkinson, Melville Gary. Born 14 November, 1835 in Scottsburg, New York. New York. 1st Lieutenant 123rd New York Infantry 16 May 1861; resigned 7 November 1861; 1st Lieutenant 107th New York Infantry 28 July 1862; Captain 9 August 1862; resigned 26 January 1863; 1st Lieutenant Veteran Reserve Corps 13 August 1863; Captain 10 December 1863.; honorably mustered out 30 June 1866; 2nd Lieutenant 42nd U.S. Infantry 28 July 1866; transferred to 6th U.S. Infantry 22 April 1869; unassigned 28 June 1869; assigned to 3rd U.S. Infantry 3 August 1870; 1st It 1 January 1871; Captain 24 April 1886; brevet 1st Lieutenant 2 March 1867 for gallant and meritorious service in the battle of Antietam Maryland; Captain 2 March 1867 for gallant and meritorious service during the war; Major 27 February 1890 for gallant service in action against Indians at the Clearwater Idaho Territory 11 and 12 July 1877 and at Kamiah Idaho Territory 13 July 1877; killed 5 October 1898 in action with Indians at Bear Island Leech Lake Minnesota.[79]

— Buried: Fort Snelling National Cemetery,
South Minneapolis, Minnesota

(0077) Wilson, Benjamin Swift. Born 24 November 1843 in Pepperell Massachusetts. New Hampshire. Private Co. K 5th New Hampshire Infantry 19 September 1861; Sergeant Major 27 October 1863; discharged 20 April 1864; 1st Lieutenant 1st U.S. Volunteer Infantry 23 April 1864; died 2 June 1865 of wounds received 26 May 1865 in action with Sioux Indians near Fort Rice Dakota Territory.[80]

— Buried: Pine Hill Cemetery, Hillsborough, New Hampshire

(0078) Wright, Thomas Forster. Born in Missouri in 1831. California. Cadet U.S. Military Academy 1 July 1848 to 17 November 1849; 1st Lieutenant Regimental Quartermaster 2nd California Cavalry 2 October 1861; resigned 31 January 1863; Major 6th California Infantry 1 February 1863; Major 2nd California Infantry 3 October 1864; Lieutenant Colonel 23 November 1864; Colonel 6 January 1865; brevet Brigadier General Volunteers 13 Mar 1865 for faithful and meritorious service; honorably mustered out 16 April 1866; 1st Lieutenant 32nd U.S. Infantry28 July 1866; Regimental Quartermaster 15 July 1867 to 12 May 1869; unassigned 12 May 1869; assigned to 12th U.S. Infantry 31 Jan 1870; Regimental Adjutant 8 March to 8 June 1870; killed 26 April 1873 in action with Modoc Indians at the Lava Beds California.[81]

— Buried: Sacramento City Cemetery, Sacramento, California

(0079) Yates, George Wilhelmus Mancius. Born 26 February 1843 in Albany, New York. New York. Private 4th Michigan Infantry 20 June 1861; Quartermaster Sergeant 1 November 1861; 1st Lieutenant 26 September 1862; honorably mustered out 28 June 1864; 1st Lieutenant 45th Missouri Infantry 24 August 1864; Captain 13th Missouri Cavalry 22 September 1864; brevet Major Volunteers 13 March 1865 for gallant and meritorious service during the war and Lieutenant Colonel Volunteers 13 March 1865 for conspicuous gallantry at Fredericksburg and Beverly Ford Virginia and at Gettysburg Pennsylvania; honorably mustered out 11 January 1866; 2nd Lieutenant 2nd U.S. Cavalry 26 March 1866; Regimental Quartermaster 12 May to 28 October 1867; Captain 7th U.S. Cavalry 12 June 1867; killed 25 June 1876 in action with Sioux Indians at the Little Big Horn Rive Montana Territory.[82]

— Buried: Fort Leavenworth National Cemetery,
Fort Leavenworth, Kansas

[73] Heitman (Volume 1), 953; Thrapp, *Encyclopedia of Frontier Biography (Volume 3)*, 1417.
[74] Heitman (Volume 1), 956-957; Otis, *Report of Surgical Cases*, 23, 54.
[75] Heitman (Volume 1), 958-959; Cullum, *Biographical Register (Volume 2)*, 638; Sprague, *Massacre*, 181-182; Thrapp, *Encyclopedia of Frontier Biography (Volume 3)*, 1425-1426.
[76] Heitman (Volume 1), 987.
[77] Heitman (Volume 1), 998; Cullum, *Biographical Register (Volume 3)*, 438; Mackintosh, *Custer's Southern Officer*; Thrapp, *Encyclopedia of Frontier Biography (Volume XY)*, 1505.
[78] Heitman (Volume 1), 1015; Cullum, *Biographical Register (Volume 3)*, 407.
[79] Heitman (Volume 1), 1037; Thrapp, *Encyclopedia of Frontier Biography (Volume 3)*, 1565.
[80] *Revised Register of the Soldiers and Sailors in New Hampshire*, 278; *Vital Records of Pepperell, Massachusetts*, 119
[81] Heitman (Volume 1), 1063; Altshuler, *Cavalry Yellow*, 382; Thrapp, *Encyclopedia of Frontier Biography (Volume 3)*, 1603.
[82] Heitman (Volume 1), 1065; Nichols, *Men with Custer*, 365; Thrapp, *Encyclopedia of Frontier Biography (Volume 3)*, 1607.

—ENLISTED—

LAST NAME	FIRST	RANK	REGIMENT	DEATH
(0080) Aarons	Henry	Private	18th U.S. Infantry	12-21-1866
(0081) Ackerman	Frederick	Private	18th U.S. Infantry	12-21-1866
(0082) Acrons	Henry	Private	18th U.S. Infantry	12-21-1866
(0083) Adams	George	Private	7th U.S. Cavalry	06-25-1876
(0084) Alberts	James	Sergeant	7th U.S. Cavalry	09-30-1877
(0085) Alcorn	Charles	Sergeant	5th U.S. Cavalry	05-13-1869
(0086) Alder	Philip	Private	7th Iowa Cavalry	06-14-1865
(0087) Allan	Fred	Private	7th U.S. Cavalry	06-25-1876
(0088) Allen	William	Private	3rd U.S. Cavalry	06-17-1876
(0089) Amberson	Thomas	Private	2nd U.S. Cavalry	12-21-1866
(0090) Amish	Frank	Private	3rd U.S. Cavalry	01-09-1879
(0091) Anderson	Thomas	Private	18th Kansas Volunteer Cavalry	08-21-1867
(0092) Andrews	William	Private	7th U.S. Cavalry	06-25-1876
(0093) Antram	Jesse	Private	11th Kansas Cavalry	07-26-1865
(0094) Archer	Edson	Blacksmith	7th U.S. Cavalry	09-14-1877[1]
(0095) Armstrong	Charles	Private	1st U.S. Cavalry	06-17-1877
(0096) Armstrong	John	Private	7th U.S. Cavalry	06-25-1876
(0097) Assadaly	Anthony	Private	7th U.S. Cavalry	06-25-1876
(0098) Atcheson	Thomas	Private	7th U.S. Cavalry	06-25-1876
(0099) Atkins	Philip	Private	9th U.S. Infantry	07-29-1866
(0100) Austin	Charles	Private	2nd California Cavalry	02-15-1866
(0101) Ayers	Lorenzo	Private	3rd U.S. Cavalry	03-17-1876
(0102) Baader	Leo	Private	2nd U.S. Cavalry	04-05-1879
(0103) Babcock	Elmer	Private	7th U.S. Cavalry	06-25-1876
(0104) Backus	William	Corporal	10th U.S. Cavalry	10-28-1880
(0106) Bacon	Fred	Private	7th U.S. Cavalry	06-21-1867
(0107) Bailey	Henry	Blacksmith	7th U.S. Cavalry	06-25-1876
(0108) Baird	James	Private	4th U.S. Cavalry	11-25-1876
(0109) Baker	James	Sergeant	2nd U.S. Cavalry	12-21-1866
(0110) Baker	Ralston	Private	2nd U.S. Cavalry	05-01-1867
(0111) Baker	William	Private	7th U.S. Cavalry	06-25-1876
(0112) Ballew	James	Private	11th Kansas Cavalry	07-26-1865
(0113) Barber	Amos	Private	3rd U.S. Cavalry	01-17-1879
(0114) Barry	Charles	Private	7th U.S. Infantry	09-15-1869
(0115) Barry	John	Private	7th U.S. Cavalry	06-25-1876
(0116) Barth	Robert	Private	7th U.S. Cavalry	06-25-1876
(0117) Batrick	George	Private	13th U.S. Infantry	07-31-1866
(0118) Batty	William	Private	5th U.S. Infantry	01-03-1877
(0119) Bauer	Gustave	Corporal	18th U.S. Infantry	12-21-1866
(0120) Beals	George	Private	31st U.S. Infantry	08-20-1868
(0121) Bennett	James	Private	7th U.S. Cavalry	07-05-1876[2]
(0122) Bennett	Richard	Private	3rd U.S. Cavalry	06-17-1876
(0123) Benson	John	Private	21st U.S. Infantry	01-17-1873
(0124) Betzler	William	Private	18th U.S. Infantry	12-21-1866
(0125) Bird	Henry	Private	6th U.S. Cavalry	08-30-1881
(0126) Bissel	Ephraim	Sergeant	18th U.S. Infantry	12-21-1866
(0127) Black	Joseph	Corporal	5th U.S. Cavalry	08-27-1872
(0128) Bladt	Peter	Private	12th U.S. Infantry	08-31-1881
(0129) Blaine	Joseph	Private	1st U.S. Cavalry	06-17-1877
(0130) Blake	Michael	Private	21st U.S. Infantry	10-05-1869
(0131) Blum	George	Private	6th U.S. Cavalry	07-12-1870
(0132) Bobo	L.Edwin	First Sergeant	7th U.S. Cavalry	06-25-1876
(0133) Bodine	George	Private	11th Ohio Cavalry	06-08-1865
(0134) Bone	Albert	Corporal	7th U.S. Cavalry	12-29-1890
(0135) Bonwell	William	Private	11th Ohio Cavalry	06-03-1865
(0136) Boothe	Jerome	Private	14th U.S. Infantry	11-02-1868
(0137) Botzer	Edward	Sergeant	7th U.S. Cavalry	06-25-1876
(0138) Bourke/Rourke	Thomas	Private	18th U.S. Infantry	03-18-1868
(0139) Bowers	George	Sergeant	18th U.S. Infantry	12-06-1866
(0140) Boyer	Eli	Private	9th U.S. Cavalry	12-26-1867
(0141) Boyle	Owen	Private	7th U.S. Cavalry	06-25-1876
(0142) Bradshaw	Elijah	Private	12th Missouri Cavalry	09-07-1865
(0143) Brady	William	Private	7th U.S. Cavalry	06-25-1876
(0144) Brandon	Benjamin	Farrier	7th U.S. Cavalry	06-25-1876
(0145) Branner	John	Private	21st U.S. Infantry	01-17-1873
(0146) Braun	Frank	Private	7th U.S. Cavalry	10-04-1876[3]
(0147) Braus	John	Private	23rd U.S. Infantry	09-26-1867
(0148) Brightfield	John	Private	7th U.S. Cavalry	06-25-1876
(0149) Briody	John	Corporal	7th U.S. Cavalry	06-25-1876
(0150) Broadhurst	Joseph	Private	7th U.S. Cavalry	06-25-1876
(0151) Brodson	Lewis	Private	3rd U.S. Cavalry	10-03-1866
(0152) Brogan	James	Private	7th U.S. Cavalry	06-25-1876
(0153) Broglin	Thomas	Private	2nd U.S. Cavalry	12-21-1866
(0154) Brooks	Bernard	Trumpeter	1st U.S. Cavalry	08-20-1877
(0155) Brooks	Edward	Private	9th U.S. Infantry	03-29-1869
(0156) Broutz	Herman	Private	7th U.S. Infantry	08-09-1877
(0157) Brown	Benjamin	Private	7th U.S. Cavalry	06-25-1876
(0158) Brown	George	Corporal	7th U.S. Cavalry	06-25-1876

[1] WIA 09-13-1877.
[2] WIA 06-25-1876.
[3] WIA 06-25-1876.

(0159) Brown	George	Farrier	3rd U.S. Cavalry	01-22-1879
(0160) Brown	James	Private	9th U.S. Cavalry	08-19-1881
(0161) Brown	John	Private	1st Oregon Volunteers	01-17-1873
(0162) Brown	Moses	Private	11th Kansas Cavalry	07-26-1865
(0163) Brown	Nathan	Private	7th U.S. Cavalry	09-13-1877
(0164) Brown	William	Private	11th Kansas Cavalry	07-26-1865
(0165) Brown	William	Private	7th U.S. Cavalry	06-25-1876
(0166) Bruchert	Charles	First Sergeant	1st U.S. Cavalry	09-26-1867
(0167) Buchanan	Henry	Private	18th U.S. Infantry	12-21-1866
(0168) Buck	Augustine	Private	3rd U.S. Infantry	05-31-1870
(0169) Bugbee	William	Private	2nd U.S. Cavalry	12-21-1866
(0170) Burgess	William	Private	32nd U.S. Infantry	04-20-1869
(0171) Burke	Thomas	Private	18th U.S. Infantry	12-21-1866
(0172) Burke	William	Corporal	14th U.S. Cavalry	02-23-1866
(0173) Burkel	Caspar	Private	37th U.S. Infantry	06-14-1867
(0174) Burrell	George	Private	18th U.S. Infantry	12-21-1866
(0175) Bruce	Patrick	Private	7th U.S. Cavalry	06-25-1876
(0176) Bucknell	Thomas	Trumpeter	7th U.S. Cavalry	06-25-1876
(0177) Buford	Albert	Sergeant	8th U.S. Infantry	10-01-1881
(0178) Burch	Frank	Private	1st U.S. Cavalry	06-17-1877
(0179) Burk	John	Private	1st U.S. Cavalry	07-03-1877
(0180) Burnham	Lucien	Private	7th U.S. Cavalry	06-25-1876
(0181) Burns	Carter	Private	10th U.S. Cavalry	10-28-1880
(0182) Burns	John	Private	5th U.S. Cavalry	09-29-1879
(0183) Burton	Francis	Blacksmith	4th U.S. Cavalry	09-14-1878
(0184) Bustard	James	Sergeant	7th U.S. Cavalry	06-25-1876
(0185) Butler	James	First Sergeant	7th U.S. Cavalry	06-25-1876
(0186) Butler	James	Sergeant	3rd U.S. Infantry	10-04-1898
(0187) Butterly	Matthew	Private	7th U.S. Infantry	08-09-1877
(0188) Byrne	James	Private	5th U.S. Artillery	07-11-1894
(0189) Cable	Joseph	Sergeant	5th U.S. Infantry	09-30-1877
(0190) Callahan	John	Corporal	7th U.S. Cavalry	06-25-1876
(0191) Callery	Terrence	Private	18th U.S. Infantry	07-21-1866
(0192) Camp	George	Private	11th Kansas Cavalry	07-26-1865
(0193) Carlin	Charles	Corporal	21st U.S. Infantry	07-13-1877
(0194) Carney	James	Private	7th U.S. Cavalry	06-25-1876
(0195) Carr	Andrew	Private	5th U.S. Cavalry	09-30-1872
(0196) Carrick	William	Corporal	7th U.S. Cavalry	11-27-1868
(0197) Carroll	David	Private	1st U.S. Cavalry	07-03-1877
(0198) Carry	Bryan	Private	1st U.S. Cavalry	09-26-1867
(0199) Carty	William	Private	3rd U.S. Cavalry	10-18-1867
(0200) Casey	Richard	Sergeant	3rd U.S. Cavalry	04-29-1882
(0201) Cashan	William	Sergeant	7th U.S. Cavalry	06-25-1876
(0202) Cather	Armantheus	Private	7th U.S. Cavalry	06-25-1876
(0203) Chapman	Silas	Sergeant	9th U.S. Cavalry	09-04-1879
(0204) Charley	Vincent	Farrier	7th U.S. Cavalry	06-25-1876
(0205) Cheever	Ami	Private	7th U.S. Cavalry	06-25-1876
(0206) Christie	Thomas	Private	7th U.S. Cavalry	11-27-1868
(0207) Christopher	Alexander	Private	6th U.S. Cavalry	05-22-1872
(0208) Christy	William	Sergeant	10th U.S. Cavalry	08-02-1867
(0209) Clancy	Patrick	Private	2nd U.S. Cavalry	12-21-1866
(0210) Clark	Charles	Private	21st U.S. Infantry	07-11-1877
(0211) Clark	Joseph	Private	14th U.S. Infantry	05-07-1869[4]
(0212) Clark	Peter	Private	5th U.S. Artillery	07-11-1894
(0213) Clarke	Charles	Bugler	7th U.S. Cavalry	06-26-1867
(0214) Clear	Elihu	Private	7th U.S. Cavalry	06-25-1876
(0215) Cleveland	John	Private	7th U.S. Cavalry	09-30-1877
(0216) Close	Oscar	Sergeant	2nd U.S. Cavalry	07-02-1867
(0217) Clover	Eugene	Private	7th U.S. Cavalry	11-27-1868
(0218) Cochlovius	Reinhold	Private	6th U.S. Cavalry	10-27-1879
(0219) Cody	Henry	Corporal	7th U.S. Cavalry	06-25-1876
(0220) Coffey	Dora	First Sergeant	7th U.S. Cavalry	12-29-1890
(0221) Cohen	Mayer	Private	1st U.S. Cavalry	07-12-1877
(0222) Colbert	John	Private	1st U.S. Cavalry	06-17-1877
(0223) Coleman	Charles	Corporal	7th U.S. Cavalry	06-25-1876
(0224) Collins	Daniel	Blacksmith	8th U.S. Cavalry	12-19-1885
(0225) Collins	Hugh	Private	4th U.S. Cavalry	08-23-1867
(0226) Compton	Elson	Private	21st U.S. Infantry	07-12-1877
(0227) Connell	Michael	Private	2nd U.S. Cavalry	07-02-1867
(0228) Connelly	Patrick	Private	1st U.S. Cavalry	06-17-1877
(0229) Connerlin	John	Private	3rd U.S. Infantry	05-31-1870
(0230) Connor	Brooks	Private	3rd U.S. Cavalry	06-17-1876
(0231) Connor	Edward	Private	7th U.S. Cavalry	06-25-1876
(0232) Connors	Thomas	Private	7th U.S. Cavalry	06-25-1876
(0233) Conradi	John	Blacksmith	4th U.S. Cavalry	05-15-1886
(0234) Conry	Terrence	Private	13th U.S. Infantry	04-07-1869
(0235) Considine	Martin	Sergeant	7th U.S. Cavalry	06-25-1876
(0236) Cook	James	Private	3rd U.S. Cavalry	07-09-1867
(0237) Cook	James	Private	13th U.S. Infantry	05-24-1868
(0238) Cook	Ralph	Private	7th U.S. Cavalry	12-29-1890
(0239) Cooney	David	Private	7th U.S. Cavalry	07-20-1876[5]
(0240) Coonrod		Sergeant	7th U.S. Cavalry	05-14-1884

[4] WIA 05-06-1869.
[5] WIA 06-25-1876.

(0241) Corbett	Cyrus	Private	7th U.S. Cavalry	09-13-1868
(0242) Cornoy	William	Private	2nd U.S. Cavalry	12-21-1866
(0243) Corwine	Richard	Sergeant Major	7th U.S. Cavalry	12-29-1890
(0244) Crawford	Adaluska	Private	1st U.S. Cavalry	06-17-1877
(0245) Costello	John	Private	7th U.S. Cavalry	12-29-1890
(0246) Coughlin	Cornelius	Private	31st U.S. Infantry	11-06-1867
(0247) Creighton	Hiram	Sergeant	1st Battalion Nebraska Cavalry	05-12-1865
(0248) Criddle	Christopher	Private	7th U.S. Cavalry	06-25-1876
(0249) Crisfield	William	Private	7th U.S. Cavalry	06-25-1876
(0250) Crowley	John	Private	7th U.S. Cavalry	06-25-1876
(0251) Crump	Jeremiah	Private	9th U.S. Cavalry	09-18-1879
(0252) Cuddy	Charles	Private	2nd U.S. Cavalry	12-21-1866
(0253) Cuddy	Charles	Private	7th U.S. Cavalry	11-27-1868
(0254) Cuff	Dominick	Private	3rd U.S. Cavalry	09-29-1879
(0255) Cullinane	Timothy	Private	18th U.S. Infantry	12-21-1866
(0256) Culp	Adam	Private	11th Kansas Cavalry	07-26-1865
(0257) Cummings	Pierce	Private	7th U.S. Cavalry	12-29-1890
(0258) Curles	Alfred	Private	11th Ohio Cavalry	05-28-1865
(0259) Curran	James	Private	3rd U.S. Infantry	09-11-1868
(0260) Curran	Michael	Corporal	1st U.S. Cavalry	06-17-1877
(0261) Curry	Bernard	Private	6th U.S. Cavalry	09-22-1868
(0262) Curry	Roger	Private	2nd U.S. Cavalry	07-02-1867
(0263) Cusack	Bernard	Private	5th U.S. Cavalry	10-14-1868
(0264) Custard	Amos	C. Sergeant[6]	11th Kansas Cavalry	07-26-1865
(0265) Dalious	James	Corporal	7th U.S. Cavalry	06-25-1876
(0266) Daly	Thomas	Private	1st California Veteran Infantry	01-17-1866
(0267) Daniel	Robert	Private	2nd U.S. Cavalry	12-21-1866
(0268) Darragh	Joseph	Private	1st U.S. Cavalry	12-11-1869[7]
(0269) Darris	John	Private	7th U.S. Cavalry	06-25-1876
(0270) Dauch	Lawrence	Private	1st U.S. Cavalry	06-17-1877
(0271) Davis	George	Private	18th U.S. Infantry	12-21-1866
(0272 Davis	Martin	Private	10th U.S. Cavalry	07-30-1880
(0273) Davis	William	Private	7th U.S. Cavalry	06-25-1876
(0274) Dawsey	David	Private	7th U.S. Cavalry	09-30-1877
(0275) Deblois	Henry	Private	3rd U.S. Cavalry	01-24-1879[8]
(0276) Demig	Harvey	Private	2nd U.S. Cavalry	12-21-1866
(0277) Densham	William	Private	8th U.S. Cavalry	11-06-1874
(0278) Deuterman	George	Private	1st U.S. Cavalry	07-03-1877
(0279) Devine	Charles	Private	1st California Veteran Infantry	01-17-1866
(0280) Devine	John	Private	3rd U.S. Cavalry	07-09-1867
(0281) Devoe	James	Sergeant	31st U.S. Infantry	08-23-1868
(0282) DeVreede	James	Private	7th U.S. Cavalry	12-29-1890
(0283) Dihring	Maximilian	Private	18th U.S. Infantry	12-21-1866
(0284) Dohman	Anton	Private	7th U.S. Cavalry	06-25-1876
(0285) Dolan	John	First Sergeant	5th U.S. Cavalry	09-29-1879
(0286) Dolan	Perry	Private	18th U.S. Infantry	12-21-1866
(0287) Donahue	William	Private	1st U.S. Cavalry	12-22-1872[9]
(0288) Donjon	John	Private	11th Ohio Cavalry	04-21-1865
(0289) Donnelly	Peter	Private	27th U.S. Infantry	11-06-1867[10]
(0290) Donnelly	Timothy	Private	7th U.S. Cavalry	06-25-1876
(0291) Doral	John	Private	4th U.S. Cavalry	09-29-1872
(0292) Doran	U.B.	Private	2nd U.S. Cavalry	12-21-1866
(0293) Dorman	John	Private	6th U.S. Cavalry	08-31-1881
(0294) Dorn	Richard	Private	7th U.S. Cavalry	06-25-1876
(0295) Dorsey	Frank	Private	9th U.S. Cavalry	05-29-1879
(0296) Dose	Henry	Trumpeter	7th U.S. Cavalry	06-25-1876
(0297) Dougan	Wesley	Private	5th U.S. Artillery	07-11-1894
(0298) Dougherty	William	Sergeant	23rd U.S. Infantry	04-28-1876
(0299) Douglas	George	Private	2nd U.S. Cavalry	02-07-1880
(0300) Douglas	James	Corporal	7th U.S. Cavalry	06-26-1867
(0301) Doune	John	Private	1st U.S. Cavalry	06-17-1877
(0302) Dowdy	Peter	Private	3rd U.S. Cavalry	03-17-1876
(0303) Downey	Thomas	Private	7th U.S. Cavalry	11-27-1868
(0304) Downing	Thomas	Private	7th U.S. Cavalry	06-25-1876
(0305) Doyle	Patrick	Private	21st U.S. Infantry	07-11-1877
(0306) Doyle	Thomas	Private	27th U.S. Infantry	08-02-1867
(0307) Drake	McKindra	Private	7th U.S. Infantry	08-09-1877
(0308) Drinan	James	Private	7th U.S. Cavalry	06-25-1876
(0309) Driscoll	Edward	Private	7th U.S. Cavalry	06-25-1876
(0310) Drouch	Joseph	Private	37th U.S. Infantry	09-29-1867
(0311) Drummond	George	Saddler	8th U.S. Cavalry	04-18-1867
(0312) Ducket	Orlando	Private	11th Ohio Cavalry	06-08-1865
(0313) Duggan	George	Private	8th U.S. Cavalry	12-17-1867[11]
(0314) Duggan	John	Private	7th U.S. Cavalry	06-25-1876
(0315) Duke	Thomas	Private	9th U.S. Cavalry	04-30-1881
(0316) Dummel	William	Sergeant	7th U.S. Cavalry	06-21-1867
(0317) Durleson	Otto	Sergeant	7th U.S. Cavalry	09-30-1877
(0318) Dute	William	Corporal	18th U.S. Infantry	12-21-1866
(0319) Dye	William	Private	7th U.S. Cavalry	06-25-1876
(0320) Dyer	Arthur	Sergeant	7th U.S. Cavalry	12-29-1890
(0321) Eagan	Harry	Private	2nd U.S. Cavalry	08-20-1879
(0322) Eagan	Thomas	Corporal	7th U.S. Cavalry	06-25-1876

---

[6] Commissary Sergeant.
[7] WIA 12-10-1869.
[8] WIA 01-22-1879.
[9] WIA 12-21-1872.
[10] WIA 11-04-1867.
[11] WIA 11-08-1867.

(0323) Easter	Jesse	Private	2nd Missouri Light Artillery	09-01-1865
(0324) Eberhard	Nathan	Private	8th U.S. Cavalry	06-16-1869
(0325) Edgeworth	Robert	First Sergeant	7th U.S. Infantry	08-09-1877
(0326) Edstrome	Charles	Corporal	3rd U.S. Cavalry	12-21-1891
(0327) Edwards	Albert	Private	18th U.S. Infantry	12-02-1867
(0328) Edwards	George	Corporal	1st California Veteran Infantry	11-22-1865
(0329) Edwards	Valentine	Private	1st U.S. Cavalry	06-17-1877
(0330) Eiseman	George	Private	7th U.S. Cavalry	06-25-1876
(0331) Eisenhut	Isaac	Corporal	7th U.S. Infantry	08-09-1877
(0332) Emery	Russell	Private	4th U.S. Infantry	04-06-1869
(0333) Engle	Gustave	Private	7th U.S. Cavalry	06-25-1876
(0334) Ensner	August	Recruit	6th U.S. Cavalry	10-02-1881
(0335) Erustberger	Charles	Private	27th U.S. Infantry	04-26-1867
(0336) Everett	William	Private	3rd U.S. Cavalry	01-11-1879
(0337) Farrand	James	Private	7th U.S. Cavalry	06-25-1876
(0338) Farrell	Richard	Private	7th U.S. Cavalry	06-25-1876
(0339) Ferguson	John	Private	37th U.S. Infantry	05-31-1867
(0340) Finckle	George	Sergeant	7th U.S. Cavalry	06-25-1876
(0341) Finley	Jeremiah	Sergeant	7th U.S. Cavalry	06-25-1876
(0342) Firestone	Michael	Private	5th U.S. Cavalry	09-29-1879
(0343) Fitzgerald	Andrew	Private	2nd U.S. Cavalry	12-21-1866
(0344) Fitzpatrick	Thomas	Private	18th U.S. Infantry	09-20-1866
(0345) Fitzpatrick	Thomas	Farrier	7th U.S. Cavalry	11-27-1868
(0346) Flood	Bernard	Private	14th U.S. Infantry	03-21-1868
(0347) Floyed	William	Private	2nd U.S. Cavalry	07-02-1867
(0348) Flynn	Eugene	Private	3rd U.S. Cavalry	06-17-1876
(0349) Foley	John	Corporal	7th U.S. Cavalry	06-25-1876
(0350) Fonda	Charles	Private	23rd U.S. Infantry	04-30-1868[12]
(0351) Foran	Thomas	Private	6th U.S. Cavalry	08-30-1881
(0352) Forbes	John	Private	7th U.S. Cavalry	06-25-1876
(0353) Ford	John	Sergeant	5th U.S. Cavalry	05-13-1869
(0354) Foreman	Nathan	Private	2nd U.S. Cavalry	12-21-1866
(0355) Forrest	Harry	Corporal	7th U.S. Cavalry	12-29-1890
(0356) Foster	Larkin	Bugler	10th U.S. Cavalry	09-19-1871
(0357) Franceshetti	Dominick	Private	7th U.S. Cavalry	12-30-1890
(0358) Franklin	Louis	Musician	14th U.S. Infantry	12-11-1866
(0359) French	Henry	Corporal	7th U.S. Cavalry	06-25-1876
(0360) Frey	Henry	Private	7th U.S. Cavalry	12-29-1890
(0361) Gale	Henry	C. Sergeant[13]	11th Kansas Cavalry	07-05-1865[14]
(0362) Gallagher	Daniel	Private	1st U.S. Cavalry	12-12-1872[15]
(0363) Gallagher	Michael	Musician	7th U.S. Infantry	08-09-1877
(0364) Gallagher	Patrick	Corporal	18th U.S. Infantry	12-21-1866
(0365) Galvan	James	Private	7th U.S. Cavalry	06-25-1876
(0366) Galvin	John	Saddler	1st U.S. Cavalry	06-17-1877
(0367) Garber	George	Sergeant	1st Oregon Cavalry	04-18-1865[16]
(0368) Gardner	William	Private	7th U.S. Cavalry	06-25-1876
(0369) Garrison	Abner	Private	2nd Missouri Light Artillery	09-01-1865
(0370) Gates	William	Private	21st U.S. Infantry	10-05-1869
(0371) Gaudmeyer	Frederick	Private	1st U.S. Cavalry	07-11-1877
(0372) Gebhart	James	Private	7th U.S. Cavalry	06-25-1876
(0373) Geogehgan	Thomas	Private	5th U.S. Infantry	09-30-1877
(0374) George	John	Private	7th U.S. Cavalry	11-27-1868
(0375) George	William	Private	7th U.S. Cavalry	06-25-1876
(0376) Gibson	George	Private	8th U.S. Cavalry	12-19-1885
(0377) Gilbert	William	Corporal	7th U.S. Cavalry	06-25-1876
(0378) Gilchrist	Allande	Private	18th U.S. Infantry	09-14-1866
(0379) Gillette	David	Private	7th U.S. Cavalry	06-25-1876
(0380) Gitter	John	Private	2nd U.S. Cavalry	12-21-1866
(0381) Given	John	Corporal	6th U.S. Cavalry	07-12-1870
(0382) Glaemon	Carl	Private	21st U.S. Infantry	01-17-1873
(0383) Glass	Samuel	Farrier	2nd U.S. Cavalry	08-24-1877[17]
(0384) Glockowsky	Frank	Private	2nd U.S. Cavalry	05-07-1877
(0385) Godfrey	Isaac	Private	1st Nevada Cavalry	05-20-1865
(0386) Golden	Patrick	Private	7th U.S. Cavalry	06-25-1876
(0387) Golding	Thomas	Saddler	9th U.S. Cavalry	08-19-1881
(0388) Goldrick	William	Private	6th U.S. Cavalry	04-28-1882
(0389) Good	William	Private	3rd U.S. Cavalry	01-10-1879
(0390) Goodall	George	Private	18th U.S. Infantry	12-21-1866
(0391) Gordon	Francis	Private	18th U.S. Infantry	12-21-1866
(0392) Gordon	Henry	Private	7th U.S. Cavalry	06-25-1876
(0393) Graddon	Silas	Private	9th U.S. Cavalry	09-04-1879
(0394) Graff	Joseph	Private	1st U.S. Cavalry	08-01-1870
(0395) Graham	Charles	Private	7th U.S. Cavalry	06-25-1876
(0396) Gray	William	Private	11th Kansas Cavalry	07-26-1865
(0397) Green	Daniel	Private	2nd U.S. Cavalry	12-21-1866
(0398) Green	Martin	Private	11th Kansas Cavalry	07-26-1865
(0399) Green	Martin	Private	3rd U.S. Cavalry	05-05-1871
(0400) Gregg	Seander	Private	4th U.S. Cavalry	10-11-1871
(0401) Griffen	Patrick	Private	7th U.S. Cavalry	06-25-1876
(0402) Griffin	Asa	Private	18th U.S. Infantry	12-21-1866
(0403) Griffin	Daniel	Sergeant	6th U.S. Cavalry	05-08-1880[18]
(0404) Griffin	Jeremiah	Private	10th U.S. Cavalry	10-28-1880

[12] WIA 04-29-1868.
[13] Commissary Sergeant.
[14] WIA 07-04-1865.
[15] WIA 11-29-1872.
[16] WIA 04-17-1865.
[17] WIA 08-20-1877
[18] WIA 05-07-1880.

(0405) Groesbeck	John	Sergeant	7th U.S. Cavalry	06-25-1876
(0406) Groger	Richard	Private	7th Iowa Cavalry	06-14-1865
(0407) Groman	Michael	Private	2nd U.S. Cavalry	07-02-1867
(0408) Griffin	Daniel	Sergeant	6th U.S. Cavalry	05-08-1880[19]
(0409) Griffin	Jeremiah	Private	10th U.S. Cavalry	10-28-1880
(0410) Groesbeck	John	Sergeant	7th U.S. Cavalry	06-25-1876
(0411) Gross	Daniel	Sergeant	9th U.S. Cavalry	01-12-1880
(0412) Gross	George	Private	7th U.S. Cavalry	06-25-1876
(0413) Gruntzinger	Peter	Corporal	1st U.S. Cavalry	06-23-1878
(0414) Gumford	Charles	Private	2nd U.S. Cavalry	12-21-1866
(0415) Gunn	Patrick	Sergeant	1st U.S. Cavalry	06-17-1877
(0416) Haag	Herman	Private	4th U.S. Cavalry	05-22-1885
(0417) Hackett	Charles	Private	18th U.S. Infantry	10-01-1866[20]
(0418) Haddo	John	Corporal	5th U.S. Infantry	09-30-1877
(0419) Hagan	Michael	Sergeant	7th U.S. Infantry	08-09-1877
(0420) Hagemann	Otto	Corporal	7th U.S. Cavalry	06-25-1876
(0421) Haggerty	Henry	Private	27th U.S. Infantry	08-02-1867
(0422) Haines	George	Private	27th U.S. Infantry	08-02-1867
(0423) Haines	Peter	Private	9th U.S. Cavalry	09-18-1879
(0424) Haley	Michael	Private	2nd U.S. Cavalry	07-02-1867
(0425) Hamilton	Henry	Private	7th U.S. Cavalry	06-25-1876
(0426) Hamilton	Rice	Private	11th Ohio Cavalry	07-26-1865
(0427) Hammon	George	Private	7th U.S. Cavalry	06-25-1876
(0428) Hardick	Charles	Private	7th U.S. Cavalry	09-30-1877
(0429) Hardy	Wesley	Private	10th U.S. Cavalry	08-06-1880
(0430) Harrington	Weston	Private	7th U.S. Cavalry	06-25-1876
(0431) Harris	Charles	Private	21st U.S. Infantry	07-13-1871
(0432) Harris	James	Private	1st U.S. Cavalry	11-29-1872
(0433) Harrison	Stephen	Private	7th U.S. Infantry	07-07-1875
(0434) Harrison	William	Corporal	7th U.S. Cavalry	06-25-1876
(0435) Harten	Michael	Private	18th U.S. Infantry	12-21-1866
(0436) Hathersall	James	Private	7th U.S. Cavalry	06-25-1876
(0437) Hauggi	Louis	Private	7th U.S. Cavalry	06-25-1876
(0438) Haynes	Charles	Corporal	2nd U.S. Cavalry	07-02-1867
(0439) Haywood	Charles	Private	9th U.S. Cavalry	12-30-1890
(0440) Heath	William	Farrier	7th U.S. Cavalry	06-25-1876
(0441) Hedgecock	Thomas	Private	37th U.S. Infantry	11-17-1867
(0442) Hedges	William	Sergeant	7th U.S. Cavalry	12-29-1890
(0443) Heil	George	Private	11th Kansas Cavalry	07-26-1865
(0444) Heim	John	Private	7th U.S. Cavalry	06-25-1876
(0445) Helmer	Julius	Trumpeter	7th U.S. Cavalry	06-25-1876
(0446) Henchey	B.	Private	4th U.S. Cavalry	05-24-1872
(0447) Henderson	Henry	Private	31st U.S. Infantry	08-20-1868
(0448) Henderson	John	Private	7th U.S. Cavalry	06-25-1876
(0449) Henderson	Sykes	Private	7th U.S. Cavalry	06-25-1876
(0450) Henry	John	Private	7th California Infantry	07-22-1865
(0451) Herford	August	Private	2nd California Cavalry	07-26-1865
(0452) Herman	Andrew	Sergeant	5th U.S. Infantry	12-11-1865
(0453) Herrigan	Thomas	Corporal	2nd U.S. Cavalry	12-21-1866
(0454) Hetesimer	Adam	Private	7th U.S. Cavalry	06-25-1876
(0455) Hibbard	Ruffus	Private	8th U.S. Cavalry	11-06-1874
(0456) Hickman	Samuel	Private	4th U.S. Cavalry	10-10-1885
(0457) Hiffin	Michael	Private	31st U.S. Infantry	08-23-1868
(0458) Hinshaw	Silas	Private	11th Kansas Cavalry	06-16-1865
(0459) Hoffman	James	Private	4th U.S. Volunteer Infantry	07-28-1865
(0460) Hoffman	John	Private	6th U.S. Cavalry	11-20-1868[21]
(0461) Hogged	Christopher	Wagoner	5th U.S. Infantry	09-23-1867
(0462) Hohmeyer	Frederick	First Sergeant	7th U.S. Cavalry	06-25-1876
(0463) Hoke	Lafayette	Private	9th U.S. Cavalry	09-04-1879
(0464) Holcomb	Edward	Private	7th U.S. Cavalry	06-25-1876
(0465) Hollas	George	Private	1st U.S. Cavalry	01-17-1873
(0466) Hollis	Joseph	Private	10th U.S. Cavalry	05-03-1886
(0467) Holt	Larkin	Sergeant	2nd Missouri Light Artillery	09-01-1865
(0468) Holt	John	Private	7th U.S. Infantry	09-14-1869
(0469) Hoppe	August	Private	11th Kansas Cavalry	07-26-1865
(0470) Horn	Marion	Private	7th U.S. Cavalry	06-25-1876
(0471) Horton	John	Private	11th Kansas Cavalry	07-26-1865
(0472) Housen	Edward	Private	7th U.S. Cavalry	06-25-1876
(0473) Houser	Ferdinand	Private	2nd U.S. Cavalry	12-21-1866
(0474) Howard	Henry	Sergeant	7th U.S. Cavalry	01-30-1891[22]
(0475) Howell	George	Saddler	7th U.S. Cavalry	06-25-1876
(0476) Howell	James	Private	8th U.S. Cavalry	08-03-1869[23]
(0477) Huber	William	Private	7th U.S. Cavalry	06-25-1876
(0478) Hufstudler	James	Private	4th U.S. Volunteer Infantry	07-28-1865
(0479) Hughes	Francis	Private	7th U.S. Cavalry	06-25-1876
(0480) Hughes	Robert	Sergeant	7th U.S. Cavalry	06-25-1876
(0481) Hughes	William	Private	1st U.S. Volunteer Infantry	04-12-1865
(0482) Hulse	Peter	Private	3rd U.S. Cavalry	01-24-1879[24]
(0483) Humphries	William	Private	2nd U.S. Cavalry	07-02-1867
(0484) Hunter	Louis	Private	1st California Veteran Infantry	01-17-1866
(0485) Hurlbert	William	Private	1st U.S. Cavalry	06-17-1877
(0486) Hutchinson	William	Private	21st U.S. Infantry	07-11-1877

[19] WIA 05-07-1880.
[20] WIA 09-21-1866.
[21] WIA 11-19-1868.
[22] WIA 12-29-1890.
[23] WIA 07-06-1869.
[24] WIA 01-09-1879.

(0487) Hutton	Frank	Wagoner	8th U.S. Cavalry	12-19-1885
(0488) Irwin	William	Private	21st U.S. Infantry	04-17-1872
(0489) Irving	John	Private	2nd U.S. Cavalry	10-01-1877[25]
(0490) James		Private	9th U.S. Cavalry	01-12-1880
(0491) James	Isaac	Farrier	9th U.S. Cavalry	04-06-1880
(0492) James	William	Sergeant	7th U.S. Cavalry	06-25-1876
(0493) Jameson	Horace	Corporal	Brackett's Battalion[26]	08-27-1865
(0494) Johnson	George	Private	7th U.S. Cavalry	12-29-1890
(0495) Johnson	John	Private	9th U.S. Cavalry	09-30-1879
(0496) Johnson	Jonathan	Private	4th U.S. Infantry	12-02-1869[27]
(0497) Johnson	Joseph	Sergeant	2nd U.S. Cavalry	04-01-1880
(0498) Johnson	Nathan	Private	9th U.S. Cavalry	12-05-1867
(0499) Johnson	Peter	Private	18th U.S. Infantry	09-16-1866
(0500) Johnston	William	Private	7th U.S. Cavalry	10-02-1868
(0501) Jones	E.T.	Private	9th U.S. Cavalry	10-01-1867
(0502) Jones	Frank	Private	2nd U.S. Cavalry	12-21-1866
(0503) Jones	John	Private	1st California Cavalry	07-14-1865
(0504) Jones	John	Corporal	9th U.S. Infantry	07-29-1866
(0505) Jones	John	Trumpeter	1st U.S. Cavalry	06-17-1877
(0506) Jones	Julien	Private	7th U.S. Cavalry	06-25-1876
(0507) Jones	William	Private	9th U.S. Cavalry	01-25-1881
(0508) Jordan	Thomas	Private	2nd U.S. Cavalry	05-23-1867
(0509) Karston	Frank	Corporal	18th U.S. Infantry	12-21-1866
(0510) Kavanagh	Laurence	Private	1st U.S. Cavalry	06-17-1877
(0511) Kavanagh	Thomas	Private	7th U.S. Cavalry	06-25-1876
(0512) Kean	James	Private	18th U.S. Infantry	12-21-1866
(0513) Keil	Herrman	Private	18th U.S. Infantry	12-21-1866
(0514) Keller	Alexander	Private	4th U.S. Cavalry	11-25-1876
(0515) Kelley	Bernard	Private	3rd U.S. Cavalry	01-12-1879[28]
(0516) Kellner	August	Private	7th U.S. Cavalry	12-29-1890
(0517) Kelly	James	Corporal	2nd U.S. Cavalry	12-21-1866
(0518) Kelly	James	Private	7th U.S. Cavalry	12-29-1890
(0519) Kelly	John	Private	4th U.S. Cavalry	09-29-1872
(0520) Kelly	John	Private	7th U.S. Cavalry	06-25-1876
(0521) Kelly	Lewis	Private	7th U.S. Cavalry	09-30-1877
(0522) Kelly	Martin	Private	18th U.S. Infantry	12-21-1866
(0523) Kelly	Patrick	Private	7th U.S. Cavalry	06-25-1876
(0524) Kelly	William	Sergeant	7th California Infantry	07-22-1865
(0525) Kenna	George	Private	2nd U.S. Cavalry	11-06-1869
(0526) Kennedy	J.W.	Private	5th U.S. Cavalry	09-09-1876
(0527) Kenney	Michael	First Sergeant	7th U.S. Cavalry	06-25-1876
(0528) Kennedy	Walter	Sergeant-Major	7th U.S. Cavalry	11-27-1868
(0529) Kerr	William	Private	3rd U.S. Cavalry	07-09-1867
(0530) Killiher	Patrick	Private	2nd U.S. Cavalry	05-23-1867
(0531) King	George	Corporal	7th U.S. Cavalry	07-02-1876[29]
(0532) King	John	Blacksmith	7th U.S. Cavalry	06-25-1876
(0533) King	Robert	Private	32nd U.S. Infantry	05-26-1868
(0534) Kinney	Michael	Private	18th U.S. Infantry	12-21-1866
(0535) Kittridge	Horace	Private	27th U.S. Infantry	08-02-1867
(0536) Klein	Gustav	Private	7th U.S. Cavalry	06-25-1876
(0537) Kleis	John	Private	7th U.S. Infantry	08-09-1877
(0538) Klotzbucher	Henry	Private	7th U.S. Cavalry	06-25-1876
(0539) Knaupp	Frank	Private	7th U.S. Cavalry	09-30-1877
(0540) Knauth	Herman	Private	7th U.S. Cavalry	06-25-1876
(0541) Knecht	Andy	Private	7th U.S. Cavalry	06-25-1876
(0542) Knowles	George	Private	32nd U.S. Infantry	05-26-1868
(0543) Kohler	Joseph	Private	5th U.S. Infantry	10-01-1877[30]
(0544) Korn	Gustav	Blacksmith	7th U.S. Cavalry	12-29-1890
(0545) Kramer	William	Trumpeter	7th U.S. Cavalry	06-25-1876
(0546) Kranberg	Herman	Private	7th U.S. Cavalry	12-29-1890
(0547) Kreiger	Charles	Private	7th U.S. Cavalry	09-15-1868[31]
(0548) Kuhn	Joseph	Private	2nd Colorado Cavalry	05-20-1865
(0549) Kurtz	William	Private	4th U.S. Cavalry	04-25-1882[32]
(0550) Lampman	Charles	Sergeant	1st U.S. Cavalry	07-03-1877
(0551) Lang	Augustus	First Sergeant	18th U.S. Infantry	12-21-1866
(0552) Laroren	George	Private	7th U.S. Infantry	07-07-1875
(0553) Lavelle	Charles	Private	1st U.S. Cavalry	01-17-1873
(0554) Lawler	James	Private	7th U.S. Cavalry	09-18-1877[33]
(0555) Lawler	Michael	Private	2nd U.S. Cavalry	07-02-1867
(0556) Lee	John	Private	3rd U.S. Cavalry	07-09-1867
(0557) Lee	Remin	Corporal	1st U.S. Cavalry	06-17-1877
(0558) Lehman	Henry	Private	7th U.S. Cavalry	06-25-1876
(0559) Lehmann	Frederick	Private	7th U.S. Cavalry	06-25-1876
(0560) Lell	George	Corporal	7th U.S. Cavalry	06-25-1876
(0561) Lemon	Joseph	Sergeant	1st U.S. Cavalry	06-16-1868
(0562) Lennon	Robert	Corporal	18th U.S. Infantry	12-21-1866
(0563) Lennon	Thomas	Private	37th U.S. Infantry	06-05-1867
(0564) Lerock	William	Private	7th U.S. Cavalry	06-25-1876
(0565) Lewis	Edward	Private	37th U.S. Infantry	09-29-1867
(0566) Lewis	James	Private	1st U.S. Cavalry	06-17-1877
(0567) Lewis	John	Private	7th U.S. Cavalry	06-25-1876
(0568) Liddiard	Herod	Private	7th U.S. Cavalry	06-25-1876

[25] WIA 09-30-1877.
[26] Bracket's Battalion Minnesota Cavalry.
[27] WIA 12-01-1869.
[28] WIA 01-11-1879.
[29] WIA 06-25-1876.
[30] WIA 09-30-1877.
[31] WIA 09-14-1868.
[32] WIA 04-23-1882.
[33] WIA 09-13-1877.

(0569) Liebsnow	Gustav	Private	4th U.S. Cavalry	05-15-1886
(0570) Liehman	Max	Private	31st U.S. Infantry	08-20-1868
(0571) Liemann	Werner	Private	6th U.S. Cavalry	06-25-1876
(0572) Lindercrantz	Anton	Private	6th U.S. Cavalry	10-02-1881
(0573) Lineback	Ferdinand	Private	7th U.S. Cavalry	11-27-1868
(0574) Liston	William	Private	1st U.S. Cavalry	06-17-1877
(0575) Livelsberger	George	Private	18th U.S. Infantry	07-19-1866[34]
(0576) Livingstone	Edward	Private	6th U.S. Cavalry	08-30-1881
(0577) Lloyd	Edward	Private	7th U.S. Cavalry	06-25-1876
(0578) Lobering	Louis	Private	7th U.S. Cavalry	06-25-1876
(0579) Long	Robert	Private	21st U.S. Infantry	01-17-1873
(0580) Long	Silas	Private	7th California Infantry	07-21-1865
(0581) Long	William	Private	11th Kansas Cavalry	07-26-1865
(0582) Lord	William	Corporal	1st U.S. Cavalry	07-18-1866
(0583) Lowe	Edward	Private	3rd U.S. Infantry	10-04-1898
(0584) Logan	James	Private	7th U.S. Cavalry	12-29-1890
(0585) Lorentz	George	Private	7th U.S. Cavalry	06-25-1876
(0586) Lossee	William	Private	7th U.S. Cavalry	06-25-1876
(0587) Louys	Peter	Private	2nd U.S. Cavalry	05-07-1877
(0588) Lubberden	George	Private	5th U.S. Artillery	07-11-1894
(0589) Lynch	Michael	Private	5th U.S. Cavalry	09-29-1879
(0590) Lynch	Patrick	Corporal	4th U.S. Cavalry	09-13-1878
(0591) Lyons	James	Private	1st U.S. Cavalry	09-26-1867
(0592) Madden	Thomas	Private	18th U.S. Infantry	12-21-1866
(0593) Madsen	Christian	Private	7th U.S. Cavalry	06-25-1876
(0594) Maginnis	James	Private	7th U.S. Infantry	08-09-1877
(0595) Mahan	Patrick	Private	27th U.S. Infantry	02-27-1867
(0596) Maher	John	Private	18th U.S. Infantry	12-21-1866
(0597) Maher	Patrick	Private	1st U.S. Cavalry	01-22-1873[35]
(0598) Mahoning	Bartholomew	Private	7th U.S. Cavalry	06-25-1876
(0599) Manning	James	Blacksmith	7th U.S. Cavalry	06-25-1876
(0600) Maroney	John	Private	4th U.S. Cavalry	08-22-1867
(0601) Marquardt	Charles	Corporal	4th U.S. Artillery	07-12-1877
(0602) Marriott	William	Private	1st U.S. Cavalry	06-23-1878
(0603) Marshall	Daniel	Sergeant	3rd U.S. Cavalry	06-17-1876
(0604) Marshall	Frank	Trumpeter	1st U.S. Cavalry	06-17-1877
(0605) Martin	Byron	Private	7th U.S. Infantry	09-23-1877
(0606) Martin	James	Corporal	7th U.S. Cavalry	06-25-1876
(0607) Martin	James	Private	1st U.S. Cavalry	06-17-1877
(0608) Martin	Lewis	Private	31st U.S. Infantry	08-23-1868
(0609) Martin	Michael	First Sergeant	7th U.S. Cavalry	09-30-1877
(0610) Martin	William	Sergeant	7th U.S. Infantry	08-09-1877
(0611) Martindale	Charles	Private	2nd U.S. Cavalry	05-07-1877
(0612) Mask	George	Private	7th U.S. Cavalry	06-25-1876
(0613) Mason	Henry	Corporal	7th U.S. Cavalry	06-25-1876
(0614) Masterson	J.D.	Private	18th Kansas Volunteer Cavalry	08-21-1867
(0615) Mautz	Gottileb	Private	7th U.S. Infantry	08-09-1877
(0616) Maxwell	Thomas	Private	7th U.S. Cavalry	06-25-1876
(0617) McAllister	John	Private	2nd U.S. Cavalry	11-06-1869
(0618) McArty	Edmund	Private	3rd U.S. Infantry	06-15-1867
(0619) McCafferey	David	Corporal	7th U.S. Infantry	08-09-1877
(0620) McCann	Bernard	Private	22nd U.S. Infantry	01-12-1877[36]
(0621) McCannon	Michael	Private	3rd U.S. Cavalry	03-17-1876
(0622) McCarthy	Charles	Private	7th U.S. Cavalry	12-21-1866
(0623) McCasey	Benjamin	Private	7th U.S. Cavalry	11-30-1868[37]
(0624) McClarren	James	Sergeant	7th U.S. Infantry	08-14-1872
(0625) McClernan	John	Private	7th U.S. Cavalry	11-27-1868
(0626) McClintock	William	Private	7th U.S. Cavalry	12-29-1890
(0627) McClure	Samuel	Sergeant	27th U.S. Infantry	02-27-1867
(0628) McCue	John	Private	7th U.S. Cavalry	12-29-1890
(0629) McDermott	George	First Sergeant	7th U.S. Cavalry	09-30-1877
(0630) McDonald	George	Private	11th Kansas Cavalry	07-26-1865
(0631) McDonald	James	Private	7th U.S. Cavalry	06-25-1876
(0632) McDougal	John	Sergeant	4th U.S. Cavalry	11-14-1867
(0633) McElroy	Thomas	Trumpeter	7th U.S. Cavalry	06-25-1876
(0634) McFarland	Alexander	Private	5th U.S. Cavalry	11-28-1876[38]
(0635) McFee	William	Private	4th U.S. Cavalry	09-07-1880
(0636) McGinnis	John	Private	7th U.S. Cavalry	06-25-1876
(0637) McGregor	John	Private	4th U.S. Cavalry	03-12-1867
(0638) McGucker	John	Trumpeter	7th U.S. Cavalry	06-25-1876
(0639) McGue	Peter	Private	7th U.S. Cavalry	06-25-1876
(0640) McGuire	James	Private	2nd U.S. Cavalry	12-21-1866
(0641) McGully	George	Private	12th Missouri Cavalry	09-05-1865
(0642) McIlhargey	Archibald	Private	7th U.S. Cavalry	06-25-1876
(0643) McIntyre	Samuel	Private	7th U.S. Cavalry	09-30-1877
(0644) McKay	Walter	Private	2nd U.S. Cavalry	01-23-1870
(0645) McKee	Samuel	Private	5th U.S. Cavalry	09-29-1879
(0646) McKeever	Joseph	Private	27th U.S. Infantry	11-08-1867[39]
(0647) McKolly	John	Private	2nd U.S. Cavalry	12-21-1866
(0648) McLernon	Joseph	Private	6th U.S. Cavalry	07-17-1882
(0649) McMahon	Edward	Private	7th Iowa Cavalry	06-14-1865

---

[34] WIA 07-17-1866.
[35] WIA 01-17-1873.
[36] WIA 01-08-1877.
[37] WIA 11-27-1868.
[38] WIA 11-25-1876.
[39] WIA 11-04-1867.

(0650) McMillan	Harry	Private	8th U.S. Cavalry	12-19-1885
(0651) McNally	David	Private	21st U.S. Infantry	07-11-1877
(0652) Meador	Thomas	Private	7th U.S. Cavalry	06-25-1876
(0653) Meara	Michael	Sergeant	1st U.S. Cavalry	09-26-1867
(0654) Meighan	Henry	Private	1st California Veteran Infantry	11-22-1865
(0655) Meier	Frederick	Private	7th U.S. Cavalry	06-25-1876
(0656) Menges	Joseph	Private	5th U.S. Cavalry	11-25-1876
(0657) Mercer	Harry	Corporal	7th U.S. Cavalry	11-27-1868
(0658) Merrill	Benson	Private	1st U.S. Cavalry	06-16-1868
(0659) Mers	William	Private	3rd U.S. Volunteer Infantry	05-18-1865
(0660) Metzger	Adolph	Bugler	2nd U.S. Cavalry	12-21-1866
(0661) Meyer	Albert	Corporal	7th U.S. Cavalry	06-25-1876
(0662) Meyer	August	Private	7th U.S. Cavalry	06-25-1876
(0663) Meyer	Frederick	Private	1st U.S. Cavalry	07-03-1877
(0664) Meyer	John	Private	5th U.S. Cavalry	05-13-1869
(0665) Meyer	William	Private	7th U.S. Cavalry	06-25-1876
(0666) Mezo	William	Private	7th U.S. Cavalry	12-29-1890
(0667) Mielke	Max	Sergeant	7th U.S. Cavalry	09-30-1877
(0668) Miller	Amos	Wagoner	5th U.S. Cavalry	09-29-1879
(0669) Miller	C.C.	Sergeant	8th U.S. Cavalry	09-29-1867
(0670) Miller	Curtin	Sergeant	8th U.S. Cavalry	12-11-1868
(0671) Miller	Jacob	Private	3rd U.S. Infantry	06-11-1867
(0672) Miller	John	Private	7th U.S. Cavalry	06-25-1876
(0673) Miller	William	Corporal	11th Kansas Cavalry	07-26-1865
(0674) Miller	William	Private	6th U.S. Cavalry	08-30-1881
(0675) Milner	Cyrus	Private	5th U.S. Cavalry	09-14-1876
(0676) Mills	George	Private	10th U.S. Cavalry	10-28-1880
(0677) Milton	Francis	Private	7th U.S. Cavalry	06-25-1876
(0678) Mitchell	Allen	Private	3rd U.S. Cavalry	06-17-1876
(0679) Mitchell	John	Private	7th U.S. Cavalry	06-25-1876
(0680) Monroe	James	Private	1st Nevada Cavalry	05-20-1865
(0681) Monroe	Joseph	Private	7th U.S. Cavalry	06-25-1876
(0682) Montaudon	Frederick	Private	4th U.S. Artillery	07-11-1877
(0683) Moodie	William	Private	7th U.S. Cavalry	06-25-1876
(0684) Moody	Franklin	Private	1st U.S. Cavalry	07-03-1877
(0685) Mooney	Thomas	Private	5th U.S. Cavalry	09-29-1879
(0686) Moonie	George	Trumpeter	7th U.S. Cavalry	06-25-1876
(0687) Moore	Andrew	Private	7th U.S. Cavalry	06-25-1876
(0688) Moore	Lawrence	Private	21st U.S. Infantry	08-18-1870
(0689) Morby	Harry	Sergeant	4th U.S. Cavalry	04-23-1882
(0690) Morris	George	Corporal	7th U.S. Cavalry	06-25-1876
(0691) Morgan	William	Sergeant	18th U.S. Infantry	12-21-1866
(0692) Morris	James	Private	12th Missouri Cavalry	09-05-1865
(0693) Morrisey	James	Private	1st U.S. Cavalry	06-17-1877
(0694) Mosforth	John	Private	1st U.S. Cavalry	06-17-1877
(0695) Mularky	James	Sergeant	14th U.S. Infantry	05-02-1872
(0696) Mulligan	William	Private	7th U.S. Cavalry	11-27-1868
(0697) Munich	Peter	Sergeant	4th U.S. Cavalry	06-08-1885
(0698) Munroe	James	Private	21st U.S. Infantry	01-17-1873
(0699) Murphy	Hugh	First Sergeant	18th U.S. Infantry	12-21-1866
(0700) Murphy	James	Private	1st U.S. Cavalry	06-16-1868
(0701) Murphy	John	Private	1st U.S. Cavalry	06-16-1868
(0702) Murphy	John	Private	1st U.S. Cavalry	06-17-1877
(0703) Murphy	Joseph	Private	7th U.S. Cavalry	12-29-1890
(0704) Murphy	William	Private	9th U.S. Cavalry	09-04-1879
(0705) Myers	Carson	Private	7th U.S. Cavalry	11-27-1868
(0706) Myers	John	Private	7th U.S. Cavalry	11-27-1868
(0707) Nation	William	Private	5th U.S. Cavalry	09-30-1872
(0708) Navin	Thomas	Private	27th U.S. Infantry	08-01-1867
(0709) Nehring	Sebastian	Private	11th Kansas Cavalry	07-26-1865
(0710) Nelson	Anthony	Private	1st Battalion Dakota Cavalry	08-15-1865
(0711) Nelson	George	Private	3rd U.S. Cavalry	01-22-1879
(0712) Nettles	Robert	Sergeant	7th U.S. Cavalry	12-29-1890
(0713) Newell	Charles	Corporal	7th U.S. Cavalry	12-29-1890
(0714) Newkirken	Antoine	Sergeant	3rd U.S. Cavalry	06-17-1876
(0715) Niehouse	Henry	Saddler	4th U.S. Cavalry	06-08-1885
(0716) Nielson	Olaf	Private	1st U.S. Cavalry	06-17-1877
(0717) Nix	Robert	Private	14th U.S. Infantry	10-21-1868
(0718) Noshing	Jacob	Private	7th U.S. Cavalry	06-25-1876
(0719) Nugens	George	Private	2nd U.S. Cavalry	12-21-1866
(0720) Nursey	Frederick	Sergeant	7th U.S. Cavalry	06-25-1876
(0721) Oberly	Christian	Private	18th U.S. Infantry	10-03-1866
(0722) O'Brien	F. John	Private	7th U.S. Infantry	08-09-1877
(0723) O'Bryan	John	Private	7th U.S. Cavalry	06-25-1876
(0724) O'Connell	David	Private	2nd California Cavalry	11-17-1865
(0725) O'Connell	David	Private	7th U.S. Cavalry	06-25-1876
(0726) O'Conner	Patrick	Private	7th U.S. Cavalry	06-25-1876
(0727) O'Connor	Daniel	Private	6th U.S. Cavalry	09-22-1868
(0728) O'Connor	Dominick	Corporal	7th U.S. Infantry	08-09-1877
(0729) Odum	John	Private	1st U.S. Volunteer Infantry	04-12-1865
(0730) O'Garra	Michael	Private	18th U.S. Infantry	12-21-1866
(0731) Ogden	John	Sergeant	7th U.S. Cavalry	06-25-1876
(0732) O'Harra	Miles	Sergeant	7th U.S. Cavalry	06-25-1876
(0733) Olmstead	John	Private	3rd U.S. Infantry	10-04-1898
(0734) Omling	Sebastian	Private	7th U.S. Cavalry	06-25-1876
(0735) O'Neil	John	Private	4th California Infantry	10-29-1865

(0736) Ore	Henry	Corporal	3rd U.S. Cavalry	01-12-1879[40]
(0737) O'Toole	Lawrence	Sergeant	1st U.S. Cavalry	12-28-1866[41]
(0738) Overstreet	Monroe	Private	9th U.S. Cavalry	08-19-1881
(0739) Owsley	Jerry	Private	9th U.S. Cavalry	01-26-1875
(0740) Page	Edward	Sergeant	2nd U.S. Cavalry	08-09-1877
(0741) Papier	Theodore	Sergeant	6th U.S. Cavalry	04-23-1875
(0742) Pardee	Oscar	Private	7th U.S. Cavalry	06-25-1876
(0743) Parker	Kenny	Corporal	8th U.S. Cavalry	01-30-1869[42]
(0744) Parker	John	Private	7th U.S. Cavalry	06-25-1876
(0745) Parrick	Peter	Private	4th U.S. Infantry	09-12-1869
(0746) Partenheimer	Harold	Private	27th U.S. Infantry	11-04-1867
(0747) Patton	John	Trumpeter	7th U.S. Cavalry	06-25-1876
(0748) Payne	Franklin	Private	2nd U.S. Cavalry	12-21-1866
(0749) Payne	John	Farrier	3rd U.S. Cavalry	12-29-1868
(0750) Payne	William	Corporal	7th U.S. Infantry	08-09-1877
(0751) Peabody	Washington	Private	21st U.S. Infantry	08-18-1870
(0752) Perkins	Charles	Saddler	7th U.S. Cavalry	06-25-1876
(0753) Percival	Ambram	Private	9th U.S. Cavalry	09-04-1879
(0754) Perry	Charles	Private	9th U.S. Cavalry	08-12-1881
(0755) Peshall	Richard	Private	5th U.S. Cavalry	09-30-1877
(0756) Phillips	Edgar	Private	7th U.S. Cavalry	06-25-1876
(0757) Phillips	George	Corporal	18th U.S. Infantry	12-21-1866
(0758) Phillips	William	Corporal	1st Oregon Cavalry	05-27-1866
(0759) Pitter	Felix	Private	7th U.S. Cavalry	06-25-1876
(0760) Plater	Juan	Private	1st U.S. Cavalry	07-11-1877
(0761) Pollock	Oscar	Hospital[43]	7th U.S. Cavalry	12-29-1890
(0762) Pommeroy	William	Private	7th U.S. Infantry	08-09-1877
(0763) Porter	James	Private	11th Kansas Cavalry	07-26-1865
(0764) Post	George	Private	7th U.S. Cavalry	06-25-1876
(0765) Potts	George	Private	3rd U.S. Cavalry	06-17-1876
(0766) Powell	John	Private	14th U.S. Infantry	03-22-1866
(0767) Powell	Thomas	Private	11th Kansas Cavalry	07-26-1865
(0768) Prall	Elias	Wagoner	22nd U.S. Infantry	03-16-1869
(0769) Queswelle	Constand	Private	13th U.S. Infantry	05-24-1868
(0770) Quinn	James	Private	7th U.S. Cavalry	06-25-1876
(0771) Quinn	John	Corporal	18th U.S. Infantry	12-21-1866
(0772) Quinn	Patrick	Private	1st U.S. Cavalry	07-03-1877
(0773) Quinlan	David	Private	1st U.S. Cavalry	06-17-1877
(0774) Rae	Robert	Sergeant	4th U.S. Infantry	04-06-1869
(0775) Raichel	Henry	Sergeant	7th U.S. Cavalry	09-30-1877
(0776) Randall	William	Private	7th U.S. Cavalry	09-30-1877
(0777) Rapp	John	Private	7th U.S. Cavalry	06-25-1876
(0778) Rauter	John	Private	7th U.S. Cavalry	06-25-1876
(0779) Raymeyer	Henry	Private	2nd U.S. Cavalry	05-23-1876
(0780) Raymond	Francis	Sergeant	18th U.S. Infantry	12-21-1866
(0781) Reach	George	Private	2nd U.S. Cavalry	07-19-1868
(0782) Reahme	Frank	Private	7th U.S. Cavalry	06-26-1867
(0783) Reed	Delos	Private	18th U.S. Infantry	12-21-1866
(0784) Reed	William	Private	7th U.S. Cavalry	06-25-1876
(0785) Rees	William	Private	7th U.S. Cavalry	06-25-1876
(0786) Regan	Michael	Private	7th U.S. Cavalry	12-29-1890
(0787) Reibold	Christian	Private	7th U.S. Cavalry	06-25-1876
(0788) Reinecky	Frank	Private	7th U.S. Cavalry	12-29-1890
(0789) Richards	Charles	Private	14th U.S. Infantry	03-22-1866
(0790) Rickie	Henry	Private	7th U.S. Cavalry	09-10-1868
(0791) Ricter	Otto	Private	1st U.S. Cavalry	07-03-1877
(0792) Riley	James	Private	27th U.S. Infantry	02-27-1867
(0793) Rix	Edward	Private	7th U.S. Cavalry	06-25-1876
(0794) Roach	William	Private	1st U.S. Cavalry	07-03-1877
(0795) Roberts	Franklin	Corporal	27th U.S. Infantry	08-14-1867
(0796) Roberts	Henry	Private	7th U.S. Cavalry	06-25-1876
(0797) Robinson	Matthew	Private	2nd Texas Cavalry	05-13-1865
(0798) Rodenburgh	Henry	Private	5th U.S. Infantry	01-08-1877
(0799) Roe	Gilbert	Private	3rd U.S. Cavalry	06-17-1876
(0800) Rogers	Benjamin	Private	7th U.S. Cavalry	06-25-1876
(0801) Rogers	Jeremiah	Private	37th U.S. Infantry	05-31-1867
(0802) Rogers	Walter	Private	7th U.S. Cavalry	06-25-1876
(0803) Rollins	Richard	Private	7th U.S. Cavalry	06-25-1876
(0804) Ronan	Thomas	Private	1st California Veteran Infantry	01-17-1866
(0805) Rood	Edward	Private	7th U.S. Cavalry	06-25-1876
(0806) Rooney	Patrick	Sergeant	18th U.S. Infantry	12-21-1866
(0807) Rosenberg	Jacob	Private	18th U.S. Infantry	12-21-1866
(0808) Rossbury	John	Private	7th U.S. Cavalry	06-25-1876
(0809) Roth	Francis	Private	7th U.S. Cavalry	09-30-1877
(0810) Rothman	Augustus	Corporal	5th U.S. Infantry	01-08-1877
(0811) Rouse	John	Private	1st Battalion Dakota Cavalry	08-15-1865
(0812) Rudden	Patrick	Private	7th U.S. Cavalry	06-25-1876
(0813) Russell	James	Private	7th U.S. Cavalry	06-25-1876
(0814) Ryan	Daniel	Corporal	7th U.S. Cavalry	06-25-1876
(0815) Ryan	Daniel	Private	1st U.S. Cavalry	07-03-1877
(0816) Ryan	James	Private	2nd U.S. Cavalry	12-21-1866
(0817) Ryan	Patrick	Corporal	4th U.S. Cavalry	11-25-1876

---

[40] WIA 01-11-1879.
[41] WIA 12-26-1866.
[42] WIA 01-25-1869.

[43] Hospital Steward.

(0818) Ryan	Thomas	Sergeant	1st U.S. Cavalry	06-17-1877
(0819) Sale	Robert	Corporal	7th U.S. Infantry	08-09-1877
(0820) Sampson	Charles	Corporal	1st U.S. Cavalry	11-05-1887
(0821) Saunders	Richard	Private	7th U.S. Cavalry	06-25-1876
(0822) Saunders	William	Private	9th U.S. Cavalry	04-06-1880
(0823) Schafer	Ferdinand	Private	11th Kansas Cavalry	07-26-1865
(0824) Schele	Henry	Private	7th U.S. Cavalry	06-25-1876
(0825) Schmidt	Carl	Private	9th U.S. Infantry	07-29-1866
(0826) Schmidt	Charles	Private	7th U.S. Cavalry	06-25-1876
(0827) Schmidt	Frank	Private	3rd U.S. Cavalry	01-22-1879
(0828) Schneider	George	Private	2nd U.S. Cavalry	03-17-1876
(0829) Schullein	Peter	Private	1st U.S. Cavalry	06-17-1877
(0830) Schultz	Joseph	Saddler	1st U.S. Cavalry	06-23-1878
(0831) Schwallen....[44]	John	Private	3rd U.S. Infantry	10-04-1898
(0832) Schwenkey	Philip	Private	7th U.S. Cavalry	12-29-1890
(0833) Scott	Charles	Private	7th U.S. Cavalry	06-25-1876
(0834) Seafferman	Henry	Private	7th U.S. Cavalry	06-25-1876
(0835) Seiler	John	Corporal	7th U.S. Cavalry	06-25-1876
(0836) Selby	Crawford	Saddler	7th U.S. Cavalry	06-25-1876
(0837) Shade	Samuel	Private	7th U.S. Cavalry	06-25-1876
(0838) Shannon	Patrick	Private	18th U.S. Infantry	12-21-1866
(0839) Sharkey	Michael	Corporal	18th U.S. Infantry	12-21-1866
(0840) Sharpe	Cal	Private	7th U.S. Cavalry	11-27-1868
(0841) Sharpe	William	Private	9th U.S. Cavalry	12-26-1867
(0842) Sharrow	William	Sergeant Major	7th U.S. Cavalry	06-25-1876
(0843) Shaw	Andrew	Private	1st U.S. Cavalry	06-17-1877
(0844) Shay	John	Private	1st U.S. Cavalry	06-17-1877
(0845) Shea	Jeremiah	Private	7th U.S. Cavalry	06-25-1876
(0846) Shellberger		Private	21st U.S. Infantry	10-05-1869
(0847) Sheridan	Phillip	Private	7th U.S. Cavalry	09-10-1868
(0848) Shields	Dennis	Private	6th U.S. Infantry	08-23-1876
(0849) Short	Nathan	Private	7th U.S. Cavalry	06-25-1876
(0850) Shrenger	Charles	Private	2nd U.S. Cavalry	05-07-1877
(0851) Sicfous	Francis	Private	7th U.S. Cavalry	06-25-1876
(0852) Siemon	Charles	Blacksmith	7th U.S. Cavalry	06-25-1876
(0853) Siemonson	Bent	Private	7th U.S. Cavalry	06-25-1876
(0854) Simonds	Charles	Private	4th U.S. Artillery	07-12-1877
(0855) Simpson	John	Private	1st U.S. Cavalry	06-17-1877
(0856) Slagle	Cornelius	Private	27th U.S. Infantry	05-30-1867
(0857) Slocum	John	Private	21st U.S. Infantry	10-05-1869
(0858) Smallwood	William	Private	7th U.S. Cavalry	06-25-1876
(0859) Smith	Albert	Private	7th U.S. Cavalry	06-25-1876
(0860) Smith	Alexander	First Sergeant	18th U.S. Infantry	12-21-1866
(0861) Smith	George	Private	6th U.S. Cavalry	09-13-1874
(0862) Smith	George	Private	7th U.S. Cavalry	06-25-1876
(0863) Smith	James (#1)	Private	7th U.S. Cavalry	06-25-1876
(0864) Smith	James (#2)	Private	7th U.S. Cavalry	06-25-1876
(0865) Smith	John	Private	7th U.S. Infantry	08-09-1877
(0866) Smith	Patrick	Private	18th U.S. Infantry	09-29-1866
(0867) Smith	Patrick	Private	18th U.S. Infantry	12-21-1866
(0868) Smith	Richard	Private	1st U.S. Cavalry	07-08-1878
(0869) Smith	Robert	Private	9th U.S. Cavalry	09-01-1880
(0870) Smith	Sidney	Private	1st U.S. Cavalry	12-21-1872
(0871) Smith	Thomas	Private	10th U.S. Cavalry	08-21-1867
(0872) Snow	Andrew	Private	7th U.S. Cavalry	06-25-1876
(0873) Snowdon	Andrew	Private	14th U.S. Infantry	05-16-1866[45]
(0874) Song	Hermana	Private	27th U.S. Infantry	08-02-1867
(0875) Soudegger	John	Private	6th U.S. Cavalry	08-30-1881
(0876) Spillman	James	Private	7th U.S. Cavalry	06-13-1867[46]
(0877) Sproul	Samuel	Private	11th Kansas Cavalry	07-26-1865
(0878) St. John	Ludwick	Private	7th U.S. Cavalry	06-25-1876
(0879) Stafford	Benjamin	Private	7th U.S. Cavalry	06-25-1876
(0880) Stahlnecker	Tillmon	Private	11th Kansas Cavalry	06-03-1865
(0881) Stanley	Edward	Private	7th U.S. Cavalry	06-25-1876
(0882) Stanley	James	Private	10th U.S. Cavalry	10-28-1880
(0883) Stanton	Daniel	Private	9th U.S. Cavalry	09-01-1880
(0884) Staples	Alvah	Corporal	18th U.S. Infantry	09-20-1866
(0885) Staples	Samuel	Corporal	7th U.S. Cavalry	06-25-1876
(0886) Stella	Alexander	Private	7th U.S. Cavalry	06-25-1876
(0887) Stern	George	Private	38th U.S. Infantry	12-29-1868
(0888) Stewart	George	Sergeant	5th U.S. Cavalry	09-30-1872
(0889) Stewart	Perry	Private	11th Ohio Cavalry	06-08-1865
(0890) Stinebacker	Thomas	Musician	7th U.S. Infantry	08-09-1877
(0891) Stocabus	Frederick	Private	7th U.S. Cavalry	11-27-1868
(0892) Stoker	Augustus	Private	2nd U.S. Cavalry	05-23-1876
(0893) Stone	Harry	Private	7th U.S. Cavalry	01-13-1891[47]
(0894) Stone	John	Sergeant	5th U.S. Cavalry	05-13-1869
(0895) Stortz	F.J.	First Sergeant	7th U.S. Infantry	08-09-1877
(0896) Stressinger	Frederick	Corporal	7th U.S. Cavalry	06-25-1876
(0897) Struad	Frank	Private	4th U.S. Cavalry	09-13-1878
(0898) Stuart	Alpheus	Private	7th U.S. Cavalry	06-25-1876
(0899) Stungewitz	Ygnatz	Private	7th U.S. Cavalry	06-25-1876

---

[44] Schwallenstocker.
[45] WIA 03-22-1866.
[46] WIA 06-12-1867.

[47] WIA 12-29-1890.

(0900) Sullivan	Charles	Private	1st U.S. Cavalry	06-17-1877
(0901) Sullivan	Frank	Private	18th U.S. Infantry	12-21-1866
(0902) Sullivan	John	Private	7th U.S. Cavalry	06-25-1876
(0903) Sullivan	John	Private	4th U.S. Cavalry	11-25-1876
(0904) Sullivan	John	Private	6th U.S. Cavalry	08-30-1881
(0905) Summers	David	Private	7th U.S. Cavalry	06-25-1876
(0906) Summers	Edwin	Private	11th Kansas Cavalry	07-26-1865
(0907) Swayer	Willoughby	Private	1st U.S. Cavalry	09-26-1867
(0908) Sweetser	Thomas	Private	7th U.S. Cavalry	06-25-1876
(0909) Symms	Darwin	Private	7th U.S. Cavalry	06-25-1876
(0910) Taggent	James	Sergeant	3rd U.S. Cavalry	01-22-1879
(0911) Tarbox	Byron	Private	7th U.S. Cavalry	06-25-1876
(0912) Taylor	Charles	Private	18th U.S. Infantry	12-21-1866
(0913) Taylor	William	Private	10th U.S. Cavalry	08-04-1880
(0914) Teeman	William	Corporal	7th U.S. Cavalry	06-25-1876
(0915) Teltow	Charles	Private	2nd U.S. Cavalry	07-02-1867
(0916) Temple	Guy	Private	9th U.S. Cavalry	08-12-1881
(0917) Tessier	Edward	Private	7th U.S. Cavalry	06-25-1876
(0918) Thadus	John	Private	7th U.S. Cavalry	06-25-1876
(0919) Theims	Robert	Private	6th U.S. Cavalry	04-23-1875
(0920) Thimpson	John	Private	18th U.S. Infantry	12-21-1866
(0921) Thomas	Joseph	Private	18th U.S. Infantry	12-21-1866
(0922) Thompson	John	Corporal	1st U.S. Cavalry	06-17-1877
(0923) Thorrey	Daniel	Private	18th U.S. Infantry	12-21-1866
(0924) Timmons	Leonard	Private	11th Ohio Cavalry	04-23-1865
(0925) Tockes	George	Private	10th U.S. Cavalry	08-03-1880
(0926) Torrey	William	Private	7th U.S. Cavalry	06-25-1876
(0927) Tragesor	Conrad	Private	8th U.S. Cavalry	03-10-1870[48]
(0928) Train	Edwin	Bugler	2nd U.S. Cavalry	06-12-1867
(0929) Trevor	Harry	Private	2nd U.S. Cavalry	10-04-1877[49]
(0930) Trial	Nathan	Private	7th U.S. Cavalry	06-26-1867
(0931) Trimble	Andrew	Private	9th U.S. Cavalry	12-26-1867
(0932) Trimble	Frank	Private	1st Oregon Volunteers	01-17-1873
(0933) Troy	David	Private	14th U.S. Infantry	03-21-1868
(0934) Troy	James	Private	7th U.S. Cavalry	06-25-1876
(0935) Tull	Samuel	Private	11th Kansas Cavalry	07-26-1865
(0936) Turley	Henry	Private	7th U.S. Cavalry	06-25-1876
(0937) Turner	Moses	Private	9th U.S. Cavalry	01-26-1875
(0938) Tweed	Thomas	Private	7th U.S. Cavalry	06-25-1876
(0939) Twohig	Daniel	Private	7th U.S. Cavalry	12-29-1890
(0940) Van Allen	Garret	Private	7th U.S. Cavalry	06-25-1876
(0941) Van Bramer	Charles	Private	7th U.S. Cavalry	06-25-1876
(0942) Van Elyff	George	Private	37th U.S. Infantry	12-30-1868[50]
(0943) Van Sant	Cornelius	Private	7th U.S. Cavalry	06-25-1876
(0944) Vane	John	Private	22nd U.S. Infantry	09-26-1868
(0945) Vanousky	Erwin	Sergeant	7th U.S. Cavalry	11-27-1868
(0946) Varden	Frank	First Sergeant	7th U.S. Cavalry	06-25-1876
(0947) Vetter	Johann	Private	7th U.S. Cavalry	06-25-1876
(0948) Vislaoki	D.	Private	4th U.S. Cavalry	06-08-1885
(0949) Voight	Henry	Private	7th U.S. Cavalry	06-25-1876
(0950) Voss	Henry	Chief....[51]	7th U.S. Cavalry	06-25-1876
(0951) Walker	George	Private	7th U.S. Cavalry	06-25-1876
(0952) Walsh	Frederick	Trumpeter	7th U.S. Cavalry	06-25-1876
(0953) Walsh	John	Private	5th U.S. Cavalry	09-30-1872
(0954) Walters	Albert	Private	18th U.S. Infantry	12-21-1866
(0955) Ward	Thomas	Private	8th U.S. cavalry	04-29-1868
(0956) Warner	Oscar	Private	7th U.S. Cavalry	06-25-1876
(0957) Warren	Amos	Sergeant	7th U.S. Cavalry	06-25-1876
(0958) Warren	George	Private	7th U.S. Cavalry	06-25-1876
(0959) Wasser	John	Private	18th U.S. Infantry	10-03-1866
(0960) Waterbury	George	Private	18th U.S. Infantry	12-21-1866
(0961) Watson	William	Sergeant	7th U.S. Infantry	08-19-1877[52]
(0962) Way	Thomas	Trumpeter	7th U.S. Cavalry	06-25-1876
(0963) Weaver	George	Private	7th U.S. Infantry	07-07-1875
(0964) Weaver	John	Private	18th U.S. Infantry	12-21-1866
(0965) Wells	Benjamin	Farrier	7th U.S. Cavalry	06-25-1876
(0966) Welsh	John	Private	7th U.S. Cavalry	06-26-1867
(0967) Welsh	Thomas	Private	6th U.S. Cavalry	10-01-1881
(0968) Werner	Albert	Private	1st U.S. Cavalry	06-17-1877
(0969) West	William	Private	11th Kansas Cavalry	07-26-1865
(0970) Weusserman	Henry	Private	6th U.S. Cavalry	05-22-1872
(0971) Whaley	William	Private	7th U.S. Cavalry	06-25-1876
(0972) Whitcomb	Joseph	Private	8th U.S. Cavalry	01-07-1869[53]
(0973) White	Edward	Private	3rd U.S. Cavalry	07-09-1867
(0974) Whitlow	William	Private	7th U.S. Cavalry	09-30-1877
(0975) Whittig	John	Private	7th California Infantry	07-21-1865
(0976) Wild	John	Corporal	7th U.S. Cavalry	06-25-1876
(0977) Wilde	Otto	First Sergeant	7th U.S. Cavalry	09-30-1877
(0978) Wilkinson	John	Sergeant	7th U.S. Cavalry	06-25-1876
(0979) Williams	James	Corporal	7th U.S. Cavalry	11-27-1868

[48] WIA 03-09-1870.
[49] WIA 08-20-1877.
[50] WIA 12-25-1868.

[51] Chief Trumpeter.
[52] WIA 08-09-1877.
[53] WIA 09-05-1869.

(0980) Williams	John	Private	34th Indiana Infantry	05-13-1865
(0981) Williams	Oliver	Private	2nd U.S. Cavalry	12-21-1866
(0982) Wilson	George	Private	8th U.S. Cavalry	07-07-1867
(0983) Winkler	Paul	Private	12th U.S. Infantry	08-31-1881
(0984) Winney	DeWitt	First Sergeant	7th U.S. Cavalry	06-25-1876
(0985) Winzel	John	Private	3rd U.S. Cavalry	09-09-1876
(0986) Woldruff	Joseph	Private	3rd U.S. Infantry	06-15-1867
(0987) Woodard	Major	Private	9th U.S. Cavalry	09-30-1879
(0988) Woodruff	John	Private	18th U.S. Infantry	12-21-1866
(0989) Workman	James	Sergeant	4th U.S. Artillery	07-12-1877
(0990) Wright	Charles	Private	5th U.S. Cavalry	09-29-1879
(0991) Wright	Emanuel	Private	9th U.S. Cavalry	10-01-1867
(0992) Wright	James	Corporal	21st U.S. Infantry	06-02-1870
(0993) Wright	Willis	Private	7th U.S. Cavalry	06-25-1876
(0994) Wurm	Daniel	Private	4th U.S. Cavalry	08-22-1867
(0995) Wurmser	Martin	Private	4th U.S. Cavalry	09-30-1870
(0996) Wykoff	Edward	Private	21st U.S. Infantry	07-11-1877
(0997) Wyllyams	Frederick	Sergeant	7th U.S. Cavalry	06-26-1867
(0998) Wyman	Henry	Private	7th U.S. Cavalry	06-25-1876
(0999) Yandell	John	Private	8th U.S. Infantry	10-01-1881
(1000) Young	Thomas	Private	11th Kansas Cavalry	07-26-1865
(1001) Younge	Charles	Corporal	3rd U.S. Cavalry	05-07-1869
(1002) Zehell	Albert	Private	3rd U.S. Infantry	10-04-1898
(1003) Zinn	Jacob	Private	11th Kansas Cavalry	07-26-1865
(1004) Zinn	John	Private	11th Kansas Cavalry	07-26-1865
(1005) Zolinder	Bernhard	Private	7th U.S. Cavalry	12-29-1890

— INDIAN SCOUTS —

(1006) Abraham Brooks	Indian Scout	07-17-1877
(1007) Aichovio	Indian Scout	11-07-1885
(1008) Amongst	Indian Scout	08-26-1872
(1009) Barrajo	Indian Scout	09-18-1879
(1010) Black Eagle	Indian Scout	03-09-1880
(1011) Bloody Knife	Indian Scout	06-25-1876
(1012) Bob Tailed Bull	Indian Scout	06-25-1876
(1013) Ceguania	Indian Scout	04-23-1882
(1014) Chief Youngman	Indian Scout	10-02-1872
(1015) Chilchuene	Indian Scout	02-03-1880
(1016) Coppinger	Indian Scout	08-22-1867
(1017) Crow's Tail	Indian Scout	10-02-1872
(1018) Dick	Indian Scout	09-07-1880
(1019) Hat-Ta-Hu-Mah	Indian Scout	12-15-1872
(1020) Humme	Indian Scout	10-27-1879
(1021) John Levi	Indian Scout	07-17-1877
(1022) Kaloh Vichajo	Indian Scout	04-23-1882
(1023) Little Brave	Indian Scout	06-25-1876
(1024) Little Horse	Indian Scout	03-09-1880
(1025) Magpie	Indian Scout	07-17-1879
(1026) Medicine Stand	Indian Scout	07-17-1879
(1027) Monte Jack	Indian Scout	09-07-1880
(1028) Panocho	Indian Scout	07-17-1882
(1029) Pete	Indian Scout	07-17-1882
(1030) Qual-Ten-E-Quam-Yah	Indian Scout	10-25-1872
(1031) Red Bead	Indian Scout	07-02-1867
(1032) Red Bear	Indian Scout	10-02-1872

(1033) Rock		Indian Scout	09-04-1878
(1034) Sam		Indian Scout	09-18-1879
(1035) Shadow Comes Out		Indian Scout	07-18-1879[54]
(1036) Sicon-al-Toga		Indian Scout	09-22-1885
(1037) Simon Olgin		Indian Scout	06-11-1880
(1038) Skilly		Indian Scout	10-27-1879
(1039) Spotted Eagle		Indian Scout	08-26-1872
(1040) Squalth		Indian Scout	07-13-1867
(1041) Yah-to-Et		Indian Scout	05-22-1885
(1042) Yuma Bill		Indian Scout	04-23-1882

— INDIAN POLICE—

(1043) Afraid-of-Soldier		Indian Police	12-15-1890
(1044) Albert Sterling		Indian Police	04-19-1882
(1045) Bull Head		Indian Police	12-15-1890
(1046) Gway-Bah-Be-Pung		Indian Police	10-04-1898
(1047) Hawk Man #2		Indian Police	12-15-1890
(1048) John Armstrong		Indian Police	12-15-1890
(1049) John Colvig		Indian Police	07-06-1882
(1050) Little Eagle		Indian Police	12-15-1890
(1051) Sagotal		Indian Police	04-19-1882
(1052) Shave Head		Indian Police	12-15-1890

— CITIZENS —

(1053) Armstrong	John	Citizen	08-09-1877
(1054) Baliran	Augustus	Citizen	08-04-1873
(1055) Blewett	Charles	Citizen	07-03-1877
(1056) Bostwick	Henry	Citizen	08-09-1877
(1057) Bouyer	Mitch	Citizen	06-25-1876
(1058) Bradley	Edmund	Citizen	09-25-1877
(1059) Brockmeyer	Wesley	Citizen	08-02-1876
(1060) Brownley	John	Citizen	05-02-1868
(1061) Campbell		Citizen	07-02-1878
(1062) Clark	Sam	Citizen	07-11-1894
(1063) Culver	George	Citizen	09-17-1868
(1064) Custer	Boston	Citizen	06-25-1876
(1065) Daly	George	Citizen	08-19-1881
(1066) Davis		Citizen	11-20-1868
(1067) DeWolf	James	Citizen	06-25-1876
(1068) Dorman	Isaiah	Citizen	06-25-1876

---

[54] WIA 07-17-1879.

(1069) Elliot	Lynde	Citizen	08-09-1877
(1070) Evans	Benjamin	Citizen	07-05-1877
(1071) Farley	Louis	Citizen	09-25-1868
(1072) Fisher	Isaac	Citizen	12-21-1866
(1073) Foster	William	Citizen	07-03-1877
(1074) Frohman	A.A.	Citizen	07-20-1878
(1075) Gould	John	Citizen	08-08-1867
(1076) Hadsell	Charles	Citizen	05-26-1868
(1077) Hagan	Jack	Citizen	09-18-1879
(1078) Hanson	Rufus	Citizen	01-29-1867
(1079) Harris	William	Citizen	03-26-1868
(1080) Hauser	D.H.	Citizen	07-17-1877[55]
(1081) Hedges	Nathaniel	Citizen	08-13-1865
(1082) Hoag	Daniel	Citizen	05-01-1868
(1083) Hollister	John	Citizen	08-02-1867[56]
(1084) Holt	John	Citizen	09-14-1869
(1085) Honsinger	John	Citizen	08-04-1873
(1086) Hovey	Eugene	Citizen	04-15-1873
(1087) Howser	D.	Citizen	07-05-1877
(1088) Huffman	George	Citizen	08-19-1874
(1089) Kellogg	Marcus	Citizen	06-25-1876
(1090) Lockwood	Alvin	Citizen	08-09-1877
(1091) Lowry	Charlie	Citizen	09-29-1879
(1092) Mann	Frank	Citizen	06-25-1876
(1093) Marshall	Nate	Citizen	11-20-1868
(1094) McGuire	Thomas	Citizen	09-29-1879
(1095) McKinstry	William	Citizen	09-29-1879
(1096) Mitchell	Campbell	Citizen	08-09-1877
(1097) Mooers	John	Citizen	09-18-1868
(1098) Morrow	David	Citizen	08-09-1877
(1099) Myers	William	Citizen	06-23-1878
(1100) Nus	Wendolen	Citizen	11-29-1872
(1101) O'Donnell	Thomas	Citizen	11-18-1868[57]
(1102) Olgin	Simon	Citizen	06-11-1880
(1103) Parks	Thomas	Citizen	08-16-1867
(1104) Patino	Severino	Citizen	03-12-1867
(1105) Quinn	James	Citizen	05-23-1876
(1106) Randall	Darius	Citizen	07-05-1877
(1107) Reed	Harry	Citizen	06-25-1876
(1108) Reynolds	Charles	Citizen	06-25-1876
(1109) Saffel	Charles	Citizen	08-16-1867
(1110) Simpson	William	Citizen	05-05-1871
(1111) Slater	John	Citizen	11-05-1867
(1112) Thomas	Eleasar	Citizen	04-11-1873
(1113) Thurber	Jack	Citizen	11-29-1872
(1114) Warfield	Joseph	Citizen	07-26-1865
(1115) Webber	Lewis	Citizen	04-26-1873
(1116) Wheatley	James	Citizen	12-21-1866
(1117) White	Jonathan	Citizen	09-09-1876
(1118) Whitney	Robert	Citizen	10-24-1871
(1119) Wilson	William	Citizen	09-17-1868

[55] WIA 07-05-1877.
[56] WIA 08-01-1867.
[57] WIA 09-17-1868.

APPENDIX B: MEDAL OF HONOR (1865-1898)

LAST NAME	FIRST	REGIMENT	ACTION	RECEIVED
(0001) Albee	George	41st U.S. Infantry	10-28-1869	01-18-1894
(0002)	Alchesay	Indian Scouts	Winter 1872 to 1873	04-12-1875
(0003) Allen	William	23rd U.S. Infantry	03-27-1873	04-12-1875
(0004) Anderson	James	6th U.S. Cavalry	10-05-1870	11-19-1870
(0005) Aston	Edgar	8th U.S. Cavalry	05-30-1868	07-28-1868
(0006) Austin	William	7th U.S. Cavalry	12-29-1890	06-27-1891
(0007) Ayers	James	6th U.S. Cavalry	04-23-1875	11-16-1876
(0008) Babcock	John	5th U.S. Cavalry	05-16-1869	09-18-1897
(0009) Bailey	James	5th U.S. Cavalry	Winter 1872 to 1873	04-12-1875
(0010) Baird	George	5th U.S. Infantry	09-30-1877	11-27-1894
(0011) Baker	John	5th U.S. Infantry	10-1876 to 01-1877	04-27-1877
(0012) Bancroft	Neil	7th U.S. Cavalry	06-25-1876	10-05-1878
(0013) Barnes	Will	Signal Corps	09-11-1881	11-08-1882
(0014) Barrett	Richard	1st U.S. Cavalry	05-23-1872	04-12-1875
(0015) Beauford	Clay	5th U.S. Cavalry	Winter 1872 to 1873	04-12-1875
(0016) Bell	James	7th U.S. Infantry	07-09-1875	12-02-1876
(0017) Bergerndahl	Frederick	4th U.S. Cavalry	12-08-1874	10-13-1875
(0018) Bertram	Heinrich	8th U.S. Cavalry	1868	07-24-1869
(0019) Bessey	Charles	3rd U.S. Cavalry	01-13-1877	05-15-1890
(0020) Bishop	Daniel	5th U.S. Cavalry	03-25-1873	04-12-1875
(0021) Blair	James	1st U.S. Cavalry	Winter 1872 to 1873	04-12-1875
(0022)	Blanquet	Indian Scouts	Winter 1872 to 1873	04-12-1875
(0023) Bowden	Samuel	6th U.S. Cavalry	10-05-1870	11-19-1870
(0024) Bowman	Alonzo	6th U.S. Cavalry	08-30-1881	11-04-1882
(0025) Boyne	Thomas	9th U.S. Cavalry	05-29-1879	01-06-1882
(0026) Bradbury	Sanford	8th U.S. Cavalry	07-03-1869	03-03-1870
(0027) Branagan	Edward	4th U.S. Cavalry	09-29-1872	11-19-1872
(0028) Brant	Abram	7th U.S. Cavalry	06-25-1876	10-05-1878
(0029) Bratling	Frank	8th U.S. Cavalry	07-08-1873 to 08-12-1875	07-11-1873
(0030) Brett	Lloyd	2nd U.S. Cavalry	04-01-1880	02-07-1895
(0031) Brogan	James	6th U.S. Cavalry	12-14-1877	01-09-1880
(0032) Brophy	James	8th U.S. Cavalry	1868	07-24-1869
(0033) Brown	Benjamin	24th U.S. Infantry	05-11-1889	02-19-1890
(0034) Brown	James	5th U.S. Cavalry	08-27-1872	12-04-1874
(0035) Brown	Lorenzo	7th U.S. Infantry	08-09-1877	05-08-1878
(0036) Bryan	William	Hospital Steward	03-17-1876	06-15-1899
(0037) Burkard	Oscar	Hospital Corps	10-05-1898	08-21-1899
(0038) Burke	Patrick	8th U.S. Cavalry	1868	07-24-1869
(0039) Burke	Richard	5th U.S. Infantry	10-1876 to 01-1877	04-27-1877
(0040) Burnett	George	9th U.S. Cavalry	08-16-1881	07-23-1897
(0041) Butler	Edmond	5th U.S. Infantry	01-08-1877	11-27-1894
(0042) Byrne	Denis	5th U.S. Infantry	10-1876 to 01-1877	04-27-1877
(0043) Cable	Joseph	5th U.S. Infantry	10-1876 to 01-1877	04-27-1877
(0044) Callen	Thomas	7th U.S. Cavalry	06-25-1876	10-24-1896
(0045) Calvert	James	5th U.S. Infantry	10-1876 to 01-1877	04-27-1877
(0046) Canfield	Heth	2nd U.S. Cavalry	05-15-1870	06-22-1870
(0047) Carpenter	Louis	10th U.S. Cavalry	09-1868 to 10-1868	04-08-1898
(0048) Carr	John	8th U.S. Cavalry	10-29-1869	02-14-1870
(0049) Carroll	Thomas	8th U.S. Cavalry	08-1868 to 10-1868	07-24-1869
(0050) Carter	George	8th U.S. Cavalry	08-1868 to 10-1868	07-24-1869
(0051) Carter	Mason	5th U.S. Infantry	09-30-1877	11-27-1894
(0052) Carter	Robert	4th US. Cavalry	10-10-1871	02-27-1900
(0053) Carter	William	6th U.S. Cavalry	08-30-1881	09-17-1891
(0054) Casey	James	5th U.S. Infantry	01-08-1877	11-27-1894
(0055) Chapman[1]	Amos	Citizen	09-12-1874	11-04-1874
(0056) Cheever	Benjamin	6th U.S. Cavalry	01-01-1891	04-25-1891
(0057)	Chiquito	Indian Scout	Winter 1872 to 1873	04-12-1875
(0058) Clancy	John	1st U.S. Artillery	12-29-1890	01-23-1892
(0059) Clark	Wilfred	2nd U.S. Cavalry	08-09-1877 and 02-28-1878	08-20-1877
(0060) Clarke	Powhatan	10th U.S. Cavalry	05-03-1886	03-12-1891
(0061) Cody[2]	William	Citizen	04-26-1872	UNKNOWN
(0062) Comfort	John	4th U.S. Cavalry	11-05-1874	10-13-1875
(0063) Connor	John	6th U.S. Cavalry	07-12-1870	08-25-1870
(0064) Coonrod	Aquilla	5th U.S. Infantry	10-1876 to 01-1877	04-27-1877
(0065) Corcoran	Michael	8th U.S. Cavalry	08-25-1869	03-03-1870
(0066)	Co-Rux-Re-Chod-Ish[3]	Indian Scouts	07-08-1869	08-24-1869
(0067) Craig	Samuel	4th U.S. Cavalry	05-15-1886	04-27-1887
(0068) Crandall	Charles	8th U.S. Cavalry	08-1868 to 10-1868	07-24-1869

[1] In 1916, the general review of all Medals of Honor deemed 900 unwarranted. This recipient was one of them. In June 1989, the U.S. Army Board of Correction of Records restored the medal to this recipient.
[2] In 1916, the general review of all Medals of Honor deemed 900 unwarranted. This recipient was one of them. In June 1989, the U.S. Army Board of Correction of Records restored the medal to this recipient.
[3] Mad Bear.

LAST NAME	FIRST	REGIMENT	ACTION	RECEIVED
0069) Crist	John	8th U.S. Cavalry	11-26-1869	03-03-1870
0070) Criswell	Benjamin	7th U.S. Cavalry	06-25-1876	10-05-1878
0071) Cruse	Thomas	6th U.S. Cavalry	07-17-1882	07-12-1892
0072) Cubberly	William	8th U.S. Cavalry	05-30-1868	07-28-1868
0073) Cunningham	Charles	7th U.S. Cavalry	06-25-1876	10-05-1876
0074) Daily	Charles	8th U.S. Cavalry	08-1868 to 10-1868	07-24-1869
0075) Daniels	James	4th U.S. Cavalry	03-07-1890	05-15-1890
0076) Dawson	Michael	6th U.S. Cavalry	04-23-1875	11-16-1876
0077) Day	Matthias	9th U.S. Cavalry	09-18-1879	05-07-1890
0078) Day	William	5th U.S. Cavalry	1872 to 1873	04-12-1875
0079) De Armond	William	5th U.S. Cavalry	09-09-1874 to 04-23-1875	09-11-1874
0080) Deary	George	5th U.S. Cavalry	04-02-1874	04-12-1875
0081) Deetline	Frederick	7th U.S. Cavalry	06-25-1876	10-15-1878
0082) Denny	John	9th U.S. Cavalry	08-18-1879	11-27-1891
0083) Dickens	Charles	8th U.S. Cavalry	10-20-1869	02-14-1870
0084) Dixon4	William	Citizen	09-12-1874	11-04-1874
0085) Dodge	Francis	9th U.S. Cavalry	09-29-1879	04-02-1898
0086) Donahue	John	8th U.S. Cavalry	10-20-1869	02-14-1870
0087) Donavan	Cornelius	8th U.S. Cavalry	08-25-1869	03-03-1870
0088) Donelly	John	5th U.S. Infantry	10-1876 to 01-1877	04-27-1877
0089) Doshier	James	Citizen	10-05-1870	11-19-1870
0090) Dougherty	William	8th U.S. Cavalry	08-1868 to 10-1868	07-24-1869
0091) Dowling	James	8th U.S. Cavalry	08-1868 to 10-1868	07-24-1869
0092) Edwards	William	7th U.S. Infantry	08-09-1877	12-02-1878
0093) Eldridge	George	6th U.S. Cavalry	07-12-1870	08-25-1870
0094)	Elsatsoosu	Indian Scout	Winter 1872 to 1873	04-12-1875
0095) Elwood	Edwin	8th U.S. Cavalry	10-20-1869	02-14-1870
0096) Emmet	Robert	9th U.S. Cavalry	09-18-1879	08-24-1899
0097) Evans	William	7th U.S. Infantry	07-09-1876	12-02-1876
0098) Factor	Pompey	Indian Scouts	04-25-1875	05-28-1875
0099) Falcott	Henry	8th U.S. Cavalry	08-1868 to 10-1868	07-24-1869
0100) Farren	Daniel	8th U.S. Cavalry	08-1868 to 10-1868	07-24-1869
0101) Feaster	Mosheim	7th U.S. Cavalry	12-29-1890	06-23-1891
0102) Fegan	James	3rd U.S. Infantry	03-1868	10-19-1878
0103) Ferrari	George	8th U.S. Cavalry	09-23-1869	11-23-1869
0104) Fichter	Hermann	3rd U.S. Cavalry	05-05-1871	11-13-1871
0105) Foley	John	3rd U.S. Cavalry	04-26-1872	05-22-1872
0106) Folly	William	8th U.S. Cavalry	08-1868 to 10-1868	07-24-1869
0107) Foran	Nicholas	8th U.S. Cavalry	08-1868 to 10-1868	07-24-1869
0108) Forsyth	Thomas	4th U.S. Cavalry	11-25-1876	07-14-1891
0109) Foster	William	4th U.S. Cavalry	09-29-1872	11-19-1872
0110) Freemeyer	Christopher	5th U.S. Infantry	10-21-1876 to 04-27-1877	01-08-1877
0111) Gardiner	Peter	6th U.S. Cavalry	04-23-1875	11-16-1876
0112) Gardner	Charles	8th U.S. Cavalry	08-1868 to 10-1868	07-24-1869
0113) Garland	Harry	2nd U.S. Cavalry	05-07-1877 and 02-28-1878	08-29-1877
0114) Garlington	Ernest	7th U.S. Cavalry	12-29-1890	09-26-1893
0115) Gates	George	8th U.S. Cavalry	06-04-1869	03-03-1870
0116) Gay	Thomas	8th U.S. Cavalry	08-1868 to 10-1868	07-24-1869
0117) Geiger	George	7th U.S. Cavalry	06-25-1876	10-05-1878
0118) Georgian	John	8th U.S. Cavalry	10-20-1869	02-14-1870
0119) Gerber	Frederick	U.S. Engineers	1839 to 1871	11-08-1871
0120) Given	John	6th U.S. Cavalry	07-12-1870	08-25-1870
0121) Glavinski	Albert	3rd U.S. Cavalry	03-17-1876	10-16-1876
0122) Glover	T.B.	2nd U.S. Cavalry	04-10-1879 and 11-20-1897	02-10-1880
0123) Glynn	Michael	5th U.S. Cavalry	07-13-1872	12-04-1874
0124) Godfrey	Edward	7th U.S. Cavalry	09-30-1877	11-27-1894
0125) Golden	Patrick	8th U.S. Cavalry	08-1868 to 10-1868	07-24-1869
0126) Goldin	Theodore	7th U.S. Cavalry	06-25-1876	12-21-1895
0127) Goodman	David	8th U.S. Cavalry	10-14-1869	03-03-1870
0128) Grant	George	18th U.S. Infantry	02-1867	05-06-1871
0129) Greaves	Clinton	9th U.S. Cavalry	01-24-1877	06-26-1879
0130) Green	Francis	8th U.S. Cavalry	1868 to 1869	09-06-1869
0131) Green	John	1st U.S. Cavalry	01-17-1873	11-18-1897
0132) Gresham	John	7th U.S. Cavalry	12-29-1890	03-25-1895
0133) Grimes	Edward	5th U.S. Cavalry	09-29-1879 to 01-17-1880	10-05-1879
0134) Gunther	Jacob	8th U.S. Cavalry	1868 to 1869	09-06-1869
0135) Haddoo	John	5th U.S. Infantry	10-1876 to 04-27-1877	01-08-1877
0136) Hall	John	8th U.S. Cavalry	08-1868 to 10-1868	07-24-1869
0137) Hall	William	5th U.S. Cavalry	10-20-1879	09-18-1897
0138) Hamilton	Frank	8th U.S. Cavalry	08-25-1869	03-03-1870
0139) Hamilton	Matthew	7th U.S. Cavalry	12-29-1890	05-25-1891

[4] In 1916, the general review of all Medals of Honor deemed 900 unwarranted. This recipient was one of them. In June 1989, the U.S. Army Board of Correction of Records restored the medal to this recipient.

[5] In 1916, the general review of all Medals of Honor deemed 900 unwarranted. This recipient was one of them. In June 1989, the U.S. Army Board of Correction of Records restored the medal to this recipient.

LAST NAME	FIRST	REGIMENT	ACTION	RECEIVED
(0140) Hanley	Richard	7th U.S. Cavalry	06-25-1876	10-05-1878
(0141) Harding	Mosher	8th U.S. Cavalry	10-20-1869	02-14-1870
(0142) Harrington	John	6th U.S. Cavalry	09-12-1874	11-04-1874
(0143) Harris	Charles	8th U.S. Cavalry	09-23-1869	11-23-1869
(0144) Harris	David	7th U.S. Cavalry	06-25-1876	10-05-1878
(0145) Harris	William	7th U.S. Cavalry	06-25-1876	10-05-1878
(0146) Hartzog	Joshua	1st U.S. Artillery	12-29-1890	03-24-1891
(0147) Haupt	Paul	8th U.S. Cavalry	07-03-1869	03-03-1870
(0148) Hawthorne	Harry	2nd U.S. Artillery	12-29-1890	10-11-1892
(0149) Hay	Fred	5th U.S. Infantry	09-09-1874	04-23-1875
(0150) Heartery	Richard	6th U.S. Cavalry	08-30-1881	07-20-1888
(0151) Heise	Clamor	8th U.S. Cavalry	08-1868 to 10-1868	07-24-1869
(0152) Herron	Leander	3rd U.S. Infantry	09-02-1868	UNKNOWN
(0153) Heyl	Charles	23rd U.S. Infantry	04-28-1876	10-26-1897
(0154) Higgins	Thomas	8th U.S. Cavalry	08-1868 to 10-1868	07-24-1869
(0155) Hill	Frank	5th U.S. Cavalry	09-08-1872	08-12-1875
(0156) Hill	James	5th U.S. Cavalry	03-25-1873	08-12-1875
(0157) Hillock	Marvin	7th U.S. Cavalry	06-25-1876	10-05-1878
(0158) Himmelsback	Michael	2nd U.S. Cavalry	05-15-1870	06-22-1870
(0159) Hinemann	Lehmann	1st U.S. Cavalry	Winter 1872 to 1873	08-12-1875
(0160) Hobday	George	7th U.S. Cavalry	12-29-1890	06-23-1891
(0161) Hogan	Henry	5th U.S. Infantry	10-1876 to 06-26-1894	01-08-1877
(0162) Hogan	Henry	5th U.S. Infantry	09-30-1877	UNKNOWN
(0163) Holden	Henry	7th U.S. Cavalry	06-25-1876	10-05-1878
(0164) Holland	David	5th U.S. Infantry	10-1876 to 06-26-1894	01-08-1877
(0165) Hooker	George	5th U.S. Cavalry	01-22-1873	08-12-1875
(0166) Hoover	Samuel	1st U.S. Cavalry	05-06-1873	08-12-1875
(0167) Hornaday	Simpson	6th U.S. Cavalry	04-23-1875	11-16-1876
(0168) Howze	Robert	6th U.S. Cavalry	01-01-1891	07-25-1891
(0169) Hubbard	Thomas	2nd U.S. Cavalry	05-15-1870	06-22-1870
(0170) Huff	James	1st U.S. Cavalry	Winter 1872 to 1873	04-12-1876
(0171) Huggins	Eli	2nd U.S. Cavalry	04-01-1880	11-27-1894
(0172) Humphrey	Charles	4th U.S. Artillery	07-11-1877	03-02-1897
(0173) Hunt	Fred	5th U.S. Infantry	10-21-1876 to 06-26-1894	01-08-1877
(0174) Hutchinson	Rufus	7th U.S. Cavalry	06-25-1876	10-05-1878
(0175) Hyde	Henry	1st U.S. Cavalry	Winter 1872 to 1873	08-12-1875
(0176) Irwin	Bernard	Assistant Surgeon	02-13-1861 to 01-24-1894	02-14-1861
(0177) Jackson	James	1st U.S. Cavalry	08-20-1877	04-17-1896
(0178) James	John	5th U.S. Infantry	09-09-1874 to 04-23-1875	09-11-1874
(0179) Jarvis	Frederick	1st U.S. Cavalry	10-20-1869	02-14-1870
(0180) Jetter	Bernhard	7th U.S. Cavalry	Sioux Campaign-December 1890	04-24-1891
(0181)	Jim	Indian Scouts	Winter 1871 to 1873	04-12-1875
(0182) Johnson	Henry	9th U.S. Cavalry	10-02-1878 to 09-22-1890	10-05-1878
(0183) Johnston	Edward	5th U.S. Infantry	10-1876 to 04-27-1877	01-08-1877
(0184) Jones	William	2nd U.S. Cavalry	05-07-1877 and 02-28-1878	08-20-1877
(0185) Jordan	George	9th U.S. Cavalry	05-14-1880 and 05-07-1890	08-12-1881
(0186) Kay	John	8th U.S. Cavalry	10-21-1868	03-03-1870
(0187) Keating	Daniel	6th U.S. Cavalry	10-05-1870	11-19-1870
(0188) Keenan	Bartholomew	1st U.S. Cavalry	10-20-1869	02-14-1870
(0189) Keenan	John	8th U.S. Cavalry	08-1868 to 10-1868	07-24-1869
(0190) Kelley	Charles	1st U.S. Cavalry	10-20-1869	02-14-1870
(0191) Kelly	John	5th U.S. Infantry	09-09-1874	04-23-1875
(0192) Kelly	Thomas	5th U.S. Infantry	09-09-1874	04-23-1875
(0193)	Kelsay	Indian Scouts	Winter 1872 to 1873	04-12-1875
(0194) Kennedy	Phillip	5th U.S. Infantry	10-21-1876 to 04-27-1877	01-08-1877
(0195) Kerr	John	6th U.S. Cavalry	01-01-1891	04-25-1891
(0196) Kerrigan	Thomas	6th U.S. Cavalry	07-12-1870	08-25-1870
(0197) Kilmartin	John	3rd U.S. Cavalry	05-05-1871	11-13-1871
(0198) Kirk	John	6th U.S. Cavalry	07-12-1870	08-25-1870
(0199) Kirkwood	John	3rd U.S. Cavalry	09-09-1876	10-16-1877
(0200) Kitchen	George	6th U.S. Cavalry	09-09-1874	04-23-1875
(0201) Knaak	Albert	8th U.S. Cavalry	08-1868 to 10-1868	07-24-1869
(0202) Knight	Joseph	6th U.S. Cavalry	01-01-1891	05-01-1891
(0203) Knox	John	5th U.S. Infantry	09-09-1874	04-23-1875
(0204) Koelpin	William	5th U.S. Infantry	09-09-1874	04-23-1875
(0205)	Kosoha	Indian Scouts	Winter 1872 to 1873	04-12-1875
(0206) Kreher	Wendelin	5th U.S. Infantry	10-21-1876 to 06-27-1877	01-08-1877
(0207) Kyle	John	5th U.S. Cavalry	07-08-1869	08-24-1869
(0208) Larkin	David	4th U.S. Cavalry	09-29-1872	11-19-1872
(0209) Lawrence	James	8th U.S. Cavalry	08-1868 to 10-1868	07-24-1869
(0210) Lawton	John	5th U.S. Cavalry	09-29-1879	06-07-1880
(0211) Lenihan	James	5th U.S. Cavalry	01-02-1873	04-12-1875

LAST NAME	FIRST	REGIMENT	ACTION	RECEIVED
(0212) Leonard	Patrick	2nd U.S. Cavalry	05-15-1870	06-22-1870
(0213) Leonard	Patrick	23rd U.S. Infantry	04-28-1876	08-26-1876
(0214) Leonard	William	2nd U.S. Cavalry	05-07-1877	08-08-1877
(0215) Lewis	William	3rd U.S. Cavalry	01-20-1877 to 03-28-1879	01-22-1877
(0216) Little	Thomas	8th U.S. Cavalry	08-1868 to 10-1868	07-24-1869
(0217) Lohnes	Francis W.	1st Neb. Vet. Cavalry	05-12-1865	07-24-1865
(0218) Long	Oscar	5th U.S. Infantry	09-30-1877	03-22-1895
(0219) Lowthers	James	6th U.S. Cavalry	04-23-1875	11-16-1876
(0220) Loyd	George	7th U.S. Cavalry	12-29-1890	04-16-1891
(0221) Lytle	Leonidas	8th U.S. Cavalry	07-08-1873 to 04-12-1875	07-11-1873
(0222) Lytton	Jeptha	23rd U.S. Infantry	04-28-1876	08-26-1876
(0223)	Machol	Indian Scouts	1872 to 1873	04-12-1875
(0224) Mahers	Herbert	8th U.S. Cavalry	08-25-1869	03-03-1870
(0225) Mahoney	Gregory	4th U.S. Cavalry	09-26-1874 to 10-13-1875	09-28-1874
(0226) Martin	Patrick	5th U.S. Cavalry	06-1873 to 07-1873	04-12-1875
(0227) Matthews	David A.	8th U.S. Cavalry	1868 to 1869	09-06-1869
(0228) Maus	Marion	1st U.S. Infantry	01-11-1886	11-27-1894
(0229) May	John	6th U.S. Cavalry	07-12-1870	08-25-1870
(0230) Mays	Isaiah	24th U.S. Infantry	05-11-1889	02-19-1890
(0231) McBride	Bernard	8th U.S. Cavalry	08-1868 to 10-1868	07-24-1869
(0232) McBryar	William	10th U.S. Cavalry	03-07-1890	05-15-1890
(0233) McCabe	William	4th U.S. Cavalry	09-26-1874 to 10-13-1875	09-28-1874
(0234) McCann	Bernard	22nd U.S. Infantry	10-21-1876 to 04-27-1877	01-08-1877
(0235) McCarthy	Michael	1st U.S. Cavalry	06-1877 to 01-1878	11-20-1897
(0236) McClernand	Edward	2nd U.S. Cavalry	09-30-1877	11-27-1894
(0237) McCormick	Michael	5th U.S. Infantry	10-21-1876 to 04-27-1877	01-08-1877
(0238) McDonald	Franklin	11th U.S. Infantry	08-05-1872	08-31-1872
(0239) McDonald	James	8th U.S. Cavalry	08-1868 to 10-1868	07-24-1869
(0240) McDonald	Robert	5th U.S. Infantry	01-08-1877	11-27-1894
(0241) McGann	Michael	3rd U.S. Cavalry	06-17-1876	08-09-1880
(0242) McGar	Owen	5th U.S. Infantry	10-21-1876 to 04-27-1877	01-08-1877
(0243) McHugh	John	5th U.S. Infantry	10-21-1876 to 04-27-1877	01-08-1877
(0244) McKinley	Daniel	8th U.S. Cavalry	08-1868 to 10-1868	07-24-1869
(0245) McLennon	John	7th U.S. Infantry	08-09-1877	12-02-1878
(0246) McLoughlin	Michael	5th U.S. Infantry	10-21-1876 to 04-27-1877	01-08-1877
(0247) McMasters	Henry	4th U.S. Cavalry	09-29-1872	11-19-1872
(0248) McMillan	Albert	7th U.S. Cavalry	12-29-1890	06-23-1891
(0249) McNally	James	8th U.S. Cavalry	1868 to 1869	09-06-1869
(0250) McNamara	William	4th U.S. Cavalry	09-29-1872	11-19-1872
(0251) McPhelan	Robert	5th U.S. Infantry	10-21-1876 to 04-27-1877	01-08-1877
(0252) McVeagh	Charles	8th U.S. Cavalry	08-1868 to 10-1868	07-24-1869
(0253) Meaher	Nicholas	1st U.S. Cavalry	10-20-1869	02-14-1870
(0254) Mechlin	Henry	7th U.S. Cavalry	06-25-1876	08-29-1879
(0255) Merrill	John	5th U.S. Cavalry	09-29-1879	06-07-1880
(0256) Miller	Daniel	3rd U.S. Cavalry	05-05-1871	11-13-1871
(0257) Miller	George	8th U.S. Cavalry	08-1868 to 10-1868	07-24-1869
(0258) Miller	George	5th U.S. Infantry	10-21-1876 to 04-27-1877	01-08-1877
(0259) Mitchell	John	5th U.S. Infantry	09-09-1874 to 04-23-1875	09-11-1874
(0260) Mitchell	John	8th U.S. Cavalry	07-03-1869	03-03-1870
(0261) Montrose	Charles	5th U.S. Infantry	10-21-1876 to 04-27-1877	01-08-1877
(0262) Moquin	George	5th U.S. Cavalry	09-29-1878 to 01-27-1880	10-05-1879
(0263) Moran	John	8th U.S. Cavalry	08-25-1869	03-03-1870
(0264) Morgan	George	3rd U.S. Cavalry	07-17-1882	07-15-1891
(0265) Moriarity	John	8th U.S. Cavalry	1868 to 1869	09-06-1869
(0266) Morris	James	8th U.S. Cavalry	07-08-1873 to 08-12-1875	07-11-1873
(0267) Morris	William	6th U.S. Cavalry	09-09-1874 to 04-23-1875	09-11-1874
(0268) Mott	John	3rd U.S. Cavalry	05-05-1871	11-13-1874
(0269) Moylan	Myles	7th U.S. Cavalry	09-30-1877	11-27-1894
(0270) Murphy	Edward	1st U.S. Cavalry	10-20-1869	UNKNOWN
(0271) Murphy	Edward	5th U.S. Cavalry	09-29-1879	04-23-1880
(0272) Murphy	Jeremiah	3rd U.S. Cavalry	03-17-1876	10-16-1877
(0273) Murphy	Philip	8th U.S. Cavalry	08-25-1869	03-03-1870
(0274) Murphy	Thomas	8th U.S. Cavalry	08-25-1869	03-03-1870
(0275) Murray	Thomas	7th U.S. Cavalry	06-25-1876	10-05-1876
(0276) Myers	Fred	6th U.S. Cavalry	01-01-1891	02-04-1891
(0277)	Nannasaddie	Indian Scouts	1872 to 1873	04-12-1875
(0279) Neal	Solon	6th U.S. Cavalry	07-12-1870	08-25-1870
(0280) Neder	Adam	7th U.S. Cavalry	Sioux Campaign-December 1890	04-25-1891
(0281) Neilon	Frederick	6th U.S. Cavalry	09-09-1874 to 04-23-1875	09-11-1874
(0282) Newman	Henry	5th U.S. Cavalry	07-13-1872	12-04-1874
(0283) Nihill	John	5th U.S. Cavalry	07-13-1872	12-04-1874
(0284) Nolan	Richard	7th U.S. Cavalry	12-30-1890	04-01-1891

LAST NAME	FIRST	REGIMENT	ACTION	RECEIVED
(0285) O'Callaghan	John	8th U.S. Cavalry	08-1868 to 10-1868	07-24-1869
(0286) Oliver	Francis	1st U.S. Cavalry	10-20-1869	02-14-1870
(0287) O'Neill	William	4th U.S. Cavalry	09-29-1872	11-19-1872
(0288) O'Regan	Michael	8th U.S. Cavalry	08-1868 to 10-1868	07-24-1869
(0289) Orr	Moses	1st U.S. Cavalry	Winter 1872 to 1873	04-12-1875
(0290) Osborne	William	1st U.S. Cavalry	Winter 1872 to 1873	04-12-1875
(0291) O'Sullivan	John	4th U.S. Cavalry	12-08-1874	10-13-1875
(0292) Paine	Adam	Indian Scouts	09-26-1874 to 10-13-1875	09-27-1874
(0293) Parnell	William	1st U.S. Cavalry	06-17-1877	09-16-1897
(0294) Payne	Isaac	Indian Scouts	04-25-1875	05-28-1875
(0295) Pengally	Edward	8th U.S. Cavalry	10-20-1869	02-14-1870
(0296) Pennsyl	Josiah	6th U.S. Cavalry	09-11-1874	04-23-1875
(0297) Phife	Lewis	8th U.S. Cavalry	08-1868 to 10-1868	07-24-1869
(0298) Philipsen	Wilhelm	5th U.S. Cavalry	09-29-1879	12-12-1894
(0299) Phillips	Samuel	2nd U.S. Cavalry	05-07-1877	08-08-1877
(0300) Phoenix	Edwin	4th U.S. Cavalry	09-26-1874 to 10-13-1875	09-27-1874
(0301) Platten	Frederick	6th U.S. Cavalry	04-23-1875	11-16-1876
(0302) Poppe	John	5th U.S. Cavalry	09-29-1879 to 01-27-1880	10-05-1879
(0303) Porter	Samuel	6th U.S. Cavalry	07-12-1870	08-25-1870
(0304) Powers	Thomas	1st U.S. Cavalry	10-20-1869	02-14-1870
(0305) Pratt	James	4th U.S. Cavalry	09-29-1872	11-19-1872
(0306) Pym	James	7th U.S. Cavalry	06-25-1876	10-05-1878
(0307) Raerick	John	8th U.S. Cavalry	10-14-1869	03-03-1870
(0308) Ragnar	Theodore	7th U.S. Cavalry	12-30-1890	04-13-1891
(0309) Rankin	William	4th U.S. Cavalry	09-29-1872	11-19-1872
(0310) Reed	James	8th U.S. Cavalry	04-29-1868	07-24-1869
(0311) Richman	Samuel	8th U.S. Cavalry	1868 to 1869	09-06-1869
(0312) Roach	Hampton	5th U.S. Cavalry	09-29-1879 to 01-27-1880	10-05-1879
(0313) Robbins	Marcus	6th U.S. Cavalry	04-23-1875	11-16-1876
(0314) Robinson	Joseph	3rd U.S. Cavalry	06-17-1876	01-23-1880
(0315) Roche	David	5th U.S. Infantry	10-21-1876 to 04-27-1877	01-08-1877
(0316) Rodenburg	Henry	5th U.S. Infantry	10-21-1876 to 04-27-1877	01-08-1877
(0317) Rogan	Patrick	7th U.S. Infantry	08-09-1877	12-02-1878
(0318) Romeyn	Henry	5th U.S. Infantry	09-30-1877	11-27-1894
(0319) Rooney	Edward	5th U.S. Infantry	10-21-1876 to 04-27-1877	01-08-1877
(0320) Roth	Peter	6th U.S. Cavalry	09-12-1874	11-04-1874
(0321) Rowalt	John	8th U.S. Cavalry	10-14-1869	03-03-1870
(0322)	Rowdy	Indian Scouts	03-07-1890	05-15-1890
(0323) Roy	Stanislaus	7th U.S. Cavalry	06-25-1876	10-05-1878
(0324) Russell	James	1st U.S. Cavalry	10-20-1869	02-14-1870
(0325) Ryan	David	5th U.S. Infantry	10-21-1876 to 04-27-1877	01-08-1877
(0326) Ryan	Dennis	6th U.S. Cavalry	12-02-1874	04-23-1875
(0327) Sale	Albert	8th U.S. Cavalry	06-29-1869	03-03-1870
(0328) Schnitzer	John	4th U.S. Cavalry	04-23-1882	08-17-1896
(0329) Schou	Julius	22nd U.S. Infantry	Sioux Campaign 1870	11-19-1884
(0330) Schroeter	Charles	8th U.S. Cavalry	10-20-1869	02-14-1870
(0331) Scott	George	7th U.S. Cavalry	06-25-1876 to 10-05-1878	06-26-1876
(0332) Scott	Robert	8th U.S. Cavalry	10-20-1869	02-14-1870
(0333) Shaffer	William	8th U.S. Cavalry	08-1868 to 10-1868	07-24-1869
(0334) Sharpless	Edward	6th U.S. Cavalry	09-09-1874 to 04-23-1875	09-11-1874
(0335) Shaw	Thomas	9th U.S. Cavalry	08-12-1881	12-07-1890
(0336) Sheerin	John	8th U.S. Cavalry	07-08-1873 to 08-12-1875	07-11-1873
(0337) Sheppard	Charles	5th U.S. Infantry	10-21-1876 to 04-27-1877	01-08-1877
(0338) Shingle	John	3rd U.S. Cavalry	06-17-1876	06-01-1880
(0339) Skinner	John	Contract Surgeon	01-17-1873	UNKNOWN
(0340) Smith	Andrew	8th U.S. Cavalry	10-20-1869	02-14-1870
(0341) Smith	Charles	6th U.S. Cavalry	07-12-1870	08-25-1870
(0342) Smith	Cornelius	6th U.S. Cavalry	01-01-1891	02-04-1891
(0343) Smith	George	6th U.S. Cavalry	09-12-1874	11-04-1874
(0344) Smith	Otto	8th U.S. Cavalry	1868 to 1869	09-06-1869
(0345) Smith	Robert	3rd U.S. Cavalry	09-09-1876	10-16-1877
(0346) Smith	Theodore	1st U.S. Cavalry	10-20-1869	02-14-1879
(0347) Smith	Thomas	1st U.S. Cavalry	10-20-1869	02-14-1870
(0348) Smith	Thomas	1st U.S. Cavalry	10-20-1869	02-14-1870
(0349) Smith	William	8th U.S. Cavalry	10-20-1869	02-14-1870
(0350) Smith	William	1st U.S. Cavalry	10-20-1869	02-14-1870
(0351) Snow	Elmer	3rd U.S. Cavalry	06-17-1876	10-16-1877
(0352) Spence	Orizoba	8th U.S. Cavalry	10-20-1869	02-14-1870
(0353) Springer	George	1st U.S. Cavalry	10-20-1869	02-14-1870
(0354) Stance	Emanuel	9th U.S. Cavalry	05-20-1870	06-28-1870
(0355) Stanley	Eben	5th U.S. Cavalry	03-25-1873 and 04-12-1875	03-27-1873
(0356) Stanley	Edward	8th U.S. Cavalry	08-26-1869	03-03-1870
(0357) Stauffer	Rudolph	5th U.S. Cavalry	1872	07-30-1875
(0358) Steiner	Christian	8th U.S. Cavalry	10-20-1869	02-14-1870

LAST NAME	FIRST	REGIMENT	ACTION	RECEIVED
(0359) Stewart	Benjamin	7th U.S. Infantry	07-09-1876	12-02-1876
(0360) Stickoffer	Julius	8th U.S. Cavalry	11-11-1868	03-03-1870
(0361) Stivers	Thomas	7th U.S. Cavalry	06-25-1876 to 10-05-1878	06-26-1876
(0362) Stokes	Alonzo	6th U.S. Cavalry	07-12-1870	08-25-1870
(0363) Strayer	William	3rd U.S. Cavalry	04-26-1872	05-22-1872
(0364) Strivson	Benoni	8th U.S. Cavalry	08-1868 to 10-1868	07-24-1869
(0365) Sullivan	Thomas	1st U.S. Cavalry	10-20-1869	02-14-1870
(0366) Sullivan	Thomas	7th U.S. Cavalry	12-29-1890	12-17-1891
(0367) Sumner	James	1st U.S. Cavalry	10-20-1869	02-14-1870
(0368) Sutherland	John	8th U.S. Cavalry	08-1868 to 10-1868	07-24-1869
(0369) Taylor	Bernard	5th U.S. Cavalry	11-01-1874	04-12-1875
(0370) Taylor	Charles	3rd U.S. Cavalry	07-17-1882	12-16-1882
(0371) Taylor	Wilbur	8th U.S. Cavalry	1868 and 1869	09-06-1869
(0372) Tea	Richard	6th U.S. Cavalry	04-23-1875	11-16-1876
(0373) Thomas	Charles	11th Ohio Cavalry	09-17-1865	08-24-1894
(0374) Thompson	George	2nd U.S. Cavalry	05-15-1870	06-22-1870
(0375) Thompson	John	1st U.S. Cavalry	10-20-1869	02-14-1870
(0376) Thompson	Peter	7th U.S. Cavalry	06-25-1876	10-05-1878
(0377) Tilton	Henry	U.S. Army	09-30-1877	03-22-1895
(0378) Tolan	Frank	7th U.S. Cavalry	06-25-1876	10-05-1878
(0379) Toy	Frederick	7th U.S. Cavalry	12-29-1890	05-26-1891
(0380) Tracy	John	8th U.S. Cavalry	10-20-1869	02-14-1870
(0381) Trautman	Jacob	7th U.S. Cavalry	12-29-1890	03-27-1891
(0382) Turpin	James	5th U.S. Cavalry	1872 to 1874	04-12-1875
(0383) Varnum	Charles	7th U.S. Cavalry	12-30-1890	09-22-1897
(0384) Veuve	Ernest	4th U.S. Cavalry	11-03-1874	10-13-1875
(0385) Voit	Otto	7th U.S. Cavalry	06-25-1876	10-05-1878
(0386) Vokes	Leroy	3rd U.S. Cavalry	04-26-1872	05-22-1872
(0387) Von Medem	Rudolph	5th U.S. Cavalry	1872 to 1873	04-12-1875
(0388) Walker	Allen	3rd U.S. Cavalry	12-30-1891	04-25-1892
(0389) Walker	John	8th U.S. Cavalry	09-23-1869	11-23-1869
(0390) Wallace	William	5th U.S. Infantry	10-21-1876 to 04-27-1877	01-08-1877
(0391) Walley	Augustus	9th U.S. Cavalry	08-16-1881	10-01-1890
(0392) Ward	Charles	1st U.S. Cavalry	10-20-1869	02-14-1870
(0393) Ward	James	7th U.S. Cavalry	12-29-1890	04-16-1891
(0394) Ward	John	24th U.S. Infantry	04-25-1875	05-28-1875
(0395) Warrington	Lewis	4th U.S. Cavalry	12-08-1874	04-12-1875
(0396) Watson	James	6th U.S. Cavalry	07-12-1870	08-25-1870
(0397) Watson	Joseph	8th U.S. Cavalry	06-04-1869	03-03-1870
(0398) Weaher	Andrew	8th U.S. Cavalry	08-1868 to 10-1868	07-24-1869
(0399) Weinert	Paul	1st U.S. Artillery	12-29-1890	03-24-1891
(0400) Weiss	Enoch	1st U.S. Cavalry	10-20-1869	02-14-1870
(0401) Welch	Charles	7th U.S. Cavalry	06-25-1876 to 10-05-1878	06-26-1876
(0402) Welch	Michael	6th U.S. Cavalry	10-05-1870	11-19-1870
(0403) West	Frank	6th U.S. Cavalry	07-17-1882	07-12-1892
(0404) Whitehead	Patton	5th U.S. Infantry	10-21-1876 to 04-27-1877	01-08-1877
(0405) Widmer	Jacob	5th U.S. Cavalry	09-29-1879	05-04-1880
(0406) Wilder	Wilber	4th U.S. Cavalry	04-23-1882	08-17-1896
(0407) Wilkens	Henry	2nd U.S. Cavalry	05-07-0877 and 02-28-1878	08-20-1877
(0408) Williams	Moses	9th U.S. Cavalry	08-16-1881	11-12-1896
(0409) Wills	Henry	8th U.S. Cavalry	07-08-1873 to 08-12-1875	07-11-1873
(0410) Wilson	Benjamin	6th U.S. Cavalry	10-05-1870	11-19-1870
(0411) Wilson	Charles	5th U.S. Infantry	10-21-1876 to 04-27-1877	01-08-1877
(0412) Wilson	Milden	7th U.S. Infantry	08-09-1877	12-02-1878
(0413) Wilson	William	4th U.S. Cavalry	03-28-1872	04-27-1872
(0414) Wilson	William	4th U.S. Cavalry	09-29-1872	UNKNOWN
(0415) Wilson	William	9th U.S. Cavalry	Sioux Campaign-1890	09-17-1891
(0416) Windolph	Charles	7th U.S. Cavalry	06-25-1876 to 10-05-1878	06-26-1876
(0417) Windus	Claron	6th U.S. Cavalry	07-12-1870	08-25-1870
(0418) Winterbottom	William	6th U.S. Cavalry	07-12-1870	08-25-1870
(0419) Witcome	Joseph	8th U.S. Cavalry	08-1868 to 10-1868	07-24-1869
(0420) Wood	Leonard	U.S. Army	Apache Campaign-Summer 1886	04-18-1898
(0421) Woodall	Zachariah	6th U.S. Cavalry	09-12-1874	11-07-1874
(0422) Woods	Brent	9th U.S. Cavalry	08-19-1881	07-12-1894
(0423) Wortman	George	8th U.S. Cavalry	08-1868 to 10-1868	07-24-1869
(0424) Yount	John	3rd U.S. Cavalry	05-05-1871	11-13-1871
(0425) Ziegner	Hermann	7th U.S. Cavalry	12-29-1890 to 06-23-1891	12-30-189

APPENDIX C: BREVETS (1865-1898)

	LAST NAME	FIRST	RANK	ACTION	RECEIVED
(0001)	Abbott	Lemuel	Major	07-17-1882	02-27-1890
(0002)	Adam	Emil	Major	09-25-1872	02-27-1890
(0003)	Albee	George	Captain	09-16-1869 to 10-28-1869	02-27-1890
(0004)	Alexander	Charles	Colonel	07-11-1877	02-27-1890
(0005)	Babbitt	Lawrence	Major	07-11-1877	02-27-1890
(0006)	Babcock	John	Lt. Colonel	06-16-1873 to 01-16-1874	02-27-1890
(0007)	Bacon	John	Lt. Colonel	06-07-1869 to 10-28-1869	02-27-1890
(0008)	Bailey	Harry	1st Lieutenant	07-11-1877	02-27-1890
(0009)	Bailey	Hobart	1st Lieutenant	11-08-1874	02-27-1890
(0010)	Baird	George	Captain		02-27-1890
(0011)	Baker	Eugene	Colonel	1866, 1867, 1868	12-01-1868
(0012)	Baldwin	Frank	Captain	08-30-1874 ; 11-08-1874	02-27-1890
(0013)	Baldwin	Frank	Major	12-18-1876 ; 01-08-1877	02-27-1890
(0014)	Bancroft	Eugene	Major	07-11-1877	02-27-1890
(0015)	Bankhead	Henry C.	Brigadier General	09-1868	10-01-1868
(0016)	Barnitz	Albert	Colonel	11-27-1868	11-27-1868
(0017)	Bell	James	Lt. Colonel	09-13-1877	02-27-1890
(0018)	Bendire	Charles	Major	09-13-1877	02-27-1890
(0019)	Benson	Henry	Captain	08-20-1877	02-27-1890
(0020)	Benteen	Frederick	Colonel	08-13-1868	08-13-1868
(0021)	Benteen	Frederick	Brigadier General	06-25-1876 ; 09-13-1877	02-27-1890
(0022)	Bernard	Reuben	Brigadier General	10-20-1869 06-28-1878 07-08-1878	02-27-1890
(0023)	Blocksom	Augustus	1st Lieutenant	05-07-1880	02-27-1890
(0024)	Boehm	Peter M.	Captain	10-28-1869 10-10-1871 09-29-1872	02-27-1890
(0025)	Bomus	Peter	1st Lieutenant	12-13-1872	02-27-1890
(0026)	Bouetelle	Frazier	1st Lieutenant	11-29-1872	02-27-1890
(0027)	Bourke[1]	John	Captain	12-28-1872	02-27-1890
(0028)	Bourke[2]	John	Major	03-17-1876 06-17-1876	02-27-1890
(0029)	Braden	Charles	1st Lieutenant	08-11-1873	02-27-1890
(0030)	Brayton	George	Lt. Colonel	06-25-1875 07-04-1875 01-10-1877 01-30-1877	02-27-1890
(0031)	Brown	William	1st Lieutenant	08-19-1879 08-17-1879 09-25-1879	02-27-1890
(0032)	Bullis	John	Captain	05-18-1873 04-26-1875	02-27-1890
(0033)	Bullis	John	Major	07-30-1876 05-03-1881	02-27-1890
(0034)	Burton	George H.	Major	01-17-1873 07-11-1877	02-27-1890
(0035)	Butler	Edmond	Major	01-08-1877	02-27-1890
(0036)	Carpenter	Louis H.	Colonel	10-18-1868	10-18-1868
(0037)	Carr	Camillo	Major	08-20-1877	02-27-1890
(0038)	Carroll	Henry	Major	09-16-1869 04-07-1880	02-27-1890
(0039)	Carter	Mason	Captain	09-19-1867	10-18-1867
(0040)	Carter	Mason	Major	09-30-1877	02-27-1890
(0041)	Carter	Robert	1st Lieutenant	10-10-1871	02-27-1890
(0042)	Carter	Robert	Captain	05-18-1873	02-27-1890
(0043)	Casey	Edward	1st Lieutenant	05-07-1877	02-27-1890
(0044)	Casey	James	Lt. Colonel	01-08-1877	02-27-1890
(0045)	Chaffee	Adna	Major	03-07-1868	03-07-1868
(0046)	Chaffee	Adna	Lt. Colonel	08-30-1874 07-17-1882	02-27-1890
(0047)	Clarke	Powhatan	1st Lieutenant	05-03-1886	02-27-1890
(0048)	Comba	Richard	Lt. Colonel	08-09-1877	02-27-1890
(0049)	Compton	Charles	Colonel	08-30-1874	02-27-1890
(0050)	Conline	John	Captain	04-07-1880	02-27-1890
(0051)	Converse Jr.	George	1st Lieutenant	07-17-1882	02-27-1890
(0052)	Conway	William	Captain	10-15-1876	02-27-1890
(0053)	Coolidge	Charles	Major	08-09-1877	02-27-1890
(0054)	Coppinger	John	Colonel	1866, 1867, 1868	12-01-1868
(0055)	Cresson	Charles	Lt. Colonel	04-17-1873 08-20-1877	02-27-1890
(0056)	Cruse	Thomas	1st Lieutenant	07-17-1882	02-27-1890
(0057)	Cusack	Patrick	Captain	09-12-1868	09-12-1868
(0058)	Cusack	Patrick	Major	04-07-1880	02-27-1890

[1] Bourke declined his brevet promotion. *Army and Navy Journal*, 26 January 1895.
[2] Bourke declined his brevet promotion. *Army and Navy Journal*, 26 January 1895.

	LAST NAME	FIRST	RANK	ACTION	RECEIVED
(0059)	Davis	Wirt	Lt. Colonel	09-29-1872	02-27-1890
				11-25-1876	
(0060)	Dawson	Byron	Captain	06-07-1869	02-27-1890
				10-28-1869	
(0061)	Day	Mathias	Captain	08-07-1885	02-27-1890
				09-22-1885	
(0062)	DeLany	Hayden	1st Lieutenant	05-01-1868	05-01-1868
(0063)	DeLany	Hayden	Captain	11-25-1876	02-27-1890
(0064)	Dimmick	Eugene	Captain	09-23-1879	02-27-1890
(0065)	Dodge	Francis	Major	09-29-1879	02-27-1890
(0066)	Duncan	Joseph	1st Lieutenant	07-11-1877	02-27-1890
(0067)	Eagan	Charles	Captain	04-17-1873	02-27-1890
(0068)	Ebstein	Frederick	Captain	07-04-1877	02-27-1890
				08-20-1877	
				07-13-1878	
(0069)	Eltonhead	Francis	1st Lieutenant	07-11-1877	02-27-1890
(0070)	Eskridge	Richard	Captain	09-26-1867	09-26-1867
(0071)	Evans	Andrew	Colonel	12-25-1868	12-25-1868
(0072)	Evans	Andrew	Brigadier General	07-17-1882	02-27-1890
(0073)	Ewers	Ezra	Major	01-08-1877	02-27-1890
(0074)	Farrow	Edward	1st Lieutenant	08-19-1879	02-27-1890
				10-08-1879	
(0075)	Fetcher	Robert	Captain	07-11-1877	02-27-1890
				09-13-1877	
(0076)	Forbush	William	1st Lieutenant	10-25-1868	02-27-1890
(0077)	Forsyth	George	Brigadier General	09-17-1868	09-17-1867
(0078)	Fuller	Alfred	1st Lieutenant	05-07-1877	02-27-1890
(0079)	Fuller	Ezra	Captain	09-13-1877	02-27-1890
(0080)	Godfrey	Edward	Major	09-30-1877	02-27-1890
(0081)	Gordon	David S.	Lt. Colonel	05-04-1870	02-27-1890
(0082)	Graham	George	Captain	09-17-1868	09-17-1868
(0083)	Green	John	Colonel	04-30-1869	02-27-1890
(0084)	Green	John	Brigadier General	01-17-1873	02-27-1890
				Modoc War	
(0085)	Guilfoyle	John	1st Lieutenant	07-19-1881	02-27-1890
				07-25-1881	
				08-03-1881	
(0086)	Hall	William	Captain	07-11-1877	02-27-1890
(0087)	Hamilton	John	Major	01-16-1873	02-27-1890
(0088)	Hamilton	Louis	Major	11-27-1868	11-27-1868
(0089)	Hardin	Edward	1st Lieutenant	08-09-1877	02-27-1890
(0090)	Hasbrouck	Henry	Major	05-10-1873	02-27-1890
(0091)	Hasson	Patrick	1st Lieutenant	11-08-1867	02-27-1890
(0092)	Hatfield	Charles	Major	05-16-1886	02-27-1890
(0093)	Haughey	James	Captain	07-11-1877	02-27-1890
(0094)	Hayes	Edward	Captain	10-25-1868	02-27-1890
(0095)	Henry	Guy	Brigadier General	06-17-1876	02-27-1890
(0096)	Heyl	Charles	1st Lieutenant	05-24-1874	02-27-1890
				04-28-1876	
(0097)	Heyl	Edward	Major	06-07-1869	02-27-1890
				09-16-1869	
				09-24-1869	
(0098)	Hooton	Mott	Major	10-15-1876	02-27-1890
(0099)	Howard	Guy	1st Lieutenant	08-20-1877	02-27-1890
(0100)	Hughes	Martin	Captain	04-07-1880	02-27-1890
(0101)	Humphrey	Charles	Captain	07-11-1877	02-27-1890
(0102)	Hunt	James	Lt. Colonel	01-27-1867	01-27-1867
(0103)	Inman	Henry	Lt. Colonel	02-11-1869	02-11-1869
(0104)	Jackson	Allan	Lt. Colonel	08-09-1877	02-27-1890
(0105)	Jackson	James	Lt. Colonel	11-29-1872	02-27-1890
				07-12-1877	
(0106)	Jacobs[3]	Joshua	Captain	08-08-1877	02-27-1890
(0107)	Jocelyn	Stephen	Major	07-11-1877	02-27-1890
(0108)	Kell	William	1st Lieutenant	10-15-1876	02-27-1890
(0109)	Kelly	William	Major	04-05-1868	04-05-1868
(0110)	Ketchum	Hiram	Captain	08-11-1873	02-27-1890
(0111)	King[4]	Charles	Captain	05-21-1874	02-27-1890
(0112)	Kramer	Adam	Major	05-06-1880	02-27-1890
(0113)	Kress	John	Lt. Colonel	07-08-1878	02-27-1890
(0114)	Lafferty	John	Captain	02-15-1867	02-27-1890
				10-20-1869	

---

[3] Jacobs declined his brevet promotion. *Army Register (1901)*, 350.
[4] King declined his brevet promotion. *Army Register (1901)*, 350.

	LAST NAME	FIRST	RANK	ACTION	RECEIVED
(0115)	Latimer	Alfred	Lt. Colonel	09-29-1872	02-27-1890
(0116)	Leary, Jr.	Peter	Captain	04-15-1873	02-27-1890
(0117)	Lewis	Granville	Captain	09-09-1874	02-27-1890
(0118)	Lockwood	Benjamin	Captain	10-15-1876	02-27-1890
(0119)	Lyman	Wyllys	Lt. Colonel	09-11-1874	02-27-1890
(0120)	MacGowan	Alexander	Major	09-01-1881	02-27-1890
(0121)	Madigan	John	Captain	09-27-1867	09-27-1867
(0122)	Manning	William	Captain	12-13-1872	02-27-1890
(0123)	Mason	Edwin	Brigadier General	04-17-1873 07-11-1877	02-27-1890
(0124)	McClernand	Edward	1st Lieutenant	09-30-1877	02-27-1890
(0125)	McDonald[5]	Robert	Captain	01-08-1877	02-27-1890
(0126)	McElderry	Henry	Major	05-07-1869 01-17-1869	02-27-1890
(0127)	McGonnigle	Andrew J.	Colonel	Indian Campaign	02-11-1869
(0128)	McGregor	Thomas	Major	05-06-1873	02-27-1890
(0129)	McLellan	Curwen B.	Lt. Colonel	08-30-1874 04-07-1880	02-27-1890
(0130)	Merrill	Lewis	Brigadier General	09-13-1877	02-27-1890
(0131)	Michler	Francis	1st Lieutenant	09-25-1872 01-22-1873	02-27-1890
(0132)	Miles	Evan	Major	07-11-1877 07-13-1878	02-27-1890
(0133)	Miller	William	1st Lieutenant	04-17-1873	02-27-1890
(0134)	Miller	Marcus	Colonel	04-17-1873 07-11-1877	02-27-1890
(0135)	Mills	Anson	Colonel	09-09-1876	02-27-1890
(0136)	Mills	Stephen	1st Lieutenant	04-07-1880 04-28-1882	02-27-1890
(0137)	Miner	Charles	Major	10-15-1876	02-27-1890
(0138)	Montgomery	Robert H.	Major	09-25-1872	02-27-1890
(0139)	Morgan	George	1st Lieutenant	07-17-1882	02-27-1890
(0140)	Morris	Arthur	Major	07-11-1877	02-27-1890
(0141)	Morton[6]	Charles	1st Lieutenant	06-05-1871	02-27-1890
(0142)	Moylan	Myles	Major	09-30-1877	02-27-1890
(0143)	Nickerson[7]	James	1st Lieutenant	10-15-1876	02-27-1890
(0144)	Norwood	Randolph	Major	05-07-1877 08-20-1877	02-27-1890
(0145)	Nowlan	Henry	Major	09-13-1877	02-27-1890
(0146)	Orleman	Louis	1st Lieutenant	10-18-1868 08-22-1874	02-27-1890
(0147)	Overton	Gilbert	Captain	11-08-1874	02-27-1890
(0148)	Parnell	William	Lt. Colonel	09-26-1867	09-26-1867
(0149)	Parnell	William	Colonel	06-17-1877	02-29-1890
(0150)	Payne	John	Major	09-29-1879	02-29-1890
(0151)	Perry	David	Lt. Colonel	12-26-1866	12-26-1866
(0152)	Perry	David	Colonel	04-05-1868	04-05-1868
(0153)	Pollock	Robert	Major	07-11-1877	02-27-1890
(0154)	Porter	Charles	Major	08-15-1876 01-01-1878 04-03-1878	02-27-1890
(0155)	Powell	James	Lt. Colonel	08-02-1867	08-02-1867
(0156)	Price	William	Colonel	12-10-1868	12-10-1868
(0157)	Rafferty	William	Major	10-05-1870 04-28-1882	02-27-1890
(0158)	Randall	George	Lt. Colonel	03-27-1873 04-22-1873	02-27-1890
(0159)	Randall	George	Colonel	03-08-1874 Arizona 1874	02-27-1890
(0160)	Reynolds	Bainbridge	1st Lieutenant	06-17-1876	02-27-1890
(0161)	Romeyn	Henry	Major	09-30-1877	02-27-1890
(0162)	Royall	William	Brigadier General	06-17-1876	02-27-1890
(0163)	Sanno	James	Major	08-08-1877	02-27-1890
(0164)	Schuyler	Walter	1st Lieutenant	09-25-1872 06-26-1873 04-14-1874 04-28-1874	02-27-1890
(0165)	Schuyler	Walter	Captain	11-25-1876	02-27-1890
(0166)	Sharpe	Alfred	1st Lieutenant	10-15-1876	02-27-1890
(0167)	Shurley	Edmund	Captain	11-04-1867	02-27-1890
(0168)	Sibley	Frederick	1st Lieutenant	07-07-1876	02-27-1890

[5] McDonald declined his brevet promotion. *Army Register (1901)*, 379.
[6] Morton declined his brevet promotion. *Army and Navy Journal*, 26 January 1895.
[7] Nickerson declined his brevet promotion. *Army Register (1901)*, 359.

	LAST NAME	FIRST	RANK	ACTION	RECEIVED
(0169)	Slocum	Herbert	1st Lieutenant	09-13-1877	02-27-1890
(0170)	Small	John	Captain	09-08-1867	09-08-1867
(0171)	Smith	Abiel	Captain	07-1866 to 09-1866	02-27-1890
(0172)	Smith	Oskaloosa	Captain	10-15-1876	02-27-1890
(0173)	Snyder	Simon	Major	09-30-1877	02-27-1890
(0174)	Somerby	Rufus	1st Lieutenant	08-30-1868	08-30-1868
(0175)	Somerby	Rufus	Captain	10-07-1868	10-07-1868
(0176)	Spencer	James	Captain	03-22-1869	02-27-1890
(0177)	Sprole	Henry	Captain	10-14-1874	02-27-1890
				11-29-1874	
(0178)	Stanton	Alexander	Captain	04-05-1868	04-05-1868
(0179)	Stanton	Thadeus	Lt. Colonel	03-17-1876	02-27-1890
(0180)	Sternberg	George	Lt. Colonel	07-12-1877	02-27-1890
(0181)	Stewart	William	Captain	07-11-1877	02-27-1890
(0182)	Sumner	Samuel	Lt. Colonel	07-11-1869	02-27-1890
(0183)	Taylor	Alfred	Major	12-28-1872	02-27-1890
(0184)	Taylor	Charles	1st Lieutenant	04-07-1880	02-27-1890
(0185)	Taylor	Sydney	Captain	1873	02-27-1890
(0186)	Thomas	Earl	1st Lieutenant	06-08-1870	02-27-1890
(0187)	Thomas	Earl	Captain	12-28-1872	02-27-1890
				1874	
(0188)	Thompson	William	Captain	09-27-1874	02-27-1890
				11-05-1874	
(0189)	Tupper	Tullius	Lt. Colonel	08-30-1874	02-27-1890
				04-28-1882	
(0190)	Van Orsdale	John	1st Lieutenant	08-09-1877	02-27-1890
(0191)	Wainwright	Robert	1st Lieutenant	07-13-1878	02-27-1890
(0192)	Walsh	Robert	1st Lieutenant	06-06-1886	02-27-1890
(0193)	Watson	James	Captain	03-07-1890	02-27-1890
(0194)	Wesendorf	Max	Captain	09-30-1872	02-27-1890
(0195)	West	Frank	1st Lieutenant	09-09-1874	02-27-1890
(0196)	Wheelan	James	Major	05-07-1877	02-27-1890
(0197)	Whipple	Stephen	Major	07-11-1877	02-27-1890
(0198)	Wilder	Wilber	Captain	04-23-1882	02-27-1890
(0199)	Wilkinson	Melville	Major	07-11-1877	02-27-1890
				07-13-1877	
(0200)	Wilkinson	John	Captain	09-13-1877	02-27-1890
(0201)	Williams	Charles	1st Lieutenant	07-11-1877	02-27-1890
(0202)	Williams	Constant	Major	08-09-1877	02-27-1890
(0203)	Williams	Ephraim	Captain	09-23-1867	09-23-1867
(0204)	Williams	James	Major	04-16-1867	07-09-1867
				06-14-1867	
				07-09-1867	
(0205)	Wood	Abram	Captain	09-21-1878	02-27-1890
				09-27-1878	
(0206)	Woodbridge	Charles	1st Lieutenant	08-09-1877	02-27-1890
(0207)	Woodruff	Charles	Captain	08-08-1877	02-27-1890
(0208)	Woodruff	Thomas	1st Lieutenant	09-30-1877	02-27-1890
(0209)	Wright	Henry	1st Lieutenant	01-24-1877	02-27-1890
				07-29-1878	
				05-29-1879	
(0210)	Young	Robert H.	1st Lieutenant	03-22-1869	02-27-1890

APPENDIX D: CERTIFICATE OF MERIT (1865-1898)

	LAST NAME	FIRST	RANK	ACTION	RECEIVED
(0001)	Angel	Jeremiah	Private	6th U.S. Cavalry	04-28-1882
(0002)	Arrington	George	Private	24th U.S. Infantry	05-11-1889
(0003)	Bannon	Andrew	Corporal	3rd U.S. Artillery	08-12-1892
(0004)	Bell	Frank	Private	7th U.S. Cavalry	11-03-1893
(0005)	Bell	James	Private	7th U.S. Infantry	07-09-1876
(0006)	Bell	James	Sergeant	7th U.S. Infantry	08-09-1877
(0007)	Benson	John	Private	2nd U.S. Infantry	07-29-1879
(0008)	Brennan	John	Private	3rd U.S. Cavalry	09-29-1879
(0009)	Bresnahan	Maurice	Private	3rd U.S. Cavalry	01-13-1877
(0010)	Bundy	Thomas	Private	7th U.S. Cavalry	08-09-1877
(0011)	Burge	Benjamin	Private	24th U.S. Infantry	05-11-1889
(0012)	Capron	Harry	Corporal	7th U.S. Cavalry	12-29-1890
(0013)	Carpenter	Clarence	Private	5th U.S. Cavalry	09-29-1879
(0014)	Clark	Charles	Private	5th U.S. Cavalry	09-29-1879
(0015)	Clarke	Henry	Private	3rd U.S. Cavalry	08-12-1892
(0016)	Cleary	Patrick	Private	2nd U.S. Cavalry	08-07-1880
(0017)	Coghlan	John	Private	4th U.S. Cavalry	05-15-1886
(0018)	Combs	Kenrick	Private	5th U.S. Cavalry	09-29-1879
(0019)	Costner	Richard	Private	Hospital Corps	12-30-1890
(0020)	Crowley	John	Private	3rd U.S. Cavalry	09-29-1879
(0021)	Donley	Elwood	Blacksmith	3rd U.S. Cavalry	08-12-1890
(0022)	Donnelly	James	Private	18th U.S. Infantry	03-31-1892
(0023)	Drennan	Daniel	Private	General Service	1870 and 1871
(0024)	DuBois	William	Private	3rd U.S. Cavalry	09-09-1876
(0025)	Eakle	Samuel	Private	5th U.S. Cavalry	09-29-1879
(0026)	Fellman	Nathan	Private	7th U.S. Cavalry	12-29-1890
(0027)	Foley	Timothy	Private	6th U.S. Cavalry	07-17-1882
(0028)	Gannon	Michael	Sergeant	3rd U.S. Artillery	08-12-1892
(0029)	Garvean	William	Private	21st U.S. Infantry	07-11-1877
(0030)	Girdwood	William	Private	Hospital Corps	12-30-1890
(0031)	Grover	Sylvester	Private	4th U.S. Cavalry	10-10-1885
(0032)	Hagerman	Samuel	Private	4th U.S. Infantry	09-29-1879
(0033)	Hale	John	Private	3rd U.S. Cavalry	09-09-1876
(0034)	Hams	Thornton	Private	10th U.S. Cavalry	05-11-1889
(0035)	Harrington	John	Private	6th U.S. Cavalry	09-12-1874
(0036)	Harrison	Julius	Private	24th U.S. Infantry	05-11-1889
(0037)	Hoffman	Oskar	Musician	23rd U.S. Infantry	08-12-1892
(0038)	Hogan	Thomas	Private	3rd U.S. Cavalry	09-29-1879
(0039)	Hubbard	John	Private	6th U.S. Cavalry	04-28-1882
(0040)	Johnson	Oliver	Private	7th U.S. Infantry	08-09-1877
(0041)	Jordan	George	Sergeant	9th U.S. Cavalry	08-12-1881
(0042)	Kaine	Patrick	First Sergeant	3rd U.S. Infantry	06-16-1893
(0043)	Klingensmith	Samuel	Private	5th U.S. Cavalry	09-29-1879
(0044)	Lawrence	Samuel	Private	6th U.S. Cavalry	04-02-1882
(0045)	LeMay	William	Private	4th U.S. Artillery	07-11-1877
(0046)	Lewis	Hamilton	Private	24th U.S. Infantry	05-11-1889
(0047)	Lewis	Thomas	Private	3rd U.S. Cavalry	09-29-1879
(0048)	Long	John	Artificer	3rd U.S. Artillery	08-12-1892
(0049)	Lynch	Edward	Private	6th U.S. Cavalry	04-28-1882
(0050)	Madison	Ingoman	Sergeant	9th U.S. Cavalry	01-23-1881
(0051)	Magerlein	Marcus	Private	3rd U.S. Cavalry	01-22-1879
(0052)	Mahoney	John	Private	3rd U.S. Cavalry	09-29-1879
(0053)	Maloney	John	Private	3rd U.S. Cavalry	09-29-1879
(0054)	Martin	John	Blacksmith	6th U.S. Cavalry	08-30-1881
(0055)	McDonald	John	Private	5th U.S. Cavalry	09-29-1879
(0056)	McKiernan	Edward	Private	3rd U.S. Cavalry	09-09-1876
(0057)	McNamara	Thomas	Private	3rd U.S. Cavalry	09-29-1879
(0058)	Moloney	John	Private	22nd U.S. Infantry	10-14-1876
(0059)	Mullica	James	Private	6th U.S. Cavalry	07-17-1882
(0060)	Murray	William	Corporal	3rd U.S. Artillery	08-12-1892
(0061)	Nihill	John	Private	5th U.S. Cavalry	07-13-1872
(0062)	Nowlin	Newcomb	Private	23rd U.S. Infantry	08-12-1892
(0063)	Patterson	Eugene	Private	5th U.S. Cavalry	09-29-1879
(0064)	Patterson	Joseph	Private	3rd U.S. Cavalry	09-29-1879
(0065)	Quinn	James	Private	3rd U.S. Cavalry	09-08-1876
(0066)	Rogers	John	Trumpeter	9th U.S. Cavalry	08-16-1881
(0067)	Ryan	Thomas	Private	4th U.S. Cavalry	11-25-1876
(0068)	Schnitzer	John	Private	4th U.S. Cavalry	06-08-1885
(0069)	Schwarz	Adolphus	Private	3rd U.S. Cavalry	04-22-1896
(0070)	Settlers	James	Private	9th U.S. Cavalry	07-19-1889
(0071)	Sudsburger	Joseph	Private	4th U.S. Cavalry	09-27-1878
(0072)	Sullivan	Timothy	Private	7th U.S. Cavalry	09-17-1887
(0073)	Taggert	James	Private	3rd U.S. Cavalry	01-13-1877
(0074)	Taylor	John	Private	3rd U.S. Cavalry	09-09-1876
(0075)	Trittle	John	Sergeant	7th U.S. Cavalry	12-29-1890
(0076)	Tschan	Paul	Private	21st U.S. Infantry	07-11-1877
(0077)	Volkmar	Walter	Sergeant	Signal Corps	03-15-1898
(0078)	Watts	George	Private	2nd U.S. Cavalry	07-06-1876
(0079)	Wheeler	James	Private	10th U.S. Cavalry	05-11-1889
(0080)	Williams	Squire	Private	24th U.S. Infantry	05-11-1889
(0081)	Witt	John	Private	6th U.S. Cavalry	07-17-1882
(0082)	Woodall	Zachariah	Sergeant	6th U.S. Cavalry	09-12-1874
(0083)	Young	James	Private	24th U.S. Infantry	05-11-1889
(0084)	Young	John	Sergeant Major	3rd U.S. Infantry	11-19-1896

> *"It is a wonderful consolation that each…*
> *met a soldier's death in defense of the government and laws of their country.*
> *Of the men in the ranks who were killed or wounded,*
> *it is perhaps sufficient to say they proved their bravery with their blood…."* [1]

BIBLIOGRAPHY

Registers of Deaths, Regular Army, 1860-1889 (Entry 643). Record Group 94, Records of the Adjutant General's Office, 18 Volumes. National Archives and Records Administration, Washington, D.C.

Reports of Diseases and Individual Cases "File F", 1861-1889 (Entry 624). Record Group 94, Records of the Adjutant General's Office. National Archives and Records Administration, Washington, D.C.

Reports of Diseases and Individual Cases "SSD File", 1861-1888 (Entry 627). Record Group 94, Records of the Adjutant General's Office. National Archives and Records Administration, Washington, D.C.

Reports of Diseases and Individual Cases Special Reports on Individual Soldiers 1871-1886 (Entry 631). Record Group 94, Records of the Adjutant General's Office. National Archives and Records Administration, Washington, D.C.

ARCHIVAL — MICROFILM

Burial Registers for Military Posts, Camps and Stations, 1768-1921. Microfilm (M2014), Compiled by Claire Prechtel-Kluskens, National Archives and Records Administration, Washington, D.C. 1996.

Reports and Correspondence Relating to the Army Investigations of the Battle of Wounded Knee and to the Sioux Campaign, 1890-1891. Microfilm (M983), National Archives and Records Administration, Washington D.C.

Returns of U.S. Army Posts, 1865-1898. Microfilm (M617), National Archives and Records Administration, Washington D.C.

U.S. Army Regimental Monthly Returns — Artillery, 1865-1898. Microfilm (M727), National Archives and Records Administration, Washington D.C.

U.S. Army Regimental Monthly Returns — Cavalry, 1865-1898. Microfilm (M744), National Archives and Records Administration, Washington D.C.

U.S. Army Regimental Monthly Returns — Infantry, 1865-1898. Microfilm (M665), National Archives and Records Administration, Washington D.C.

GOVERNMENT PUBLICATIONS

Annual Report of the Commissioner of Indian Affairs to the Secretary of the Interior, 1865-1898. Washington, D.C.: Government Printing Office.

Annual Report of the Secretary of War, 1865-1898. Washington, D.C.: Government Printing Office.

Heitman, Francis B. *Historical Register and Dictionary of the United States Army, From Its Organization, September 29, 1789, to March 2, 1903* (2 Volumes). Washington, D.C.: Government Printing Office, 1903.

Official Army Register of the Volunteer Force of the United States Army for the Years 1861, 62, 63, 64, 65 (8 Volumes). Washington, D.C.: Government Printing Office, 1867.

Official Army Register for 1901. Washington, D.C.: Adjutant General's Office, 1900.

Otis, George A. *A Report of Surgical Cases Treated in the Army of the United States from 1865 to 1871.* Washington DC: War Department Surgeon General's Office, 1871.

Reports of the Committees of the Senate of the United States for the Second Session Thirty-Ninth Congress, 1866-67. Washington, D.C.: Government Printing Office, 1867.

War of the Rebellion: a Compilation of the Official Records of the Union and Confederate Armies. Washington, D.C.: Government Printing Office, 1880-1901.

BOOKS

Adams, Gerald M. *The Post Near Cheyenne: A History of Fort D.A. Russell, 1867-1930.* Boulder, Colorado: Pruett Publishing Co., 1989.

Aleshire, Peter. *Reaping the Whirlwind: The Apache Wars.* New York, New York: Facts on File, Inc, 1998.

Alexander, David V. *Arizona Frontier Military Place Names, 1846-1912.* Las Cruces, New Mexico: Yucca Tree Press, 1998.

Allred, B.W. *Great Western Indian Fights.* Garden City, New York: Doubleday, 1960.

Altshuler, Constance W. *Cavalry Yellow and Infantry Blue: Army Officers in Arizona Between 1851 and 1886.* Tucson, Arizona: Arizona Historical Society, 1991.

Altshuler, Constance W. *Chains of Command: Arizona and the Army, 1856-1875.* Tucson, Arizona: Arizona Historical Society, 1981.

Altshuler, Constance W. *Starting with Defiance: Nineteenth Century Arizona Military Posts.* Tucson, Arizona: Arizona Historical Society, 1983.

Armes, George A. *Ups and Downs of an Army Officer.* Washington, D.C., 1900.

Arnold, R. Ross. *Indian Wars of Idaho.* Caldwell, Idaho: Caxton Printers, Ltd., 1932.

Athearn, Robert, G. *William Tecumseh Sherman and the Settlement of the West.* Norman, Oklahoma: University of Oklahoma Press, 1956.

Ayling, Augustus D. *Revised Register of the Soldiers and Sailors in New Hampshire in the War of the Rebellion, 1861-1866.* Concord, New Hampshire: Ira C. Evans, Public Printer, 1895.

Ball, Larry D. *Ambush at Bloody Run: The Wham Paymaster Robbery of 1889.* Tucson, Arizona: Arizona Historical Society, 2000.

Barnett, Louise. *Touched by Fire: The Life, Death, and Mythic Afterlife of George Armstrong Custer.* New York, New York: Henry Holt and Company, 1996.

Barnitz, Albert. *Life in Custer's Cavalry: Diaries and Letters of Albert and Jennie Barnitz, 1867-1868.* New Haven Connecticut: Yale University Press, 1977.

Billington, Monroe L. *New Mexico's Buffalo Soldiers 1866-1900.* Niwot, Colorado: University Press of Colorado, 1991.

Bourke, John G. *Apache Campaign in the Sierra Madre: An Account of the Expedition in Pursuit of the Hostile Chiricahua Apaches in the Spring of 1883.* Lincoln, Nebraska: University of Nebraska Press, 1987.

Bourke, John G. *Mackenzie's Last Fight with the Cheyennes: A Winter Campaign in Wyoming and Montana.* New York, New York: Argonaut Press Ltd., 1966.

Bradley, James H. *The March of the Montana Column.* Norman, Oklahoma: University of Oklahoma Press, 1961.

Brennan, Irene J. *Fort Mojave, 1859-1890: Letters of the Commanding Officers.* Manhattan, Kansas: MA/AH Publishing, Kansas State University, 1980.

Brimlow, George F. *The Bannock Indian War of 1878.* Caldwell, Idaho: Caxton, 1938.

Brimlow, George F. *Cavalryman out of the West: The Life of William Carey Brown.* Caldwell, Idaho: Caxton, 1944.

Broome, Jeff. *Dog Soldier Justice: The Ordeal of Susanna Alderdice in the Kansas Indian War.* Lincoln, Kansas: Lincoln County Historical Society, 2003.

Brown, Dee A. *Fort Phil Kearny: An American Saga.* New York, New York: G.P. Putnam's Sons, 1962.

---

[1] *San Francisco Daily Evening Bulletin,* 29 April 1873.

Brown, Dee A. *The Galvanized Yankees.* Urbana, Illinois: University of Illinois Press, 1963.

Brown, Mark H. *The Flight of the Nez Perce.* Lincoln, Nebraska: University of Nebraska Press, 1967.

Brown, Mark H. *The Plainsmen of the Yellowstone: A History of the Yellowstone Basin.* New York, New York: G.P. Putnam's Sons, 1961.

Buecker, Thomas R. *Fort Robinson and the American West, 1874-1899.*

Burton, Art T. *Black, Buckskin, and Blue: African American Scouts and Soldiers on the Western Frontier.* Austin, Texas: Eakin Press, 1999.

Butts, Michele T. *Galvanized Yankees on the Upper Missouri: The Face of Loyalty.* Boulder, Colorado: University Press of Colorado, 2003.

Carlson, Paul H. *"Pecos Bill": A Military Biography of William R. Shafter.* College Station, Texas: Texas A&M University Press, 1989.

Carranco, Lynnwood and Estle Beard. *Genocide and Vendetta: The Round Valley Wars of Northern California.* Norman, Oklahoma: University of Oklahoma Press, 1981.

Carriker, Robert C. *Fort Supply, Indian Territory: Frontier Outpost on the Plains.* Norman, Oklahoma: University of Oklahoma Press, 1970.

Carrington, Margaret I. *Absaraka: Home of the Crows Being the Experience of an Officer's Wife on the Plains.* Philadelphia, Pennsylvania: J.B. Lippincott and Co., 1868. Reprint, Lincoln, Nebraska: University of Nebraska Press, 1983.

Carter, R.G. *On the Border with Mackenzie or Winning West Texas From the Comanches.* New York, 1935. Reprint, New York, New York: Antiquarian Press, Ltd., 1961.

Carter, W.H. *From Yorktown to Santiago with the Sixth U.S. Cavalry.* Austin Texas, Statehouse Press, 1989.

Casebier, Dennis G. *The Battle of Camp Cady, Tales of the Mojave Road No. 2.* Norco, California: The King's Press, 1972.

Cashin, Herschel V. *Under Fire with the Tenth U.S. Cavalry.* Niwot, Colorado: University Press of Colorado, 1993.

Cashion, Ty. *A Texas Frontier: The Clear Fork Country and Fort Griffin, 1849-1887.* Norman, Oklahoma: University of Oklahoma Press, 1996.

Chalfant, William Y. *Cheyennes at Dark Water Creek: The Last Fight of the Red River War.* Norman, Oklahoma: University of Oklahoma Press, 1997.

Chalfant, William Y. *Hancock's War: Conflict on the Southern Plains.* Norman, Oklahoma: Arthur H. Clark Company, 2010.

Chalfant, William Y. *Without Quarter: The Wichita Expedition and the Fight on Crooked Creek.* Norman, Oklahoma: University of Oklahoma Press, 1991.

Chandler, Melbourne C. *Of Garryowen in Glory: The History of the 7th U.S. Cavalry.* Annandale, Virginia: Turnpike Press, 1960.

Collins, Charles. *Apache Nightmare: The Battle at Cibecue Creek.* Norman, Oklahoma: University of Oklahoma Press, 1999.

Counties of LaGrange and Noble, Indiana: Historical and Biographical. Chicago, Illinois: F.A. Battey & Co., 1882.

Cozzens, Peter. *Eyewitness to the Indian Wars, 1865-1890 (5 Volumes).* Mechanicsburg, Pennsylvania: Stackpole Books, 2003.

Crawford, Samuel J. *Kansas in the Sixties.* Chicago, Illinois: A.C. McClurg & Co., 1911.

Criqui, Orvel A. *Fifty Fearless Men: The Forsyth Scouts and Beecher Island.* Marceline, Missouri: Walsworth Publishing Company, 1993.

Cruse, J. Brett. *Battles of the Red River War: Archeological Perspectives on the Indian Campaign of 1874.* College Station, Texas: Texas A&M University Press, 2008.

Cruse, Thomas. *Apache Days and After.* Caldwell, Idaho: Caxton Press, Ltd., 1941.

Cullum, George W. *Biographical Register of the Officers and Graduates of the U.S. Military Academy at West Point, N.Y., from its Establishment, March 16, 1802, to the Army Reorganization of 1866-67 (2 Volumes).* New York, New York: D. Van Nostrand, 1868.

Cullum, George W. *Biographical Register of the Officers and Graduates of the U.S. Military Academy, from 1802 to 1867, Revised Edition, with a Supplement Continuing the Register of Graduates to January 1, 1879 (Volume 3).* New York, New York: James Miller, Publisher, 1879.

Cullum, George W. *Biographical Register of the Officers and Graduates of the U.S. Military Academy at West Point, New York Since its Establishment in 1802 (Volume 4).* Cambridge, Massachusetts: The Riverside Press, 1901.

Dary, David. *The Santa Fe Trail: Its History, Legends, and Lore.* New York, New York: Alfred A. Knopf, 2000.

Davis, Britton. *The Truth About Geronimo.* New Haven, Connecticut: Yale University Press, 1929. Reprint, Lincoln, Nebraska: University of Nebraska Press, 1976.

Dawson, Joseph G. *The Late 19th Century U.S. Army, 1865-1898: Research Guides in Military Studies, Number 3.* New York, New York: Greenwood Press, 1990.

Day, Carl F. *Tom Custer: Ride to Glory.* Spokane, Washington: Arthur H. Clark Company, 2002.

Dillon, Richard. *Burnt-Out Fires.* Englewood Cliffs, New Jersey: Prentice-Hall, Inc., 1973.

Di Silvestro, Roger L. *In the Shadow of Wounded Knee: The Untold Final Chapter of the Indian Wars.*

Dixon, David. *Hero of Beecher Island: The Life and Military Career of George A. Forsyth.* Lincoln, Nebraska: University of Nebraska Press, 1994.

Dobak, William A. and Thomas D. Phillips. *The Black Regulars, 1866-1898.* Norman, Oklahoma: University of Oklahoma Press, 2001.

Donovan, James. *A Terrible Glory: Custer and the Little Bighorn, the Last Great Battle of the American West.* New York, New York: Little, Brown and Company, 2008.

Downey, Fairfax. *Indian-Fighting Army.* New York, New York: Scribner, 1941.

Dunlay, Thomas W. *Wolves for the Blue Soldiers: Indian Scouts and Auxiliaries with the United States Army, 1860-1890.* Lincoln, Nebraska: University of Nebraska Press, 1982.

Ege, Robert J. *"Tell Baker to Strike Them Hard!": Incident on the Marias, 23 January 1870.* Bellevue, Nebraska: Old Army Press, 1970.

Emmett, Chris. *Fort Union and the Winning of the Southwest.* Norman, Oklahoma: University of Oklahoma Press, 1965.

Emmitt, Robert. *The Last War Trail: The Utes and the Settlement of Colorado.* Norman, Oklahoma: University of Oklahoma Press, 1954.

Farish, Thomas E. *History of Arizona (8 Volumes).* San Francisco, California: Filmer Brothers Electrotype Co., 1916.

Faulk, Odie B. *Crimson Desert: Indian Wars of the American Southwest.* New York, New York: Oxford University Press, 1974.

Faulk, Odie B. *The Geronimo Campaign.* New York, New York: Oxford University Press, 1969.

Fougera, Katherine G. *With Custer's Cavalry.* Caldwell, Idaho: The Caxton Printers, Ltd., 1940.

Fowler, Arlen L. *The Black Infantry in the West, 1869-1891.* Westport, Connecticut: Greenwood publishing Corporation- A Negro Universities Press, Publication, 1971.

Frink, Maurice. *Fort Defiance and the Navajos.* Boulder, Colorado: Pruett Press, 1968.

Frost, Lawrence A. *Custer's 7th Cav and the Campaign of 1873.* El Segundo, California: Upton and Sons Publishers, 1986.

Gatewood, Charles and Kraft, Louis. *Lt. Charles Gatewood and His Apache Wars Memoir.* Lincoln, Nebraska: University of Nebraska Press, 2005.

Glass, E.L.N. *The History of the Tenth Cavalry.* Fort Collins, Colorado: The Old Army Press, 1972.

Glassley, Ray H. *Indian Wars of the Pacific Northwest.* Portland, Oregon: Binfords & Mort, Publishers, 1953.

Gleim, Albert F. *The Certificate of Merit: U.S. Army Distinguished Service Award, 1847-1918.* Arlington, Virginia, 1979.

Goodrich, Thomas. *Scalp Dance: Indian Warfare on the High Plains, 1865-1879.* Mechanicsburg, Pennsylvania: Stackpole Books, 1997.

Gottfredson, Peter. *History of Indian Depredations in Utah.* Salt Lake City, Utah: Skelton Publishing Co., 1919.

Gray, John S. *Centennial Campaign: The Sioux War of 1876.* Norman, Oklahoma: University of Oklahoma Press, 1988.

Gray, John S. *Custer's Last Campaign: Mitch Boyer and the Little Bighorn Reconstructed.* Lincoln, Nebraska: University of Nebraska Press, 1991.

Greene, Jerome A. *Battles and Skirmishes of the Great Sioux War, 1876-1877.* Norman, Oklahoma: University of Oklahoma Press, 1993.

Greene, Jerome A. *Morning Star Dawn: The Powder River Expedition and the Northern Cheyennes, 1876.* Norman, Oklahoma: University of Oklahoma Press, 2003.

Greene, Jerome A. *Nez Perce Summer, 1877: The U.S. Army and the Nee-Me-Poo Crisis.* Helena, Montana: Montana Historical Society Press, 2000.

Greene, Jerome A. *Slim Buttes, 1876: An Episode of the Great Sioux War.* Norman, Oklahoma: University of Oklahoma Press, 1982.

Greene, Jerome A. *Washita: The U.S. Army and the Southern Cheyennes, 1867-1869.* Norman, Oklahoma: University of Oklahoma Press, 2004.

Greene, Jerome A. *Yellowstone Command: Colonel Nelson A. Miles and the Great Sioux War, 1876-1877.* Norman, Oklahoma: University of Oklahoma Press, 2006.

Griffith, A. Kinney. *Mickey Free, Manhunter.* Caldwell, Idaho: The Caxton Printers, Ltd., 1969.

Grinnell, George B. *The Fighting Cheyennes.* Norman, Oklahoma: University of Oklahoma Press, 1915.

Grinnell, George B. *Two Great Scouts and Their Pawnee Battalion: The Experiences of Frank J. North and Luther H. North, Pioneers in the Great West, 1856-1882, and Their Defense of the Building of the Union Pacific Railroad.* Spokane, Washington: Arthur H. Clark Company, 1928. Reprint, Lincoln, Nebraska: University of Nebraska Press, 1973.

Guinn, Jeff. *Our Land Before We Die: The Proud Story of the Seminole Negro.* New York, New York: Penguin Group, 2002.

Gwynne, S.C. *Empire of the Summer Moon: Quanah Parker and the Rise and Fall of the Comanches, the Most Powerful Indian Tribe in American History.* New York, New York: Scribner, 2010.

Hafen, Leroy R. and Ann W. Hafen. *Powder River Campaigns and Sawyers Expedition of 1865: A Documentary Account Comprising Official Reports, Diaries, Contemporary Newspaper Accounts, and Personal Narratives.* Glendale, California: The Arthur H. Clark Company, 1961.

Hagan, Barry J. *Exactly in the Right Place: A History of Fort C.F. Smith, Montana Territory, 1866-1868.* El Segundo, California: Upton and Sons, Publishers, 1999.

Haines, Aubrey L. *The Battle of the Big Hole: The Story of the Landmark Battle of the 1877 Nez Perce War.* Guilford, Connecticut: The Globe Pequot Press, 2007.

Hamilton, Allen L. *Sentinel of the Southern Plains: Fort Richardson and the Northwest Texas Frontier, 1866-1878.* Fort Worth, Texas: Texas Christian University Press, 1988.

Hardorff, Richard G. *Washita Memories: Eyewitness Views of Custer's Attack on Black Kettle's Village.* Norman, Oklahoma: University of Oklahoma Press, 2006.

Hathaway, Edward E. *The War Nobody Won: The Modoc War from the Army's Point of View.* Show Low, Arizona: American Eagle Publications , Inc., 1998.

Hayes, Jess G. *Apache Vengeance.* Albuquerque, New Mexico: University of New Mexico Press, 1954.

Hebard, Grace R. and Brininstool, E.A. *The Bozeman Trail: Historical Accounts of the Blazing of the Overland Routes into the Northwest and the Fights with Red Cloud's Warriors (2 Volumes).* Cleveland, Ohio: The Arthur H. Clark Company, 1922.

Hedren, Paul L. *Fort Laramie in 1876: Chronicle of a Frontier Post at War.* Lincoln, Nebraska: University of Nebraska Press, 1988.

Hedren, Paul L. *Great Sioux War Orders of Battle: How the United States Army Waged War on the Northern Plains, 1876-1877.* Norman, Oklahoma: The Arthur H, Clark Company, 2011.

Heyman, Max L., Jr. *Prudent Soldier: A Biography of Major General E.R.S. Canby, 1817-1873.* Glendale, California: The Arthur H. Clark Company, 1959.

Hoig, Stan. *Fort Reno and the Indian Territory Frontier.* Fayetteville, Arkansas: University of Arkansas Press, 2000.

Hoig, Stan. *Perilous Pursuit: The U.S. Cavalry and the Northern Cheyennes.* Boulder, Colorado: University Press of Colorado, 2002.

Hoig, Stan. *Tribal Wars of the Southern Plains.* Norman, Oklahoma: University of Oklahoma Press, 1993.

Howard, Oliver O. *My Life and Experiences Among Our Hostile Indians: A Record of Personal Observations, Adventures, and Campaigns Among the Indians of the Great West with Some Account of Their Life, Habits, Traits, Religion, Ceremonies, Dress, Savage Instincts, and Customs in Peace and War.* Hartford, Connecticut: A.T. Worthington and Co., 1907. Reprint, New York, New York: Da Capo Press Inc., 1972.

Howe, Elizabeth M. *Frontiersmen.* Cambridge, Massachusetts: Harvard University Press, 1931.

Hunt, Aurora. *The Army of the Pacific: Its Operations in California, Texas, Arizona, New Mexico, Utah, Nevada, Oregon, Washington, Plains Region, Mexico, etc., 1860-1866.* Glendale, California: Arthur H. Clark Company, 1951.

Hunt, Jeffrey W. *The Last Battle of the Civil War.* Austin, Texas: University of Texas Press, 2002.

Hutton, Paul A. *Phil Sheridan and His Army.* Lincoln, Nebraska: University of Nebraska Press, 1985.

Jackson, Donald. *Custer's Gold: The United States Cavalry Expedition of 1874.* New Haven, Connecticut: Yale University Press, 1966.

Johnson, Dorothy M. *The Bloody Bozeman: The Perilous Trail to Montana's Gold.* New York, New York: McGraw-Hill Book Company, 1971.

Johnson, Randy and Nancy Allan. *A Dispatch to Custer: The Tragedy of Lieutenant Kidder.* Missoula, Montana: Mountain Press Publishing Company, 1999.

Keleher, William A. *Turmoil in New Mexico, 1846-1868.* Santa Fe, New Mexico: The Rydal Press, 1952.

Kennedy, W.J.D. *On the Plains with Custer and Hancock: The Journal of Isaac Coates, Army Surgeon.* Boulder, Colorado: Johnson Printing, 1997.

King, James T. *War Eagle: A Life of General Eugene A. Carr.* Lincoln, Nebraska: University of Nebraska Press, 1963.

Kirshner, Ralph. *The Class of 1861: Custer, Ames, and Their Classmates after West Point.* Carbondale, Illinois: Southern Illinois University Press, 1999.

Lang, George; Collins, Raymond L.; White, Gerard F. *Medal of Honor Recipients, 1863-1994 (2 Volumes).* New York, New York: Facts on File, Inc, 1995.

Leckie, William H. *The Buffalo Soldiers: A Narrative of the Negro Cavalry in the West.* Norman, Oklahoma: University of Oklahoma Press, 1967.

Leckie, William H. *The Military Conquest of the Southern Plains.* Norman, Oklahoma: University of Oklahoma Press, 1963.

Leckie, William H. and Shirley A. Leckie. *Unlikely Warriors: General Benjamin Grierson and His Family.* Norman, Oklahoma: University of Oklahoma Press, 1984.

Lee, Robert. *Fort Meade and the Black Hills.* Lincoln, Nebraska: University of Nebraska Press, 1991.

Lekson, Stephen H. *Nana's Raid: Apache Warfare in Southern New Mexico, 1881.* El Paso, Texas: Texas Western Press, 1987.

Lindmier, Tom. *Drybone: A History of Fort Fetterman, Wyoming.* Glendo, Wyoming: High Plains Press, 2002.

Lockwood, Frank C. *The Apache Indians.* New York, New York: Macmillan Publishing, 1938. REPRINT Lincoln, Nebraska: University of Nebraska Press, 1987.

Ludwig, Larry L. and Stute, James L. *The Battle of K-H Butte: Apache Outbreak - 1881: Arizona Territory.* Tucson, Arizona: Westernlore Press, 1993.

Lubetkin, M. John. *Jay Cooke's Gamble: The Northern Pacific Railroad, the Sioux and the Panic of 1873.* Norman, Oklahoma: University of Oklahoma Press, 2006.

Mackintosh, John D. *Custer's Southern Officer: Captain George D. Wallace, 7th U.S. Cavalry.* Lexington, South Carolina: Cloud Creek Press, 2002.

Maddux, Albert G. and Vernon R. Maddux. *In Dull Knife's Wake: The True Story of the Northern Cheyenne Exodus of 1878.* Norman, Oklahoma: Horse Creek Publications, Inc., 2003.

Mangum, Neil C. *Battle of the Rosebud: Prelude to the Little Bighorn.* El Segundo, California: Upton and Sons, 1987.

McChristian, Douglas C. *Fort Bowie, Arizona: Combat Post of the Southwest, 1858-1894.* Norman, Oklahoma: University of Oklahoma Press, 2005.

McChristian, Douglas C. *Fort Laramie: Military Bastion of the High Plains.* Norman Oklahoma: Arthur H. Clark Company, 2008.

McConnell, H.H. *Five Years a Cavalryman; Or Sketches of Regular Army Life on the Texas Frontier, 1866-1871.* Jacksboro, Texas: J.N. Rogers and Company, 1889. REPRINT Norman, Oklahoma: University of Oklahoma Press, 1996

McDermott, John D. *Circle of Fire: The Indian War of 1865.* Mechanicsburg, Pennsylvania: Stackpole Books, 2003.

McDermott, John D. *Forlorn Hope: The Battle of White Bird Canyon and the Beginning of the Nez Perce War.* Boise, Idaho: Idaho State Historical Society, 1978.

McDermott, John D. *General George Crook's 1876 Campaigns.* Sheridan, Wyoming: Frontier Heritage Alliance, 2000.

McDermott, John D. *Red Cloud's War: The Bozeman Trail, 1866-1868 (2 Volumes).*

Michno, Gregory F. and Susan J. *A Fate Worse Than Death: Indian Captivities in the West, 1830-1885.* Caldwell, Idaho: Caxton Press, 2007.

Michno, Gregory F. And Susan J. Michno. *Circle the Wagons! Attacks on Wagon Trains in History and Hollywood Films.* Jefferson, North Carolina: McFarland & Company, Inc., Publishers, 2009.

Michno, Gregory F. *Encyclopedia of Indian Wars: Western Battles and Skirmishes, 1850 - 1890.* Missoula, Montana: Mountain Press Publishing Company, 2003.

Miles, Nelson A. *Personal Recollections and Observations of General Nelson A. Miles: Embracing a Brief View of the Civil War or From New England to the Golden Gate and the Story of his Indian Campaigns with Comments on the Exploration, Development and Progress of our Great Western Empire.* Chicago, Illinois: The Werner Company, 1896. REPRINT New York, New York: Da Capo Press, Inc., 1969.

Miller, Mark E. *Hollow Victory: The White River Expedition of 1879 and the Battle of Milk Creek.* Niwot, Colorado: University Press of Colorado, 1997.

Monnett, John H. *Massacre at Cheyenne Hole: Lieutenant Austin Henley and the Sappa Creek Controversy.* Niwot, Colorado: University Press of Colorado, 1999.

Monnett, John H. *Tell Them We Are Going Home: The Odyssey of the Northern Cheyennes.* Norman, Oklahoma, University of Oklahoma Press, 2001.

Monnett, John H. *The Battle of Beecher Island and the Indian War of 1867- 1869.* Niwot, Colorado: University of Colorado Press, 1992.

Monnett, John H. *Where a Hundred Soldiers Were Killed: The Struggle for the Powder River Country in 1866 and the Making of the Fetterman Myth.* Albuquerque, New Mexico: University of New Mexico Press, 2008.

Moore, William H. *Chiefs, Agents & Soldiers: Conflict on the Navajo Frontier, 1868-1882.* Albuquerque, New Mexico: University of New Mexico Press, 1994.

Mulroy, Kevin. *Freedom on the Border: The Seminole Maroons in Florida, the Indian Territory, Coahuila, and Texas.* Lubbock, Texas: Texas Tech University Press, 1993.

Murray, Keith A. *The Modocs and Their War.* Norman, Oklahoma: University of Oklahoma Press, 1959.

Nankivell, John. *Buffalo Soldier Regiment: History of the Twenty-fifth United States Infantry, 1869-1925.*

Nelson, Kurt R. *Fighting for Paradise: A Military History of the Pacific Northwest.* Yardley, Pennsylvania: Westholme Publishing, 2007.

North, Luther. *Man of the Plains: Recollections of Luther North, 1856-1882.* Lincoln, Nebraska: University of Nebraska Press, 1961.

Nye, Wilbur S. *Carbine and Lance: The Story of Old Fort Sill.* Norman, Oklahoma: University of Oklahoma Press, 1942.

Official Roster of the Soldiers of the State of Ohio in the War of the Rebellion. 1861-1866 (12 Volumes). Akron, Ohio: Werner Ptg. & Litho. Co., 1891.

Orton, Richard H. *Record of California Men in the War of the Rebellion.* Sacramento, California: Adjutant General's Office, 1890.

Overfield, Loyd J. *The Little Big Horn, 1876: The Official Communications, Documents and Reports, with Rosters of the Officers and Troops of the Campaign.* Lincoln, Nebraska: University of Nebraska Press, 1971.

Paul, R. Eli. *Nebraska Indian Wars Reader: 1865-1877.* Lincoln, Nebraska: University of Nebraska Press, 1998.

Peters, Joseph P. *Indian Battles and Skirmishes on the American Frontier, 1790 - 1898.* New York, New York: Argonaut Press Ltd, 1966.

Porter, Joseph C. *Paper Medicine Man: John Gregory Bourke and His American West.* Norman, Oklahoma: University of Oklahoma Press, 1986.

Price, George F. *Across the Continent with the Fifth Cavalry.* New York, New York: Antiquarian Press, 1959.

Proceedings of Reunions Held at Pittsburgh, Pa., Sept. 11-12, 1894, Crawfish Springs, Ga., Sept. 18-19, 1895, St. Paul, Minn., Sept. 1-2, 1896, Columbus, Ohio, Sept. 22-23, 1897. Columbus, Ohio: Press of John L. Trauger, 1898.

Randall, Kenneth A. *Only the Echoes: The Life of Howard Bass Cushing.* Las Cruces, New Mexico: Yucca Tree Press, 1995.

Rathbun, Daniel C.B. *Nevada Military Place Names of the Indian Wars and Civil War.* Las Cruces, New Mexico: Yucca Tree Press, 2002.

Rathbun, David C.B. and David V. Alexander. *New Mexico Frontier Military Place Names.* Las Cruces, New Mexico: Yucca Tree Press, 2003.

Reedstrom, E. Lisle. *Apache Wars: An Illustrated Battle History.* New York, New York: Sterling Publishing Co, Inc., 1990.

Report of the Adjutant General of the State of Kansas, 1861-1865 (2 Volumes). Leavenworth, Kansas: Bullentine Co-Operative Printing Company, 1867.

Rice, George A. *Vital Records of Pepperell, Massachusetts to the Year 1850.* Boston, Massachusetts: New England Historic Genealogical Society, 1985.

Rickey, Don, Jr. *Forty Miles a Day on Beans and Hay.* Norman, Oklahoma: University of Oklahoma Press, 1963.

Rister, Carl C. *Fort Griffin on the Texas Frontier.* Norman, Oklahoma: University of Oklahoma Press, 1956.

Roberts, David. *Once They Moved Like the Wind: Cochise, Geronimo, and the Apache Wars.* New York, New York: Touchstone, 1993.

Robinson, Charles M., III. *Bad Hand: A Biography of General Ranald S. Mackenzie.* Austin, Texas: State House Press, 1993.

Rockwell, Ronald V. *The U.S. Army in Frontier Montana.* Helena, Montana: Sweetgrass Books, 2009.

Rodenbough, Theophilus F. *From Everglade to Canyon with the Second United States Cavalry.* New York, New York: D. Van Nostrand, 1875. Reprint, Norman, Oklahoma: University of Oklahoma Press, 2000.

Rodenbough, Theophilus F. and William L. Haskins. *The Army of the United States: Historical Sketches of Staff and Line with Portraits of Generals-in-Chief.* New York, New York: Maynard, Merrill, & Co., 1896.

Russell, Don. *Campaigning with King: Charles King, Chronicler of the Old Army.* Omaha: University of Nebraska Press, 1991.

Russell, Don. *One Hundred and Three Fights and Scrimmages: The Story of General Reuben F. Bernard.* Mechanicsburg, Pennsylvania: Stackpole Books, 2003.

Simmons, Marc. *Massacre on the Lordsburg Road: A Tragedy of the Apache Wars.* College Station, Texas: Texas A&M University Press, 1997.

Smallwood, James M. *The Feud That Wasn't: The Taylor Ring, Bill Sutton, John Wesley Hardin, and Violence in Texas.* College Station, Texas: Texas A&M University Press, 2008.

Smith, Cornelius C., Jr. *Fort Huachuca: The True Story of a Frontier Post.* Washington, D.C.: Government Printing Office, 1976.

Smith, Shannon D. *Give Me Eighty Men: Women and the Myth of the Fetterman Fight.* Lincoln, Nebraska: University of Nebraska Press, 2008.

Smith, Sherry L. *Sagebrush Soldier: Private William Earl Smith's View of the Sioux War of 1876.* Norman, Oklahoma: University of Oklahoma Press, 1989.

Smith, Sherry L. *The View From Officers' Row: Army Perceptions of Western Indians.* Tucson, Arizona: University of Arizona Press, 1990.

Smith, Thomas T. *Fort Inge: Sharps, Spurs and Sabers on the Texas Frontier 1849-1869.* Austin, Texas: Eakin Press, 1993.

Smith, Thomas T. *The Old Army in Texas: A Research Guide to the U.S. Army in Nineteenth-Century Texas.* Austin, Texas: Texas State Historical Association, 2000.

Sprague, Marshall. *Massacre: The Tragedy at White River.* Boston, Massachusetts: Little, Brown and Company, 1957.

Spring, Agnes W. *Caspar Collins: The Life and Exploits of an Indian Fighter of the Sixties.* New York, New York: AMS Press, Inc., 1967.

Stanley, F. *Fort Craig.* Pampa, Texas: Pampa Print Shop, 1963.

Stewart, Edgar I. *Custer's Luck.* Norman, Oklahoma: University of Oklahoma Press, 1955.

Stout, Jospeh A, Jr. *Apache Lightning: The Last Great Battles of the Ojo Calientes.* New York, New York: Oxford University Press, 1974.

Strate, David Kay. *Sentinel to the Cimarron: The Frontier Experience of Fort Dodge, Kansas.* Dodge City, Kansas: High Plains Publishers, Inc., 1970.

Sweeney, Edwin R. *Cochise: Chiricahua Apache Chief.* Norman, Oklahoma: University of Oklahoma Press, 1991.

Sweeney, Edwin R. *Cochise to Geronimo: The Chiricahua Apaches, 1874-1886.* Norman, Oklahoma: University of Oklahoma Press, 2010.

Tate, Michael L. *The Frontier Army in the Settlement of the West.* Norman, Oklahoma: University of Oklahoma Press, 1999.

Thompson, Erwin N. *Modoc War: Its Military History and Topography.* Sacramento, California: Argus Books, 1971.

Thompson, Gerald. *The Army and the Navajo: The Bosque Redondo Reservation Experiment.* Tucson, Arizona: University of Arizona Press, 1976.

Thrapp, Dan L. *Al Sieber, Chief of Scouts.* Norman, Oklahoma: University of Oklahoma Press, 1964.

Thrapp, Dan L. *The Conquest of Apacheria.* Norman, Oklahoma: University of Oklahoma Press, 1967.

Thrapp, Dan L. *Encyclopedia of Frontier Biography (4 volumes).* Spokane, Washington: Arthur H. Clark Co., 1994.

Thrapp, Dan L. *Victorio and the Mimbres Apaches.* Norman, Oklahoma: University of Oklahoma Press, 1974.

Uglow, Loyd M. *Standing in the Gap: Army Outposts, Picket Stations, and the Pacification of the Texas Frontier, 1866-1886.* Fort Worth, Texas: Texas Christian University Press, 2001.

Unrau, William E. *Tending the Talking Wire: A Buck Soldiers View of Indian Country, 1863-1866.* Salt Lake City, Utah: University of Utah Press, 1979.

Upton, Richard. *The Indian as a Soldier at Fort Custer.* El Segundo, California: Upton and Sons, 1983.

Utley, Robert M. *Cavalier in Buckskin: George Armstrong Custer and the Western Military Frontier.* Norman, Oklahoma: University of Oklahoma Press, 1988.

Utley, Robert M. *Frontier Regulars: The United States Army and the Indian, 1866-1891.* Lincoln, Nebraska: University of Nebraska Press, 1973.

Utley, Robert M. *The Lance and the Shield: The Life and Times of Sitting Bull*. New York, New York: Henry Holt and Company, Inc, 1993.

Utley, Robert M. *The Last Days of the Sioux Nation*. New Haven, Connecticut: Yale University Press, 1963.

Van de Logt, March. *War Party in Blue: Pawnee Scouts in the U.S. Army*. Norman, Oklahoma: University of Oklahoma Press, 2010.

Vaughn, J.W. *Indian Fights: New Facts on Seven Encounters*. Norman, Oklahoma: University of Oklahoma Press, 1966.

Vaughn, J.W. *The Battle of Platte Bridge*. Norman, Oklahoma: University of Oklahoma Press, 1963.

Vaughn, J.W. *The Reynolds' Campaign on Powder River*. Norman, Oklahoma: University of Oklahoma Press, 1961.

Vaughn, J.W. *With Crook at the Rosebud*. Harrisburg, Pennsylvania: Stackpole, 1956.

Wagner and David E. Wagner. *Patrick Connor's War: The 1865 Powder River Indian Expedition*. Norman, Oklahoma: University of Oklahoma Press, 2010.

Wagner, David E. *Powder River Odyssey: Nelson Cole's Western Campaign of 1865, the Journals of Lyman G. Bennett and Other Eyewitness Accounts*. Norman, Oklahoma: The Arthur H. Clark Company, 2009.

Wallace, Ernest. *Ranald S. Mackenzie on the Texas Frontier*. College Station, Texas: Texas A&M University Press, 1993.

Walling, A.G. *History of Southern Oregon, Comprising Jackson, Josephine, Douglas, Curry and Coos Counties, Compiled from the Most Authentic Sources*. Portland, Oregon: Printing and Lithograph House of A.G. Walling, 1884.

Webb, George. *Chronological List of Engagements Between the Regular Army of the United States and Various Tribes of Hostile Indians Which Occurred During the Years 1790 to 1898, Inclusive*. St. Joseph, Missouri: Wing Printing and Publishing Co., 1939.

Wert, Jeffry D. *Custer: The Controversial Life of George Armstrong Custer*. New York, New York: Simon and Schuster, 1996.

Wellman, Paul I. *Death in the Desert: The Fifty Years' War for the Great Southwest*. Lincoln, Nebraska: University of Nebraska Press, 1935.

White, Lonnie J. *Hostiles and Horse Soldiers: Indian Battles and Campaigns in the West*. Boulder, Colorado: Pruett, 1972.

Wilbarger, J.W. *Indian Depredations in Texas*. Austin, Texas: Hutchings Printing House, 1889.

Williams, Clayton. *Texas' Last Frontier: Fort Stockton and the Trans-Pecos, 1861-1895*.

Williams, Dallas. *Fort Sedgwick, C.T.: Hell Hole on the Platte*. Julesburg, Colorado: Fort Sedgwick Historical Society, 1996.

Wittenberg, Eric J. *One of Custer's Wolverines: The Civil War Letters of Brevet Brigadier General James H. Kidd, 6th Michigan Cavalry*. Kent, Ohio: Kent State University Press, 2000.

Wooster, Robert. *Frontier Crossroads: Fort Davis and the West*. College Station, Texas: Texas A&M University Press, 2006.

Wooster, Robert. *History of Fort Davis, Texas*. Santa Fe, New Mexico: Division of History, Southwest Cultural Resources Center, 1990.

Wooster, Robert. *The Military and United States Indian Policy, 1865-1903*. New Haven, Connecticut: Yale University Press, 1988.

Zesch, Scott. *The Captured: A True Story of Abduction by Indians on the Texas Frontier*. New York, New York: St. Martin's Press, 2004.

Zimmer, William F. *Frontier Soldier: An Enlisted Man's Journal of the Sioux and Nez Perce Campaigns, 1877*. Helena, Montana: Montana Historical Society Press, 1998.

JOURNALS - MAGAZINES

Archambeau, Ernest R. (ed) "The Battle of Lyman's Wagon Train." *Panhandle-Plains Historical Review* 36 (1963): 89-101.

Barnes, Will C. "The Apaches' Last Stand in Arizona: The Battle of Big Dry Wash." *Arizona Historical Review* 3 (January 1931): 36-59.

Buecker, Thomas R. "Confrontation at Sturgis: An Episode in Civil-Military Relations, 1885." *South Dakota History* 14 (Fall 1984): 238-261.

Calloway, Colin G. "Sword Bearer and the 'Crow Outbreak', 1887." *Montana, the Magazine of Western History* 36 (Autumn 1986): 38-51.

Cunningham, Bob. "The Calamitous Career of Lt. Royal E. Whitman." *Journal of Arizona History* 29 (Summer 1988): 149-162.

Dinges, Bruce J. "Leighton Finley: A Forgotten Soldier of the Apache Wars." *Journal of Arizona History* 29 (Summer 1988): 163-184.

Ellis, Richard N. "The Humanitarian Generals." *Western Historical Quarterly* 3 (April 1972): 169-178.

Filipiak, John D. "The Battle of Summit Springs." *Colorado Magazine* 41 (Fall 1964): 343-354.

Fisher, John R. "The Royall and Duncan Pursuits: Aftermath of the Battle of Summit Springs, 1869." *Nebraska History* 50 (Fall 1969): 293-308.

Gale, Jack C. "Hatfield Under Fire, May 15, 1886: An Episode of the Geronimo Campaigns." *Journal of Arizona History* 18 (Winter 1977): 447-468.

Gale, Jack C. "Lebo in Pursuit." *Journal of Arizona History* 21 (Spring 1980): 11-24.

Garfield, Marvin H. " Defense of the Kansas Frontier, 1866-1867." *Kansas Historical Quarterly* 1 (August 1932): 326-344.

Garfield, Marvin H. " Defense of the Kansas Frontier, 1868-1869." *Kansas Historical Quarterly* 1 (November 1932): 451-473.

Hamilton, Doug, Berndt Kuhn and Larry Ludwig "Death in the Desert: Apache Ambush at Cottonwood Wash." *Wild West* (October 2010): 44-49.

Leckie, William H. "Buell's Campaign [in the Red River War, 1874-1875]." *Red River Valley Historical Review* 3 (Spring 1978): 186-193.

Leonard, Thomas C. "The Reluctant Conquerors: How the Generals Viewed the Indians." *American Heritage* 27 (August 1976): 34-41.

McChristian, Douglas C. "Grierson's Fight at Tinja de las Palmas: An Episode of the Victorio Campaign." *Red River Valley Historical Review* 7 (May 1982): 45-63.

Mehren, Lawrence L. "Scouting for Mescaleros: The Price Campaign of 1873." *Arizona and the West* 10 (Summer 1968): 171-190.

Niderost, Eric. "Cheyenne Fall: The Battle of Red Fork." *Wild West* (October 2011): 26-33.

Pate, J'Nell. "The Battles of Adobe Walls." *Great Plains Journal* 16 (Fall 1976): 3-44.

Porter, Kenneth W. "The Seminole-Negro Indian Scouts, 1870-1881." *Southwestern Historical Quarterly* 55 (January 1952): 358-377.

Rickey, Don, Jr. "The Battle of Wolf Mountain." *Montana, the Magazine of Western History* 13 (Spring 1963): 44-54.

Robertson, Francis B. "'We Are Going to Have a Big Sioux War': Colonel David S. Stanley's Yellowstone Expedition, 1872." *Montana, the Magazine of Western History* 34 (January 1984): 2-15.

Roddis, Louis H. "The Last Indian Uprising in the United States." *Minnesota History Bulletin* 3 (February 1920): 272-290.

Russell, Don. "How Many Indians Were Killed? White Man versus Red Man: The Facts and the Legend." *American West* 10 (July 1973): 42-47, 61-63.

Russell, Don. "The Duel on the War Bonnet." *Journal of the American Military Foundation* (Summer 1937): 55-69.

Schubert, Frank N. "The Sugg's Affray: The Black Cavalry in the Johnson County War. " *Western Historical Quarterly*. Vol. 4, No. 1 (January 1973): 57-68.

Shearer, George M. "The Battle of Vinegar Hill." *Idaho Yesterday* 12 (Spring 1968): 16-21.

Taylor, Morris F. "Plains Indians on the New Mexico-Colorado Border: The Last Phase, 1870-1876." *New Mexico Historical Review* 46 (October 1971): 315-336.

Thane, James L. "The Montana 'Indian War' of 1867." *Arizona and the West* 10 (Summer 1968): 153-170.

Underhill, Lonnie E. And Daniel F. Littlefield, Jr. "The Cheyenne 'Outbreak' of 1897." *Montana, the Magazine of Western History* 24 (October 1974): 30-41.

Utley, Robert M. "A Chained Dog: The Indian Fighting Army." *American West* (July 1973): 18-24, 61.

West, G. Derek. "The Battle of Adobe Walls, 1874." *Panhandle-Plains Historical Review* 36 (1963):1-36.

White, Lonnie J. "The Battle of Beecher Island: The Scouts Hold Fast on the Arickaree." *Journal of the West* 5 (January 1966): 1-24.

White, Lonnie J. "The Cheyenne Barrier on the Texas Frontier, 1868-1869." *Arizona and the West* 4 (Spring 1962): 51-64.

White, Lonnie J. "General Sully's Expedition to the North Canadian, 1868." *Journal of the West* 11 (January 1972): 75-98.

White, Lonnie J. "The Hancock and Custer Expeditions of 1867." *Journal of the West* 5 (July 1966): 355-378.

White, Lonnie J. "Indian Raids on the Kansas Frontier, 1869." *Kansas Historical Quarterly* 38 (Winter 1972): 369-388.

White, Lonnie J. "Warpaths on the Southern Plains: The Battles of the Saline River and Prairie Dog Creek." *Journal of the West* 4 (October 1965): 485-503.

NEWSPAPERS

Arizona Citizen

Arizona Miner

Arizona Star

Army and Navy Journal

Buffalo Courier and Republic

Daily State Journal

Frontier Scout

Highland Weekly News

Indianapolis Sentinel

LaGrange Standard

Lancaster Gazette

Montana Post

New Southwest and Grant County Herald

New York Herald

New York Times

Owyhee Avalanche

Sacramento Bee

Sacramento Union

San Francisco Daily Evening Bulletin

INTERNET

www.itd.nps.gov/cwss/index.html Civil War Soldiers and Sailor System

www.findagrave.com Find a Grave Nationwide Gravesite Locator

www.history.army.mil/moh.html U.S. Army Center of Military History Medal of Honor Citations

www.cem.va.gov U.S. Department of Veterans Affairs Nationwide Gravesite Locator

THOS. J. C. MADDOX.

Assistant Surgeon U.S.A.
son of
Thomas and Mary P. Maddox.
Born December 28, 1832.
Killed in a skirmish with
APACHE INDIANS
Near Alma, N.M.
December 19, 1885.

MADDOX

WILLIAMS

SIGISMUND
STERNBERG
—
DISTRICT OF COLUMBIA
—
2 LT. 27 U. S. INF.
AUGUST 1, 1867